Core Concepts in
HUMAN
SEXUALITY

Bryan Strong

University of California, Santa Cruz

Christine DeVault

Cabrillo College

Barbara Werner Sayad, MPH, CHES

California State University, Monterey Bay

MAYFIELD PUBLISHING COMPANY

Mountain View, California

London • Toronto

With gratitude and love, to my husband, Bob, my children, Sarah, Elizabeth, and Sam, and my parents, Robert and Elsie.　　　　　　　　　—Barbara Werner Sayad

Copyright © 1996 by Mayfield Publishing Company

Library of Congress Cataloging-in-Publication Data

Strong, Bryan.
　　Core concepts in human sexuality / Bryan Strong, Christine
DeVault, Barbara Werner Sayad.
　　　　p.　　cm.
　　Includes bibliographical references and index.
　　ISBN 1-55934-508-X
　　1. Sex.　2. Sex customs.　3. Hygiene, Sexual.　4. Gender identity.
5. Sex role.　I. DeVault, Christine.　II. Sayad, Barbara Werner
III. Title.
HQ21.S8124　1996
306.7--dc20　　　　　　　　　　　　　　　　　　　　　　　　　95-35035
　　　　　　　　　　　　　　　　　　　　　　　　　　　　　　CIP

Manufactured in the United States of America
10　9　8　7　6　5　4

Mayfield Publishing Company
1280 Villa Street
Mountain View, California 94041

Sponsoring editor, Franklin C. Graham; production editor, Melissa Kreischer; developmental editor, Kathleen Engelberg; manuscript editor, Carol Dondrea; art director, Jeanne M. Schreiber; text and cover designer, Donna Davis; art editor, Susan Breitbard; photo researcher, Brian Pecko; illustrators, Jennifer Hagerman, Natalie Hill, Marilyn Kreiger, and Kevin Somerville; manufacturing manager, Randy Hurst. The text was set in 10.5/12 Goudy by GTS Graphics, Inc. and printed on 45# Optimatte by Banta Company.

Cover art: © Thom Sevalrud.
Photo credits appear at the back of the book on page 571, which constitutes a continuation of the copyright page.

 This book is printed on recycled paper.

Brief Contents

Contents

iv

CHAPTER THIRTEEN

Preface

We wrote this textbook to make the study and teaching of human sexuality a meaningful and rewarding experience for both students and instructors. We present the study of human sexuality in such a manner as to enlarge both the student's personal and intellectual understanding. A personal approach does not exclude scholarship; nor does scholarship exclude personal understanding. Instead, scholarship allows the student to see beyond his or her own experience; and personal exploration breathes life into academic research.

The primary goal of this textbook is to integrate the personal and intellectual foundations of human sexuality. This goal led us to ask two fundamental questions. First, if we were college students, what would we want and need to know and understand about human sexuality? Second, what do we, as instructors and researchers, believe is important for an educated person to know about human sexuality? With these questions in mind, we formulated the structure and direction of this textbook. There are six important aspects to this textbook, described below.

Popular Culture. As we thought about the context in which students would read this textbook, we were struck by how powerful popular culture is in shaping attitudes, beliefs, and ideas about sexuality. In contemporary America, Dr. Ruth, Abigail van Buren, Oprah, Donahue, Geraldo, as well as Sharon Stone, Sylvester Stallone, Dana Carvey, RuPaul, and Madonna, are among the most significant sources of sexual information, ideas, stereotypes, and values. It is important that students think about the depictions of sexuality in popular culture and critically evaluate their impact on our lives. Just as any research finding on human sexuality is subject to critical thought, so too is every image given to us by our popular culture.

Integration of Gay/Lesbian/Bisexuality Research. As we considered the subject of sexual orientation, we decided that it is important to integrate gay/lesbian/bisexual research into the text rather than segregate these issues into a separate chapter. There are no compelling intellectual reasons to segregate research on gay, lesbian, and bisexual men and women from general discussions per se of communication, love, cohabitation, sexual expression, and so on. Such segregation implies differences where none may exist. It distorts our common humanity and relegates gay men, lesbians, and bisexuals to a "special" category. Such segregation, we believe, unintentionally encourages continued stigmatization.

Ethnic Diversity. As we looked at the demographic composition of our classes, colleges, and universities, we were struck by their increasing ethnic diversity. This diversity reflects the diversity of our nation in which over 20% of Americans are from African American, Latino, Asian America, Native American, or other ethnic descent. To reflect this diversity, we have integrated scholarship on ethnicity and sexuality as much as possible. This scholarship, however, is limited, and much of it is problem-oriented. But we believe it is important in our ethnically diverse society to expand the study of human sexuality to include all distinct ethnic groups.

HIV/AIDS Crisis. We are acutely aware of the HIV/AIDS epidemic. Because of its severity, we have devoted a chapter to examining its various aspects, including not only the biological and health aspects but also the personal, social, and psychological aspects.

Research Based. We are deeply committed to scholarship and to presenting cutting-edge research in the field of human sexuality. In writing this book we carefully evaluated the current literature, using bibliographic databases and communicating with scholars around the country. We include what we believe to be the most up-to-date, important, and interesting research findings available. Our own research on love and sexuality continues to remind us of the joys (and limits) of research.

Teaching Support. We want to provide as much support as we can to the instructor teaching human sexuality. We believe a textbook's effectiveness as a teaching tool is dramatically increased when the text is systematically integrated with supplementary instructional material. We have developed a comprehensive, integrated teaching package that dovetails with the text and with classroom needs. Included in this package (described in detail below) are an instructor's resource book, a printed test bank, corresponding computerized test bank, a student study guide, supplemental videos and audiocassettes, and biannual newsletters.

PEDAGOGICAL AIDS

Core Concepts in Human Sexuality is written in an accessible style at a level appropriate for most undergraduates. To support both teaching and learning, we have incorporated several learning aids in the text. Each chapter begins with a **chapter preview,** a self-quiz that challenges students' preconceptions about the topic presented in that chapter. The preview is followed by a **chapter outline,** designed to give the student an overview of topics discussed in the chapter. Reinforcing these two aids is an **"In this chapter"** paragraph, describing the chapter's contents.

Providing students with greater understanding of particular timely, high-interest topics are boxes called **"Think About It."** Sample titles include "A Change in the Quality of Sperm," "Body Play: Tattooing and Piercing," "Women and Condom Use," "Gay and Lesbian Parents," and "AIDS Myths, AIDS Facts." Also featured are boxes called **"You and Your Sexual Well-Being."** These boxes give students the opportunity to reflect on their personal attitudes, beliefs, and behaviors and to evaluate their own experiences in light of knowledge gained through reading the chapter. Sample titles include "Sexual Communication Satisfaction Questionnaire," "Choosing a Birth Control Method," "Discovering Your Conditions for Good Sex," and "How to Tell If You Are in an Abusive Situation."

Important **key terms** are printed in boldface type and defined in context. Terms are also defined in a **running glossary** on the text page where they first appear. Appearing at the ends of chapters are chapter **summaries,** designed to assist students in understanding main ideas and in reviewing chapter material. An annotated listing of **suggested readings** is included at the end of every chapter as well, providing the student with sources of additional information and resources for research projects. Together, these pedagogical aids support and facilitate effective teaching and successful learning.

INTEGRATED TEACHING PACKAGE

As noted above, *Core Concepts in Human Sexuality* includes an integrated package of materials designed to increase its effectiveness as a teaching tool. At the heart of this package is the **Instructor's Resource Guide,** which we have developed using a new approach. The resource book begins with course planning material, such as reference tools and resources; suggestions for background reading; bibliographies of materials on human sexuality and ethnicity; and suggested films, videos, transparency masters, and student worksheets. Material for each chapter follows: chapter outlines, selected bibliographies, discussion questions, activities, and sample test questions.

A **computerized test bank** of close to 2,000 test items has been prepared by Grace Galliano, Kennesaw State College, and Kina Leitner, New York University. Together they bring substantial experience in teaching and in testing and measurement to this element of the package. Each chapter contains approximately 100 test items, including multiple choice questions, true-false questions, fill-in questions tied to key terms, short-answer questions, and essay questions. The test bank can be used with either IBM or Macintosh computers. The test bank is also printed and bound into one volume.

A student **study guide** has been prepared by Bobbi Mitzenmacher, Long Beach State University, and Barbara Sayad. The study guide contains detailed learning objectives, practice tests, activities, personal involvement assessments, and a step-by-step guide to preparing a personal and meaningful gender identity paper.

Our selection of **videotapes** gives instructors the opportunity to illustrate and extend coverage of the most current and compelling topics treated in the text. For information about the videos, instructors should contact their Mayfield representative or call 1-800-433-1279.

Finally, a biannual **newsletter** provides updates to the text, information on new research and relevant current events, suggestions for lectures and activities, and perspectives on the latest issues in human sexuality.

ACKNOWLEDGMENTS

Many people contributed to the creation and development of this book. We are grateful, first of all, for the kind assistance of the reference staff at the Dean McHenry Library at the University of California, Santa Cruz. Reference librarians Alan Ritch, Deborah Murphy, Paul Machlis, and Jaquelyn Maria were very helpful in compiling bibliographies, answering questions, verifying citations, obtaining books and journals through interlibrary loans, and assisting us in the use of on-line and CD-ROM bibliographic systems. The reference staff at the Santa Cruz and Seaside Public Libraries also provided much-appreciated assistance.

Ruth Gunn Mota, Director of Education, Santa Cruz AIDS Project (SCAP), provided valuable information about HIV and AIDS. She is deeply committed to increasing AIDS awareness among students and members of the community, as are the SCAP staff and a number of people living with AIDS in our community. We applaud their work.

Our friend and colleague Art Aron, one of the leading researchers in the social psychology of love, assisted us in developing Chapter 9, "Communicating About Sex." Terence Crowley, professor of library science at San Jose State University, continues to assist us—and entertain us—when we have difficult questions to research. Pepper Schwartz at the University of Washington has shared her ideas with us about the relationship between sex research and its popularization in the media. Fran Bussard, formerly of California State University, Chico, is an ever-thoughtful friend who provides ongoing insight into human relationships. Herb Colston and Michael Santos contributed greatly to the development of the instructor's manual. Special thanks to William Yarber of Indiana University for allowing us to use his health assessment instruments. We also thank James Barbour of the University of Maine for allowing us to reprint in the resource book his essay on human sexuality discussion groups. Zoe Sodja, Nona William, and Cheryl VanDeVeer patiently and cheerfully helped us input the text. To all, we express our deep appreciation.

Of those at Mayfield Publishing Company, we particulary wish to acknowledge Frank Graham, our editor, and thank him for his inspiration, knowledge, and hard work. We also wish to thank Kate Engelberg, Managing Development Editor, for her insights, sensitivity, patience, and professionalism. We thank our production editor, Melissa Kreischer, who also did outstanding work in developing our photo program; Susan Breitbard skillfully managed the art program, Brian Pecko managed the photos, and Pamela Trainer competently secured the permissions. Linda Toy, vice president and director of production, has been a constant source of encouragement in producing the book and especially in developing the art program. Thanks also to our editorial assistant, Julie Wildhaber. Dick Greenberg, president of Mayfield, has offered support and encouragement; it has been a pleasure working with him.

We also thank our children—Gabe, Willy, Maria, and Kristin—whose continued development from toddlerhood to young adulthood is an ever-rich source of challenge, delight, and insight.

Finally, we wish to thank the instructors and researchers, listed here alphabetically, whose ideas and feedback contributed to the final shape of this book: Betty Sue Benison, Texas Christian University; Dennis M. Dailey, University of Kansas; Grace Galliano, Kennesaw State College; Richard A. Kaye, Kingsborough Community College of CUNY; Molly Laflin, Bowling Green State University; William L. Yarber, Indiana University.

Prologue

Being sexual is an essential part of being human. Through our sexuality, we are able to connect with others on the most intimate levels, revealing ourselves and creating strong bonds. Sexuality is a source of great pleasure and profound satisfaction. It is the means by which we reproduce—bringing new life into the world, and transforming ourselves into mothers and fathers. Paradoxically, sexuality can also be a source of guilt and confusion, a pathway to infection, and a means of exploitation and aggression. Examining the multiple aspects of human sexuality will help you understand your own sexuality and that of others. It will provide the basis for enriching your relationships.

Throughout our lives, we make sexual choices based on our experience, attitudes, values, and knowledge. The decisions many of us may face include whether to become or keep on being sexually active; whether to establish, continue, or end an intimate relationship; whether to practice safer sex consistently; and how to resolve conflicts, if they exist, between our values and our sexual desires, feelings, and behaviors. The choices we make may vary at different times in our lives. Our sexuality changes and evolves as we ourselves change.

STUDYING HUMAN SEXUALITY

Students begin studying sexuality for many reasons: to gain insight into their sexuality and relationships, to explore personal sexual issues, to dispel anxieties and doubts, to resolve traumatic sexual experiences, to prepare for the helping professions, or to increase their general knowledge. Many students find the study of sexuality empowering. They discover their ability to make intelligent sexual choices based on their own needs, desires, and values rather than on guilt, ignorance, pressure, fear, or conformity.

The study of human sexuality differs from the study of accounting, plant biology, and medieval history because human sexuality is surrounded by a vast array of taboos, fears, prejudices, and hypocrisy. For many Americans, sexuality creates feelings of stress. It is linked not only with intimacy and pleasure, but also with stress, guilt, and discomfort. As a result, you may find yourself confronted with society's mixed feelings about sexuality as you study it. You may find, for example, that others perceive you as somehow "different" for taking a course in human sexuality. Some may feel threatened in a vague, undefined way. Parents, partners, or spouses (not to mention your own children, if you are a parent) may wonder why you want to take a "sex class"; they may want to know why you don't take something

1

You and Your Sexual Well-Being

WHAT STUDENTS WANT TO LEARN IN A HUMAN
SEXUALITY COURSE: THE PERSONAL DIMENSION

Students begin the study of human sexuality for a multitude of reasons. When we asked our students to tell us what they wanted to learn in our class, their answers emphasized the personal dimension of learning. The student responses below are representative.

My biggest issue is setting my own sexual guidelines, rather than accepting those of others, such as my friends, society, etc.   —*a 20-year-old woman*

I want to know the difference between sex and love. When I have sex with a woman, I think I'm in love with her, or at least want to be. Am I kidding myself?   —*a 21-year-old man*

I have a hard time telling my boyfriend what I want him to do. I get embarrassed and end up not getting what I need. —*a 19-year-old woman*

I lost my virginity last week. What do you do when you sleep with someone for the first time?   —*an 18-year-old man*

I recently separated from my husband and am beginning to date again. I'd like to know what the proper sexual etiquette is today. Such as, do you kiss or have sex on the first date . . . or what?   —*a 37-year-old woman*

I'm gay, but my family would disown me if they found out. What can I do to make my parents understand that it's OK to be gay?   —*a 20-year-old man*

My parents continue to hassle me about sex. They want me to be a virgin when I marry (which is next to impossible, since I lost my virginity when I was 16). Any suggestions on how to raise parents?   —*a 19-year-old woman*

Is it wrong to masturbate if you have a regular partner?   —*a 22-year-old man*

Why do women get called "sluts" if they have more than one partner, and it doesn't matter for guys? In fact, the more women they "have," the more points they get.   —*an 18-year-old woman*

How do I know if I'm normal? What is normal? And why do I care?   —*a 21-year-old man*

I'm a sexy 70-year-old. How come young people think sex stops when you're over 40? We don't spend all day just knitting, you know.   —*a 70-year-old woman*

Some of these questions relate to facts, some concern attitudes or relationships, and still others concern values. But all of them are within the domain of human sexuality. As you study human sexuality, you may find answers to many of these questions, as well as those of your own. You will also find that your class will raise questions the textbook or instructor cannot answer. Part of the reason we cannot answer all your questions is that there is insufficient research available to give an adequate response. But part of the reason also may be that it is not the domain of social science to answer questions of value. As social scientists, it is our role to provide you with knowledge, analytical skills, and insights for making your own moral evaluations. It is you who is ultimately responsible for determining your sexual value system.

more "serious"—as if sexuality were not one of the most important issues we face as individuals and as a society. Sometimes this uneasiness manifests itself in humor, one of the ways in which we deal with ambivalent feelings: "You mean you have to take a *class* on sex?" "Are there labs?" "Why don't you let me show you?"

Ironically, despite societal ambivalence, you may quickly find that your human sexuality textbook becomes the most popular book in your dormitory or apartment. "I can never find my textbook when I need it," one of our students complained. "My roommates are always reading it. And they're not even taking the course!" Another student observed: "My friends used to kid me about taking the class, but now the first thing they ask when they see me is what we discussed in class." "People borrow my book so often without asking," wrote one student, "that I hide it now."

What these responses signify is simple: Despite their ambivalence, people *want* to learn about human sexuality. On some level, they understand that what they have learned may have been haphazard, unreliable, stereotypical, incomplete, unrealistic, irrelevant—or dishonest. As adults, they are ready to move beyond "sperm meets egg" stories.

As you study human sexuality, you will discover yourself exploring areas not ordinarily discussed in other classes. Sometimes they are rarely talked about even among friends. They may be prohibited by parental or religious teaching. The more an area is judged to be in some way "bad" or "immoral," the less likely it is to be discussed. Ordinary behaviors such as masturbation and sexual fantasies are often the source of considerable guilt. But in your human sexuality course, they will be examined objectively. You may be surprised to discover, in fact, that part of your learning consists in *unlearning* myths, half-truths, factual errors, and distortions you learned earlier.

You may feel uncomfortable when you go to the first class meetings. That's not at all uncommon. When I (Bryan Strong) went to the first day of my human sexuality class as a student in 1970, I felt embarrassed, out of place. The class was in a darkened auditorium, which gave me the uncomfortable sense I was in an adult movie house. Because I was nervous, I went with a friend; I slouched low in my seat. In retrospect, these feelings are not surprising. Sexuality may be the most tabooed subject we study as undergraduates. (Highly respected sex researchers have been investigated by the FBI because of their research.) Your comfort level in class will probably increase as you recognize that you and your fellow students have a common purpose in learning about sexuality. Your sense of ease may also increase as you and your classmates get to know each other and discuss sexuality, both inside and outside class.

You may find that as you become used to using the accepted sexual vocabulary, you become more comfortable discussing various topics. Perhaps you may find that you have never before used the words "masturbation," "sexual intercourse," "vulva," "penis," "heterosexuality," or "homosexuality" in a class setting (or any kind of setting, for that matter). But after a while, they may become second nature to you. You may discover that discussing sex academically becomes as easy as discussing geography, accounting, or literature. You may even find yourself, as many students do, telling your friends what you learned in class while on a bus or in a restaurant, as other passengers or diners gasp in shock or lean toward you to hear better!

Studying sexuality requires respect for your fellow students. You'll discover that the experiences and values of your classmates vary greatly. Some students have little sexual experience, while others have substantial experience; some students hold liberal sexual values, while others hold conservative ones. Some students are gay, lesbian, or bisexual, while the majority are heterosexual. Most students are young, others middle-aged, some old— each in a different stage of life and with different development tasks before them. Furthermore, the presence of students from any of the more than 124 ethnic groups in the United States reminds us that there is no single behavioral, attitudinal, value, or belief system that encompasses sexuality in contemporary America.

Because of America's diversity in terms of experience, values, orientation, age, and ethnicity, the study of sexuality calls for us to be openminded: to be receptive to new ideas and to differentness; to seek to understand what we have not understood before; to reexamine old assumptions, ideas, and beliefs; to encompass the humanity in each of us. In our quest for knowledge and understanding, we need to be intellectually curious. As writer Joan Nestle observes, "Curiosity builds bridges. . . . Curiosity is not trivial; it is the respect one life pays to another."

THE AUTHORS' PERSPECTIVE

We developed this textbook along several themes, which we believe will help you better understand your sexuality and that of others.

Psychosocial Orientation

Although we are creatures rooted in biology, hormones and the desire to reproduce are not the most important factors shaping our sexuality. We believe that the most significant factor is the interplay between our individual personality and social factors. As a result, we use a psychosocial perspective in explaining human sexuality. A psychosocial perspective emphasizes the role of psychological factors (such as motivation, emotions, and attitudes) and social learning (the process of learning from others and society). We look at how sexuality is shaped in our culture; we examine how it differs in different historical periods and between different ethnic groups in our culture. We also examine how sexuality takes different forms in other cultures throughout the world.

In addition, because we want students to apply the concepts presented in this book to their own lives, we have presented information and ideas in ways that encourage students to become proactive in their own sexual well-being. We have highlighted sexual health-related topics in boxes called "Think About It" and asked questions that prompt students to examine their own values and the ways they express their sexuality in boxes called "You and Your Sexual Well-Being."

Sex as Intimacy

We believe that sex in our culture is basically an expressive and intimate activity. It is a vehicle for expressing feelings, whether positive or negative. It is also a means for establishing and maintaining intimacy. Sex is also important as a means of reproduction, but because of the widespread use of birth control, reproduction has become increasingly a matter of choice.

Gender Roles

Gender roles are societal expectations of how women and men are expected to behave in a particular culture. Among other things, gender roles tell us how we are to act sexually. Although women and men differ, we believe most differences are rooted more in social learning than in biology.

Traditionally, our gender roles have viewed men and women as "opposite" sexes. Men were active, women passive; men were sexually aggressive, women sexually receptive; men sought sex, women sought love. Research, however, suggests that we are more alike than different as men and women. To reflect our commonalities rather than differences, we refer not to the "opposite" sex, but to the "other" sex.

Sexuality and Popular Culture

Much of what we learn about sexuality from popular culture and the media—from so-called sex experts, magazine articles, how-to-do-it books, and TV and the movies—is wrong, half-true, or stereotypical. Prejudice may masquerade as fact. Scholarly research may also be flawed for various reasons. Throughout the textbook, we look at how we can evaluate what we read and see, both in popular culture and in scholarly research. We compare scholarly findings to sexual myths and beliefs, including research about gay men and lesbians and ethnic groups.

Homosexuality as a Normal Sexual Variation

We recognize the normality of gay and lesbian sexual orientations. Gay men and lesbians have been subjected to discrimination, prejudice, and injustice for centuries because of their orientation. But as society has become more enlightened, it has discovered that lesbians and gay men do not differ from heterosexuals in any significant aspect except in their choice of sexual partners. In 1972, the American Psychiatric Association removed homosexuality from its list of mental disorders. Today, the major professional psychological, sociological, and health associations in the United States regard homosexuality as a normal sexual variation. For this reason, we have integrated discussions of lesbians and gay men throughout the book.

The Significance of Ethnicity

Until recently, Americans have ignored ethnicity as a factor in studying human sexuality. We have acted as if being white, African American, Latino, Asian American, or Native American made no difference in terms of sexual attitudes, behaviors, and values. But there are important differences, and we discuss these throughout the textbook. It is important to examine these differences within their cultural context. Ethnic differences, therefore, should not be interpreted as "good" or "bad," "healthy" or "deficient," but as reflections of culture. Our understanding of the role of ethnicity, however, is limited because ethnic research is only now beginning to emerge.

Over the years, we have asked our students to briefly state what they learned or gained in our human sexuality class. Here are some of their answers.

I learned to value the exploration of my sexuality much more. I learned that sexuality comes in many forms, and I'm one of them. The class gave me a forum or safe place to explore sexuality, especially since I have not yet had a fully sexual relationship.

I found the psychological, historical, and anthropological elements of sexuality we discussed to be very valuable. I see homosexuality in a totally new light.

I learned that being sexual is OK, that basically we are all sexual beings and that it is normal to want to have sex. I am no longer afraid to talk about sex with my boyfriend.

The information about AIDS cleared up many misconceptions and fears I had. I will always practice safer sex from now on.

The class has helped me come to terms with things that have happened over the last few months that are disturbing to me.

I have paid more attention to the erotic nature of things, not just the physical aspects of sex.

We believe that the knowledge you gain from studying human sexuality will be something you will carry with you the rest of your life. We hope it will help you understand and appreciate not only yourself but those who differ from you, and that it will enrich, expand, and enliven your experiences and your relationships.

Chapter One

PERSPECTIVES ON HUMAN SEXUALITY

P R E V I E W : SELF-QUIZ

1. The division of sexual behavior into natural and unnatural acts is based on the biological sciences. True or false?

2. Sexual themes often run through family-oriented situation comedies. True or false?

3. Value judgments, such as "good" and "bad," are useful tools for scientifically describing sexual behavior. True or false?

4. High levels of sexual desire are found in all cultures. True or false?

5. All cultures divide human beings into only two genders: male and female. True or false?

6. The media increasingly depict sexuality as it exists in the real world. True or false?

7. Sexual relationships between men are universally condemned. True or false?

8. College students' sexual ideas tend to reflect popular culture. True or false?

9. Using sexual images in advertising is an effective device for all products. True or false?

10. The most explicit TV sex is usually found on crime shows. True or false?

ANSWERS 1. F, 2. T, 3. F, 4. F, 5. F, 6. F, 7. F, 8. T, 9. F, 10. F

Chapter Outline

Sexuality was once hidden from view in our culture: Fig leaves covered the "private parts" of nudes; poultry breasts were renamed "white meat"; censors prohibited the publication of the works of D. H. Lawrence, James Joyce, and Henry Miller; and homosexuality was called "the love that dares not speak its name." But over the last few generations, sexuality has become more open. In recent years, popular culture and the media have transformed what we "know" about sexuality. Not only is sexuality *not* hidden from view, it often seems to surround us.

In this chapter, we examine popular culture and the media to see how they shape our ideas about sexuality. Then we look at how sexuality has been treated in different cultures and at different times in history. Finally, we examine how society defines various aspects of our sexuality as natural or normal.

SEXUALITY, POPULAR CULTURE, AND THE MEDIA

Much of our sexuality is influenced and shaped by popular culture, especially the mass media. Popular culture presents us with myriad images of what it means to be sexual. But what kind of sexuality is portrayed by the media—and consumed by us? What are media messages about sex to children, adolescents, adults, and the aged? To men? To women? To whites, African

Americans, Latinos, Asian Americans, and other ethnic groups? Perhaps as important as what the media portray sexually is what is not portrayed—for example, masturbation, condom use, and erotic marital interactions.

Media Portrayals of Sexuality

Media depictions of sexuality are not as obvious and straightforward as we may initially think. On television, for example, we are usually presented with visual images that suggest but do not show sexual activities other than kissing. In the movies, a wider range of sexual behaviors are shown more explicitly. "Steamy" sex scenes and female nudity (often combined with violence) are part of the Hollywood formula for success. ("How can we put more tits and c— [sic] into this movie?" the director of *Basic Instinct* reportedly asked, upon walking onto the set [Zevin, 1992].)

The music industry is awash with sexual images. Contemporary pop music, from rock 'n' roll to hip hop, bursts with lyrics about sexuality mixed with love, rejection, violence, and loneliness. Heavy metal often reinforces negative attitudes toward women (St. Lawrence & Joyner, 1991). Popular music is transmitted through CD or cassette players or through television and radio. MTV, VH1, and music video programs televise videos filled with sexually suggestive lyrics, images, and dance. Because of censorship issues, the most overtly sexual music is not played on radio, except for some college stations. Disk jockeys, "shock jocks" such as Howard Stern (who was recently fined by the FCC for sexually offensive and racist remarks), weather reporters, and sportscasters make numerous sexual references. They also reinforce conformist gender roles by calling men "guys," "mister," or "sir," while referring to women in terms of family roles, such as "wife," "mother," "daughter," "sister," or "ladies" (Lont, 1990).

Magazines, tabloids, and books contribute to the sexualization of our environment. Sexual references (measured as the ratio of references per page) tripled between 1950 and 1980 in such magazines as *Reader's Digest,*

Shock jocks such as Howard Stern are popular radio personalities whose programs are filled with sexual references and innuendos. What messages do they suggest about sexuality? Men? Women? Homosexuality?

Women's magazines, such as Cosmopolitan, Redbook, *and* Mademoiselle, *use sex to sell their publications. How do these magazines differ from men's magazines, such as* Playboy *and* Penthouse, *in their treatment of sexuality?*

Time, and *Newsweek* (Scott, 1986b). Popular novels, romances, and self-help books, such as *The ESO Ecstasy Program* (Brauer, Brauer, & Rhodes, 1991) and *Women, Sex, and Addiction* (Kasl, 1989) help disseminate popular ideas and values about sexuality. Supermarket tabloid headlines exploit the unusual ("Woman with Two Vaginas Has Multiple Lovers") or sensational ("Televangelist's Love Tryst Exposed").

Men's magazines have been singled out for their sexual sell. *Playboy* and *Penthouse,* with their Playmates of the Month, Pets of the Month, and other nude pictorials, are among the most popular magazines in the world (Wolf & Kielwasser, 1991). Playboy sells about 10 million issues monthly, including 2 million to women (Martin, 1992). (One-quarter of the top 40 best-selling videocassettes are usually produced by *Playboy* and *Penthouse.*) *Sports Illustrated*'s annual swimsuit edition sells over 5 million copies, twice as many as its other issues. But it would be a mistake to think that only male-oriented magazines focus on sex.

Women's magazines, such as *Cosmopolitan* and *Redbook,* have their own sexual content (McMahon, 1990). These magazines feature romantically staged photographs of lovers to illustrate stories with such titles as "Sizzling Sex Secrets of the World's Sexiest Women," "Making Love Last: If Your Partner Is a Premature Ejaculator," and "Turn on Your Man with Your Breasts (Even If They Are Small)."

Katherine McMahon (1990) found that almost all the articles she surveyed over a 12-year period in *Cosmopolitan* magazine dealt directly or indirectly with sex.

Advertising in all media uses the sexual sell, promising sex, romance, popularity, and fulfillment provided the consumer purchases the right soap, perfume, cigarettes, alcohol, toothpaste, jeans, or automobile. An advertisement for Infiniti, for example, claims: "It's not a car. It's an aphrodisiac." In reality, not only does one *not* become "sexy" or popular by consuming a certain product, the product may actually be detrimental to one's sexual well-being. It is ironic, in fact, to link cigarettes and alcohol with sex. Heavy smoking, for example, is associated with erectile dysfunction, the inability of the penis to become erect, and with lowered fertility in both men and women (Rosen et al., 1991). Alcohol consumption is linked to both male and female sexual problems and severe birth defects in the children of heavy drinkers (see Chapter 12).

Over the last generation, the degree of nudity has increased in magazine advertising. The level of sexually provocative attire is greater for female models than for males; the level of provocation has also been increasing (Soley & Reid, 1986).

Media images of sexuality permeate all areas of life. They are more important than family in influencing the sexual attitudes and behavior of adolescents and college students. Studies indicate that movies are one of the leading sources of sex information for Anglo, Latino, and Native American male adolescents. They appear to learn more from movies than from their female peers (Davis & Harris, 1982). Half of the college men (but fewer women) in a recent study reported that pornography had been a source of information for them on masturbation, oral-genital sex, and anal intercourse (Duncan, 1990). Overall, only peers are as important as the media in transmitting sexual knowledge (Courtright & Baran, 1980; Moffatt, 1989).

Television is one of the most pervasive media affecting our views of sexuality. What ideas and images about sexuality do your favorite programs convey?

Sexual images are used to sell products. What ideas are conveyed by this advertisement? How does its appeal differ according to whether one is male or female?

Mass-media depictions of sexuality are meant to entertain, not to inform. As a result, the media do not present us with "real" depictions of sexuality. Sexual activities, for example, are usually not explicitly acted out or described in mainstream media. The various media present the social *context* of sexuality (C. Smith, 1991); that is, the programs, plots, movies, stories, articles, newscasts, and vignettes tell us *what* behaviors are appropriate (e.g., kissing or sexual intercourse), *with whom* they are appropriate (e.g., girlfriend/boyfriend, partner, among heterosexuals), and *why* they are appropriate (e.g., attraction, love, loneliness, exploitation).

Television

Television is the most pervasive and influential medium affecting our views of sexuality. The visual depiction of explicit sexual behavior on network television, however, is limited. We generally see nothing more than kissing and occasional fondling and only between heterosexuals. Other sexual behaviors, such as coitus or oral sex, may be suggested through words ("Oh, it feels so good") or visual or sound cues (closeups of faces tensing during orgasm or music from Ravel's *Bolero* playing on the soundtrack). Sexual behavior is never overtly depicted, as it is in sexually oriented films. References to masturbation are rarely made; when they are, they are usually negative and consigned to an adolescent context, suggesting that such behavior is "immature." Female breasts may be shown, but usually in tight garments, with suggestive cleavages or nipples outlined through clothing; nipples themselves are taboo.

Subscriber cable television, however, offers more sexually oriented programs than network programs. The Playboy Channel offers explicit films. But most cable stations do not show X-rated films. One hard-core cable company, The Exxxtasy Channel, was forced out of business as a result of government obscenity prosecutions. Because of concern about community reaction, sexually oriented films are generally R-rated (no penetration, ejaculation, or gay/lesbian sex).

Today television helps form our sexual perceptions through its depiction of stereotypes and its reinforcement of **norms,** which are cultural rules or standards. Television shapes our perceptions differently, however, depending on the TV genre (the type of program). There are five major TV genres in which sexual stereotyping and norms are especially influential: situation comedies, soap operas, crime/action-adventure programs, made-for-TV movies, and music videos. In addition, TV commercials can be considered a genre.

Each genre has a different formula for what is sexually permissible and how to depict sex. The formulas are influenced by network censors and conservative advocacy groups, such as Donald Wildmon's American Family Association (Montgomery, 1989). These groups exert pressure on networks and advertisers to present morally correct programming. Positive references to birth control, abortion, and gays and lesbians, for example, are considered to be promoting immorality. The effectiveness of pressure groups can be seen if you think of the last time you saw a condom advertisement or heard the word "condom" on any of the major networks.

Situation Comedies Sex in situation comedies? When asked, most people think there is none. After all, sitcoms usually deal with families or familylike relationships; children are often the major characters. Because they are family-oriented, sitcoms do not deal with explicit depictions of sex (C. Smith, 1991; Taylor, 1989). Instead, they deal with sexuality in the form of taboos centering around marital or family issues. The taboos are mild, such as the taboo against a married person flirting with another man or woman. If a sitcom dealt with a major taboo, such as incest, the program would go beyond the sitcom's normal boundaries; it would not be funny.

In sitcoms, the formula is to put a character in a situation in which he or she unknowingly violates a conventional social rule, thereby creating chaos. The chaos, however, is resolved by the show's end, and everyone "lives happily ever after" until the next episode. Thus, a married man can be getting an eyelash out of his sister-in-law's eye when his wife comes home early and becomes jealous, suspecting her husband and sister of kissing. While the laugh track plays, the husband tries to explain that "she had something in her eye."

Sitcoms are sexually stereotypical. Their range of sexual standards and implied behaviors is limited, although the sexual references have increased considerably since the days of "I Love Lucy" (Cantor, 1991). Despite the increase in sexual references, sitcoms barely touch on the variety of values and behaviors found in the real world. Billy Crystal's breakthrough gay character in "Soap" and Martin Mull's in "Roseanne" are examples of sympathetic gay characters in mainstream sitcoms, but they remain the exception. Conservative advocacy groups continue to oppose depictions of gay

norm A cultural rule or standard of behavior.

men and lesbians as normal (Montgomery, 1989). Although sitcoms have a limited range, they are nevertheless affirming of connectedness and family values. They provide a context of intimacy for sexuality. Whatever transgression occurs, it is forgotten by the next episode.

Soap Operas Soap operas are one of the most popular TV genres. One soap, "Days of Our Lives," is among the top ten most-watched television programs among college students (Cary, 1992). Although sexual transgressions are soon forgotten in sitcoms, they are never forgotten in soap operas. Transgressions are the lifeblood of soaps: jealousy and revenge are ever-present. Most characters are now, or once were, involved with each other. The ghosts of past loves haunt the mansions and townhouses; each relationship carries a heavy history with it. Infidelity, pregnancy alarms, wild affairs, betrayals, and jealousy punctuate every episode. Depictions of sexual behavior are fairly frequent. One study of soaps found one reference to sexual intercourse every 40 minutes; scenes of sexual intercourse were depicted every 90 minutes (Greenberg & D'Alessio, 1985).

Gender roles tend to be stereotypical, with men generally more dominant and aggressive than women. Few characters over age 40 are depicted as sexually active (Greenberg & D'Alessio, 1985). African Americans have been notably absent in soaps. When a black does appear, it is generally as a single character in the context of dealing with racial issues, such as discrimination. African American characters often are engaged in interracial affairs. These affairs do not last long, and the characters generally find other black men or women to be partners (Geraghty, 1990). No major American soap incorporates representative numbers of African Americans, Latinos, Asian Americans, or other ethnic groups. Only "EastEnders," the popular English soap opera shown on many PBS stations, thoroughly integrates ethnic characters and families into its story lines.

In recent years, *telenovelas*, Spanish-speaking soaps such as "La Fuerza del Amor" ("The Force of Love"), "Destino" ("Destiny"), and "Muchachitas" ("Girls") from Latin America, have become increasingly popular in the Latino population. The content and messages of Latino soaps, however, do

Soap operas offer distinct visions of sexuality. Sexuality is portrayed as intense and inspires jealousy. Women are the primary audience. Why?

not differ significantly from soaps produced in the United States. They differ mainly in presenting fewer scenes suggestive of sexual activities, such as characters in bed (Raisbaum, 1986).

The most explicit nudity is seen on the soaps: frontal shots of nude male torsos (genitals are not shown) and back shots of nude female torsos (to avoid the taboo naked female breast). Characters lounge in bed, wrapped in sheets; they are either about to engage in sex or are basking in its pleasurable aftermath. At the same time, no one seems to use contraception or take measures to prevent sexually transmitted diseases (STDs). By the odds, one would expect many pregnancies and an epidemic of STDs (Lowry & Towles, 1989).

Although there is also intimacy in the world of soaps, it is intense, unstable, and desperate. Relationships are usually stormy and short-lived, setting the scene for jealousy and revenge in subsequent episodes. There is no satisfaction or fulfillment in most soap relationships.

Crime/Action-Adventure Programs In crime and action-adventure programs, there are few intimate relationships. Instead, relationships are fundamentally sexual, based on attraction. They are the backdrop to crime and adventure, which form the main plot of the story. The basic theme of a crime program is disorder (a crime) that must be resolved so that order can be restored. Often the disorder is caused by a sexual act or a sexually related issue, such as prostitution, pornography, rape, cross-dressing, sexual blackmail, or seduction for criminal purposes. As such, we see the underside of sex. Plots involve police searching for female killers who turn out to be cross-dressers, prostitutes who are murdered by sociopaths, runaways lured into pornography, and so on. Detectives and police go undercover, leading the audience into the underworld of prostitutes, pimps, and johns.

The detectives live remote, emotional lives. Their involvements are ephemeral, usually not lasting beyond a single episode. Often their love interests are murdered; other times, the women themselves prove to be criminals. Detectives are portrayed as loners. The only intimacy they may find is with their detective partners or with secretaries (Clark, 1992).

Made-for-TV Movies Made-for-TV movies focus on "problem" themes. In contrast to most series, TV movies revolve around more controversial topics. When plots center on sexuality, they generally focus on sex as a social issue rather than sex as intimacy. Their plots feature such issues as adolescent pregnancy, extramarital affairs, rape, sexual harassment, and AIDS. (TV movies about AIDS have introduced, for the first time, non-stereotypical gay and lesbian characters who display a fuller range of human emotions.) But because TV seeks to entertain rather than inform, most sexual topics lend easily to sensationalism, which TV often exploits.

TV movies in which rape occurs often place rape within the context of entertainment. Such movies may use gratuitous sexual aggression as a means of "hooking" an audience. In the process, these movies may distort the seriousness of rape (Wilson, 1988). Rape movies may present misleading stereotypes, such as a woman being sexually provocative, "deserving" to be raped, or "leading the man on." By using a certain type of music, they make rape seem titillating (Pfaus, Myronuk, & Jacobs, 1986). Although most rapists are known to the victim, TV films generally depict rapists as strangers. And although most rapes take place between members of the same ethnic group, rape movies on TV disproportionately depict African American men preying on white women (South & Felson, 1990; Wilson, 1988).

Music Videos: MTV and VH1 MTV, VH1, and music-video programs such as "Friday Night Videos" and "Night Track" are some of the most popular programs among adolescents and young adults. Most viewers, however, do not watch them for longer than 15 minutes at a time because the videos are repetitive.

Unlike audio-recorded music, music videos play upon the eye as well as the ear. Some productions, such as those of Michael Jackson and Madonna, are exceptionally artistic. Cindy Lauper's "Girls Just Want to Have Fun" was a breakthrough video with its affirmation of female freedom (Lewis, 1992). More recently, Madonna's blending of musical and visual components, especially dance, brings an erotic female presence to music videos.

Sexuality is an ever-present theme in rock and rap. What image are the Red Hot Chili Peppers communicating about themselves, their music, and their fans?

In fact, according to one critic, Madonna's videos represent powerful affirmations of female sexuality and power (Lewis, 1992; McClary, 1990).

But most videos are of average quality, relying on flashing visual images to sustain audience interest. Because TV prohibits the explicit depiction of sexual acts, music videos use sexual innuendos and suggestiveness to impart sexual meaning (Baxter et al., 1985; Sherman & Dominick, 1986). There is considerable aggression against both men and women. But contrary to popular images, in music videos women are more likely to initiate aggression against men (Kalis & Neuendorf, 1989). Women are often portrayed condescendingly; they are usually provocatively dressed. A study of 110 music videos aired on MTV revealed that 57% of the videos depicted women as sexual objects; another 17% showed women being "kept in place." Only 14% portrayed women as the equal of men (Vincent et al., 1987). In contrast to videos featuring whites, those featuring African Americans are more likely to depict blacks in caring roles (Brown & Campbell, 1986).

TV Commercials   Commercials form a unique genre of TV programming. Although they are not part of a television program per se, because they are inserted before, after, and during the program, they become a free-floating part of the program. In commercials, television advertisers may manipulate sexual images to sell products. The most sexually explicit commercials generally advertise jeans, beer, and perfume.

These commercials present a story told visually through a series of brief scenes or images. They do not pretend to explain the practical benefits of their product, such as cost or effectiveness. Instead, they offer the consumer an image or attitude. Directed especially toward adolescents and young adults, these commercials play upon fantasies of attractiveness, sexual success, and fun. The consumer will supposedly acquire these attributes as a result of using a particular product.

Other TV Genres   Sex is present in other TV genres, too. Game shows often play on sexual themes, either suggestively ("The Dating Game") or explicitly ("Studs"). Among the staples of daytime talk shows, such as "Donahue," "Oprah," "Sally Jesse Raphael," "Geraldo," and "Cristina," are unconventional guests and topics, such as women married to gay men or transsexuals, so-called sex addicts, and polygamists. Such talk shows use unconventional sexuality to provoke viewer interest. Although their prime purpose remains entertainment, talk shows can provide first-hand accounts of atypical sexual behavior that differs from the more common forms of sexual expression. These shows reveal the diversity of human sexuality, as well as give its participants a human face. As critic Walter Goodman (1992) observes: "They carry a gospel of tolerance, preaching openness for the unusual and encouraging greater acceptance of groups and behavior that have long been the objects of ignorance and fear." A few syndicated programs, such as Ruth (Dr. Ruth) Westheimer's "Good Sex," offer more thoughtful (though still entertaining) discussions of sexuality from a therapeutic perspective (Buxton, 1991).

News programs continuously report rapes, child sexual abuse, pornography, sex therapies, and opinion polls on sexuality. TV news magazines examine various sexual issues in more "depth" (i.e., they devote more time, not thought). Both types of news programs usually deal with atypical or controversial aspects of sexuality.

In addition to mainstream television broadcasting, religious television networks and programs have wide-scale appeal. Religious programming, such as "The 700 Club," broadcasts Christian fundamentalist visions of sex, sin, and morality (Shepard, 1989; Wills, 1989, 1990). These programs stress conservative family themes, such as adolescent chastity, opposition to sex education based on choice rather than abstinence, pro-life appeals, and homophobia. Of the most important televangelists during the 1980s, only Pat Robertson, who ran for the Republican presidential nomination in 1988, and Jerry Falwell remain active. The other powerful televangelists, Jim Bakker and Jimmy Swaggart, lost their ministries because of sexual improprieties.

Hollywood Films

American motion pictures follow different rules from those of television regarding sexuality. Movies generally are permitted greater license in graphically depicting sexual behavior. But films are still limited by censorship. Like television, films tend to depict sexual stereotypes and to adhere to mainstream sexual norms.

Mainstream Films From their very inception, motion pictures have dealt with sexuality. In 1896, a film entitled *The Kiss* outraged moral guardians when it showed a couple stealing a quick kiss. "Absolutely disgusting," complained one critic. "The performance comes near being indecent in its emphasized indecency. Such things call for police action" (quoted in Webb, 1983). Today, by contrast, film critics use "sexy," a word independent of artistic value, to praise a film. "Sexy" films are movies in which the requisite "sex scenes" are sufficiently titillating to overcome their lack of aesthetic merit. *Basic Instinct,* for example, was most noted for its "hot" sex scenes involving Sharon Stone, who subsequently achieved stardom based on her "sexiness" rather than her acting ability. Interestingly, sex scenes do not create equally famous male stars.

In Hollywood films of the 1990s, there is considerable female nudity, especially above the waist. But men are never filmed nude in the same manner as women. Men are generally clothed or partially covered; if they are fully nude, the scene takes place at night, the scene is blurred, or we see only his backside. Except on rare occasions, the penis is never visible; if it is visible, it is limp, not erect, according to one film director (Toback, 1992). In *Basic Instinct*, the director reported that the motion picture ratings board permitted him to show the penis of a murdered man "because it was dead" (Andrews, 1992). (In the more liberal European version of the film, however, a scene reveals Michael Douglas's penis in a frontal nude shot; the shot was cut for the American release.) A film psychologist notes: "People have gotten accustomed to wanting to see women nude. They don't think a nude woman looks vulnerable anymore. When a man is uncovered . . . the reaction is that he is extremely vulnerable" (Andrews, 1992).

Although there is more naked flesh, the old war-between-the-sexes theme continues with a significant variation. In today's film comedies and dramas, men pursue women and women resist, as they did before. What is new, however, is that the man's persistence awakens the woman's sexual desire. They fall in love, make love (or vice versa), and have passionate sex happily ever after. In these films, sex takes place outside of marriage (usually premaritally), reflecting the widespread acceptance of nonmarital intercourse. Such scenarios reflect traditional male/female stereotypes of the active man and passive woman. At the same time, however, they validate premarital sexual intercourse as a social norm.

Shots suggesting sexual intercourse and oral sex are commonplace in today's films. But scenes of sexual intercourse are generally filmed from a male perspective; the camera explores the woman's body and her reaction (Andrews, 1992). Even family-centered films have scenes intimating oral sex (such as *Parenthood* [1990], when Steve Martin's screen wife performs fellatio on him, causing a car crash). But other common forms of sexual behavior, such as masturbation, are virtually absent from contemporary films. Director Richard Benjamin's acting career came to a virtual halt after he played a comic masturbation scene in *Portnoy's Complaint* (1972).

In films, dangerous men and dangerous women are depicted differently. As film critic Jerome Weeks (1993) notes:

> Masculine menace on screen and stage is usually seen as a generalized threat: Anyone would fear this particular male because he's a master of violence or dangerously out of control. But if female performers are dangerous, they're dangerous only "to men." It's practically unheard of for a female character to be intimidating in any terms that are not sexual. If they're killers, they kill their husbands, lovers, or the patsies they need and therefore seduce.

Violence among men, however, is portrayed. The horrifying rape of the character Marselles in *Pulp Fiction* (1994) interweaves violence and aggression with sex. Only a few female stars, such as Linda Hamilton in *The Terminator* movies and Sigourney Weaver in the *Alien* movies, dispense violence with the ease of a Clint Eastwood, Arnold Schwartzenegger, or Jean-Claude van Damme.

Gay Men and Lesbians in Film
Gay men and lesbians are generally absent from mainstream films. When gay men and lesbians do appear, they are consistently defined in terms of their sexual orientation, as if there was nothing more to their lives than sexuality. Gay men are generally stereotyped as effeminate, flighty, or "arty." Lesbians are often stereotyped as humorless, mannish, or "butch." (The popular *Fried Green Tomatoes* [1992] muted the lesbian relationship between the central female characters found in the novel.)

If gay men and lesbians are not seen as effeminate or butch, they are portrayed as sinister beings. Their sexual orientation is symptomatic of a dangerous pathology. In *The Silence of the Lambs,* the best of the recent psychothrillers, the killer is a gay cross-dresser (Tharp, 1991). Film director Tom Kalin notes that films about obsessive love and murder between men and women, such as *Double Indemnity* (1944) and *Body Heat* (1981), never "argue that heterosexuals are inherently pathological, driven to crime by their sexuality" (Kalin, 1992). And one film critic (Weir, 1992) notes:

> In Hollywood movies, heterosexuals are never defined as evil or irrelevant simply *because* of their sexuality. Whether they act nobly or ignominiously, other aspects of their personalities are brought to bear. Gay men and lesbians, on the other hand, are consistently characterized solely in terms of their homosexuality—when they are depicted at all. What's more, in American movies, homosexuality seems invariably to signal that a character is either sinister or irrelevant.

Recently, gay and lesbian films have been increasingly integrating their characters' gayness into a wider focus. The poignant *Torch Song Trilogy* (1989), based on the Tony award-winning play about a gay female impersonator, and *Desert Hearts* (1986), an insightful love story about two women, are not as much films about being gay or lesbian as they are about being human. Foreign films, by contrast, often treat gay men and lesbians more realistically than American films do. *My Beautiful Laundrette* (1985), *Maurice* (1986), and *The Crying Game* (1992) all include gay themes, but

Gay men and lesbians are largely absent in Hollywood films, unless they are depicted stereotypically. In the novel Fried Green Tomatoes, *the love relationship between the two main women characters is depicted as a lesbian one. In the film, however, their love relationship was changed to a friendship. Why did Hollywood change the nature of their relationship? How would it have affected the story if the film had remained true to the novel?*

the films are not about homosexuality per se. Instead, they touch on universal themes, such as love, loyalty, and self-discovery. Film historian Vito Russo (1987) observed:

> The fact they are movies about self-identified gays often confuses people into thinking that they are films by gays about homosexuality. This confusion will end when gayness is no longer a controversial topic. As Quentin Crisp has said, "Homosexuality won't be accepted until it is completely seen as boring—a mundane, inconsequential part of everyday life."

There is no more need to identify *Desert Hearts* as being about lesbians than there is to identify *Pretty Woman* as being about heterosexuals.

SEXUALITY ACROSS CULTURES AND TIMES

What we have learned to call "natural" in our culture may be viewed as unnatural in other cultures. Few Americans would disagree about the erotic potential of kissing. But other cultures perceive kissing as the exchange of saliva. To the Mehinaku of the Amazonian rain forests, for example, "kiss-

The sensual movements of Latin American dancing have become popular in American culture, evidenced in films featuring the "Lambada," and by the thousands enrolled in Latin American dance classes. These dancers are celebrating their culture in a Latin American Heritage festival.

ing" is a disgusting sexual abnormality. No Mehinaku engages in it (Gregor, 1985). The fact that whites press their lips against each other, salivate, *and* become sexually excited merely confirms their "strangeness" to the Mehinaku.

Culture takes our **sexual impulses**—our incitements or inclinations to act sexually—and molds and shapes them, sometimes celebrating sexuality, other times condemning it. Sexuality can be viewed as a means of spiritual enlightenment, as in the Hindu tradition, where the gods themselves engage in sexual activities; or it can be at war with the divine, as in the Judeo-Christian tradition, where the flesh is the snare of the devil (Parrinder, 1980).

Among the variety of factors that shape how we feel and behave sexually, culture is the most powerful. A brief exploration of sexual themes across cultures and times will give you a sense of the diverse shapes and meanings human beings have given to sexuality.

sexual impulse An inclination to act sexually.

Sexual Impulse

All cultures assume that adults have the *potential* for becoming sexually aroused and for engaging in sexual intercourse for the purpose of reproduction (Davenport, 1987). But cultures differ considerably in terms of how strong they believe sexual impulses are. These beliefs, in turn, affect the level of desire expressed in each culture.

You and Your Sexual Well-Being

EXPLORING YOUR SEXUAL ATTITUDES

As you study human sexuality, you may find yourself reassessing or changing some of your attitudes or beliefs as a result of what you learn. To get a sense of how you change, answer the questions below on a separate sheet of paper. Save your responses. At the end of the course, answer the questions again and compare your responses. You may wish to copy and share this inventory with a trusted friend or partner.

The abridged Eysenck Inventory of Sexual Attitudes reprinted below has been widely used by researchers to study sexual attitudes. It will take 5–10 minutes to complete.

Read each statement carefully, then circle Yes or No, depending on your views. If you cannot decide, circle the question mark. There are no right or wrong answers. Don't think too long over each question; try to give an immediate answer that represents your feeling on each issue. Some questions are similar to others; there are good reasons for getting at the same attitude in slightly different ways.

1.	Members of the opposite sex will respect you more if you are not too familiar with them.	Yes	?	No
2.	Sex without love ("impersonal sex") is highly unsatisfactory.	Agree	?	Disagree
3.	Conditions have to be just right to get me excited sexually.	Yes	?	No
4.	All in all I am satisfied with my sex life.	Yes	?	No
5.	Virginity is a girl's most valuable possession.	Yes	?	No
6.	I think only rarely of sex.	Agree	?	Disagree
7.	Sometimes it has been a problem to control my sex feelings.	Yes	?	No
8.	Masturbation is unhealthy.	Yes	?	No
9.	If I love a person I could do anything with him or her.	Yes	?	No
10.	I get pleasant feelings from touching my sexual parts.	Yes	?	No
11.	I have been deprived sexually.	Yes	?	No
12.	I am sexually rather unattractive.	Yes	?	No
13.	Sex contacts have never been a problem to me.	True	?	False
14.	It is disturbing to see necking in public.	Yes	?	No
15.	Sexual feelings are sometimes unpleasant to me.	Yes	?	No
16.	Something is lacking in my sex life.	Yes	?	No
17.	My sexual behavior has never caused me any problems.	True	?	False
18.	My love life has been disappointing.	Yes	?	No
19.	I never had many dates.	True	?	False
20.	I consciously try to keep sexual thoughts out of my mind.	Yes	?	No
21.	It wouldn't bother me if the person I married were not a virgin.	True	?	False
22.	At times I have been afraid of myself for what I might do sexually.	Yes	?	No
23.	I have had conflicts about my sexual feelings toward a person of my own sex.	Yes	?	No
24.	I have many friends of the opposite sex.	Yes	?	No
25.	I have strong sex feelings, but when I get a chance I can't seem to express myself.	Yes	?	No
26.	My parents' influence has inhibited me sexually.	Yes	?	No
27.	People of my own sex frequently attract me.	Yes	?	No
28.	There are some things I would not want to do with anyone.	True	?	False
29.	Children should be taught about sex.	Yes	?	No
30.	I think about sex almost every day.	Yes	?	No

31.	I get excited sexually very easily.	Yes	?	No
32.	It is better not to have sexual relations until you are married.	True	?	False
33.	I like to look at sexy pictures.	Yes	?	No
34.	My conscience bothers me too much.	Yes	?	No
35.	My religious beliefs are against sex.	Yes	?	No
36.	Sometimes sexual feelings overpower me.	Yes	?	No
37.	I feel nervous with members of the opposite sex.	Yes	?	No
38.	When I get excited I can think of nothing else but satisfaction.	Yes	?	No
39.	I feel ill at ease with people of the opposite sex.	Yes	?	No
40.	It is hard to talk with people of the opposite sex.	Yes	?	No
41.	I feel more comfortable when I am with members of my own sex.	Yes	?	No
42.	I enjoy petting.	Yes	?	No
43.	I worry a lot about sex.	Yes	?	No
44.	Seeing a person nude doesn't interest me.	True	?	False
45.	Sometimes thinking about sex makes me very nervous.	Yes	?	No
46.	I am embarrassed to talk about sex.	Yes	?	No
47.	Young people should learn about sex through their own experience.	Yes	?	No
48.	A person should learn about sex gradually by experimenting with it.	Yes	?	No
49.	I have sometimes felt like humiliating my sex partner.	Yes	?	No
50.	(M) I get very excited when touching a woman's breast. (F) I get very excited when men touch my breasts.	Yes	?	No
51.	I have been involved with more than one sexual affair at the same time.	Yes	?	No
52.	Homosexuality is normal for some people.	Yes	?	No
53.	I have sometimes felt hostile toward my sex partner.	Yes	?	No
54.	I like to look at pictures of nudes.	Yes	?	No
55.	If I had a chance to see people making love, without being seen, I would like it.	Yes	?	No
56.	Prostitution should be legally permitted.	Yes	?	No
57.	Decisions about abortion should be the concern of no one but the woman concerned.	Yes	?	No
58.	The dual standard of morality, allowing men greater freedom, is natural, and should be continued.	Yes	?	No
59.	Sex is far and away my greatest pleasure.	Yes	?	No
60.	Sexual permissiveness threatens to undermine the entire foundation of civilized society.	Yes	?	No
61.	Sex should be used for the purpose of reproduction, not for personal pleasure.	True	?	False
62.	It is all right for children to see their parents naked.	Yes	?	No
63.	Women who get raped are partly responsible themselves.	Yes	?	No
64.	Buttocks excite me.	Yes	?	No
65.	Men marry to have intercourse; women have intercourse for the sake of marriage.	Yes	?	No

Source: Adapted from Eysenck, H. J. *Sex and Personality*. London: Open Books, 1976.

The Mangaia Among the Mangaia in Polynesia, both sexes, beginning in early adolescence, experience high levels of sexual desire (Marshall, 1971). Around age 13 or 14, following a circumcision ritual, boys are given instruction in the ways of pleasing a girl: erotic kissing, cunnilingus, breast fondling and sucking, and techniques for bringing a partner to multiple orgasm. After two weeks, an older, sexually experienced woman has sexual intercourse with the boy to instruct him further on how to sexually satisfy a woman. Girls the same age are instructed by older women on how to be orgasmic: how to thrust their hips and rhythmically move their vulvas in order to have multiple orgasms. A girl finally learns to be orgasmic through the efforts of a "good man." If the woman's partner fails to satisfy her, she is likely to leave him; she may also ruin his reputation with other women by denouncing his lack of skill. Young men and women are expected to have many sexual experiences prior to marriage.

This adolescent paradise, however, does not last forever. Mangaian culture believes sexuality is strongest during youth. As a result, when they leave young adulthood, youths experience a rapid decline in sexual desire and activity. They cease to be aroused as passionately as they once were. They attribute this swift decline to the workings of nature and settle into a sexually contented adulthood.

The Dani In contrast to the Mangaia, the New Guinean Dani show little interest in sexuality. To them, sex is a relatively unimportant aspect of life. The Dani express no concern about sexual techniques or enhancing erotic pleasure. Sexual affairs and jealousy are rare. As their only sexual concern is reproduction, sexual intercourse is performed quickly, ending with male orgasm. Female orgasm appears to be unknown to them. Following childbirth, both mothers and fathers go through five years of sexual abstinence. The Dani are an extreme example in which culture rather than biology shapes sexual impulses.

Victorian Americans In the nineteenth century, white middle-class Americans believed that women had little sexual desire. If they experienced desire at all, it was "reproductive desire," the wish to have children. Reproduction entailed the unfortunate "necessity" of engaging in sexual intercourse. A leading reformer (Alcott, 1868) wrote that in her "natural state" a woman never makes advances based on sexual desires, for the "very plain reason that she does not feel them." Those women who did feel desire were "a few exceptions amounting in all probability to diseased cases." Such women were classified by a prominent physician as suffering from "Nymphomania, or Furor Uterinus" (Bostwick, 1860).

Although women were viewed as asexual, men were believed to be driven by raging sexual appetites. Men, driven by lust, sought to satisfy their desires on innocent women. Both men and women believed that male sexuality was dangerous, uncontrolled, and animal-like. It was part of a woman's duty to tame unruly male sexual impulses.

The polar beliefs about the nature of male and female sexuality created destructive antagonisms between angelic women and demonic men. These beliefs provided the rationale for a "war between the sexes." They also led to the separation of sex from love. Intimacy and love had nothing to do with male sexuality. In fact, male lust always lingered in the background of married life, threatening to destroy love by its overbearing demands.

Although almost 100 years have passed since the end of the Victorian era, many Victorian sexual beliefs and attitudes continue to influence us. Some of these include the belief that men are "naturally" sexually aggressive and women sexually passive, the sexual double standard, and the value placed on women being sexually "inexperienced."

Sexual Orientation

Sexual orientation is the pattern of sexual and emotional attraction based on the gender of one's partner. **Heterosexuality** refers to sexual relationships between men and women. **Homosexuality** refers to same-sex sexual relationships. In contemporary American culture, heterosexuality is the only sexual orientation receiving full social legitimacy. Although same-sex relationships are relatively common, they do not receive general social acceptance. Many other cultures, however, view same-sex relationships as normal, acceptable, or preferable. Marriage between members of the same sex is recognized in 15 to 20 cultures throughout the world (Gregersen, 1986).

Ancient Greece In ancient Greece, the birthplace of European culture, the Greeks accepted same-sex relationships as naturally as Americans today

sexual orientation The pattern of sexual and emotional attraction based on the gender of one's partner.

heterosexuality Sexual orientation in which emotional and sexual attraction are directed toward members of the other sex.

homosexuality Sexual orientation in which emotional and sexual attraction are directed toward members of the same sex.

In ancient Greece, the highest form of love was that expressed between males.

accept heterosexuality. For the Greeks, same-sex relationships between men represented the highest form of love.

The male-male relationship was based on love and reciprocity; sexuality was only one component of it. In this relationship, the code of conduct called for the older man to initiate the relationship. The youth initially resisted; only after the older man courted the young man with gifts and words of love would the youth reciprocate. The two men formed a close, emotional bond. The older man was also the youth's mentor as well as his lover. He introduced the youth to men who would be useful for his advancement later; he assisted him in learning his duties as a citizen. As the youth entered adulthood, the erotic bond between the two evolved into a deep friendship. After the youth became an adult, he married a woman and later initiated a relationship with an adolescent boy.

Greek male-male relationships, however, were not substitutes for male-female marriage. The Greeks discouraged exclusive male-male relationships because marriage and children were required to continue the family. Men regarded their wives primarily as domestics and the bearers of children (Keuls, 1985). (The Greek word for woman, *gyne,* literally translates as "childbearer.") Husbands did not turn to their wives for sexual pleasure but to *hetaerae (hi-TIR-ee),* highly regarded courtesans who were usually educated slaves.

The Sambians of New Guinea Among Sambian males of New Guinea, sexual orientation is very malleable (Herdt, 1987). Young boys begin sexual activities with older boys, move to sexual activities with both sexes during adolescence, and engage in exclusively male-female activities in adulthood. Sambians believe that a boy can grow into a man only by the ingestion of semen, which is, they say, like mother's milk. At age 7 or 8, boys begin their sexual activities with older boys; as they get older, they seek multiple partners to accelerate their growth into manhood. At adolescence, their role changes, and they must provide semen to boys to enable them to develop. At first they worry about their own loss of semen, but they are taught to drink tree sap, which magically replenishes their semen. During adolescence, boys are betrothed to preadolescent girls with whom they engage in sexual activities. When the girls mature, the boys give up their sexual involvement with other males. They become fully involved with adult women, losing their desire for men. They become sexually interested only in women from then on.

Gender

gender The social and cultural characteristics associated with being male or female.

Although sexual impulses and orientation may be influenced by culture, it is difficult to imagine that culture has anything to do with **gender,** the characteristics associated with being male or female. There are, after all, only two sexes: male and female. These appear solidly rooted in our biological nature. But is being male or female *really* biological? The answer is yes *and* no. Having male or female genitalia is anatomical. But the possession of a penis does not *always* make a person a man, nor does the possession of a vulva and vagina *always* make a person a woman. Men who consider themselves women, "women with penises," are accepted or honored in many cultures throughout the world (Bullough, 1991).

Transsexuals Within the United States there are approximately 15,000 **transsexuals,** people whose genitalia and identities as men or women are discordant. In transsexuality, a person with a penis, for example, identifies as a woman, or a person with a vulva and vagina identifies as a man. In the psychiatric literature, transsexuals are considered psychologically impaired.

In order to make their genitalia congruent with their gender identity, many transsexuals have their genitalia surgically altered. If being male or female depends on genitalia, then postsurgical transsexuals have changed their sex—men have become women and women have become men. But defining sex in terms of genitalia presents problems, as has been shown in the world of sports. In the 1970s, Renee Richards, whose genitalia had been surgically transformed from male to female, began competing on the women's professional tennis circuit. Protests began immediately. Although Ms. Richards's genitalia were female, her body and musculature were male. Despite the surgery, she remained genetically male because her sex chromosomes were male. Her critics insisted that genetics, not genitalia, defined one's sex; anatomy could be changed, but chromosomes could not. Richards, however, maintained that she was a woman by any common definition of the word. (Issues of sex, gender, and biology are discussed in Chapter 5.)

Two-Spirit Most Americans consider transsexuality problematical at best. But this is not necessarily true in all cultures. In some cultures, an anatomical man identifying as a woman might be considered a "man-woman" and accorded high status and special privileges. He would be identified as a two-spirit. A **two-spirit** is a man who assumes female dress, gender role, and status. Two-spirit is regarded as a third gender (Callendar et al., 1983). It is neither transsexuality, transvestism (wearing the clothes, or passing as a member, of the other sex), nor a form of same-sex relationship (Callendar & Kochems, 1985; Forgey, 1975; Roscoe, 1991). Two-spirit is found in numerous cultures throughout the world, including Native American, Filipino, Lapp, and East Indian cultures. It is almost always men who become two-spirits, although there are a few cases of women assuming male roles in a similar fashion (Blackwood, 1984). Two-spirits are often considered shamans, individuals who possess great spiritual power.

Among the Zuni of New Mexico, two-spirits are considered a third sex (Roscoe, 1991). Despite the existence of transsexuals and pseudohermaphrodites, Western beliefs about gender focus on gender as biological. The Zuni, by contrast, believe that gender is socially acquired.

Two-spirits were suppressed by missionaries and the government as "unnatural" or "perverts." Their ruthless repression led anthropologists to believe that two-spirits had been driven out of existence in Native American cultures. But there is evidence that two-spirits continue to hold ceremonial and social roles in some tribes, such as the Lakota Sioux. Understandably, two-spirit activities are kept secret from outsiders for fear of reprisals (Williams, 1985). Among gay and lesbian Native Americans, the two-spirit provides historical continuity with their traditions (Roscoe, 1991).

transsexual A person whose genitals and gender identity as male or female are discordant.

two-spirit In many cultures, a male who assumes female dress, gender role, and status.

In some cultures, men who dress or identify as women are considered shamans. We'wha was a Zuni man-woman who lived in the nineteenth century.

SOCIETAL NORMS AND SEXUALITY

The immense diversity across cultures and times immediately calls into question the appropriateness of labeling sexual behaviors as *inherently* natural or unnatural, normal or abnormal. Too often we give such labels to sexual behaviors without thinking about the basis on which we make those judgments. Such categories discourage knowledge and understanding because they are value judgments, evaluations of right and wrong. As such, they are not objective descriptions about behaviors but statements of how we feel about those behaviors.

Natural Sex

How do we decide if a sexual behavior is natural or unnatural? To make this decision, we must have some standard of nature against which to compare the behavior. But what is "nature"? On the abstract level, nature is the essence of all things in the universe. Or, personified as Nature, it is the force regulating the universe. These definitions, however, do not give us much information for deciding what is natural or unnatural.

When we asked our students to identify their criteria for determining which sexual behaviors they considered "natural" or "unnatural," there was a variety of responses. These included the following:

> If a person feels something instinctive, I believe it is a natural feeling.

> Natural and unnatural have to do with the laws of nature. What these parts were intended for.

> I decide by my gut instincts.

> I think all sexual activity is natural as long as it doesn't hurt yourself or anyone else.

> Everything possible is natural. Everything natural is normal. If it is natural and normal, it is moral.

When we label sexual behavior as "natural" or "unnatural," we are actually indicating whether the behavior conforms to our culture's sexual norms. Our sexual norms appear natural because we have internalized them since infancy. These norms are part of the cultural air we breathe, and, like the air, they are invisible. We have learned our culture's rules so well that they have become a "natural" part of our personality, a "second nature" to us. They seem "instinctive."

Normal Sex

Closely related to the idea that sexual behavior is natural or unnatural is the belief that sexuality is either normal or abnormal. More often than not, describing behavior as "normal" or "abnormal" is merely another way of making value judgments. Although "normal" has often been used to imply "healthy" or "moral" behavior, among social scientists it is used strictly as

HUMAN SEXUALITY: IT'S MORE THAN PLUMBING

Think back to the first time you learned about sex. Who was doing the teaching and what was said? How old were you? How accurate and thorough was the information? How did you feel as a result of what you learned?

If you are typical of most Americans, you probably obtained your earliest information from a friend, and only much later—if at all—received formal education, probably about anatomy and physiology, sexually transmitted diseases, and sexual decision making. You may also remember discussions of dating, marriage and parenthood, and sexual abstinence (de Mauro, 1990; Forrest & Silverman, 1989; Sonenstein & Pittman, 1984). But you probably didn't hear much about homosexuality, masturbation, birth control, abortion, or a host of other topics.

Less than 10% of American children receive comprehensive sexuality education from kindergarten through adulthood. Most notably absent in the typical sex education curriculum are discussions of the social, psychological, and spiritual components of sexuality. These are the very components that contribute the most to the acceptance of oneself as a sexual being and to the understanding of others.

The physical aspects of human sexuality are the least open to debate. They are also the least complicated and the ones with which we are most familiar: "I am female because I have a vagina," "I am male because I have a penis."

Discussions become more complex and subjective when we ask the question, What is normal? Normality is something determined by society: Society defines how "normal" people express their sexual feelings. Religious and cultural influences come into play here, too, as we consider who does what with whom, under what circumstances, and for what reasons. At this level of discussion, topics in sexuality become controversial and subject to debate.

The psychological aspects of sexuality include feelings, values, needs, expectations, beliefs, and ideas about sex. How we view ourselves and our relationships, what we value, and what we wish to communicate to the world all contribute to our sexual self-image. The sexual self is both personal and public; it is dynamic and subject to change; and it is probably, along with the spiritual component, at the core of our sexual behavior and expression.

In order to understand, apply, and evaluate human sexuality, we must explore each of these components. This means addressing topics that are controversial and open to varying interpretations and opinions. It means looking at different ideas and beliefs about sex within the context of individual value systems. And it means making personal decisions and choices about sex based on a thorough understanding of our own background, expectations, and values. A full appreciation of human sexuality is built on this multidimensional foundation.

---

a statistical term. For them, **normal sexual behavior** is behavior that conforms to a group's average or median patterns of behavior. Normality has nothing to do with moral or psychological deviance.

Ironically, although we may feel pressure to behave like the average person (the statistical norm), most of us don't actually know how others behave sexually. People don't ordinarily reveal much about their sexual activities. If they do, they generally reveal only their most conformist sexual behaviors, such as sexual intercourse. They rarely disclose their masturbatory activities, their sexual fantasies, their anxieties or feelings of guilt.

normal sexual behavior Behavior that conforms to a group's average or median patterns of behavior.

Kissing is "natural" and "normal" in our culture. It is an expression of intimacy, love, and passion for young and old, heterosexuals, gay men, and lesbians.

All that most people present of themselves—unless you know them well—is the conventional self that masks their actual sexual feelings, attitudes, and behaviors.

The only guidelines most of us have for determining our normality are given to us by our friends, partners, and parents (who usually present conventional sexual images of themselves) through stereotypes, media images, religious teachings, customs, and cultural norms. None of these, however,

AM I NORMAL?

The question Am I normal? seems to haunt many people. For some, it causes a great deal of unnecessary fear, guilt, and anxiety. For others, it provides the motivation to study the literature, consult with a trusted friend or therapist, or take a course in sexuality.

What is normal? We commonly use several criteria in deciding whether to label different sexual behaviors "normal" or "abnormal." These criteria are conventional, biological, psychological, and moral. Regardless of what criteria we use, they ultimately reflect societal norms.

• *Conventionally "normal" behavior.* People engage in certain forms of sexual behavior more than others because cultural norms, customs, and laws encourage them to do so. The fact that a behavior is not widely practiced does not make it abnormal except in a statistical sense. **Fellatio** (fel-AY-she-o) (oral stimulation of the penis) and **cunnilingus** (cun-i-LIN-gus) (oral stimulation of the female genitalia), for example, are widely practiced today because they have become "acceptable" behaviors. But a generation ago, oral sex was tabooed as something "dirty" or "shameful." As a result, only a minority engaged in it (Kinsey, Pomeroy, & Martin, 1948; Kinsey, Pomeroy, Martin, & Gebhard, 1953; Rubin, 1990; Simon & Gagnon, 1986).

• *Biologically "normal" behavior.* Human beings have sexual impulses that are rooted in our biological makeup. But simply having sexual impulses does not mean that these impulses have to be expressed through a specific type of behavior. The idea that the "natural" purpose of sex is reproduction reflects religious dogma rather than biology. If our sexuality could only be expressed legitimately in sexual intercourse, erotic kissing would be considered biologically abnormal. For men and women alike, sexual intercourse with a woman who has gone through menopause would similarly be considered abnormal because conception is not possible. When it comes to specific behaviors, what is biologically normal is what culture defines as normal.

• *Psychologically "normal" behavior.* Sexual behavior that enhances our satisfaction or sense of psychological well-being is often identified as normal or healthy. Behavior that creates feelings of guilt, shame, anxiety, tension, or frustration is often regarded as abnormal. But such "psychologically healthy" sexual behavior makes us feel good because we have learned to feel satisfied when we act in socially approved ways. If we feel guilty about masturbating, it is because we have been taught to feel guilty about masturbation, not because masturbation is intrinsically unhealthy.

• *Morally "normal" behavior.* If "normal" sexual behavior is "moral" sexual behavior, the morality of any act depends on *whose* morality we choose to use—yours, mine, or someone else's. Morality is culturally relative; there are no universal moral absolutes regarding sexuality. Even within contemporary Judeo-Christian traditions, unanimity about sexual matters does not exist. Catholics, for example, condemn birth control as a sin, while Protestants do not. Many American religious groups regard same-sex relations as sinful, while some Lutheran churches and Reformed Jewish synagogues ordain gay men and lesbians as ministers or rabbis. All find justification for their beliefs in their scriptures but interpret the passages differently; they emphasize some passages and ignore others.

These four criteria form the basis of what we usually consider normal behavior. Often the different interpretations of "normal" conflict with each other. How does a person determine whether he or she is normal if conventionally "normal" behavior, such as oral sex, is condemned as immoral by one's religion? Such dilemmas are commonplace and lead many people to question their normality. However, they should not question, their normality as much as their *concept* of normality.

---

fellatio   Oral stimulation of the penis.

cunnilingus   Oral stimulation of the female genitals.

tells you much about how people *actually* behave. Because we don't know how people really behave, it is easy for us to imagine that we are abnormal if we differ from our cultural norms and stereotypes. We wonder if our desires, fantasies, and activities are normal: Is it normal to fantasize? To masturbate? To enjoy erotica? To be attracted to someone of the same sex? Some of us believe that everyone else is "normal" and that only we are "sick" or "abnormal."

Because culture determines what is normal, there is a vast range of normal behaviors across different cultures. What is considered the normal sexual urge for the Dani would send most of us into therapy for treatment of low sexual desire. And the idea of teaching sexual skills to early adolescents, as the Mangaia do, would horrify most American parents.

Typical and Atypical Sexual Behavior

Sex researchers have generally rejected the traditional sexual dichotomies of natural/unnatural, normal/abnormal, moral/immoral, and good/bad. Regarding the word "abnormal," Ira Reiss (1989) writes:

> We need to be aware that people will use those labels to put distance between themselves and others they dislike. In doing so, these people are not making a scientific diagnosis but are simply affirming their support of certain shared concepts of proper sexuality.

Instead of classifying behavior into what are essentially moralistic normal/abnormal and natural/unnatural categories, researchers view human sexuality as characterized by **sexual variation**—that is, sexual variety and diversity. As human beings, we vary enormously in terms of our sexual orientation, our desires, our fantasies, our attitudes, and our behaviors. Kinsey (1948) succinctly stated the matter like this: "The world is not to be divided into sheep and goats."

To understand our sexual diversity, researchers believe that the best way to examine sexual behavior is to view our activities as existing on a continuum. On this continuum, the frequency with which individuals engage in different sexual activities, such as sexual intercourse, masturbation, and oral sex, ranges from "Never" to "Always." Significantly, there is no point on the continuum that marks normal or abnormal behavior. In fact, the difference between one individual and the next on the continuum is minimal (Kinsey et al., 1948, 1953). The most that can be said of a person is that his or her behaviors are more or less typical or atypical of the group average. Furthermore, nothing can be inferred about an individual whose behavior differs significantly from the group average except that his or her behavior is atypical. The individual who differs is not sick, abnormal, or perverse; rather, he or she is a sexual nonconformist (Reiss, 1986, 1989). Except for engaging in sexually atypical behavior, a person may be indistinguishable from any other person.

Many activities that are usually thought of as **deviant sexual behavior**—activities diverging from the norm, such as exhibitionism, voyeurism, and fetishism—exist in most of us to some degree or another. We may delight in displaying our bodies on the beach or in "dirty dancing" in crowded clubs (exhibitionism). We may like watching ourselves make love, viewing erotic videos, or seeing our partner undress (voyeurism). Or we may enjoy kissing

sexual variation Sexual variety and diversity in terms of sexual orientation, attitudes, behaviors, desires, fantasies, and so on.

deviant sexual behavior Sexual behavior that diverges from the norm.

our lover's photograph, keeping a lock of hair, or sleeping with an article of his or her clothing (fetishism). Most of the time these feelings or activities are only one aspect of our sexual selves; they are not especially significant in our overall sexuality. Such atypical behaviors represent nothing more than sexual nonconformity when they occur between mutually consenting adults and do not cause distress (Reiss, 1989).

The rejection of natural/unnatural, normal/abnormal, and moral/immoral categories by sex researchers does not mean that standards for evaluating sexual behavior do not exist. There are many sexual behaviors that are harmful to oneself (e.g., masturbatory asphyxia, suffocating or hanging oneself during masturbation to increase sexual arousal) and to others (e.g., rape, child molestation, exhibitionism, and obscene phone calling). Current psychological standards for determining the harmfulness of sexual behaviors center around the issues of coercion, grave potential for inflicting harm on oneself or others, or personal distress. (These issues are discussed in greater detail in Chapter 10.)

As social scientists, the role of sex researchers is to *describe* sexual behavior, not evaluate it as good or bad, moral or immoral. It is up to the individual to evaluate the ethical or moral aspect of sexual behavior in accordance with his or her ethical or religious values. At the same time, however, understanding diverse sexual attitudes, motives, behaviors, and values will help deepen the individual's own value system.

Popular culture both encourages and discourages sexuality. It promotes stereotypical sexual interactions between men and women that fail to touch on the deeper significance sexuality holds for us. Marital love and sexuality are infrequently depicted in contrast to casual or nonmarital sex. (By ignoring marital sex, popular culture implies that marriage is a sexual wasteland. Yet it is within marriage that the overwhelming majority of sexual interactions between men and women takes place.) The media ignore or disparage the wide array of sexual behaviors and choices, from masturbation to gay and lesbian relationships, that are significant in many people's lives. It discourages the linking of sex and intimacy, contraceptive responsibility, and the acknowledgment of STD risks.

What is clear from examining other cultures is that sexual behaviors and norms vary from culture to culture and, within our own society, from one time to another. The variety of sexual behaviors even within our own culture testifies to diversity not only between cultures but within cultures as well. Understanding diversity allows us to acknowledge that there is no such thing as inherently "normal" or "natural" sexual behavior. Rather, sexual behavior is strongly influenced by culture—including our own.

SUMMARY

Sexuality, Popular Culture, and the Media

• Popular culture, especially the media, strongly influences our sexuality through the depiction of sexual stereotypes and norms. Mainstream media do not explicitly depict sexual behavior.

• Each television genre depicts sexuality according to its formula. Situation comedies focus on the violation of minor taboos centering on marital and family issues. Soap operas deal with sexual transgressions, jealousy, and power linked to sex. Crime/action-adventure programs depict relationships that are based on attraction and are short-lived; detective heroes form close relationships primarily with their detective partners or secretaries. Made-for-TV movies focus on "problem" themes, such as rape or adolescent pregnancy. Music videos rely on suggestiveness and innuendo to depict sexuality; women are usually portrayed as sex objects. TV commercials may promote a product by suggesting that consuming the product will lead to attractiveness or sexual success.

• Although Hollywood films depict sexual behavior more graphically than television does, sex scenes are often gratuitous. Sexuality tends to be stereotypical. Gay men and lesbians have generally been absent from films except in stereotypical roles. More recently, a few non-stereotypical gay and lesbian characters have been introduced.

Sexuality Across Cultures and Times

• The most powerful force shaping human sexuality is culture. Culture molds and shapes our sexual impulses.

• The Mangaia of Polynesia and the Dani of New Guinea represent cultures at the opposite ends of a continuum, with the Mangaia having an elaborate social and cultural framework for instructing adolescents in sexual technique and the Dani downplaying the importance of sex.

• Middle-class Americans in the nineteenth century believed that men had strong sexual drives while women had little sexual desire. Because sexuality was considered animalistic, the Victorians separated sex and love.

• In ancient Greece, same-sex relationships between men represented the highest form of love. Among the Sambians of New Guinea, boys have sexual relations with older boys, believing that the ingestion of semen is required for growth. When the girls to whom they are betrothed reach puberty, adolescent boys cease sexual relations with other boys.

• A transsexual has the genitalia of one sex but identifies as a member of the other sex. A pseudohermaphrodite may identify as one sex with the genitalia of that sex but has the chromosomes of the other sex. In our culture, transsexuality is considered a psychological disorder, but such individuals may be highly regarded in other cultures.

• A two-spirit is a person of one sex who identifies with the other sex; in some cultures, such as the Zuni, a two-spirit is considered a third gender and is believed to possess great spiritual power.

Societal Norms and Sexuality

• Sexuality tends to be evaluated according to categories of natural/unnatural, normal/abnormal, and moral/immoral. These terms are value judgments, reflecting social norms rather than any quality inherent in the behavior itself.

• There is no commonly accepted definition of natural sexual behavior. Normal sexual behavior is what a culture defines as normal. We commonly use four criteria to categorize sexual behavior as normal or abnormal: conventionally normal, biologically normal, psychologically normal, and morally normal.

• Human sexuality is characterized by sexual variation. Researchers believe that the best way to examine sexual behavior is by using a continuum. On the continuum, the frequency with which people engage in different sexual activities ranges from "Never" to "Always." Most people fall somewhere in between these two extremes. Many activities that are considered deviant sexual behavior exist in most of us to some degree or another. These include exhibitionism, voyeurism, and fetishism.

• Behaviors are not abnormal or unnatural; rather they are more or less typical or atypical of the group average. Those whose behaviors are atypical may be regarded as sexual nonconformists rather than abnormal or perverse.

SUGGESTED READINGS

Bullough, Vern. *Sexual Variance in Society and History*. New York: Wiley, 1976. A thorough examination of attitudes toward sexuality in Western and non-Western cultures.

Chapple, Steve, and David Talbot. *Burning Desires: Sex in America. A Report from the Field*. New York: Doubleday, 1989. An entertaining and informative work on contemporary sexuality and popular culture by two journalists.

D'Emilio, John, and Estelle Freedman. *Intimate Matters: A History of Sexuality in America*. New York: Harper & Row, 1988. An important study of American sexuality, especially in the nineteenth century.

Suggs, David N., and Andrew Miracle, eds. *Culture and Human Sexuality*. Pacific Grove, CA: Brooks/Cole, 1993. A collection of essays on sexuality in diverse cultures throughout the world.

Chapter Two

STUDYING HUMAN SEXUALITY

PREVIEW: SELF-QUIZ

1. "College students should engage in premarital sexual intercourse to gain experience" is an example of a value judgment. True or false?

2. Attitudes accurately predict behaviors. True or false?

3. Research on the role of ethnicity has been generally limited to problem areas, such as adolescent pregnancy. True or false?

4. Because of ethical considerations, it is impossible to conduct experimental studies in human sexuality. True or false?

5. Sexual stereotypes usually reflect positive images of men and women. True or false?

6. The sexual values of inner-city and middle-class African Americans are quite similar. True or false?

7. "Latino men are macho" is an example of a stereotypical statement. True or false?

8. Because they place a high value on children, African Americans of all classes tend to believe there is no such thing as an "illegitimate" or "illegally born" child. True or false?

9. Since the turn of the century, the most influential sex researchers have considered masturbation normal. True or false?

10. Gay and lesbian studies tend to focus on the causes of homosexuality. True or false?

ANSWERS 1. T, 2. F, 3. T, 4. F, 5. F, 6. F, 7. T, 8. T, 9. T, 10. F

Chapter Outline

An important discovery about orgasm was announced today by Harvard researchers. . . . But first, a message from. . . ." So begins a commercial lead-in on the ten o'clock news report, reminding us that sex research is often part of both news and entertainment. In fact, most of us learn about the results of sex research from TV and magazines rather than from scholarly journals and books. After all, the mass media are more entertaining than most scholarly research. And unless we are studying human sexuality, few of us have the time to read the scholarly journals in which scientific research is regularly published.

But how accurate is what the mass media tell us about sex and sex research? In this chapter, we discuss the dissemination of sex information by the various media. Then we look at the critical-thinking skills that help us evaluate how we discuss and think about sexuality. When are we making objective statements? When are we reflecting biases or opinions? Next, we examine sex research methods, as they are critical to the scientific study of human sexuality. Then, we look at the leading sex researchers to see how they have influenced our understanding of sexuality. Finally, we examine feminist, gay/lesbian, and ethnic sex research to see how they enrich our knowledge of sexuality.

SEX, ADVICE COLUMNISTS, AND POP PSYCHOLOGY

As we saw in Chapter 1, the mass media convey seemingly endless sexual images. But in addition to the various television, film, and advertising genres, there is another genre that we might call the sex information/advice genre, which transmits *information* rather than images. The **sex information/ advice genre** is a media genre that transmits information and norms about sexuality to a mass audience to both inform and entertain in a simplified manner. For most college students, as well as many others, the sex information/advice genre is a major source of their sexual knowledge (Moffatt, 1989).

A veritable industry exists to support the sex information/advice genre. It produces sex manuals, self-help books, advice columns, radio and television shows, as well as numerous articles in magazines and newspapers. Sex information comes in torrents. But what do we really learn about sexuality from the sex information/advice genre?

This genre is ostensibly concerned with transmitting information that is factual and accurate. In newspapers, it is represented by such popular national columnists as Abigail Van Buren (whose column "Dear Abby" is now written by a man), Ann Landers, Beth Winship, and Pat Califia. Sexual self-help and pop sex books written by "experts" frequent the best-seller lists, ranging from David Reuben's *Everything You Ever Wanted to Know About Sex—But Were Afraid to Ask* (1969) to Naura Hayden's recent *How to Satisfy a Woman Every Time* (1991). On radio and television, Ruth Westheimer, a professional therapist, has hosted shows dispensing sex information and advice.

Newspaper columns, magazine articles, and TV programs share several features. First, their primary purpose is to sell newspapers and magazines or to raise program ratings. This goal is in marked contrast to scholarly research, whose primary purpose is to pursue knowledge. Even the inclusion of survey questionnaires in magazines asking readers to respond about their sexual attitudes or behaviors is ultimately designed to promote sales. We fill out the questionnaires for fun, much as we would crossword puzzles or anagrams. Then we buy the subsequent issue or watch a later program to see how we compare to others.

Second, the media must entertain while disseminating information about sexuality. The success of media personalities such as Ruth Westheimer does not rest as much on their expertise as it does on their ability to present information as entertainment (Buxton, 1991). Because the genre seeks to entertain, sex information and advice must be simplified. Complex explanations and analyses must be avoided because they would interfere with the entertainment purpose. Furthermore, the genre relies on high-interest or

Popular advice columnists and sex experts, such as Dr. Ruth, dispense information while they entertain.

sex information/advice genre
A media genre that transmits information and norms about sexuality to a mass audience.

bizarre material to attract readers or viewers. Consequently, we are more likely to read or view stories about increasing sexual attractiveness or unusual sexual practices than stories about new research methods or the process of sexual stereotyping.

Third, the genre focuses on how-to information or on morality. The how-to material advises us on how to improve our sex lives. Westheimer's book, *Dr. Ruth's Guide to Good Sex* (1988), for example, advises its readers on oral sex:

> Not everybody has to be engaging in oral sex. So after saying that, if your husband likes it a lot and really craves for that, then one of the ways you might try . . . eat an ice-cream cone. . . . Then when you do perform oral sex, think of that ice-cream cone. Don't tell your husband. Just put an ice-cream cone in your head.

Advice columnists often give advice on issues of sexual morality. "Is it all right to have sex without commitment?" "Yes, if you love him/her" or "No, casual sex is empty," and so on. Advice columnists act as moral arbiters, much as ministers, priests, and rabbis.

The line between media sex experts and advice columnists is often blurred. Ruth Westheimer, for example, mixes information and normative judgments. In her discussion of oral sex and ice cream cones, for example, not only does Westheimer suggest ways to engage in oral sex, she also implies two contradictory norms: (1) Oral sex is a matter of individual choice, and (2) a woman should do what a man wants. The use of the word "good" in the title of her book (as well as in her radio and television programs) is significant. "Good" can be interpreted in two ways: good as sexually satisfying or good as virtuous.

Fourth, the genre uses the trappings of social science and psychiatry without their substance. Writers and columnists interview social scientists and therapists to give an aura of scientific authority to their material. They rely especially heavily on therapists whose background is clinical rather than academic. Because clinicians tend to deal with people with problems, they often see sexuality as problematical.

In order to reinforce their authority, the media also incorporate statistics, which are key features of social science research. But as Susan Faludi (1991) notes:

HOW TO EVALUATE SEX INFORMATION

With the media awash with sex information and advice, how can we evaluate what is presented to us? Here are some important guidelines:

- *Be skeptical.* Remember, much of what you read or see is meant is to entertain you. If it seems superficial, it probably is.

- *Search for biases, stereotypes, and lack of objectivity.* Information is often distorted by points of view. Is there any reason to suspect bias in the selection of subjects? What conflicting information may have been omitted? How are women and ethnicity portrayed?

- *Look for moralizing.* Many times what passes as fact is really disguised moral judgment. What are the underlying values of the article or program?

- *Go to the original source or sources.* The media always simplify. Find out for yourself what the studies really reported. What were the backgrounds and credentials of the persons or organizations who conducted the research? How large were the samples? How valid were the methodologies used in the studies? What were their strengths and limitations?

- *Seek additional information.* The whole story is probably not told. Look for additional information in scholarly books and journals, reference books, or textbooks.

Keeping questions like these in mind will help you steer a course between blind acceptance and offhand dismissal of a given research study.

The statistics that the popular culture chooses to promote most heavily are the very statistics we should view with the most caution. They may well be in wide circulation not because they are true but because they support widely held media preconceptions.

Even such renowned sex researchers as William Masters and Virginia Johnson could sometimes be guilty of "statistical excess." Without a shred of evidence, for example, they made the oft-quoted claim that "half of American marriages are sexual disaster areas" (Masters & Johnson, 1974). The media unquestioningly repeated this statistic for years because it reinforced the popular conception that sex and marriage don't mix. In the 1980s, the media also popularized the G-spot, a supposedly highly erotic area within the vagina, supported by questionable scientific evidence. The media publicized the G-spot as an incontrovertible fact, while its existence and significance continue to be disputed among sex researchers (Tavris, 1992). (The G-spot is discussed further in Chapter 3.) A few years later, the media promoted the idea of an infertility "epidemic" occurring because women delayed childbearing until their thirties. Although there was an increase in infertility, it was due not as much to aging as to STDs going undetected and untreated (Faludi, 1991).

The media frequently quote or describe social science research, but they may do so in an oversimplified or distorted manner. Scholars tend to qualify their findings as tentative or limited to a certain group. They are very cautious about making generalizations. By contrast, the media tend to make results sound more certain and generalizable. The media may report, for example, a study finding that premarital sexual intercourse generally results in feelings of guilt, although a later study finds no relationship between the two. On what basis do you decide which study to believe? Many of us think all studies are equal, that one is as good as another as long as they are conducted by experts who presumably know what they are doing. But all studies are not necessarily comparable or equally well done. One study may have drawn its sample from the fundamentalist Bob Jones University, while the other drew its sample from the more liberal Harvard University. In one case, information may have been drawn from a clinical study of students being treated for depression, while the other may have been based on a cross section of nondepressed students. Often such critical information about studies is missing in media research accounts.

THINKING (CRITICALLY) ABOUT SEX

Although each of us has his or her own perspective, values, and beliefs regarding sexuality, as students, instructors, and researchers, we are committed to the scientific study of sexuality. Basic to any scientific study is a fundamental commitment to **objectivity,** the observation of things as they exist in reality as opposed to our feelings or beliefs about them. Objectivity calls for us to suspend the beliefs, biases, or prejudices we have about a subject in order to understand it (Reiss, 1980).

objectivity The observation of things as they exist in reality as opposed to our feelings or beliefs about them.

Objectivity is not always easy, for sexuality is the focal point of powerful emotions, moral ambivalence, anxiety, and fear. We experience sex very subjectively. But whether we find it easy or difficult to be objective, objectivity is the prerequisite for studying sexuality.

Most of us think about sex, but thinking about it critically requires us to think with logic and objectivity. We make common errors when discussing sexuality that inhibit our understanding and comprehension. Some of these mistakes are discussed in the following sections.

Value Judgments Versus Objectivity

For many of us, objectivity about sex is difficult because our culture has traditionally viewed sexuality in moral terms: Sex is moral or immoral, right or wrong, good or bad. When examining sexuality, we tend, therefore, to make **value judgments,** evaluations based on moral or ethical standards rather than objective ones. Unfortunately, value judgments are often blinders to understanding. They do not tell us about motivations, how frequently a behavior is practiced, or how its participants feel. Value judgments do not tell us anything about sexuality except how we ourselves feel. In studying human sexuality, then, we need to put aside value judgments as incompatible with the pursuit of knowledge.

value judgment An evaluation as "good" or "bad" based on moral or ethical standards rather than objective ones.

How does one tell the difference between a value judgment and an objective statement? Examine the following two statements. Which is a value judgment? Which is an objective statement?

1. College students should not engage in premarital sexual intercourse.

2. The majority of students engage in premarital sexual intercourse sometime during their college careers.

The first is a value judgment; the second is an objective statement. There is a simple rule of thumb for telling the difference between the two: Value judgments imply how a person *ought* to behave, whereas objective statements describe how people *actually* behave. The first statement is a value judgment because it makes a judgment about premarital sexual behavior. The second is an objective statement because it describes how people act.

There is a second difference between value judgments and objective statements: Value judgments cannot be empirically validated, while objective statements can be validated. The truth or accuracy of an objective statement can be measured and tested. Despite claims of universality, these standards are generally regarded by social scientists as culturally relative. (**Cultural relativity** is an important anthropological concept meaning that the positive or negative appropriateness of any custom or activity must be evaluated in terms of how it fits in with the culture as a whole.)

cultural relativity The perspective that any custom must be evaluated in terms of how it fits within the culture as a whole.

Opinions, Biases, and Stereotypes

Value judgments obscure our search for understanding. They substitute judgment for objective description of the world as it exists. Opinions, biases, and stereotypes also interfere with the pursuit of knowledge.

An **opinion** is an unsubstantiated belief or conclusion about what seems to be true according to an individual's personal thoughts. Opinions are not based on positive knowledge or concrete evidence. Because opinions are unsubstantiated, they often reflect the individual's personal values or biases.

A **bias** is a personal leaning or inclination. Biases lead to selecting information that supports our views or beliefs while ignoring information that does not. We need not be victims, however, of our biases. We can make a concerted effort to discover what they are and overcome them. Indeed, as William Simon (1992) writes of scientific research:

opinion An unsubstantiated belief or conclusion above what seems to be true according to an individual's personal thoughts.

bias A personal leaning or inclination.

> Science as an enduring institution is essentially an ethical posture. It is a pledge that while we cannot control or ever be fully aware of our biases, we will not knowingly lie, we will not fudge the data.

To avoid personal bias, scholars apply the objective methods of social science research.

A **stereotype** is a set of simplistic, rigidly held, overgeneralized beliefs about an individual, a group of people, an idea, and so on. Stereotypical beliefs are resistant to change. Although men may think that their perceptions of women have changed, research indicates that they continue to hold the same stereotypical beliefs about women today as they did 20 years ago (Bergen & Williams, 1991). Furthermore, stereotypes—especially sexual ones—are often negative.

stereotype A set of simplistic, rigidly held, overgeneralized beliefs about a person or group of people.

Common sexual stereotypes include the following:

- Men are "animals."
- "Nice" women are not interested in sex.
- Virgins are uptight and asexual.
- Gay men are child molesters.
- Lesbians hate men.

- African Americans are sexually uninhibited.
- Latino men are macho.

Psychologists believe that stereotypes structure knowledge. They affect the ways in which we process information: what we see, what we notice, what we remember, and how we explain things (Hamilton, 1979). Or, as humorist Ashleigh Brilliant said, "Seeing is believing. I wouldn't have seen it if I hadn't believed it." A stereotype is a type of **schema,** a way in which we organize knowledge in our thought processes. Schemas help us channel or filter the mass of information we receive in order for us to make sense of it. They determine what we will regard as important. Although these mental plans are useful, they can also create blind spots. With stereotypes, we see what we expect to see and ignore what we don't expect to see.

Sociologists point out that sexual stereotyping is often used to justify discrimination. Targets of stereotypes are usually members of subordinate social groups, such as women, low-income groups, and members of ethnic groups. As we will see, sexual stereotyping is especially powerful in stigmatizing African Americans, Latinos, and gay men and lesbians.

We all have opinions and biases; most of us to varying degrees think stereotypically. But the commitment to objectivity requires us to become aware of these opinions, biases, and stereotypes and to put them aside in the pursuit of knowledge.

Confusing Attitudes and Behavior

An **attitude** is a predisposition a person has to act, think, or feel in certain ways toward particular things. A **behavior** is the way a person acts. There are two problems we commonly experience when discussing sexual attitudes and behavior: (1) We fail to identify whether we are discussing attitudes or behavior, and (2) we assume attitudes reflect behavior and vice versa.

Failure to identify whether we are discussing attitudes or behavior can lead to confusion and an endless round of disagreement. Imagine, for example, two friends discussing premarital sex without either specifying whether he or she is talking about attitudes or behavior. One says, "Everyone I know accepts premarital sex." The other disagrees: "That's not so. Almost all our friends are virgins." The fact is, both may be correct. But the first person is talking about premarital sexual *attitudes* while the second is talking about actual premarital sexual *behavior*. The two may never be able to find agreement because they are both talking about different things.

There is often a discrepancy between attitudes and behavior. As a result, we cannot infer a person's behavior from his or her attitudes about sexuality, or vice versa. A person may disapprove of premarital sexual intercourse, for example, but nevertheless engage in it. A woman may oppose abortion but may terminate her own pregnancy.

Common Fallacies: Egocentric and Ethnocentric Thinking

A **fallacy** is an error in reasoning that affects our understanding of a subject. Fallacies distort our thinking, leading us to false or erroneous conclusions. In the field of sexuality, egocentric and ethnocentric fallacies are common.

schema A set of interrelated ideas that helps us process information by organizing it in useful ways.

attitude The predisposition to act, think, or feel in certain ways toward particular things.

behavior The way a person acts.

fallacy An error in reasoning that affects our understanding of a subject.

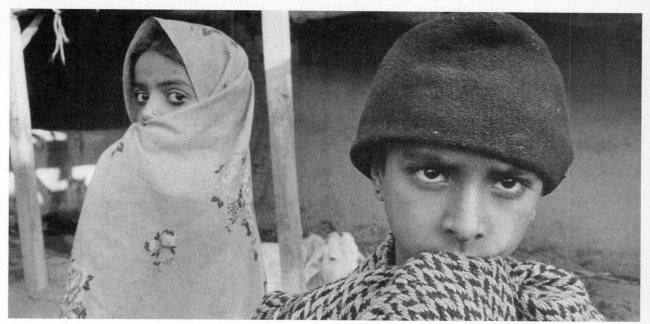

The **egocentric fallacy** is the mistaken belief that one's own personal experience and values are held by others in general. As a result of this false consensus, we use our own beliefs and values to explain the attitudes, motivations, and behaviors of others. Of course, our own experiences and values are important; they are the source of personal strength and knowledge. They are often valuable in giving us insight into others. But we cannot necessarily generalize from our own experience to that of others. Our own personal experiences are limited and may be unrepresentative; sometimes they are merely opinions or disguised value judgments.

The **ethnocentric fallacy,** also known as **ethnocentrism,** is the belief that one's own ethnic group, nation, or culture is innately superior to others. Ethnocentrism is reinforced by opinions, biases, and stereotypes about other groups and cultures. As members of a group, we tend to share similar values and attitudes with other group members. But the mere fact that we share these beliefs with others is not sufficient proof of their truth.

Ethnocentrism has been increasingly evident as a reaction to the increased awareness of **ethnicity,** ethnic affiliation or identity. For many Americans, a significant part of their sense of self comes from identification with their ethnic group. An **ethnic group** is a group of people distinct from other groups because of cultural characteristics, such as language, religion, and customs that are transmitted from one generation to another. Contemporary American ethnic groups include African Americans, Latinos (Hispanics), Native Americans, Japanese Americans, and Chinese Americans.

Although there has been little research on ethnicity and sexuality until recently, evidence suggests that there is significant ethnic variation in terms of sexual attitudes and behavior (Cortese, 1989; Staples, 1991; Staples & Johnson, 1993). For example, it appears that whites are less sexually per-

Ethnocentrism views one's own culture or ethnic group as superior to that of others. Although child marriage is prohibited in our society, it is acceptable in many cultures throughout the world, including India. Such marriages generally do not include cohabitation or sexual relations until the couple is old enough in the eyes of their society.

egocentric fallacy An erroneous belief that one's own personal experience and values are held by others in general.

ethnocentric fallacy or **ethnocentrism** The belief that one's own ethnic group, nation, or culture is innately superior to others.

ethnicity Ethnic affiliation or identity.

ethnic group A group of people distinct from other groups because of cultural characteristics transmitted from one generation to the next.

missive than African Americans, and Latinos are less permissive than either whites or African Americans. From a white ethnocentric viewpoint, the greater acceptance of premarital sex among African Americans may be evidence that blacks are "promiscuous." From an African American point of view, whites may be viewed as sexually "uptight." Latinos may see both groups as "immoral."

Ethnocentrism is also expressed in stereotyping other cultures as "primitive," "innocent," "inferior," or "not as advanced." We may view the behavior of other peoples as strange, exotic, unusual, or bizarre, but to them it is normal. Their attitudes, behaviors, values, and beliefs form a unified sexual system, which makes sense within their culture. In fact, we engage in many activities that appear peculiar to those outside our culture. For example, Amazonian people do not understand why young men or women would masturbate. As a Mehinaku youth asked incredulously: "Having sex with the hand? Why would anyone bother? There are plenty of women around" (Gregor, 1985).

SEX RESEARCH METHODS

One of the key factors that distinguishes the findings of social science from beliefs, prejudice, bias—and pop psychology—is its commitment to the scientific method. The **scientific method** is the method by which a hypothesis is formed from impartially gathered data and tested empirically. The scientific method relies on **induction**—that is, forming arguments whose premises are intended to provide some support, but not conclusive support, for their conclusions. The scientific method seeks to describe the world rather than evaluate or judge it.

Although sex researchers use the same methodology as other social scientists, they are constrained by ethical concerns and taboos that those in other fields do not experience. Because of the taboos surrounding sexuality, some traditional research methods are inappropriate.

Sex research, like most social science research, uses different methodological approaches. These include the following:

- Clinical research
- Survey research: questionnaires and interviews
- Observational research
- Experimental research

Research Concerns

Researchers face two general concerns in conducting their work. The first concern is ethical, centering around the use of human beings as subjects. The second concern is methodological, regarding sampling techniques and their accuracy. Without a representative sample, the conclusions drawn by these methodologies are limited.

Ethical Issues Ethics are important in any scientific endeavor. They are especially important in such an emotional and value-laden subject as

scientific method A systematic approach to acquiring knowledge by collecting data, forming a hypothesis, testing it empirically, and observing the results.

induction A type of reasoning in which arguments are formed from a premise to provide support for its conclusion.

sexuality. Among the most important ethical issues are (1) informed consent, (2) protection from harm, (3) confidentiality, and (4) the use of deception.

Informed consent is the full disclosure to an individual of the purpose, potential risks, and benefits of participating in a research project. The individual must be at least age 18 and without mental impairment. Under informed consent, people are free to decide whether to participate in a project without coercion or deceit. Once a study begins, a person has the right to withdraw at any time without penalty.

Each research participant is entitled to protection from harm. Some sex research, such as the viewing of explicit films to measure physiological responses, may cause some people psychological distress. The identity of research subjects is to be confidential. Because of the highly charged nature of sexuality, participants need to be guaranteed anonymity.

Of all the ethical issues surrounding research, the use of deception is the most problematic. Sometimes it is necessary to deceive subjects in order for the experiment to work. If participants in a study on the role of attractiveness at first meetings knew they were being studied in terms of their response to attractive people rather than, say, opening lines, their responses might be different. The issue of deception is generally resolved by requiring the researcher to debrief an individual following the experiment.

Most colleges and universities have review boards or human subject committees to make sure that research follows ethical guidelines. Proposed research is submitted to the committee prior to the project's beginning. If the committee believes the research poses ethical problems, the project will not be approved until the problems are corrected.

Sampling In each research approach, the choice of a sample—a portion of a larger group of people observed or studied—is critical. To be useful, a sample should be a **random sample**—that is, a sample collected in an unbiased way. Further, the sample should be a **representative sample,** a small group representing the larger group in terms of age, sex, ethnicity, social class, orientation, and so on. Samples that are not representative of the larger group are known as **biased samples.** Using samples is important. It would be impossible, for example, to study the sexual behaviors of all college students in the United States. But we can select a representative sample of college students from various schools and infer from their behavior how other college students behave. Using the same sample to infer the sexual behavior of Americans in general, however, would be a biased sample. We cannot infer the sexual activities of Americans from studying college students because the sample would be biased in terms of age (young), education (college), socioeconomic status (middle class), and ethnicity (white).

Most samples in sex research are limited for several reasons:

1. They depend on volunteers or clients. Because these samples are generally self-selected, we cannot assume that they are representative of the population as a whole (Morokoff, 1986; Harry, 1986). Volunteers for sex research are generally more sexually experienced, more liberal, and less religious than the population as a whole. They are more likely, for example, to be tolerant of premarital sex than those who do not participate.

2. Most sex research takes place in a university or college setting with

informed consent Assent given by a mentally competent individual at least 18 years old with full knowledge of the purpose and potential risks and benefits of participation.

random sample A portion of a larger group collected in an unbiased way.

representative sample A small group representing a larger group in terms of age, sex, ethnicity, socioeconomic class, orientation, and so on.

biased sample A nonrepresentative sample.

student volunteers. College students, however, are generally in late adolescence or early adulthood and are single; they are at the beginning of their sexual lives. Is the value they place on sexuality in marriage, for example, likely to be the same as older, married adults?

3. Ethnic groups are generally underrepresented. Representative samples of African Americans, Latinos, Native Americans, and some Asian Americans are not easily found because they are underrepresented in colleges and universities where subjects are generally recruited.

4. The study of gay men and lesbians presents unique sampling problems. Are gay men and lesbians who have come out (publicly identified themselves as gay or lesbian) different from those who have not? How does one find and recruit subjects who have not come out?

Because these factors limit most studies, one must be careful in making generalizations from them.

Clinical Research

clinical research The in-depth examination of an individual or group by a clinician who assists with psychological or medical problems.

Clinical research is the in-depth examination of an individual or group who come to a psychiatrist, psychologist, or social worker for assistance with psychological or medical problems or disorders. Clinical research is descriptive. Inferences of cause and effect cannot be drawn from it. The individual is interviewed and treated for a specific problem. At the same time the person is being treated, he or she is being studied. In their evaluations, clinicians attempt to determine the causes of a disorder and how it may be treated. They may also try to infer from dysfunctional people how healthy people develop.

Clinical research focuses largely on what is considered deviant, abnormal, inadequate, or unhealthy sexual behavior, such as transsexuality (individuals who feel they are trapped in bodies of the wrong sex) and sexual dysfunctions (such as lack of desire, premature ejaculation, erectile difficulties, or lack of orgasm).

pathological behavior Behavior deemed diseased by current medical standards.

A major limitation of clinical research is its emphasis on unhealthy or **pathological behavior** (diseased behavior). Such an emphasis makes clinical research dependent on cultural definitions of what is "unhealthy" or "pathological." These definitions, however, change over time and are dependent on prevailing social norms.

Survey Research

survey research A method of gathering information from a small group to make inferences about a larger group.

Survey research is a method used to gather information from a small group and to make inferences about a larger group. The survey method uses questionnaires or interviews to gather information. Questionnaires offer anonymity, may be completed fairly quickly, and are relatively inexpensive to administer; however, they usually do not allow an in-depth response. A person must respond with a short answer or a limited choice. Interview techniques avoid some of the shortcomings of questionnaires, as interviewers are able to probe in greater depth and follow paths suggested by the subject.

Although the survey method is an important source of information, it has several limitations. First, people tend to be poor reporters of their own sexual behavior. Men may exaggerate their number of sexual partners, while women may minimize their casual encounters. Members of both sexes

You and Your Sexual Well-Being

THE KINSEY INSTITUTE/ROPER ORGANIZATION
NATIONAL SEX KNOWLEDGE TEST

This self-assessment was given to a representative sample of Americans in 1990. It was found that the average American knows little about sexuality, contraception, or STDs. Worse, they were misinformed.

Circle one answer after reading each question carefully. If you have trouble or want advice about any of these issues, look them up in the text and/or discuss them with a professional.

1. **Nowadays, what do you think is the age at which the *average or typical* American *first* has sexual intercourse?**

   a. 11 or younger   d. 14   g. 17   j. 20

   b. 12   e. 15   h. 18   k. 21 or older

   c. 13   f. 16   i. 19   l. Don't know

2. **Out of every ten married American men, how many would you estimate have had an extramarital affair—that is, have been sexually unfaithful to their wives?**

   a. Less than one out of ten   e. Four out of ten (40%)   i. Eight out of ten (80%)

   b. One out of ten (10%)   f. Five out of ten (50%)   j. Nine out of ten (90%)

   c. Two out of ten (20%)   g. Six out of ten (60%)   k. More than nine out of ten

   d. Three out of ten (30%)   h. Seven out of ten (70%)   l. Don't know

3. **Out of every ten American women, how many would you estimate have had anal (rectal) intercourse?**

   a. Less than one out of ten   e. Four out of ten (40%)   i. Eight out of ten (80%)

   b. One out of ten (10%)   f. Five out of ten (50%)   j. Nine out of ten (90%)

   c. Two out of ten (20%)   g. Six out of ten (60%)   k. More than nine out of ten

   d. Three out of ten (30%)   h. Seven out of ten (70%)   l. Don't know

4. **A person can get AIDS by having anal (rectal) intercourse even if neither partner is infected with the AIDS virus.**

   True   False   Don't know

5. **There are over-the-counter spermicides people can buy at the drugstore that will kill the AIDS virus.**

   True   False   Don't know

6. **Petroleum jelly, Vaseline Intensive Care, baby oil, and Nivea are *not* good lubricants to use with a condom or diaphragm.**

   True   False   Don't know

7. **More than one out of four (25%) of American men have had a sexual experience with another male during either their teens or adult years.**

   True   False   Don't know

8. **It is usually difficult to tell whether people *are or are not* homosexual just by their appearance or gestures.**

   True   False   Don't know

9. **A woman or teenage girl can get pregnant during her menstrual flow (her "period").**

   True   False   Don't know

(continued)

SEX KNOWLEDGE TEST (*continued*)

10. **A woman or teenage girl can get pregnant even if a man withdraws his penis before he ejaculates (before he "comes").**

    True   False   Don't know

11. **Unless they are having sex, women do not need to have regular gynecological examinations.**

    True   False   Don't know

12. **Teenage boys should examine their testicles ("balls") regularly just as women self-examine their breasts for lumps.**

    True   False   Don't know

13. **Problems with erection are most often started by a physical problem.**

    True   False   Don't know

14. **Almost all erection problems can be successfully treated.**

    True   False   Don't know

15. **Menopause, or change of life as it is often called, does *not* cause most women to lose interest in having sex.**

    True   False   Don't know

16. **Out of every ten American women, how many would you estimate have masturbated either as children or after they were grown up?**

    a. Less than one out of ten   e. Four out of ten (40%)   i. Eight out of ten (80%)

    b. One out of ten (10%)   f. Five out of ten (50%)   j. Nine out of ten (90%)

    c. Two out of ten (20%)   g. Six out of ten (60%)   k. More than nine out of ten

    d. Three out of ten (30%)   h. Seven out of ten (70%)   l. Don't know

generally underreport experiences considered deviant or immoral, such as same-sex experiences, bondage, and so on. Second, interviewers may allow their own preconceptions to influence the way in which they frame questions and to bias their interpretations of responses as well. Third, some respondents may feel uncomfortable about revealing information—such as masturbation or incestuous experiences—in a face-to-face interview. Fourth, the interviewer's gender may also influence how comfortable respondents are in disclosing information about themselves. Finally, some ethnic groups, because of their cultural values, may be reluctant to reveal sexual information about themselves. Recent findings suggest, however, that African Americans and Latinos are willing to participate in research and to answer sensitive questions (Jackson, 1991; Marin & Marin, 1989, 1991).

17. What do you think is the length of the average man's *erect* penis?

a. 2 inches	d. 5 inches	g. 8 inches	j. 11 inches
b. 3 inches	e. 6 inches	h. 9 inches	k. 12 inches
c. 4 inches	f. 7 inches	i. 10 inches	l. Don't know

18. Most women prefer a sexual partner with a larger-than-average penis.

True   False   Don't know

Scoring the Test

Each question is worth one point. So, the total possible number of points you can get is 18. Using this chart, score each item and then add up your total number of points. When a range of possible answers is correct, according to currently available research data, all respondents choosing one of the answers in the correct range are given a point.

Question number	Give yourself a point if you circled any of the following answers	Circle the number of points you received		Question number	Give yourself a point if you circled any of the following answers	Circle the number of points you received
1	f,g	0 1		11	False	0 1
2	d,e	0 1		12	True	0 1
3	d,e	0 1		13	True	0 1
4	False	0 1		14	True	0 1
5	(any answer, everyone gets a point as explained in discussion of question)	1		15	True	0 1
				16	g,h,i	0 1
				17	d,e,f	0 1
6	True	0 1		18	False	0 1
7	True	0 1				
8	True	0 1			Total Number of Points: _____	
9	True	0 1				
10	True	0 1				

Source: Reinisch, J. *The New Kinsey Report,* New York: St. Martin's Press, 1990, pp. 3–5.

Observational Research

Observational research is the method by which a researcher unobtrusively observes and makes systematic notes about people's behavior without trying to manipulate it. The observer does not want to affect the subject's behavior by his or her presence. But because sexual behavior is regarded as significantly different from other behaviors, there are serious ethical concerns involved in observing people's sexual behavior without their knowledge and consent. (Even with their knowledge and consent, such observation may be considered voyeuristic and subject to criminal prosecution.) Because researchers cannot observe sexual behavior as they might observe flirting at a party, dance, or bar, such observations usually take place in a

observational research A method of gathering information in which a researcher systematically and unobtrusively observes behavior.

laboratory setting. In such instances, the setting is not a natural environment; participants are aware that their behavior is under observation.

Probably the largest observational study in human sexuality was William Masters and Virginia Johnson's work on sexual response in which they observed and measured more than 10,000 orgasms in a hospital's soundproof laboratory. (The soundproofing was necessary to prevent physicians and nurses from eavesdropping; some even placed stethoscopes against the walls in an attempt to listen.) In such studies, volunteer bias may be a particularly critical issue. Are individuals who participate in such studies exhibitionistic? How does awareness that they are being observed affect their behavior? Masters and Johnson tried to eliminate bias by extensive interviews with their volunteers. They allowed their participants practice sessions in the laboratories to familiarize them with the setting.

Experimental Research

Experimental research is the systematic manipulation of the environment to learn the effect of such manipulation on behavior. It enables researchers to isolate a single factor under controlled circumstances to determine its influence. Researchers are able to control their experiments by using **variables,** aspects or factors that can be manipulated in experiments. There are two types of variables: independent variables and dependent variables. **Independent variables** are factors that can be manipulated or changed by the experimenter; **dependent variables** are factors that are affected by changes in the independent variable.

Because it controls variables, experimental research differs from the previous methods we have examined. Clinical studies, surveys, and observational research are correlational in nature. **Correlational studies** measure two or more naturally occurring variables to determine their relationship to each other. Because these studies do not manipulate the variables, they cannot tell us which variable *causes* the other to change. But experimental studies manipulate the independent variables, so researchers *can* reasonably determine what variables cause the other variables to change.

Much experimental research on sexuality depends on measuring physiological responses. These responses are usually measured by **plethysmographs,** devices attached to the genitals to measure physiological response. Researchers use either a penile plethysmograph or a **strain gauge** (a rubberbandlike device) for men and a vaginal plethysmograph for women. Both the penile plethysmograph and strain gauge are placed around the penis; they measure changes in the circumference of the penis that accompany sexual arousal. The vaginal plethysmograph is about the size of a menstrual tampon and is inserted into the vagina like a tampon. The vaginal plethysmograph measures the amount of blood within the vaginal walls, which increases as a woman becomes aroused.

Imagine that researchers want to study the influence of alcohol on sexual response. They would use a plethysmograph to measure sexual response, the dependent variable. In this study, the independent variables would be the levels of alcohol consumption: no alcohol consumption, moderate alcohol consumption, and high alcohol consumption. In such experiments, subjects may view an erotic film. To get a baseline measurement, researchers measure the genitals' physiological patterns in an unaroused state prior to viewing the film or drinking. Then they measure sexual arousal (dependent

experimental research The systematic manipulation of an individual or the environment to learn the effect of such manipulation on behavior.

variable An aspect or factor that can be manipulated in an experiment.

independent variable A factor that can be manipulated or changed in a experiment.

dependent variable In an experiment, a factor that is affected by changes in the independent variable.

correlational study The measurement of two or more naturally occurring variables to determine their relationship to each other.

plethysmograph A device attached to the genitals to measure physiological response.

strain gauge A rubberbandlike device placed over the penis to measure physiological response.

variable) to erotica as they increase the levels of alcohol consumption (independent variables).

Good experiments are difficult to design because the experimental situation must resemble the real world. There are four important concerns about experimental research. (1) To what degree does the experiment replicate the complexities and settings of real-life sexuality? Does a laboratory setting radically alter responses? (2) Do the devices used to measure sexual response affect the subject's sexual responsiveness? (3) The measuring devices measure only genital response, while the overall sexual response includes increased heart rate, muscle tension, changed brain-wave patterns, sexual fantasies and thoughts, and so on. (4) Can the results from the experiment be generalized to nonlaboratory conditions? Because there are so many variables outside controlled laboratory conditions, many researchers believe that experimental findings are highly limited when applied to the real world.

THE SEX RESEARCHERS

It was not until the nineteenth century that Western sexuality began to be studied using a scientific framework. Prior to that time, sexuality was claimed by religion rather than science; sex was the subject of moral rather than scientific scrutiny. From the earliest Christian era, treatises, canon law, papal bulls, as well as sermons and confessions catalogued the sins of the flesh. Reflecting this Christian tradition, the early students of sexuality were concerned with the excesses and deviances of sexuality rather than its healthy functioning. They were fascinated by what they considered the pathologies of sex, such as fetishism, sadism, masturbation, and homosexuality—the very behaviors that religion condemned as sinful. Alfred Kinsey ironically noted that nineteenth-century researchers created "scientific classifications . . . nearly identical with theological classifications and with moral pronouncements . . . of the fifteenth century" (Kinsey et al., 1948).

But as we will see, there has been a liberalizing trend in our thinking about sexuality. Both Richard von Krafft-Ebing and Sigmund Freud viewed sexuality as inherently dangerous and needing repression. But Havelock Ellis, Alfred Kinsey, William Masters and Virginia Johnson, and a number of more recent researchers have viewed sexuality more positively; in fact, historian Paul Robinson (1976) regards these later researchers as modernists ("sexual enthusiasts," he calls them). Three themes are evident in their work. First, they believed that sexual expression was essential to an individual's well-being. Second, they sought to broaden the range of legitimate sexual activity, including homosexuality. Third, they believed that female sexuality was the equal of male sexuality.

As much as possible, sex researchers attempt to examine sexuality objectively. But, like all of us, many of their views are intertwined with the beliefs and values of their times. This is especially apparent among the early sex researchers.

Richard von Krafft-Ebing (1840–1902)

Richard von Krafft-Ebing, a Viennese professor of psychiatry, was probably the most influential of the early researchers. In 1886, he published his most famous work, *Psychopathia Sexualis*, a collection of case histories of fetishists,

Richard von Krafft-Ebing (1840–1902) viewed most sexual behavior other than marital coitus as a sign of pathology.

neurosis A psychological disorder characterized by anxiety or tension.

repression A psychological mechanism that keeps people from becoming aware of hidden memories and motives because they arouse guilt or pain.

psychoanalysis A psychological system developed by Sigmund Freud that traces behavior to unconscious motivations.

id In Freudian theory, the instinct.

libido The sex drive.

pleasure principle In Freudian theory, the principle that organisms (including people) seek pleasure and avoid pain.

ego In Freudian theory, the self.

Sigmund Freud (1856–1939) was the founder of psychoanalysis and one of the most influential European thinkers of the first half of the twentieth century. Freud viewed sexuality with suspicion.

sadists, masochists, and homosexuals. (He invented the words "sado-masochism" and "transvestite.")

Krafft-Ebing traced variations in Victorian sexuality to "hereditary taint," "moral degeneracy," and, in particular, to masturbation. He intermingled descriptions of fetishists who became sexually excited by kid gloves with those of sadists who disemboweled their victims. For Krafft-Ebing, the origins of fetishism and murderous sadism, as well as most variations, lay in masturbation, the sexual sin of the nineteenth century.

In our time, Krafft-Ebing's theories on the origins, nature, and dangers of sexual aberrations are little more than amusing stories or strange curiosities. Much of what he considered degeneracy, such as masturbation, is today considered normal sexual behavior. His *Psychopathia Sexualis,* however, brought to public attention and discussion an immense range of sexual behaviors that had never before been documented in a dispassionate, if erroneous, manner. A darkened region of sexual behavior was brought into the open for public examination (Bullough, 1976).

Sigmund Freud (1856–1939)

Few people have had as dramatic an impact on the way we think about the world as the Viennese physician Sigmund Freud. In his attempt to understand the **neuroses,** psychological disorders characterized by anxiety or tension, plaguing his patients, Freud explored the unknown territory of the unconscious. If unconscious motives were brought to consciousness, a person could change his or her behavior. But, he believed, **repression,** a psychological mechanism that keeps people from becoming aware of hidden memories and motives because they arouse guilt, prevents such knowledge.

To explore the unconscious, Freud used various techniques; in particular, he analyzed the meaning of dreams. His journeys into the mind led to the development of **psychoanalysis,** a psychological system that traces behavior to unconscious desires. He fled Vienna when Hitler annexed Austria in 1938 and died a year later in England.

The Theory of Personality His clinical work led Freud to develop a theory of personality in which sexuality played a critical role. (For the best concise discussion of Freudian psychology, see Hall, 1980.) According to Freud's theory, personality consists of three parts: the id, the ego, and the superego. The **id** represents the instincts and is driven by the **libido,** which seeks pleasure, especially sexual pleasure. The libido, or sexual drive, pursues pleasure regardless of the cost; it follows what Freud called the **pleasure principle,** the idea that organisms seek pleasure and avoid pain. The **ego,** however, deals with reality. It acts as an intermediary between the demands of the id and those of society. It is governed by the **reality principle,** the control the external world exerts on the organism, which postpones pleasure. The **superego** acts as the individual's conscience. It is an internalization of society's demands, which the individual learns from birth. These various elements are in constant conflict with each other. The id is constantly seeking gratification; the superego is constantly seeking to repress it. The repression of instinctive desires often leads to neurosis.

The Theory of Psychosexual Development Freud believed that sexuality begins at birth. His belief in infant and child sexuality set him apart from other researchers. Freud described five stages in psychosexual development. The first stage is the **oral stage,** lasting from birth to age 1. During this time, the infant's eroticism is focused on the mouth; thumb-sucking produces an erotic pleasure. Freud believed the "most striking character of this sexual activity . . . is that the child gratifies himself on his own body; . . . he is autoerotic" (Freud, 1938). The second stage, between ages 1 and 3, is the **anal stage.** The erotic activities continue to be autoerotic, but the region of pleasure shifts to the anus. From age 3 through 5, the child is in the **phallic stage,** in which he or she exhibits interest in the genitals. At age 6, children enter a **latency stage,** in which their sexual impulses are no longer active. At puberty, they enter the **genital stage,** at which point the adolescent becomes interested in genital sexual activities, especially sexual intercourse.

The phallic stage is the critical stage in both male and female development. The boy develops sexual desires for his mother, leading to the **Oedipal complex.** He simultaneously desires his mother and fears his father. This fear leads to **castration anxiety,** the belief that the father will cut off his penis because of jealousy. Girls follow a more complex development, according to Freud. A girl develops an **Electra complex,** desiring her father while fearing her mother. Upon discovering that she does not have a penis, she feels deprived and develops **penis envy.** By age 6, both boys and girls resolve their Oedipal and Electra complexes by relinquishing their desires for the parent of the other sex and identifying with their same-sex parent. In this manner, they develop their masculine and feminine identities. But because girls never acquire their "lost penis," Freud believed, they fail to develop an independent character like that of boys.

Critique In many ways, such as in his commitment to science and his explorations of the unconscious, Freud seems the embodiment of twentieth-century thought. But over the last generation, his influence among American sex researchers has dwindled. Two of the most important reasons are his lack of empiricism and his inadequate description of female development.

Because of its limitations, Freud's work has become mostly of historical interest to mainstream sex researchers. It continues to exert influence in some fields of psychology but has been greatly modified by others. Even among contemporary psychoanalysts, his work has been radically revised.

Havelock Ellis (1859–1939)

Havelock Ellis, who became one of the most influential sexual thinkers and reformers in the twentieth century, was a child of the Victorian era. A native of England, his youth was marked by the sexual repression and fears of that time. He set himself against these sexual inhibitions in order to free humanity from ignorance. He was among the first modern affirmers of sexuality. "Sex lies at the root of life," he wrote, "and we can never learn to reverence life until we know how to understand sex" (Ellis, 1900). He believed that the negators of sexuality used morality and religion to twist and deform sex until it became little more than sin and degradation.

Ellis was the earliest important modern sexual thinker. His *Studies in the Psychology of Sex* (the first six volumes of which were published between 1897 and 1910) consisted of case studies, autobiographies, and personal letters. One

reality principle In Freudian theory, the principle by which the external world exerts influence on the organism.

superego In Freudian theory, the conscience.

oral stage In Freudian theory, the period lasting from birth to age 1 in which infant eroticism is focused on the mouth.

anal stage In Freudian theory, the period from age 1 to 3, during which the child's erotic activities center on the anus.

phallic stage In Freudian theory, the period from age 3 to 6, during which both male and female children exhibit interest in the genitals.

latency stage In Freudian theory, the period from age 6 to puberty in which sexual impulses are no longer active.

genital stage In Freudian theory, the period in which adolescents become interested in genital sexual activities, especially sexual intercourse.

Oedipal complex In Freudian theory, the male child's erotic desire for his mother and simultaneous fear of his father.

castration anxiety In Freudian theory, the belief that the father will cut off the child's penis because of rivalry for the mother/wife.

Electra complex In Freudian theory, the female child's erotic desire for the father and simultaneous fear of the mother.

penis envy In Freudian theory, female desire to have a penis.

of his most important contributions was pointing out the relativity of sexual values. In the nineteenth century, Americans and Europeans alike believed that their society's dominant sexual beliefs were the only morally and naturally correct standards. But Ellis demonstrated that Western sexual standards were not the only moral standards and that they were not necessarily rooted in nature. In doing so, he was among the first researchers to appeal to studies in animal behavior, anthropology, and history.

Ellis also challenged the view that masturbation was abnormal. He argued that masturbation was widespread and that there was no evidence linking it with any serious mental or physical problems. He recorded countless men and women who masturbated without ill effect. In fact, he argued, masturbation provided a positive function: It relieved tension.

The nineteenth century viewed women as essentially "pure beings" who possessed reproductive rather than sexual desires. Men, by contrast, were driven by such strong sexual passions that their sexuality had to be severely controlled and repressed. In countless case studies, Ellis documented that women possessed sexual desires no less intense than those of men.

Ellis argued that a wide range of behaviors was normal, including much behavior that the Victorians considered abnormal. He argued that both masturbation and female sexuality were normal behaviors and that even the so-called abnormal elements of sexual behavior were simply exaggerations of the normal.

He also reevaluated homosexuality. The nineteenth century viewed homosexuality as the essence of sin and perversion. It was dangerous, lurid, and criminal. Ellis insisted that it was not a disease or vice but a congenital condition: A person was born homosexual; one did not *become* homosexual. By insisting that homosexuality was congenital, Ellis denied that it could be considered a vice or a form of moral degeneracy because a person did not *choose* it. If homosexuality was both congenital and harmless, then, Ellis reasoned, it should not be considered immoral or criminal.

Alfred Kinsey (1894–1956)

In 1948, Alfred A. Kinsey, a biologist at Indiana University and America's leading authority on gall wasps, destroyed forever the belief in American sexual innocence and virtue. He accomplished this through two books, *Sexual Behavior in the Human Male* (Kinsey et al., 1948) and *Sexual Behavior in the Human Female* (Kinsey et al., 1953). These two volumes statistically documented the actual sexual behavior of Americans. In massive detail, they demonstrated the great discrepancy between *public* standards of sexual behavior and *actual* sexual behavior. In the firestorm that accompanied the publication of Kinsey's books (popularly known as the *Kinsey Reports*), many Americans protested the destruction of their cherished ideals and illusions.

Sexual Diversity and Variation What Kinsey discovered in his research was an extraordinary diversity in individual sexual behaviors. Among men, he found individuals who had orgasms daily and others who went months without orgasms. Among women, he found those who had never had orgasms and those who had them several times a day. He discovered one male who had ejaculated only once in 30 years and another who climaxed 30 times a week on average. "This is the order of variation,"

Alfred Kinsey (1894–1956) shocked Americans by revealing how they actually behaved sexually. His scientific efforts led to the termination of his research funding because of political pressure.

he commented dryly, "which may occur between two individuals who live in the same town and who are neighbors, meeting in the same place of business and coming together in common social activities" (Kinsey et al., 1948).

Reevaluation of Masturbation Kinsey's work aimed at a reevaluation of the role of masturbation in a person's sexual adjustment. Kinsey made three points about masturbation: (1) It is harmless, (2) it is not a substitute for sexual intercourse but a distinct form of sexual behavior that provides sexual pleasure, and (3) it plays an important role in women's sexuality because it is a more reliable source of orgasm than heterosexual intercourse, and because its practice seems to facilitate women's ability to become orgasmic during intercourse. Indeed, Kinsey believed that masturbation was the best way to measure a woman's inherent sexual responsiveness because it did not rely on another person.

Same-Sex Behavior Prior to Kinsey's work, an individual was identified as homosexual if he or she engaged in a single sexual act with a member of the same sex. Kinsey found, however, that many people had sexual experiences with members of both sexes. He reported that 50% of the men and 28% of the women in his studies had same-sex experiences; 38% of the men and 13% of the women had orgasms during these experiences (Kinsey et al., 1948, 1953). Furthermore, he discovered that sexual preferences could change over the course of a person's lifetime. Kinsey's research led him to believe that it was erroneous to classify people as either heterosexual or homosexual. A person's sexuality was significantly more complex and fluid.

Kinsey wanted to eliminate the concept of heterosexual and homosexual *identities*. He did not believe that homosexuality, any more than heterosexuality, existed as a fixed psychological identity. Instead, he argued, there were only sexual acts, and acts alone did not make a person gay, lesbian, or heterosexual. It was more important to determine what proportion of behaviors were same-sex and other-sex than to label a person as gay, lesbian, or heterosexual.

He devised the Kinsey scale to represent the proportion of an individual's sexual behaviors with the same or other sex (Figure 2.1). This scale charted behaviors from no behaviors with the same sex to behaviors exclusively with members of the same sex. These behaviors existed on a continuum. His scale radicalized the categorization of human sexual behavior (McWhirter, 1990).

Rejection of Normal/Abnormal Dichotomy As a result of his research, Kinsey insisted that the distinction between normal and abnormal was meaningless. Like Ellis, he argued that sexual differences were a matter of degree, not kind. Almost any sexual behavior could be placed alongside another that differed from it only slightly. His observations led him to be a leading advocate of the toleration of sexual differences.

Critique Although Kinsey's statistical methodology has been criticized, the two most important criticisms of his work are (1) his emphasis on the quantification of sexual behavior, and (2) his rejection of the psychological dimension.

Because Kinsey wanted to quantify behaviors, he studied only those

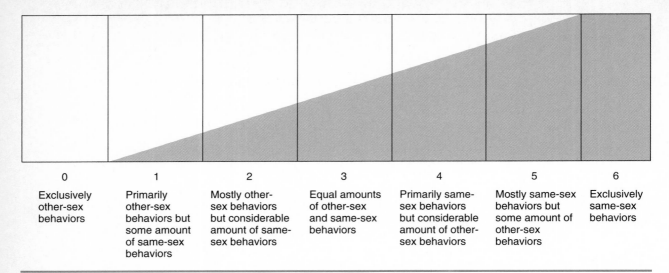

0	1	2	3	4	5	6
Exclusively other-sex behaviors	Primarily other-sex behaviors but some amount of same-sex behaviors	Mostly other-sex behaviors but considerable amount of same-sex behaviors	Equal amounts of other-sex and same-sex behaviors	Primarily same-sex behaviors but considerable amount of other-sex behaviors	Mostly same-sex behaviors but some amount of other-sex behaviors	Exclusively same-sex behaviors

FIGURE 2.1 The Kinsey scale focused on the degree to which a person engaged in other-sex and same-sex sexual behaviors.

behaviors that could be objectively measured. Thus, he defined sexual behaviors as those that lead to orgasm. By defining sexuality in this way, Kinsey reduced sexual behavior to genital activity. He excluded from his research sexual activities, such as kissing and erotic fantasies, that do not ordinarily lead to orgasm.

He also neglected the psychological dimension of sexuality. Motivation and attitudes did not interest him because he did not believe they could be objectively measured. As a consequence, the role of emotions, such as love, did not enter into his discussion of sexuality.

Kinsey's lack of interest in the psychological dimension of human sexuality led him to reject homosexual/heterosexual *identities* as meaningless. Although a person's sexual behaviors may not correspond to his or her identity as homosexual or heterosexual, this identity is nevertheless a critical aspect of self-concept. By ignoring these elements, Kinsey seriously limited his understanding of human sexuality.

William Masters and Virginia Johnson

In the 1950s, William Masters, a St. Louis physician, became interested in treating sexual inadequacy—such problems as premature ejaculation and erection difficulties in men, and lack of orgasm in women. As a physician, he felt that a systematic study of human sexual response was necessary, but none existed. To fill this void, he decided to conduct his own research. Masters was joined several years later by Virginia Johnson. Later they married, and in 1992 they divorced.

Masters and Johnson detailed the sexual response cycles of 382 men and 312 women during over 10,000 acts of sexual behavior, including masturbation and sexual intercourse. The researchers combined observation with direct measurement of changes in male and female genitals using electronic devices.

William Masters and Virginia Johnson detailed the sexual response cycle in the 1960s and revolutionized sex therapy in the 1970s.

Human Sexual Response (1966), their first book, became an immediate success among both researchers and the public at large. What made their work significant was not only the detailed description of physiological responses, but the articulation of several key ideas. First, Masters and Johnson discovered that, physiologically, male and female sexual responses were very similar. Second, they demonstrated that women achieved orgasm primarily through clitoral stimulation. Penetration of the vagina was not needed for orgasm to occur. By demonstrating the primacy of the clitoris, Masters and Johnson destroyed once and for all the Freudian distinction between vaginal and clitoral orgasms. (Freud believed that a woman's orgasm experienced through masturbation was somehow physically and psychologically inferior to one experienced through sexual intercourse. He made no such distinction for men.) By destroying the myth of the vaginal orgasm, Masters and Johnson legitimized female masturbation.

In 1970, Masters and Johnson published *Human Sexual Inadequacy*, which revolutionized sex therapy by treating sexual problems as simply difficulties that could be easily treated using behavioral therapy. They argued that sexual problems were not the result of underlying neuroses or personality disorders. More often than not, problems resulted from a lack of information, poor communication between couples, or marital conflict. Their behavioral approach, which included "homework" exercises such as clitoral or penile stimulation, led to an astounding increase in the successful treatment of sexual problems. Their work made them pioneers in modern sex therapy.

Although Masters and Johnson continued to publish work on sexuality, their later books have not been as well received as their early pioneering efforts. In fact, some of their subsequent work has been highly criticized as unscientific. Their work on homosexuality, for example, advocated methods for "reversing" homosexuality (Masters & Johnson, 1979). Critics pointed out that mainstream psychologists reject the idea of reversing homosexuality; instead, the customary treatment is directed toward healthy adjustment and acceptance. Their book on AIDS (Masters, Johnson, & Kolodny, 1988) was rejected by sex researchers and public-health authorities alike (Irvine, 1990; Randolph, 1988; Specter, 1988).

EMERGING RESEARCH PERSPECTIVES

Although sex research continues to explore diverse aspects of human sexuality, some scholars have felt their particular interests have been given insufficient attention. Feminists and gay and lesbian scholars have focused their research on issues that mainstream scholars have largely ignored. And ethnic research, only now beginning to be undertaken, points to the lack of knowledge about the sexuality of African Americans, Latinos, Asian Americans, and other ethnic Americans. These emerging research perspectives enrich our knowledge of sexuality.

Feminist Scholarship

The initial feminist research generated an immense amount of groundbreaking work on women in almost every field of the social sciences and humanities. Feminists made gender and gender-related issues significant

Magnus Hirschfeld (1868–1935) was a leading European sex reformer who championed homosexual rights. He founded the first institute for the study of sexuality. The institute was burned when the Nazis took power in Germany; he fled for his life.

research questions in a multitude of academic disciplines. In the field of sexuality, feminism expanded the scope of research to include the subjective experience and meaning of sexuality for women, sex and power, pornography, and issues of female victimization, such as rape, the sexual abuse of children, and sexual harassment.

There is no single feminist perspective; instead, there are several feminist perspectives. Nevertheless, feminist research focuses on gender issues, assumes that the female experience of sex has been devalued, believes power is a critical element in male-female relationships, and stresses the importance of ethnic diversity.

Gay and Lesbian Research

During the nineteenth century, sexuality became increasingly perceived as the domain of science, especially medicine. Physicians competed with ministers, priests, and rabbis in defining what was "correct" sexual behavior. But medicine's so-called scientific conclusions were not scientific; rather, they were morality disguised as science. "Scientific" definitions of healthy sex closely resembled religious definitions of moral sex. In studying sexual activities between men, they "invented" and popularized the distinction between heterosexuality and homosexuality (Gay, 1986; Weeks, 1986).

Early Researchers and Reformers Although most physician-moralists condemned same-sex relationships as pathological as well as immoral, a few individuals stand out in their attempt to understand same-sex sexuality.

Magnus Hirschfeld (1868–1935) was a leading crusader in Germany, especially for homosexual rights. He was both a homosexual and possibly a transvestite. He eloquently presented the case for the humanity of transvestites (Hirschfeld, 1991). And in defense of homosexual rights, he argued that homosexuality was not a perversion but the result of the hormonal development of inborn traits. His defense of homosexuality led to the popularization of the word "homosexual." Hirschfeld's importance, however, lies not so much in his theory of homosexuality as in his sexual reform efforts (Bullough, 1976). In Berlin in 1897, he helped found the first organization for homosexual rights, and he began the first journal devoted to the study of sexuality.

Psychologist Evelyn Hooker was an important American researcher. As a result of Kinsey's research, Americans learned that same-sex sexual relationships were widespread among both men and women. A few years later, Hooker startled her colleagues by demonstrating that homosexuality in itself was not a psychological disorder. She found that ordinary gay men did not differ significantly in personality characteristics from similar heterosexual men (Hooker, 1957). The reverberations of her work continue to this day (McWhirter, 1990).

Contemporary Research By the mid-1960s, political activism and a growing body of scientific literature, based on the work of Ellis, Kinsey, and Hooker, began challenging the traditional psychopathological model of homosexuality (Bayer, 1981). In 1973, the American Psychiatric Association (APA) removed homosexuality from its list of psychological disorders

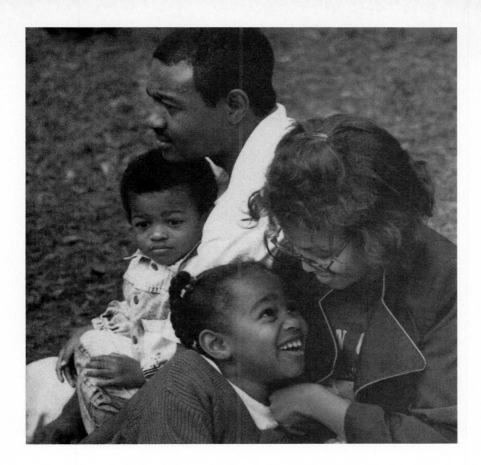

Culture and social class help to shape values and behaviors.

in its *Diagnostic and Statistical Manual of Mental Disorders (DSM-II)*. The APA decision was reinforced by similar resolutions by the American Psychological Association and the American Sociological Association.

As a result of the rejection of the psychopathological model, social and behavioral research on gay men and lesbians has moved in a new direction (Herek, 1984). Research no longer focuses primarily on the causes and cures of homosexuality. Most of the new research approaches homosexuality in a neutral manner. The only major exception to the shift in perspective is found in psychoanalytic literature.

Ethnicity and Sexuality

Over the last few years, researchers have begun to recognize the significance of ethnicity in various aspects of American life, including sexuality. Although little research is available, we will attempt to provide some background to assist an understanding of sexuality and ethnicity.

African Americans African Americans represent the largest ethnic group in America. In studying the sexuality of African Americans, we must consider several factors: (1) sexual stereotypes, (2) socioeconomic status, (3) black subculture, and (4) number of single adults.

Sexual stereotypes greatly distort our understanding of black sexuality. One of the most common stereotypes is the depiction of African Americans as sexually driven (Murry, 1991). Although this is an age-old stereotype dating back to the fifteenth century, it continues to hold considerable strength among nonblacks. Discussing African American men, Robert Staples (1991) writes: "Black men are saddled with a number of stereotypes that label them as irresponsible, criminalistic, hypersexual, and lacking in masculine traits."

Socioeconomic status is a person's ranking in society based on a combination of occupational, educational, and income levels. It is an important element in African American sexual values and behaviors (Staples & Johnson, 1993). Although stereotypes suggest that *all* blacks have a low income, at least 37% are middle class in lifestyle and income (Staples, 1988). Middle-class blacks share many sexual attitudes and values with middle-class whites (Howard, 1988; Staples, 1988). For example, the overwhelming majority of births to single mothers are among low-income African Americans. But as income level increases among blacks, births to single mothers decrease significantly (Staples, 1988).

Values and behaviors are shaped by culture and social class. The subculture of blacks of low socioeconomic status is deeply influenced by poverty, discrimination, and structural subordination. In contrast to middle-class whites and blacks, low-income blacks are more likely to engage in sexual intercourse at an earlier age and to have children outside of marriage. Because of the poverty, violence, and prejudice of inner-city life, low-income black children do not experience a prolonged or "innocent" childhood. They are forced to become adults at an early age.

Premarital sexual activity is not considered immoral or stigmatized, as it is in middle-class communities. Because sexual activity is regarded as natural, premarital sex is considered appropriate as relationships become more involved. Furthermore, as mere survival is not even guaranteed, adolescents may see no reason to wait for a future they may never have. In the inner-city subculture, boys tend to use sex exploitively and competitively. For them, sex is not so much a means of achieving intimacy with partners as it is a way of achieving status among their male peers. For girls, sex is a means of demonstrating their maturity; it is a sign of their womanhood.

For inner-city black adolescents, one becomes a woman by becoming a mother (Zinn & Eitzen, 1990). The black community, which values children highly, generally does not stigmatize the unmarried mother. For blacks of all classes, there is no such thing as an "illegitimate" or "illegally born" child. All children are considered valuable (Collins, 1991; Stack, 1974).

A high proportion of African American women are single (Staples & Johnson, 1993). There are 1.5 million more African American women than men. This gender imbalance is the result of high death rates, incarceration, and drug use among black men, often attributable to the effects of discrimination (see Chapter 6). If they wish to have children, many African American women are likely to be unmarried single parents. Furthermore, the single lifestyle, whether white or black, is associated with more sexual partners, a lack of contraceptive responsibility, and a greater likelihood of contracting STDs.

Although there has been a significant increase in African American research over the last decade, much still needs to be done (Bryant & Coleman, 1988; Taylor, Chatters, Tucker, & Lewis, 1991). For example, we need

socioeconomic status Ranking in society based on a combination of occupational, educational, and income levels.

In studying Latino sexuality, it is important to remember that Latinos come from diverse ethnic groups, including Mexican American, Cuban American, and Puerto Rican, each with its own unique background and set of cultural values.

to (1) explore the sexual attitudes and behaviors of the general African American population, not merely adolescents; (2) examine black sexuality from an African American cultural context; and (3) utilize a cultural equivalency perspective that rejects differences between blacks and whites as signs of inherent deviance. (The **cultural equivalency perspective** is the view that the attitudes, values, and behaviors of one ethnic group are similar to those of another ethnic group.)

cultural equivalency perspective The view that attitudes, behaviors, and values of diverse ethnic groups are basically similar, with differences resulting from adaptation to historical and social forces, such as slavery, discrimination, or poverty.

Latinos Latinos are the fastest-growing and second-largest ethnic group in the United States. Between 1980 and 1990, the Latino population increased by 35%, mostly as a result of immigration from Mexico. There is very little research, however, about Latino sexuality.

Two common stereotypes depict Latinos as sexually permissive and Latino males as pathologically *macho,* or hypermasculine (Becerra, 1988; Espín, 1984). Like African Americans, Latino males are stereotyped as being promiscuous, engaging in excessive and indiscriminate sexual activities. No research, however, validates this stereotype. In fact, one study concludes that in contrast to the dominant stereotype, they are significantly less experienced sexually than their Anglo peers (Padilla & O'Grady, 1987).

The macho stereotype paints Latino males as hypermasculine—swaggering and domineering. But the stereotype of machismo distorts its cultural meaning among Latinos. (The Spanish word was originally incorporated into English in the 1960s as a slang term to describe any male who was sexist.) Within its cultural context, however, **machismo** is a positive concept, characterized by a man's courage, strength, generosity, politeness, and respect for others. And in day-to-day functioning, relations between Latino men and women are significantly more egalitarian than the macho stereo-

machismo In Latino culture, highly prized masculine traits.

type suggests. This is especially true among Latinos who are more acculturated (Becerra, 1988; Griswold del Castillo, 1984). (**Acculturation** is the process of adaptation of an ethnic group to the values, attitudes, and behaviors of the dominant culture.)

In studying Latino sexuality, we must consider three important factors: (1) diversity of ethnic groups, (2) significance of socioeconomic status, and (3) degree of acculturation.

Latinos comprise numerous ethnic subgroups, the largest of which are Mexican American, Puerto Rican, and Cuban (Vega, 1991). Each group has its own unique background and set of cultural traditions that affect sexual attitudes and behaviors. For example, Latino adolescents differ in their contraceptive use according to their ethnic background (Durant, Pendergast, & Seymore, 1990). Fertility rates also differ between groups. The fertility rate of Mexican Americans, for example, is almost one-third higher than that of Anglos; by contrast, the fertility rate for Cuban Americans is lower than that of Anglos (Staples, 1988).

Socioeconomic status is important, as middle-class Latino values appear to differ from those of low-income Latinos. The birth rate for single women, for example, is significantly higher among low-income Latinas than among middle-class Latinas (Bean & Tienda, 1987). Furthermore, Latino ethnic groups rank differently on the socioeconomic scale. The middle class is largest among Cuban Americans, followed by Puerto Ricans, and then Mexican Americans.

The degree of acculturation may be the most important factor affecting sexual attitudes and behavior among Latinos. This can be viewed on a continuum: traditional at one pole, bicultural in the middle, and acculturated at the other pole (Guerrero Pavich, 1986). (This same continuum may also be used with other ethnic groups, such as Europeans, Asian Americans, and Caribbean and Pacific Islanders.)

In traditional Latino culture, Catholicism plays an important role, especially in the realm of sexuality. The Church teaches premarital virginity and prohibits both contraception and abortion. For traditional Latinas, using contraception may lead to "considerable guilt and confusion on the part of the individual woman who feels she is alone in violating the cultural taboos against contraception" (Guerrero Pavich, 1986). Traditional Latinas are more negative toward birth control and are less likely to use it than more acculturated women (Ortiz & Casas, 1990). Abortion is out of the question. Only the most acculturated Latinas view abortion as an option.

Among bicultural Latinos, there may be gender-role conflict (Salgado de Snyder, Cervantes, & Padilla, 1990). Emma Guerrero Pavich describes the conflicts some Latinas experience: "She observes the freedom and sexual expression 'Americanas' have. At first she may condemn them as 'bad women'; later she may envy their freedom. Still later she may begin to want those freedoms for herself" (Guerrero Pavich, 1986).

For bicultural Latinos, sexual values and attitudes appear to lie at different points along the continuum, depending on the degree of acculturation. Research, however, is lacking.

There is significantly greater flux among Latinos as a result of continuing high rates of immigration and the acculturation process. Much current research on Latinos focuses on the acculturation of new immigrants. We know less, however, about bicultural Latinos and even less about acculturated Latinos. The habits, beliefs, and values of Asian Americans and other ethnic minorities are rarely discussed. But we know next to nothing about the sexuality of all these groups.

Popular culture surrounds us with sexual images disseminated through advertising, music, television, and film that form a backdrop to our daily living. Much of what is conveyed is simplified, stereotypical, shallow—and entertaining. But through sex research, we can gain tools for evaluating the mass of sex information disseminated through the media. Studying sex research enables us to understand how research is conducted and to be aware of its strengths and its limitations. Traditional sex research has been expanded in recent years by feminist and gay and lesbian research, which provides fresh insights and perspectives. Although the study of sexuality and ethnicity is only now beginning to emerge, it promises to enlarge our understanding of the diversity of attitudes, behaviors, and values in contemporary America.

SUMMARY

Sex, Advice Columnists, and Pop Psychology

• The sex information/advice genre transmits information to both entertain and inform; the information is generally oversimplified so that it does not interfere with the genre's primary entertainment purpose. Much of the information or advice conveys social norms. Although it uses the social science framework, it tends to overgeneralize and distort.

Thinking (Critically) About Sex

• Objective statements are based on observations of things as they exist in themselves. Value judgments are evaluations based on moral or ethical standards. Opinions are unsubstantiated beliefs based on an individual's personal thoughts. Biases are personal leanings or inclinations. Stereotypes, rigidly held beliefs about the personal characteristics of a group of people, are a type of schema, the organization of knowledge through thought processes.

• Attitudes are predispositions to acting, thinking, or feeling certain ways toward things. Behaviors are the ways people act. Behaviors cannot necessarily be inferred from attitudes, or vice versa.

• Fallacies are errors in reasoning. The egocentric fallacy is the belief that others necessarily share one's own values, beliefs, and attitudes. The ethnocentric fallacy is the belief that one's own ethnic group, nation, or culture is inherently superior to any other.

Sex Research Methods

• Ethical issues are important concerns in sex research. The most important issues are informed consent, protection from harm, confidentiality, and the use of deception.

• In sex research, sampling is a particularly acute problem. To be meaningful, samples should be representative of the larger group from which they are drawn. But most samples are limited by volunteer bias, dependence on college students, underrepresentation of ethnic groups, and difficulties in sampling gay men and lesbians.

• The most important methods in sex research are clinical, survey, observational, and experimental. Clinical research relies on in-depth examinations of individuals or groups who come to the clinician seeking treatment for psychological or medical problems. Survey research uses questionnaires or interviews to gather information from a small representative sample of people. Observational research requires the researcher to observe interactions carefully in as unobtrusive a manner as possible. Experimental research presents subjects with various stimuli under controlled conditions in which their responses can be measured.

• Experiments are controlled through the use of independent variables (which can be changed by the experimenter) and dependent variables (which are changes dependent on changes in the independent variable). Clinical, survey, and observational research efforts, by contrast, are correlational studies that infer relationships between variables without manipulating them. In experimental research, physiological responses are often measured by plethysmographs or strain gauges.

The Sex Researchers

• Richard von Krafft-Ebing, who published his *Psychopathia Sexualis* in 1886, was one of the earliest sex researchers. His work emphasized the pathological aspects of sexuality. Although his theories are now out of date, he documented a vast range of sexual behaviors and brought them into public discussion.

• Sigmund Freud was one of the most influential thinkers in Western civilization. According to Freud's theory, personality consisted of three parts: the id, ego, and superego. Freud believed there were five stages in psychosexual development: the oral stage, anal stage, phallic stage, latency stage, and genital stage.

• Havelock Ellis was the earliest modern sexual thinker. His ideas included the relativity of sexual values, the normality of masturbation, a belief in the sexual equality of men and women, the redefinition of "normal," and a reevaluation of homosexuality.

• Alfred Kinsey applied statistical techniques to the study of human sexuality. His work documented enormous diversity in sexual behavior, emphasized the role of masturbation in sexual development, and argued that the distinction between normal and abnormal behavior was meaningless. The Kinsey scale charts sexual activities along a continuum ranging from exclusive heterosexual behaviors to exclusive same-sex behaviors.

• William Masters and Virginia Johnson detailed the physiology of the human sexual response cycle. Their physiological studies demonstrated the similarity between male and female sexual responses; they demonstrated that women achieved orgasms through clitoral stimulation. Their work on sexual inadequacy revolutionized sex therapy through the use of behavioral techniques.

Emerging Research Perspectives

• There is no single feminist perspective in sex research.

• Research on homosexuality has rejected the moralistic-pathological approach. The pioneers of gay/lesbian research included Magnus Hirschfeld and Evelyn Hooker. Contemporary gay/lesbian research approaches homosexuality in a neutral manner.

• The role of ethnicity in human sexuality has been largely overlooked until recently.

• Socioeconomic status is important in the study of African American sexuality. Other factors include stereotyping of blacks as hypersexual and promiscuous, the importance of the African American subculture, and the large number of single adults.

• Two common stereotypes about Latinos are that they are sexually permissive and that males are pathologically macho. Factors in studying Latino sexuality include the diversity of ethnic groups, such as Mexican American, Cuban American, and Puerto Rican; the role of socioeconomic status; and the degree of acculturation.

SUGGESTED READINGS

Geer, James, and William O'Donohue, eds. *Theories of Human Sexuality*. New York: Plenum Press, 1987. A collection of essays briefly describing various theories of human sexuality.

Haberstein, Charles, and Robert Mindel. *Ethnic Families in America: Patterns and Variations*, 3rd ed. New York: Elsevier North Holland, 1988. An important collection of essays on different ethnic groups, including historical background and current status. Excellent background for understanding sexual values and the dynamics of diverse groups.

Irvine, Janice. *Disorders of Desire: Sex and Gender in Modern American Sexology*. Philadelphia: Temple University Press, 1990. A critical examination, from a feminist perspective, of sexology, including the Kinsey studies, the work of Masters and Johnson, sex therapy, and gender research, especially gay/lesbian sexuality and transsexuality.

McKinney, Kathleen, and Susan Sprecher, eds. *Human Sexuality: The Societal and Interpersonal Context*. New York: Ablex, 1989. Sociologically oriented essays on human sexuality.

Minton, Henry, ed. *Gay and Lesbian Studies: Emergence of a Discipline*. Binghamton, NY: Harrington Press, 1992. A collection of essays on the development of gay/lesbian studies.

Vance, Carole. *Pleasure and Danger: Exploring Female Sexuality*. Boston: Routledge & Kegan Paul, 1984. A provocative collection of essays dealing with female sexuality from a feminist perspective.

Weeks, Jeffrey. *Sexuality and Its Discontents: Meanings, Myths, and Modern Sexualities*. London: Routledge & Kegan Paul, 1985. An excellent study on the changing meanings of sexuality.

Chapter Three

FEMALE SEXUAL ANATOMY, PHYSIOLOGY, AND RESPONSE

PREVIEW: SELF-QUIZ

1. Early in their development, all embryos appear as female. True or false?

2. The female reproductive organs are collectively known as the vagina. True or false?

3. The center of sexual arousal in women is the clitoris. True or false?

4. Many women can tell when they are ovulating by the consistency of the mucus secreted by the cervix. True or false?

5. At birth, the ovaries of the human female contain about 25,000 immature eggs. True or false?

6. Women's ovaries produce estrogen and testosterone. True or false?

7. Menstrual cramps are often psychosomatic (induced by the mind or by emotions). True or false?

8. A common cause of a missed menstrual period is pregnancy. True or false?

9. For women, orgasms from intercourse are generally more physically intense than orgasms from masturbation. True or false?

10. The sex drive of men and women is influenced by the hormone testosterone. True or false?

ANSWERS 1. T, 2. F, 3. T, 4. T, 5. F, 6. T, 7. F, 8. T, 9. F, 10. T

Chapter Outline

Although women and men are similar in many more ways than they are different, we tend to focus on the differences rather than the similarities. Various cultures hold diverse ideas about exactly what it means to be female or male, but just about the only differences that are consistent are actual physical differences, most of which relate to sexual structure and function. In this chapter and the following one, we discuss both the similarities and differences in the anatomy (body structures), physiology (body functions), and sexual response of males and females. This chapter introduces the sexual structures and functions of women's bodies, including the influence of hormones and the menstrual cycle. We also look at models of sexual arousal and response, the relationship of these to women's experiences of sex, and the role of orgasm. In Chapter 4, we discuss male anatomy and physiology, and in Chapter 5, we move beyond biology to look at gender and the meanings we ascribe to being male and female.

FEMALE SEX ORGANS: WHAT ARE THEY FOR?

Anatomically speaking, all embryos appear as females when their reproductive organs begin to develop. If it does not receive certain genetic and hormonal signals, the fetus will continue to develop as a female. In humans

Mons pubis

Labia majora

Urethral opening

Prepuce of clitoris

Clitoris (glans)

Labia minora

Vaginal opening

Perineum

Anus

FIGURE 3.1 External Female Sexual Structures (Vulva).

and most other mammals, the female, in addition to providing half the genetic instructions for the offspring, provides the environment in which it can develop until it becomes capable of surviving as a separate entity. She also nourishes the offspring, both during gestation (the period of carrying the young in the uterus) via the placenta and following birth via the breasts through lactation (milk production).

It is clear that the female sex organs serve a reproductive function. But they perform other functions as well. Some sexual parts serve to bring pleasure to their owners; they may also serve to attract potential sexual partners. Because of the mutual pleasure partners give each other, we can see that sexual structures also serve an important role in human relationships. People demonstrate their affection for one another by sharing sexual pleasure and generally form enduring partnerships at least partially on the basis of mutual sexual sharing. Let's look at the features of human female anatomy and physiology that provide pleasure to women and their partners and enable them to conceive and give birth.

External Structures (The Vulva)

The sexual and reproductive organs of both men and women are also called **genitals,** or genitalia, from the Latin *genere*, to beget. The external female genitals are the mons pubis, the clitoris, the labia majora, and the labia minora, collectively known as the **vulva** (Figure 3.1). (People often use the word "vagina" when they are actually referring to the vulva. The vagina is an internal structure.)

genitals The reproductive and sexual organs of males and females. Also known as genitalia.

vulva The collective term for the external female genitalia.

mons pubis In the female, the mound of fatty tissue covering the pubic bone; the pubic mound. Also known as mons veneris.

mons veneris The pubic mound; literally, mountain of Venus. Also known as mons pubis.

clitoris An external sexual structure that is the center of arousal in the female; located above the vagina at the meeting of the labia minora.

glans clitoridis The erotically sensitive tip of the clitoris.

clitoral hood A fold of skin covering the glans of the clitoris.

labia majora (singular, *labium majus*) Two folds of spongy flesh extending from the mons pubis and enclosing the labia minora, clitoris, urethral opening, and vaginal entrance. Also known as major lips.

labia minora (singular, *labium minus*) Two small folds of skin within the labia majora that meet above the clitoris to form the clitoral hood. Also known as minor lips.

vestibule The area enclosed by the labia minora.

Bartholin's gland One of two small ducts on either side of the vaginal opening that secretes a small amount of moisture during sexual arousal. Also known as vestibular gland.

vagina In females, a flexible, muscular organ that begins between the legs and extends diagonally toward the small of the back. It encompasses the penis during sexual intercourse and is the pathway (birth canal) through which an infant is born.

The Mons Pubis The **mons pubis** (pubic mound) or **mons veneris** (mound of Venus) is a pad of fatty tissue that covers the area of the pubic bone about 6 inches below the navel. Beginning in puberty, the mons is covered with pubic hair. In some women, this area is sensitive to sexual stimulation.

The Clitoris The **clitoris** is the center of sexual arousal in the female. It contains a high concentration of nerve endings and is exquisitely sensitive to stimulation, especially at the tip of its shaft, the **glans clitoridis.** A fold of skin called the **clitoral hood** covers the glans when the clitoris is not engorged. Although the clitoris is structurally analogous to the penis (it is formed from the same embryonic tissue), its sole function is sexual arousal. (The penis serves the additional functions of urine excretion and semen ejaculation.) When stimulated, the clitoris enlarges initially, then retracts beneath the hood just before and during orgasm. With repeated orgasms, it follows the same pattern of engorgement and retraction, although its swellings may not be as pronounced after the initial orgasm.

The Labia Majora and Labia Minora The **labia majora** (major lips) are two folds of spongy flesh extending from the mons pubis and enclosing the labia minora clitoris, urethral opening, and vaginal entrance. The **labia minora** (minor lips) are smaller folds within the labia majora that meet above the clitoris to form the clitoral hood. They are smooth, hairless, and vary quite a bit in appearance from woman to woman. They are sensitive to the touch and swell during sexual arousal, doubling or tripling in size. The area enclosed by the labia minora is referred to as the **vestibule.** Within the vestibule, on either side of the vaginal opening, are two small ducts from the **Bartholin's glands** (or vestibular glands), which secrete a small amount of moisture during sexual arousal.

Internal Structures

The internal female sexual structures and reproductive organs include the vagina; the uterus and its lower opening, the cervix; the ovaries; and the fallopian tubes (Figure 3.2).

The Vagina The **vagina,** from the Latin word for sheath, is a flexible, muscular structure that begins between the legs and extends diagonally toward the small of the back. The vagina serves two reproductive functions: It encompasses the penis during **coitus** (sexual intercourse) so that sperm will be deposited near the entrance of the uterus, and it is the **birth canal** through which an infant is born. Normally the walls of the vagina are relaxed and collapsed together, but during sexual arousal, the inner two-thirds of the vagina expand. Mucous membranes line the vagina, providing lubrication during arousal. The opening of the vagina is known as the **introitus.** Prior to first intercourse or other intrusion, the introitus is partially covered by a thin membrane, the **hymen** (named for the Roman god of marriage). (Maintaining good vaginal health is discussed in Chapter 13.)

The hymen typically has one or several perforations, allowing menstrual blood and mucous secretions to flow out of the vagina (and generally allowing for tampon insertion). In many cultures, it is (or was) important for a

FIGURE 3.2 Internal Female Sexual Structures.

woman's hymen to be intact on her wedding night. Blood on the nuptial sheets is taken as proof of her virginity. (Even in some developed countries today, plastic surgeons do a brisk trade reconstructing the hymens of brides-to-be.) The stretching or tearing of the hymen may or may not be painful. According to one study of first intercourse, 25% of women experienced no pain, 40% had moderate pain, and 33% felt severe pain (Weis, 1985). The women who experienced pain tended to be younger than those who did not; they held more conservative sexual values, had more negative feelings toward their partners and toward intercourse with them, and more often expected intercourse to be painful. Prior to first intercourse, the hymen may be stretched somewhat by tampon insertion, by the woman's self-manipulation, or by a partner during noncoital sexual activity.

Fairly recently, controversial research has asserted that an erotically sensitive area, the **Grafenberg spot,** is located on the front wall of the vagina midway between the introitus and the cervix (on the vaginal side of the urethra). This area, also known as the **G-spot,** is described as being about the size of a small bean during its unaroused state and growing to the size of a dime during arousal (Ladas, Whipple, & Perry, 1982). Stimulation of the G-spot is said to lead to orgasm, and, in some women, the ejaculation of a clear fluid from the urethra. Masters and Johnson noted, however, in a study of 100 women, that fewer than 10% experienced any special sensitivity in that area (Masters, Johnson, & Kolodny, 1992). They suggest that additional research is necessary.

The Uterus and Cervix

The **uterus,** or womb, is a hollow, thick-walled, muscular organ held in the pelvic cavity by a number of flexible ligaments and supported by several muscles. It is pear-shaped, with the tapered

coitus Sexual intercourse.

birth canal The passageway through which an infant is born; the vagina.

introitus The opening of the vagina.

hymen A thin membrane partially covering the introitus prior to first intercourse or other breakage.

Grafenberg spot According to some researchers, an erotically sensitive area on the front wall of the vagina midway between the introitus and the cervix. Also known as G-spot.

uterus A hollow, thick-walled, muscular organ held in the pelvic cavity by flexible ligaments and supported by several muscles. Also known as womb.

VAGINAL SECRETIONS AND LUBRICATION

The mucous membranes lining the walls of the vagina normally produce clear, white, or pale yellow secretions. These secretions pass from the cervix through the vagina and vary in color, consistency, odor, and quantity depending on the phase of the menstrual cycle, a woman's health, and her unique physical characteristics. It is important for you to observe your secretions periodically and note any changes, especially if symptoms accompany them. Call a health practitioner if you feel uncertain, suspicious, and/or have been exposed to a sexually transmittable disease.

Although the vaginal walls are generally moist, sexual excitement causes lubrication to increase substantially. This lubrication serves two biological purposes. First, it increases the possibility of conception by alkalinizing the normally acidic chemical balance in the vagina, thus making it more hospitable to sperm, which die faster in acid environments. Second, it makes coitus easier and more pleasurable for both you and your partner, as friction between the vaginal walls and penis is reduced.

Use the following chart to compare your personal observations with those of other women.

Vaginal Mucus and Secretions Chart

Color	Consistency	Odor	Other Symptoms	Possible Cause	What To Do
clear	slightly rubbery; stretchy	normal	—	ovulation; sexual stimulation	nothing
milky	creamy	normal	—	preovulation	nothing
white	sticky, curdlike	normal	—	postovulation; the pill	nothing
brownish	watery and sticky	normal or slightly different	—	last days of period; spotting	nothing
white	thin, watery, creamy	normal to foul or fishy	itching	Gardnerella bacteria or nonspecific bacterial infection	see health practitioner
white	curdlike or flecks, slight amount of discharge	yeasty or foul	itching or intense itching	overgrowth of yeast cells, yeast infection	apply yogurt or vinegar solution; see health practitioner
yellow, yellow-green	smooth or frothy	usually foul	itchy; may have red dots on cervix	possible Trichomonas infection	see health practitioner
yellow, yellow-green	thick, mucous	none to foul	pelvic cramping or pelvic pain	possible infection of fallopian tubes	see health practitioner right away

SOURCE: Strong, Bryan, and Christine DeVault. The Marriage and Family Experience. St. Paul, MN: West, 1992.

end, the **cervix,** extending down and opening into the vagina. If a woman has not given birth, the uterus is about 3 inches long and 3 inches wide at the top; it is somewhat larger in women who have given birth. The uterus expands during pregnancy to the size of a volleyball or larger, to accommodate the developing fetus. The lining of the uterine walls, the **endometrium,** is filled with tiny blood vessels. During the menstrual cycle, this tissue is built up, then shed and expelled through the cervical **os** (opening), unless fertilization has occurred. In the event of pregnancy, the pre-embryo is embedded in the nourishing endometrium.

In addition to the more-or-less monthly menstrual discharge, mucous secretions from the cervix also flow out through the vagina. These secretions tend to be somewhat white, thick, and sticky following menstruation, becoming thinner as ovulation approaches. At ovulation, the mucous flow tends to increase and to be clear, slippery, and stretchy, somewhat like egg white. (Birth control using cervical mucus to determine the time of ovulation is discussed in Chapter 11.)

The Ovaries　On each side of the uterus, held in place by several ligaments, is one of a pair of ovaries. The **ovary** is a **gonad,** an organ that produces **gametes,** the sex cells containing the genetic material necessary for reproduction. Female gametes are called **oocytes,** from the Greek words for egg and cell. (Oocytes are commonly referred to as eggs or **ova** [singular, **ovum**]. Technically, however, the cell does not become an egg until it completes its final stages of division following fertilization.) The ovaries are the size and shape of large almonds. In addition to producing oocytes, they serve the important function of hormone production. The basic female hormones, estrogen and progesterone, are discussed later in this chapter.

At birth the human female's ovaries contain 400,000–700,000 oocytes (Marieb, 1992; Masters, Johnson, & Kolodny, 1992). During childhood, many of these degenerate; then, beginning in puberty and ending after menopause, a total of about 400 oocytes mature and are released on a more-or-less monthly basis. The release of an oocyte is called **ovulation.** The immature oocytes are embedded in saclike structures called **ovarian follicles.** The fully ripened follicle is called a **vesicular** or **Graffian follicle.** At maturation, the follicle ruptures, releasing the oocyte to begin its journey. After the oocyte emerges, the ruptured follicle becomes the **corpus luteum** (from Latin for yellow body), a producer of important hormones; it eventually degenerates.

The Fallopian Tubes　At the top of the uterus, one on each side, are two tubes known as **fallopian tubes,** uterine tubes, or oviducts. The tubes are about 4 inches long. They extend toward the ovaries but are not attached to them. Instead, the funnel-shaped end of each tube (the **infundibulum**) fans out into fingerlike **fimbriae,** which drape over the ovary but may not actually touch it. Tiny, hairlike **cilia** on the fimbriae become active during ovulation. Their waving motion conducts the oocyte that has been released from the ovary into the fallopian tube. Just within the infundibulum is the **ampulla,** the widened part of the tube in which fertilization normally occurs if sperm and oocyte are there at the same time. (The process of ovulation and the events leading to fertilization are discussed later in this chapter; fertilization is covered in Chapter 12.)

cervix　The end of the uterus, opening toward the vagina.

endometrium　The lining of the uterine walls.

os　The cervical opening.

ovary　One of a pair of organs that produces oocytes.

gonad　An organ (ovary or testis) that produces gametes.

gamete　A sex cell containing the genetic material necessary for reproduction; an oocyte (ovum) or sperm.

oocyte　The female gamete, referred to as an egg or ovum.

ovum　(plural, *ova*) An egg; an oocyte; the female gamete.

ovulation　The release of an oocyte from the ovary during the ovarian cycle.

ovarian follicle　A saclike structure in which an oocyte develops.

vesicular follicle or **Graffian follicle**　A fully ripened ovarian follicle.

corpus luteum　The tissue formed from a ruptured ovarian follicle that produces important hormones after the oocyte emerges.

fallopian tube　One of two uterine tubes extending toward an ovary.

infundibulum　The funnel-shaped end of a fallopian tube.

fimbriae　The fingerlike ends of the fallopian tubes, extending toward the ovary.

cilia　(singular, *cilium*) Tiny, hairlike fibers on fimbriae whose waving motion conducts the oocyte into the fallopian tube.

ampulla　The widened part of the fallopian tube or the vas deferens.

Other Structures

There are several other important anatomical structures in the genital areas of both men and women. Although they may not serve reproductive functions, they may be involved in sexual activities. Some of these areas may also be affected by sexually transmitted diseases. In women, these structures include the urethra, anus, and perineum. The **urethra** is the tube through which urine passes; the **urethral opening** is located between the clitoris and the vaginal opening. Between the vagina and the **anus**—the opening of the rectum, through which excrement passes—is a diamond-shaped region called the **perineum.** This area of soft tissue covers the muscles and ligaments of the **pelvic floor,** the underside of the pelvic area extending from the top of the pubic bone (above the clitoris) to the anus. (To learn more about this muscle and Kegel exercises, see Chapter 14.) The anus consists of two sphincters, circular muscles that open and close like valves. The tissue that rings the opening is tender and is erotically sensitive for some people.

In sex play or intercourse involving the anus or rectum, care must be taken not to rupture the delicate tissues. Anal sex, insertion of the penis into the rectum, is not considered safe, because abrasions of the tissue provide easy access for pathogens, such as HIV (the virus that causes AIDS), into the bloodstream (see Chapter 16).

The Breasts

Both women and men have breasts. At puberty, the female breasts begin to develop in response to hormonal stimuli (Figure 3.3). At maturity, the left breast is often slightly larger than the right (Rome, 1992).

The reproductive function of the breasts is to nourish the offspring through **lactation,** or milk production. A mature female breast, also known as a **mammary gland,** is composed of fatty tissue and 15–25 lobes that radiate around a central protruding nipple. Around the nipple is a ring of darkened skin called the **areola.** Tiny muscles at the base of the nipple cause it to become erect in response to touch, cold, or sexual arousal.

When a woman is pregnant, the structures within the breast undergo further development. Directly following childbirth, in response to hormonal signals, small glands within the lobes called **alveoli** begin producing milk. The milk passes into ducts, each of which has a dilated region for storage; the ducts open to the outside at the nipple. (Breast-feeding is discussed in detail in Chapter 12.) During lactation, a woman's breasts increase in size from enlarged glandular tissues and stored milk. In women who are not lactating, breast size depends mainly on fat content, often determined by hereditary factors.

FEMALE SEXUAL PHYSIOLOGY

The female reproductive cycle can be viewed as having two components (although, of course, multiple biological processes are involved): the ovarian cycle, in which eggs develop, and the menstrual or uterine cycle, in which the womb is prepared for pregnancy. These cycles repeat approximately every month for about 35 or 40 years. The task of directing these processes belongs to a class of chemicals called hormones.

urethra The tube through which urine passes.

urethral opening The opening in the urethra through which urine is expelled.

anus The opening of the rectum, consisting of two sphincters, circular muscles that open and close like valves.

perineum An area of soft tissue between the genitals and the anus that covers the muscles and ligaments of the pelvic floor.

pelvic floor The underside of the pelvic area, extending from the top of the pubic bone to the anus.

lactation The production of milk in the breasts (mammary glands).

mammary gland A mature female breast.

areola A ring of darkened skin around the nipple.

alveoli (singular, *alveolus*) Small glands within the female breast that begin producing milk following childbirth.

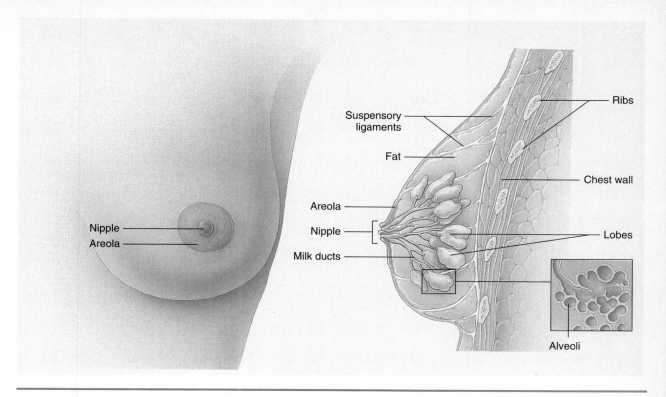

FIGURE 3.3 The Female Breast.

The Role of Hormones

Hormones are chemical substances that serve as messengers, traveling within the body through the bloodstream. Most hormones are composed of either amino acids (building blocks of proteins) or steroids (derived from cholesterol). They are produced by the ovaries and the endocrine glands—the adrenals, pituitary, and hypothalamus. Hormones assist in a variety of tasks, including development of the reproductive organs and secondary sex characteristics during puberty, regulation of the menstrual cycle, maintenance of pregnancy, initiation and regulation of childbirth, and initiation of lactation. Hormones that act directly on the gonads are known as **gonadotropins.** Among the most important of the female hormones is **estrogen,** which affects the maturation of the reproductive organs, menstruation, and pregnancy. The principal hormones involved in a woman's reproductive and sexual life and their functions are described in Table 3.1.

The Ovarian Cycle

The development of female gametes is a complex process that begins even before a woman is born. In infancy and childhood, the cells that will develop into ova (eggs) undergo no further development. During puberty,

hormone A chemical substance that acts as a messenger within the body, regulating various functions.

gonadotropin A hormone that acts directly on the gonads.

estrogen The principal female hormone, regulating reproductive functions and the development of secondary sex characteristics.

TABLE 3.1 Female Reproductive Hormones

Hormone	Where Produced	Functions
Estrogen (including estradiol, estrone, estriol)	Ovaries, adrenal glands, placenta (during pregnancy)	Promotes maturation of reproductive organs, development of secondary sex characteristics, and growth spurt at puberty; regulates menstrual cycle; sustains pregnancy
Progesterone	Ovaries, adrenal glands	Promotes breast development, maintains uterine lining, regulates menstrual cycle, sustains pregnancy
Gonadotropin-releasing hormone (GnRH)	Hypothalamus	Promotes maturation of gonads, regulates menstrual cycle
Follicle-stimulating hormone (FSH)	Pituitary	Regulates ovarian function and maturation of ovarian follicles
Luteinizing hormone (LH)	Pituitary	Assists in production of estrogen and progesterone, regulates maturation of ovarian follicles, triggers ovulation
Human chorionic gonadotropin (HCG)	Embryo and placenta	Helps sustain pregnancy
Testosterone	Ovaries, adrenal glands	Helps stimulate sexual interest
Oxytocin	Hypothalamus	Stimulates uterine contractions during childbirth
Prolactin	Pituitary	Stimulates milk production
Prostaglandins	All body cells	Mediate hormone response, stimulate muscle contractions

oogenesis The production of oocytes; the ovarian cycle.

ovarian cycle The more-or-less monthly process during which oocytes are produced.

hormones trigger the completion of the process of **oogenesis** (oh-uh-JEN-uh-sis), literally, "egg beginning." This process, called the **ovarian cycle,** continues until a woman reaches menopause.

The ovarian cycle averages 28 days in length, although there is considerable variation among women, ranging from 21 to 40 days. In their own particular cycle length after puberty, however, most women experience little variation. Generally, ovulation occurs in only one ovary each month, alternating between the right and left sides with each successive cycle. If a single ovary is removed, the remaining one begins to ovulate every month (Fox, 1987). The ovarian cycle has three phases, called follicular, ovulatory,

(a) Follicular Phase

Fallopian tube

Oocyte disintegrates

Uterine lining

Ovary

Fimbriae

Uterine lining sloughs off and passes out of the body through the cervix and vagina

Uterus

Cervix

Vagina

(MENSTRUATION)

Uterine lining renews

Maturing oocyte in follicle

Immature oocytes

(FOLLICLE DEVELOPMENT)

(b) Ovulatory Phase

Uterine lining thickens

Oocyte is released

(c) Luteal Phase

Oocyte travels through tube

Remaining cells of follicle develop into corpus luteum

Lining continues to thicken

FIGURE 3.4 Ovarian and Menstrual Cycles. The ovarian cycle consists of the activities within the ovaries and the development of oocytes; it includes the follicular, ovulatory, and luteal phases. The menstrual cycle consists of events in the uterus. Hormones regulate these cycles.

and luteal (Figure 3.4). As an ovary undergoes its changes, corresponding changes occur in the uterus. These changes, called the uterine, or menstrual, cycle are discussed after the ovarian cycle.

Follicular Phase On the first day of the cycle, **gonadotropin-releasing hormone (GnRH)** is released from the hypothalamus. GnRH begins to stimulate the pituitary to release **follicle-stimulating hormone (FSH)** and **luteinizing hormone (LH),** initiating the **follicular phase.** During the first ten days, 10 to 20 ovarian follicles begin to grow, stimulated by FSH and LH. In 98–99% of cases, just one of the follicles will mature completely during this period. (The maturation of more than one oocyte is one factor in multiple births.) All the developing follicles begin secreting estrogen. Under the influence of FSH and estrogen, the oocyte matures; it begins to bulge from the surface of the ovary.

Ovulatory Phase The **ovulatory phase** begins at about day 11 and culminates with ovulation at about day 14. Stimulated by an increase of LH from the pituitary, the primary oocyte undergoes cell division and becomes ready for ovulation. The ballooning follicle wall thins and ruptures, and the

gonadotropin-releasing hormone (GnRH) A hormone that stimulates the pituitary gland to release follicle-stimulating hormone (FSH) and luteinizing hormone (LH), initiating the follicular phase of the ovarian cycle.

follicle-stimulating hormone (FSH) A hormone that regulates ovulation.

luteinizing hormone (LH) A hormone involved in ovulation.

follicular phase The phase of the ovarian cycle during which a follicle matures.

ovulatory phase The phase of the ovarian cycle during which ovulation occurs.

Think About It

MEDICAL CARE: WHAT DO WOMEN NEED?

It is a fact that women have special needs and face difficulties in the medical system. Whereas men are apt to receive medical care from one practitioner, women often receive either uncoordinated care from several physicians or care from a physician insensitive to, or untrained to, find health problems peculiar to women. Gender bias is observed in the male-to-female ratio of physicians, the research decisions that are based on male subjects, and the observations that many male physicians are less focused on women's than men's medical needs. Recent studies have shown that, compared with women who see female practitioners, those who see male practitioners are less likely to have such diagnostic procedures as Pap smears and mammograms. They are also less likely to receive thorough diagnosis and treatment for coronary heart disease.

For those reasons and more, it is important for women to be aware and proactive in their medical care. That means selecting a male or female physician who is knowledgeable and sensitive to their needs, who knows what services to expect and makes sure they get them. The basic services unique to women are annual pelvic exams, Pap smears, and breast exams (including a mammogram every one to two years between ages 40 and 50, and annually thereafter).

To avoid duplication and maximize observations and opinions, the best option—though not the cheapest—is for a woman to have both a gynecologist and a primary care physician and be sure they communicate with each other. Either kind of physician alone can fulfill a woman's health care needs; however, the combination is a better choice. Women should not be afraid to get a second (or third) opinion if they are confused, do not get a response to their symptoms, or are faced with differing diagnoses. It is important that women interview a new physician before seeking his or her care and be sure that the physician's attitude about women's health is similar to their own.

_____

Adapted from Lipman, M. (1994, May). "Office Visit: What Do Women Need?" *Consumer Reports on Health*.

---

oocyte enters the abdominal cavity near the beckoning fimbriae. Ovulation is now complete. Some women experience a sharp twinge on one side of the lower abdomen during ovulation.

Luteal Phase Following ovulation, estrogen levels drop rapidly, and the ruptured follicle, still under the influence of increased LH, becomes a corpus luteum, which secretes **progesterone** and small amounts of estrogen. Increasing levels of these hormones serve to inhibit pituitary release of FSH and LH. Unless fertilization has occurred, the corpus luteum deteriorates, becoming a mass of scar tissue. In the event of pregnancy, the corpus luteum maintains its hormonal output, helping to sustain the pregnancy. The hormone human chorionic gonadotropin (HCG)—similar to LH—is secreted by the embryo and signals the corpus luteum to continue until the placenta has developed sufficiently to take over hormone production.

The **luteal phase** typically lasts from day 14 (immediately after ovulation) through day 28 of the ovarian cycle. Even when cycles are more or less than 28 days, the duration of the luteal phase remains the same; the time between ovulation and the end of the cycle is always 14 days. At this

progesterone A female hormone that helps regulate the menstrual cycle and sustain pregnancy.

luteal phase The phase of the ovarian cycle during which a follicle becomes a corpus luteum and then degenerates.

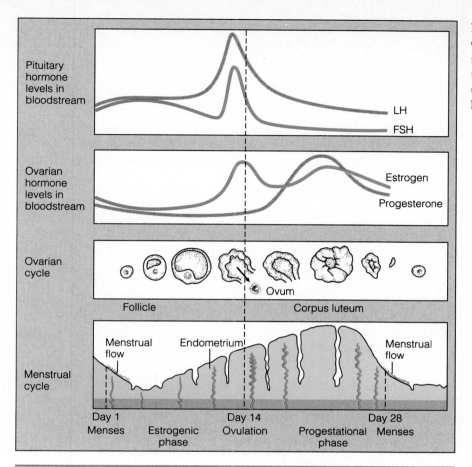

FIGURE 3.5 The Menstrual Cycle, Ovarian Cycle, and Hormone Levels. This chart compares the activities of the ovaries and uterus and shows the relationship of hormone levels to these activities.

point, the ovarian hormone levels are at their lowest, GnRH is released, and FSH and LH levels begin to rise.

The Menstrual Cycle

As estrogen levels fall following the degeneration of the corpus luteum, the uterine lining (endometrium) is shed because it will not be needed to help sustain a fertilized ovum. The shedding of endometrial tissue and the bleeding that accompanies it are, collectively, a monthly event in the lives of women from puberty through menopause. Cultural and religious attitudes as well as personal experience influence our feelings about this phenomenon. (The physical and emotional effects of menstruation are discussed later in this section. The onset of menstruation and its effect on a woman's psychosexual development is discussed in Chapter 6. Menopause is discussed in Chapter 13.)

The **menstrual cycle** (or uterine cycle), like the ovarian cycle, is divided into three phases. What occurs within the uterus is inextricably related to what is happening in the ovaries, but only in their final phases do the two cycles actually coincide (Figure 3.5). The menstrual cycle consists of the menstrual, proliferative, and secretory phases.

menstrual cycle The more-or-less monthly process during which the uterus is readied for implantation of a fertilized ovum. Also known as uterine cycle.

You and Your Sexual Well-Being

RELIEVING MENSTRUAL SYMPTOMS

To date, the causes of premenstrual syndrome (PMS) are unknown, and there are no universally effective ways to relieve PMS symptoms. For women, recognizing their menstrual patterns, learning about their bodies, and recognizing and dealing with existing difficulties can be useful in heading off or easing potential problems. Different remedies work for different women. We suggest you try varying combinations of them and keep a record of your response to each. Following are suggestions for relieving the more common premenstrual and menstrual symptoms; both self-help and medical treatments are included.

For Premenstrual Symptoms

- *Diet.* Moderate amounts of protein and substantial amounts of carbohydrates (such as fresh fruits and vegetables, whole-grain breads and cereals, beans, rice, and pasta) are recommended. Reduce or avoid salt, sugar, and caffeine products such as coffee and colas (Rossignol, Zhang, Chen, & Xiang, 1989). Keep in mind that although you may crave chocolate, it may have a negative effect on you; try fruit or popcorn instead, and see how you feel. Frequent small meals may be better than two or three large meals. Some women find relief by taking a maximum 300 mg per day dose of vitamin B6 during their menstrual period. Excessive doses of this vitamin over prolonged periods, however, can cause neurological problems.

- *Alcohol and tobacco.* Avoid them.

- *Exercise.* Moderate exercise is suggested, but be sure to include about 30 minutes of aerobic movement three or four times per week (Hatcher et al., 1990). Aerobic exercise brings oxygen to body tissues and stimulates the production of endorphins, chemical substances that help promote feelings of well-being. Yoga may also be helpful, especially the "cobra" position.

- *Medical treatments.* For severe PMS, progesterone therapy is sometimes recommended (Dalton, 1984). There is much controversy within the medical profession about the actual effectiveness of this therapy, however. Hormonal contraceptives are sometimes prescribed to relieve premenstrual (and menstrual) distress. Prostaglandin inhibitors, discussed below, may help relieve premenstrual headaches and cramping. If eliminating salt from the diet does not work to reduce fluid retention, diuretics may be prescribed.

---

menstrual phase The shedding of the endometrium during the menstrual cycle.

menses The menstrual flow, in which the endometrium is discharged.

menarche The onset of menstruation.

proliferative phase The building up of the endometrium in response to increased estrogen during the menstrual cycle.

Menstrual Phase With hormone levels low because of the degeneration of the corpus luteum, the outer layer of the endometrium becomes detached from the uterine wall. The shedding of the endometrium marks the beginning of the **menstrual phase.** This endometrial tissue, along with mucus, other cervical and vaginal secretions, and a small amount of blood (2–5 oz per cycle) is expelled through the vagina. The menstrual flow, or **menses,** generally occurs over a period of 3–5 days. FSH and LH begin increasing around day 5, marking the end of this phase. A girl's first menstruation is known as **menarche.**

Proliferative Phase The **proliferative phase** lasts about 9 days. During this time, the endometrium builds up in response to increased estrogen. The mucous membranes of the cervix secrete a clear, thin mucus with a crys-

---

- *Support groups.* Therapy or support groups may help some women deal with the ways PMS affects their lives. They may also help women deal with issues that may be exacerbated by the stress of coping with PMS.

For Cramps

- *Relaxation.* Rest, sleep, and relaxation exercises can help reduce pain from uterine and abdominal cramping, especially in combination with one or more of the remedies listed below.
- *Heat.* A heating pad, hot-water bottle (or, in a pinch, a cat) applied to the abdominal area may help relieve cramps; a warm bath may also help.
- *Massage.* Lower back massage, or other forms of massage, such as acupressure, Shiatsu, or polarity therapy, are quite helpful for many women. See *The New Our Bodies, Ourselves* (Boston Women's Health Book Collective, 1992) for guidelines for menstrual massage.
- *Herbal remedies.* Herbal teas, especially raspberry leaf, are helpful for some women. Health food stores carry a variety of teas, tablets, and other preparations. Use them as directed, and stop using them if you experience additional discomfort or problems.
- *Prostaglandin inhibitors.* Antiprostaglandins reduce cramping of the uterine and abdominal muscles. Aspirin is a mild prostaglandin inhibitor. Ibuprophen, a highly effective prostaglandin inhibitor, was often prescribed for menstrual cramps (as Motrin) before it became available over the counter. Aspirin increases menstrual flow slightly, whereas ibuprophen reduces it (Speroff, Glass, & Kase, 1989). Stronger antiprostaglandins may be prescribed. Taking medication at the first sign of cramping—as opposed to waiting until the pain is severe—increases its effectiveness greatly.
- *Orgasm.* Some women report relief of menstrual congestion and cramping at orgasm (with or without a partner).

If pain cannot be controlled with these methods, further medical evaluation is needed. The symptoms may indicate an underlying problem such as endometriosis or pelvic inflammatory disease (PID).

talline structure that facilitates the passage of sperm. The proliferative phase ends with ovulation.

Secretory Phase During the first part of the **secretory phase,** with the help of progesterone, the endometrium begins to prepare for the arrival of a fertilized ovum. Glands within the uterus enlarge and begin secreting glycogen, a cell nutrient. The cervical mucus thickens and starts forming a plug to seal off the uterus, in the event of pregnancy. If fertilization does not occur, the corpus luteum begins to degenerate, as LH levels decline. Progesterone levels then fall, and the endometrial cells begin to die. The secretory phase lasts 14 days, corresponding with the luteal phase of the ovarian cycle. It ends with the shedding of the endometrium.

secretory phase The phase of the menstrual cycle during which the endometrium begins to prepare for the arrival of a fertilized ovum; without fertilization, the corpus luteum begins to degenerate.

During ovulation, the ovarian follicle swells and ruptures, releasing the mature oocyte to begin its journey through the fallopian tube.

Menstrual Effects   For some women, menstruation is a problem. For others, it is simply a fact of life that creates little disruption. For individual women, the problems associated with their menstrual period may be physiological, emotional, or practical. Various studies report that about 70% of menstruating women notice at least one emotional, physical, or behavioral change in the week or so prior to menstruation (Hopson & Rosenfeld, 1984). Most women describe the changes negatively: breast tenderness and swelling, abdominal bloating, irritability, cramping, depression, or fatigue. Some women also report positive changes, such as increased energy, heightened sexual arousal, or a general feeling of well-being. For most women, changes during the menstrual cycle are usually mild to moderate; they appear to have little impact on their lives. (Toxic shock syndrome, a blood infection associated with menstruation, is discussed in Chapter 13.) The most common problems associated with menstruation are discussed below.

premenstrual syndrome (PMS)
A set of severe symptoms associated with menstruation.

Premenstrual Syndrome   More severe menstrual problems have been attributed to what is commonly called **premenstrual syndrome (PMS),** a term used to describe the most commonly reported cluster of severe physical and emotional symptoms. About 3–12% of menstruating women report a dozen or more negative changes that severely affect their lives (Hopson & Rosenfeld, 1984). Some studies, however, suggest that the number of seriously affected women may be as high as 30% (Laube, 1985). But because of the variety of symptoms and the difficulty involved in evaluating them, studies on PMS are contradictory and inconclusive (Reid, 1986). In 1994 the American Psychiatric Association included "premenstrual dysphoric disorder" in the fourth edition of its *Diagnostic and Statistical Manual of Mental Disorders* (*DSM-IV*), which is used for psychiatric diagnosis. The most common symptoms leading to a diagnosis of premenstrual syndrome include dysphoria (depression, nervousness, irritability, anxiety), fluid retention (bloating, swelling, weight gain), breast tenderness, headache, fatigue, and food cravings (especially for salt, sugar, chocolate) (Hatcher et al., 1990).

The greatest difficulty in understanding PMS is knowing how to separate information that clearly indicates premenstrual symptoms from other aspects of a woman's physical and emotional health (González, 1981). Certain questions need to be answered before firm conclusions can be drawn.

Dysmenorrhea Some women experience pelvic cramping and pain during the menstrual cycle; this condition is called **dysmenorrhea.** There are two basic types. *Primary dysmenorrhea* is characterized by pain that begins with uterine shedding (or just before) and by the absence of pain at other times in the cycle. It can be very severe and may be accompanied by nausea, weakness, or other physical symptoms. In *secondary dysmenorrhea,* the symptoms may be the same, but there is an underlying condition or disease causing them; pain may not be limited to the menstrual phase alone. Secondary dysmenorrhea may be caused by pelvic inflammatory disease (PID), endometriosis, endometrial cancer, or other conditions (see Chapters 13 and 15).

The effects of dysmenorrhea can totally incapacitate a woman for several hours or even days. Primary dysmenorrhea is often caused by high levels of **prostaglandins,** a type of hormone with a fatty-acid base that is found throughout the body. One type of prostaglandin is synthesized in the uterus and stimulates uterine contractions; excessive amounts cause tighter and longer contractions and keep oxygen from reaching the uterus and abdominal muscles (Rome, 1992). The discovery of a hormonal basis for dysmenorrhea has resulted in gynecologists taking menstrual pain more seriously in recent years (González, 1980). Previously, (male) physicians had often dismissed menstrual pain as being in the head, not the body (although women, of course, had a different opinion).

Amenorrhea When women do not menstruate for reasons other than aging, the condition is called **amenorrhea.** A principal cause of amenorrhea is pregnancy. Lack of menstruation, if not a result of pregnancy, is categorized as either primary or secondary amenorrhea. Women who have passed the age of 16 and never menstruated are diagnosed as having *primary amenorrhea.* It may be that they have not yet reached their critical weight (when an increased ratio of body fat triggers menstrual cycle-inducing hormones), or that they are hereditarily late maturers. But it can also signal hormonal deficiencies, abnormal body structure, or hermaphroditism. Most primary amenorrhea can be treated with hormone therapy.

Secondary amenorrhea exists when a previously menstruating woman stops menstruating for several months. If it is not due to pregnancy, breast-feeding, or the use of hormonal contraceptives, the source of secondary amenorrhea may be found in stress, lowered body fat, heavy athletic training, or hormonal irregularities. Anorexia (discussed in Chapter 13) is a frequent cause of amenorrhea (Benson, 1980). If a woman is not pregnant, is not breast-feeding, and can rule out hormonal contraceptives as a cause, she should see her health practitioner if she has gone six months without menstruating.

dysmenorrhea Pelvic cramping and pain experienced by some women during menstruation.

prostaglandins A type of hormone with a fatty-acid base that stimulates muscle contractions.

amenorrhea The absence of menstruation, unrelated to aging.

Sexuality and the Menstrual Cycle There is a general taboo in our culture, as in many others, against sexual intercourse during menstruation. This taboo may be based on religious beliefs. Among Orthodox Jews, for example, women are required to refrain from intercourse for seven days following the end of menstruation. They may then resume sexual activity after a ritual bath, the *mikvah*. Contact with blood may make some people squeamish. A man may view menstrual blood as "somehow dangerous, magical, and apparently not something he wants to get on his penis" (Delaney, Lupton, & Toth, 1977). Many women, especially at the beginning of their period, feel bloated or uncomfortable; they may experience breast tenderness or a general feeling of not wanting to be touched. Others may find that lovemaking helps relieve menstrual discomfort.

For some couples, just dealing with the logistics of bloodstains, bathing, and laundry may be enough to discourage them from intercourse at this time. For many people, however, menstrual blood holds no special connotation. It is important to note that although unusual, conception can occur during menstruation, especially if the woman has short or irregular cycles. Some women find that a diaphragm holds back the flow and facilitates lovemaking. Although it is not recommended that women engage in intercourse while a tampon is inserted because of possible injury to the cervix, cunnilingus is a possibility. And inventive lovers can, of course, find many ways to give each other pleasure that do not require putting the penis into the vagina.

Sexual intercourse during menstruation may carry health risks for women who have multiple sexual partners or whose partners may have been exposed to a sexually transmitted disease. Organisms, including HIV, have an easy pathway into a woman's bloodstream through the uterine walls exposed by endometrial shedding. Moreover, a woman with a pathogen in her blood, such as the hepatitis virus or HIV, can pass it to a partner in her menstrual blood. Therefore, during menstruation, as well as at other times, safer sex practices, including condom use, are strongly recommended. (See Chapter 15 for safer sex guidelines.)

FEMALE SEXUAL RESPONSE

Scientific research has contributed much to our understanding of sexual arousal and response. One way in which researchers investigate and describe phenomena is through the creation of models, hypothetical descriptions used to study or explain something. However, although models are useful as tools for general understanding or for assisting in the treatment of specific clinical problems (lack of arousal, for example), we should remember that they are only models.

Sexual Response Models

The **Masters and Johnson Four-Phase Model of Sexual Response** identifies the significant stages of response as excitement, plateau, orgasm, and resolution (Figure 3.6). Helen Singer Kaplan (1979) collapses the excitement and plateau phases into one, eliminates the resolution phase, and adds

Masters and Johnson Four-Phase Model of Sexual Response A model that divides sexual response into four phases: excitement, plateau, orgasm, and resolution.

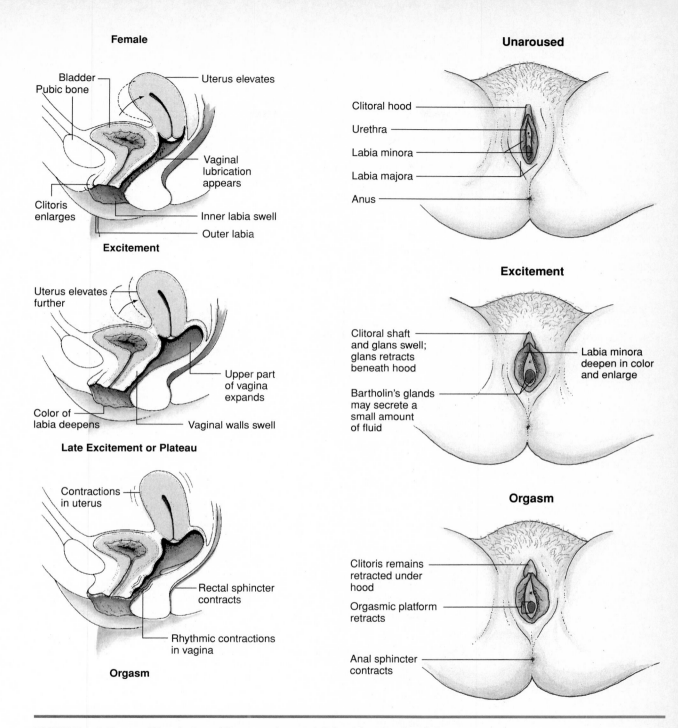

FIGURE 3.6 Stages of Female Sexual Response (internal, left; and external, right).

TABLE 3.2 Sexual Response Models Compared: Masters/Johnson and Kaplan

Psychological/Physiological Process	Name of Phase	
Some form of thought, fantasy, or erotic feeling causes us to seek sexual gratification. (An inability to become sexually aroused may be due to a lack of desire, which can have a variety of causes.)	Desire (Kaplan)	
Physical and/or psychological stimulation produces characteristic physical changes. In men, increased amounts of blood flow to the genitals produces erection of the penis; the scrotal skin begins to smooth out, and the testicles draw up toward the body. Later in this phase, the testes increase slightly in size. In women, vaginal lubrication begins, the upper vagina expands, the uterus is pulled upward, and the clitoris becomes engorged. In both women and men, the breasts enlarge slightly, and the nipples may become erect. Both men and women experience increasing muscular contractions.	Excitement (Masters/Johnson)	Excitement (Kaplan)
Sexual tension levels off. In men, the testes swell and continue to elevate. The diameter of the head of the penis swells slightly and may deepen in color. In women, the outer third of the vagina swells, lubrication may slow down, and the clitoris pulls back. Coloring and swelling of the labia increase. In both men and women, muscular tension, breathing, and heart rate increase.	Plateau (Masters/Johnson)	
Increased tension peaks and discharges, affecting the whole body. Rhythmic muscular contractions affect the uterus and outer vagina in women. In men, there are contractions of the tubes that produce and carry semen, the prostate gland, and the urethral bulb, resulting in the expulsion of semen (ejaculation).	Orgasm (Masters/Johnson and Kaplan)	
The body returns to its unaroused state. In women, this phase may not occur until after multiple orgasms.	Resolution (Masters/Johnson)	

Kaplan's Tri-Phasic Model of Sexual Response A model that divides sexual response into three phases: desire, excitement, and orgasm.

a phase to the beginning of the process. **Kaplan's Tri-Phasic Model of Sexual Response** includes the desire, excitement, and orgasm phases. These models are described and compared in Table 3.2.

Desire: Mind or Matter?

Desire is the psychological component of sexual arousal. Although we can experience desire without becoming aroused, and in some cases become aroused without feeling desire, some form of erotic thought or feeling is usually involved in our sexual behavior. The physical manifestations of sexual arousal involve a complex interaction of thoughts and feelings, sensory organs, neural responses, and hormonal reactions involving various parts of the body, including the cerebral cortex and limbic system of the brain, the nervous system, the circulatory system, the endocrine glands—as well as the genitals.

The Neural System and Sexual Stimuli   The brain is crucial to sexual response, yet relatively little is known about the manner in which the brain functions to create these responses. Through the neural system, the brain receives stimuli from the five senses plus one: sight, smell, touch, hearing, taste, *and* the imagination.

The Brain   The brain, of course, plays a major role in all of our body's functions. Nowhere is its role more apparent than in our sexual functioning. The relationship between our thoughts and feelings and our actual behavior is not well understood (and what is known would require a course in neurophysiology to satisfactorily explain it). Cultural influences, as well as expectations, fantasies, hopes, and fears, combine with sensory inputs and hormonal messages to bring us to where we are ready, willing, and able to be sexual. Even then, potentially erotic messages may be short-circuited by the brain itself, which may inhibit as well as excite sexual responses. It is not known how the inhibitory mechanism works, but guilt, anxiety, fear, and negative conditioning will prevent the brain from sending messages to the genitals. In fact, the reason moderate amounts of alcohol and marijuana appear to enhance sexuality is because they reduce the control mechanisms of the brain that act as inhibitors (Kaplan, 1974).

Anatomically speaking, the areas of the brain that appear to be involved most in sexual behaviors of both men and women are the cerebral cortex and the limbic system. The cerebral cortex is the convoluted covering of most of the brain area. It is the area that is associated with conscious behavior such as perception, memory, communication, understanding, and voluntary movement. Beneath the cortex, the **limbic system,** which consists of several separate parts, is involved with emotions and feelings. There are extensive connections between the limbic system and the cerebral cortex, explaining perhaps why "emotions sometimes override logic and, conversely, why reason can stop us from expressing our emotions in inappropriate situations" (Marieb, 1992). Some parts of the limbic system have been dubbed "pleasure centers" (Olds, 1956) because their stimulation produces sexual arousal (Heath, 1972).

limbic system   A group of structures in the brain associated with emotions and feelings; involved with producing sexual arousal.

The Senses   An attractive person (sight), a body fragrance or odor (smell), a lick or kiss (taste), a loving caress (touch), and erotic whispers (hearing) are all capable of sending sexual signals to the brain. Many of the connections we experience between sensory data and emotional responses are probably products of the limbic system. Some sensory inputs may evoke sexual arousal without a lot of conscious thought or emotion. Certain areas of the skin, called **erogenous zones,** are highly sensitive to touch. These areas may include the genitals, breasts, mouth, ears, neck, inner thighs, and buttocks; erotic associations with these areas vary from culture to culture and individual to individual. Our olfactory sense (smell) may bring us sexual messages below the level of our conscious awareness. Scientists have isolated chemical substances, called **pheromones,** that are secreted into the air by many kinds of animals including ants, moths, pigs, dogs, and monkeys. One function of pheromones, in animals at least, appears to be to arouse sexual interest. Definitive research on human pheromones, however, has yet to be developed.

erogenous zone   Any area of the body that is highly sensitive to touch and associated with sexual arousal.

pheromone   A sexually arousing chemical substance secreted into the air by many kinds of animals.

Sensory inputs such as the sight, touch, or smell of someone we love, or the sound of his or her voice, may evoke desire and sexual arousal.

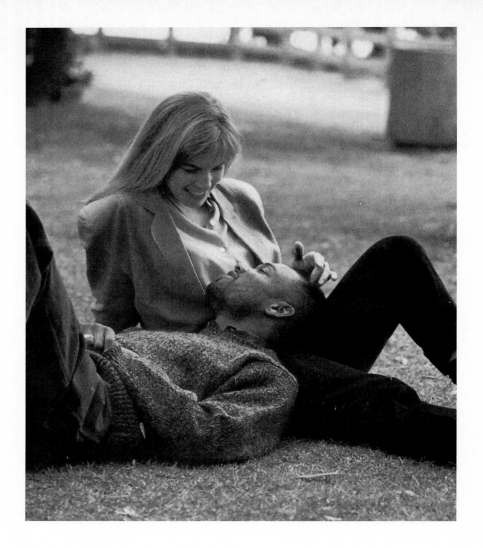

Hormones   The sex drive, or *libido*, in both men and women is biologically influenced by the hormone *testosterone*. In men, testosterone is produced mainly in the testes. In women, it is produced in the ovaries and adrenal glands. Although women produce much less testosterone than men, this does not mean they have less sexual interest; apparently, women are much more sensitive than men to its effects (Persky et al., 1982). The relationship between testosterone level and sexual interest is not well understood. Although a drop in testosterone often reduces sexual interest or functioning, this is not always the case. Estrogen also plays a role in sexual functioning. In women, estrogens help maintain the vaginal lining; it is not clear how much of a role, if any, estrogen plays in maintaining the libido. Men also produce small amounts of estrogen, but its particular function is not known. Too much estrogen, however, can induce erection difficulties.

Experiencing Sexual Arousal

For both males and females, physiological changes during sexual excitement depend on two processes: vasocongestion and myotonia. **Vasocongestion** is the concentration of blood in body tissues. For example, blood fills the genital regions of both males and females, causing the penis to become erect and the clitoris to swell. **Myotonia** is increased muscle tension accompanying the approach of orgasm; upon orgasm, the body undergoes involuntary muscle contractions and then relaxes. The sexual response pattern remains the same for all forms of sexual behavior, whether autoerotic or coital experiences, heterosexual or homosexual (Masters & Johnson, 1966, 1979).

Sexual Excitement For women, the first sign of sexual excitement is the moistening of the vaginal walls through a process called **sweating.** These secretions lubricate the vagina, enabling it to encompass the penis easily. The inner two-thirds of the vagina expands in a process called **tenting;** the vagina expands about an inch in length and doubles its width. Vasocongestion affects the labia differently depending on whether the woman has borne children. The minor lips begin to protrude outside the major lips during sexual excitement. Breathing and heart rate increase. These signs do not occur on a specific timetable; each woman has her own pattern of arousal, which may vary under different conditions, with different partners, and so on.

Contractions raise the uterus, but the clitoris remains virtually unchanged during this early phase. Although the clitoris responds more slowly than the penis to vasocongestion, it is, nevertheless, affected. The initial changes, however, are minor. Clitoral tumescence (swelling) occurs simultaneously with engorgement of the minor lips. During masturbation and oral sex, the clitoris is generally stimulated directly. During intercourse, clitoral stimulation is mostly indirect, caused by the clitoral hood being pulled over the clitoris or pressure in the general clitoral area. At the same time that these changes are occurring in the genitals, the breasts are also responding. The nipples become erect, and the breasts may enlarge somewhat because of the engorgement of blood vessels; the areolae may also enlarge. About 25% of women experience a **sex flush,** a rash that temporarily appears as a result of blood rushing to the skin's surface during sexual excitement.

As excitement increases, the clitoris retracts beneath the clitoral hood and virtually disappears. The minor lips become progressively larger until they double or triple in size. They deepen in color, becoming pink, bright red, or a deep wine-red color. This intense coloring is sometimes referred to as the "sex skin." When it appears, orgasm is imminent. Meanwhile, the vaginal opening decreases by about one-third. Its outer third becomes more congested with blood; the congested walls are known as the **orgasmic platform.** The vagina expands further, but lubrication decreases or may even stop. The uterus becomes fully elevated through muscular contractions.

Changes in the breasts continue. The areolae become larger, while, in contrast, the nipples decrease in relative size. If the woman has not breastfed, her breasts may increase by up to 25% of their unaroused size; women

vasocongestion Blood engorgement of body tissues.

myotonia Increased muscle tension.

sweating The moistening of the vagina by secretions from its walls.

tenting The expansion of the inner two-thirds of the vagina during sexual arousal.

sex flush A rash that temporarily appears as a result of blood rushing to the skin's surface during sexual excitation.

orgasmic platform A portion of the vagina that undergoes vasocongestion during sexual arousal.

who have breast-fed may have little change in size. An additional 75% of women experience a sex flush during this stage of response.

orgasm The climax of sexual excitement, including rhythmic contractions of muscles in the genital area and intensely pleasurable sensations; usually accompanied by ejaculation in males beginning in puberty.

Orgasm Continued stimulation brings **orgasm,** rhythmic contractions of the vagina, uterus, and pelvic muscles, accompanied by intensely pleasurable sensations. The inner two-thirds of the vagina does not contract; instead, it continues its tenting effect. The labia do not change during orgasm. The breasts also remain unchanged. Heart and respiratory rates along with blood pressure also reach their peak during orgasm.

After orgasm, the orgasmic platform rapidly subsides. The clitoris re-emerges from beneath the clitoral hood. (If a woman does not have an orgasm once she is sexually aroused, the clitoris may remain engorged for several hours, possibly creating a feeling of frustration.) The labia slowly return to their unaroused state, and the sex flush gradually disappears. About 30–40% of women perspire as the body begins to cool.

Following orgasm, men experience a refractory period, in which they are unable to become aroused. By contrast, women are often physiologically able to be orgasmic immediately following the previous orgasm. As a result, women can have multiple orgasms if they continue to be stimulated. Kinsey (Kinsey et al., 1953) estimated that 13% of the women in his study experienced multiple orgasms.

In the next chapter, we discuss the anatomical features and physiological functions that characterize men's sexuality and sexual response. The information in these two chapters should serve as a comprehensive basis for understanding the material that follows.

SUMMARY

Female Sex Organs: What Are They For?

• All embryos appear as female at first. Genetic and hormonal signals trigger the development of male organs in those embryos destined to be male.

• Sex organs serve a reproductive purpose, but they perform other functions also: giving pleasure, attracting sex partners, and bonding in relationships.

• The external female genitals are known collectively as the vulva. The mons pubis is a pad of fatty tissue that covers the area of the pubic bone. The clitoris is the center of sexual arousal in the female. The labia majora are two folds of spongy flesh extending from the mons pubis and enclosing the other external genitals. The labia minora are smooth, hairless folds within the labia majora that meet above the clitoris.

• The internal female sexual structures and reproductive organs include the vagina, the uterus, the cervix, the ovaries, and the fallopian tubes. The vagina is a flexible muscular organ that encompasses the penis during sexual intercourse and is the birth canal through which an infant is born. The opening of the vagina, the introitus, is partially covered by a thin, perforated membrane, the hymen, prior to first intercourse or other intrusion.

• Controversial research has posited the existence of an erotically sensitive area, the Grafenberg spot (G-spot), on the front wall of the vagina midway between the introitus and the cervix.

• The uterus, or womb, is a hollow, thick-walled, muscular organ; the tapered end, the cervix, extends downward and opens into the vagina. The lining of the uterine walls, the endometrium, is built up, then shed and expelled through the cervical os (opening) during menstruation. In the event of pregnancy, the pre-embryo is embedded in the nourishing endometrium. On each side of the uterus is one of a pair of ovaries, the female gonads (organs that produces gametes, sex cells containing the genetic material necessary for reproduction). At the top of the uterus are the fallopian tubes or uterine tubes. They extend toward the ovaries but are not attached to them. The funnel-shaped end of each tube (the infundibulum) fans out into fingerlike fimbriae, which drape over the ovary. Hairlike cilia on the fimbriae conduct the ovulated oocyte into the fallopian tube. The ampulla is the widened part of the tube in which fertilization normally occurs. Other important structures in the area of the genitals include the urethra, anus, and perineum.

• The reproductive function of the female breasts, or mammary glands, is to nourish the offspring through lactation, milk production. A breast is composed of fatty tissue and 15–25 lobes that radiate around a central protruding nipple. Alveoli within the lobes produce milk. Around the nipple is a ring of darkened skin called the areola.

Female Sexual Physiology

• Hormones are chemical substances that serve as messengers, traveling through the bloodstream. Important hormones that act directly on the gonads (gonadotropins) are follicle-stimulating hormone (FSH) and luteinizing hormone (LH). Hormones produced in the ovaries are estrogen, which helps regulate the menstrual cycle, and progesterone, which helps maintain the uterine lining.

• In a woman's lifetime, about 400 oocytes will mature and be released, beginning in puberty when hormones trigger the completion of oogenesis, the production of oocytes, commonly called eggs or ova.

• The activities of the ovaries and the development of oocytes for ovulation, the expulsion of the oocyte, are described as the three-phase ovarian cycle, which is usually about 28 days long. The phases are follicular (maturation of the oocyte), ovulatory (expulsion of the oocyte), and luteal (hormone production by the corpus luteum).

• The menstrual cycle (or uterine cycle), like the ovarian cycle, is divided into three phases. The shedding of the endometrium marks the beginning of the menstrual phase. The menstrual flow, or menses, generally occurs over a period of 2–5 days. Endometrial tissue builds up during the proliferative phase; it produces nutrients to sustain an embryo in the secretory phase.

• The most severe menstrual problems have been attributed to premenstrual syndrome (PMS), a cluster of physical and emotional symptoms, which are not agreed upon because of contradictory studies. Some women experience pelvic cramping and pain during the menstrual cycle (dysmenorrhea). When women do not menstruate for reasons other than aging, the condition is called amenorrhea. A principal cause of amenorrhea is pregnancy.

Female Sexual Response

• The Masters and Johnson Four-Phase Model of Sexual Response identifies the significant stages of response as excitement, plateau, orgasm, and resolution. Kaplan's Tri-Phasic Model of Sexual Response consists of three phases: desire, excitement, and orgasm.

• The physical manifestations of sexual arousal involve a complex interaction of thoughts and feelings, sensory perceptions, neural responses, and hormonal reactions occurring in many parts of the body. For both males and females, physiological changes during sexual excitement depend on two processes: vasocongestion, the concentration of blood in body tissues, and myotonia, increased muscle tension with approaching orgasm.

• For women, the first sign of sexual excitement is the moistening of the vaginal walls, or sweating. The inner two-thirds of the vagina expands in a process called tenting; the labia may enlarge or flatten and separate; the clitoris swells. Breathing and heart rate increase. The nipples become erect, and the breasts may enlarge somewhat. The uterus elevates. As excitement increases, the clitoris retracts beneath the clitoral hood. The vaginal opening decreases by about one-third, and its outer third becomes more congested, forming the orgasmic platform.

• Continued stimulation brings orgasm, rhythmic contractions of the vagina, uterus, and pelvic muscles, accompanied by very pleasurable sensations. Women are often able to be orgasmic following a previous orgasm if they continue to be stimulated.

SUGGESTED READINGS

Boston Woman's Health Book Collective. (1992). *The New Our Bodies, Ourselves*. New York: Simon and Shuster. A thorough, accurate, and proactive women's text covering a broad range of health issues.

Dan, Alice J., and Linda L. Lewis. *Menstrual Health in Women's Lives*. Urbana/Chicago: University of Illinois Press, 1992. A practical, positive self-help guide.

Ladas, Alice Kahn, Beverly Whipple, and John D. Perry. *The G Spot and Other Recent Discoveries About Human Sexuality*. New York: Dell, 1983. Controversial studies of the Grafenberg spot and female ejaculation.

Lark, Susan. *Premenstrual Syndrome Self-Help Book: A Woman's Guide to Feeling Good All Month*. Berkeley, CA: Celestial Arts, 1989. Helpful information and advice for women who experience PMS or other menstruation-related discomfort.

Madaras, Lynda, and Jane Patterson. *Womancare: A Gynecological Guide to Your Body*. New York: Avon Books, 1984. A thorough, very readable guide to women's gynecological health.

Sloane, Ethel. *Biology of Women*. Albany, NY: Delmar, 1985. A feminist perspective on female anatomy and physiology.

Chapter Four

MALE SEXUAL ANATOMY, PHYSIOLOGY, AND RESPONSE

PREVIEW: SELF-QUIZ

1. Erection of the penis is caused by muscle contractions. True or false?

2. An erection is not always a sign of sexual interest. True or false?

3. Semen is produced within the testicles. True or false?

4. Male breasts basically consist of the same structures as female breasts. True or false?

5. It has been scientifically proven that the hormone testosterone causes aggression. True or false?

6. Men as well as women experience mood cycles. True or false?

7. It takes about a day for a sperm to be created. True or false?

8. An important function of semen is to provide nourishment for sperm. True or false?

9. Men may experience orgasm without ejaculation and vice versa. True or false?

10. The average number of sperm expelled in an ejaculation is around one million. True or false?

ANSWERS: 1. F, 2. T, 3. F, 4. T, 5. F, 6. T, 7. F, 8. F, 9. T, 10. F

Chapter Outline

It's clear that male sexual structures and functions differ in many ways from those of females. What may not be as apparent, however, is that there are also a number of similarities in the functions of the sex organs and the sexual response patterns of both men and women. In the previous chapter, we learned that the sexual structures of both females and males derive from the same embryonic tissue. But when this tissue receives the signals to begin differentiation into a male, the embryonic reproductive organs begin to change their appearance dramatically.

MALE SEX ORGANS: WHAT ARE THEY FOR?

Like female sex organs, male sex organs serve several functions. In their reproductive role, a man's sex organs manufacture and store gametes and deliver them to a woman's reproductive tract. Some of the organs, especially the penis, provide a source of physical pleasure for both their owners and their owners' partners.

External Structures

The external male sexual structures are the penis and the scrotum.

The Penis The **penis** (from the Latin word for tail) is the organ through which both sperm and urine pass. It is attached to the male perineum, the diamond-shaped region extending from the base of the scrotum to the anus.

The penis consists of three main sections: the root, the shaft, and the head (Figure 4.1). The **root** attaches the penis within the pelvic cavity, while

penis The male organ through which semen and urine pass.

root The portion of the penis attached to the pelvic cavity.

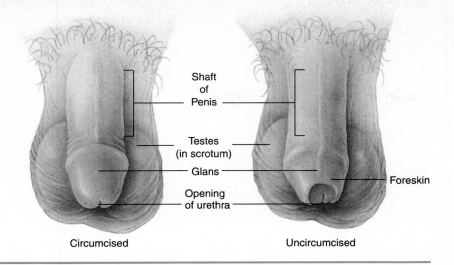

FIGURE 4.1 External Sexual Structures.

Shaft
of
Penis

Testes
(in scrotum)

Glans

Foreskin

Opening
of urethra

Circumcised

Uncircumcised

the body of the penis, the **shaft,** hangs free. At the end of the shaft is the enlarged head of the penis, the **glans penis,** and at its tip is the urethral opening. The rim at the base of the glans is known as the **corona.** On the underside of the penis is a triangular area of sensitive skin called the **frenulum,** which attaches the glans to the foreskin. The glans penis is particularly important in sexual arousal because it contains a relatively high concentration of nerve endings, making it especially responsive to stimulation.

A loose skin covers the shaft of the penis and extends to cover the glans penis; the sleevelike covering of the glans is known as the **foreskin** or **prepuce.** It can be pulled back easily to expose the glans. In the United States, the foreskins of male infants are often surgically removed by a procedure called **circumcision.** As a result of this procedure, the glans penis is left exposed. The reasons for circumcision seem to be rooted more in tradition, hospital profits, and religious beliefs (it is an important ritual in Judaism and Islam) than in any firmly established health principles (see Chapter 12). Beneath the foreskin are several small glands that produce an oily substance called **smegma.** If smegma accumulates, it thickens and produces a foul odor. It is important for uncircumcised adult men to observe good hygiene by periodically retracting the skin and washing the glans to remove the smegma. Lack of proper hygiene may be associated with sexually transmitted diseases, urinary infections, and penile cancer (McAninch, 1989; Rotolo & Lynch, 1991).

The shaft of the penis contains three parallel columns of erectile tissue. The two that extend along the front surface are known as the **corpora cavernosa** (cavernous bodies), and the third, which runs beneath them, is called the **corpus spongiosum** (spongy body). At the root of the penis, the corpora cavernosa form the **crura,** which are anchored by muscle to the pubic bone. The **urethra,** a tube that transports both urine and semen, runs from the bladder (where it expands to form the **urethral bulb**), through the spongy body, to the tip of the penis, where it opens to the outside. Inside

shaft   The body of the penis.

glans penis   The head of the penile shaft.

corona   The rim of tissue between the glans and the penile shaft.

frenulum   The triangular area of sensitive skin on the underside of the penis, attaching the glans to the foreskin.

foreskin or **prepuce**   The sleevelike skin covering the shaft of the penis and extending over the glans penis.

circumcision   The surgical removal of the foreskin covering the glans penis.

smegma   An oily substance produced by several small glands beneath the foreskin of the penis and hood of the clitoris.

corpora cavernosa   The hollow chambers in the shaft of the clitoris or penis that fill with blood and swell during arousal.

corpus spongiosum   A column of erectile tissue within the penis enclosing the urethra.

crura   (singular, *crus*) The internal branches of the clitoral or penile shaft.

urethra   The tube through which urine and semen pass.

urethral bulb   The expanded portion of the urethra.

The penis is a prominent symbol in both ancient and modern art. Here we see a contemporary phallic sculpture in Frogner Park, Oslo, Norway, and a pair of well-endowed ceremonial figures from Nigeria.

the three chambers are a large number of blood vessels through which blood freely circulates when the penis is flaccid (relaxed). During sexual arousal, these vessels fill with blood and expand, causing the penis to become erect. (Sexual arousal, including erection, is discussed in greater detail later in the chapter.)

In an unaroused state, the *average* penis is slightly under 4 inches long, although there is a great deal of individual variation. When erect, penises become more uniform in size, as the percentage of volume increase is greater with smaller penises than with larger ones. But even in an unaroused state, penis size may vary. Cold air, water, fear, or anxiety, for example, often cause the penis to be pulled closer to the body and decrease in size. When the penis is erect, the urinary duct is temporarily blocked, allowing for the ejaculation of semen. But erection does not necessarily mean sexual excitement. A man may have erections at night during REM sleep, the phase of the sleep cycle when dreaming occurs (Chung & Choi, 1990; Marshall, Surridge, & Delva, 1981) or when he is anxious, for example.

Myths and misconceptions about the penis abound, especially among men. Many people believe that the size of a man's penis is directly related to his masculinity, aggressiveness, sexual ability, or sexual attractiveness.

FIGURE 4.2 Internal Male Sexual Structures.

Underside of penis
(cross section)

Others believe there is a relationship between the size of a man's penis and the size of his hand, foot, thumb, or nose. In fact, the size of the penis is not specifically related to body size, weight, muscular structure, race or ethnicity, or sexual orientation; it is determined by individual heredity factors. Furthermore, there is no relationship between penis size and a man's ability to have sexual intercourse or to satisfy his partner (Masters & Johnson, 1966).

The Scrotum Hanging loosely at the root of the penis is the **scrotum,** a pouch of skin that holds the two testicles. The skin of the scrotum is more heavily pigmented than the skin elsewhere on the body; it is sparsely covered with hair and divided in the middle by a ridge of skin. The skin of the scrotum varies in appearance under different conditions. When a man is sexually aroused, for example, or when he is cold, the testicles are pulled close to the body, causing the skin to wrinkle and become more compact. The changes in the surface of the scrotum help maintain a fairly constant temperature within the testicles (about 93°F).

Internal Structures

Male internal reproductive organs and structures include the testes (testicles), seminiferous tubules, epididymis, vas deferens, ejaculatory ducts, seminal vesicles, prostate gland, and Cowper's (bulbourethral) glands (Figure 4.2).

scrotum A pouch of skin that holds the two testicles.

FIGURE 4.3 Cross Section of a Testicle.

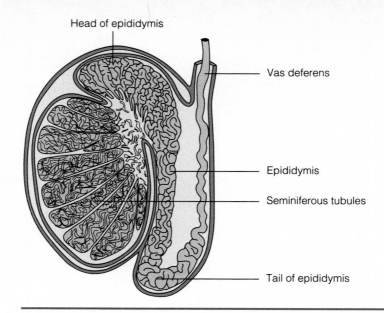

Head of epididymis

Vas deferens

Epididymis

Seminiferous tubules

Tail of epididymis

testicle or **testis** (plural, *testes*) One of the paired male gonads inside the scrotum.

spermatic cord A tube suspending the testicle within the scrotal sac, containing nerves, blood vessels, and a vas deferens.

seminiferous tubule Tiny, tightly compressed tubes in which spermatogenesis takes place.

epididymis The coiled tube formed by the merging of the seminiferous tubules, where sperm mature.

vas deferens (plural, *vasa deferentia*) One of two tubes that transport sperm from the epididymis to the ejaculatory duct within the prostate gland.

ampulla The widened part of the fallopian tube or the vas deferens.

ejaculatory duct One of two structures within the prostate gland connecting with the vasa deferentia.

The Testes Inside the scrotum are the male reproductive glands or gonads, which are called **testicles** or **testes** (singular, *testis*). The testes have two major functions: sperm production and hormone production. Each olive-shaped testis is about 1.5 inches long and 1 inch in diameter and weighs about 1 ounce; as a male ages, the testis decreases in size and weight. The testicles are usually not symmetrical; the left testicle generally hangs slightly lower than the right one. Within the scrotal sac, each testicle is suspended by a **spermatic cord** containing nerves, blood vessels, and a vas deferens, the tube that carries sperm from the testicle (Figure 4.3). Within each testicle are around 1000 **seminiferous tubules,** tiny, tightly compressed tubes 1–3 feet long (they would extend several hundred yards if laid end to end). Within these tubes, the process of spermatogenesis, the production of sperm, takes place.

As a male fetus grows, the testes develop within the pelvic cavity; toward the end of the gestation period, the testes usually descend into the scrotum. In about 3–4% of cases, however, one or both of the testes fail to descend, a condition that usually corrects itself in a year or two. (McClure, 1988).

The Epididymis and Vas Deferens The epididymis and vas deferens (or ductus deferens) are the ducts that carry sperm from the testicles to the urethra for ejaculation. The seminiferous tubules merge to form the **epididymis,** a comma-shaped structure consisting of a coiled tube about 20 feet long, where the sperm finally mature. Each epididymis merges into a **vas deferens,** a tube about 18 inches long, extending into the abdominal cavity, over the bladder, and then downward, widening into the flask-shaped **ampulla.** The vas deferens joins the **ejaculatory duct** within the prostate gland. The vas deferens can be felt easily in the scrotal sac. Because it is easily accessible and is crucial for sperm transport, it is usually the point of sterilization for men. The operation is called a vasectomy (it is discussed fully in Chapter 11). A vasectomy does not affect the ability to ejaculate since only the sperm are transported through the vas deferens. Most of the semen that is ejaculated comes from the prostate gland and the seminal vesicles.

The Seminal Vesicles, Prostate Gland, and Cowper's Glands At the back of the bladder lie two glands, each about the size and shape of a finger. These **seminal vesicles** secrete a fluid that makes up about 60% of the seminal fluid. Encircling the urethra just below the bladder is a small muscular gland about the size and shape of a chestnut. The **prostate gland** produces about 30–35% of the seminal fluid that makes up the ejaculated semen. These secretions flow into the urethra through a system of tiny ducts. Some men who enjoy receiving anal sex experience erotic sensations when the prostate is gently stroked; others find that contact with the prostate is uncomfortable (Morin, 1986). Men, especially if they are older, may be troubled by a variety of prostate problems, ranging from relatively benign conditions to more serious inflammations and prostate cancer. (Problems and diseases of the prostate are covered in Chapter 13.)

Below the prostate gland are two pea-sized glands connected to the urethra by tiny ducts. These are **Cowper's glands** or **bulbourethral glands,** which secrete a thick, clear mucus prior to ejaculation. This fluid may appear at the tip of the erect penis; its alkaline content may help buffer the acidity within the urethra and provide a more hospitable environment for sperm. Fluid from the Cowper's glands may contain sperm that have remained in the urethra since a previous ejaculation or that have leaked in from the ampullae.

The Breasts and Other Structures

Male anatomical structures that do not serve a reproductive function but may be involved in or affected by sexual activities include the breasts, urethra, buttocks, rectum, and anus.

Although the male breast contains the same basic structures as the female breast—nipple, areola, fat, and glandular tissue—the amounts of underlying fatty and glandular tissues are much smaller in men. Our culture appears to be ambivalent about the erotic function of a man's breasts. We usually do not even call them breasts, but refer to the general area as the chest. Some men find stimulation of their breasts to be sexually arousing, while others do not. **Gynecomastia,** the swelling or enlargement of the male breast, can occur during adolescence or adulthood. In puberty, gynecomastia is a normal response to hormonal changes, as we discuss in Chapter 6. In adulthood, its causes may include alcoholism, liver or thyroid disease, or cancer.

In men, the urethra serves as the passageway for both urine and semen. Because the urinary opening is at the tip of the penis, it is vulnerable to injury and infection. The sensitive mucous membranes around the opening may be subject to abrasion and can provide an entrance into the body for infectious organisms. Condoms, properly used, provide an effective barrier

seminal vesicle One of two glands at the back of the bladder that secrete about 60% of the seminal fluid.

prostate gland A muscular gland encircling the urethra that produces about one-third of the seminal fluid.

Cowper's gland or **bulbourethral gland** One of two small structures below the prostate gland that secrete a clear mucus into the urethra prior to ejaculation.

gynecomastia Swelling or enlargement of the male breast.

Male breasts, which are usually referred to euphemistically as "the chest," may or may not be considered erotic areas. Men are allowed to display their naked breasts in certain public settings. Whether or not the sight is sexually arousing depends on the viewer and the context.

between this vulnerable area and potentially infectious secretions or other substances. Men's buttocks may be a source of sexual attraction. For both women and men, the buttocks, anus, and rectum may be erotically sensitive. Both men and women may enjoy oral stimulation of the anus ("rimming"); the insertion of fingers, a hand ("fisting"), a dildo, or a penis into the rectum may bring erotic pleasure to both the receiver and the giver. (Anal sex is discussed more fully in Chapter 9; safer sex guidelines appear in Chapter 15.)

MALE SEXUAL PHYSIOLOGY

The reproductive processes of the male body include the production of hormones and the production and delivery of sperm, the male gametes. Although men do not have a monthly reproductive cycle comparable to that of women, they do experience regular fluctuations of hormone levels; there is also some evidence that men's moods follow a cyclical pattern.

The Role of Hormones

Leydig cell Cell within the testes that secretes androgens. Also known as an interstitial cell.

androgen Any of the male hormones, including testosterone.

testosterone A steroid hormone associated with sperm production, the development of secondary sexual characteristics in males, and the sex drive in both males and females.

Within the connective tissues of a man's testes are **Leydig cells** (also called interstitial cells), which secrete **androgens** (male hormones). The most important of these is testosterone, which triggers sperm production and regulates the sex drive. Other important hormones in male reproductive physiology are GnRH, FSH, and LH. In addition, men produce the protein hormone *inhibin* and small amounts of estrogen (see Table 4.1).

Testosterone As discussed in Chapter 3, **testosterone** is a steroid hormone synthesized from cholesterol. In men, it is produced principally within the testes; small amounts are also secreted by the adrenal glands. During puberty, besides acting on the seminiferous tubules to produce sperm, testosterone targets other areas of the body. It causes the penis, testicles, and other reproductive organs to grow and is responsible for the development of secondary sex characteristics, such as pubic, facial, and underarm hair, and for the deepening of the voice. It also influences the growth of bones and increase of muscle mass and causes the skin to thicken and become oilier (leading to acne in many teenage boys). In addition to stimulating sexual interest, testosterone may also play a role in aggressiveness, according to some studies. Researcher Hilary Lips suggests, however, that these studies need to be carefully interpreted. Although there is some evidence that prenatal exposure to excess testosterone leads to increased rough-and-tumble play among children of both sexes (Hines, 1982; Reinisch, Ziemba-Davis, & Saunders, 1991), the connection between such play and actual aggressive behavior has not been adequately demonstrated (Lips, 1992).

Male Cycles Studies comparing men and women have found that both sexes are subject to changes in mood and behavior patterns (Lips, 1992). Whereas such changes in women are often attributed (rightly or wrongly) to menstrual cycle fluctuations, it is not clear that male changes are related to levels of testosterone or other hormones, although there may well be a connection. Men do appear to undergo cyclic changes, although their

TABLE 4.1 Male Reproductive Hormones

Hormone	Where Produced	Functions
Testosterone	Testes, adrenal glands	Stimulates sperm production in testes, triggers development of secondary sex characteristics, regulates sex drive
GnRH	Hypothalamus	Stimulates pituitary during sperm production
FSH	Pituitary	Stimulates sperm production in testes
ICSH (LH)	Pituitary	Stimulates testosterone production in interstitial cells within testes
Inhibin	Testes	Regulates sperm production by inhibiting release of FSH
Relaxin	Prostate	Increases sperm motility

testosterone levels do not fluctuate as dramatically as do women's estrogen and progesterone levels. On a daily basis, men's testosterone levels appear to be lowest around 8:00 P.M. and highest around 4:00 A.M. (Gorman, 1992). Moreover, their overall levels appear to be relatively lower in the spring and higher in the fall.

Spermatogenesis

Within the testes, from puberty on, **spermatogenesis,** the production of **sperm,** is an ongoing process. Every day, a healthy, fertile man produces several hundred million sperm within the seminiferous tubules of his testicles (Figure 4.4). After they are formed in the seminiferous tubules, which takes 64–72 days, immature sperm are stored in the epididymis. It then takes about 20 days for the sperm to travel the length of the epididymis, during which time they become fertile and motile (able to move). Upon ejaculation, sperm in the tail section of the epididymis are expelled by muscular contractions of its walls into the vas deferens; similar contractions within the vas deferens propel the sperm into the urethra, where they are mixed with semen and then expelled from the urethral opening.

The sex of the zygote produced by the union of egg and sperm is determined by the chromosomes of the sperm. The ovum always contributes a female sex chromosome (X), whereas the sperm may contribute either a female or a male sex chromosome (Y). The combination of two X chromosomes (XX) means that the zygote will develop as a female; with an X and a Y chromosome (XY), it will develop as a male. In some cases, combinations of sex chromosomes other than XX or XY occur, causing sexual development to proceed differently; these variations are discussed in Chapter 5.

spermatogenesis The process by which a sperm develops from a spermatid.

sperm The male gamete. Also known as a spermatozoon.

Between 100 million and 600 million sperm are present in the semen from a single ejaculation. Typically, following ejaculation during intercourse, fewer than 100 will get as far as a fallopian tube, where an ovulated oocyte is present. It takes just one sperm, however, to ultimately achieve fertilization.

Acrosome — Head
Midpiece —
Flagellum (tail)

FIGURE 4.4 The human spermatozoon (sperm) consists of three sections: head, midpiece, and whiplike tail (flagellum). The head contains the sperm's nucleus, including the chromosomes, and is encased in a helmetlike acrosome. *SOURCE:* Spermatozoon from Stuart Ira Fox, *Human Physiology*, 4th edition. Copyright © 1993 Wm. C. Brown Communications, Inc., Dubuque, Iowa. All rights reserved. Reprinted by permission.

semen The ejaculated fluid containing sperm. Also known as seminal fluid.

Semen Production

Semen, or seminal fluid, is the ejaculated liquid that contains sperm. The function of semen is to nourish sperm and provide them with a hospitable environment and means of transport when they are deposited within the vagina. Sperm is mainly made up of secretions from the seminal vesicles and prostate gland, which mix together in the urethra during ejaculation. Immediately after ejaculation, the semen is somewhat thick and sticky from clotting factors in the fluid. This consistency keeps the sperm together initially; then the semen becomes liquefied, allowing the sperm to swim out. Semen ranges in color from opalescent or milky white to yellowish or grayish tones upon ejaculation, but it becomes clearer as it liquefies. Normally, about 2–6 milliliters (about 1 teaspoonful) of semen are ejaculated at one time; this amount of semen generally contains between 100 million and 600 million sperm.

MALE SEXUAL RESPONSE

At this point, it might be useful to review the material on sexual arousal and response in Chapter 3, including the models of Masters and Johnson and of Kaplan. Even though their sexual anatomy is quite different, women and men follow roughly the same pattern of excitement and orgasm, with

A CHANGE IN THE QUALITY OF SPERM

Young men today have significantly poorer quality sperm than their fathers. One French study of 1351 healthy sperm donors found an unequivocal decline in sperm counts over the past 20 years, with the youngest men having the poorest semen (lower sperm count and poorer quality sperm) (Auger et al., 1995).

Although there is a great deal of debate about the quality and implications of such research findings, many people are concerned and have asked why this decline is occurring. Researchers cannot explain their findings, but they have raised a variety of possibilities, including environmental pollution, male fetuses' exposure to estrogen in the womb, and unspecified changes in diet and lifestyle.

Richard Sharp, a male fertility specialist at the Medical Research Council's Reproductive Biology Unit in Edinburgh, Scotland, points out that more than 30 synthetic chemicals are known to have "estrogenic" properties, including dioxin, DDT, PCB, some detergents, and common substances in plastic. The danger, he notes, is that many of these can accumulate in body fat. Other scientists believe that household products such as plastic food wrappings and floor polishers may be just as dangerous.

It is important to note that a host of problems in studying male fertility make conclusions difficult to obtain. These problems vary from the wide range of factors that can influence sperm production (including tight underwear) to the vast difference in sperm counts among men and even in the same man, depending on the time in his life the sperm is obtained. The method by which the sperm counting is done may also be a factor.

Nevertheless, the research findings do have implications for future male fertility. Noting an annual fall in sperm counts of 2–3%, J. Auger of Cochin Hospital Group in Paris notes, "If this trend continues, it will create fertility problems, especially if the sperm are poor quality."

What additional side effects might be associated with these "estrogenic" properties and products? Because research is sketchy and much is still not understood about the role of diet or environmental factors on fertility, it is difficult to answer this question. How can people protect themselves and their families? Staying abreast of the research and being aware of products containing such additives as DDT and PCB might prove helpful.

Despite the concern of researchers about declining male fertility, two cautions are in order. First, sperm counts usually range from 20 million to 150 million per milliliter of semen. Men with sperm counts below 5 million per milliliter are classified as subfertile or infertile. Because it only takes one sperm to fertilize an egg, however, even a man who has spent his life around suspicious substances needs to use or support the use of birth control if he wishes to prevent a pregnancy.

Second, all information must be critically evaluated. This is especially true when the topic is one as emotional and as open to sensationalization as male fertility.

two exceptions: (1) Generally (but certainly not always), men become fully aroused and ready for penetration in a shorter amount of time than women do; and (2) once men experience orgasm, they usually cannot have another one for some time, whereas women may experience multiple orgasms.

Sexual arousal in men includes the processes of myotonia (increased muscle tension) and vasocongestion (engorgement of the tissues with blood). Vasocongestion in men is most apparent in the erection of the penis.

FIGURE 4.5 Stages of Male
Sexual Response.

Male

Vasocongestion
of penis results
in erection

Partial
erection

Unstimulated state

Testes elevate toward
perineum

Skin of scrotum
tenses, thickens,
and elevates

Excitement

Color of
penile glans
deepens

Prostate
enlarges

Cowper's
gland
secretion

Testes increase
in size and are
fully elevated

Scrotum
thickens

Cowper's
gland

Late Excitement or Plateau

Internal sphincter of
bladder contracts

Vas deferens
contracts

Seminal vesicles
contract

Penile
contractions

Sperm and semen
expelled by rhythmic
contractions of urethra

Prostate
gland
contracts

Rectal sphincter
contracts

Orgasm

Erection

erection   The process of the
penis becoming rigid through
vasocongestion; an erect penis.

When a male becomes aroused, the blood circulation within the penis
changes dramatically (Figure 4.5). During the process of **erection,** the blood
vessels expand, increasing the volume of blood, especially within the corpora cavernosa. At the same time, expansion of the penis compresses the
veins that normally carry blood out, so the penis becomes further engorged.
(There are no muscles in the penis that make it erect, nor is there a bone
in it.) Secretions from the Cowper's glands appear at the tip of the penis
during erection.

Ejaculation and Orgasm

ejaculation   The process by
which semen is forcefully
expelled from the penis.

Increasing stimulation of the penis generally leads to **ejaculation,** the
process by which semen is forcefully expelled from a man's body. When the

You and Your Sexual Well-Being

CAN AN ERECTION BE WILLED?

The **erection reflex** can be triggered by various sexual and nonsexual stimuli, including tactile stimulation (touching) of the penis or other erogenous areas; sights, smells, or sounds (usually words or sexual vocalizations); and emotions or thoughts. Even negative emotions, such as fear, can produce an erection. Conversely, emotions and thoughts can also inhibit erections, as can unpleasant or painful physical sensations. The erectile response is controlled by the parasympathetic nervous system, and as such, it cannot be consciously willed.

The length of time an erection lasts varies greatly from individual to individual and from situation to situation. With experience, most men are able to gauge the amount of stimulation that will either maintain the erection without reaching orgasm or cause orgasm to occur too soon. Failure to attain erection when one is desired is something most men experience at one time or another. (Erectile difficulties are discussed further in Chapter 14.)

There are, however, some things you can do to maximize your chances of producing viable erections. Because you need a steady flow of blood to your penis, you should get enough aerobic exercise to maintain your circulation. A diet low in fat and cholesterol and high in fiber and complex carbohydrates may also prevent hardening of the arteries, which restricts blood flow.

Some conditions may have an adverse effect on blood flow and erectile capacity, including diabetes, tension, and abnormalities in blood pressure as well as some medications that treat the abnormalities. If any of these conditions are present, or if the failure to attain an erection is persistent, see your physician.

What can you do about unwanted erections at inappropriate times? Distract yourself with unpleasant thoughts or unsightly images. Remember, the brain is the most erotic (and unerotic) organ of the body.

---

impulses that cause erection reach a critical point, a spinal reflex sets off a massive discharge of nerve impulses to the ducts, glands, and muscles of the reproductive system. Ejaculation then occurs in two stages.

Emission   In the first stage, **emission,** contractions of the walls of the tail portion of the epididymis send sperm into the vas deferens. Rhythmic contractions also occur in the vasa deferentia, ampullae, seminal vesicles, and ejaculatory ducts, which spill their contents into the urethra. The bladder's sphincter muscle closes to prevent urine from mixing with the semen and semen from entering the bladder, and another sphincter below the prostate also closes, trapping the semen in the expanded urethral bulb. At this point, the man feels a distinct sensation of **ejaculatory inevitability,** the point at which ejaculation *must* occur (Masters & Johnson, 1966). These events are accompanied by increased heart rate and respiration, elevated blood pressure, and general muscular tension. About 25% of men experience a sex flush.

Expulsion   In the second stage of ejaculation, **expulsion,** there are rapid, rhythmic contractions of the urethra, the prostate, and the muscles at the base of the penis. The first few contractions are the most forceful, causing

erection reflex   The response to arousal in which the penis becomes erect; may be triggered by a variety of stimuli.

emission   The first stage of ejaculation, in which sperm and semen are propelled into the urethral bulb.

ejaculatory inevitability   The point at which ejaculation *must* occur.

expulsion   The second stage of ejaculation, characterized by rapid, rhythmic contraction of the urethra, prostate, and muscles at the base of the penis, causing semen to spurt from the urethral opening.

semen to spurt from the urethral opening. Gradually, the intensity of the contractions decreases and the interval between them lengthens. Breathing rate and heart rate may reach their peak at expulsion.

Some men experience **retrograde ejaculation,** the "backward" expulsion of semen into the bladder rather than out of the urethral opening. This malfunctioning of the urethral sphincters may be temporary (induced by tranquilizers, for example), but if it persists, the man should seek medical counsel to determine if there is an underlying problem. Retrograde ejaculation is not normally harmful; the semen is simply collected in the bladder and eliminated during urination.

retrograde ejaculation The backward expulsion of semen into the bladder rather than out of the urethral opening.

Orgasm The intensely pleasurable physical sensations and general release of tension that accompany ejaculation constitute the experience of *orgasm*. Orgasm does not always occur with ejaculation, however. It is possible to ejaculate without having an orgasm and to experience orgasm without ejaculating. Following orgasm, men experience a **refractory period,** during which they are not capable of becoming erect or having an orgasm again. Refractory periods vary greatly in length, ranging from a few minutes to many hours (or even days, in the cases of some older men). Other changes occur immediately following orgasm. Erection diminishes as blood flow returns to normal, the sex flush (if there was one) disappears, and fairly heavy perspiration may occur. Men who experience intense sexual arousal without orgasm may feel some heaviness or discomfort in the testicles; this is generally not as painful as the common term "blue balls" implies. If discomfort persists, however, it may be relieved by a period of rest or by ejaculation through manual stimulation (by either the man or his partner). There is no harm to a man's health if he does not ejaculate frequently or at all. When the seminal vesicles are full, feedback mechanisms diminish the quantity of sperm produced. Excess sperm die and are absorbed by the body.

refractory period For men, a period following orgasm during which they are not capable of becoming erect or having an orgasm again.

In this chapter and the previous one, we have looked at the *physical* characteristics that designate us as female or male. But, as we will discover in the following chapter, there's more to gender than mere chromosomes or reproductive organs. How we feel about our male or female anatomy and how we act (our gender roles) also determine our identities as men or women.

SUMMARY

Male Sex Organs: What Are They For?

• In their reproductive role, a man's sex organs produce and store gametes and deliver them to a woman's reproductive tract. The penis is the organ through which both sperm and urine pass. The shaft of the penis contains two corpora cavernosa and a corpus spongiosum, which fill with blood during arousal, causing an erection. The head is called the glans penis; in uncircumcised men it is covered by the foreskin. Myths about the penis equate its size with masculinity and sexual prowess. The scrotum is a pouch of skin that hangs at the root of the penis. It holds the testes.

• The paired testes or testicles have two major functions: sperm production and hormone production. Within each testicle are about 1000 seminiferous tubules, where the production of sperm takes place. The seminiferous tubules merge to form the epididymis, a coiled tube where the sperm finally mature, and each epididymis merges into a vas deferens, which joins the ejaculatory duct within the prostate gland. The seminal vesicles and prostate gland produce semen, which nourishes and transports the sperm. Two tiny glands called Cowper's or bulbourethral glands secrete a thick, clear mucus prior to ejaculation.

• Male anatomical structures that do not serve a reproductive function but that may be involved in or affected by sexual activities include the breasts, urethra, buttocks, rectum, and anus.

Male Sexual Physiology

• The reproductive processes of the male body include the production of hormones and the production and delivery of sperm, the male gametes. Although men do not have a monthly reproductive cycle comparable to that of women, they do experience regular fluctuations of hormone levels; there is also some evidence that men's moods follow a cyclical pattern. The most important male hormone is testosterone, which triggers sperm production and regulates the sex drive. Other important hormones in male reproductive physiology are GnRH, FSH, LH, and inhibin.

• Sperm carry either an X chromosome, which will produce a female zygote, or a Y chromosome, which will produce a male.

• Semen, or seminal fluid, is the ejaculated liquid that contains sperm. The function of the semen is to nourish sperm and provide them with a hospitable environment and means of transport when they are deposited within the vagina. It is mainly made up of secretions from the seminal vesicles and prostate gland. The semen from a single ejaculation generally contains between 100 million and 600 million sperm.

Male Sexual Response

• Male sexual response, like that of females, involves the processes of vasocongestion and myotonia. Erection of the penis occurs when sexual or tactile stimuli cause its chambers to become engorged with blood. Continuing stimulation leads to ejaculation, which occurs in two stages. In the first stage, emission, semen mixes with sperm in the urethral bulb. In the second stage, expulsion, semen is forcibly expelled from the penis, generally resulting in orgasm.

SUGGESTED READINGS

Castleman, Michael. *Sexual Solutions: A Guide for Men and Women Who Love Them*. New York: Touchstone Books, 1989. For heterosexual men (and women), the ins and outs of lovemaking; includes a reassuring section on penis size.

Diagram Group Staff. *Man's Body*. New York: Bantam Books, 1983. Good drawings and diagrams of male anatomy.

Masters, William H., and Virginia E. Johnson. *Human Sexual Response*. Boston: Little, Brown, 1966. The groundbreaking (if sometimes flawed) work, based on observational studies of men and women, that describes in detail the physiological processes involved in sexual arousal and response.

Strage, Mark. *The Durable Fig Leaf: A Historical, Cultural, Medical, Social, Literary, and Iconographic Account of Man's Relations with His Penis*. New York: William Morrow, 1980. An entertaining book, well-rooted in scholarship.

Zilbergeld, Bernie. *The New Male Sexuality*. New York: Bantam Books, 1992. Explains both male and female anatomy and sexual response, plus communication, sexual problem solving, and much more. Authoritative, interesting, and readable; written for men (but recommended for women as well).

Chapter Five

GENDER AND
GENDER ROLES

PREVIEW: SELF-QUIZ

1. Gender roles reflect the inherent natures of women and men. True or false?

2. Psychologists believe the increasing similarity of male and female gender roles reflects a decline in mental health. True or false?

3. A person's femininity or masculinity is independent of his or her sexual orientation. True or false?

4. Males and females are opposites in terms of aggression and nurturance. True or false?

5. One's gender identity as female or male is inborn. True or false?

6. Transsexuality and homosexuality are distinctly different phenomena. True or false?

7. In adulthood, men and women tend to become more similar in their gender roles. True or false?

8. Being independent has traditionally been a component of the female gender role among African American women. True or false?

9. It is next to impossible to tell an infant's gender by behavior alone. True or false?

10. In traditional Latina gender roles, women subordinate themselves because of the belief that males are dominant. True or false?

ANSWERS 1. F, 2. F, 3. T, 4. F, 5. F, 6. T, 7. T, 8. T, 9. T, 10. T

Chapter Outline

How can you tell the difference between a man and a woman? Everyone knows that women and men are very basically distinguished by their genitals. But accurate as this answer may be academically, it is not particularly useful in social situations. In most social situations—except in nudist colonies and hot tubs, and while sunbathing *au naturel*—one's genitals are usually not visible to the casual observer. One does not expose himself or herself (or ask another to do so) for gender verification. We are more likely to rely on secondary sex characteristics, such as breasts and body hair, or on bone structure, musculature, and height. But even these characteristics are not always reliable, given the great variety of shapes and sizes we come in as human beings. And farther away than a few yards, we cannot always distinguish these characteristics. Instead of relying entirely on physical characteristics to identify males and females, we often look for other clues.

Culture provides us with an important clue for recognizing whether a person is female or male in most situations: dress. In almost all cultures, male and female clothing differs to varying degrees so that we can easily identify a person's gender (Bullough, 1991). Some cultures, such as our own,

*Lisa Lyon, 1981 Copyright ©
1981 The Estate of Robert
Mapplethorpe.*

may accentuate secondary sex characteristics, especially for females. One study found that of the different types of male/female differences, both men and women found appearance to be the greatest (Martin et al., 1991). Traditional feminine clothing, for example, emphasizes a woman's gender: dress or skirt, a form-fitting or low-cut top revealing the breasts (a secondary sex characteristic), high heels, and so on. For adventuresome women, lacy bustiers, garter belts, and brassieres, once considered undergarments, may be worn as outerwear, emphasizing "femaleness." Most clothing, in fact, that emphasizes or exaggerates secondary sex characteristics is female. Makeup (red lipstick, rouge, eyeliner) and hairstyle also serve to mark or exaggerate the differences between females and males. Even smells (perfume and after-shave cologne) and colors (blue for boys, pink for girls) help distinguish females and males.

Clothing and other aspects of appearance exaggerate the physical differences between women and men. And culture encourages us to accentuate (or invent) psychological, emotional, mental, and behavioral differences. But are men and women as different as we ordinarily think?

In this chapter, we examine some of the critical ways being male or female affects us both as human beings and as sexual beings. We look at the connection between our genitals, our identity as female or male, and our feelings of being feminine or masculine. We also examine the relationship between femininity, masculinity, and sexual orientation. Then we look at whether masculine and feminine traits are the result of biology or socialization. Because we believe socialization is the most significant factor, we next focus on theories of socialization and how we learn to act masculine and feminine in our culture. Then we look at traditional, contemporary, and androgynous gender roles. Finally, we examine hermaphroditism and transsexuality, two phenomena that raise complex issues pertaining to gender and gender identity.

STUDYING GENDER AND GENDER ROLES

Let's define some key terms, to provide us with a common terminology. If we keep these definitions in mind, it will make our discussion clearer.

Sex, Gender, and Gender Roles: What's the Difference?

The word **sex** refers to whether we are biologically female or male, based on our genetic and anatomical sex. Our **genetic sex** refers to our chromosomal and hormonal sex characteristics, such as whether our chromosomes are XY or XX, and whether estrogens or testosterone dominate our hormonal system. **Anatomical sex** refers to our physical sex, such as our gonads, uterus, vulva, vagina, or penis.

Whereas "sex" and "gender" have often been used interchangeably, gender is not the same as biological sex. **Gender** is our femininity or masculinity, the social and cultural characteristics associated with our biological sex. Whereas sex is rooted in biology, gender is rooted in culture. Our **assigned gender** is the gender given us by others, usually at birth. When we are born, someone looks at our genitals and exclaims, "It's a boy!" or "It's a girl!" With that single utterance, we are transformed from an "it" into a "male" or a "female." Our **gender identity** is the gender we *feel* ourselves to be.

Gender roles are the roles a person is expected to perform as a result of being female or male in a particular culture. The term "gender role" is gradually replacing the traditional term "sex role," because sex role continues to suggest a connection between biological sex and behavior (Unger, 1991). Biological males are expected to act out masculine gender roles; biological females are expected to act out feminine gender roles. A **gender-role stereotype** is a rigidly held, oversimplified, and overgeneralized belief that all males and all females possess distinct psychological and behavioral traits. Stereotypes tend to be false or misleading, not only for the group as a whole ("women are more interested in relationships than sex") but for any individual in the group (Jane may be more interested in sex than relationships). Even if a generalization is statistically valid in describing a group average (males are generally taller than females), such generalizations do not necessarily predict whether Roberto will be taller than Tanya. **Gender-role attitude** refers to the beliefs we have of ourselves and others regarding appropriate female and male personality traits and activities. **Gender-role behavior** refers to the actual activities or behaviors we engage in as females

sex Identification as male or female based on genetic and anatomical sex characteristics.

genetic sex Identification as male or female according to chromosomal and hormonal sex characteristics.

anatomical sex Identification as male or female based on physical sex characteristics, such as gonads, uterus, vulva, vagina, or penis.

gender The social and cultural characteristics associated with being male or female.

assigned gender The gender ascribed by others, usually at birth.

gender identity The gender one feels himself or herself to be.

gender role The role a person is expected to perform as a result of being male or female in a particular culture. Preferred over the term *sex role*.

gender-role stereotype A rigidly held, oversimplified, and overgeneralized belief that all males and all females possess distinct psychological and behavioral traits.

gender-role attitude Beliefs about appropriate male and female personality traits and activities.

gender-role behavior The activities in which individuals engage in accordance with their gender.

The moment we are born, we are identified as male or female and are socialized to fulfill masculine and feminine gender roles.

and males. When we discuss gender roles, it is important not to confuse stereotypes with reality and attitudes with behavior.

There are three central aspects of our identity as men or women: biological sex, gender identity, and gender role. Together they form our identity as female or male. For most of us, the three are in agreement. Our male or female anatomy usually coincides with our belief that we are male or female. And as male or female, we more or less act out the masculine or feminine gender role dictated by our culture.

Sex and Gender Identity

We develop our gender through the interaction of its biological and psychosocial components. The biological component includes genetic and anatomical sex, while the psychosocial component includes assigned gender and gender identity.

Assigned Gender When we were born, based on anatomical appearance, we were given our assigned gender. We had no sense of ourselves as females or males. Assigned gender is significant because it tells *others* how to respond to us. After all, one of the first questions an older child or adult asks upon seeing an infant is whether it's a girl or boy. We *learned* that we were girls and boys from the verbal responses of others. "What a pretty *girl*" or "What a good *boy*," our parents and others would say. We are constantly given signals about our gender. Our birth certificates state our sex; our names, such as Paul or Paula, are most likely gender-coded. Our clothes, even in infancy, reveal our gender.

By the time we were 2 years old, we were probably able to identify ourselves as a girl or a boy based on what we had internalized from what others told us. But we didn't really know *why* we were a girl or a boy. We didn't associate our gender with our genitals. In fact, until the age of 3 or so, most children identify girls or boys by hairstyles, clothing, or other nonanatomical signs. At around age 3, children begin to learn that the genitals are what makes a person male or female. It still takes them a while to understand that they are *permanently* a boy or a girl. They often believe that they can become the other sex later.

Gender Identity By about 24 months, we internalize and identify with our gender. We *feel* we are a girl or a boy. This feeling of our femaleness or maleness is our gender identity. Once a child's gender identity is established, he or she will often react strongly if someone mistakes that identity. For most people, gender identity is permanent and is congruent with their sexual anatomy and assigned gender. Furthermore, it is virtually impossible to develop a personal identity without a gender identity as a female or a male (Money & Tucker, 1976). Our sense of femaleness or maleness is a core component of our identity.

Some cultures, however, defer instilling gender identity in males until later. They believe in a latent or dormant femaleness in males. As a consequence, such cultures institute rituals or ceremonies in childhood to ensure that males will identify themselves as males (Whiting, 1979). In some East African societies, for example, male children are referred to as "woman-child"; there appear to be few social differences between boys and girls. Around age 7, the boy undergoes male initiation rites, such as circumcision, whose avowed purpose is to "make" the child into a man. Such ceremonies "may act as a form of therapeutic 'brainwashing,' helping the young male make the transition to a new gender identity with new role expectations" (Whiting, 1979). Other cultures allow older males to act out a latent female identity with such practices as the couvade, in which husbands mimic their wives giving birth. And in our own society, into the early years of this century, boys were dressed in gowns and wore their hair in long curls until age 2. At age 2 or 3, their dresses were replaced by pants and their hair cut. From then on, masculine socialization was stressed (Garber, 1991).

Masculinity and Femininity: Opposites or Similar?

The traditional view of masculinity and femininity sees men and women as polar opposites. Our popular terminology, in fact, reflects this view. Women and men refer to each other as the "opposite sex." But this implies that women and men are opposites, that we have little in common with each other. Our gender stereotypes fit this pattern of polar differences: Men are aggressive, women are passive; men embody **instrumentality** and are task-oriented; women embody **expressiveness** and are emotion-oriented; men are rational, women are irrational; men want sex, women want love; and so on.

It is important to recognize that gender stereotypes, despite their depiction of men and women as opposites, are usually not all-or-nothing notions. Most of us do not think that only men are assertive or only women nurturing. As individuals, along with our friends and family, we probably dis-

instrumentality Being oriented toward tasks and problem solving.

expressiveness Revealing or demonstrating one's emotions.

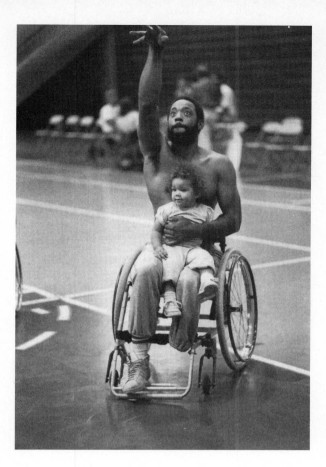

Despite traditional gender-role stereotypes that depict men as instrumental, men can be nurturing as well.

approve of this all-or-nothing notion. Stereotypes reflect *probabilities* that a woman or man will have a certain characteristic based on his or her gender. When we say that men are more independent than women, we mean there is a greater probability that a man will be more independent than a woman (Deaux, 1984).

As technology becomes more available, we are beginning to learn about what contributes to making the sexes different. We are already beginning to get hints that our identities as men and women are a combination of nature and nurture. It is through new technology that researchers can catch brains in the act of cogitating, feeling, or remembering. The most current research suggests that women engage more of their brains than men when they think sad thoughts, but possibly less when they solve SAT math problems (Begley, 1995). Other evidence has found that some differences between men and women may be due to differences in the part of the brain that controls emotional processing. In men, the part controlling action-oriented responses was more active; in women, the part thought to control more symbolic emotional responses was more active (Gur, Mozley, Mozley et al., 1995). With continued interest in this subject, differences and similarities that we once

The perception of male/female psychological differences is far greater than they are in fact.

attributed to learning or culture may be found to be biologically based. Add to this our choices, sense of identities, and life experiences, and we can begin to get a picture of what contributes to making each person unique.

Gender and Sexual Orientation

Gender, gender identity, and gender role are conceptually independent of sexual orientation (Lips, 1992). But, in many people's minds, these concepts are closely related to sexual orientation, discussed at greater length in Chapter 6. Our traditional notion of gender roles assumes that heterosexuality is a critical component of masculinity and femininity (Riseden & Hort, 1992). A "masculine" man is attracted to women and a "feminine" woman is attracted to men. From this assumption follow two beliefs about homosexuality: (1) If a man is gay, he cannot be masculine, and if a woman is lesbian, she cannot be feminine; and (2) if a man is gay, he must have some feminine characteristics, and if a woman is lesbian, she must have some masculine characteristics (Ross, 1983a). What these beliefs imply is that homosexuality is somehow associated with a failure to fulfill traditional gender roles (DeCecco & Elia, 1993). A "real" man is not gay; therefore, gay men are not "real" men. Similarly, a "real" woman is not a lesbian; therefore, lesbians are not "real" women.

Stereotypes of gay men often link them with "feminine" characteristics such as weakness, emotionality, and submissiveness. Such stereotypes can be traced back to the turn of the century, when both Havelock Ellis and Sigmund Freud (discussed in Chapter 2) believed that homosexuality was the result of inversion, reversed gender roles. There are no conclusive findings on the relationship between sexual orientation and gender roles, however (Paul, 1993). Gay and lesbian roles may emphasize certain personality traits or behaviors during one time period and different ones at another time. These traits and behaviors are not necessarily inherent to being gay or lesbian. Like gender roles, gay and lesbian roles may reflect views on how people are expected to act.

Studies on attitudes toward gay men and lesbians indicate a relationship between negative attitudes and gender roles (Herek, 1984; Kite, 1984). A comparison between individuals who hold negative attitudes toward gay men and lesbians and those who hold neutral or positive attitudes found some evidence of differences. Those holding negative attitudes were more likely to (1) adhere to traditional gender roles, (2) stereotype men and women, and (3) support the sexual double standard, granting men greater sexual freedom than women. Males tended to be more negative than women toward gay men and lesbians. And heterosexual men tended to be more negative toward gay men than toward lesbians; heterosexual women were more negative toward lesbians than toward gay men.

GENDER-ROLE LEARNING

As we have seen, gender is a social construct, rooted in culture. How do individuals learn what their society expects of them as males or females?

Theories of Socialization

Although there are a number of ways of examining how we acquire our gender roles, two of the most prominent are cognitive social learning theory and cognitive development theory.

Cognitive social learning theory is derived from behaviorist psychology. In explaining our actions, behaviorists emphasize observable events and their consequences, rather than internal feelings and drives. According to behaviorists, we learn attitudes and behaviors as a result of social interactions with others (hence the term "social learning").

> **cognitive social learning theory** A child development theory that emphasizes the learning of behavior from others, based on the belief that consequences control behavior.

The cornerstone of cognitive social learning theory is the belief that consequences control behavior. Acts that are regularly followed by a reward are likely to occur again; acts that are regularly followed by a punishment are less likely to recur. Girls are rewarded for playing with dolls ("What a nice mommy!"), but boys are not ("What a sissy!").

This behaviorist approach has been modified recently to include **cognition**—mental processes that intervene between stimulus and response, such as evaluation and reflection. The cognitive processes involved in social learning include our ability to (1) use language, (2) anticipate consequences, and (3) make observations. By using language, we can tell our daughter that we like it when she does well in school and that we don't like it when she hits someone. A person's ability to anticipate consequences affects behavior. A boy doesn't need to wear lace stockings in public to know that such dressing will lead to negative consequences. Finally, children observe what others do. A girl may learn that she "shouldn't" play video games by seeing that the players in video arcades are mostly boys.

> **cognition** Mental processes that intervene between stimulus and response, such as evaluation and reflection.

We also learn gender roles by imitation. Learning through imitation is

modeling The process of learning through imitation of others.

cognitive development theory A child development theory that views growth as the mastery of specific ways of perceiving, thinking, and doing that occurs at discrete stages.

called **modeling.** Most of us are not even aware of the many subtle behaviors that make up gender roles—the ways in which men and women use different mannerisms and gestures, speak differently, use different body language, and so on. We don't "teach" these behaviors by reinforcement. Children tend to model friendly, warm, and nurturing adults; they also tend to imitate adults who are powerful in their eyes—that is, adults who control access to food, toys, or privileges. Initially, the most powerful models that children have are their parents. As children grow older and their social world expands, so do the number of people who may act as their role models: siblings, friends, teachers, media figures. Children sift through the various demands and expectations associated with the different models to create their own unique selves.

In contrast to social learning theory, **cognitive development theory** focuses on the child's active interpretation of the messages he or she receives from the environment. Whereas social learning assumes that children and adults learn in fundamentally the same way, cognitive development theory stresses that we learn differently depending on our age. At age 2, children can correctly identify themselves and others as boys or girls, but they tend to base this identification on superficial features such as hair and clothing. Girls have long hair and wear dresses; boys have short hair and never wear dresses. Some children even believe they can change their gender by changing their clothes or hair length.

When children are 6 or 7, they begin to understand that gender is permanent; it is not something you can alter in the same way you can change your clothes. They acquire this understanding because they are capable of grasping the idea that basic characteristics do not change. A woman can be a woman even if she has short hair and wears pants. Although children can understand the permanence of gender, they tend to insist on rigid adherence to gender-role stereotypes.

Gender-Role Learning in Childhood and Adolescence

It is difficult to analyze the relationship between biology and personality because learning begins at birth. Evidence shows, for example, that infant females are more sensitive than infant males to pain and to sudden changes of environment. Such responses may be encouraged by learning that begins immediately after birth.

In our culture, infant girls are usually held more gently and treated more tenderly than boys, who are ordinarily subjected to rougher forms of play. The first day after birth, parents characterize their daughters as soft, fine-featured, and small, and their sons as hard, large-featured, big, and attentive. Fathers tend to stereotype their sons more extremely than mothers do (Fagot & Leinbach, 1987; Rubin, Provanzano, & Luria, 1974). Although it is impossible for strangers to know the sex of a diapered baby, once they learn the baby's sex, they respond accordingly.

Parents as Socializing Agents During infancy and early childhood, a child's most important source of learning is the primary caretaker, whether the mother, father, grandmother, or someone else. Most parents are not aware that their words and actions contribute to their children's gender-role socialization (Culp, Cook, & Housley, 1983). Nor are they aware that they treat their daughters and sons differently because of their gender. Although parents may recognize that they respond differently to sons than to daughters, they usually have a ready explanation: the "natural" differences in the temperament and behavior of girls and boys. Parents may also believe they adjust their responses to each particular child's personality.

Children are socialized in gender roles through four very subtle processes: manipulation, channeling, verbal appellation, and activity exposure (Oakley, 1985).

- *Manipulation*. Parents manipulate their children from infancy onward. They treat a daughter gently, tell her she is pretty, and advise her that nice girls do not fight. They treat a son roughly, tell him he is strong, and advise him that big boys do not cry. Eventually, children incorporate their parents' views in such matters as integral parts of their personalities.

- *Channeling*. Children are channeled by directing their attention to specific objects. Toys, for example, are differentiated by sex. Dolls are considered appropriate for girls, cars for boys.

- *Verbal appellation*. Parents use different words with boys and girls to describe the same behavior. A boy who pushes others may be described as "active," whereas a girl who does the same is usually called "aggressive."

- *Activity exposure*. The activity exposure of girls and boys differs markedly. Although both are usually exposed to feminine activities early in life, boys are discouraged from imitating their mothers, whereas girls are encouraged to be "mother's little helper."

It is generally accepted that parents socialize their children differently according to gender (Block, 1983; Fagot & Leinbach, 1987). Fathers, more than mothers, pressure their children to behave in gender-appropriate ways. Fathers set higher standards of achievement for their sons than for their daughters; for their daughters, fathers emphasize the interpersonal aspect of their relationship. But mothers also reinforce the interpersonal aspect of the parent-daughter relationship (Block, 1983).

Various studies have indicated that ethnicity and class are important in influencing gender roles (Zinn, 1990). Working-class families tend to differentiate more sharply between boys and girls in terms of appropriate behavior than middle-class families; they tend to place more restrictions on girls. In contrast to white families, African American families tend to socialize their daughters to be more independent (Gump, 1980; E. Smith, 1982). Indeed, among African Americans, the "traditional" female role model may never have existed. The African American female role model in which the woman is both wage-earner and homemaker is more typical and more accurately reflects African American experience (Basow, 1986).

As children grow older, their social world expands, and so do their sources of learning. Around the time children enter day care or kindergarten, teachers and peers become important influences.

Teachers as Socializing Agents Day-care centers, nursery schools, and kindergartens are often the child's first experience in the wider world outside the family. Teachers become important role models for their students.

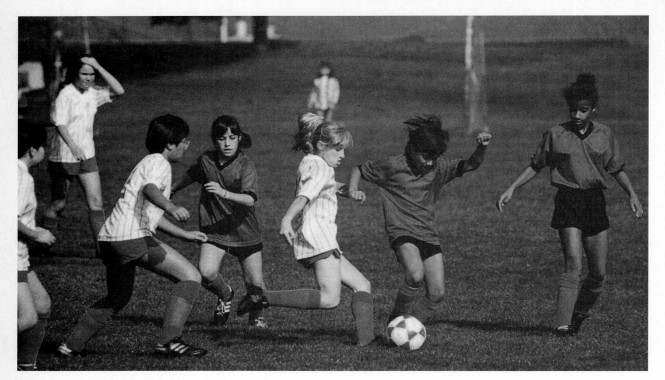

When boys and girls participate in sports together, they develop comparable athletic skills. Segregation of boys and girls encourages the development of differences that otherwise might not occur.

peer An age-mate.

Because most day-care, kindergarten, and elementary school teachers are women, children tend to think of child-adult interactions as primarily the province of women. In this sense, schools reinforce the idea that women are concerned with children, whereas men are not (Koblinsky & Sugawara, 1984). Teachers also tend to be conventional in the gender-role messages they convey to children (Wynn & Fletcher, 1987).

Peers as Socializing Agents **Peers,** a person's age-mates, become especially important when children enter school. By granting or withholding approval, friends and playmates influence what games children play, what they wear, what music they listen to, what television programs they watch, and even what cereal they eat. Peers provide standards for gender-role behavior in several ways (Absismaan, Crombie, & Freeman, 1993; Carter, 1987; Moller, Hymel, & Rubin, 1992):

- Peers provide information about gender-role norms through play activities and toys. Girls play with dolls that cry and wet or glamorous dolls with well-developed figures and expensive tastes. Boys play with dolls known as "action figures," such as GI-Joe and Power Rangers with guns, nunchuks, and bigger-than-life biceps.

- Peers influence the adoption of gender-role norms through verbal approval or disapproval. "That's for boys!" or "Only girls do that!" is a severe negative message when a girl plays with a football or a boy plays with dolls.

- Children's perceptions of their friends' gender-role attitudes, behaviors, and beliefs encourage them to adopt similar ones in order to be accepted. If a girl's friends play soccer, she is more likely to play soccer. If a boy's same-sex friends display feelings, he is more likely to display feelings.

Even though parents tend to fear the worst from peers, peers provide important positive influences. It is within their peer groups, for example, that adolescents learn to develop intimate relationships (Gecas & Seff, 1991). Adolescents in peer groups tend to be more egalitarian than parents, especially fathers (Thornton, 1989).

Media Influences Much of television programming promotes or condones negative stereotypes about gender, ethnicity, age, and gay men and lesbians. Images of women have improved somewhat in recent years, but television continues to depict rigid gender-role stereotypes. Ninety percent of the narrators in commercials are men.

Not surprisingly, research indicates that heavy TV viewers, in contrast to light viewers, hold more stereotypical gender-role views (Lips, 1992). Parents need to supervise their children's TV watching, limiting their access and teaching them how to recognize stereotypes. It is especially important to lay the groundwork during childhood because once a child reaches adolescence, such supervision is next to impossible.

Gender-Role Learning in Adulthood

Researchers have generally neglected gender-role learning in adulthood (Losh-Hesselbart, 1987; Sinnott, 1986), but people do continue to change and develop their gender-role identity over their life span. As mentioned earlier, young children have not clearly differentiated their activities into those considered appropriate for males or females. As the children enter school, however, they begin to identify behaviors as masculine and feminine. They tend to polarize masculinity and femininity as they test the appropriate roles for themselves. As they enter young adulthood, they begin slowly to shed the rigid male/female polarization as they are confronted with the realities of relationships. As they mature and grow older, women and men transcend traditional femininity and masculinity. They combine femininity and masculinity into a more complex transcendent role.

CHANGING GENDER ROLES

Within the past generation, there has been a significant shift from traditional toward more egalitarian gender roles. Although women have changed more than men, men are also changing. These changes seem to affect all socioeconomic classes. Those from conservative religious groups, such as Mormons, Catholics, and fundamentalist and evangelical Protestants, adhere most strongly to traditional gender roles (Spence et al., 1985). Despite the continuing disagreement, it is likely that the egalitarian trend will continue (Mason & Lu, 1988; Thornton, 1989).

Traditional Gender Roles

Most gender-role studies have focused on the white middle class. Very little is known about gender roles among African Americans, Latinos, Asian Americans, and other ethnic groups (Binion, 1990; Reid & Comas-Diaz, 1990; True, 1990; see *Sex Roles* 22: 7–8 [April 1990] for a special issue on gender roles and ethnicity). As a result, white middle-class students and researchers need to be careful not to project gender-role concepts or aspirations based on their values onto other groups. Too often such projections can lead to distortions or moral judgments. There is evidence, for example, that the feelings of low self-esteem and dependence often associated with traditional female roles do not apply to African American women. In contrast to middle-class whites, African Americans have traditionally valued strong, independent women (Gump, 1980; E. Smith, 1982). And among Latinos, "machismo" has a positive meaning.

The Traditional Male Gender Role What is it to be a "real" man in America? Bruce Feirstein (1982) parodied him in his book, *Real Men Don't Eat Quiche*:

Question: How many Real Men does it take to change a light bulb?

Answer: None. Real Men aren't afraid of the dark.

Question: Why did the Real Man cross the road?

Answer: It's none of your damn business.

Central personality traits associated with the traditional male role—whether white, African American, Latino, or Asian American—include aggressiveness, emotional toughness, independence, feelings of superiority, and decisiveness. Males are generally regarded as being more power-oriented than females. Men demonstrate higher degrees of aggression, especially violent aggression (such as assault, homicide, and rape), dominance, and competitiveness. Although these tough, aggressive traits may be useful in the corporate world, politics, and the military (or in hunting sabre-toothed tigers), such characteristics are rarely helpful to a man in his intimate relationships, which require understanding, cooperation, communication, and nurturing.

Males from ethnic groups must move between dominant and ethnic cultures with different role requirements. They are expected to conform not only to the gender-role norms of the dominant group but to those of their own group as well. Black males, for example, must conform to dominant stereotype expectations (success, competition, and aggression) as well as expectations of the African American community, most notably cooperation and the promotion of ethnic survival (Hunter & Davis, 1992). They must also confront negative stereotypes about black masculinity, such as hypersexuality and violence.

Male Sexual Scripts In sociology, a **script** refers to the acts, rules, and expectations associated with a particular role. It is like the script handed out to an actor. Unlike dramatic scripts, however, social scripts allow considerable improvisation within their general boundaries. We are given many scripts in life according to the various roles we play. Among them are sex-

script In sociology, the acts, rules, and expectations associated with a particular role.

ual scripts that outline how we are to behave sexually when acting out our gender roles. See Chapter 9 for further discussion on sexual scripts.

Bernie Zilbergeld (1992) suggests that the male sexual script includes the following:

- *Men should not have (or at least should not express) certain feelings.* Men should not express doubts; they should be assertive, confident, and aggressive. Tenderness and compassion are not masculine feelings.

- *Performance is the thing that counts.* Sex is something to be achieved, to win at. Feelings only get in the way of the job to be done. Sex is not for intimacy but for orgasm.

- *The man is in charge.* As in other things, the man is the leader, the person who knows what is best. The man initiates sex and gives the woman her orgasm. A real man doesn't need a woman to tell him what women like; he already knows.

- *A man always wants sex and is ready for it.* It doesn't matter what else is going on, a man wants sex; he is always able to become erect. He is a machine.

- *All physical contact leads to sex.* Because men are basically sexual machines, any physical contact is a sign for sex. Touching is seen as the first step toward sexual intercourse, not an end in itself. There is no physical pleasure except sexual pleasure.

- *Sex equals intercourse.* All erotic contact leads to sexual intercourse. Foreplay is just that: warming up, getting your partner excited for penetration. Kissing, hugging, erotic touching, and oral sex are only preliminaries to intercourse.

- *Sexual intercourse leads to orgasm.* The orgasm is the proof of the pudding. The more orgasms, the better the sex. If a woman does not have an orgasm, she is not sexual. The male feels that he is a failure because he was not good enough to give her an orgasm. If she requires clitoral stimulation to have an orgasm, she has a problem.

Common to all these myths is a separation of sex from love and attachment. Sex is seen as performance.

The Traditional Female Gender Role

Although many of the features of the traditional male gender role are the same across ethnic lines, such as being in control, there are striking ethnic differences in the female role.

Among whites, the traditional female gender role centers around women as wives and mothers. When a woman leaves adolescence, she is expected to get married and have children. Although a traditional woman may work prior to marriage, she is not expected to defer marriage for work goals.

In recent years, the traditional role has been modified to include work and marriage. Work roles, however, are clearly subordinated to marital and family roles. Upon the birth of the first child, the woman is expected to remain home, if economically feasible, to become a full-time mother.

The traditional white female gender role does not extend to African American women. This may be attributed to a combination of the African heritage, slavery, which subjugated women to the same labor and hardships as men, and economic discrimination, which forced women into the labor

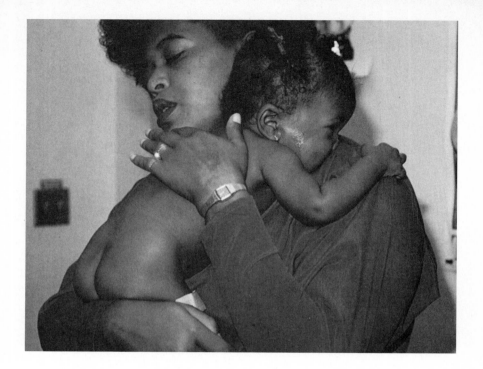

force (Hatchett, 1991). African American men are generally more supportive than white or Latino men of more egalitarian gender roles for both women and men.

In traditional Latina gender roles, women subordinate themselves to males (Vasquez-Nuthall, Romero-Garcia, & DeLeon, 1987). But this subordination is based more on respect for the man's role as provider than on dominance (Becerra, 1988). Unlike in the Anglo culture, gender roles are strongly affected by age roles, in which the young subordinate themselves to the old. In this dual arrangement, notes Rosina Becerra (1988), "females are viewed as submissive, naive, and somewhat childlike. Elders are viewed as wise, knowledgeable, and deserving of respect." As a result of this intersection of gender and age roles, older women are treated with greater deference than younger women.

Female Sexual Scripts Whereas the traditional male sexual script focuses on sex over feelings, the traditional female sexual script focuses on feelings over sex, on love over passion. The traditional female sexual script cited by Lonnie Barbach (1982) includes the following ideas:

- *Sex is good and bad.* Women are taught that sex is both good and bad. What makes sex good? Sex in marriage or a committed relationship. What makes sex bad? Sex in a casual or uncommitted relationship. Sex is "so good" that you need to save it for your husband (or for someone with whom you are deeply in love). Sex is bad; if it is not sanctioned by love or marriage, you'll get a bad reputation.

- *Don't touch me "down there."* Girls are taught not to look at their genitals, not to touch them, especially not to explore them. As a result, women know very little about their genitals. They are often concerned about vaginal odors, making them uncomfortable about cunnilingus.

- *Sex is for men.* Men want sex, women want love. Women are sexually passive, waiting to be aroused. Sex is not a pleasurable activity as an end in itself; it is something performed by women *for* men.

- *Men should know what women want.* This script tells women that men know what they want, even if women don't tell them. Women are supposed to remain pure and sexually innocent. It is up to the man to arouse the woman, even if he doesn't know what a particular woman finds arousing. To keep her image of sexual innocence, she does not tell him what she wants.

- *Women shouldn't talk about sex.* Many women cannot talk about sex easily because they are not expected to have strong sexual feelings. Some women may know their partners well enough to have sex with them but not well enough to communicate their needs to them.

- *Women should look like "Playmates."* The media present ideally attractive women as beautiful models with slender hips, supple breasts, no fat; they are always young, with never a pimple, wrinkle, or gray hair in sight. As a result of these cultural images, many women are self-conscious about their physical appearance. They worry that they are too fat, too plain, too old. They often feel awkward without their clothes on to hide their imagined flaws.

- *Women are nurturers.* Women give, men receive. Women give themselves, their bodies, their pleasures to men. Everyone else's needs come first; his desire over hers, his orgasm over hers. If a woman always puts her partner's enjoyment first, she may be depriving herself of her own enjoyment. As Barbach (1982) points out, "If our attention is so totally riveted on another person, or on external events rather than on ourselves, it is impossible to experience the full pleasure and sensation of the sexual event."

- *There is only one right way to have an orgasm.* Women often "learn" that there is only one "right" way to have an orgasm: during sexual intercourse as a result of penile stimulation. But there are many ways to have an orgasm: through oral sex; manual stimulation before, during, or after intercourse; masturbation; and so on. For women who rarely or never have an orgasm during heterosexual intercourse to believe that this is the only legitimate way to have one deprives them of expressing themselves sexually in other ways.

Contemporary Gender Roles

Until recently, most Americans tended to look at women and men as if they were each a distinct species that shared few traits, behaviors, and attitudes. Males traditionally suppressed "feminine" traits in themselves, and females suppressed "masculine" traits. What is apparently happening today, especially among women, is that gender roles are becoming more androgynous—that is, incorporating both masculine and feminine traits. The

Although attitudes toward motherhood are changing, especially among middle-class whites, it continues to be highly valued in our culture.

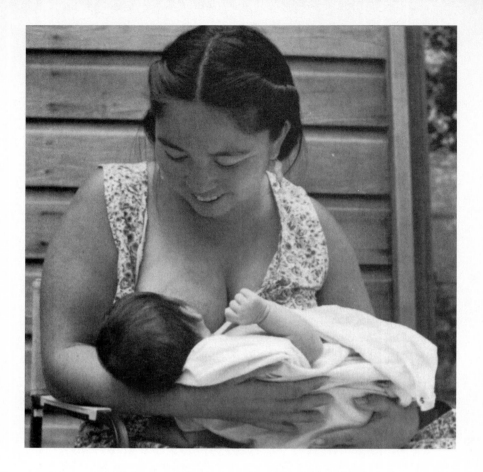

identification of masculinity with instrumentality and femininity with expressiveness appears to be breaking down. In part, this is because the instrumental/expressive dichotomy was a false dichotomy to begin with.

Contemporary gender roles are also evolving from traditional hierarchical gender roles (in which one sex is subordinate to the other) to more egalitarian roles (in which both sexes are treated equally). Thus, contemporary gender roles often display traditional elements as well as egalitarian and androgynous ones.

Questioning Motherhood Changes in women's roles profoundly reinforce the contemporary trend to separate sex from reproduction. Record numbers of women are rejecting motherhood because of the conflicts child rearing creates with marriage and work. It is estimated that 20–25% of female "baby boomers" are choosing to remain childfree to maximize work opportunities and time with their husbands (Nock, 1987). This contrasts with an approximately 10% childlessness rate in the previous generation. Similarly, women are having fewer children than ever before.

Women from ethnic and minority status groups, however, are less likely to view motherhood as an impediment. African American women and Latinas tend to place greater value on motherhood than the white (Anglo) majority. For African Americans, the tradition has generally combined work and motherhood; the two are not viewed as necessarily antithetical (Basow, 1986). For Latinas, the cultural and religious emphasis on family, the higher status conferred on motherhood, and their own familial attitudes have contributed to high fertility rates (Jorgensen & Adams, 1988).

Contemporary Sexual Scripts As gender roles change, so do sexual scripts. Traditional sexual scripts have been challenged by more liberal and egalitarian ones. Sexual attitudes and behaviors have become increasingly liberal for both white and African American males and females, although African American attitudes and behaviors continue to be somewhat more liberal than those of whites (Belcastro, 1985; Gutherie, 1988; Peters & Wyatt, 1988; Weinberg & Wilson, 1988; Wilson, 1986). Many college-age women have made an explicit break with the more traditional scripts, especially the good girl/bad girl dichotomy and the older belief that "nice" girls don't enjoy sex (Moffatt, 1989). Older professional women who are single also appear to reject the old images (Davidson & Darling, 1988). We do not know how Latino sexuality and Asian American sexuality have changed, as there is almost no research on their sexual scripts, values, and behaviors.

Contemporary sexual scripts include the following elements for both sexes (Gagnon & Simon, 1987; Reed & Weinberg, 1984; Rubin, 1990; Seidman, 1989):

- Sexual expression is a positive good.
- Sexual activities are a mutual exchange of erotic pleasure.
- Sexuality is equally involving, and both partners are equally responsible.
- Legitimate sexual activities are not limited to sexual intercourse but also include masturbation and oral-genital sex.
- Sexual activities may be initiated by either partner.
- Both partners have a right to experience orgasm, whether through intercourse, oral-genital sex, or manual stimulation.
- Premarital sex is acceptable within a relationship context.

These contemporary scripts give increasing recognition to female sexuality. They are increasingly relationship-centered rather than male-centered. Women, however, are still not granted full sexual equality with males (Williams & Jacoby, 1989).

Androgyny

Some scholars have challenged the traditional masculine/feminine gender-role dichotomy, arguing that such models are unhealthy and fail to reflect the real world. Instead of looking at gender roles in terms of polarized opposites, they suggest examining them in terms of androgyny (Roopnarine & Mounts, 1987). **Androgyny** refers to flexibility in gender roles and the unique combination of instrumental and expressive traits as influenced by individual differences, situations, and stages in the life cycle (Bem, 1975; Kaplan, 1979). (The term "androgyny" is derived from the Greek *andros*, man, and *gyne*, woman.) An androgynous person combines both the instru-

androgyny The unique and flexible combination of instrumental and expressive traits in accordance with individual differences, situations, and stages in the life cycle.

Androgyny encourages men and women to express both instrumental and expressive qualities.

mental traits previously associated with masculinity and the expressive traits associated with traditional femininity. An androgynous lifestyle allows men and women to choose from the full range of emotions and behaviors, according to their temperament, situation, and common humanity, rather than their gender. Men are permitted to cry and display tenderness; they can touch, feel, and nurture without being considered effeminate. Women can be aggressive or career-oriented; they can seek leadership and can be mechanical or physical.

Flexibility and integration are important aspects of androgyny. Individuals who are rigidly instrumental or expressive, despite the situation, are not considered androgynous. A woman who is always aggressive at work and passive at home, for example, would not be considered androgynous, as work may call for compassion and home life for assertion.

It is not clear what proportion of individuals may be identified as androgynous or traditional. Although it has been suggested that androgyny is a white middle-class concept, one study of African American women (Binion, 1990) indicated that 37% identified themselves as androgynous, 18%

Think About It

ANDROGYNY AND HEALTH: A CLOSER LOOK

Did you ever wonder what effect being androgynous might have on relationships, self-esteem, and even one's willingness to exercise? There is considerable evidence that androgynous individuals and couples have a greater ability to form and sustain intimate relationships and adopt a wide range of behaviors and values (Ickes, 1993). Androgynous college students and older people tend to have greater confidence in social situations than individuals who are **sex-typed,** following gender-role stereotypes (Puglisi & Jackson, 1981). Masculine and androgynous people of both sexes are more independent and less likely to have their opinions influenced than are those who label themselves highly feminine (Bem, 1975). At the same time, feminine and androgynous people of both sexes appear to be more nurturing than those who describe themselves as typically masculine (Bem et al., 1976).

In addition, androgynous people have shown greater resilience to stress (Ross & Cohen, 1987).

They are more aware of feelings of love and more expressive of them (Ganong & Coleman, 1987). Androgynous couples may have greater satisfaction in their relationships than sex-typed couples. Transcending traditional female and male behaviors and values, androgynous couples are more flexible in their responses to each other and to the environment. Androgyny even seems to affect health behaviors. Androgynous individuals, for example, are more likely to exercise and not to smoke (Shifren, Bauserman, & Carter, 1993).

Androgyny, however, does not necessarily equate to better. Some studies have indicated that androgyny may increase job-related stress and adversely affect emotional adjustment (Lee & Schurer, 1983; Rotherman & Weiner, 1983). As in many areas of human sexuality, more research needs to be conducted before we can make conclusive statements about the affects of androgyny on mental, marital, and physical health.

as feminine, and 24% as masculine. (The remaining women did not identify themselves.) That such a large percentage was androgynous or masculine, the study argues, is not surprising, given the demanding family responsibilities and cultural expectations that require instrumental and active traits. Another study of college students from India indicated a high degree of androgyny, suggesting cross-cultural validity (Ravinder, 1987).

Androgyny, like other personality theories, assumes that masculinity and femininity are basic aspects of an individual's personality. It assumes that when we are active, we are expressing our masculine side, and when we are sensitive, we are expressing the feminine side of our personality. Androgyny retains the concept of masculinity and femininity, and thus it retains some of the categories of bipolar gender-role thinking (Willemsen, 1993).

Living up to an androgynous gender role, however, may be just as stultifying to an individual as trying to be traditionally feminine or masculine. In advocating the expression of both feminine and masculine traits, perhaps we are imposing a new form of gender-role rigidity on ourselves. Bem, one of the leading proponents of androgyny, has become increasingly critical of the idea. She believes now that androgyny replaces "a prescription

sex-typed Following gender-role stereotypes.

You and Your Sexual Well-Being

MASCULINITY, FEMININITY, AND ANDROGYNY

Increased interest in androgynous gender roles has led to the development of a number of instruments to measure masculinity, femininity, and androgyny in individuals. The one below is patterned after the Bem Sex Role Inventory (BSRI), which is one of the most widely used tests (Bem, 1974, 1981).

To get a rough idea of how androgynous you are, examine the 21 personality traits below. Use a scale of 1 to 5 to indicate how well a personality trait describes you.

1	2	3	4	5
NOT AT ALL	SLIGHTLY	SOMEWHAT	QUITE A BIT	VERY MUCH

1. Aggressive
2. Understanding
3. Helpful
4. Decisive
5. Nurturing
6. Happy
7. Risk-taker
8. Shy
9. Unsystematic
10. Strong
11. Affectionate
12. Cordial
13. Assertive
14. Tender
15. Moody
16. Dominating
17. Warm
18. Unpredictable
19. Independent-minded
20. Compassionate
21. Reliable

Scoring

Your masculinity, femininity, and androgyny scores may be determined as follows:

1. To determine your masculinity score, add up your answers for numbers 1, 4, 7, 10, 13, 16, and 19, and divide the sum by seven.
2. To determine your femininity score, add up your answers for numbers 2, 5, 8, 11, 14, 17, and 20, and divide the sum by seven.
3. To determine your androgyny score, subtract the femininity score from the masculinity score.

The closer your score is to zero, the more androgynous you are. A high positive score indicates masculinity; a high negative score indicates femininity. A high masculine score not only indicates masculine attributes but also a rejection of feminine attributes. Similarly, a high feminine score indicates not only feminine characteristics, but a rejection of masculine attributes.

Source: Strong, Bryan, and Christine DeVault. *The Marriage and Family Experience*. St. Paul, MN: West, 1992.

to be masculine or feminine with the doubly incarcerating prescription to be masculine *and* feminine. The individual now has not one but two potential sources of inadequacy to contend with" (Bem, 1983).

GENDER PROBLEMS: HERMAPHRODITISM AND TRANSSEXUALITY

For most of us, there is no question about our gender: We *know* we are female or male. We may question our femininity or masculinity, but rarely do we question being female or male. For hermaphrodites and transsexuals, however, "What sex am I?" is a real and painful question. Their dilemma, however, reinforces the fact that our gender identity as male or female is not "natural" but learned.

The genitals of a fetally adrogenized female may resemble those of a male.

Hermaphroditism: Chromosomal and Hormonal Errors

Unusual genital or physical development can make a person's sex unclear. Usually such ambiguity is caused by chromosomal or hormonal errors during prenatal development. Sometimes a child is born with an underdeveloped penis or an enlarged clitoris, making it unclear whether the child is male or female. The most common chromosomal and hormonal errors in prenatal development are discussed below. They are summarized in Table 5.1.

Many of these individuals are **hermaphrodites,** males or females possessing the sex characteristics of both sexes, as mentioned in Chapter 1. A *true hermaphrodite* develops both male and female gonads: either one of each, two of each, or two ovotestes (gonads that have both ovarian and testicular tissue in the same gland). The external appearance of a true hermaphrodite is ambiguous, with genital and other physical characteristics of both sexes. *Pseudohermaphrodites,* as we saw in Chapter 1, have two testes or two ovaries but an ambiguous genital appearance. (Although rare among humans, hermaphroditism is fairly common in the animal world, where snails, for example, possess the reproductive organs of both sexes, changing "genders" for the purpose of copulation.)

hermaphrodite A person with both male and female gonads: either one of each, two of each, or two ovotestes (gonads that have both ovarian and testicular tissue in the same gland). Also known as true hermaphrodite.

Chromosomal Errors Chromosomal errors are common. One study of 35,000 Danish newborns found that the incidence of sex chromosome errors was 1 in 426 children, or 2.34 in 1000 (Nielsen & Wohlert, 1991). Chromosomal errors occur when an individual has fewer or more X or Y chromosomes than normal. Two syndromes resulting from erroneous chromosomal patterns may result in gender confusion: Turner syndrome and Klinefelter syndrome. In both of these, the body develops with some marked physical characteristics of the other sex.

Females with **Turner syndrome** are born lacking an X chromosome (notated as 45, XO). It is one of the most common chromosomal errors among females, occurring about once in 2500 live births (Mullins, Lynch, Orten, & Youll et al., 1991).

Infants and young girls with Turner syndrome appear normal externally, but they have no ovaries. At puberty, changes initiated by ovarian hormones cannot take place. The body does not gain a mature look or height,

Turner syndrome A chromosomal error affecting females born lacking an X chromosome, resulting in the failure to develop ovaries.

TABLE 5.1 Abnormalities in Prenatal Development

	Chromosomal Sex*	Gonads	Internal Reproductive Structures	External Reproductive Structures	Secondary Sex Characteristics	Gender Identity
Chromosomal						
Turner syndrome	Female (45, XO)	Nonfunctioning or absent ovaries	Normal female except for ovaries	Underdeveloped genitals	No breast development or menstruation at puberty	Female
Klinefelter syndrome	Male (47, XXY)	Testes	Normal male	Small penis and testes	Female secondary sex characteristics develop at puberty	Male, but frequent gender confusion at puberty
Hormonal Errors						
Androgen-insensitivity syndrome	Male (46, XY)	Testes, but body unable to utilize androgen (testosterone)	Shallow vagina, lacks normal male structures	Labia	Female secondary sex characteristics develop at puberty; no menstruation	Female
Congenital adrenal hyperplasia (pseudohermaphroditism)	Female (46, XX)	Ovaries	Normal female	Ambiguous tending toward male appearance; fused vagina and enlarged clitoris may be mistaken for empty scrotal sac and micropenis	Female secondary sex characteristics develop at puberty	Usually male unless condition discovered at birth and rectified by hormonal therapy

*Chromosomal sex refers to 46, XX (female) or 46, XY (male). Sometimes a chromosome will be missing, as in 45, XO, or there will be an extra chromosome, as in 47, XXY. In these notations, the number refers to the number of chromosomes (46, in 23 pairs, is normal); the letters X and Y refer to chromosomes and O refers to a missing chromosome.

and menstruation cannot occur. The adolescent girl may question her femaleness because she does not menstruate or develop breasts like her peers. Hormonal therapy, including estrogen therapy and human growth hormone (HGH) therapy, can replace the hormones necessary to produce normal adolescent changes, such as growth and menstruation (LaFranchi, 1992; Rongen-Westerlaken, Vanes, Wit, Otten, & Demuinkkeizer-Schrama,

1992; Rosenfeld, Frane, Attie, Brasel, Bursten, & Clara, 1992). Even with hormonal therapy, however, women with Turner syndrome will likely remain infertile, although they may successfully give birth through embryo transfer following in vitro fertilization with donated ova (Rogers, Murphy, Leeton, Hoise, & Beaton, 1992).

Males with **Klinefelter syndrome** have one or more extra X chromosomes (47, XXY; 48, XXXY; or 49, XXXXY). One study estimated the incidence as 1 in 576 boys (Nielsen & Wohlert, 1991). The presence of the Y chromosome designates a person as male. It causes the formation of testes and ensures a masculine physical appearance. However, the presence of a double X chromosome pattern, which is a female trait, adds some female physical traits. At puberty, female secondary sex characteristics such as breasts and hips develop, and male characteristics tend to be weak: small penis and testes; scanty, soft body hair. The XXY male is often confused about his gender identity. He may be subject to teasing or ridicule by others. If the condition is identified early, many of the problems associated with it will respond to hormonal treatment (Mandoki, Sumner, Hoffman, & Riconda, 1991). Because of low testosterone levels, the vast majority of males with the syndrome are unable to experience erections; virtually all are sterile.

Klinefelter syndrome A condition in which a male has one or more extra X chromosomes, causing the development of female secondary sex characteristics.

Hormonal Errors Hormonal imbalances may result in males and females developing physical characteristics associated with the other sex.

Androgen-insensitivity syndrome or **testicular feminization** is a hereditary condition passed through X chromosomes (Williams, Patterson, & Hughes, 1993; see Kaplan & Owett, 1993, for female androgen-deficiency syndrome.) A genetic male is born with testes, but because of his body's inability to absorb testosterone, the estrogen influence prevails. From the earliest stages, therefore, his body tends toward a female appearance, failing to develop male internal and external reproductive structures. Externally the infant is female, with labia and vagina, but the internal female structures are not present. At puberty, the body develops breasts, hips, and other secondary female sex characteristics. The testes remain in the abdomen and are sterile. People with androgen insensitivity are usually assigned female gender status at birth (Gooren & Cohen-Kettenis, 1991; Shah, Wooley, & Costin, 1992).

Physically, individuals with androgen-insensitivity syndrome develop as typical females, except for their inability to menstruate. It is often not until puberty that the physical anomaly is discovered. Usually the person is comfortable about her female gender identity. She can enjoy sex and orgasm (Money & Tucker, 1975).

androgen-insensitivity syndrome or **testicular feminization** A hereditary condition passed through X chromosomes in which a genetic male is born with testes but is unable to absorb testosterone; as a result, the estrogen influence prevails, and his body tends toward a female appearance, failing to develop male internal and external sex organs.

In **congenital adrenal hyperplasia** (formerly known as adrenogenital syndrome), a genetic female with ovaries and vagina develops externally as a male, the result of a malfunctioning adrenal gland. The adrenal gland produces androgen instead of androgen-inhibiting cortisone.

At birth, the child appears to be a male with a penis and an empty scrotum. The appearance, however, may be ambiguous. Some have only an enlarged clitoris, with or without a vaginal opening, some a micropenis, and some a complete penis and scrotum. When the situation is discovered at birth, the child is usually assigned female status, and treatment is given to promote female development. The child develops as a female. If the con-

congenital adrenal hyperplasia A condition in which a genetic female with ovaries and vagina develops externally as a male as a result of malfunctioning adrenal gland. Previously known as adrenogenital syndrome.

Think About It

TRANSSEXUAL SURGERY

Many transsexuals do not view their dilemma as a psychological problem but as a medical one. As a result, they tend to seek surgeons who may change their genitalia rather than psychiatrists who can help them to examine and then to match their gender identity with their physical body. Sexual reassignment is not about sex but rather about matching one's gender identity to one's physiological status.

Gender dysphoric individuals seeking **sex reassignment surgery (SRS),** the surgical process by which the reproductive organs are surgically altered from one sex to the other, go through a comprehensive treatment program prior to their operation. The goal of the surgery is to reduce the needless suffering and psychological adjustment problems that occur when the genitals do not conform to the brain's gender. There are four basic steps to treatment:

1. *Gender dysphoria therapy.* The client meets with a therapist or group of other gender dysphoric individuals regularly for a period of six months. The client must demonstrate to the therapist that a persistent desire to be rid of his or her assigned gender and genitals has existed for at least two years prior to hormonal treatment (Chong, 1990). The therapist, in making a diagnosis of transsexualism, must also exclude mental disorders, such as schizophrenia or borderline personalities. One study reported that 23% of those attending a gender dysphoric clinic eventually were referred to sex reassignment surgery (Burns, Farrell, & Christie-Brown, 1990).

2. *Hormonal treatment.* Preoperative male-to-female transsexuals receive estrogen therapy and preoperative female-to-male transsexuals receive testosterone therapy. These therapies induce the appropriate secondary sex characteristics, such as breasts for male-to-female transsexuals, and facial and body hair and penises (enlarged clitorises) for female-to-male transsexuals. Dramatic changes are observable in the female-to-male therapies, such as male patterned baldness (if the gene is present), facial hair, and shifts of body weight.

3. *Living as a member of the preferred gender.* The client must live successfully for a year as a mem-

sex reassignment surgery (SRS) The surgical process by which the reproductive organs are surgically altered from one sex to the other.

gender dysphoria Dissatisfaction with one's gender.

transsexual A person whose genitals and gender identity as male or female are discordant. Postsurgical transsexuals have surgically altered their genitals to fit their gender identity.

dition is discovered after the child establishes a male gender identity, a decision must be made to support the male gender identity or to initiate a sex change.

Transsexuality

Gender dysphoria is the state of dissatisfaction individuals experience when they feel they are trapped in the body of the "wrong" sex (Freund & Watson, 1993; Pauly, 1990). They feel they are not *really* the gender to which their genitals have "condemned" them. Gender dysphoric people who wish to have, or have had, their genitals surgically altered to conform to their gender identity are known as **transsexuals.** Transsexuals are classified as preoperative transsexuals and postoperative transsexuals.

In transsexuality, the individual's gender identity and sexual anatomy are at war. Transsexuals are convinced that by some strange quirk of fate they ber of the preferred gender. This is not an easy task, for such subtle gender clues as mannerisms, voice inflections, and body movement, learned in childhood, must be altered.

4. *Sex reassignment surgery.* For former males, SRS involves the removal of the penis and testes and the construction of a clitoris from the former penis, vaginal lips from excess skin and tissue, and an artificial vagina (Hage et al., 1993). For former females, the clitoris is refashioned into a penis, removable penile implants are used for erections, and a scrotum is built with artificial testes (Eldh, 1993; Fang, Chen, & Imperato–McGinley, 1992). Some are able to experience orgasm (Lief & Hubschman, 1993).

Of the estimated 10,000–15,000 transsexuals in the United States, about 3000–4000 have undergone surgery to correct nature's anatomical "mistake." Unfortunately, there have been few long-term studies of the impact of SRS on adjustment. Several factors appear to affect the satisfaction of postoperative transsexuals. First, the surgery must be skillfully done so that the transsexual will have a positive body image

(Ross & Need, 1989). Second, gay men and lesbians are generally more satisfied with their transsexual status than are heterosexuals (Blanchard et al., 1989). Third, female-to-male transsexuals appear to be more satisfied than male-to-female transsexuals in terms of sexual satisfaction and intimate relationships, both preoperatively and postoperatively (Kockott & Fahrner, 1988). Fourth, primary transsexuals have an easier adjustment than secondary transsexuals because of their greater amount of experience in their preferred gender (Leavitt & Berger, 1990).

Going public with the change involves significant risk for the transsexual, both personally and professionally. Because they are not specifically protected from discrimination in the workplace under the categories of "race, creed, color, ancestry, age, sex, sexual orientation, disability, or place of birth," transsexuals have good reason to be apprehensive. This situation is changing in a handful of cities where laws have been enacted to protect transsexuals. Legally, most states will issue new birth certificates, or amend existing ones, so they match the new status of the individual.

have been given the body of the wrong sex. They generally want to change their sex, not their personality. Many have little interest in sexual relationships. It is more important for them to acquire the anatomy of the desired gender than to have greater sexual satisfaction (Arndt, 1991; Braunthal, 1981).

As transsexuality revolves around issues of gender identity, it is a distinctly different phenomenon from cross-dressing, transvestism, or homosexuality. Transvestites, cross-dressers, gay men, and lesbians are not transsexuals (Garber, 1991). In contrast to transsexuals, members of the latter group feel confident of their female or male identity. Being lesbian or gay reflects sexual orientation rather than gender questioning. A study of female-to-male transsexuals and lesbians, for example, revealed that most members of both groups had sexual experiences with males, but the female-to-male transsexuals fantasized being males, while the lesbians completely identified with being female (McCauley & Ehrhardt, 1980). Furthermore,

The genitals of a postoperative female-to-male transsexual, left, and the genitals of a postoperative male-to-female transsexual, right.

postoperative transsexuals may or may not change their sexual orientation, whether it is toward members of the same, the other, or both sexes.

Estimates of the prevalence of transsexuality vary greatly, ranging from 1 in 100,000 to 1 in 37,000 for males and from 1 in 400,000 to 1 in 100,000 for females. In countries where there is greater tolerance of transsexuality, such as the Netherlands, estimates of male transsexuals range from 1 in 29,000 to 1 in 18,000 (Arndt, 1991). Some cultures, however, accept a gender identity that is not congruent with sexual anatomy and create an alternative third sex, as we saw in Chapter 1. "Men-women"—Native American two-spirits, Indian *hijas,* and Burmese *acaults*—are considered a third gender (Bullough, 1991; Coleman, Colgan, & Gooren, 1992; Roscoe, 1991). Members of these third genders are often believed to possess spiritual powers because of their "specialness." Our culture, however, provides no similar category, and such discordance in gender identity is considered pathological.

There are no known definitive causes of transsexuality (Arndt, 1991; Bullough, 1991; Money, 1980). Among those known as *primary transsexuals,* transsexuality may begin in childhood; it is detectable sometimes in the first two years after birth. *Secondary transsexuals* experience gender dysphoria later, usually in adulthood. Parents of primary transsexuals often remark that their male children, who by age 4 or 5 identified themselves psychologically as girls, had acted as girls from the very beginning. Throughout childhood, these children engaged in girls' activities, play, and dress; they moved, walked, and ran as girls. Their playmates were girls. By the time the transsexual child reaches late adolescence, he may request an operation to change his genitals to those of a woman; male-to-female operations vastly outnumber female-to-male by a ratio of 3 to 1. By this time, the adolescent has usually learned the roles associated with femininity so well that he can easily pass as a woman in most situations.

Because primary transsexuals have lived much of their lives in their preferred gender (despite their genitals), they are often able to move into their "new" gender with relative ease. Secondary transsexuals, however, who have lived most of their lives in their assigned gender, have more difficulty in making the transition to the behaviors associated with their preferred gender (Leavitt & Berger, 1990).

Preoperative transsexuals vary in their interest in sexual activity. One study of preoperative male-to-female transsexuals who were attracted to males found that 44% abstained from sexual activity, 19% were sexually active but avoided using their penises, and 37% were sexually active with their penises and enjoyed their experiences (Leavitt & Berger, 1990).

We ordinarily take our gender as female or male for granted. The making of gender, however, is a complex process involving both biological and psychological elements. Biologically, we are male or female in terms of genetic and anatomical makeup. Psychologically, we are male or female in terms of our assigned gender and our gender identity. Only in rare cases, as with chromosomal and hormonal errors or gender dysphoria, is our gender identity problematical. For most of us, gender identity is rarely a source of concern. More often, what concerns us is related to our gender roles: Am I sufficiently masculine? Feminine? What it means to be feminine or masculine differs from culture to culture. Although femininity and masculinity are regarded as opposites in our culture, there are relatively few significant inherent differences aside from males impregnating and females giving birth and lactating. The majority of social and psychological differences are exaggerated or culturally encouraged. All in all, women and men are more similar than different.

SUMMARY

Studying Gender and Gender Roles

• Sex is the biological aspect of being female or male. Gender is the social and cultural characteristics associated with biological sex. Normal gender development depends on both biological and psychological factors. Psychological factors include assigned gender and gender identity. Gender roles are the roles that tell us how we are to act as men and women in a particular culture.

• Although our culture encourages us to think that men and women are "opposite" sexes, they are more similar than dissimilar. Innate gender differences are generally minimal; differences are encouraged by socialization.

• Masculine and feminine stereotypes assume heterosexuality. If men or women do not fit the stereotypes, they are likely to be considered gay or lesbian. Gay men and lesbians, however, are as likely as heterosexuals to be masculine or feminine.

Gender-Role Learning

• The two most important socialization theories are cognitive social learning theory and cognitive development theory. Cognitive social learning theory emphasizes learning behaviors from others through cognition and modeling. Cognitive development theory asserts that once children learn gender is permanent, they independently strive to act like "proper" girls and boys because of an internal need for congruence.

• Children learn their gender roles from parents through manipulation, channeling, verbal appellation, and activity exposure. Parents, teachers, peers, and the media are the most important agents of socialization during childhood and adolescence.

Changing Gender Roles

• The traditional male gender role emphasizes aggression, independence, instrumentality, and sexual prowess. Traditional male sexual scripts include the denial of the expression of feelings, an emphasis on performance and being in charge, the belief that men always want sex and that all physical contact leads to sex, and assumptions that sex equals intercourse and that sexual intercourse always leads to orgasm.

• Traditional female roles emphasize passivity, compliance, physical attractiveness, and being a wife and mother. Among African Americans, women are expected to be instrumental; there is no conflict between work and motherhood. Among Latinos, women are deferential to men generally from respect rather than subservience; elders, regardless of gender, are afforded respect.

• Female sexual scripts suggest that sex is good and bad (depending on the context); genitals should not be touched; sex is for men; men should know what women want; women shouldn't talk about sex; women should look like "Playmates"; women are nurturers; and there is only one right way to experience an orgasm.

• Contemporary gender roles are more egalitarian. Important changes affecting today's gender roles include increasing questioning, especially among white women, of motherhood as a core female identity; and the breakdown of the instrumental/expressive dichotomy.

• Contemporary sexual scripts are more egalitarian and include the belief that sex is a positive good, that it involves a mutual exchange, and that it may be initiated by either partner.

• *Androgyny* combines traditional female and male characteristics into a more flexible pattern of behavior, rather than seeing them as opposites. Evidence suggests that androgyny contributes to psychological and emotional health.

Gender Problems: Hermaphroditism and Transsexuality

• A number of hormonal and chromosomal errors can affect gender development. Some of these errors can result in people who are known as hermaphrodites or pseudohermaphrodites. Chromosomal errors include Turner syndrome and Klinefelter syndrome. Hormonal errors include androgen-insensitivity syndrome and congenital adrenal hyperplasia.

• Gender dysphoria is the state of dissatisfaction individuals may experience about their gender. People who have (or plan to have) surgery to construct the "appropriate" gender are known as transsexuals. This surgery is known as sex reassignment surgery (SRS). Transsexuals are not gay or lesbian. The causes of transsexuality are not known.

SUGGESTED READINGS

Fausto-Sterling, Anne. *Myths of Gender: Biological Theories About Women and Men*. New York: Basic Books, 1985. A well-written book by a developmental geneticist arguing that most biological explanations of gender differences are unscientific justifications for traditional gender roles that subordinate women to men.

Kimmel, Michael S., and Michael A. Messner. *Men's Lives*, 2nd ed. New York: Macmillan, 1992. A collection of essays on contemporary multiethnic masculinity.

Messner, M., and D. Sabo. *Sex, Violence and Power in Sports*. Freedom, CA: The Crossing Press, 1994. The book examines and discusses controversial issues in sports and challenges the values boys have been taught.

Money, J. *The Adam Principle: Genes, Genitals, Hormones and Gender: Selected Readings in Sexology*. Amhurst, NY: Prometheus Books, 1993. A provocative book that examines the interrelationships among gender identity, genetics, hormones, sexual orientation, and behavior.

Tavris, Carol. *The Mismeasure of Woman*. New York: Simon & Schuster, 1992. An examination of various misconceptions and biases that affect our understanding of women; includes critiques of sociobiology, the G-spot, premenstrual and postmenstrual syndromes, and the codependency and addiction movements.

Wainrib, Barbara Rubin, ed. *Gender Issues Across the Life Cycle*. New York: Springer, 1992. Clinically oriented essays on developmental issues facing men and women from adolescence through old age.

Chapter Six

SEXUALITY OVER THE LIFE SPAN

PREVIEW: SELF-QUIZ

1. Our education about what's "right" and "wrong" sexually begins in infancy. True or false?

2. Masturbation is not healthy, and children should be discouraged from engaging in it. True or false?

3. Peer pressure does not actually have as much influence on teenagers as is commonly believed. True or false?

4. Many gay and lesbian teenagers are aware of their sexual orientation but are very fearful of revealing it. True or false?

5. The United States has the highest teenage pregnancy rate among developed countries. True or false?

6. Most teenagers use contraceptives when they begin having intercourse. True or false?

7. Among college students, premarital sexual intercourse generally is considered acceptable even if it takes place outside a loving context. True or false?

8. The frequency of marital sex tends to decline over time but is not considered especially problematical if the overall relationship is judged good. True or false?

9. Cohabitating gay men and lesbians tend to divide labor along age lines. True or false?

10. Despite stereotypes, extramarital affairs tend to be more emotional than sexual. True or false?

ANSWERS 1. T, 2. F, 3. F, 4. T, 5. T, 6. F, 7. F, 8. T, 9. F, 10. F

Chapter Outline

As we consider the human life cycle from birth to death, we cannot help but be struck by how profoundly sexuality weaves its way through our lives. From the moment we are born, we are rich in sexual and erotic potential, which begins to take shape in our sexual experimentations of childhood. As children, we were still unformed, but the world around us helped shape our sexuality. In adolescence, our education continued as a random mixture of learning and yearning. But as we enter adulthood, with greater experience and understanding, we develop a potentially mature sexuality. We establish our sexual orientation as heterosexual, gay, lesbian, or bisexual; we integrate love and sexuality; we forge intimate connections and make commitments; we make decisions regarding our fertility; we develop a coherent sexual philosophy. Then, in our middle years, we redefine sex in our intimate relationships, accept our aging, and reevaluate our sexual philosophy. Finally, as we become elderly, we reinterpret the meaning of sexuality in accordance with the erotic capabilities of our bodies. We come to terms with the possible loss of our partner and our own eventual decline. In all these stages, sexuality weaves its bright and dark threads through our lives.

In this chapter, we discuss both the innate and the learned aspects of sexuality, from infancy through late adulthood. We discuss both physical development and **psychosexual development,** which involves the psychological aspects of sexuality. We see how culture, the family, the media, and other factors affect children's feelings about their bodies and influence their sexual feelings and activities. We look at how the physical changes experienced by teenagers affect their sexual awareness and sexual identity as heterosexual, gay, or lesbian. We discuss adolescent sexual behaviors, sex education, teenage pregnancy, and teenage parenthood. Next, we turn to middle adulthood, where we look at developmental concerns, marital and extramarital sexuality, and divorce and sexuality. Finally, we look at sexuality in late adulthood, examining developmental issues, age, stereotypes, differences in aging between men and women, and the role of the partner in sustaining health.

psychosexual development
Development of the psychological components of sexuality.

INFANT SEXUALITY AND CHILDHOOD SEXUALITY

Infants cannot talk to us about their lives, and most of us don't remember what happened or how we felt when we were babies. Our understanding of infant sexuality is based on observation and inference. It is obvious that babies derive sensual pleasure from stroking, cuddling, bathing, and other tactile stimulation. Ernest Borneman, a researcher of children's sexuality since the 1950s, suggests that the first phase of sexual development be called the cutaneous phase (from the Greek *kytos,* skin). During this period, an infant's skin can be considered a "single erogenous zone" (Borneman, 1983).

The young child's healthy psychosexual development lays the foundation for further stages of growth (Constantine & Martinson, 1981). Psychosexual maturity, including the ability to love, begins to develop in infancy, when babies are lovingly touched all over their appealing little bodies (which appear to be designed to attract the caresses of their elders).

Kissing and cuddling are essential to an infant's healthy psychosexual development.

Infants and very young children communicate by smiling, gesturing, crying, and so on. Before they understand our words, they learn to interpret our movements, facial expressions, body language, and tone of voice. Our earliest lessons are conveyed in these ways. During infancy, we begin to learn how we "should" feel about our bodies. If a parent frowns, speaks sharply, or spanks an exploring hand, the infant quickly learns that a particular activity—touching the genitals, for example—is not right. The infant may or may not continue the activity, but if he or she does, it will be in secret, probably accompanied by the beginnings of guilt and shame (Renshaw, 1988).

Infants also learn about the gender role they are expected to fulfill. In our culture, baby girls are often handled more gently than baby boys. They are dressed up more and given soft toys and dolls to play with. Baby boys are expected to be "tough." Their dads may roughhouse with them and speak more loudly to them than to their sisters. They will be given "boy toys"—blocks, cars, and tiny plastic "superheroes." This gender-role learning is reinforced as the child grows older (see Chapter 5).

Children become aware of sex and sexuality much earlier than many people realize. They generally learn to disguise their interest rather than risk the disapproval of their elders, but they continue as small scientists—collecting data, performing experiments, and attending conferences with their colleagues.

Curiosity and Sex Play

Starting as early as age 3, when they begin playful interaction with their peers, children begin to explore their bodies together. They may play

EXPRESSING AFFECTION

Families vary in the amount and type of physical contact they encourage and allow. Some families hug and kiss, give back rubs, sit and lean on each other, and generally maintain a high degree of physical closeness. Some parents extend this closeness to their sleeping habits, allowing their infants and small children in their beds each night. (In many cultures, this is the rule rather than the exception.) Other families limit their contact to hugs and tickles. Variations of this kind are normal. Concerning children's needs for physical contact, we can make the following generalizations:

- All children (and adults) need a certain amount of freely given physical affection from those they love. Although there is no prescription for the right amount or form of such expression, its quantity and quality both affect children's emotional well-being and the emotional and sexual health of the adults they will become (Kagan, 1976; Montauk & Clasen, 1989).

- Children should be told, in a nonthreatening way, what kind of touching by adults is "good" and what is "bad." They need to feel that they are in charge of their own bodies, that parts of their bodies are "private property," and that no adult has the right to touch them with sexual intent.

- It is not necessary to frighten a child by going into great detail about the kind of things that might happen. A better strategy is to instill a sense of self-worth and confidence in children, so they will not allow themselves to be victimized (Pogrebin, 1983).

- We should also learn to listen to children and trust them. They need to know that if they are sexually abused, it is not their fault. They need to feel that they can tell about it and still be worthy of love.

"mommy and daddy" and hug and kiss and lie on top of each other; they may play "doctor" so that they can look at each other's genitals (Golden, 1989). Letty Cottin Pogrebin (1983) suggests that we think of children as "students" rather than "voyeurs." It is important for them to know what others look like in order to feel comfortable about themselves.

Dr. Mary Calderone (1983b) stresses that children's sexual interest should never be labeled "bad," but that it may be called inappropriate for certain times, places, or persons. According to Calderone, "the attitude of the parents should be to socialize for privacy rather than to punish or forbid."

Children who participate in sex play generally do so with members of their own sex. Most go on to develop heterosexual orientations; some do not. But whatever a person's sexual orientation, it seems clear that childhood sex play does not create the orientation. The origins of homosexuality are not well understood; in some cases, there may indeed be a biological basis, but at this point there is more speculation than hard evidence. Many gay men and lesbians say they first became aware of their attraction to members of the same sex during childhood, but many heterosexuals also

Children are naturally curious about bodies. Although the playground may not be considered the appropriate place to satisfy such curiosity, it is important that these kinds of explorations not be labeled "bad." Many sex educators advise parents to allow young children to observe each other naked in such settings as the bathroom or the beach.

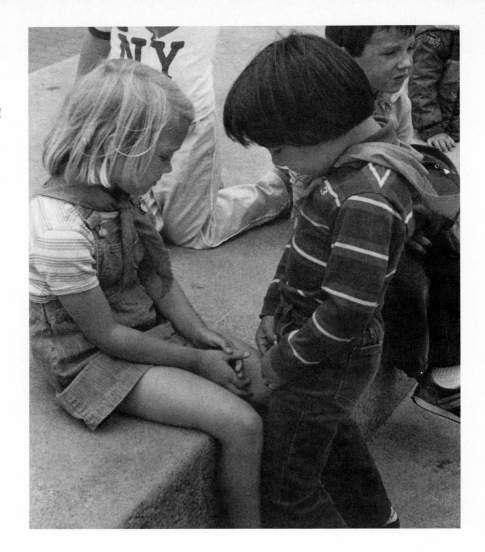

report these feelings. Such feelings and behaviors appear to be quite common and congruent with healthy psychological development in heterosexuals, lesbians, and gays (Van Wyk & Geist, 1984).

If children's natural curiosity about their sexuality is satisfied, they are likely to feel comfortable with their own bodies as adults (Renshaw, 1988). This is especially important for little girls, whose parents rarely discuss their daughters' genitals or teach the proper names for them (vulva, vagina, clitoris, urethra). Girls may learn to devalue their sexuality not because of the "mysterious and concealed nature" of their anatomy but because of the "mysterious and concealed nature of [their parents'] communication about it" (Lerner, 1976; Pogrebin, 1983).

Masturbation and Permission to Feel Pleasure

It is a safe bet to say that most of us masturbate; it is also safe to say that most of us were raised to feel guilty about it. Research shows that although most parents accept that their children masturbate, many of them still respond negatively when confronted with it (Gagnon, 1985). The message "If it feels good, it's bad" is often internalized at an early age, leading to psychological and sexual disorders in later life. Virtually all sex researchers and therapists advise that masturbation is not harmful. Some also suggest that there are physically harmful effects from "early sexual deprivation" (Money, 1980; Pogrebin, 1983; Vaughter, 1976). (Masturbation is discussed further in Chapter 9.)

Children need to understand that pleasure from self-stimulation is normal and acceptable (Feitel, 1990). They also should know that it is something we do in private, something that some people are uncomfortable with. It is important for young children to know the proper names of their genitals and what they are for (pleasure, elimination, future reproduction).

SEXUALITY IN ADOLESCENCE

Puberty is the stage of human development when the body becomes capable of reproduction. For legal purposes (laws relating to child abuse, for example), puberty is considered to begin at age 12 for girls and age 14 for boys. **Adolescence** is the social and psychological state that occurs during puberty.

puberty The stage of human development when the body becomes capable of reproduction.

adolescence The social and psychological state occurring during puberty.

Psychosexual Development

Adolescents are sexually mature (or close to it) in a physical sense, but they are still learning their gender roles and social roles, and they still have much to learn about their sexual scripts (see Chapter 5). They may also be struggling to understand the meaning of their sexual feelings for others and their sexual orientation.

Physical Changes During Puberty The physical changes of puberty are centered around the development of secondary sex characteristics (in both sexes) and the onset of menstruation (in girls) and ejaculation (in boys).

In girls, physical changes usually begin between ages 9 and 14. These include a rapid increase in height (called the growth spurt), the beginnings of breast development, the growth of pubic and underarm hair, and the onset of vaginal mucous secretions. Menarche, the onset of menstruation, follows within a year or two. The average age of menstruation is 12 or 13, although girls may begin menstruating as early as age 9 or as late as age 17 (Calderone & Johnson, 1989; Zacharias et al., 1976). Although menstruation is a basic part of female maturation, a study by the manufacturers of Tampax tampons, conducted in the early 1980s, revealed that one-third of the girls and women polled did not know what was happening to them when they got their first menstrual period (Sarrel & Sarrel, 1984).

THE "ORIGINS" OF HOMOSEXUALITY

What causes homosexuality? What causes heterosexuality? Many have asked the first question, but few have asked the second. Although researchers don't understand the origins of sexual orientation in general, they have nevertheless focused almost exclusively on homosexuality. Their explanations generally fall into either biological or psychological categories.

Biological Theories

The earliest researchers, including Krafft-Ebing, Hirschfeld, and Ellis, believed that homosexuality was something hereditary. The biological perspective, however, lost influence over the years; it was replaced by psychological theories, most notably psychoanalytic theories. Recently, there has been some renewed interest in the biological perspective. Today, many researchers, as well as many gay men and lesbians, believe that homosexuality is innate—people are "born" homosexual. Researchers point to possible genetic or hormonal factors.

In the first controlled genetic study of homosexuality in 40 years, researchers found a strong genetic link in male homosexuality (Bailey & Pillard, 1991). The researchers matched 157 identical and fraternal twin brothers and adopted brothers the same age to determine if there was a genetic component in homosexuality. (Identical twins are genetic clones, having developed from a single egg that split after fertilization.

Fraternal twins develop simultaneously from two separate eggs.) The study found that if one identical twin was gay, there was a 52% chance that his brother was also gay, compared to 22% likelihood among fraternal twins and an 11% likelihood among genetically unrelated (adopted) brothers. The researchers estimated that the genetic contribution to male homosexuality could range from 30% to 70%. Next they conducted a study of lesbian and heterosexual twins that came to similar conclusions. They found that if one identical twin was lesbian, there was about a 50% chance that her sister was also lesbian (Bailey, Pillard, Neale, & Agyei, 1993). For those genetically predisposed to homosexuality, social learning remains an important factor in their sexual expression.

Other researchers have explored the possibility that homosexuality could have a hormonal basis. As hormonal levels are sensitive to such factors as general health, diet, smoking, and stress, it is very difficult to control studies measuring sexual orientation. A review by researcher John Money (1988) of controlled studies comparing hormone levels of adult gay men, lesbians, and heterosexuals found no difference in circulating hormones.

Because it is unethical to experiment with living fetuses, we cannot come to any meaningful conclusions about the effect of hormones on fetal brain development. There are some relevant studies, however.

Breast development is a visible symbol of approaching womanhood. Some girls who develop early may feel awkward and embarrassed. Those who develop slowly may feel anxious and insecure.

In boys, physical changes include a growth spurt, hand and foot growth, muscle-mass growth, voice deepening, and hair growth on the face, the underarms, the pubic area, and sometimes other parts of the body. The boy's penis and testicles also develop. Some boys reach puberty around the time they enter junior high school (about age 12); others, not until their later

An analysis of maternal stress found no correlation among stress, hormonal fluctuation, and sexual orientation (Bailey, Willerman, & Parks, 1991). But it has been found that women who took the synthetic estrogen DES when pregnant were more likely to have daughters with bisexual or homosexual tendencies (Fagin, 1995). No such increase was found in males. The results suggest that although exposure to estrogenic chemicals in the womb is not a dominant cause of homosexuality, it may be one of many causes—some inborn and some learned.

In a study conducted by Simon LeVay (1991) on gay men and heterosexual men and women, LeVay found that the brain's anterior hypothalamus, which influences sexual behavior, was smaller among gay men than among those he assumed were heterosexuals. But as the study was conducted on the cadavers of gay men who had died from AIDS, the smaller hypothalamic size may have resulted from the disease. It may also have resulted from their behavior.

Psychological Theories

Psychoanalysis provided the earliest psychological theory accounting for the development of homosexuality. Freud believed that human beings were initially bisexual but gradually developed heterosexuality. But if children did not successfully resolve their Oedipus or Electra complex, their development would be arrested. In the 1960s, psychoanalyst Irving Bieber (1962), reflecting popular stereotypes, proposed that men became homosexual because they were afraid of women. In a study of 200 heterosexual and gay men, Bieber found that gay men tended to have overprotective, dominant mothers and passive or absent fathers in contrast to heterosexuals. A review of Bieber's and similar studies found that there was some evidence to support the view that males from such families are slightly more likely to be gay (Marmor, 1980c). But one woman (Price, 1993) asks, tongue-in-cheek: "If having a dominant mother and a weak or absent father were truly a recipe for homosexuality, wouldn't most Americans be gay?" Most gay men and lesbians appear to come from families no different from those of heterosexuals. Their siblings (except for identical twins) are not especially likely to be gay (Gagnon, 1977; Masters & Johnson, 1979).

Because research on the origins of sexual orientation examines homosexuality and not heterosexuality as well, there tends to be an underlying bias that homosexuality is not an acceptable or normal sexual variation. This bias has skewed research studies, especially psychoanalytic studies. As homosexuality has become increasingly accepted by researchers as a normal sexual variation, scholars have shifted their research from determining the "causes" of homosexuality to understanding the nature of gay and lesbian relationships.

teens. Generally, however, they lag about two years behind girls in pubertal development.

At puberty, boys begin to ejaculate semen, which accompanies the experience of orgasm they may have been having for some time. Just as girls often do not know what is happening when they begin to menstruate, many boys are unnerved by the first appearance of semen as a result of masturbation, or by nocturnal emissions during sleep ("wet dreams"). Like menstruation for girls, the onset of ejaculation is a sexual milestone for boys. It

In addition to biological factors, social forces strongly influence young teenagers. Peers are very important, especially for boys, whose self-esteem and social status may be linked to evaluations from their friends. Because certain types of violence and aggression are considered "manly" by our society, the boys in this photograph take great pleasure in an arcade game featuring simulated warfare.

For adolescent girls, the physical and hormonal changes of puberty often result in a great deal of interest (some would say obsession) with personal appearance. Cultural norms and media influences emphasizing female beauty reinforce this interest.

is the beginning of their fertility. Kinsey called first ejaculation the most important psychosexual event in male adolescence (Kinsey et al., 1948).

Influences on Psychosexual Development Besides biological forces, many other influences are involved in adolescent psychosexual development. Peer pressure, the perceived attitudes and opinions of their friends, is the single most powerful social influence on adolescents. One educator (De Armand, 1983) found that ninth-graders ranked "Friends/Peer Group" and "Everybody's Doing It" as their leading influences. Parents were ranked fifth or sixth by most. Other research has found the media, especially television, to be highly influential in shaping adolescent values, attitudes, and behavior.

Parental Influence   Children learn a great deal about sexuality from their parents. For the most part, however, they don't learn because their parents set out to teach them but because they are avid observers of their parents' behavior. Much of what they learn concerns the hidden nature of sexuality.

As they enter adolescence, young people are especially concerned about their own sexuality, but they are often too embarrassed to ask their parents directly about these "secret" matters. And most parents are ambivalent about their children's developing sexual nature. They are often fearful that their children (daughters especially) will become sexually active if they have "too much" information. They tend to indulge in wishful thinking: "I'm sure Jenny's not really interested in boys yet"; "I know Joey would never do anything like that." Parents may put off talking seriously with their children about sex, waiting for the "right time." Or they may bring up the subject once, make their points, breathe a sigh of relief, and never mention it again. Sociologist John Gagnon calls this the "inoculation" theory of sex education: "Once is enough" (Roberts, 1983). But children need frequent "boosters" where sexual knowledge is concerned. When a parent does undertake to educate a child about sex, it is usually the mother. Thus, most children grow up believing that sexuality is an issue that men don't deal with unless they have a specific problem (Roberts, 1983).

Recent research indicates that parental concern and involvement with sons and daughters is a key factor in preventing teenage pregnancy (Hanson, Myers, & Ginsburg, 1987). Parental influence in instilling values, such as respect for others and responsibility for one's actions, provides a context in which young people can use their knowledge about sex. A strong bond with parents appears to lessen teenagers' dependence on the approval of their peers and their need for interpersonal bonding, which may lead to sexual relationships (DiBlasio & Benda, 1992; Miller & Fox, 1987). But parents also need to be aware of the importance of friends in their teenagers' lives. Families that stress familial loyalty and togetherness over interactions with others outside the family may set the stage for rebellion. Traditional Latino families, for example, may expect that daughters will spend most of their time at home, often caring for their siblings. This can lead to conflict, as the "mainstream culture" expects teenagers of both sexes to be socially active (Guerrero Pavich, 1986).

Parents can also contribute to their children's feelings of self-worth by their ongoing demonstrations of acceptance and affection. Adolescents need to know that their sexuality is OK and that they are loved in spite of the changes they are going through (Gecas & Seff, 1991). Whereas low self-esteem increases vulnerability to peer pressure, high self-esteem increases adolescents' confidence and can enhance their sense of responsibility regarding their sexual behavior.

Peer Influence Adolescents garner a wealth of misinformation from each other about sex. They also put pressure on each other to carry out traditional sex roles. Boys encourage other boys to be sexually active even if they are unprepared or uninterested. They must camouflage their inexperience with bravado, which increases misinformation; they cannot reveal sexual ignorance. Bill Cosby (1968) recalled the pressure to have sexual intercourse as an adolescent: "But how do you find out how to do it without blowin' the fact that you don't know how to do it?" On his way to his first sexual encounter, he realized that he didn't have the faintest idea of how to proceed:

> So now I'm walkin', and I'm trying to figure out what to do. And when I get there, the most embarrassing thing is gonna be when I have to take my pants down. See, right away, then, I'm buck naked . . . buck naked in front of this girl. Now, what happens then? Do . . . do you just . . . I don't even know what to do . . . I'm gonna just stand there and she's gonna say, "You don't know how to do it." And I'm gonna say, "Yes, I do, but I forgot." I never thought of her showing me, because I'm a man and I don't want her to show me. I don't want nobody to show me, but I wish somebody would kinda slip me a note.

Even though many teenagers find their early sexual experiences less than satisfying, they still seem to feel a great deal of pressure to conform, which means continuing to be sexually active (DiBlasio & Benda, 1992). The following are typical statements from a group of teenagers in a study by Children's Home Society (De Armand, 1983): "I had to do it. I was the only virgin" (from a 15-year-old girl); "If you want a boyfriend, you have to put out" (from a 13-year-old girl); "You do what your friends do or you will be bugged about it" (from a 12-year-old boy). The students interviewed also said that "everyone" has to make the decision about having sexual intercourse by age 14. Researcher Charlotte De Armand comments that although, of course, "not 'everyone' is involved, certainly a large number of young people are making this decision at 14 or younger."

The Media Extensive, controlled research on the effects of sexual portrayals in the mass media has not been done. We can speculate with some degree of certainty, however, that unrealistic, stereotypical presentations of the roles of men and women have a negative effect on the attitudes and understanding of those who view them, especially if the viewers are young and impressionable. We know that erotic portrayals—nudity, sexually provocative language, and displays of sexual passion—are of great interest to the American viewing public. This public includes many curious and malleable children and adolescents. To the extent that these erotic images or actions outside a real-life context are mistaken for reality, they are potentially confusing at best and dangerously misleading at worst. A survey of 391 adolescents found a strong correlation between sexual activity and watching TV shows with high sexual content. It did not determine, however, if the viewing led to sexual activity, or whether the sexual activity led to increased interest in viewing such programs (Brown & Newcomer, 1991).

Although some would choose to protect young viewers by censoring what is shown on television or played on the radio, a more viable solution to sexual hype in the media is to balance it with information about real life. Parents can help their children understand that sexuality occurs in a context,

Lesbian and gay teenagers often have an especially difficult time coming to terms with their sexuality because society generally disapproves of their orientation. The young people in this photograph may be more fortunate than most, as they attend a school specifically for gay and lesbian youth. They have teachers who understand them and friends for mutual support.

that it is complex, and that it entails a great deal of personal responsibility. Themes from television can be used by parents to initiate discussions about sex, love, and desire (including the desire of advertisers to sell their products).

Most important of all, perhaps, parents can encourage their children to think for themselves. Because adolescents generally feel a strong need to conform to the ideals of their subculture, it can be especially hard for them to discriminate between what they think they should do and what they actually feel comfortable doing. Much of the process of becoming a mature adult involves the rejection of these images and the discovery and embracing of one's own unique identity.

Gay and Lesbian Adolescents During adolescence and early adulthood, sexual orientation may become an issue. Many young people experience sexual fantasies involving others of their own sex; some engage in same-sex play. For most, these feelings of sexual attraction are transitory, but for 4–10% of the population the realization of a romantic attraction to members of their own sex will begin to grow. Some gay men and lesbians report that they began to be aware of their "difference" in middle or late childhood. Some, but not all, gay men report "feminine" behaviors or occurrences, such as a preference for girls' games, playing with dolls, imagining themselves as a model or dancer, or being called a sissy. (A number of heterosexual men also report these childhood behaviors, however.) More predictive of adult gay orientation is a lack of "masculine" behaviors, such as a preference for boys' games, rough-and-tumble play, a desire to grow up like one's father, and imagining oneself to be a sports figure (Hockenberry & Billingham, 1987; Phillips & Over, 1992; Whitam, 1977). Gay and lesbian adolescents usually have heterosexual dating experiences during their teens, but they report ambivalent feelings about them.

Society in general has difficulty dealing with the fact of adolescent sexuality. The fact of gay and lesbian (or bisexual) adolescent sexuality has been virtually impossible for society to deal with. The "assumed heterosexuality" of society, which includes social scientists, educators, health-care providers, and so on, has resulted in the virtual invisibility of gay, lesbian, and bisexual youth (Savin-Williams & Rodriguez, 1993).

For virtually all gay and lesbian teens, the process of coming to terms with their sexuality and with the expectations of their parents and peers is confusing and painful. Suicide rates may be especially high among this group. A 1985 study of 29 young gay males by the University of Minnesota Adolescent Health Care Program found that ten of them had attempted suicide and all except one had considered it (Behr, 1986). Although there is more understanding of homosexuality now than in decades past, and more counseling and support services are available in some areas, young gays and lesbians are still subject to ridicule and rejection. Very few feel they can talk to their parents about their sexual orientation. Many (especially boys) leave home or are "kicked out" because their parents cannot accept their sexuality. It is sobering to think that a significant number of our children are forced into secrecy and suffering because of society's reluctance to openly acknowledge the existence of homosexual orientations.

Adolescent Sexual Behavior

Hormonal changes during puberty, which serve the human species by preparing each member for his or her reproductive function, bring about a dramatic increase in sexual interest.

Masturbation If children have not begun masturbating before adolescence, the chances are good that they will begin once the hormonal and physical changes of puberty start. By the time they enter college, about 5 out of 6 males and 7 or 8 out of 10 females masturbate (Sarrel & Sarrel, 1984). In addition to providing release from sexual tension, masturbation gives us the opportunity to learn about our own sexual functioning, knowledge that can later be shared with a sexual partner. Despite these positive aspects, adolescents, especially girls, often feel very concerned and guilty about their autoerotic activities.

First Base, Second Base: A Normative Sequence of Behaviors
Most heterosexual adolescent couples follow a normative pattern in the sequence of their sexual behaviors: hand-holding, embracing, kissing, fondling and petting, and (for some) intercourse (Miller et al., 1993). A study in the United States showed a normative behavior sequence for white adolescents (Smith & Udry, 1985). The normal progression was necking, feeling breasts through clothing, feelings breasts directly, feeling female genitals, feeling penis directly, and intercourse (occurring least often). The sequence was not predictable, however, for young blacks. For example, more African American adolescents had experienced intercourse than had engaged in unclothed petting involving either the breasts or the genitals. For

most teens, both white and black, however, increasing commitment to the relationship brought an increased desire for sexual intimacy. Emotional involvement expands the range of sexual behavior that is normatively acceptable (Thornton, 1990).

Kissing is an important activity for teenage couples. An adolescent's first erotic kiss often proves to be an unforgettable experience, "a milestone, a rite of passage, the beginning of adult sexuality" (Alapack, 1991). It is largely through kissing that we learn to be sexually intimate, to be comfortable with physical closeness, and to give and take sexual pleasure. Young couples may spend hours alternately kissing and gazing into each other's eyes.

Oral sex among teenagers, including heterosexuals, lesbians, and gays, has apparently become increasingly frequent in recent years, paralleling its growing acceptability in the culture at large (Wilson & Medora, 1990). In a study of junior high school students, cunnilingus was the most commonly reported form of oral sex. Among the girls surveyed, more had given or received oral sex than had engaged in intercourse; among the boys, more had engaged in intercourse than had given or received oral sex (Newcomer & Udry, 1985).

First Intercourse and Virginity With the advent of the "sexual revolution" in the late 1960s, adolescent sexual behavior began to change. The average age for first intercourse has dropped sharply, and almost as many girls as boys are engaging in it. By age 15 or 16, about 1 out of every 4 white girls and boys have started having intercourse, as have 5 out of 10 African American girls and 9 out of 10 African American boys (Beyette, 1986). A recent study of 13,454 Native American adolescents found that by the twelfth grade, 58% of the girls and 65% of the boys had had intercourse (Blum et al., 1992). Altogether, by age 19, 7 out of 10 girls and 8 out of 10 boys have had intercourse (Beyette, 1986).

In the past, peer pressure among girls was an important factor in limiting their sexual behavior. Today, girls' peers seem to exert the opposite effect. However, teenagers may feel compelled to act more sexually sophisticated than they actually are; they may lie to protect themselves from being thought of as immature. The context in which she "gives up" her virginity is still important for many girls; most feel that they are doing it for love (Hass, 1979).

In spite of increased social pressure to engage in intercourse, there are "significant fractions of Americans who experience first coitus after marriage" (Thornton, 1990). Among older teens and young adults who have experienced intercourse, many say they wish they had postponed first intercourse until they were more emotionally mature.

Adolescents and Contraception Most teenagers, especially younger ones, do not take measures to protect themselves against pregnancy or sexually transmitted diseases (STDs) when they begin having sexual intercourse. Teenage clients of family planning clinics have their first clinic visit an average of 13.2 months after their first intercourse (Kisker, 1984). Those who begin having sex at age 18 or 19 are much more likely to use contraception (Zelnik, Kantner, & Ford, 1981). (Adolescents and STDs are discussed in Chapters 15 and 16.)

Think About It

SEX EDUCATION TODAY

Most students today receive some type of sex education before graduating from high school. Most of these classes, however, can hardly be called comprehensive; some are referred to merely as "organ recitals." Yet a poll by Yankelovich, Clancy, and Shulman showed that 86% of the respondents were in favor of sex education in the schools ("How the Public Feels," 1986). Most of those polled also thought that information about birth control, sexually transmitted diseases (including HIV infection and AIDS), sexual intercourse, premarital sex, abortion, and homosexuality should be given to 12-year-olds in school. Sex educators say that teenagers have pressing concerns about such subjects as contraception, abortion, masturbation, and homosexuality, yet these subjects are often considered taboo by schools. What's going on here?

Different Values, Different Goals

Among parents, teachers, and school administrators, there is substantial disagreement about what a "comprehensive" course in sex education should include. Some feel that only basic reproductive biology should be taught. Others see the prevention (or at least the reduction) of STDs as legitimate goals of sex education. Still others would like the emphasis to be on the prevention of sexual activity among adolescents. Most sex educators seem to feel that *all* of these goals are worthy of pursuit. Some feel it's also important to address more controversial issues, such as gay and lesbian identities and the role of pleasure and desire in sexuality. Most also feel that young people need to develop the skills necessary to make healthful, responsible decisions regarding their sexual behavior. Strict prohibitions and threats are not at all effective in regulating teenage sexual activities (Brody, 1986; Elkind, 1984).

Although the opposition to comprehensive sex education may be small, it is very vocal. Many school administrators are simply afraid of provoking controversy. Those opposed to sex education fear that knowledge about sexuality will lead to increased sexual activity.

HIV/AIDS Education

The alarming spread of sexually transmitted diseases, especially HIV infection and AIDS, has added to the controversy. Former U.S. Surgeon General C. Everett Koop recommended that instruction about HIV begin in the third grade. He said, "We have to be as explicit as necessary to get the message across. You can't talk of the dangers of snake poisoning and not mention snakes" (quoted in Leo, 1986). The quality of HIV education is also an important issue. Misinformation or incomplete information can cause unnecessary anxiety and fears among the young.

Teaching About Homosexuality

Lessons about AIDS have brought the subject of homosexuality into the classroom. This is a highly controversial subject; some parents fear their children will "catch" it if they learn about it. Nevertheless, it is important for young people to understand that same-sex orientations are normal, for two principal reasons. One is that gay and lesbian teenagers need to have their identities validated; the other is that bias-related violence against gays and lesbians is largely perpetrated by teenage boys. Some school districts are taking steps to eliminate prejudice against gays and lesbians. In 1992, the New York City Board of Education mandated that all curricula be revised to reflect diversity, including diversity in sexual orientation. (Parent opposition, however, forced cancellation of the curriculum.) In Los Angeles, a program called Project 10 offers counseling to gay and lesbian teens in the schools. In San Francisco, each school has a "gay-sensitive" staff member to work with gay and lesbian students (Humm, 1992; Uribe & Harbeck, 1991).

Too Little, Too Late

One reason sex education doesn't succeed better at reducing sexual activity, disease, and pregnancy may be that it is too little, too late. One study showed that 52% of girls who began intercourse at age 15 had not had a sex education course prior to that time. The proportion of sexually active but "sexually uneducated" younger girls was even greater. Boys were still less likely to have taken a sex education class prior to beginning intercourse. Seventy-four percent of sexually active 15-year-old boys had not had a prior sex education course (Marsiglio & Mott, 1986).

The earlier children are introduced to sexual topics appropriate for their age, the easier it is for them to discuss such matters later on without self-consciousness and embarrassment (Uslander et al., 1973).

Secondary Virginity and Abstinence-Based Curricula

One kind of sex education curriculum that is increasing in popularity, often with the help of federal funds, stresses abstinence (chastity) for teens as the only form of birth control. Some educators teach the concept of "secondary virginity" (C. Smith, 1986). Its message is that even though someone has begun having intercourse, he or she doesn't have to continue. This message is true as far as it goes. Most teenagers, younger teens in particular, aren't mature enough to handle the emotional or physiological consequences of intercourse. Many can benefit by learning that it's all right to say "no" to sex. But the fact remains that the majority of teens continue to say "yes." Abstinence-based programs turn many teenagers off because of their emphasis on morality and "saving yourself for marriage." Although younger adolescents may be willing and able to postpone sexual involvement, many of them entertain the possibility of having intercourse by their late teens. Given these odds, educators should provide a balanced approach, supporting those who have chosen abstinence and arming others with information, decision-making skills, and a sense of responsibility for their sexuality.

Condoms in the Schools

Some school districts are attempting to address the problems of unintended pregnancies and sexually transmitted diseases among teenagers by making condoms available in the schools. Should schools be in the business of distributing condoms? This highly charged issue is creating controversy and causing moral and ideological debate among parents, clergy, and the state.

For many, especially those in the public health community, the role of schools in distributing condoms is a health issue, that of preventing the spread of HIV infection, AIDS, and other STDs, and reducing the number of unintended pregnancies. Many educators, however, view the issue with different priorities and restraints, the primary ones being staffing and liability.

Because the availability of condoms in schools is a recent phenomenon, little is known about the most effective ways to make them available or about the impact of such availability on sexual behavior or condom use. What research has established is that selling condoms through vending machines is not an effective method of distribution. Providing them free of charge through school staff, "condom bowls," or school-based health centers may, however, be very effective approaches (Kirby, 1993).

The way school officials approach the condom issue varies among communities, with a variety of factors influencing and affecting a community's interest, readiness, and ability to make condom availability a priority (Greene, 1993). The American Academy of Pediatrics (1995) has recently declared that, though sexual abstinenance should be encouraged, youth should have access to condoms in the schools. Educators still have to face the problems of distribution logistics as well as possible liability concerns.

Additional well-designed research is needed to inform future action on this issue. (For further information, see *Condoms in the Schools* [Samuels & Smith, 1993], a publication from the Kaiser Forums.)

(continued)

SEX EDUCATION TODAY *(continued)*

Does Education Lead to Sex?

Does talking about sex lead to having sex? Several studies indicate that this is not the case. Furstenberg and colleagues showed that 17% of the 15- and 16-year-olds who had taken sex education courses had intercourse, but 26% of those who had *not* taken such courses also had intercourse (Furstenberg et al., 1985). No study that we know of indicates a positive correlation between sex education and sexual intercourse.

Studies have shown that when information about birth control is included in sex education courses, contraceptive use has increased accordingly (Dawson, 1986; Marsiglio & Mott, 1986; Zabin, Hirsch, Smith, Strett, & Hardy, 1986). In California, a study of 13 high schools featuring a curriculum emphasizing both abstinence and contraception showed a 40% drop in the frequency of unprotected sexual intercourse among stu-

dents who had not previously begun having sex (Kirby, Barth, Leland, & Fettro, 1991). There was little change in contraceptive use, however, among those who were already sexually active at the time of the program. These results indicate that sex education and prevention skills should be initiated well before the age when students are likely to begin having intercourse.

One thing seems clear: Talking about sex does not cause it to happen. Learning about sex in age-appropriate increments, at home and at school, and having access to contraception and protection from STDs, seem to be the best defenses against the unhappy consequences of "too much, too soon." Young people guided by their parents and armed with knowledge and self-confidence can make informed decisions and direct their own sexual destinies.

Condoms are popular among teens who do use contraception, especially in casual relationships or the early stages of more serious ones (Kisker, 1985). Still, almost half say they did not use one the last time they had sex (CDC, 1995). Along with condoms, withdrawal (an unreliable method) is the method most frequently practiced by teenagers who use contraception, although it may be less common now than a decade ago (Blum & Resnick, 1982; Sonenstein et al., 1989).

Young women involved in serious relationships are more likely to use a reliable contraceptive method, such as the pill, than are those who are just beginning to have intercourse. Hormonal implants (Norplant) may prove to be a popular method for teenagers, although they are relatively new on the market and at present require the outlay of several hundred dollars for implantation. Implants do protect against pregnancy for five years, however.

Adolescent Pregnancy

The vast majority of births to teenage girls are unplanned. Between 1983 and 1988, 87% of births to unmarried 15- to 18-year-olds were reported by them to be unwanted or mistimed. A study by Susheela Singh (1986) of

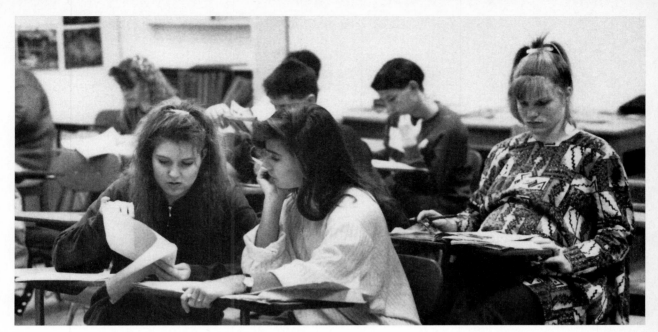

There are more than a million teenage pregnancies every year in the United States; about 60% are carried to term. Most of these births occur outside of marriage to young girls who are ill-prepared for the responsibilities of parenthood.

the Alan Guttmacher Institute, which researches family planning, indicated that about 11% of teenage girls between 15 and 19 become pregnant every year in this country. Every year, more than a million American teenagers (including about 30,000 under age 15) become pregnant.

In spite of the fact that 42% of pregnant teenagers choose abortion over childbirth (Henshaw & VanVort, 1989), teen pregnancies and births cost the U.S. more than $25 billion a year in medical, welfare, and related expenses. Such pregnancies trap most of the young mothers and fathers and their children in a downward spiral of lowered expectations and poverty. Because of poor nutrition and inadequate medical care during pregnancy, babies born to teenagers have twice the normal risk of low birth weight, which is responsible for numerous physical and developmental problems. Also, many of these children will have disrupted family lives, absent fathers, and the attendant problems of poverty, such as poor diet, violent neighborhoods, limited health care, and limited access to education. They are also at higher risk of being abused than children born to older parents.

Why Teenagers Get Pregnant
Why do teenagers begin intercourse as early as they do, and why do they rarely use contraception? The forces of their hormones, combined with pressure from peers and the media, tend to propel teenagers into sexual activity before they are emotionally prepared for it. They often don't use contraception because they are afraid to acknowledge their sexuality; or they may have difficulties in obtaining it, be too embarrassed to ask for it, not know how to use it properly, or not have it readily available. They may underestimate the risks or not fully understand their implications.

But not all teen pregnancies are accidental. About 10–20% of them are planned (De Salvo, 1985; Thompson, 1986; Wattleton, in Beyette, 1986). Some teenage girls or couples see having a baby as a way to escape from an oppressive home environment. The pull of having someone to love them exclusively and unconditionally is strong for some girls. Both girls and boys may see parenthood as a way to enhance their status, to give them an aura of maturity, or to enhance their masculinity or femininity. Some believe a baby will cement a shaky relationship. (Many adult women and men choose to have babies for these same less-than-sensible reasons.) Unfortunately, for many expectant teens, parenthood may turn out to be as much a disaster as a blessing.

Teenage Mothers Most teenage mothers feel that they are "good" girls and that they became pregnant in a moment of unguarded passion. Apparently, most also say they would "do it again," although they would counsel other girls to use birth control in similar situations (Thompson, 1986). The reality of the *boy + girl = baby* equation often doesn't sink in until pregnancy is well advanced. This lack of realism makes it difficult (emotionally and physically) or impossible to have an abortion for those who might otherwise choose one. Teenage mothers are far more likely than other mothers to live below the poverty level and to receive welfare. Only about half of them finish high school, compared to 96% of girls who are not mothers (Wallis, 1985). Planned Parenthood identifies teenage girls at greatest risk of becoming pregnant as those from single-parent homes, those whose mothers or sisters became pregnant in their teens, and those who do not do well in school (Beyette, 1986).

African American teenage girls have by far the highest fertility rate of any teenage population group in the world (Jones et al., 1985). This is partly explained by the way in which the forces of racism and poverty combine to limit the options of young people of color (Singh, 1986). (Poor whites also have disproportionately high teenage birthrates.) But additional factors contribute to pregnancy and childbirth among black teens. For one thing, African American communities are far more accepting of births to unmarried women than their white counterparts; three-generation families are much more common, with the result that grandparents often have an active role in child rearing. (This is also true of Latino communities.) For another, there is often a great deal of pressure among young African American men (especially in communities with lower socioeconomic status) to prove their masculinity by engaging in sexual activity (Staples & Johnson, 1993). Another reason may be related to a lack of role models for African American girls to identify with (Janice Anderson in Wallis, 1985).

Teenage mothers have special needs. The most pressing that can be provided within the community are health care and education (Voydanoff & Donnelly, 1990). Regular prenatal (before the birth) care is essential to monitor fetal growth and the mother's health, including diet, possible sexually transmitted disease, and possible alcohol or drug use. After the birth, both mother and child need continuing care. The mother may need contraceptive counseling and services, and the child needs regular physical checkups and immunizations. Graduation from high school is an important goal of education programs for teenage mothers, as it directly influences

REDUCING ADOLESCENT PREGNANCY

Every year, 1 out of every 10 adolescent girls in the United States becomes pregnant; half of them give birth. That equals about 500,000 babies born to teenage mothers each year. The vast majority of these births are unplanned. According to the Alan Guttmacher Institute's extensive study of teenage pregnancy in 37 countries, the United States has an astonishingly high birthrate (AGI, 1986; Jones et al., 1985). When compared to similarly developed countries (Canada, England, France, Sweden, and the Netherlands), the birthrate is nearly twice as great as that of the next highest country (England) and seven times greater than that of the Netherlands. The United States also leads these countries in abortion rates by a wide margin. These countries have similar levels of sexual activity among teenagers. What is the reason for this huge birthrate discrepancy? In a word, contraception.

A multifaceted approach to reducing teen pregnancy is suggested by family planning experts, sociologists, demographers, and others who have studied these issues:

- The underlying issues of poverty and the racism that often reinforces it must be dealt with. There must be a more equitable distribution of income so that all children can have a true variety of educational, occupational, social, and personal options in their future.

- Contraception must be made available, along with practical information and a climate of openness about sexuality. This is one of the lessons to be learned from developed countries that have low teenage birthrates. Both sex education and tolerance of teenage sexual activity prevail in Western Europe. The United States appears prudish and hypocritical by comparison.

- At the same time, schools, health-care agencies, and welfare agencies "have to be marching in the same direction, all at the same time" (Dryfoos, 1985). A concerted effort to educate young people and to help them combat feelings of worthlessness and despair must be made.

- Because parental attitudes play an important role in the sexual development of children, parents must also be educated so they become more knowledgeable and effective sex educators of their children (Darling & Hicks, 1982; Staples, 1972; Timberlake & Carpenter, 1986). An emphasis on responsibility must prevail. At the same time, an appreciation of preexisting attitudes as well as a respect for cultural and ethnic differences must be built into any program that educates parents as well as their children.

- Reliable, specific information about sex and responsibility needs to be present on television and radio, in books, magazines, music, and advertisements. This requires a major overhaul in the way our society presents sex to its children and adolescents and may demand that adults reexamine their purchasing power.

their employability and ability to support (or help support) themselves and their children. Many teenage mothers need financial assistance, at least until they complete their education. Programs such as AFDC, food stamps, Medicaid, and WIC (Women, Infants, and Children, a program that provides coupons for essential foods) are often crucial to the survival of young mothers and their children. These government progams are underfunded now and, at the publication of this book, are threatened with being cut off entirely. Even with the current programs in place, most families need additional income to survive.

The coordination of health, educational, and social services is important because it reduces costs and provides the most comprehensive support (Voydanoff & Donnelly, 1990). School-based health clinics, which provide prenatal and postnatal care, contraception, and counseling, and teenage mother education programs, which provide general education, job skills, and life skills, are examples of coordinated care (Stevens-Simon & Beach, 1992). Such programs may be costly, but the costs of not providing these services are far greater.

SEXUALITY IN EARLY ADULTHOOD

Like other passages, the one from adolescence to early adulthood offers potential for growth if one is aware and remains open to the opportunities this period brings.

Developmental Concerns

Several tasks challenge young adults as they develop their sexuality (Gagnon & Simon, 1973).

- *Establishing sexual orientation.* Children and adolescents may engage in sexual experimentation, such as playing doctor, kissing, and fondling, with members of both sexes. They do not necessarily associate these activities with sexual orientation (Gagnon & Simon, 1973). Instead, their orientation as heterosexual, gay, or lesbian is in the process of emerging.

- *Integrating love and sex.* Traditional gender roles call for men to be sex-oriented and women to be love-oriented. In adulthood, the sex-versus-love opposition needs to be addressed. Instead of polarizing love and sex, people need to develop ways of uniting them.

- *Forging intimacy and making commitments.* Young adulthood is characterized by increasing sexual experience. Through dating, courtship, and cohabitation, individuals gain knowledge of themselves and others as potential partners. As relationships become more meaningful, the degree of intimacy and interdependence increases. Sexuality can be a means of enhancing intimacy and self-disclosure as well as a means of physical pleasure. As adults become more intimate, they need to develop their ability to make commitments.

- *Making fertility/childbearing decisions.* Childbearing is socially discouraged during adolescence, but it becomes increasingly legitimate in the twenties, especially if people are married. Fertility issues are often critical but unacknowledged, especially for single young adults.

- *Evolving a sexual philosophy.* As individuals move from adolescence to adulthood, they reevaluate their moral standards, moving from moral decision making based on authority to standards based on their personal principles of right and wrong, of caring and responsibility (Gilligan, 1982; Kohlberg, 1969). They become responsible for developing their own moral code, which includes sexual issues. In doing so, they need to evolve a personal philosophical perspective to give coherence to sexual attitudes, behaviors, beliefs, and values. They need to place sexuality within the larger framework of their lives and relationships. They need to integrate their personal, religious, spiritual, or humanistic values with their sexuality (Kupersmid & Wonderly, 1980).

Premarital Sexuality

Premarital sex refers to sexual activities, especially sexual intercourse, that take place prior to marriage. However, using "premarital sex" to describe sexual behavior among all unmarried adults is becoming increasingly questioned. We use **nonmarital sex** to refer to the sexual activities occurring primarily among adults over 30 and divorced or widowed men and women. Although this guideline is not absolute, it will help clarify the differences between these groups.

Premarital Sex: From Sin to Acceptance A little more than a generation ago, virginity was the norm regarding premarital sex. Sex outside of marriage was considered sinful and immoral. In 1969, according to a Gallup survey, only 32% of the American population believed that premarital sex was acceptable (Lord, 1985). Today, however, values have shifted. Premarital intercourse among young adults (but not adolescents) in a relational context has become the norm (Sprecher & McKinney, 1993; Tanfer & Schoorl, 1992). Older Americans and groups with conservative religious backgrounds, such as Catholics and fundamentalist Protestants, continue to believe all nonmarital sex is morally wrong (Beck, Cole, & Hammond, 1991; Cochran & Beeghley, 1991; Thornton & Camburn, 1987). But religious conviction does not eliminate premarital sex. A survey of 1000 readers of the conservative *Christianity Today*, for example, found that 40% had engaged in premarital intercourse (Robinson, 1992).

The shift from sin to acceptance is the result of several factors. The advent of effective contraception, legal abortion, and changing gender roles legitimizing female sexuality have played major roles in this change. But one of the most significant factors may be traced to demography. Over the last 20 years, there has been a dramatic increase in unmarried men and women over age 18 (Cate & Lloyd, 1992). It is this group that has traditionally looked the most favorably on premarital intercourse. In 1991, the median age for first marriage for men was 26.3 years compared to 23.5 years in 1975. For women, the median age in 1991 was 24.1 years, compared to 21.1 years in 1975. On average, men and women have three additional years in which they may become sexually active prior to marriage.

Factors Leading to Premarital Sexual Involvement What factors lead individual women and men to have premarital sexual intercourse? One study indicated that among women and men who had premarital sex, the most important factors were their love (or liking) for each other, physical arousal and willingness of both partners, and preplanning and arousal prior to the encounter (Christopher & Cate, 1984). Among nonvirgins, as with virgins, love or liking between the partners was extremely important (Christopher & Cate, 1984), but feelings of obligation or pressure were about as important as actual physical arousal.

premarital sex Sexual activities, especially sexual intercourse, taking place prior to marriage or among adolescents or young adults.

nonmarital sex Sexual activities occurring primarily among single adults over 30 and widowed men and women.

Among the most important factors associated with premarital sex for both men and women are their liking and loving each other, physical arousal and willingness, preplanning, and sexual arousal prior to their encounter.

Examining the sexual decision-making process more closely, researcher Susan Sprecher identifies individual, relationship, and environmental factors affecting the decision to have premarital intercourse (Sprecher, 1989; Sprecher & McKinney, 1993). Individual factors include previous sexual experience, sexual attitudes, personality characteristics, and gender. The more premarital sexual experience a man or woman has had in the past, the more likely he or she is to engage in sexual activities in the present.

Two of the most important factors determining sexual activity are the level of intimacy in the relationship and the length of time the couple has been together. Even those who are less permissive in their sexual attitudes accept sexual involvement if the relationship is emotionally intimate and long-standing. People who are less committed (or not committed) to a relationship are less likely to be sexually involved. Finally, people in relationships that share power equally are more likely to be sexually involved than those in inequitable ones.

Environmental factors may involve either the physical or the cultural environment. In the most basic sense, the physical environment affects the opportunity for sex. Because sex is a private activity, the opportunity for it may be precluded by the presence of parents, friends, roommates, or children (Tanfer & Cubbins, 1992). The cultural environment also affects premarital sex. The values of one's parents or peers may encourage or discourage sexual involvement. A person's ethnic group also affects premarital involvement: generally, African Americans are more permissive than whites; Latinos are less permissive than Anglos (Baldwin, Whitely, & Baldwin, 1992). Furthermore, a person's subculture—such as the university or church environment, the singles world, the gay and lesbian community—exerts an important influence on sexual decision making.

Establishing Sexual Orientation

A critical task of adulthood is establishing one's sexual orientation as heterosexual, gay, or lesbian. In childhood and early adolescence, there is considerable sex play or sexual experimentation with members of the other sex and same sex. These exploratory experiences are tentative in terms of sexual orientation (Van Wyk & Geist, 1984). But in late adolescence and young adulthood, men and women are confronted with the important developmental task of establishing intimacy. And part of the task of establishing intimate relationships is solidifying one's sexual orientation as heterosexual, gay, or lesbian. A relatively small minority of individuals identify themselves as bisexual. **Bisexuality** refers to being sexually involved or attracted to members of both sexes.

bisexuality A sexual orientation in which one is equally and consistently attracted to members of both sexes.

Most people develop a heterosexual identity by adolescence or young adulthood. Their task is simplified because their development as heterosexuals is approved by society (Wilkinson & Kitzinger, 1993). But for those who are lesbian, gay, or unsure, development is filled with more doubt and anxiety. Because those who are attracted to members of the same sex are aware that they are violating deep societal taboos, confirming their sexual orientation takes longer.

The Gay/Lesbian Identity Process We do not know the numbers of men and women who are heterosexual, gay, lesbian, or bisexual. In large part, this is because homosexuality is stigmatized. Gay men and lesbians are often reluctant to reveal their identities in random surveys, and large-scale national surveys have been blocked until recently because of conservative opposition.

Studies suggest that as many as 10% of Americans are lesbian or gay. Among women, about 13% have had orgasms with other women, but only 1–3% identify themselves as lesbian (Fay et al., 1989; Kinsey et al., 1948, 1953; Laumann, Gagnon, Michael, & Michaels, 1994; Marmor, 1980b). Among males, including adolescents, as many as 20–37% have had orgasms with other males, according to Kinsey's studies. Ten percent were predominantly gay for at least 3 years; 4% were exclusively gay throughout their entire lives (Kinsey et al., 1948). A review of studies on male same-sex behavior between 1970 and 1990 estimated that a minimum of 5–7% of adult men had had sexual contact with other men in adulthood. Based on their review, the researchers suggest that about 4.5% of men are exclusively gay (Rogers & Turner, 1991). A more recent large-scale study published by the University of Chicago of 3500 men and women reported that 2.8% of men and 1.4% of women describe themselves as homosexual or bisexual (Laumann et al., 1994).

What are we to make of these differences between studies? In part, the variances may be explained by different methodologies, interviewing techniques, sampling, or definitions of homosexuality. Furthermore, sexuality is more than simply sexual behaviors; it also includes attraction and desire. One can be a virgin or celibate and still be gay or heterosexual. Finally, because sexuality is varied and changes over time, its expression at any one time is not necessarily its expression at another time or for all time.

Identifying oneself as lesbian or gay takes considerable time and includes several phases, usually beginning in late childhood or early adolescence (Blumenfeld & Raymond, 1989; Troiden, 1988). The first phase is marked by fear and suspicion that somehow one's desires are different. At first, the person finds it difficult to label these emotional and physical desires for the same sex. His or her initial reactions often include fear, confusion, or denial (Herdt & Boxer, 1992).

In the second phase, the person actually labels these feelings of attraction, love, or desire as **homoerotic,** that is, gay or lesbian. The third phase includes the person's self-definition as gay. This may be difficult, for it entails accepting a label that society generally regards as deviant. Questions then arise about whether to tell parents or friends, whether to hide one's identity ("stay in the closet"), or make it known ("come out of the closet").

Some or most gay men or lesbians may go through two additional phases. The next phase begins with a person's first gay or lesbian love affair (Troiden, 1988). This marks the commitment to unifying sexuality and affection. Most lesbians and gay men have had such love affairs. The last phase a lesbian or gay man may enter is becoming involved in the gay subculture. A gay man or lesbian may begin acquiring exclusively gay friends, going to gay bars and clubs, or joining gay activist groups. In the gay/lesbian world, gay and lesbian identities incorporate a way of being in which sexual orientation is a major part of one's identity as a person.

For many, being lesbian or gay is associated with a total lifestyle and way of thinking (Conrad & Schneider, 1980). In making gay or lesbian orientation a lifestyle, **coming out,** publicly acknowledging one's homosexuality, has become especially important as an affirmation of one's sexual orientation (Richardson, 1983). Coming out is a major decision because it may jeopardize many relationships, but it is also an important means of self-validation. By publicly acknowledging one's lesbian or gay orientation, a person begins to reject the stigma and condemnation associated with it (Friend, 1980). Generally, coming out to heterosexuals occurs in stages, first involving family members, especially the mother and siblings, and later the father.

Lesbians and gay men are often "out" to varying degrees. Some may be out to no one, not even themselves. Some are out only to their lovers, others to close friends and lovers but not to their families, employers, associates, or fellow students. Others may be out to everyone. Because of fear of reprisal, dismissal, or public reaction, gay and lesbian school teachers, police officers, members of the military, politicians, and members of other such professions are rarely out to their employers, co-workers, or the public.

Bisexuality Heterosexuality and homosexuality are terms used to categorize people according to the sex of their sexual partners. Such categories do not always adequately reflect the complexity of human sexuality, however. Bisexuals are people who are attracted to members of both sexes. Becoming bisexual requires the rejection of heterosexual and homosexual

homoeroticism Sexual attraction, desire, or impulses directed toward members of the same sex; homosexuality.

coming out The public acknowledgment of one's gay, lesbian, or bisexual orientation.

identities. Statistics on the prevalence of bisexuality range from 1% (Laumann, Gagnon, Michael, & Michaels, 1994) to an average of 4% (Janus & Janus, 1993).

Because they reject heterosexuality *and* homosexuality, bisexuals often find themselves stigmatized by gay men and lesbians as well as by heterosexuals. Among heterosexuals, bisexuals are likely to be viewed as "really" homosexual. In the gay community, they may be viewed as "fence-sitters," not willing to admit their supposed homosexuality or as simply "playing" with their orientation (Weinberg, Williams, and Pryor, 1994). In all these instances, their bisexual orientation is not taken seriously. Loraine Hutchins and Lani Kaahumanu (1991) believe that bisexuality arouses hostility because it "challenges current assumptions about the immutability of people's orientations and society's supposed divisions into discrete groups."

In contrast to research on homosexuality, there is little research on bisexual identity. The exception is research on HIV and AIDS that focuses on bisexual behavior among men who identify themselves as heterosexual. It was not until 1994 that the first model of bisexual identity formation was developed by Martin Weinberg and colleagues (1994). According to this model, bisexual men and women go through several stages in developing their identity. The first stage, often lasting years, is *initial confusion*. Many bisexuals are distressed to find they are sexually attracted to both sexes; others feel that their attraction to the same sex means an end of their heterosexuality; still others are disturbed by their inability to categorize their feelings as either heterosexual or homosexual. The second stage is *finding and applying the bisexual label*. For many, discovering there is such a thing as bisexuality is a turning point; some find that their first heterosexual or same-sex experience permits them to view sex with *both* sexes as pleasurable; others learn of the term "bisexuality" from friends and are consequently able to apply it to themselves. The third stage is *settling into the identity*. This stage is characterized as feeling at home with the label "bisexual." For many, self-acceptance is critical. The fourth stage for many bisexuals is *continued uncertainty*. Bisexuals don't have a community or social environment that reaffirms their identity. Despite being settled in their orientation, many feel persistent pressure from gay acquaintances to relabel themselves as homosexual and to engage exclusively in same-sex activities.

Being Single

Over the last 20 years, there has been a staggering increase in the numbers of unmarried adults (never married, divorced, or widowed). Most of this increase has been the result of men and women, especially young adults, marrying later.

The New Social Context of Singlehood
Some of the results of this dramatic shift affecting unmarried young adults include:

- *Greater premarital sexual experience.* As men and women are marrying later, they are more likely to have more premarital experience and sexual partners than earlier generations. Premarital sex is becoming the norm among adults.

- *Widespread acceptance of cohabitation.* As young adults are deferring marriage longer, cohabitation has become an integral part of young adult life. Because gay men and lesbians are not legally permitted to marry, cohabitation has become for many of them a form of marriage.

- *Increased unintended pregnancies.* Because greater numbers of women are single and sexually active, more single women are likely to become unintentionally pregnant as a result of unprotected sexual intercourse or contraceptive failure.

- *Increased numbers of abortions and births to single women.* The increased numbers of unintended pregnancies has led to more abortions and births to single mothers. (About 20% of marriages take place with the woman being pregnant.) In 1989, for example, single women age 20–24 accounted for approximately 30% of all abortions. During the same period, over one-third of all births were to unmarried women in the same age group (U.S. Bureau of the Census, 1992).

- *Greater numbers of separated and divorced men and women.* In 1991, over 13% of the young adults from 20 to 28 were separated or divorced; the figure rises to 29% if we include 30- to 34-year-olds (U.S. Bureau of the Census, 1992). Because of their previous marital experience, separated and divorced men and women tend to have different expectations about relationships than never-married young adults. Forty percent of all marriages are now remarriages for at least one partner (Surra, 1991).

- *Rise of single-parent families.* The rise of divorce and births to single women has led to a 61% increase of single-parent families between 1970 and 1989 (U.S. Bureau of the Census, 1991). Today, there are 6.8 million single-parent families, representing 29% of all families in 1991 (U.S. Bureau of the Census, 1992). Eighty-seven percent of single-parent families are headed by women.

The world that unmarried young adults enter is one in which greater opportunities than ever before exist for exploring intimate relationships.

The College Environment The college environment is important not only for intellectual development but also for social development. The social aspects of the college setting—classes, dormitories, fraternities and sororities, parties, mixers, and sports events—provide opportunities for meeting others. For many, college is where people search for or find mates.

Dating in college is similar to high school dating in many ways. It may be formal or informal ("getting together"); it may be for recreation or to find a mate. Some of the features that distinguish college dating from high school dating, however, are the more independent setting (away from home, diminished parental influence, and so on), the increased maturity of each partner, more role flexibility, and the increased legitimacy of sexual interactions.

There appears to be a general expectation among students that they will engage in sexual intercourse at some point during their college career (Komarovsky, 1985; Sprecher & McKinney, 1993) and that sexual involvement will occur within a loving relationship.

Sociologist Ira Reiss (1967) described four moral standards of premarital sexuality among college students. The first is the *abstinence standard*, which

The college social setting provides opportunities for students to meet and establish relationships.

was the official sexual ideology in American culture until the 1950s and early 1960s. This belief held that it was wrong for either men or women to engage in sexual intercourse before marriage regardless of the circumstances or their feelings for each other. The second is the *double standard,* widely practiced but rarely approved publicly, which permitted men to engage in premarital intercourse. Women, however, were considered immoral if they had premarital intercourse. *Permissiveness with affection* represents a third standard. It describes sex between men and women who have an affectionate, stable, and loving relationship. This standard is widely held today (Sprecher, McKinney, Walsh, & Anderson, 1988; Sprecher & McKinney, 1993). *Permissiveness without affection* is the fourth standard. It holds that people may have sexual relationships with each other even if there is no affection or commitment (see Jacoby & Williams, 1985).

Although acceptance of premarital sex is widespread among college students, there are limits. If a woman has sexual intercourse, it should take place in the context of a committed relationship. Women who "sleep around" are morally censured. Reflecting the continuing double standard, men are not usually condemned as harshly as women for having sex without commitment (Komarovsky, 1985).

For gay men and lesbians, the college environment is often liberating because many campuses are more accepting of sexual diversity than society at large is. College campuses often have lesbian and gay organizations that sponsor social events, dances, and get-togethers. There they can freely meet others in open circumstances that permit meaningful relationships to develop and mature. Although prejudice against gay men and lesbians continues to exist in colleges and universities, college life has been an important safe haven for many.

The Singles World   Men and women involved in the singles world tend to be older than college students; they range in age from 25 to 40. They have never been married, or, if they are divorced, they usually do not have primary responsibility for children. Single adults are generally working rather than attending school (Cargan & Melko, 1982).

Although young adults are remaining unmarried in record numbers, in 1991 the majority of unmarried young adults under 30 lived with their parents. Thirty-one percent of young adults age 25–29 live at home (U.S. Bureau of the Census, 1992). Young adults living with their parents often find themselves in conflict as their parents try to continue to exert control over their sexuality.

Although dating in the singles world is somewhat different from dating in high school and college, there are similarities. Singles, like their counterparts in school, emphasize recreation and entertainment, sociability, and physical attractiveness.

The problem of meeting other single people is very often central. In college, students meet each other in classes or dormitories, at school events, or through friends. There are many meeting places and large numbers of eligibles. Because they are working, singles have less opportunity to meet available people. For single adults, friends, common interests, parties, work, or talking to a stranger are the most frequent means of meeting others (Shostak, 1987).

To fill the demand for meeting other singles, the singles world has spawned a multibillion-dollar industry—bars, resorts, clubs, and housing (Shostak, 1987). Singles increasingly rely on personal classified ads where men advertise themselves as "success objects" and women advertise themselves as "sex objects" (Davis, 1990). Their ads tend to reflect stereotypical gender roles. Single men and women also often rely on their churches and church activities to meet other singles.

As a result of the growing acceptance of sexuality outside marriage, singles are presented with various sexual options. Some choose celibacy for religious or moral reasons. Others choose celibacy over casual sex; when they are involved in a committed nonmarital relationship, they may become sexually intimate. Some are temporarily celibate; they are taking "a vacation from sex." They utilize their celibacy to clarify the meaning of sexuality in their relationships (Brown, 1980).

Sexual experimentation is important for many. Although an individual may derive personal satisfaction from sexual experimentation, he or she must also manage the stress of conflicting commitments, loneliness, and a lack of connectedness.

Many single women reject the idea of casual sex (Stein, 1983). Instead, they feel that sex must take place within the context of a relationship. In relationship sex, intercourse becomes a symbol of the degree of caring between two persons. Such relationships are expected to be "leading somewhere," such as to commitment, love, cohabitation, or marriage. As men and women get older, marriage becomes an increasingly important goal of a relationship.

Gay and Lesbian Singlehood

As a result of the stigmatization of homosexuality, in the late nineteenth century, groups of gay men and lesbians began congregating in their own secretive clubs and bars. There, in relative safety, they could find acceptance and support, meet others, and socialize. Today, some neighborhoods in large cities are identified with gay men and lesbians. These neighborhoods feature not only openly gay or lesbian bookstores, restaurants, coffeehouses, and bars but also churches, clothing stores, physicians, lawyers, and hair salons.

Gay and lesbian businesses, institutions, and neighborhoods are important for affirming positive identities; they enable gay men and lesbians to interact beyond a sexual context. They help make being lesbian or gay a complex social identity consisting of many parts—student, parent, worker, professional, churchgoer—rather than being simply a sexual role (Altman, 1982).

In these neighborhoods, men and women are free to express their affection as openly as heterosexuals. They experience little discrimination or intolerance and are involved in gay and lesbian social and political organizations (Weinberg & Williams, 1974). More recently, with increasing acceptance in some areas, many middle-class gay men and lesbians are moving to suburban areas. In the suburbs, however, they remain more discreet than they do in large cities (Lynch, 1992).

The Gay Male Subculture The urban gay male subculture that emerged in the 1970s emphasized sexuality. Although relationships were important, sexual experiences and variety were even more important. Despite the emphasis on sex over relationships, however, two researchers found that most gay men in their study had at least one exclusive relationship (Weinberg & Williams, 1974). In fact, involvement in the gay subculture enhanced the likelihood of lasting relationships. The researchers speculated that closeted gay men were more likely than open gay men to avoid attachments for fear of discovery.

With the rise of the HIV/AIDS epidemic in the 1980s and 1990s, the gay subculture has placed an increased emphasis on the relationship context of sex (Carl, 1986; Isensee, 1990). Relational sex has become the norm among large segments of the gay population (Levine, 1992). Most gay men have sex within dating or love relationships. (In fact, some AIDS organizations are giving classes on gay dating in order to encourage safe sex.)

African American gay men often experience a conflict between their black and gay identities (Peterson, 1992). African Americans are less likely to disclose their gay identity because the black community is less accepting of homosexuality than the white community. At the same time, African Americans may experience racial discrimination in the predominantly white gay community. Gay African Americans whose primary identity is racial tend to socialize in the black community, where they are tolerated only as long as they are closeted. Few gay institutions are available to them.

Two women register as domestic partners. Domestic partnerships provide committed, cohabiting heterosexuals, gay men, and lesbians some of the legal protection and rights previously associated only with marriage, such as health benefits. The evolution of domestic partnership laws increases the legitimacy of cohabitation.

In most communities, they must rely on discreet friendship circles or clandestine bars to meet other gay black men.

For gay Latinos in cities with large Latino populations, there is usually at least one gay bar. Such places usually specialize in dancing or female impersonation. The extent to which a gay Latino participates in the Anglo or Latino gay world depends on the individual's degree of acculturation (Carrier, 1992).

The Lesbian Community Beginning in the 1950s and 1960s, young and working-class lesbians developed their own institutions, especially women's softball teams and exclusively female gay bars as places to socialize. During the late 1960s and 1970s, lesbian separatists, lesbians who wanted to create a separate "womyn's" culture distinct from heterosexual *and* gay men, rose to prominence. They developed their own music, literature, and erotica; they had their own clubs and bars. But by the middle of the 1980s, the lesbian community underwent a "shift to moderation" (Faderman, 1991). It became more diverse and included Latinas, African American women, Asian American women, and older women. It has developed closer ties with the gay male community. Lesbians now view gay men as sharing much in common with them because of the common prejudice directed against both groups.

Lesbians tend to value the emotional quality of relationships more than the sexual component. Lesbians usually form longer-lasting relationships than gay men (Tuller, 1988). Lesbians' emphasis on emotions over sex and

COMMON MISCONCEPTIONS ABOUT HOMOSEXUALITY

There are numerous misconceptions about being gay or lesbian. These continue to circulate, adding to the fires of prejudice. The misconceptions include:

- *Misconception No. 1: Men and women are gay or lesbian because they can't get a heterosexual partner.* This belief is reflected in such remarks about lesbians as "All she needs is a good lay" (implying a man). Similar remarks about men include "He just needs to meet the right woman." Research indicates that lesbians and gay men have about as much heterosexual high school dating experience as their peers. Furthermore, the majority of lesbians had sexual experiences with men; many of those experiences were pleasurable (Bell et al., 1981).

- *Misconception No. 2: Lesbians and gay men "recruit" heterosexuals to become gay.* People are not recruited or seduced into being gay any more than they are recruited into being heterosexual. Most gay men and lesbians have their first gay experience with a peer, either a friend or an acquaintance. They report having had homosexual feelings prior to their first experience (Bell et al., 1981).

- *Misconception No. 3: Gay men are child molesters.* This is a corollary to the recruitment misconception above. The overwhelming majority of child molesters are heterosexual males who molest girls; these men include fathers, stepfathers, uncles, and brothers. A large percentage of men who molest boys identify themselves as heterosexual (Arndt, 1991).

- *Misconception No. 4: Homosexuality can be caught.* Homosexuality is not the flu. Some parents express fear about having their children taught by homosexual teachers. They fear their children will model themselves after the teacher or be seduced by him or her. But a child's sexual orientation is well-established by the time he or she enters

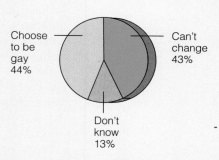

Percentage of Adults Who Believe Homosexuality Is Chosen or Can't Be Changed.

school, and a teacher would not have an impact on that child's orientation (Marmor, 1980).

- *Misconception No. 5: Gay men and lesbians could change if they wanted.* There is no evidence that gay men and lesbians can change their sexual orientation. The belief that they should reflects assumptions that homosexuality is abnormal or sinful. Most psychotherapy with gay men and lesbians who are unhappy about their orientation aims at helping them adjust to it.

- *Misconception No. 6: Homosexuality is condemned in the Bible.* The Bible condemned same-sex sexual activities between men, not homosexuality. Some biblical scholars believe that the rejection of same-sex sexual activities was based on historical factors, including the lack of the concept of sexual orientation, the exploitative and abusive nature of much same-sex activity in ancient times, the belief that the purpose of sex was procreation, and purity or holiness concerns that such acts were impure (there were similar concerns about sexual intercourse with a menstruating woman). There is increasing debate among religious groups as to whether same-sex relationships are inherently sinful.

the more enduring quality of their relationships reflects their socialization as women. Being female influences a lesbian more than being gay.

Cohabitation

In 1990, more than 2.9 million heterosexual couples and 1.5 million gay or lesbian couples were living together in the United States (U.S. Bureau of the Census, 1991). In contrast, only 523,000 heterosexual couples were cohabiting in 1970. Delaying marriage has increased the number of men and women cohabiting (Tanfer & Cubbins, 1992). For census purposes, heterosexuals who cohabit are called POSSLQs *(possel-kews)*, people of the other sex sharing living quarters.

domestic partnership A legal category granting some rights ordinarily reserved to married couples to committed, cohabiting heterosexual, gay, and lesbian couples.

A New Norm Cohabitation is increasingly accepted at almost every level of society. By age 30, about 40–50% of all young adult women will have cohabited (Surra, 1991). Currently, 4% are cohabiting (Bumpass & Sweet, 1988). As mentioned earlier, some scholars believe that cohabitation is becoming institutionalized as part of the normal mate-selection process (Gwartney-Gibbs, 1986). The concept of **domestic partnership** has led to laws granting some of the protections of marriage to men and women, including gay men and lesbians, who cohabit in committed relationships.

Living together has become more widespread and accepted in recent years for several reasons. First, the general climate regarding sexuality is more liberal than it was a generation ago. Sexuality is more widely considered to be an important part of a person's life, whether or not he or she is married. The moral criterion for judging sexual intercourse has shifted; love rather than marriage is now widely regarded as making a sexual act moral. Second, the meaning of marriage is changing. Because of the dramatic increase in divorce rates over the last two decades, marriage is no longer thought of necessarily as a permanent commitment. Permanence is increasingly replaced by **serial monogamy,** a succession of marriages. Because the average marriage now lasts only seven years, the distinction between marriage and living together is losing its clarity. Third, young adults are continuing to defer marriage. At the same time, they want the companionship found by living intimately with another person.

serial monogamy A succession of monogamous marriages.

For young adults, there are a number of advantages to cohabitation. First, because their lives are often in transition—as they finish school, establish careers, or become more secure financially—cohabitation represents a "tentatively" committed relationship. Second, in cohabiting relationships, partners tend to be more egalitarian. They do not have to deal with the more structured roles of husband and wife. They are freer to develop their own individuality independent of marital roles. Third, the couple knows they are together because they want to be, not because of the pressure of marital obligations.

Although there are a number of advantages, there may also be disadvantages. Parents may refuse to provide support for school as long as their child is living with someone; they may not welcome their child's partner into their home. Cohabiting couples also may find they cannot easily buy houses together as banks may not count their income as joint; they usually don't qualify for insurance benefits. If one partner has children, the other partner is usually not as involved as if they were married. Cohabiting couples who live together often find themselves socially stigmatized if they have a child. Finally, cohabiting relationships generally don't last more than two years; couples either break up or get married.

There is no consensus about whether cohabitation significantly increases or decreases later marital stability (Teachman & Polonko, 1990). Although couples who are living together often argue that cohabitation helps prepare them for marriage, such couples are statistically as likely to divorce as those who do not live together before marriage. Other studies have found that those who had cohabited before marriage were no more or less satisfied with their marriages than other couples (Jacques & Chason, 1979; Watson, 1983).

Gay and Lesbian Cohabitation   In 1990, there were over 1.5 million gay male or lesbian couples living together. The relationships of gay men and lesbians have been stereotyped as less committed than heterosexual couples because (1) lesbians and gay men cannot legally marry, (2) they may not appear to emphasize sexual exclusiveness, and (3) heterosexuals misperceive love between lesbian and gay couples as being somehow less real than love between heterosexuals. Numerous similarities, however, exist between gay and heterosexual couples, according to Letitia Peplau (1981, 1988). Regardless of their sexual orientation, most people want a close, loving relationship with another person. For gay men, lesbians, and heterosexuals, intimate relationships provide love, romance, satisfaction, and security. There is one important difference, however. Heterosexual couples tend to adopt a traditional marriage model, whereas gay couples tend to have a "best-friend" model.

Few lesbian and gay relationships are divided into the traditional heterosexual provider/homemaker roles. Among heterosexuals, these divisions are gender-linked as male or female. In same-sex couples, however, tasks are often divided pragmatically, according to considerations such as who likes cooking more (or dislikes it less) and work schedules (Marecek, Finn, & Cardell, 1988). Most gay couples are dual-worker couples; neither partner supports or depends on the other economically. And because gay and lesbian couples are the same sex, the economic discrepancies based on greater male earning power are absent. Although gay couples emphasize egalitarianism, if there are differences in power, they are attributed to personality; if there is an age difference, the older partner is usually more powerful (Harry, 1988).

Because they confront societal hostility, lesbians and gay men fail to receive the general social support given heterosexuals in maintaining relationships. One rarely finds parents, for example, urging their gay male or lesbian children to make a commitment to a stable same-sex relationship or, if the relationship is rocky, to stick it out.

SEXUALITY IN MIDDLE ADULTHOOD

In the middle years, family and work become especially important. Personal time is spent increasingly on marital and family matters, especially if a couple has children. Sexual expression often decreases in frequency, intensity, and significance, replaced by family and work concerns. Sometimes the change reflects a higher value placed on family intimacy. At other times, it may reflect habit, boredom, or conflict.

Developmental Concerns

In the middle adult years, some of the psychosexual developmental tasks begun in young adulthood may be continuing. These tasks may have been deferred or only partly completed in young adulthood, such as intimacy issues or childbearing decisions. Because of separation or divorce, people may find themselves facing the same intimacy and commitment tasks at age 40 they thought they had completed 15 years earlier (Cate & Lloyd, 1992). But life does not stand still; it moves steadily forward, ready or not. Other developmental issues appear, including the following ones:

- *Redefining sex in marital or other long-term relationships.* In new relationships, sex is often passionate, intense; it may be the central focus. But in long-term marital or cohabiting relationships, habit, competing parental and work obligations, fatigue, and unresolved conflicts often erode the passionate intensity associated with sex. Sex may need to be redefined as a form of intimacy and caring. Individuals may also need to decide how to deal with the possibility, reality, and meaning of extramarital or extrarelational affairs.

- *Reevaluating one's sexuality.* Single women and men may need to weigh the costs and benefits of sex in casual or lightly committed relationships. In long-term relationships, sexuality often becomes less than central to relationship satisfaction. Nonsexual elements, such as communication, intimacy, and shared interests and activities, become increasingly important to relationships. Women who have deferred their childbearing begin to reappraise their decision: Should they remain child-free, race against their biological clock, or adopt a child? Some people may redefine their sexual orientation. One's sexual philosophy continues to evolve.

- *Accepting the biological aging process.* As people age, their skin wrinkles, their flesh sags, their hair turns gray (or falls out), their vision blurs—and they become, in the eyes of society, less attractive and less sexual. By their forties, their physiological responses have begun to slow noticeably. By their fifties, society begins to "neuter" them, especially women who have been through menopause. The challenge of aging is to accept its biological mandate.

Marital Sexuality

When people marry, they may discover that their sexual lives are very different than they were before marriage. Sex is now morally and socially sanctioned. It is in marriage that the great majority of heterosexual interactions take place. Yet as a culture, we feel ambivalent about marital sex. On the one hand, marriage is the only relationship in which sexuality is legitimized. On the other hand, marital sex is an endless source of humor and ridicule.

Frequency of Sexual Interactions Sexual intercourse tends to diminish in frequency the longer a couple is married. For newly married couples,

Although stereotypes among the young desexualize middle-aged and older couples, they may be as affectionate and sexual as younger couples—or even more so.

the average rate of sexual intercourse is about three times a week. As they get older, the frequency drops. A recent study found that average Americans have sex about once per week (Laumann, Gagnon, Michael, & Michaels, 1994). This study of 3500 adults, age 18–59, found that 30% of adults have sex with a partner only a few times a year or not at all; 35% have sex once or several times a month, and about 35% have sex at least two or more times a week. A decreased frequency of intercourse, however, does not necessarily mean that sex is no longer important or that the marriage is unsatisfactory. It often means simply that one or both members are too tired. For dual-worker families and families with children, fatigue and lack of private time may be the most significant factors in the decline of frequency (Blumstein & Schwartz, 1983; Olds, 1985). Philip Blumstein and Pepper Schwartz (1983) found that most people attributed the decline in sexual intercourse to lack of time or physical energy or to "being accustomed" to each other. In addition, other activities and interests engage them besides sex.

Most married couples don't seem to feel that declining frequency is a major problem if their overall relationship is good (Cupach & Comstock, 1990; Sprecher & McKinney, 1993). Sexual intercourse is only one erotic bond among many in marriage. There are also kissing, caressing, nibbling, stroking, massaging, candlelight dinners, walking hand-in-hand, looking into each other's eyes, and intimate words.

Giving New Meaning to Sex Sexuality within marriage is significantly different from premarital sex in at least three ways. First, sex in marriage is expected to be monogamous. Second, procreation is a legitimate goal. Third, sex takes place in the everyday world. These differences present each person with important tasks.

One of the most significant factors shaping marital sexuality for most couples is the expectation of monogamy. This expectation lasts a lifetime; a person marrying at 20 commits himself or herself to 40–60 years of sex with the same person. Within a monogamous relationship, each partner must decide how to handle fantasies, desires, and opportunities for extramarital sexuality. Do you tell your spouse that you have fantasies about other people? That you masturbate? Do you flirt with others? Do you have an extramarital relationship? If you do, do you tell your spouse? How do you handle sexual conflicts or difficulties with your partner? How do you deal with sexual boredom or monotony?

Sex also takes on a procreative meaning within marriage. Although it is obviously possible to get pregnant before marriage, marriage is the only socially sanctioned setting for having children. In marriage, partners are confronted with the task of deciding whether or when to have children. It is one of the most crucial decisions they will make, for having children profoundly alters a relationship. If the couple decides to have a child, the nature of their lovemaking may change from simply an erotic activity to an intentionally reproductive act as well.

Marriage also changes the context of sex. Because married life takes place in a day-to-day living situation, sex must also be expressed in the day-to-day world. Sexual intercourse must be arranged around working hours and at times when the children are at school or asleep. One or the other partner may be tired, frustrated, or angry. The emotions associated with premarital sex may disappear. Some of the passion of romantic love eventually disappears as well, to be replaced with a love based on intimacy, caring, and commitment. Although we may tend to believe that good sex depends on good techniques, it really depends more on the quality of the marriage.

Extramarital Sexuality

A fundamental assumption in our culture is that marriages are monogamous. Each person remains the other's exclusive intimate partner, in terms of both emotional and sexual intimacy. Extramarital relationships violate that assumption.

Although we tend to think of extramarital involvements as being sexual, they actually assume several forms (Thompson, 1983). They may be (1) sexual but not emotional, (2) sexual and emotional, or (3) emotional but not sexual (Thompson, 1984). Very little research has been done on extramarital relationships in which both people are emotionally but not sexually involved. Thompson's study, however, found that of 378 married and cohabiting people, the three types of extrarelational involvement were about equally represented.

Extrarelational Sex in Dating and Cohabiting Relationships

You don't have to be married to have sex outside a relationship. Both cohabiting couples and those in committed relationships usually have expectations of sexual exclusiveness. But, like some married men and women who take vows of fidelity, they do not always remain sexually exclusive. Blumstein and Schwartz (1983) found that those involved in cohabiting relationships had similar rates of extrarelational involvement as married couples, except that cohabiting males had somewhat fewer partners than husbands did. Gay men had more partners than cohabiting and married men. And lesbians had fewer partners than any other group.

Large numbers of both women and men have sexual involvements outside dating relationships that are considered exclusive. Of those who knew of their partner's affair, a large majority felt that it had hurt their own relationship. When both partners had engaged in affairs, each believed that their partner's affair had harmed the relationship more than their own had.

Extramarital Sex in Exclusive Marriages In marriages that assume emotional and sexual exclusivity, mutuality and sharing are emphasized. Extramarital sexual relationships are assumed to be destructive of the relationship; nonsexual heterosexual relationships may also be judged threatening. The possibility of infecting one's husband or wife with an STD must also be considered.

As a result of marital assumptions, both sexual and nonsexual extramarital relationships take place without the knowledge or permission of the other partner. If the extramarital relationship is discovered, a marital crisis ensues. Many married people feel that the spouse who is unfaithful has broken a basic trust (Weiss, 1975). Sexual accessibility implies emotional accessibility. When a person learns that his or her spouse is having an affair, the emotional commitment of that spouse is brought into question. How can you prove that you still have a commitment? You cannot; commitment is assumed, it can never be proved. Furthermore, the extramarital relationship may imply to the partner (rightly or wrongly) that he or she is sexually inadequate or uninteresting.

Extramarital Sex in Nonexclusive Marriages There are several types of nonexclusive marriage (Weiss, 1983): (1) open marriage in which intimate but nonsexual friendships with others are encouraged, (2) open marriage in which outside sexual relationships are allowed, (3) swinging, and (4) group marriage/multiple relationships. The marriage relationship is considered the primary relationship in both nonconsensual extramarital relationships and in open marriages and swinging relationships. Only the group marriage/multiple relationships model rejects the primacy of the married relationship. Group marriage is the equal sharing of partners, as in polygamy; it may consist of one man and two women, one woman and two men, or two couples. The two most common types of consensual extramarital sex are swinging and sexually open marriages.

Swinging (also called mate sharing or wife swapping) is a form of consensual extramarital sex in which couples engage in sexual activities with others in a social context clearly defined as recreational sex. These contexts may include swinging parties or commercial clubs. Married swingers swing together (Weiss, 1983). Forming an intimate relationship with an extramarital partner is prohibited. In terms of health, swinging may be an especially risky form of behavior. It is estimated that 2% of adult Americans have engaged in swinging (Jenks, 1985; Weiss, 1983).

In **open marriage,** partners may mutually agree to allow sexual relationships with others. Little research has been done on open marriages. Blumstein and Schwartz (1983) found that 15–26% of the couples in their sam-

open marriage A marriage in which both partners agree to allow each other to have openly acknowledged and independent relationships with others, including sexual ones.

ple had "an understanding" that permitted extramarital relations in certain circumstances, such as the affair's occurring only out of town, never seeing the same person twice, never having sex with a mutual friend, and so on.

Two researchers found that successful sexually open marriages required: (1) a commitment to the primacy of the marriage, (2) a high degree of affection and trust between the spouses, (3) good interpersonal skills to manage complex relationships, and (4) nonmarital partners who did not compete with the married partner (Knapp & Whitehurst, 1977).

Motivation for Extramarital Sex People who engage in extramarital affairs have a number of different motivations, and affairs satisfy a number of different needs (Moultrup, 1990). John Gagnon (1977) describes the attraction extramarital affairs have for the people involved:

> Most people find their extramarital relationships highly exciting, especially in the early stages. This is a result of psychological compression: the couple gets together; they are both very aroused (desire, guilt, expectation); they have only three hours to be together. . . . Another source of attraction is that the other person is always seen when he or she looks good and is on best behavior, never when feeling tired or grubby, or when taking care of children, or when cooking dinner. . . . Each time, all the minutes that the couples has together are special because they have been stolen from all these other relationships. The resulting combination of guilt and excitement has a heightening effect, which tends to explain why people may claim that extramarital sex and orgasms are more intense.

Research by Ira Reiss (1980) suggests that extramarital affairs appear to be related to two variables: unhappiness of the marriage and/or extramarital sexual permissiveness. Generally speaking, in happy marriages, a partner is less likely to seek outside sexual relationships. If a person had premarital sex, he or she is more likely to have extramarital sex. Once the first prohibition is broken, the second holds less power.

Characteristics of Extramarital Sex It is not clear how many people become involved in extramarital sex. According to one large-scale study (Laumann et al., 1994), 25% of men and 10% of women have been unfaithful to their spouses. Most other large-scale nationwide surveys have been nonrepresentative samples of their readers by popular magazines. These studies suggest that about 50% of men and 25–50% of women have had extramarital affairs (J. Peterson et al., 1983; Rubenstein & Tavris, 1987; Tavris & Sadd, 1977; Wolfe, 1981). How many of these experiences are meaningful involvements as opposed to one-time-only experiments is not known.

Men are more likely to have extramarital sex when they are younger, women when they are older. Women in their late thirties tend to be more interested in sex than they were when younger. This difference between male and female sexual life cycles may account for women's increasing involvement in extramarital sex as they get older. The *Playboy* survey, however, found that among young marrieds, significantly more women than men had affairs (J. Peterson et al., 1983).

Think About It

CHILDREN OF DIVORCE: HOW DO THEY FARE?

Divorce has become a fact of life for many Americans today. Between 50% and 60% of all new marriages are likely to end in divorce (Martin & Bumpass, 1989). In 1991, 15.8 million Americans (8.1%) were divorced. Most Americans who divorce, however, do not stay that way for long. They usually remarry within 3–4 years (Coleman & Ganong, 1991), often acquiring stepchildren and extended families along the way.

Tens of millions of children have watched their parents split up over the past 25 years, and now these children are adults themselves. Although many report successful marriages and happy lives, they also report deep emotional wounds, with the divorce remaining a central issue throughout their lives. Others report a sense of having missed out on something seen as a birthright, the right to grow up in a house with two parents. Compared to children who have grown up with intact families, adult children of divorce are more likely to have troubled relationships and broken marriages (Kantrowitz, Wingert et al., 1992). Others fear commitment because they learned the lesson of their childhood—not to trust—all too well. They worry that they don't know how to be half of a happy couple because they've never seen one close up at home. Social scientists can't decide whether the adjustment problems grow out of the divorce experience itself, the subsequent years of living in a single-parent family, or the economic decline that follows a breakup, especially when the children are living with the mother. The answer is probably some combination of all these factors.

Apparently, there is no way to predict how children will react to parental divorce. Much depends on the child's age and sex, the relationship with each parent, and the memories of the predivorce family life. One critical factor in determining how well a child functions is the attitude of the custodial parent, who is usually the mother. According to Constance Ahrons, coauthor of *Divorced Families* (Ahrons & Rogers, 1987) and associate director of the Marriage and Family Therapy Program at the University of Southern California, "most people don't divorce well, but some parents manage to put aside their anger and put the issues of parenting first" (Conant & Wingert, August 24, 1987).

Many adult children of divorce believe they have to take aggressive action to overcome the hurt of their earlier years. It helps them to see that divorce did have a profound impact, begin to deal with it, and move into separating real problems from imagined ones. Independence and maturity are unexpected but not uncommon benefits of divorce. Children who can see beyond and learn from their parents' mistakes as well as forgive them may ultimately make stronger and more committed marriage partners.

SEXUALITY IN LATE ADULTHOOD

Sexuality is one of the least understood aspects of life in old age (Weg, 1983b). Many older people continue to adhere to the standards of activity or physical attraction they held when they were young (Creti & Libman, 1989). They need to become aware of the taboos and aging stereotypes they held when they were younger so that they can enjoy their sexuality in their later years (Kellett, 1991).

Developmental Concerns

Many of the psychosexual tasks older Americans must undertake are directly related to the aging process.

One of the most famous twentieth-century sculptures is Auguste Rodin's The Kiss, *which depicts young lovers embracing. Here, the aging model, Antoni Nordone, sits before the statue that immortalized his youth.*

- *Changing sexuality.* As older men's and women's physical abilities change with age, their sexual responses change as well. A 70-year-old, though still sexual, is not sexual in the same manner as an 18-year-old. As men and women continue to age, their sexuality tends to be more diffuse, less genital, and less insistent. Chronic illness and increasing frailty understandably result in diminished sexual activity. These considerations contribute to the ongoing evolution of the individual's sexual philosophy.

- *Loss of a partner.* One of the most critical life events is the loss of a partner. After age 60, there is a significant increase in spousal deaths. As having a partner is the single most important factor determining an older person's sexual interactions, his or her death signals a dramatic change in the survivor's sexual interactions.

These tasks are accomplished within the context of continuing aging. Their resolution helps prepare us for acceptance of our own eventual death.

Stereotypes of Aging

Our society stereotypes aging as a lonely and depressing time, but most studies of the aged find that they express relatively high levels of satisfaction and well-being. It is poverty and poor health that make old age difficult.

But even so, the aged have lower levels of poverty than most Americans, including young adults, women, and children. More important, until their mid-seventies, most older people report few if any restrictions on their activities because of health.

The sexuality of older Americans tends to be invisible. Society tends to discount their sexuality (Libman, 1989). In fact, one review of the aging literature concludes that the decline in sexual activity among aging men and women is more cultural than biological in origin (Kellett, 1991). Several factors account for this in our culture (Barrow & Smith, 1992). First, we associate sexuality with the young, assuming that sexual attraction exists only between those with youthful bodies. Interest in sex is considered normal and virile in 25-year-old men, but in 75-year-old men, it is considered lecherous (Corby & Zarit, 1983). Second, we associate the idea of romance and love with the young; many of us find it difficult to believe that the aged can fall in love or love intensely. Third, we continue to associate sex with procreation, measuring a woman's femininity by her childbearing and maternal role and a man's masculinity by the children he sires. Finally, the aged do not have as strong sexual desires as the young, and they are not expressed as openly. Intimacy is especially valued and important for an older person's well-being (Mancini & Blieszner, 1992).

Aging gay men and lesbians face a double stereotype: They are old *and* gay. But like other stereotypes of aging Americans, this one reflects myths rather than realities. Most gay men and lesbians are satisfied with their sexual orientation; about half are worried about aging (Berger, 1982; Kehoe, 1988).

Not only do stereotypes and myths of aging affect the sexuality of the aged. The narrow definition of sexuality contributes to the problem. Sexual behavior is defined by researchers and the general population in terms of masturbation, sexual intercourse, and orgasm. But sexuality has emotional, sensual, and relationship aspects that are enjoyed by all people, regardless of age.

Male and Female Differences

Aged women and men face different problems sexually (Robinson, 1983). Physiologically, men are less responsive. The decreasing frequency of intercourse and the increasing time required to attain an erection produce anxieties in many older men about erectile dysfunction (impotence)—anxieties that may very well lead to such dysfunctions. When the natural slowing down of sexual responses is interpreted as the beginning of erectile dysfunction, this self-diagnosis triggers a vicious spiral of fears and even greater difficulty in having or maintaining an erection.

Among older adults, fantasies become more diffuse, turning from those that are obviously sexual to those centering more on pleasurable experiences in general (Barclay, 1980). As some men get older, their erotic performance becomes more dependent on fantasies; they are less responsive to simple tactile stimulation of the genitals.

Women, who are sexually capable throughout their lives, have different concerns. They face greater social constraints than men (Robinson, 1983). Women are confronted with an unfavorable sex ratio (27 unmarried men per 100 unmarried women over age 65), a greater likelihood of widowhood,

WHAT PHYSICIANS (AND THE REST OF US) NEED TO KNOW ABOUT SEX AND AGING

Envision yourself now. How do you look? How do you feel about your sexuality? Move the clock ahead 45 years from now (or adjust it accordingly so that you are 70 years old). How do you feel about the way you look? Are you in a relationship? Are you sexual? If the image of you as a sexual person is dimmed by a different body image, lack of a partner, or poor health, you are not alone. Most of us (including physicians and other health professionals) have been indoctrinated by restrictive attitudes or an absence of images about older adults and their sexuality. A few facts about sex and aging are in order:

- *People remain sexual throughout their lives.* Though individuals may not be sexually active, they still have sexual histories, knowledge, and values that must not be denied. Though sexual activity declines over the decades and many older people choose abstinence as a lifestyle, physicians and health-care workers need to recognize that sexual feelings are healthy throughout life. With this understanding, they will be better able to alleviate feelings of guild and remorse among older people about their sexuality.

- *Many older people have a need for a good sexual relationship.* Loss of health, friends, partner, children, and career may cause depression and a profound sense of loneliness. An excellent antidote to the loss is a loving, intimate, secure sexual relationship.

- *Sexual physiology changes with age.* Being aware of potential changes often helps older people accept and deal with them. Males may often have less turgid erections, less forceful ejaculations, and a longer refractory period. A longer refractory period may simply mean there may be sexual relations without ejaculation. Men and their partners can learn that there can be gratifying sex without an erect penis. The slowing down of the sexual response cycle means that foreplay can be prolonged and intimacy and gratification increased.

    Although some women celebrate the arrival of menopause, finding it liberating from the concerns of pregnancy and menstruation, others find it disturbing, embarrassing, or painful. Vaginal dryness, the most common symptom and one that can make sexual intercourse quite painful, can be alleviated by an over-the-counter water-soluble lubricant or by saliva. Hormone replacement therapy or an estrogen cream can also remedy this problem. Hot flashes and bone loss leading to osteoporosis are additional problems that women must contend with and should discuss with their physician.

- *Changes in body image may have a profound impact on sexuality.* This is particularly true in our society, where image and youth are valued over age and wisdom. Older people must try to reverse the influence of years of conditioning and consciously reevaluate their images of sex and aging.

- *Use it or lose it.* This is not an empty phrase. Sexual activity is a physiological function that tends to deteriorate if not exercised; it is particularly fragile in the elderly. Sexual activity appears to keep the vagina more elastic, flexible, and lubricated. According to Masters, Johnson, and Kolodny (1992), intercourse and/or masturbation at least once per week over a period of years helps to keep the mucus secretions active, maintains muscle tone, and helps preserve the shape and size of the vagina.

- *Older people are better lovers.* Think about what experience and time bring to an individual. In the case of sexuality, experience brings awareness of self and (hopefully) sensitivity to others. Given the quantity of leisure time and the slower-paced lifestyle of many older adults, relationships can often be nurtured and enjoyed. A more accepting attitude about self, others, and life in general can help to make people better sexual partners later in life.

Adapted from Cross, R. "What doctors and others need to know; sex facts on human sexuality and aging." *SEICUS Report,* June–July 1993, 7–9.

SEXUALITY, PARTNER AVAILABILITY, AND HEALTH

As age increases, so often does the number of health problems. Hypertension, cardiovascular disease, cancer, diabetes, and arthritis may occur, causing a debilitation of overall health and sexual well-being. Therapies to control or treat these maladies may also cause adverse reactions or changed body image and may require education, support, reevaluation of the therapies, or an alternation in the sexual habits of those affected. Often, older adults indicate that they continue to feel sexual desires; they simply lack the ability to express them because of their health (Verwoerdt et al., 1969).

The greatest determinants of an aged person's sexual activity are the availability of a partner and health. A major study of older people found that only 7% of those who were single or widowed were sexually active, in contrast to 54% of those living with a partner (Verwoerdt et al., 1969). Frequency of sexual intercourse of the latter group, with an average age of 70, ranged from three times a week to once every two months. Those who described their sexual feelings as having been weak or moderate in their youth stated that they were without sexual feelings. More recently, researchers studying 800 married couples over age 60 found that over half of the sample (and 24% of those older than 76) had had sexual intercourse within the previous month (Marsiglio & Donnelly, 1991). Masturbation continued to be a pleasurable activity for those with and without partners (Pratt & Schmall, 1989).

After age 75, a significant decrease in sexual activity often takes place. In spite of the fact that 17% of men and women expressed a desire for sexual activity (White, 1982), most families, nursing homes, and society in general make no provisions for the sexuality of the aged. Instead, they actively discourage sexual expression—not only sexual intercourse but also masturbation—or try to sublimate their client's erotic interests into crafts or television, or deaden them with medication. Such manipulations, however, do little to satisfy erotic needs.

It is not the loss of sexuality alone that older people must face, or course. Many older widows do not miss the sexual aspect of their married lives as much as the social aspects. It is the companionship, the activity, the pleasure found in their partners that many older people miss most acutely (Malatesta, Chambless, Pollack, & Cantor, 1989).

and norms against marrying younger men. Grieving over the death of a partner, isolation, and depression also affect their sexuality (Rice, 1989). Finally, there is a double standard of aging. In our culture, as men age, they become distinguished; as women age, they simply get older. Femininity is connected with youth and beauty. But as women age, they tend to be regarded as more masculine. A young woman, for example, is "beautiful," but an older woman is "handsome," a term ordinarily used for men of any age.

As this chapter has shown, psychosexual development occurs on a continuum rather than as a series of discrete stages. Each person develops in his or her own way, according to personal and social circumstances and the dictates of biology. As adolescents grow toward sexual maturity, the gap between their physiological development and their psychological development begins to narrow; their emotional and intellectual capabilities begin to "grow into" their bodies. Nearing adulthood, young people become less

The greatest determinants of an aged person's sexual activity are the availability of a partner and health.

dependent on their elders and more capable of developing intimacy on a new level. In young adulthood, tasks that define adult sexuality include establishing sexual orientation, making commitments, entering long-term intimate relationships, and making childbearing decisions. None of these tasks is accomplished overnight. Nor does a task necessarily end as a person moves into a new stage of life.

In middle adulthood, individuals face new tasks involving the nature of their long-term relationships. Often these tasks involve reevaluating these relationships. As people enter late adulthood, they need to adjust to the aging process—to changed sexual responses and needs, declining physical health, the loss of a partner, and their own eventual death. Each stage is filled with its own unique meaning, which gives shape and significance to life and to sexuality.

SUMMARY

Infant Sexuality and Childhood Sexuality

• Psychosexual development begins in infancy, when we begin to learn how we "should" feel about our bodies and our gender roles. Infants need stroking and cuddling to ensure healthy psychosexual development.

• Children learn about bodies through various forms of sex play. Their sexual interest should not be labeled "bad" but may be called inappropriate for certain times, places, or persons. Children need expressions of physical affection and to be told nonthreateningly about "good" and "bad" touching by adults.

Sexuality in Adolescence

• Puberty is the biological stage when reproduction becomes possible. The psychological state of puberty is adolescence, a time of growth and often confusion as the body matures faster than the emotional and intellectual abilities. The traits of adolescence are culturally determined.

• Pubertal changes in girls begin between ages 9 and 14. They include a growth spurt, breast development, pubic and underarm hair, vaginal secretions, and menarche (first menstruation). Pubertal changes in boys generally begin about two years later than in girls. They include a growth spurt; voice deepening; hair growth; development of external genitals; and the ejaculation of semen.

• Children and adolescents often learn from their parents that sex is secretive, and bad. A strong bond between parent and child reduces the risk of early sexual involvement and pregnancy.

• Peers are the strongest influence on the values, attitudes, and behavior of adolescents. They are also a source of much misinformation regarding sex.

• The media present highly charged images of sexuality that are often out of context. Parents can counteract media distortions by discussing the context of sexuality with their children and controlling access to television.

• Young gays and lesbians are largely invisible because of society's assumption of heterosexuality. Gays and lesbians may begin to come to terms with their homosexuality during their teenage years. Because of society's reluctance to acknowledge homosexuality openly, most gay and lesbian teens suffer a great deal of emotional pain.

• Most adolescents engage in masturbation. White adolescent heterosexual couples generally follow a normative sequence of adolescent behaviors, from hand-holding to intercourse. African American teens do not necessarily follow such a sequence. For most teenagers, increased emotional involvement leads to increased sexual activity.

• The average age of first intercourse has dropped sharply in the last two decades. By age 19, 7 out of 10 girls and 8 out of 10 boys have had intercourse.

• The U.S. leads the world's developed nations in teen pregnancies, births, and abortions. Adolescents get pregnant mainly because they do not use contraception or use it improperly; some get pregnant intentionally.

• Black communities are more accepting of births outside of marriage than are white communities. Teenage mothers' principal needs are for health care, including prenatal care, and education, including parenting and life skills and job training.

• Part of the solution to reducing teenage pregnancy is to work toward eliminating the poverty and racism that limit the options and lower the self-esteem of many adolescents.

Sexuality in Early Adulthood

• Developmental tasks in young adulthood include establishing sexual orientation, integrating love and sex, forging intimacy and making commitments, making fertility/childbearing decisions, and evolving a sexual philosophy.

• Premarital sex among young adults (but not adolescents) in a relational context has become the norm. An important factor in this shift is the surge in numbers of unmarried men and women who represent 39% of the adult population.

• Factors leading to premarital sexual involvement include individual factors, relationship factors, and environmental factors. Ethnicity also affects premarital involvement.

• A critical task of adulthood is establishing one's sexual identity as heterosexual, gay, lesbian, or bisexual. As many as 10% of Americans have had a significant amount of same-sex sexual contact. Various studies suggest that 4.5–7% of men identify themselves as gay during some point in their adult lives. About 1–3% of women identify themselves as lesbian. Identifying oneself as a lesbian or a gay male, however, is complex and includes several phases. Coming out is publicly acknowledging one's homosexuality or bisexuality. Though relatively few people identify themselves as bisexual, its presence points to the fact that human sexual behavior cannot be easily categorized.

• A large increase in the number of unmarried adults has dramatically altered the nature of singlehood in our society.

• The two most widely held standards regarding premarital sexual intercourse are permissiveness with affection and the double standard. For gay men and lesbians, the college environment is often liberating because of greater acceptance.

• Among noncollege single men and women, meeting others can be a problem. Singles often meet at work, clubs, resorts, housing complexes, and churches.

• Gay neighborhoods are found in the largest cities. They are important in enabling lesbians and gay men to interact outside a sexual context. Relational sex has become the norm among large segments of the gay population.

• The contemporary lesbian community is currently more moderate and diverse than in prior years. It has closer ties with the gay community. Lesbians' emphasis on emotions over sex and the more enduring quality of their relationships reflects their socialization as women.

• Cohabitation has become more widespread and accepted in recent years. Over 1.5 million gay or lesbian couples and 2.9 million heterosexual couples cohabit. Domestic partnerships provide some legal protection for cohabitating couples in committed relationships.

Sexuality in Middle Adulthood

• Developmental issues of sexuality in middle adulthood include redefining sex in long-term relationships, reevaluating one's sexuality, and accepting the biological aging process.

• In marriage, sex tends to diminish in frequency the longer a couple is married. Most married couples don't feel that declining frequency is a major problem if their overall relationship is good.

• Extrarelational sexual involvement exists in dating, cohabiting, and marital relationships. In monogamous marriages, extramarital sexual relationships are assumed to be destructive of the relationship and are kept secret. Nonexclusive marriages permit extramarital sex. Successful sexually open marriages require commitment to the primacy of the marriage, a high degree of affection and trust, good interpersonal skills, and partners who do not compete with the married partner.

• Extramarital affairs appear to be related to two variables: unhappiness of the marriage and/or premarital sexual permissiveness. Men are more likely to have extramarital sex when they are younger, women when they are older.

Sexuality in Late Adulthood

• Many of the psychosexual tasks older Americans must undertake are directly related to the aging process, including changing sexuality and the loss of a partner. Most studies of the aged find that they express relatively high levels of satisfaction and well-being. Sexuality of the aged tends to be invisible because we associate sexuality and romance with youth and procreation.

• Sexual behavior in late adulthood often becomes more intimacy-based, involving touching and holding rather than genital activity. Physiologically, men are less responsive. Women's concerns are more social than physical; they have an unfavorable sex ratio, a greater likelihood of widowhood, and the double standard of aging.

• The greatest determinants of an aged individual's sexual activity are the availability of a partner and health. After age 75, a significant decrease in sexual activity takes place due to health problems.

SUGGESTED READINGS

The following journals contain articles on adolescent psychosexual development, sexuality education, and other issues concerning teenagers: SIECUS Reports, Family Planning Perspectives, *published by the Alan Guttmacher Institute, and* Journal of Adolescence.

Blume, Judy. *Letters to Judy: What Your Kids Wish They Could Tell You.* New York: Putnam, 1986. Letters to the popular children's book author from children who didn't think their parents would understand.

Blumstein, Philip, and Pepper Schwartz. *American Couples: Money, Work, Sex.* New York: William Morrow, 1983. A classic work examining power as expressed in money, work, and sex in cohabiting, married, gay, and lesbian relationships.

Calderone, Mary S., and Eric W. Johnson. *The Family Book About Sexuality.* Rev. ed. New York: Harper & Row, 1989. An excellent guide for parents who want to transmit humanistic values about sexuality to their children.

Gullotta, Thomas P., Gerald R. Adams, and Raymond Montemayor, eds. *Adolescent Sexuality.* Newbury Park, CA: Sage, 1993. Current research in many areas of adolescent sexuality, including sexual behavior, gay and lesbian teenagers, teenage pregnancy, and promoting sexual responsibility.

Heron, Ann, ed. *One Teenager in Ten: Writings by Gay and Lesbian Youth.* Boston: Alyson Publications, 1983. Writings by 26 lesbian and gay young people from varied ethnic, religious, and socioeconomic backgrounds.

Klein, Marty. *Ask Me Anything.* New York: Simon & Schuster, 1992. A book for adults (teachers, parents, therapists) who want to be prepared to give straightforward, knowledgeable answers to any question a child may ask about sex, concerning, for example, homosexuality, love, masturbation, or orgasm.

Rubin, Lillian. *Erotic Wars: What Happened to the Sexual Revolution?* New York: Harper & Row, 1991. An examination of changing sexual mores among young adults and married couples.

Sears, James, ed. *Sexuality and the Curriculum.* New York: Teachers College Press, 1992. This collection of essays challenges assumptions about sex education and suggests alternative strategies.

Sprecher, Susan, and Kathleen McKinney. *Sexuality.* Newbury Park, CA: Sage, 1993. A comprehensive examination of sexuality within the context of close relationships, such as dating, cohabitation, and marriage.

Weg, Ruth, ed. *Sexuality in the Later Years: Roles and Behavior.* New York: Academic Press, 1983. An excellent, multidisciplinary approach to aging and sexuality.

Chapter Seven

LOVE, INTIMACY, AND SEX

PREVIEW: SELF-QUIZ

1. Love is an exclusive emotion that cannot exist with other feelings, such as anger or boredom. True or false?

2. Love alone is sufficient to make a commitment last. True or false?

3. Love relationships are similar in many ways to parent/ infant relationships. True or false?

4. In romantic relationships, caring is less important than physical attraction. True or false?

5. Males and females, whites, African Americans, Latinos, Asians, heterosexuals, gay men and lesbians, old and young are all equally likely to fall in love. True or false?

6. In many ways, love is like the attachment an infant experiences for his or her caregiver. True or false?

7. The love that lesbians and gay men experience is similar in quality to that experienced by heterosexuals. True or false?

8. Infatuation is usually equally intense for both parties. True or false?

9. Men, in general, are more likely to separate love and sex. True or false?

10. A high degree of jealousy is a sign of true love. True or false?

ANSWERS 1. F, 2. F, 3. T, 4. F, 5. F, 6. T, 7. T, 8. F, 9. T, 10. F

Chapter Outline

L ove is one of the most profound human emotions, and it manifests itself in various forms across all cultures. In our culture, love binds us together as partners, parents, children, and friends. It is a powerful force in the intimate relationships of heterosexuals, gay men, and lesbians; it crosses all ethnic boundaries (Aron & Aron, 1991). We make major life decisions, such as whom we marry, based on love (Simpson, Campbell, & Berscheid, 1986). We make sacrifices for it, sometimes sacrificing even our lives for those we love.

Love is both a feeling and an activity. A person feels love for someone and acts in a loving manner. But we can also be angry with the person we love, or feel frustrated, bored, or indifferent. This is the paradox of love: It encompasses opposites. A loving relationship includes affection and anger, excitement and boredom, stability and change, bonds and freedom. Its paradoxical quality makes some ask whether they are really in love when they are not feeling "perfectly" in love or when their relationship is not going smoothly. Love does not give us perfection, however; it gives us meaning. In fact, as sociologist Ira Reiss (1980) suggests, a more important question to ask is not if one is feeling love, but, "Is the love I feel the kind of love on which I can build a lasting relationship or marriage?"

In this chapter, we examine the relationship between sex and love. We look at the always perplexing question of the nature of love. Then we examine the ways that social scientists study love to gain new insights into it. We then turn to the darker side of love—jealousy—to understand its dynamics. Finally, we see how love transforms itself from passion to intimacy, providing the basis for long-lasting relationships.

LOVE AND SEXUALITY

Love and sexuality are intimately intertwined (Aron & Aron, 1991). Although marriage was once the only acceptable context for sexual intercourse, for most people today, love legitimizes premarital sex. With the "sex with affection" standard of premarital intercourse, we use individualistic rather than social norms to legitimize sexual relations. Our sexual standards have become personal rather than institutional. This shift to personal responsibility makes love even more important in sexual relationships.

We can even see this connection between love and sex in our everyday use of words. Think of the words we use to describe sexual interactions. When we say that we "make love," are "lovers," or are "intimate" with someone, we generally mean that we are sexually involved. But this sexual involvement carries overtones of relationship, caring, or love. Such potential meanings are absent in such technically correct words as "sexual intercourse," "fellatio," or "cunnilingus," as well as in such obscene words as "fuck" or "screw."

Men, Sex, and Love

Men and women who are not in an established relationship have different expectations. Men are more likely than women to separate sex from affection. Studies consistently demonstrate that for the majority of men, sex and love can be easily separated (Blumstein & Schwartz, 1983; Carroll, Volk, & Hyde 1985).

Although men are more likely than women to separate sex and love, Linda Levine and Lonnie Barbach (1985) found in their interviews that men indicated that their most erotic sexual experiences took place in a relational context. Most men in the study responded that it was primarily the emotional quality of the relationship that made their sexual experiences special.

Women, Sex, and Love

Women generally view sex from a relational perspective. In the decision to have sexual intercourse, the quality and degree of intimacy of a relationship were more important for women than men (Christopher & Cate, 1984). Women were more likely to report feelings of love if they were sexually involved with their partners than if they were not sexually involved (Peplau, Rubin, & Hill, 1977). For women, love is also more closely related to feelings of self-esteem (Walsh & Balazs, 1990).

Although women generally seek emotional relationships, some men initially seek physical relationships. This difference in intentions can place women in a bind. Carole Cassell (1984) suggests that women face a "damned if you do, damned if you don't" dilemma in their sexual relationships. If a woman has sexual intercourse with a man, he says goodbye; if she doesn't, he says he respects her and still says goodbye.

Traditionally, women were labeled "good" or "bad" based on their sexual experience and values. "Good" women were virgins, sexually naive, or passive, whereas "bad" women were sexually experienced, independent, and passionate. According to Lillian Rubin (1990), this attitude has not entirely changed. Rather, we are ambivalent about sexually experienced women. One exasperated woman leaped out of her chair and began to pace the floor, exclaiming to Rubin, "I sometimes think what men really want is a sexually experienced virgin. They want you to know the tricks, but they don't like to think you did those things with anyone else."

Gay Men, Lesbians, and Love

Love is equally important for heterosexuals, gay men, lesbians, and bisexuals (Aron & Aron, 1991; Keller & Rosen, 1988; Kurdek, 1988; Peplau & Cochran, 1988). Many heterosexuals, however, perceive lesbian and gay love relationships as less satisfying and less loving than heterosexual ones. It is well documented that love is important for gay men and lesbians; their relationships have multiple emotional dimensions and are not based solely on sex, as others might believe (Adler, Hendrick, & Hendrick, 1989).

Although men in general are more likely to separate love and sex than women, gay men are especially likely to make this separation. Gay men value love, but they also value sex as an end in itself. Furthermore, they place less emphasis on sexual exclusiveness in their relationships. Many gay men appear to successfully negotiate sexually open relationships. Keeping the sexual agreements they make appears to matter most for these men. Further, the data from 560 self-selected gay couples indicate that the pursuit of outside sex should not be taken as evidence that sex between the partners is lacking (Demian, 1994).

Researchers suggest that heterosexual men are not as different from gay men in terms of their acceptance of casual sex as might be thought. Heterosexual men, they maintain, would be as likely as gay men to engage in casual sex if women were equally interested. Women, however, are not as interested in casual sex; as a result, heterosexual men do not have as many willing partners as gay men do (Foa, Anderson, Converse, & Urbansky, 1987; Symons, 1979).

For lesbians, gay men, and bisexuals, love has special significance in the formation and acceptance of their identities. Although significant numbers of men and women have had sexual experiences with members of the same sex or both sexes, relatively few identify themselves as gay or lesbian. As we saw in Chapter 6, same-sex sexual interactions are not in themselves sufficient to acquiring a gay or lesbian identity. An important element in solidifying such an identity is loving someone of the same sex. Love signifies a commitment to being lesbian or gay by unifying the emotional and physical dimensions of a person's sexuality (Troiden, 1988). For the gay man or lesbian, it marks the beginning of sexual wholeness and acceptance. In fact, some researchers believe that the ability to love someone of the same sex, rather than having sex with him or her, is the critical element that distinguishes being gay or lesbian from being heterosexual (Money, 1980).

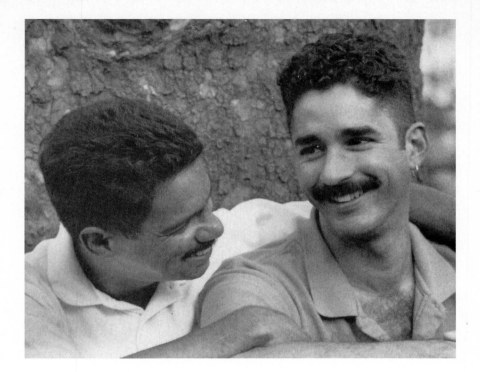

For lesbians, gay men, and bisexuals, love is an important component in the formation and acceptance of their sexual orientation. The public declaration of love and commitment is a milestone in the lives of many couples.

Sex Without Love

Is love necessary for sex? We assume that it is, but that assumption is based on motives and values. It cannot be answered by reference to empirical or statistical data (Crosby, 1985). The question becomes a more fundamental one: Is sexual activity legitimate in itself, or does it require justification? To believe that sex does not require love as a justification, argues researcher John Crosby (1985), does not deny the significance of love and affection in sexual relations. In fact, love and affection are important and desirable for enduring relationships. They are simply not necessary, Crosby believes, for affairs in which erotic pleasure is the central feature.

Ironically, although sex without love violates our overt beliefs about sexuality, it is the least threatening form of extrarelational sex. Even those who accept their partner's having sex outside the relationship find it especially difficult to accept their partner's having a meaningful affair. "They believe that two intense romantic relationships cannot co-exist and that one would have to go" (Blumstein & Schwartz, 1983).

Attitudes and Behaviors Associated with Love

A review of the research finds a number of attitudes, feelings, and behaviors associated with love (Kelley, 1983). Notice how some of these are also associated with sex.

In terms of attitudes and feelings, positive attitudes and feelings toward the other bring people together. Zick Rubin (1970, 1973) found that there

The physiological sensations accompanying sexual arousal are often identified as feelings of love.

were four feelings identifying love. These feelings, which correspond fairly well to the prototypical characteristics identified with love, are:

- *Caring for the other,* wanting to help him or her.
- *Needing the other,* having a strong desire to be in the other's presence and to have the other care for you.
- *Trusting the other,* mutually exchanging confidences.
- *Tolerating the other,* including his or her faults.

Of these, caring appears to be the most important, followed by needing, trusting, and tolerating (Steck, Levitan, McLane, & Kelley, 1982). J. R. Davitz (1969) identified similar feelings associated with love but noted, in addition, that respondents reported feeling an inner glow, optimism, and cheerfulness. They felt harmony and unity with the person they loved. They were intensely aware of the other person, feeling that they were fully concentrated on him or her.

Love is also expressed in certain behaviors. One study found that romantic love was expressed in several ways (Swensen, 1972). Notice that the expression of love often overlaps thoughts of love:

- *Verbally expressing affection,* such as saying, "I love you."
- *Self-disclosing,* such as revealing intimate facts about yourself.
- *Giving nonmaterial evidence,* such as emotional and moral support in times of need, and respecting the other's opinion.
- *Expressing nonverbal feelings,* such as feeling happier, more content, more secure when the other is present.
- *Giving material evidence,* such as gifts, flowers, small favors, or doing more than your share of something.
- *Physically expressing love,* such as hugging, kissing, making love.
- *Tolerating the other,* such as accepting his or her idiosyncrasies, peculiar routines, or forgetfulness about putting the cap on the toothpaste.

Recent research supports the belief that people "walk on air" when they are in love. Researchers have found that those in love view the world more positively than those who are not in love (Hendrick & Hendrick, 1988).

HOW DO I LOVE THEE? APPROACHES TO THE STUDY OF LOVE

Researchers have developed a number of ways of studying love (Hendrick & Hendrick, 1987). Each approach looks at love from different perspectives. Although no single perspective wholly accounts for the experience of love, together they provide considerable insight.

Styles of Love

Sociologist John Lee describes six basic styles of love (Borrello & Thompson, 1990; Lee, 1973, 1988). These styles of love, he cautions, describe relationship styles, not individual styles. The style of love may change as the relationship changes or when individuals enter different relationships.

According to sociologist John Lee, there are six styles of love: eros, mania, ludus, storge, agape, and pragma. What style do you believe this couple illustrates? Why?

1. **Eros:** Love of beauty.
2. **Mania:** Obsessive love.
3. **Ludus:** Playful love.
4. **Storge:** Companionate love.
5. **Agape:** Altruistic love.
6. **Pragma:** Practical love.

In addition to these pure forms, there are mixtures of the basic types: storgic-eros, ludic-eros, and storgic-ludus.

Eros was the ancient Greek god of love, the son of Aphrodite. (The Romans called him Cupid.) Erotic lovers delight in the tactile, the sensual, the immediate; they are attracted to beauty (though beauty is in the eye of the beholder). They love the lines of the body, its feel and touch. They are fascinated by every detail of their beloved. Their love burns brightly but soon flickers and dies.

The word "mania" comes from the Greek word for madness. For manic lovers, nights are marked by sleeplessness and days by pain and anxiety. The slightest sign of affection brings ecstasy for a short while, only to disappear. Satisfactions last but a moment before they must be renewed. Manic love is roller-coaster love.

"Ludus" is the Latin word for play. For ludic lovers, love is a game, something to play at rather than to become deeply involved in. Love is ultimately *ludic*rous. Love is for fun; encounters are casual, carefree, and often careless. "Nothing serious" is the motto of ludic lovers.

eros   In John Lee's typology of love, the love of beauty.

mania   In John Lee's typology of love, obsessive love.

ludus   In John Lee's typology of love, playful love.

storge   In John Lee's typology of love, companionate love.

agape   In John Lee's typology of love, altruistic love.

pragma   In John Lee's typology of love, practical love.

You and Your Sexual Well-Being

YOUR STYLE OF LOVE

John Lee, who developed the idea of styles of love, also developed a questionnaire that allows men and women to identify their style of love. Complete the questionnaire to identify your style of love. Then ask yourself to which style of love you find yourself drawn in others. Is it the same as your own or different?

Consider each characteristic as it applies to a current relationship that you define as love, or to a previous one if that is more applicable. For each, note whether the trait is *almost always* true (AA), *usually* true (U), *rarely* true (R), or *almost never* true (AN).

	Eros	Ludus	Storge	Mania	Ludic-Eros	Storgic-Eros	Storgic-Ludus	Pragma
1. You consider your childhood less happy than the average of peers.	R		AN	U				
2. You were discontented with life (work, etc.) at time your encounter began.	R		AN	U	R			
3. You have never been in love before this relationship.					U	R	AN	R
4. You want to be in love or have love as security.	R	AN		AA		AN	AN	U
5. You have a clearly defined ideal image of your desired partner.	AA	AN	AN	AN	U	AN	R	AA
6. You felt a strong gut attraction to your beloved on the first encounter.	AA	R	AN	R		AN		
7. You are preoccupied with thoughts about the beloved.	AA	AN	AN	AA			R	
8. You believe your partner's interest is at least as great as yours.		U	R	AN			R	U
9. You are eager to see your beloved almost every day; this was true from the beginning.	AA	AN	R	AA		R	AN	R
10. You soon believed this could become a permanent relationship.	AA	AN	R	AN	R	AA	AN	U
11. You see "warning signs" of trouble but ignore them.	R	R		AA		AN	R	R
12. You deliberately restrain frequency of contact with partner.	AN	AA	R	R	R	R	U	
13. You restrict discussion of your feelings with beloved.	R	AA	U	U	R		U	U
14. You restrict display of your feelings with beloved.	R	AA	R	U	R		U	U
15. You discuss future plans with beloved.	AA	R	R				AN	AA
16. You discuss wide range of topics, experiences with partner.	AA	R				U	R	AA

17.	You try to control relationship, but feel you've lost control.	AN	AN	AN	AA	AN	AN		
18.	You lose ability to be first to terminate relationship.	AN	AN		AA	R	U	R	R
19.	You try to force beloved to show more feeling, commitment.	AN	AN		AA		AN	R	
20.	You analyze the relationship, weigh it in your mind.			AN	U		R	R	AA
21.	You believe in the sincerity of your partner.	AA			U	R	U	AA	
22.	You blame partner for difficulties of your relationship.	R	U	R	U	R	AN		
23.	You are jealous and possessive but not to the point of angry conflict.	U	AN	R		R	AN		
24.	You are jealous to the point of conflict, scenes, threats, etc.	AN	AN	AN	AA	R	AN	AN	AN
25.	Tactile, sensual contact is very important to you.	AA		AN		U	AN		R
26.	Sexual intimacy was achieved early, rapidly in the relationship.	AA		AN	AN	U	R	U	
27.	You take the quality of sexual rapport as a test of love.	AA	U	AN		U	AN	U	R
28.	You are willing to work out sex problems, improve technique.	U	R		R	U		R	U
29.	You have a continued high rate of sex, tactile contact throughout the relationship.	U		R	R	U	R		R
30.	You declare your love first, well ahead of partner.		AN	R	AA		AA		
31.	You consider love life your most important activity, even essential.	AA	AN	R	AA		AA	R	R
32.	You are prepared to "give all" for love once under way.	U	AN	U	AA	R	AA	R	R
33.	You are willing to suffer abuse, even ridicule from partner.		AN	R	AA			R	AN
34.	Your relationship is marked by frequent differences of opinion, anxiety.	R	AA	R	AA	R	R		R
35.	The relationship ends with lasting bitterness, trauma for you.	AN	R	R	AA	R	AN	R	R

To diagnose your style of love, look for patterns across characteristics. If you consider your childhood less happy than that of your friends, were discontent with life when you fell in love, and very much want to be in love, you have "symptoms" that are rarely typical of eros and almost never true of storge, but which do suggest mania. Where a trait did not especially apply to a type of love, the space in that column is blank. Storge, for instance, is not the *presence* of many symptoms of love, but precisely their absence; it is cool, abiding affection rather than *Sturm und Drang.*

Source: Reprinted with permission from *Psychology Today Magazine,* copyright ©1974 (Sussex Publishers, Inc.).

Storge (STOR-gay), from the Greek word for natural affection, is the love between companions. It is, wrote Lee, "love without fever, tumult, or folly, a peaceful and enchanting affection." It begins usually as friendship and then gradually deepens into love. If the love ends, it also occurs gradually, and the couple often become friends once again. Of such love Theophile Gautier wrote, "To love is to admire with the heart; to admire is to love with the mind."

Agape (AH-ga-pay), from the Greek word for brotherly love, is the traditional Christian love that is chaste, patient, and undemanding; it does not expect to be reciprocated. It is the love of saints and martyrs. Agape is more abstract and ideal than concrete and real. It is easier to love all of humankind than an individual in this way.

"Pragma" is derived from the Greek word meaning business. Pragmatic lovers are, first and foremost, businesslike in their approach to looking for someone who meets their needs. They use logic in their search for a partner, seeking background, education, personality, religion, and interests that are compatible with their own. If they meet a person who satisfies their criteria, erotic, manic, or other feelings may develop. But, as Samuel Butler warned, "Logic is like the sword—those who appeal to it shall perish by it."

Two researchers (Hendrick & Hendrick, 1988) found that college students in love were more erotic and agapic and less ludic than those not in love.

The Triangular Theory of Love

The triangular theory of love, developed by Robert Sternberg (1986), emphasizes the dynamic quality of love relationships. This theory sees love as composed of three elements, as in the points of a triangle. These elements are intimacy, passion, and decision/commitment (see Figure 7.1). Each can be enlarged or diminished in the course of a love relationship, which will affect the quality of the relationship. They can also be combined in different ways. Each combination gives us a different type of love, such as romantic love, infatuation, empty love, liking, and so on. We may combine the components differently at different times in the same love relationship.

The Components of Love According to Robert Sternberg, there are three components to love: intimacy, passion, and decision/commitment. These components may combine in different proportions.

Intimacy refers to the warm, close, bonding feelings we get when we love someone. According to Sternberg and Grajek (1984), there are ten signs of intimacy:

1. Wanting to promote your partner's welfare.
2. Feeling happiness with your partner.
3. Holding your partner in high regard.
4. Being able to count on your partner in time of need.
5. Being able to understand each other.
6. Sharing yourself and your possessions with your partner.
7. Receiving emotional support from your partner.

FIGURE 7.1 According to Robert Sternberg's triangular theory of love, the three triangle points are intimacy, passion, and decision/commitment.

Are the man and woman in this photograph friends or lovers? What clues do you find to support your answer?

8. Giving emotional support to your partner.

9. Being able to communicate with your partner about intimate things.

10. Valuing your partner's presence in your life.

The passion component refers to the elements of romance, attraction, and sexuality in your relationship. These may be fueled by desires to increase self-esteem, to be sexually active or fulfilled, to affiliate with others, to dominate, or to subordinate.

The decision/commitment component consists of two separate parts, a short-term part and a long-term part. The short-term part refers to your decision that you love someone. You may or may not make the decision consciously. But it usually occurs before you decide to make a commitment to that person. The commitment represents the long-term part; it is the maintenance of love. But a decision to love someone does not necessarily entail a commitment to maintaining that love.

Kinds of Love The intimacy, passion, and decision/commitment components can be combined in eight basic ways, according to Sternberg. These combinations form the basis for classifying love:

1. Liking (intimacy only)

2. Infatuation (passion only)

3. Romantic love (intimacy and passion)
4. Companionate love (intimacy and commitment)
5. Fatuous love (passion and commitment)
6. Consummate love (intimacy, passion, and commitment)
7. Empty love (decision/commitment only)
8. Nonlove (absence of intimacy, passion, and commitment)

These types represent extremes that probably few of us experience. Not many of us, for example, experience infatuation in its purest form, in which there is absolutely *no* intimacy. (Empty love, in fact, is not really love at all.) These categories are nevertheless useful for examining the nature of love.

Liking represents the intimacy component alone. It forms the basis for close friendships but is neither passionate nor committed. As such, liking is often an enduring kind of love. Boyfriends and girlfriends may come and go, but good friends remain.

Infatuation is "love at first sight." It is the kind of love that idealizes its object; it rarely sees the other as a "real" person who sometimes has bad breath (but is worthy of being loved nonetheless). Infatuation is marked by sudden passion and a high degree of physical and emotional arousal. It tends to be obsessive and all-consuming; one has no time, energy, or desire for anything or anyone but the beloved (or thoughts of him or her). To the dismay of the infatuated individual, infatuations are usually asymmetrical: One's passion (or obsession) is rarely returned equally. And the greater the asymmetry, the greater the distress in the relationship (Sternberg & Barnes, 1985).

Romantic love combines intimacy and passion. It is similar to liking except it is more intense as a result of physical or emotional attraction. It may begin with an immediate union of the two components, with friendship that intensifies with passion, or with passion that also develops intimacy. Although commitment is not an essential element of romantic love, it may develop.

Companionate love is essential to a committed friendship. It often begins as romantic love, but as the passion diminishes and the intimacy increases, it is transformed into companionate love. Some couples are satisfied with such love, while others are not. Those who are dissatisfied in companionate love relationships may seek extrarelational affairs to maintain passion in their lives. They may also end the relationship to seek a new romantic relationship that they hope will remain romantic.

Fatuous or deceptive love is whirlwind love; it begins the day a couple meet, quickly results in cohabitation or engagement, then marriage. It goes so fast one hardly knows what happened. Often enough, nothing much really did happen that will permit the relationship to endure. As Sternberg (1988) observes, "It is fatuous in the sense that a commitment is made on the basis of passion without the stabilizing element of intimate involvement—which takes time to develop." Passion fades soon enough, and all that remains is commitment. But commitment that has had relatively little time to deepen is a poor foundation on which to build an enduring relationship. With neither passion nor intimacy, the commitment wanes.

Consummate love is born when intimacy, passion, and commitment combine to form their unique constellation. It is the kind of love we dream about but do not expect in all our love relationships. Many of us can achieve it, but it is difficult to sustain over time. To sustain it, we must nourish its different components, for each is subject to the stress of time.

The shape of the love triangle depends on the intensity of the love and the balance of the parts. Intense love relationships create triangles with greater area; such triangles occupy more of one's life. Just as love relationships can be balanced or unbalanced, so can love triangles. The balance determines the shape of the triangle (Figure 7.2). A relationship in which the intimacy, passion, and commitment components are equal forms an equilateral triangle. But if the components are not equal, unbalanced triangles form. The size and shape of a person's triangle gives a good pictorial sense of how that person feels about another. The greater the match between each person's triangle in a relationship, the more each is likely to experience satisfaction in the relationship (Sternberg & Barnes, 1985).

JEALOUSY

Many of us think that the existence of jealousy proves the existence of love. We may try to test someone's interest or affection by attempting to make him or her jealous by flirting with another person. If our date or partner becomes jealous, the jealousy is taken as a sign of love (Salovey & Rodin, 1991; White, 1980a). But provoking jealousy proves nothing except that the other person can be made jealous. Making jealousy a litmus test of love is dangerous, for jealousy and love are not necessary companions. Jealousy may be a more accurate yardstick for measuring insecurity or possessiveness than love.

It's important to understand jealousy for several reasons. First, jealousy is a painful emotion filled with anger and hurt. Its churning emotions can turn us inside out, making us feel out of control. If we can understand jealousy, especially when it is irrational, then we can eliminate some of its pain. Second, jealousy can help cement or destroy a relationship. Jealousy helps maintain a relationship by guarding its exclusiveness. But in its irrational or extreme forms, it can destroy a relationship by its insistent demands and attempts at control. We need to understand when and how jealousy is functional and when it is not. Third, jealousy is often linked to violence (Follingstad, Rutledge, Berg, & Hause, 1990; Laner, 1990). It is a factor in precipitating violence in dating relationships among both high school and college students (Burcky, Reuterman, & Kopsky, 1988; Stets & Pirog-Good, 1987). Marital violence and rape are often provoked by jealousy (Russell, 1990). It is often used by abusive spouses to justify their violence (Adams, 1990).

What Is Jealousy?

Jealousy is an aversive response that occurs because of a partner's real, imagined, or likely involvement with a third person (Bringle & Buunk, 1985). Jealousy sets boundaries for the behaviors that are acceptable in relationships; the boundaries cannot be crossed without evoking jealousy (Reiss, 1986).

a. Perfectly matched involvements

b. Closely matched involvements

c. Moderately mismatched involvements

d. Severely mismatched involvements

FIGURE 7.2 According to the triangular theory of love, the shape and size of each person's triangle indicates how well each is matched to the other.

jealousy An aversive response that occurs because of a partner's real, imagined, or likely involvement with a third person.

Think About It

LOVE AS ATTACHMENT

Human beings need to bond with other people. At the same time, many people fear bonding. Where do these contradictory impulses and emotions come from? Can they ever be resolved?

Attachment theory, the most prominent new approach to the study of love, helps us understand adult relationships, what goes wrong in them, and what to do when things do go wrong. In this theory, love is seen as a form of **attachment,** a close, enduring emotional bond that finds its roots in infancy (Hazan & Shaver, 1987; Shaver, 1984; Shaver, Hazan, & Bradshaw, 1988). Research suggests that romantic love and infant/caregiver attachment have similar emotional dynamics. These include the following:

Attachment

- Attachment bond's formation and quality depend on attachment object's (AO) responsiveness and sensitivity.
- When AO is present, infant is happier.
- Infant shares toys, discoveries, objects with AO.
- Infant coos, talks baby talk, "sings."
- Feelings of oneness with AO.

attachment The emotional tie between an infant and his or her primary caregiver.

Romantic Love

- Feelings of love are related to lover's interest and reciprocation.
- When lover is present, person feels happier.
- Lovers share experience and goods; give gifts.
- Lovers coo, sing, and talk baby talk.
- Feelings of oneness with lover.

The implications of attachment theory are far-reaching. Attachment impacts the way we process information, interact with others, and view the world. Quite basically, it influences our ability to love and see ourselves as lovable. Research shows that we can carry an attachment style with us for life; this style predisposes us to behave in certain ways in love relationships (Shaver et al., 1988).

The core elements of love appear to be the same for children as they are for adults: the need to feel emotionally safe and secure. When a partner responds to a need, for instance, adults sense the world as home, a safe place. In this respect, we don't differ greatly from children.

The most basic concept of attachment theory is that to be whole adults, we do not need to deny the fact that

The Psychological Dimension As most of us know, jealousy is a painful emotion. It is an agonizing compound of hurt, anger, depression, fear, and doubt. We feel less attractive and acceptable to our partner (Bush, Bush, & Jennings, 1988). Jealous responses are most intense in committed or marital relationships because both assume "specialness." This specialness occurs because one's intimate partner is different from everyone else. With him or her, you are most confiding, revealing, vulnerable, caring, and trusting. There is a sense of exclusiveness. To have sex outside the relationship violates that sense of exclusiveness because sex symbolizes specialness. Words such as "disloyalty," "cheating," and "infidelity" reflect the sense that an unspoken pledge has been broken. This unspoken pledge is the normative expectation that serious relationships, whether dating or marital, will be sexually exclusive (Lieberman, 1988).

As our lives become more and more intertwined, we become less and we are also vulnerable children. In a secure, intimate adult relationship, it is neither demeaning or diminishing nor pathologic to share honest emotions. It is the capacity to be vulnerable and open and accepting of others' giving that makes us lovable and human.

Based on observations made by Mary Ainsworth and colleagues (1978, cited in Shaver et al., 1988), Shaver and colleagues (1988) hypothesized that the styles of attachment developed in childhood—secure, anxious/ambivalent, and avoidant—continue through adulthood. Their surveys revealed similar styles in adult relationships.

Adults with **secure attachments,** for example, found it relatively easy to get close to others. They felt comfortable depending on others and having others depend on them. They didn't frequently worry about being abandoned or having someone get too close to them. More than avoidant and anxious/ambivalent adults, they felt that others generally liked them; they believed that people were generally well intentioned and good-hearted. Their love experiences tended to be happy, friendly, and trusting. They accepted and supported their partners. About 56% of the adults in the study were secure.

Adults with **anxious/ambivalent attachments** felt that others did not get as close as they themselves wanted. They worried that their partners didn't really love them or would leave them. They also wanted to merge completely with another, which sometimes scared others away. More than others, they felt that it is easy to fall in love. Their experiences in love were often obsessive and marked by desire for union, high degrees of sexual attraction, and jealousy. Between 19% and 20% of the adults were identified as anxious/ambivalent.

Adults with **avoidant attachments** felt discomfort in being close to others; they were distrustful and fearful of being dependent. More than others, they believed that romance seldom lasts, but at times it could be as intense as it was at the beginning. Their partners wanted more closeness than they did. Avoidant lovers feared intimacy and experienced emotional highs and lows and jealousy. Twenty-three to 25% of the adults in the study were avoidant.

What kind of adult are you? How do you feel about this label? If you wanted to change, what steps could you take to become a more secure adult?

less independent. For some, this loss of independence increases the fear of losing the partner. But it takes more than simple dependency to make a person jealous. To be jealous, we also need to lack self-esteem and have a feeling of insecurity, either about ourselves or about our relationships (Berscheid & Frei, 1977; McIntosh, 1989). Insecure people tend to feel jealous in their relationships (McIntosh & Tate, 1990). This is true for both whites and African Americans (McIntosh, 1989).

Jealous responses are most intense when they involve sexuality; Americans tend to be particularly insecure and competitive in this realm (Bringle & Buunk, 1991). Consider, for example, the different responses you might feel if you believe your partner is talking to, holding hands with, kissing, or having sexual intercourse with a potential or real rival. Which activities do you find most threatening? Least? If you are like most people, the more sexual the interaction, the higher the level of jealousy.

secure attachment A style of infant attachment characterized by feelings of security and confidence in relation to the primary caregiver.

anxious/ambivalent attachment A style of infant attachment characterized by separation anxiety and insecurity in relation to the primary caregiver.

avoidant attachment A style of infant attachment characterized by avoidance of the primary caregiver as a defense against rejection.

suspicious jealousy A type of jealousy that is groundless or that arises from ambiguous evidence.

reactive jealousy A type of jealousy that occurs because of a partner's current, past, or anticipated relationship with another person.

Types of Jealousy Social psychologists suggest that there are two types of jealousy: suspicious and reactive (Bringle & Buunk, 1991). **Suspicious jealousy** occurs when there is no reason to be suspicious, or when only ambiguous evidence exists for suspecting that a partner is involved with a third person. **Reactive jealousy** occurs when a partner is involved in a current, past, or anticipated relationship with another person.

Suspicious jealousy tends to occur most often when a relationship is in its early stages. The relationship is not firmly established, and the couple is unsure about its future. The smallest distraction, imagined slight, or inattention can be taken as evidence of interest in another person. Even without *any* evidence, a jealous partner may worry ("Is he or she seeing someone else but not telling me?"). The partner may engage in vigilance, watching his or her partner's every move ("I'd like to audit your human sexuality class"). He or she may snoop, unexpectedly appearing in the middle of the night to see if someone else is there ("I was just passing by and thought I'd say hello"). The partner may try to control the other's behavior ("If you go to your friend's party without me, we're through").

Sometimes, however, suspicions are valid. Suspicious jealousy, in fact, may be a reasonable response to circumstantial evidence. Robert Bringle and Bram Buunk believe that a certain amount of suspicious jealousy may be functional. They observe that "emotional reactions to these [circumstantial] events may forewarn the partner of what will happen if there are serious transgressions and thereby serve the role of *preventing* extradyadic involvements" (Bringle and Buunk, 1991).

At the same time, suspicious jealousy may be wholly unfounded. It can be self-defeating. The jealous man or woman may feel out of control and, as a result, his or her self-esteem suffers. "I can't help it. I know it is irrational, and I hate myself for it. I am a terrible person. But every time you are out of my sight, I think you are seeing someone else." Such jealousy may undermine the relationship. A jealous partner may try to control the other's feelings, activities, and movements until the partner feels suffocated. Such irrational jealousy can destroy the very relationship it is trying to preserve.

Reactive jealousy occurs when one learns of a partner's present, past, or anticipated sexual involvement with another person. This usually provokes the most intense jealousy. If the affair occurred during the current relationship, the discovering partner may feel that the entire relationship has been based on a lie. Trust is questioned. Every word and event must be reevaluated: "If you slept with each other when you said you were going to the library, did you also sleep with him/her when you said you were going to the laundromat?" Or, "How could you say you loved me when you were seeing him/her?" The damage can be irreparable.

If the affair is currently going on, similar questions arise but with an important difference. If the affair is over, it is clear that the partner involved in the affair has chosen to remain. But if the affair is continuing, the involved partner may be confronted with a choice: With whom will he or she remain? Sometimes, however, there is no choice. Because of the affair, the offended partner breaks off the relationship or marriage.

Boundary Markers As we noted earlier, jealousy represents a boundary marker. It points out what the boundaries are in a particular relationship.

Adults with secure attachments find it easy to get close to others.

It determines how, to what extent, and in what manner others can interact with members of the relationship. It also shows the limits to which the members of the relationship can interact with those outside the relationship. Culture prescribes the general boundaries of what evokes jealousy, but individuals adjust them to the dynamics of their own relationship.

Boundaries may vary depending on the type of relationship, gender, sexual orientation, and ethnicity. Although the majority of people believe sexual exclusiveness to be important in serious dating relationships and cohabitation, it is virtually mandatory in marriage (Blumstein & Schwartz, 1983; Buunk & van Driel, 1989; Hansen, 1985; Lieberman, 1988). Men are generally more restrictive than women; heterosexuals are more restrictive than gay men and lesbians. Although we know very little about jealousy and ethnicity, traditional Latinos and new Latino and Asian immigrants tend to be more restrictive than Anglos or African Americans (Mindel, Habenstein, & Wright, 1988). Despite variations in where the boundary lines are drawn, jealousy functions to guard those lines.

Managing Jealousy

Jealousy can be unreasonable, based on fears and fantasies, or realistic, reacting to genuine threats or events. Unreasonable jealousy can become a problem when it interferes with an individual's well-being or that of the relationship. Dealing with irrational suspicions can often be very difficult, for such feelings touch deep recesses in ourselves. As we noted earlier, jealousy is often related to personal feelings of insecurity and inadequacy. The source of such jealousy lies within ourselves, not within the relationship.

If we can work on the underlying causes of our insecurity, then we can deal effectively with our irrational jealousy. Excessively jealous people may

Think About It

THE WEB OF DECEPTION AND HOW IT AFFECTS RELATIONSHIPS

Assuming the following statements were true for you, which would you reveal to a partner or spouse?

- In order to become aroused and maintain arousal, you need to fantasize about another person or situation.

- You have had an extrarelational affair.

- You no longer find your partner physically attractive.

- (For women only) You rarely experience orgasm during intercourse.

If you would not reveal this information to your partner, are you being deceptive? Or are these just private issues? How does deception differ from privacy?

Deception involves betrayal and delusion; it often takes the form of lies, omissions, fabrications, or secrets. Counselors and psychologists agree that though deception is extremely common in intimate relationships, it has the power to destroy closeness and intimacy and ultimately to shatter trust. Whether or not a deception is revealed, it creates distance and disorientation in the relationship. It erodes bonds and blocks authentic communication and trust. Deception strips away spontaneity and often leaves a couple operating on a higher level of anxiety, states psychologist Harriet Lerner, author of *The Dance of Deception* (1993).

There are differences, some cultural and some personal, in what people consider acceptable and proper to reveal. Many people, for instance, do not reveal their sexual fantasies to their partners, considering it neither necessary nor valuable to do so. They consider this a matter of privacy rather than one of deceptiveness. Deception typically originates with betrayal or involves lies and secrets that drive couples apart.

Are you deceptive in your primary relationship? If so, in the process of identifying and confronting deception, it is valuable to understand your motivations. Are they the result of unfounded criticism by a partner? Contempt about an extramarital relationship? Boredom in the bedroom? Dissatisfaction with the quality of communication? Or stonewalling an idea or project? Perhaps you don't understand why your behavior exists. The reasons and motivations are often complex, with their expression rooted in our early life experiences and the ways we have learned to behave. For some, therapy is a way to help unravel, understand, and communicate what often seems beyond comprehension.

If one believes that truth and intimacy are connected, then truth is usually the preferred choice. Given the high cost of deception, it is worthwhile to try to understand the reason for the deceit, confront it with honesty, and communicate openly about it. This approach, though difficult and painful, will ultimately strengthen the relationship, whereas continued deception will only erode it further.

Adapted from Adler, E. (1994, August 24). "How The Tangled Web of Deception Hurts Relationships." *San Francisco Chronicle.*

deception Actions aimed at betraying, misleading, or deluding another person, including lies, omissions, fabrications, and secrets.

need considerable reassurance, but at some point they must also confront their own irrationality and insecurity. If they do not, they emotionally imprison their partner. Their jealousy may destroy the very relationship they have been desperately trying to preserve.

But jealousy is not always irrational. Sometimes there are real reasons, such as the relationship boundaries being violated. In this case, the cause lies not within ourselves but within the relationship. If the jealousy is well founded, the partner may need to modify or end the relationship with the third party whose presence initiated the jealousy. Modifying the third-party relationship reduces the jealous response and, more important, symbolizes the partner's commitment to the primary relationship. If the partner is unwilling to do this, because of a lack of commitment, unsatisfied personal needs, or problems in the primary relationship, the relationship is likely to reach a crisis. In such cases, jealousy may be the agent for profound change.

There are no set rules for dealing with jealousy. Each person must deal with it using his or her own understanding and insights. As with most of life's puzzling problems, jealousy has no simple answers.

THE TRANSFORMATION OF LOVE: FROM PASSION TO INTIMACY

Ultimately, passionate or romantic love may be transformed or replaced by a quieter, more lasting love. Otherwise, the relationship will likely break up, and each person will search for another who will once again ignite his or her passion.

Although love is one of the most important elements of our humanity, it seems to come and go. The kind of love that stays is what we might call intimate love. In intimate love, each person knows he or she can count on the other. The excitement comes from the achievement of other goals— from creativity, from work, from child rearing, from friendships—as well as from the relationship. The key to making love stay does not seem to be in love's passionate intensity but in transforming it into intimate love. Intimate love is based on commitment, caring, and self-disclosure.

Commitment is an important component of intimate love. It is a determination to continue a relationship or marriage in the face of bad times as well as good (Reiss, 1986). It is based on conscious choice rather than on feelings, which, by their very nature, are transitory. Commitment is a promise of a shared future, a promise to be together, come what may.

Commitment has become an important concept in recent years. We seem to be as much in search of commitment as we are in search of love or marriage. We speak of "making a commitment" to someone or to a relationship. A "committed" relationship has become almost a stage of courtship, somewhere between dating and being engaged or living together.

Caring is the making of another's needs as important as your own. It requires what the philosopher Martin Buber called an "I-Thou" relationship. Buber described two fundamental ways of relating to people: I-Thou and I-It. In an I-Thou relationship, each person is treated as a Thou—that is, as a person whose life is valued as an end in itself. In an I-It relationship, each person is treated as an It; the person has worth only as someone who can be used. When a person is treated as a Thou, his or her humanity and uniqueness are paramount.

Self-disclosure is the revelation of personal information that others would not ordinarily know because of its riskiness. When we self-disclose,

self-disclosure The revelation of personal information that others would not ordinarily know because of its riskiness.

Think About It

MAKING LOVE LAST: THE ROLE OF COMMITMENT

Although we generally make commitments because we love someone, love alone is not sufficient to make a commitment last. Our commitments seem to be affected by several factors that can strengthen or weaken the relationship. Ira Reiss (1980) believes that there are three important factors: the balance of costs to benefits, normative inputs, and structural constraints.

The Balance of Costs to Benefits

Whether we like it or not, human beings have a tendency to look at romantic, marital, and sexual relationships from a cost-benefit perspective. Most of the time, when we are satisfied, we are unaware that we may judge our relationships in this manner. But when there is stress or conflict, we often ask ourselves, "What am I getting out of this relationship?" Then we add up the pluses and minuses. If the result is on the plus side, we are encouraged to continue the relationship; if the result is negative, we are more likely to discontinue it, especially if the negativity continues over a long period of time. By this system, sexual interactions can have a positive or negative value. But although sex is important, it is generally not the only factor; it is not even necessarily the most important factor.

Normative Inputs

Normative inputs for relationships are the values that you, your partner, and society hold about love, relationships, marriage, and family. These values can either sustain or detract from a commitment. How do you feel about a love commitment? If you are heterosexual, a marital commitment? Do you believe that marriage is for life? If you are gay, lesbian, or bisexual, what are the values you and your partner bring to your relationship in terms of commitment? How do you create your own positive norms in the face of negative societal norms?

Structural Constraints

The structure of a relationship will add to or detract from commitment. Depending on the type of relationship—whether it is dating, living together, or marriage—there are different structural roles and expectations. In marital relationships, there are partner roles (husband/wife) and economic roles (employed worker/homemaker). There may also be parental roles (mother/father). There is usually the expectation of monogamy. In gay and lesbian relationships, the marital relationship model is replaced by the best-friends model, in which sexual exclusiveness is generally negotiable.

These different factors interact to increase or decrease commitment in a relationship. Commitments are more likely to endure in marriage than in cohabiting or dating relationships, which tend to be relatively short-lived. They are more likely to last in heterosexual relationships than in gay or lesbian relationships (Testa, Kinder, & Ironson, 1987). The reason commitments tend to endure in marriage may or may not have anything to do with a couple's being happy. Marital commitments tend to last because of norms, and structural constraints may compensate for the lack of personal satisfaction.

For most people, love seems to include commitment and commitment includes love. Though the two seem to overlap considerably, we can mistakenly assume that if someone loves us, he or she is also committed to us. It is not uncommon for one partner to believe there is more commitment in a relationship than there actually is. Even if a person is committed, it is not always clear what the commitment means: Is it a commitment to the person or to the relationship? For a short time or for a long time? Is it for better and for worse?

we reveal ourselves—our hopes, our fears, our everyday thoughts—to others. Self-disclosure deepens others' understanding of us. It also deepens our own understanding, for we discover unknown aspects as we open ourselves to others.

Without self-disclosure, we remain opaque and hidden. If others love us, such love leaves us with anxiety: Are we loved for ourselves, or for the image we present to the world?

Together, these elements help transform love. But in the final analysis, perhaps the most important means of sustaining love are our words and actions; caring words and deeds provide the setting for maintaining and expanding love (Byrne & Murnen, 1988).

The study of love is only beginning, but it is already helping us to understand the various components that make up this complex emotion. Although there is something to be said for the mystery of love, understanding how it works in the day-to-day world may help us keep our love vital and growing.

SUMMARY

Love and Sexuality

• Sexuality and love are intimately related in our culture. Sex is most highly valued in loving relationships. Sex with affection rivals marriage as an acceptable moral standard for intercourse. Love is valued by heterosexual men and women, gay men, lesbians, and bisexuals.

• Men are more likely than women to separate sex from love; women tend to view sex within a relational context. Gay men are more likely than heterosexual men to be involved in purely sexual relationships. Researchers suggest, however, that heterosexual males would have more sex-centered relationships if there were more willing women; they are constrained by the availability of consenting women.

• Attitudes and feelings associated with love include caring, needing, trusting, and tolerating. Behaviors associated with love include verbal, nonverbal, and physical expression of affection, self-disclosure, giving of nonmaterial and material evidence, and tolerance.

How Do I Love Thee? Approaches to the Study of Love

• According to John Lee, there are six basic styles of love: eros, mania, ludus, storge, agape, and pragma.

• The triangular theory of love views love as consisting of three components: intimacy, passion, and decision/commitment.

• The attachment theory of love views love as being similar in nature to the attachments we form as infants. The attachment (or love) styles of both infants and adults are secure, anxious/ambivalent, and avoidant.

Jealousy

• Jealousy is an aversive response to a partner's real, imagined, or likely involvement with a third person. Jealous responses are most likely in committed or marital relationships because of presumed "specialness" of the relationship, symbolized by sexual exclusiveness.

• As individuals become more interdependent, there is a greater fear of loss. Fear of loss, coupled with insecurity of self or the relationship, increases the likelihood of jealousy.

• There are two types of jealousy: suspicious and reactive. Suspicious jealousy occurs when there is no reason to be suspicious or only ambiguous evidence. Reactive jealousy occurs when a partner reveals a current, past, or anticipated relationship with another.

• Jealousy acts as a boundary marker for relationships. Boundaries vary according to type of relationship, gender, sexual orientation, and ethnicity.

**The Transformation of Love:
From Passion to Intimacy**

• Time affects romantic relationships. Intimate love is based on commitment, caring, and self-disclosure, the revelation of information not normally known by others.

• Love alone is not sufficient to make a commitment last. Three factors that can strengthen or weaken a relationship are the costs versus benefits, normative inputs, and structural constraints.

SUGGESTED READINGS

Buscaglia, Leo. *Loving Each Other*. New York: Ballantine Books, 1984. America's most popular proponent of love in a series of thoughtful essays about relationships.

Hendrick, Susan, and Clyde Hendrick. *Romantic Love*. Newbury Park, CA: Sage, 1991. A concise review of social science research on romantic love.

Peck, M. Scott. *The Road Less Traveled: A New Psychology of Love, Traditional Values, and Spiritual Growth*. New York: Simon & Schuster, 1978. A psychological/spiritual approach to love that sees love's goal as spiritual growth.

Sternberg, Robert, and Michael Barnes, eds. *The Psychology of Love*. New Haven: Yale University Press, 1988. An excellent collection of essays by some of the leading researchers in the area of love.

White, Greg, and Paul Mullen. *Jealousy: A Clinical and Multidisciplinary Approach*. New York: Guilford, 1989. A comprehensive examination of what we know about jealousy (and its treatment).

Chapter Eight

COMMUNICATING ABOUT SEX

PREVIEW: SELF-QUIZ

1. Most people verbally indicate their interest in initiating a sexual interaction. True or false?

2. Women often covertly signal their interest in beginning a conversation with someone. True or false?

3. Studies suggest that those couples with the highest marital satisfaction tend to disclose more than those who are unsatisfied. True or false?

4. Overall, men and women tend to touch about the same amount. True or false?

5. Conflict and intimacy go hand in hand in intimate relationships. True or false?

6. Good communication is primarily the ability to offer reasonable advice to your partner to help him or her change. True or false?

7. In ongoing relationships, women respond positively to sexual invitations at about the same rate as men. True or false?

8. Most people find that articulating their feelings about sex is quite difficult. True or false?

9. Men and women tend to use different sexual vocabularies. True or false?

10. The most effective way of expressing your desire not to have sex is by directly stating so. True or false?

ANSWERS 1. F, 2. T, 3. T, 4. T, 5. T, 6. F, 7. T, 8. T, 9. T, 10. T

Chapter Outline

Communication is the thread that connects sexuality and intimacy. The quality of the communication affects the quality of the relationship, and the quality of the relationship affects the quality of the sex (Cupach & Metts, 1991). Good relationships tend to have good sex, while bad relationships often have bad sex. Sex, in fact, frequently serves as a barometer for the quality of the relationship. The ability to communicate about sex is important in developing and maintaining both sexual and relationship satisfaction (Cupach & Comstock, 1990; Metts & Cupach, 1989). People who are satisfied with their sexual communication also tend to be satisfied with their relationship as a whole (Wheeless, Wheeless, & Baus, 1984).

Most of the time, we don't think about our ability to communicate. Only when problems arise do we consciously think about it. Then we become aware of our limitations in communicating, or more often, what we believe are the limitations of others: "You just don't get it, do you?" "You're not listening to me." And as we know, communication failures are marked by frustration.

There are generally two types of communication problems in relationships. The first problem is the failure to self-disclose. The second is poor communication skills. Although much of what we discuss here refers to interpersonal communication in general, such knowledge will enrich your ability to communicate about sexual issues as well.

It's important to realize, however, that not all of a relationship's problems are communication problems. Often we understand each other very clearly; the problem is that we are unable or unwilling to change or compromise. Good communication will not salvage a bad relationship or the "wrong" relationship. But good communication will allow us to see our differences. It will allow us to see the consequence of our actions or inactions, and it will provide us with the ability to make informed decisions.

In this chapter, we examine the characteristics of communication and how different contexts affect it. Next, we look at forms of nonverbal communication, such as touch, which are especially important in sexual relationships. Then we examine the different ways we communicate about sex in intimate relationships. Afterward, we explore ways we can develop our communication skills in order to enhance our relationships. Finally, we look at the different types of conflicts in intimate relationships and how to resolve them.

THE NATURE OF COMMUNICATION

Communication is a transactional process by which we convey symbols, such as words, gestures, and movements, to establish human contact, exchange information, and reinforce or change our attitudes and behaviors and those of others.

Communication Contexts

Our communication takes place simultaneously within cultural, social, and psychological contexts. These contexts affect our ability to communicate clearly by prescribing rules (usually unwritten or unconscious) for communicating about various subjects, including sexuality.

The Cultural Context   The cultural context refers to the language, values, beliefs, and customs in which communication takes place. On the whole, reflecting our Judeo-Christian heritage, our culture has viewed sexuality negatively. Sexual topics are often tabooed. Children and adolescents are discouraged from obtaining sexual knowledge; they learn they are not supposed to talk about sex. Censorship abounds in the media, with the ever-present "beep" on television or the "f—k" in newspapers and magazines to indicate a "forbidden" sexual word. Our language has few words for describing "the sex act" except scientific or impersonal ones ("sexual intercourse," "coitus," or "copulation"), moralistic ones ("fornication"), euphemistic ones ("doing it," "being intimate," or "sleeping with"), and tabooed ones ("fucking"). A few terms place sexual interactions in a relational category, such as "making love." But love is not always involved—as in, for example, a single encounter between strangers—and the term does not capture the erotic quality of sex. Furthermore, the gay and lesbian subculture has

communication   A transactional process in which symbols, such as words, gestures, and movements, are used to establish human contact, exchange information, and reinforce or change attitudes and behaviors.

developed its own sexual argot or slang, because society prohibits the open discussion or expression of homosexuality.

Different ethnic groups within our culture also have different language patterns that affect the way they communicate about sexuality. African American culture creates distinct communication patterns (Hecht, Collier, & Ribeau, 1993). Among African Americans, for example, language and expressive patterns are characterized by, among other things, emotional vitality, realness, and valuing direct experience (White & Parham, 1990). Emotional vitality is expressed in the animated, expressive use of words. Realness refers to "telling it like it is," using concrete, nonabstract words. Direct experience is valued because "there is no substitute in the Black ethos for actual experience gained in the course of living" (White & Parham, 1990). In sexual (and other) matters, "mother wit," practical or experiential knowledge, may be valued over knowledge gained from books or lectures.

Among Latinos, especially traditional Latinos, there is the assumption that sexual matters will not be discussed openly (Guerrero Pavich, 1986). Confrontations are to be avoided; negative feelings are not to be expressed. As a consequence, nonverbal communication is especially important. Women are expected to read men's behavior for clues to their feelings and for discovering what is acceptable. Because confrontations are unacceptable and sex cannot be openly discussed, secrets are important. They are shared between friends but not between partners. Sometimes secrets are hinted at; at times of crisis, they may be revealed through anger.

Asian Americans tend to be less individualistic than other Americans in general. Whereas mainstream American culture views the individual as self-reliant and self-sufficient, Asian American subcultures are more relationally oriented. Asian Americans are less verbal and expressive in their interactions than white Americans. They rely to a great degree on indirection and nonverbal communication, such as silence and the avoidance of eye contact as signs of respect (Del Carmen, 1990).

Because harmonious relationships are highly valued, Asian Americans have a greater tendency to avoid direct confrontation if possible. Japanese Americans, for example, "value implicit, nonverbal, intuitive communication over explicit, verbal, the rational exchange of information" (Del Carmen, 1990). In order to avoid conflict, verbal communication is often indirect or ambiguous; it skirts around issues rather than confronting them. As a consequence, Asian Americans rely on each other to interpret the meaning of a conversation or nonverbal clues.

The Social Context The social context of communication refers to the roles we play in society. These roles are derived from being members of different groups. As men and women, we play out masculine and feminine roles. As members of marital units, we act out roles of husband and wife. As members of cohabiting units, we perform heterosexual, gay, or lesbian cohabiting roles.

Roles exist in relationship to other people. Without a female role, there would be no male role; without a wife role, there would be no husband role. Because roles exist in relationship to others, **status,** a person's position in a group, is important. In traditional gender roles, men are accorded higher status than women; in traditional marital roles, husbands are superior in status to wives. And in terms of orientation, society awards higher status to

status   An individual's position in a group.

heterosexuals than to gay men, lesbians, and bisexuals. Because of this male/female disparity, heterosexual relationships tend to have a greater power imbalance than gay and lesbian couples (Lips, 1992).

The Psychological Context Although the cultural and social contexts are important factors in communication, they do not *determine* how people communicate. We are not prisoners of culture and society, but unique individuals. We may accept some cultural or social aspects, such as language taboos, but reject, ignore, or modify others, such as traditional gender roles. Because we have distinct personalities, we express our uniqueness by the way we communicate: We may be assertive or submissive, rigid or flexible, sensitive or insensitive; we may exhibit high self-esteem or low self-esteem.

Our personality characteristics affect our ability to communicate, change, or manage conflict. Rigid people, for example, are less likely to change than flexible ones, regardless of the quality of communication. People with high self-esteem may be more open to change because they do not necessarily take conflict as an attack on themselves. Personality characteristics such as having negative or positive feelings about sex affect our sexual communication more directly.

Nonverbal Communication

There is no such thing as not communicating. Even when you are not talking, you are communicating by your silence (an awkward silence, a hostile silence, a tender silence). You are communicating by the way you position your body and tilt your head, through your facial expressions, your physical distance from another person, and so on. Look around you. How are the people in your presence communicating nonverbally?

Much of our communication of feeling is nonverbal. We radiate our moods: A happy mood invites companionship; a solemn mood pushes people away. Joy infects; depression distances—all without a word being said. Nonverbal expressions of love are particularly effective—a gentle touch, a loving glance, or the gift of a flower.

One of the problems with nonverbal communication, however, is the imprecision of its messages. Is a person frowning or squinting? Does the smile indicate friendliness or nervousness? A person may be in reflective silence, but we may interpret the silence as disapproval or distance.

The ability to correctly interpret nonverbal communication appears to be an important ingredient in successful relationships. "I can tell when something is bothering him/her" reveals the ability to read nonverbal clues, such as body language. This ability is especially important in ethnic groups and cultures that rely on nonverbal expression of feelings, such as Latino and Asian cultures. Although the value placed on nonverbal expression may vary among groups and across cultures, the ability to communicate and understand nonverbally remains important in all cultures.

Three of the most important forms of nonverbal communication are proximity, eye contact, and touching.

Proximity **Proximity** is nearness in physical space and time. Where we sit or stand in relation to another person signifies a level of intimacy or relationship. Many of our words that convey emotion relate to proximity, such

proximity Nearness in terms of physical space and time.

You and Your Sexual Well-Being

SEXUAL COMMUNICATION SATISFACTION QUESTIONNAIRE

This questionnaire assesses your satisfaction with your sexual communication with your partner. Use the following scale to indicate how strongly you agree or disagree with each statement:

1 = Strongly agree   **4** = Disagree
2 = Agree   **5** = Strongly disagree
3 = Neither agree nor disagree

Feel free to ask your partner to complete the survey so that the two of you may share results.

_____   1.   I tell my partner when I am especially sexually satisfied.

_____   2.   I am satisfied with my partner's ability to communicate his/her sexual desires to me.

_____   3.   I do not let my partner know things that I find pleasing during sex.

_____   4.   I am very satisfied with the quality of our sexual interactions.

_____   5.   I do not hesitate to let my partner know when I want to have sex with him/her.

_____   6.   I do not tell my partner whether or not I am sexually satisfied.

_____   7.   I am dissatisfied over the degree to which my partner and I discuss our sexual relationship.

_____   8.   I am not afraid to show my partner what kind of sexual behavior I find satisfying.

_____   9.   I would not hesitate to show my partner what is a sexual turn-on to me.

_____ 10.   My partner does not show me when he/she is sexually satisfied.

_____ 11.   I show my partner what pleases me during sex.

_____ 12.   I am displeased with the manner in which my partner and I communicate with each other during sex.

_____ 13.   My partner does not show me things he/she finds pleasing during sex.

_____ 14.   I show my partner when I am sexually satisfied.

_____ 15.   My partner does not let me know whether sex has been satisfying or not.

_____ 16.   I do not show my partner when I am sexually satisfied.

_____ 17.   I am satisifed concerning my ability to communicate about sexual matters with my partner.

_____ 18.   My partner shows me by the way he/she touches me if he/she is satisfied.

_____ 19.   I am dissatisfied with my partner's ability to communicate his/her sexual desire to me.

_____ 20.   I have no way of knowing when my partner is sexually satisfied.

_____ 21.   I am not satisfied in the majority of our sexual interactions.

_____ 22.   I am pleased with the manner in which my partner and I communicate with each other after sex.

Source: Wheeless, Lawrence R., Virginia Eman Wheeless, and Raymond Baus. "Sexual Communication, Communication Satisfaction, and Solidarity in the Developmental Stages of Intimate Relationships," *Western Journal of Speech Communication*, 48(3), p. 224, copyright © 1984 by the Western Speech Communication Association. Reprinted by permission of the Western Speech Communication Association.

The physical distance between individuals connotes levels of intimacy or the type of relationship. The appropriate distance in face-to-face interactions may differ according to ethnicity.

as feeling "distant" or "close," or being "moved" by someone. We also "make the first move," "move in" on someone else's partner, or "move in together."

In a social gathering, the face-to-face distances between people when starting a conversation are clues to how the individuals wish to define the relationship. All cultures have an intermediate distance in face-to-face interactions that is neutral. In most cultures, decreasing the distance signifies an invitation to greater intimacy or a threat. Moving away denotes the desire to terminate the interaction. When you stand at an intermediate distance from someone at a party, you send the message, "intimacy is not encouraged." If you want to move closer, however, you risk the chance of rejection.

Because of cultural differences, there can be misunderstandings. The neutral intermediate distance for Latinos, for example, is much closer than for Anglos, who may misinterpret the same distance as "too close for comfort." In social settings, this can lead to problems. As Carlos Sluzki (1982) points out, "A person raised in a non-Latino culture will define as seductive behavior the same behavior that a person raised in a Latin culture defines as socially neutral." An Anglo may interpret the behavior as an invitation for intimacy, while the Latino may interpret it as neutral. Because of the miscue, the Anglo may withdraw or flirt, depending on his or her feelings. If the Anglo flirts, the Latino may respond to what he or she believes is the other's initiation. Additionally, among people whose culture features greater intermediate distances and less overt touching, such as Asian Americans, neutral responses may be misinterpreted negatively by those outside the culture.

Eye Contact Much can be discovered about a relationship by watching how people look at each other. Making eye contact with another person,

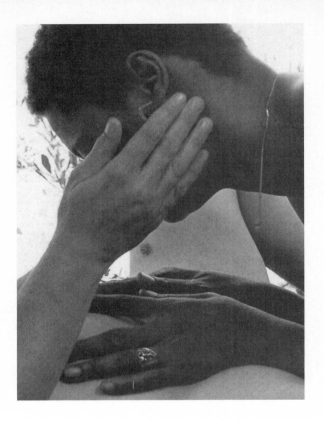

if only for a split second longer than usual, is a signal of interest. Brief and extended glances, in fact, play a significant role in women's expression of initial interest (Moore, 1985). When you can't take your eyes off another person, you probably have a strong attraction to him or her. In addition to eye contact, dilated pupils may be an indication of sexual interest.

Research suggests that the amount of eye contact between a couple in conversation can distinguish between those who have high levels of conflict and those who don't. Those with the greatest degree of agreement have the greatest eye contact with each other (Beier & Sternberg, 1977). Those in conflict tend to avoid eye contact (unless it is a daggerlike stare). As we saw earlier, however, the level of eye contact may differ by culture.

Touching It is difficult to overestimate the significance of touch. It is the most basic of all senses. Skin contains receptors for pleasure and pain, heat and cold, roughness and smoothness. "Touch is the mother sense and out of it, all the other senses have been derived," writes anthropologist Ashley Montagu (1986). Touch is a life-giving force for infants. If babies are not touched, they may fail to thrive and may even die. We hold hands with small children and those we love.

But touch can also be a violation. Strangers or acquaintances may touch as if they were more familiar than they are. Your date or partner may touch you in a manner you don't like or want. And sexual harassment includes unwelcomed touching (see Chapter 17).

TOUCH: OVERCOMING DIFFERENCES

"How can I become more openly affectionate when expressing affection was discouraged by my family when I was growing up?"

"My partner likes to touch and be touched, but I am uncomfortable with both. How can we overcome these differences?"

These are questions students ask over and over in human sexuality classes. They are aware of the deep need and value of human touch. So profound is this need that infants have been observed wasting and becoming ill, in spite of good physical care, as a result of lack of touch and cuddling. Among adults, professionals see a correlation between marital happiness and physical affection: The happiest couples often tend to be the most demonstrative couples. The response to touch is indeed physical: Biochemical reactions produced by touch can cause an increase in heart rate, a drop in blood pressure, and an easing of pain.

A variety of factors appears to contribute to each individual's need for and ability to touch. Among these, culture is a strong determinant. Studies show that Americans tend to touch less than people from many Latin American countries, the Middle East, and Russia. Families also have a key role in influencing how comfortable people are with touch. Both quantity and quality of touch among adults and between adults and children are observed by children and then translated into behavior that often repeats itself in later adulthood. Inborn differences, gender, and individual preferences also influence touching.

Regardless of where the patterns and preferences originate, problems can occur in relationships if distinct discrepancies exist between partners in sending or receiving touch. Misunderstandings, discomfort, and a widening gap in the ability of each person to emotionally connect with the other often result.

The most obvious and possibly the most difficult solution to this problem is honest communication. Communication can replace assumptions (about why someone is not being touched), ignorance (about what does and does not feel good), misplaced anger and resentment (about the importance of touch), and misinterpretation (about the meaning of touch). Communication in a nonthreatening and relaxed environment can begin to help unravel and expose in a new way existing patterns and behaviors.

Discussing what touch means to each person is a beginning. For some, touch means intimacy; for others, it represents safety; and for still others, it signals a readiness for sex. Often, the absence of touch is merely a response to previous learning. But the absence of touch can elicit feelings in another ranging from abandonment to rage. Sharing the meaning of touch may expand its definition and allow it to find a place in one's patterns of expression.

If touching is an issue in your relationship, experiment with nonsexual touching. Learn to enjoy giving and receiving touch. Give and accept feedback nondefensively. Give feedback, especially verbal cues, about what does and does not feel good. Initiate touch when it is appropriate, even though it may be awkward at first. Don't be afraid to be adventurous in learning and utilizing methods that are pleasing to both you and your partner.

At the same time, be prepared to accept individual differences. In spite of forthright and ongoing communication, people still have unique comfort levels. Again, honest feedback will help you and your partner find a mutually acceptable level. If you are both able to understand and enjoy the rich and powerful messages that touch sends, then your relationship as a whole can be enriched by yet another dimension.

As with eye contact, touching is a form of communication. The amount of contact, from almost imperceptible touches to "hanging all over each other," helps differentiate lovers from strangers. How and where a person is touched can suggest friendship, intimacy, love, or sexual interest. Levels of touching differ among cultures and ethnic groups.

What about gender differences in touching? Despite stereotypes of women touching and men avoiding touch, studies suggest that there are no consistent differences between the sexes in the amount of overall touching (Andersen, Lustig, & Andersen, 1987). Men do not seem to initiate touch with women any more than women do with men. Women are markedly unenthusiastic, however, about receiving touches from strangers and express greater concern in general about being touched. For women, there is greater touch avoidance unless there is a relational context with the man (Heslin & Alper, 1983). However, in situations with sexual overtones, men initiate more touching than women (Blumstein & Schwartz, 1983).

Growing research on touching indicates that it often signals intimacy, immediacy, and emotional closeness (Thayer, 1986). In fact, touch may very well be the *closest* form of nonverbal communication. One researcher writes: "If intimacy is proximity, then nothing comes closer than touch, the most intimate knowledge of another" (Thayer, 1986). And touching seems to go hand-in-hand with self-disclosure. Those who touch appear to self-disclose more; in fact, touch seems to be an important factor in prompting others to talk more about themselves (Heslin & Alper, 1983; Norton, 1983).

Sexual behavior relies above all else on touch: the touching of self and others; the touching of hands, faces, chests, arms, necks, legs, and genitals. (Sex is a contact sport, some say, with more truth than they realize.) In sexual interactions, touch takes precedence over sight, as we often close our eyes to caress, kiss, and make love. In fact, we close our eyes to better focus on the sensations aroused by touch; we shut out visual distractions to intensify the tactile experience of sexuality.

SEXUAL COMMUNICATION

Communication is important in understanding, developing, and maintaining sexual relationships. In childhood and adolescence, communication is critical for transmitting sexual knowledge and values and in forming our sexual identities. As we establish our relationships, communication enables us to signal sexual interest and initiate sexual interactions. In developed relationships, communication allows us to explore and maintain our sexuality as a couple.

Sexual Communication in Beginning Relationships

Our interpersonal sexual scripts provide us with "instructions" on how to behave sexually, including the initiation of potentially sexual relationships. Because as a culture we share our interpersonal sexual scripts, we know how we are supposed to act at the beginning of a relationship. The very process of acting out interpersonal scripts, in fact, communicates sexual meanings (Simon & Gagnon, 1987). But how do we begin relationships? What is it that attracts us to someone?

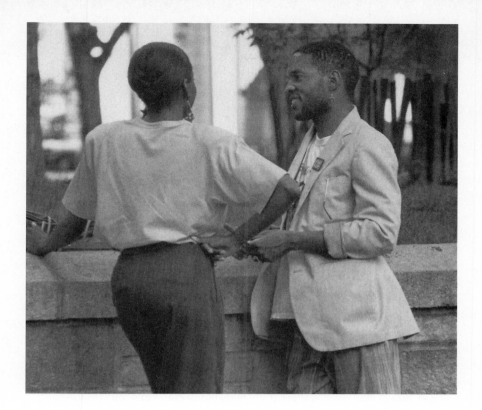

The Halo Effect Imagine yourself unattached at a party. You notice someone standing next to you as you reach for some chips. In a split second, you decide whether you are interested in him or her. On what basis do you make that decision? Is it looks, personality, style, sensitivity, intelligence, or what?

If you're like most people, you base this decision, consciously or unconsciously, on appearance. Physical attractiveness is particularly important during the initial meeting and early stages of a relationship. If you don't know anything else about a person, you tend to judge him or her on appearance.

Most people would deny that they are attracted to others just because of their looks. We like to think we are deeper than that. But looks are important unconsciously. We tend to infer qualities based on looks. This inference is based on what is known as the **halo effect,** the assumption that attractive people possess more desirable social characteristics than unattractive people. In one well-known experiment, students were shown pictures of attractive people and asked to describe what they thought these people were like (Dion, Berscheid, & Walster, 1972). Attractive men and women were assumed to be more sensitive, kind, warm, sexually responsive, strong, poised, and outgoing than others; they were assumed to be more exciting and to have better characters than "ordinary" people. Research indicates that, overall, the differences in perceptions between very attractive and average people are minimal.

halo effect   The assumption that attractive people possess more desirable social characteristics than unattractive people.

TEN RULES FOR AVOIDING INTIMACY

If you want to avoid intimacy, here are ten rules that have proved effective in nationwide testing with lovers, husbands and wives, parents, and children. Follow these guidelines, and we guarantee you'll never have an intimate relationship.

1. *Don't talk.* This is the basic rule for avoiding intimacy. If you follow this one rule, you will never have to worry about being intimate again. Sometimes, however, you may be forced to talk. But don't talk about anything meaningful. Talk about the weather, baseball, class, the stock market—anything but feelings.

2. *Never show your feelings.* Showing your feelings is almost as bad as talking, because feelings are ways of communicating. If you cry or show anger, sadness, or joy, you are giving yourself away. You might as well talk, and if you talk you could become intimate. So the best thing to do is remain expressionless (which, we admit, is a form of communication, but at least it's sending the message that you don't want to be intimate).

3. *Always be pleasant.* Always smile, always be friendly, especially if something's bothering you.

You'll be surprised at how effective hiding negative feelings from your partner is in preventing intimacy. It may even fool your partner into believing that everything's OK in your relationship.

4. *Always win.* If you can't be pleasant, try this one. Never compromise, never admit that your partner's point of view may be as good as yours. If you start compromising, it's an admission that you care about your partner's feelings, which is a dangerous step toward intimacy.

5. *Always keep busy.* Keeping busy at school or work will take you away from your partner, and you won't have to be intimate. Your partner may never figure out that you're using work to avoid intimacy. Because our culture values hard work, he or she will feel unjustified in complaining. Devoting yourself to your work will give your partner the message that he or she is not as important as your work. You can make your partner feel unimportant in your life without even talking!

6. *Always be right.* There is nothing worse than being wrong, because it is an indication that you are human. If you admit you're wrong, you might

Interest and Opening Lines After we have sized someone up based on his or her appearance, what happens next in interactions between men and women? (Gay and lesbian beginning relationships are discussed later.) Does the man initiate the encounter? On the surface yes, but in reality, the woman often "covertly initiates . . . by sending nonverbal signals of availability and interest" (Metts & Cupach, 1989). The woman will "glance" at him once or twice and "catch" his eye; she may smile or flip her hair. If the man moves into her physical space, the woman then relies on nodding, leaning close, smiling, or laughing (Moore, 1985).

If the man believes the woman is interested, he then initiates a conversation using an "opening line." The opening line tests the woman's interest and availability. There is an array of opening lines that men use. According to women, the most effective are innocuous, such as "I feel a little have to admit your partner's right, and that will make him or her as good as you. If he or she is as good as you, then you might have to consider your partner, and before you know it, you will be intimate!

7. *Never argue.* If you can't always be right, don't argue at all. If you argue, you might discover that you and your partner are different. If you're different, you may have to talk about the differences in order to make adjustments. And if you begin making adjustments, you may have to tell your partner who you really are, what you really feel. Naturally, these revelations may lead to intimacy.

8. *Make your partner guess what you want.* Never tell your partner what you want. That way, when your partner tries to guess and is wrong (as he or she often will be), you can tell your partner that he or she doesn't really understand or love you. If your partner did love you, he or she would know what you want without asking. Not only will this prevent intimacy, but it will drive your partner crazy as well.

9. *Always look out for number one.* Remember, you are number one. All relationships exist to fulfill your needs, no one else's. Whatever you feel like doing is just fine. You're OK; your partner's not

OK. If your partner can't satisfy your needs, he or she is narcissistic; after all, you are the one making all the sacrifices in the relationship.

10. *Keep the television on.* Keep the television turned on at all times: during dinner, while you're reading, when you're in bed, and while you're talking (especially if you're talking about something important). This rule may seem petty compared with the others, but it is good preventive action. Watching television keeps you and your partner from talking to each other. Best of all, it will keep you both from even noticing that you don't communicate. If you're cornered and have to talk, you can both be distracted by a commercial, a seduction scene, or the sound of gunfire. And when you actually think about it, wouldn't you rather be watching "The Simpsons" or "Home Improvement" anyway?

This list is not complete. Everyone knows additional ways for avoiding intimacy. These may be your own inventions or techniques you have learned from your boyfriend or girlfriend, husband or wife, friends, or parents. To round out this compilation, list additional rules for avoiding intimacy on a separate sheet of paper. The person with the best list wins—and never has to be intimate again.

embarrassed, but I'd like to meet you" or "Are you a student here?" The least effective are sexually blunt, such as "You really turn me on."

The First Move   After we first meet someone, we weigh each others' attitudes, values, and philosophy to see if we are compatible. We evaluate their sense of humor, their intelligence, their "partner" potential, their ability to function in a relationship, their sex appeal, and so on. Based on our overall judgment, we may continue the relationship. If the relationship continues in a romantic vein, we may move into one that includes some kind of physical intimacy. To signal this transition from nonphysical to physical intimacy, one of us must "make the first move." Making the first move marks the transition from a potentially sexual relationship to an actual one.

If the relationship develops along traditional gender-role patterns, one of the partners, usually the male, will make the first move to initiate sexual intimacy, whether it is kissing, petting, or engaging in sexual intercourse (O'Sullivan & Byers, 1992). The point at which this occurs generally depends on two factors: the level of intimacy and the length of the relationship (Sprecher, 1989). The more emotionally involved the couple, the more likely they will be sexually involved as well. The duration of the relationship also affects the likelihood of sexual involvement.

Initial sexual involvement can occur as early as the first meeting or later, as part of a well-established relationship. Although some people become sexually involved immediately ("lust at first sight"), the majority begin their sexual involvements in the context of an ongoing relationship.

In new or developing relationships, communication is generally indirect and ambiguous about sexuality. As one communication scholar notes about developing relationships, "The typical relationship process is not dominated by open, direct communication, but rather involves the construction of a web of ambiguity by which parties signal their relationship indirectly" (Baxter, 1987). Direct strategies are sometimes used to initiate sexual involvement, but these usually occur when the person is confident in the other's interest or is not concerned about being rejected.

In new relationships, we communicate *indirectly* about sex because, although we want to become sexually involved with the other person, we also want to avoid rejection. By using indirect strategies, such as turning down the lights, moving closer, touching the other's face or hair, we may test the other's interest in sexual involvement. If the other person responds positively to our cues, we can initiate a sexual encounter.

Because so much of our sexual communication is indirect, ambiguous, or nonverbal, there is a high risk of misinterpretation between women and men. There are four basic reasons for this (Cupach & Metts, 1991). First, men and women tend to disagree about *when* sexual activities should take place in a relationship. Men more than women tend to want sexual involvement earlier and with a lower level of intimacy. Second, men may be skeptical about women's refusals. Men often misinterpret women's cues, such as misinterpreting a woman's friendly touch as a sexual cue. Men also believe that women often say "no" when they actually mean "coax me." Men believe that women say "no" as token resistance.

Third, because we are indirect, women may be unclear in signaling their disinterest. They may turn their face aside, move a man's hand back to its proper place, say that it's getting late, or try to change the subject. Research indicates that women are most effective by making strong, direct verbal refusals; men become more compliant if women are persistent in such refusals (Christopher & Frandsen, 1990; Murnen, Perot, & Byrne, 1989). Fourth, men are more likely than women to interpret nonsexual behavior or cues as sexual. As William Cupach and Sandra Metts (1991) write, "Men may wear sex-colored glasses." Although both men and women flirt for fun, men are more likely to flirt with a sexual purpose. Reflecting their own tendencies, men are more likely to interpret a woman's flirtation as sexual.

Directing Sexual Activity   As we begin a sexual involvement, we have several tasks to accomplish. First, we need to practice safer sex (see Chapter 15). We should gather information about our partner's sexual history, determine whether he or she knows how to practice safer sex, and use condoms. Unlike much of our sexual communication, which is nonverbal or ambiguous, practicing safer sex requires direct verbal discussion. Second, we must discuss birth control (unless both partners have agreed to try for pregnancy). Contraceptive responsibility, like safer sex, requires verbal communication (see Chapter 11).

In addition to communicating about safer sex and contraception, we also need to communicate about what we like and what we need sexually. What kind of foreplay do we like? Afterplay? Do we like to be orally or manually stimulated during intercourse? If so, how? What does each partner need to be orgasmic? Many of our needs and desires can be communicated nonverbally by movements or by giving our partner physical cues. But if our partner does not pick up our nonverbal signals or cues, we need to discuss them directly and clearly to avoid ambiguity.

Gay and Lesbian Relationships Gay men and lesbians, like heterosexuals, rely on both nonverbal and verbal communication in expressing sexual interest in others. Unlike heterosexuals, however, they cannot necessarily assume that the person in whom they are interested is of the same sexual orientation. Instead, they must rely on specific identifying factors, such as meeting at a gay or lesbian bar, wearing a gay/lesbian pride button, participating in gay/lesbian events, or being introduced by friends to others identified as lesbian or gay (Tessina, 1989). In situations where sexual orientation is not clear, gay men and lesbians use "gaydar," gay radar, in which they look for clues as to orientation. They give ambiguous cues as to their own orientation while looking for cues from the other. These cues can include mannerisms, speech patterns, slang usage, or lingering glances. They may also include the mention of specific places for entertainment or recreation that are frequented mainly by lesbians or gay men, music or songs that can be interpreted to have "gay" meanings, such as "Strangers in the Night" or "Secret Love," or movies with gay or lesbian themes, such as *Maurice* or *Desert Hearts*. Tina Tessina (1989) writes:

> Drop a hint about your Holly Near records, or say, "I just came from the Rodeo in San Francisco." If you get a naive response, such as "Oh, who is that?" or "Are you a cowboy?" you can easily step back.

Gay men and lesbians, like heterosexuals, prefer innocuous opening lines. To prevent awkwardness, the opening line usually does not make an overt reference to orientation unless the other person is clearly lesbian or gay.

Once a like orientation is established, lesbians and gay men engage in nonverbal processes to express interest. There are mutual glances, smiles, subtle body movements; someone initiates a conversation with an opening line. In these beginning interactions, physical appearance is important, especially for gay males.

Because of their socialization as males, gay men are more likely than lesbians to initiate sexual activity earlier in the relationship. In large part, this is because both partners are free to initiate and because men are not expected to refuse sex as women are. But this same sexual socialization makes it difficult for some gay men to refuse sexual activity. Lesbians do not initiate sex as often as do gay or heterosexual men. In contrast to men, they often feel uncomfortable because women have not been socialized to sexually initiate. Philip Blumstein and Pepper Schwartz (1983) write that "many lesbians are not comfortable in the role of sexual aggressor and it is a major reason why they have sex less often than other kinds of couples."

Sexual Communication in Established Relationships

As a relationship develops and becomes established, the partners begin modifying their individual sexual scripts as they interact with each other. The scripts become less rigid and conventional as each adapts to the uniqueness of his or her partner. The couple develops a shared sexual script. Through their sexual interactions, they learn what each other likes, dislikes, wants, or needs. Much of this learning takes place nonverbally as partners in established relationships, like those in emerging relationships, tend to be indirect and ambiguous in their sexual communication. The reason that partners are indirect in established relationships is the same as for those in new relationships: They want to avoid rejection. Indirection allows them to express sexual interest while at the same time protecting themselves from loss of face.

Initiating Sexual Activity Within established relationships, men continue to overtly initiate sexual encounters more frequently than women. But women continue to signal their willingness. They pace the frequency of intercourse by showing their interest with nonverbal cues, such as giving a "certain look" or lighting candles by the bed. They may also overtly suggest "doing the wild thing." Their partners pick up on the cues and "initiate" sexual interactions. In marital relationships, many women feel more comfortable with overtly initiating sex. In part, this may be related to the decreasing significance of the double standard as relationships continue. In a new relationship, the woman initiating intercourse may be viewed negatively, as a sign of promiscuity. But in an established relationship, the woman's initiation may be viewed positively, as an expression of love. The increase may also be the result of couples becoming more egalitarian in their gender-role attitudes. Not surprisingly, sexual initiations are more often successful in marital relationships than in new or dating relationships.

Unlike new relationships, sexual disinterest is communicated verbally in established relationships (Byers & Heinlein, 1989). In established relationships, a direct refusal is not viewed as much of a threat to the relationship as it is in new relationships. In an established relationship, refusals are usually accompanied by a face-saving explanation, "I would like to but am too tired." "You are pretty sexy, but I have to finish studying for my human sexuality exam." "Let's wait until after the kids go over to their friend's." Such direct refusals are also more effective than indirect ones.

Lesbian and Gay Interactions In both lesbian and gay relationships, the more emotionally expressive partner is likely to initiate sexual interaction (Blumstein & Schwartz, 1983). The gay or lesbian partner who talks more about feelings, who spontaneously gives his or her partner hugs or kisses, is the one who most often begins sexual activity.

One of the key differences between heterosexuals and gay males and lesbians, however, is how they handle extrarelational sex. In marriage and committed heterosexual relationships, both partners are expected to be sexually exclusive; when heterosexual men and women engage in affairs, they ordinarily keep such matters secret. In gay and lesbian culture, by contrast,

Partners in established relationships tend to develop a shared sexual script. Touching and sharing feelings (by smiling or laughing, for example) are two forms of nonverbal communication that help people learn about each other.

sexual exclusivity is often negotiable. Sexual exclusiveness is not necessarily equated with commitment or fidelity. It is acceptable, sometimes expected, to be open with one's partner about extrarelational sex.

As a result of these differing norms, lesbians and gay men must decide early in the relationship whether they will be sexually exclusive (Isensee, 1990). If they choose to have a nonexclusive relationship, they need to discuss how outside sexual interests will be handled. They must decide whether to tell each other, whether to have affairs with friends; they should discuss what degree of emotional involvement is acceptable, and how to deal with jealousy. They need to deal with STD and HIV risks resulting from a third person's being in the relationship.

Gender Differences in Marital Communication For some time, researchers have been aware of gender differences in general communication patterns. More recently, they have discovered specific gender differences in marital communication (Noller & Fitzpatrick, 1991; Thompson & Walker, 1989).

- *Wives send clearer messages to their husbands than their husbands send to them.* Wives tend to be more sensitive and responsive to their husbands' messages, both during conversation and during conflict. They are more likely to reply to either positive messages or negative messages than are their husbands, who may not reply at all to such statements.

COMMUNICATION PATTERNS AND MARITAL SATISFACTION

Researchers studying marital satisfaction have found a number of communication patterns that offer clues to enhancing our intimate relationships (Hendrick, 1981; Noller & Fitzpatrick, 1991; Schaap, Buunk, & Kerkstra, 1988). They found that men and women in satisfied relationships tended to have the following common characteristics regarding communication:

- *The ability to disclose or reveal private thoughts and feelings, especially positive ones, to each other.* Dissatisfied spouses tend to disclose mostly negative thoughts to their partners. Satisfied couples say such things as "I love you," "You're sexy," or "I feel vulnerable, please hold me." Unhappy couples may also say they love each other, but more often they say things like "Don't touch me; I can't stand you," "You turn me off," or "This relationship makes me miserable and frustrated."

- *The expression by both partners of more-or-less equal levels of affective disclosures.* Both are likely to say such words as "You make me feel happy," "I love you more than I can ever say," or "I love the way you touch me."

- *More time spent talking, discussing personal topics, and expressing feelings in positive ways.* They talk about their sexual feelings, the fun they have in bed together.

- *A willingness to accept conflict but to engage in conflict in nondestructive ways.* They view conflict as a natural part of intimate relationships. When they have sexual disagreements, they do not accuse or blame; instead, they seek common ground and are willing to compromise.

- *Less frequent conflict and less time spent in conflict.* Both satisfied and unsatisfied couples, however, experience conflicts about the same topics, especially about communication, sex, and personality characteristics.

- *The ability to accurately encode (send) verbal and nonverbal messages and accurately decode (understand) such messages from their spouses.* This is especially important for men. In satisfied couples, for example, if a man wants his partner to initiate sex more often, he can say, "I'd like you to initiate sex more often," and his partner will understand the message correctly. In dissatisfied couples, the man may stop initiating sex, hoping his partner will be forced to initiate more often in order to have sex. Or he may ask his partner to initiate sex more often, but his partner may mistakenly interpret it as a personal attack.

Many of these communication patterns appear to hold true for gay and lesbian relationships as well.

- *Husbands more than wives tend to give neutral messages.* An example would be, "It doesn't matter to me." Wives give more positive or negative messages. Because women tend to smile or laugh when they send messages, however, they send fewer clearly neutral messages. The neutral responses of husbands make it more difficult for wives to decode what their partners are really trying to say. Imagine a wife responding to her husband's sexual overture by saying, "Let's do it later, when I'm not so tired." Her husband gives a neutral response: "Whatever." But the response is unclear: Does the husband really not care, or is he pretending he doesn't to avoid possible conflict?

- *Wives tend to set the emotional tone of an argument.* Although communication differences in arguments between husbands and wives are usually small, wives escalate conflict with negative verbal and nonverbal messages ("Don't give me that!") or deescalate arguments by setting an atmosphere of agreement ("I understand your feelings"). Husbands' inputs are less important in setting the climate for resolving or escalating conflicts. Wives tend to use emotional appeals and threats more than husbands, who tend to reason, seek conciliation, and try to postpone or end an argument.

DEVELOPING COMMUNICATION SKILLS

Studies suggest that poor communication skills precede the outset of marital problems (Markman, 1981; Markman et al., 1987). The material that follows will help you understand and develop your skills in communicating about sexual matters.

Developing Self-Awareness

Before we can communicate with others, we must first know how we feel ourselves. Yet we often place obstacles in the way. First, we suppress "unacceptable" feelings, especially anger, hurt, frustration, and jealousy. After a while, we don't even consciously experience them. Second, we deny our feelings. If we are feeling hurt and our partner looks at our pained expression and asks us what we're feeling, we may reply, "Nothing." We may feel nothing because we have anesthetized our feelings. Third, we displace our feelings. Instead of recognizing that we are jealous, we may accuse our partner of being jealous; instead of feeling hurt, we may say our partner is hurt.

Becoming aware of ourselves requires us to become aware of our feelings. Perhaps the first step toward this self-awareness is realizing that feelings are simply emotional states—they are neither good nor bad in themselves. As feelings, however, they need to be felt, whether they are warm or cold, pleasurable or painful. They do not necessarily need to be acted out or expressed. We do not need to censor our feelings or deny them. It is the acting out that holds the potential for problems or hurt.

Feelings are valuable guides for action. If we feel irritated at our partner, the irritation is a signal that something is wrong, and we can work toward change. But if we suppress or deny our feeling, perhaps because we are fearful of conflict, we do not have the impetus for change. The cause remains, and the irritation increases until it is blown out of proportion; a minor annoyance becomes a major source of anger.

Obstacles to Sexual Discussions

The process of articulating our feelings about sex can be very difficult. There are several reasons for this. First, we rarely have models for talking about sex. As children and adolescents, we probably never spoke with our parents about sex. If we talked about sex in their presence, they probably discouraged it or felt uncomfortable. We learned that sex is not an appropriate subject of conversation in "polite" company.

Second, talking about sexual matters defines us as being interested in sex, and interest in sex is often identified with being sexually obsessive, immoral, prurient, or "bad." If the sexual topic is tabooed, we risk further danger of being labeled "bad."

Third, we may feel that talking about sex will threaten our relationship. We don't talk about tabooed sexual feelings, fantasies, or desires because we fear our partner may be repelled or disgusted. We also are reluctant to talk about sexual difficulties or problems because of their inherent riskiness.

Sexual vocabulary can also be a problem. We shift our sexual vocabulary depending on the context or to whom we are talking. Some words are uncomfortable or inappropriate in different contexts. To describe sexuality, we have medical terms that objectify and deeroticize it: "penis," "vulva," "vagina," "sexual intercourse." These are the words we use in formal situations, as in medical or academic settings or when talking with our parents or our children; they are the acceptable terms for the printed page and for talk shows.

Slang words retain their sexual connotations: "cock," "cunt," "screw." These are the "dirty" words of our language. They are most often used in informal settings, among friends or peers. Gay men and lesbians have developed their own colloquial or slang terms.

Colloquial and slang words have powerful connotations. To modify their power, we have euphemisms, terms such as "making love" and "sleeping together," whose emotional impact stands somewhere between medical and slang terms. And, finally, we have our own private vocabulary of "pet names" for sexual body parts, such as "Miss Muff" or "Wilbur," that may develop within a relationship and be shared only with our partner (Cornog, 1986).

Because a man and a woman tend to use a different sexual vocabulary, it can be difficult for them to communicate with each other about sexual matters. A woman may be offended by the vocabulary her boyfriend uses among his friends; the man may think his girlfriend is unduly reticent because she uses euphemisms to describe sexuality. A couple must often negotiate the language they will use in order not to offend each other. Sometimes this problem will be resolved into open, acceptable communication; at other times, it may result in silence.

The Keys to Good Communication

The three principal keys to good communication are self-disclosure, trust, and feedback. Self-disclosure creates the environment for mutual understanding (Derlega, Metts, Petronio, & Margulis, 1993). Most people know us only through the conventional roles we play as female/male, wife/husband, parent/child. These roles, however, do not necessarily reflect our deepest selves. If we act as if we are nothing more than our roles, we may reach a point at which we no longer know who we are.

Through the process of self-disclosure we not only reveal ourselves to others, we also discover who we are. We discover the depths of feeling we have hidden, repressed, or ignored. We nurture forgotten aspects of ourselves by bringing them to the surface. Moreover, self-disclosure is reciprocal. In the process of our sharing, others share themselves with us. Men are less likely than women, however, to disclose intimate aspects of themselves. Because they have been taught to be strong, they are more reluctant to express tenderness or feelings of vulnerability. Women find it easier to disclose their feelings because they have been taught from childhood to express themselves (Notarius & Johnson, 1982). These differences can drive wedges between men and women. Even when people live together or are married, they feel lonely because there is no contact. And the worst kind of loneliness is feeling alone when we are with someone with whom we want to feel close.

Trust is the belief in the reliability and integrity of a person. It is the primary characteristic we associate with love. When a person says, "Trust me," he or she is asking for something that does not easily occur. For trust to develop, three conditions must exist. First, a relationship has to exist with the likelihood of continuing. Second, we must be able to predict how a person is likely to behave. If we are married or in a committed relationship, we trust that our partner will not do something that will hurt us, such as have an affair. Third, the other person must also have acceptable options available to him or her. If we were marooned on a desert island alone with our partner, he or she would have no choice but to be sexually monogamous. But if a third person, sexually attractive to our partner, swam ashore a year later, our partner would have an alternative. Our partner would then have a choice of being sexually exclusive or nonexclusive; his or her behavior would then be evidence of trustworthiness—or the lack of it.

Trust is critical in close relationships for two reasons. First, self-disclosure requires trust because it makes you vulnerable. A person will not self-disclose if he or she believes the information may be misused, by mocking or revealing a secret, for example. Second, the degree to which you trust a person influences the way you are likely to interpret ambiguous or unexpected messages from him or her. If your partner says he or she wants to study alone tonight, you are likely to take the statement at face value if you have a high level of trust. But if you have a low level of trust, you may believe he or she is going to be meeting someone else.

Feedback is the third key to good communication. Self-disclosure is reciprocal. If we self-disclose, we expect our partner to self-disclose as well. As we self-disclose, we build trust; as we withhold self-disclosure, we erode trust. To withhold ourselves is to imply that we don't trust the other person, and if we don't, he or she will not trust us.

Thus, **feedback**—the ongoing process in which participants and their messages create a given result and are subsequently modified by that result—is a critical element in communication. If my partner self-discloses to me, my response to that self-disclosure is my feedback. My partner's response is feedback to my feedback. It is a continuous process. The most important form of feedback for improving relationships is *constructive* feedback. Constructive feedback focuses on self-disclosing information that will help your partner understand the consequences of his or her actions on you and on the relationship. For example, if your partner discloses his or her doubts about the relationship, you can respond in a number of ways. Among these are remaining silent, venting anger, expressing indifference, or giving constructive feedback. Of these responses, constructive feedback is the most likely to encourage positive change.

trust Belief in the reliability and integrity of another person, process, thing, or institution.

feedback The ongoing process in which participants and their messages create a given result and are subsequently modified by that result.

CONFLICT AND INTIMACY

conflict   A communication
process in which people perceive
incompatible goals and interference from others in achieving
those goals.

Conflict is a special type of communication. **Conflict** is the communication process in which people perceive interference from others in achieving their goals.

We expect love to unify us, but sometimes it doesn't. Two people do not become one when they love each other, although at first they may have this feeling. Their love may not be an illusion, but their sense of ultimate oneness is. In reality, we retain our individual identities, needs, wants, and pasts—even while loving one another. It is a paradox that the more inti-mate two people become, the more likely they may be to experience con-flict. But it is not conflict itself that is dangerous to intimate relationships; it is the manner in which the conflict is handled. The presence of conflict does not necessarily indicate that love is going or has gone. It may mean that love is *growing*.

Conflict in relationships is expressed differently by different ethnic groups. Non-Latino whites tend to seek either dominance, which is con-frontational and controlling, or integration, which is solution-oriented. They seem to believe that conflict is more natural and expected in a rela-tionship, perhaps because of the high value placed on individualism. Both African Americans and Mexican Americans view conflict less positively; they believe that conflict has both short-term and long-term negative effects. A comparison between whites and African Americans found that whites tend to be more solution-oriented than blacks, who tend to be more controlling. In interpersonal relationships, both groups tend to identify con-flict in terms of issues and goals. By contrast, Mexican Americans view con-flict more in relationship terms; conflict occurs when a relationship is out of balance or harmony (Collier, 1991).

These differing views of conflicts and conflict resolution affect each group's willingness to deal with sexual conflicts. Understanding these dif-ferences will help in resolving sexual problems and issues.

Fighting About Sex

Fighting and sex can be intertwined in several different ways. A couple may have a disagreement about sex that leads to a fight. For example, if one per-son wants to have sexual intercourse and the other does not, they may fight.

Sex can also be used as a scapegoat for nonsexual problems. If man is angry because his wife has called him a lousy provider, he may take it out on her sexually by calling her a lousy lover. They fight about their love-making rather than about the real issue, his provider role.

Finally, a fight can be a cover-up. If a man feels sexually inadequate and does not want to have sex as often as his partner, he may pick a fight and make his partner so angry that the last thing she would want to do is to be sexual with him.

It's hard to tell during a fight if there are deeper causes than the one about which a couple is currently fighting. If you repeatedly fight about sex-ual issues without getting anywhere, the ostensible cause may not be the real one. If fighting does not clear the air and make intimacy possible again, you should look for other reasons for the fights. It may be useful to talk with your partner about why the fights do not seem to accomplish anything.

Conflict is natural in intimate relationships because each person has her or his own unique identity, values, needs, and history.

Step back and look at the circumstances of the fight, what patterns occur, and how each of you feels before, during, and after a fight.

Sex and Power

In power struggles, sexuality can be used as a weapon, but this is generally a destructive tactic (Szinovacz, 1987). A classic strategy for the weaker person in a relationship is to withhold something that the more powerful one wants. In male-female struggles, this is often sex. By withholding sex, a woman gains a certain degree of power (Kaplan, 1979). Men also use sex in its most violent form: They use rape (including date rape and marital rape) to overpower and subordinate women (see Chapter 17).

In long-term gay male relationships, refusing sex can take on symbolic meaning. Refusing sex is sometimes associated with power struggles occurring as a result of having two sexual initiators (Blumstein & Schwartz, 1983). Because initiating sex is associated with power and dominance, two men being sexually assertive can become a form of competition. The man who feels himself less powerful can try to reassert his power by refusing his partner's sexual advances. In many lesbian relationships, power issues are often disguised because of each partner's commitment to equality. In these

GUIDELINES FOR GIVING EFFECTIVE FEEDBACK

Giving constructive, effective feedback is an important skill in any intimate relationship. The following guidelines (developed by David Johnston for the Minnesota Peer Program) will help you engage in constructive dialogue and feedback with your partner:

- *Focus on "I" statements.* An "I" statement is a statement about *your* feelings: "I feel unloved." By contrast, "You" statements tell another person how *he* or *she* is, feels, or thinks: "You don't love me." "You" statements are often blaming or accusatory. Because "I" messages don't carry blame, the recipient is less likely to be defensive or resentful.

- *Focus on behavior rather than on the person.* If you focus on a person's behavior rather than on the person, you are more likely to secure change, because a person can change behaviors, but not himself or herself. If you want your partner to stimulate your clitoris during intercourse, say, "I'd like you to touch my clitoris while we're making love because it would help me have an orgasm." This statement focuses on behavior that can be changed. If you say, "You're not a particularly hot lover," you are attacking the person, and he is likely to respond defensively: "Talk about crummy lovers, how come you need my help to have an orgasm? What's wrong with you?"

- *Focus feedback on observations rather than on inferences or judgments.* Focus your feedback on what you actually observe rather than what you think the behavior means. "I don't receive enough stimulation during intercourse to have an orgasm" is an observation. "You don't really care about how I feel because you never try to help me have an orgasm" is an inference that our partner's sexual interactions indicate a lack of regard. The inference moves the discussion from sexual stimulation to the partner's caring.

- *Focus feedback on observations based on a more-or-less continuum.* Behaviors fall on a continuum. Your partner doesn't *always* do or not do a particular thing. When you say your partner does something sometimes, or even most of the time, you are *measuring* behavior. "The last three times you wanted to make love I didn't want to because of the way you smelled" is a measuring statement; its accuracy can be tested. But if you say your partner *always* (or *never*) does something, you are probably distorting reality. "You *always* smell when you come to bed" or "You *never* take a shower before sex" are probably exaggerations that may provoke hostile responses. "What do you mean? I showered last month. You got some kind of hang-up?"

- *Focus feedback on sharing ideas or offering alternatives rather than giving advice.* No one likes being told what to do. Unsolicited advice often produces anger or resentment, because advice implies that you know more about what a person needs to do than he or she does. Advice implies a lack of respect. But by sharing ideas and offering alternatives, you give the other person the freedom to decide based on his or her own perceptions and goals. "What you need to do is pay attention to some of my needs" is advice. "I wish I could be more orgasmic in intercourse. Let's try some other things. If I had more clitoral stimulation, like your rub-

---

cases, power struggles are often indirect and obscure (Burch, 1987). Sexual rejection or lack of interest may hide issues of power.

The problem with power imbalances or the blatant use of power is the negative effect on intimacy. As Ronald Sampson (1966) observed in his study of the psychology of power, "to the extent that power is the prevailbing my clitoris when we are making love . . . something like that would be great. . . . Or I could stimulate myself. What do you think?" Such responses offer alternatives.

- *Focus feedback according to its value for the recipient.* If your partner says something that upsets you, your initial response may be to lash back. A cathartic response may make you feel better for the time being, but it may not be useful for your partner. For example, your partner says that he or she has been faking orgasms. You can respond with anger or accusations, or you can express concern and try to find out why he or she felt it was necessary.

- *Focus feedback on the amount the recipient can process.* Don't overload your partner with your response. Your partner's disclosure may touch deep, pent-up feelings in you, but he or she may not be able to comprehend all that you say. If you respond to your partner's revelation of doubts about your relationship with a listing of all the doubts you have *ever* experienced about it, you may overwhelm your partner.

- *Focus feedback at the appropriate time and place.* When you discuss anything of importance, choose an appropriate time and place so that nothing will distract you. Choose a time when you are not likely to be interrupted. Turn the television off, and put the answering machine on. Also, choose a time that is relatively stress-free. Talking about something of great personal importance just before an exam or a business meeting is likely to sabotage any attempt at communication. Finally, choose a place that will provide privacy; don't start an important conversation if you are worried about people overhearing or interrupting you. A crowded dormitory lounge during "Ren and Stimpy," a kitchen filled with kids, a football stadium during a big game, or a car full of people on the way to the beach are inappropriate places.

Building these behaviors into your communication patterns will help you nurture your relationships in both the short and the long term. Research has shown that happily married couples use conflict resolution strategies that incorporate constructive feedback. In one study, communication behaviors of happily married couples displayed the following traits (Ting-Toomey, 1983):

- *Summarizing.* Each person summarized what the other said. "Let me see if I can repeat the different points you were making."

- *Paraphrasing.* Each put what the other said into his or her own words. "What you are saying is that you feel badly when I don't acknowledge your feelings."

- *Validation.* Each affirmed the other's feelings. "I can understand how you feel."

- *Clarification.* Each asked for further information to make sure that he or she understood what the other was saying. "Can you explain what you mean a little bit more to make sure that I understand you?"

ing force in a relationship—whether between husband and wife or parent and child, between friends or between colleagues—to that extent love is diminished." If partners are not equal, self-disclosure may be inhibited, especially if the powerful person believes his or her power will be lessened by sharing feelings (Glazer-Malbin, 1975). Genuine intimacy appears to require equality in power relationships. Decision making in the happiest marriages seems to be based not on coercion or "tit for tat" but on caring, mutuality, and respect for the other person. Women who feel vulnerable to their mates may withhold feelings or pretend to feel what they do not. Unequal power in marriage may encourage power politics, as each partner struggles to keep or gain power.

It is not easy to change unequal power relationships after they become embedded in the overall structure of a relationship, yet they can be changed. Talking, trying to understand, and negotiating are the best approaches. Still, in attempting changes, a person may risk estrangement or the breakup of a relationship. He or she must weigh the possible gains against the possible losses in deciding whether change is worth the risk.

Strategies for Resolving Conflicts

There are several ways to end conflicts. You can give in, but unless you believe that the conflict ended fairly, you are likely to feel resentful. You can try to impose your will through the use of power, force, or the threat of force. But using power to end conflict leaves your partner with the bitter taste of injustice. Or you can end the conflict through negotiation. In negotiations, both partners sit down and work out their differences until they can come to a mutually acceptable agreement.

Sometimes, even if we sincerely commit ourselves to working out our problems, it is difficult to see our own role in sustaining a pattern of interaction. If a couple is unable to resolve their conflicts, they should consider entering relationship counseling. A therapist or other professional can often help identify underlying problems, as well as help a couple develop negotiating skills.

Conflicts can be solved through negotiation in three major ways: agreement as a gift, bargaining, and coexistence. If you and your partner disagree on an issue, you can freely agree with your partner as a gift. If a woman wants her partner to stimulate her clitoris, and he doesn't want to because he feels it reflects badly on him, he can agree to try it because he cares about his partner. Similarly, a woman who does not want to try oral sex can try as a gift of caring. (Neither the man nor the woman, however, needs to continue if the activity continues to be objectionable.)

Agreement as a gift is different from giving in. When you give in, you do something you don't want to do. But when you agree without coercion or threats, the agreement is a gift of love. As in all exchanges of gifts, there will be reciprocation. Your partner will be more likely to give you a gift of agreement in return.

Bargaining means making compromises. But bargaining in relationships is different from bargaining in the marketplace or in politics. In relationships, you don't want to get the best deal for yourself, but the most equitable deal for both you *and* your partner. At all points during the bargaining process, you need to keep in mind what is best for the relationship, as well as for yourself, and trust your partner to do the same. In a relationship, both partners need to win. The purpose of conflict resolution in a relationship is to solidify the relationship, not to make one partner the winner and the other the loser. Achieving your end by exercising coercive power or withholding love, affection, or sex is a destructive form of bargaining. If you get what you want, how will that affect your partner and the relationship? Will your partner feel you're being unfair and become resentful? A solution has to be fair to both of you, or it won't enhance the relationship.

Sometimes differences can't be resolved, but they can be lived with. If a relationship is sound, differences can be absorbed without undermining the basic ties. All too often we regard differences as threatening rather than as the unique expression of two personalities. If one person likes to masturbate, the partner can accept it as an expression of his or her unique sexuality.

If you can't talk about what you like and what you want, there is a good chance you won't get either one. Communication is the basis for good sex and good relationships. Communication and intimacy are reciprocal: Communication creates intimacy, and intimacy, in turn, creates good communication.

If we fail to communicate, we are likely to turn our relationships into empty facades. Each person acts according to a role rather than revealing his or her deepest self. But communication is learned behavior. If we have learned *not* to communicate, we can learn *how* to communicate. Communication allows us to expand ourselves and to maintain our relationships.

SUMMARY

The Nature of Communication

• The ability to communicate is important in developing and maintaining ongoing relationships. Couples satisfied with their sexual communication tend to be satisfied about their relationships as a whole.

• Communication is a transactional process by which we convey symbols, such as words, gestures, and movements, to establish human contact, exchange information, and reinforce or change the attitudes and behaviors of ourselves and others.

• Communication takes place within cultural, social, and psychological contexts. The cultural context refers to the language, values, beliefs, and customs in which communication takes place. Ethnic groups communicate about sex differently, depending on their language patterns and values. The social context refers to the roles we play in society that influence our communication. The most important roles affecting sexuality are those relating to gender and sexual orientation. The psychological context refers to our personality characteristics, such as having positive or negative feelings about sex.

• Communication includes both verbal and nonverbal communication. The ability to correctly interpret nonverbal messages is important in successful relationships.

Proximity, eye contact, and touching are especially important forms of nonverbal communication.

Sexual Communication

• In initial encounters, physical appearance is especially important. Because of the halo effect, we infer positive qualities about people based on their appearance. Women typically send nonverbal cues to men indicating interest; men then begin a conversation with an "opening line."

• The "first move" marks the transition to physical intimacy; the male generally initiates. In initiating the first sexual interaction, communication is generally nonverbal, ambiguous, and indirect. Sexual disinterest is usually communicated nonverbally. With sexual involvement, the couple must communicate verbally about contraception, STD prevention, and sexual likes and dislikes.

• Unless there are definite clues as to orientation, gay men and lesbians try to determine through nonverbal cues whether others are appropriate partners. Because of male gender roles, gay men initiate sex earlier than heterosexuals; for parallel reasons, lesbians initiate sex later.

• In established relationships, many women feel more comfortable in initiating sexual interactions. Sexual initiations are more likely to be accepted in established relationships; sexual disinterest is communicated verbally. Women do not restrict sexual activities any more than men.

• Research indicates that happily married couples disclose private thoughts and feelings to partners, express equal levels of affective disclosure, spend more time together talking or expressing feelings in positive ways, are willing to engage in conflict in nondestructive ways, have less frequent conflict and spend less time in conflict, and accurately encode and decode messages.

• There are gender differences in marital communication. Wives send clearer messages; husbands tend to give neutral messages, whereas wives tend to give more positive or negative messages; and wives tend to set the emotional tone and escalate arguments more than husbands.

Developing Communication Skills

• Achieving self-awareness is an important first step in developing communication skills. Obstacles to talking about sex include a lack of role models, fear of being identified as "bad," cultural and personal taboos on unacceptable sexual subjects, and a lack of adequate vocabulary. Sexual vocabulary shifts according to context.

• The keys to effective communication are self-disclosure, trust, and feedback. Self-disclosure is the revelation of intimate information about ourselves. Trust is the belief in the reliability and integrity of another person. Feedback is a constructive response to another's self-disclosure.

Conflict and Intimacy

• Conflict is natural in intimate relationships. Conflicts about sex can be specific disagreements about sex, arguments that are ostensibly about sex but that are really about nonsexual issues, or disagreements about the wrong sexual issue.

• Conflict resolution may be achieved through negotiation in three ways: agreement as a freely given gift, bargaining, or coexistence. Counseling is often helpful in improving a couple's conflict resolution skills.

SUGGESTED READINGS

Derlega, Valerian, Sandra Metts, Sandra Petronio, and Steven Margulis. *Self-Disclosure*. Newbury Park, CA: Sage Publications, 1993. How self-disclosure affects intimate relationships in terms of closeness, privacy, feelings of vulnerability, and love.

Hecht, Michelle, Mary Jane Collier, and Sidney Ribeau. *African American Communication*. Newbury Park, CA: Sage Publications, 1993. A synthesis of research on African American communication and culture, including effective and ineffective communication patterns.

Satir, Virginia. *The New Peoplemaking*, rev. ed. Palo Alto, CA: Science and Behavior Books, 1988. One of the most influential (and easy to read) books of the last 25 years on communication and family relationships.

Tannen, Deborah. *You Just Don't Understand: Women and Men in Conversation*. New York: William Morrow, 1990. A best-selling, intelligent, and lively discussion of how women use communication to achieve intimacy and men use communication to achieve independence.

Ting-Toomey, Stella, and Felipe Korzenny, eds. *Cross-Cultural Interpersonal Communication*. Newbury Park, CA: Sage Publications, 1991. A ground-breaking collection of scholarly essays on communication and relationships among different ethnic and cultural groups, including African American, Latino, Korean, and Chinese ethnic groups and cultures.

Chapter Nine

SEXUAL EXPRESSION

PREVIEW: SELF-QUIZ

1. Americans believe that attractive people are more sexually permissive and responsive than unattractive people. True or false?

2. Women and gay men share many of the same ideas about ideal male body types. True or false?

3. Whites, African Americans, Latinos, and Asian Americans hold more or less the same attitudes toward oral-genital sex. True or false?

4. Fantasies about others during sexual intercourse generally indicate a lack of sexual interest in one's partner. True or false?

5. Sexual behaviors may be defined as heterosexual, gay, or lesbian. True or false?

6. Rape fantasies do not indicate an underlying desire to be raped. True or false?

7. Oral-genital sex is more widely practiced by whites than by African Americans. True or false?

8. About the same percentage of males and females masturbate. True or false?

9. Nineteenth-century physicians believed that masturbation and sexual intercourse could both lead to death. True or false?

10. Both men and women rank buttocks as the body's most sexually attractive feature. True or false?

ANSWERS 1. T, 2. T, 3. F, 4. F, 5. F, 6. T, 7. T, 8. F, 9. T, 10. T

Chapter Outline

Sexual expression is a complex process through which we reveal our sexual selves. Sexual expression involves more than simply sexual behaviors. It involves our feelings as well. "Behavior can never be unemotional," one scholar observed (Blechman, 1990). As human beings, we do not separate feelings from behavior, including sexual behavior. Our sexual behaviors are rich with emotions, ranging from love to anxiety, from desire to antipathy.

To fully understand our sexuality, we need to examine our sexual behaviors *and* the emotions we experience along with them. If we studied sexual activities apart from our emotions, we would distort the human meaning of sexuality. It would make them appear mechanistic, nothing more than genitals rubbing against each other.

In this chapter, we first discuss sexual attraction, for it motivates our sexual behaviors. Next, we turn to sexual scripts that give form to our sexual drives. Then we examine the most common sexual behaviors, both autoerotic behaviors, such as fantasies and masturbation, and interpersonal behaviors, such as oral-genital sex, sexual intercourse, and anal eroticism.

SEXUAL ATTRACTION

The concept that beauty is in the eye of the beholder is quite true when it comes to sexual attractiveness. Culture, gender, and ethnicity all influence what is considered attractive. Researchers have been particularly interested in this concept and how it affects sexual behavior.

Sexual Attractiveness

In a landmark cross-cultural study of sexuality, Cleland Ford and Frank Beach (1972) demonstrated that there is no universal standard of sexual attractiveness. In fact, the study found that there was considerable variation from culture to culture as to what parts of the body were considered erotic. In some cultures, the eyes were the key to sexual attraction; in others, height and weight; and in still others, the size and shape of the genitals. In our culture, breasts are considered erotic; in others, they are not.

Cultures that agree on which body parts are erotic may still disagree on what constitutes attractiveness. In terms of female beauty, American culture considers the slim body attractive. But worldwide, Americans are in the minority, for the type of female body most desired cross-culturally is plump. Similarly, we prefer slim hips, but the majority of cultures in Ford and Beach's study found wide hips most attractive. In our culture, large breasts are ideal, but others prefer small breasts, and still others, long and pendulous breasts. In the last decade, well-defined pectoral and arm muscles have become part of the ideal male body.

What is it that men and women find attractive in each other? One survey found that women regarded men's most attractive features as small and sexy buttocks (39%), slimness (15%), flat stomach (13%), and expressive eyes (11%) (cited in Gagnon, 1977). Interestingly, men misperceived what women found attractive about them. Men believed that women thought the most sexually attractive parts of men's bodies were, in descending order, muscular chest and shoulders (21%), muscular arms (18%), and large penis (15% [only 2% of the women indicated that a large penis was important]).

An informal classroom survey found that men were most interested in women's buttocks (25%), faces (20%), and breasts (17%) (cited in Luria et al., 1987). Women, however, misperceived men's interests. Forty-nine percent felt that men were most interested in breasts, and only 7% felt that men were interested in faces. Only the women's perception of male interest in buttocks—17%—approximated actual male interest.

Another study found that gay men and heterosexual women shared many of the same perceptions about what made men sexually attractive (Bell, 1974). Thirty-seven percent of gay men found male buttocks attractive. Where gay men and heterosexual women differed most markedly was that 42% of the gay men found a male's naked chest attractive, and 12% thought a large penis was important.

For bisexual men and women, the question of attractiveness is more complex. What is it that attracts bisexuals to certain people? Is a bisexual man, for example, attracted to women in the same manner as heterosexuals and to men in the same way as gay men? There is some evidence that gender is not as important as other physical and personality characteristics (Kaplan

& Rogers, 1984). Bisexuals may be attracted to men and women, for example, with similar physical characteristics, such as being slight or heavy-set, dark- or light-skinned. Personality characteristics may also be similar, such as being assertive or passive, traditionally masculine or feminine, or androgynous.

The Halo Effect Revisited   As discussed in Chapter 8, attractive people are surrounded by a halo effect. The halo effect extends to assumptions about sexuality. A study of men from two universities found that among the various traits attributed to attractive women, the trait most affected by their appearance was their sexual behavior (Tanke, 1982). Attractive women were viewed as more sexually warm, exciting, and permissive than unattractive ones.

Although most studies on sexuality and attractiveness relate to beliefs about attractive people, an intriguing study of 100 college women found some evidence indicating a relationship between attractiveness and actual sexual behavior (Stelzer, Desmond, & Price, 1987). Attractive women were significantly more likely to engage in sexual intercourse and oral sex than the other women. This finding suggests that the halo effect may create a self-fulfilling expectation about sexual behavior. Because attractive women are *expected* to be more sexually active, they *become* more sexually active.

Another study found that attractive women are more likely to be on top during sexual intercourse and to engage in cunnilingus and fellatio (Blumstein & Schwartz, 1983). The researchers speculate that attractiveness bestows sexual power on women. Being attractive increases women's self-esteem and permits them to express themselves more freely.

How Important Is Attractiveness? Although attractiveness is important, it's good to remember that looks aren't everything. Looks are most important to certain types or groups of people and in certain situations or locations, such as classes, parties, and bars, where people do not interact extensively with each other daily. Looks are less important to those in ongoing relationships and to adults over 30 or so (Hatfield & Sprecher, 1986). Attractiveness remains important, however, in established relationships as well. Blumstein and Schwartz (1983) found that the happiest people in cohabiting and married relationships thought of their partners as attractive. People who found their partners attractive had the best sex lives. Another study found that as husbands and wives aged, changes in the wife's physical appearance seemed to have a greater impact on the quality of marital sexuality than changes in the husband's appearance (Margolin & White, 1987). These changes led to greater sexual disinterest, a decline in sexual satisfaction, and, to a lesser extent, unfaithfulness, especially on the part of the husband.

Sexual Desire: Erotophilia and Erotophobia

Of all the sexual emotions we experience, desire may be the most important, simply because it motivates us to be sexual. Desire is affected by erotophilia and erotophobia. **Erotophilia** is a positive emotional response to sex, and **erotophobia** is a negative emotional response to sex. In recent years, researchers have hypothesized that the place where someone falls on the erotophilic/erotophobic continuum strongly influences his or her overt sexual behavior (Fisher, 1986). In contrast to erotophobic individuals, for example, erotophilic men and women accept and enjoy their sexuality, seek out sexual situations, engage in more autoerotic and interpersonal sexual activities, enjoy talking about sex, and are more likely to obtain and use contraception. Furthermore, erotophilic people are more likely to have positive sexual attitudes, to engage in more involved sexual fantasies, and to have seen more erotica than erotophobic people.

A person's emotional response to sex is also linked to how he or she evaluates other aspects of sex. Erotophilic individuals, for example, tend to evaluate sexually explicit material more positively. In fact, one study found that erotophilics identified explicit movies as erotic, while erotophobics described the same films as pornographic (Byrne, Fisher, Lambreth, & Mitchell, 1974).

Researchers have found intriguing evidence of a relationship between erotophilia/erotophobia and personality traits. Erotophobic individuals tend to be more authoritarian, believing in rules and order. They experience higher levels of guilt about sexual matters, feeling guilty about masturbation and premarital sex. They are more rigid in their gender roles, believing that men and women are basically different, especially about sexual matters (Fisher, Byrne, White, & Kelley, 1988).

But erotophilic and erotophobic traits are not fixed. Positive experiences can alter erotophobic responses over time. In fact, some therapy programs

erotophilia A positive emotional response to sexuality.

erotophobia A negative emotional response to sexuality.

You and Your Sexual Well-Being

SEXUAL DESIRE: WHEN APPETITES DIFFER

How much sexual desire is "normal," and what can couples do when one partner has more—or less—desire than the other?

Although there is a great deal of variability in sexual desire, it is generally held that "healthy" individuals experience desire regularly and take advantage of appropriate opportunities for sexual expression when they arise. Individuals who are persistently uninterested in sexual expression and do not report sexual fantasies are said to be experiencing hypoactive sexual desire disorder (American Psychiatric Association, 1994). For such individuals, therapy may be recommended.

Of course, terms like "regularly," "appropriate," and "persistent" are very subjective. The DSM-IV uses these terms to avoid defining low desire in terms of frequency of sexual activity, because some people have sex out of feelings of obligation or coercion rather than interest or desire (Wincze & Carey, 1991). Instead, the manual defines desire in terms of the individual's feelings and encourages clinical evaluation when a problem is experienced. (Note that sexual abstinence—deliberately refraining from sexual expression—is not considered a disorder and should not be labeled as such.)

Regardless of measurements and clinical judgments, it is apparent to couples when one individual is more inter-ested in sex than the other. Sometimes differences stem from such issues as timing, cleanliness, and appropriate stimulation techniques; issues like these can often be resolved through honest discussion, feedback, and practice. Elements contributing to a successful outcome in any discussion of sex include awareness, taking enough time to talk about it, using positive communication, and having a sense of humor.

Often, problems arise because individuals' expectations are based on fantasy, media influences, or lack of infor-mation. A woman may, for instance, ask herself why she is unable to reach orgasm during intercourse, or a man may wonder why his erection fails even though he wants to have intercourse. In the case of the woman, is she aware of the effects of clitoral stimulation? Has she practiced stimulation techniques on herself and effectively demonstrated them to her partner? Does she position herself during intercourse in such a way as to maximize the opportunities for stimulation? If she knows that most women require prolonged and effective amounts of stimulation up to and through orgasm, she may be able to enjoy intercourse more fully and may then feel more desire.

In the case of the man, does he know that lack of desire is a fairly common and often temporary problem? Does he know what kinds and amounts of stimulation are most effective for him? Does he feel comfortable using fantasy? Has he told his partner what he likes? Has he tried to discover noncoital means of pleasure with his partner? Once again, open and honest communication is the key to successful sexual interactions.

---

work on the assumption that consistent positive feelings, such as love, affir-mation, caring, touching, and communication, can do much to diminish the fear of sex. Positive sexual experiences can help dissolve much of the anxiety that underlies erotophobia.

SEXUAL SCRIPTS

As you recall from Chapter 5, gender roles have an immense impact on how we behave sexually, for sexual behavior and feelings depend more on learning than on biological drives. Our sexual drives can be molded into

When the situation is partner-specific—that is, each person masturbates successfully and/or desires or fantasizes about others but does not desire or respond to a given partner—the problem is obviously more complex and difficult to solve. The couple may be bored with each other or with the way they make love, or they may fear pregnancy or STDs. Other factors that interfere with desire and arousal are anger, depression, an imbalance of power between the partners, and an inability to associate love with sexual desire. Some men (and perhaps women) experience what is referred to as the "madonna-whore syndrome." They report low sexual desire with their regular partners (usually their wives) but are aroused and can function with women they consider "slutty." Trying a few of the techniques listed below may help with this problem. Some prescription drugs have been shown to reduce sexual desire and inhibit orgasm. When this is the case, individuals and couples may require the help of a physician or therapist to overcome their differences.

If you and your partner are experiencing problems stemming from differences in desire, there are some simple techniques you can use to increase interest and provide novelty in the bedroom. To set the stage, find a place where you are assured of no interruptions or distractions. Allow enough time to discover each other again. Approach lovemaking with an open mind and a sense of humor and fun. And try some of these techniques:

- Find a different location to make love—the bathroom or shower; on the floor or in the pool; or in a hotel room.
- Undress each other slowly, taking time to touch and enjoy the removal of each article of clothing.
- Use erotic films that appeal to each of you. If you don't have the same taste, alternate videos from time to time.
- Prolong pleasuring and foreplay by using body oils and lotions; give each other erotic massages.
- Bathe together, taking the time to wash and enjoy each other.
- If you are comfortable doing so, use "sex toys," such as vibrators or feathers.
- Share sexual fantasies, using graphic language if you are comfortable with it.
- Tell each other what feels good.

Because fluctuations in desire are a normal part of life, as are differences in desire between partners, individuals may choose masturbation as an acceptable and pleasurable outlet for sexual desire. Like all areas of sexual functioning, the important thing to remember when sexual appetites differ, is that open and honest communication paves the way to fulfillment.

almost any form. What is "natural" is what society calls natural; there is very little spontaneous, unlearned behavior (Gagnon & Simon, 1973). Sexual behavior, like all other forms of social behavior (such as courtship, classroom behavior, and sports), relies on scripts.

Scripts are like plans that organize and give direction to our behavior. The sexual scripts we receive strongly influence our sexual activities as men and women in our culture. As William Gagnon (1977) writes:

A script is simpler than the activity we perform. . . . It is like a blueprint or roadmap or recipe, giving directions but not specifying everything that must be done. Regardless of its sketchiness, the script is often more important than the concrete acts. It is our script that we carry from action to action, modified by our concrete acts, but not replaced by them. Scripts do change, as new elements are added and old elements are reworked, but very few people have the desire, energy, or persistence to create highly innovative or novel scripts.

Our sexual scripts have three main components: cultural, intrapersonal, and interpersonal.

- *Cultural component.* The cultural component provides the general pattern that sexual behaviors are expected to take. Our general cultural script, for example, emphasizes heterosexuality, gives primacy to sexual intercourse, discourages masturbation, and so on.

- *Intrapersonal component.* The intrapersonal component deals with the internal and physiological states that lead to, accompany, or identify sexual arousal, such as a pounding heart, erection or vaginal lubrication, and so on.

- *Interpersonal component.* The interpersonal component deals with the shared conventions and signals that enable two people to engage in sexual behaviors, such as body language, words, and erotic touching.

Cultural Scripting

Our culture sets the general contours of our sexual scripts. It tells us which behaviors are acceptable ("moral" or "normal") and which are unacceptable ("immoral" or "abnormal"). Among middle-class white Americans, the norm is a sequence of sexual events consisting of kissing, genital caressing, and sexual intercourse. If large numbers of people did not share these conventions, there would be sexual chaos. Imagine a scenario in which two people from different cultures try to initiate a sexual encounter. The one from our culture follows our culture's sexual sequence, and the other from a different culture follows a sequence beginning with sexual intercourse, moving to genital caressing, and ending with passionate kissing. At least initially, such a couple might experience endless frustration and confusion as one tried to initiate the sexual encounter with kissing and the other with sexual intercourse.

We may believe that everyone shares our own particular script, projecting our experiences onto others and assuming that they share our erotic definitions of objects, gestures, and situations. But often, they initially do not. Our partner may have come from a different socioeconomic group or religious background and may have had far different learning experiences. Each has to learn the other's sexual script and be able to complement and adjust to it. If our scripts are to be integrated, we must make our needs known through words, gestures, or movements. This is the reason many people view their first intercourse as somewhat of a comedy or tragedy—or perhaps a little bit of both.

Intrapersonal Scripting

On the intrapersonal level, sexual scripts enable people to give meaning to their physiological responses. The meaning depends largely on the situation. An erection, for example, does not always mean sexual excitement.

Very little of our sexual life is displayed in public. When we encounter public displays of passion, we often avert our eyes to avoid acknowledging it. What would you do if you were walking past this couple? Would your response be different if they were gay or lesbian?

Young boys sometimes have erections when they are frightened, anxious, or worried. In the morning, men may experience erections that are unaccompanied by arousal. Adolescent girls sometimes experience sexual arousal without knowing what their sensations mean. They report them as funny, weird kinds of feelings; or as anxiety, fear, or an upset stomach. The sensations are not linked to a sexual script until the girl becomes older and physiological states acquire a definite erotic meaning.

The intrapersonal, internal script also determines what physiological events our minds will become aware of. During masturbation or intercourse, for example, an enormous number of physiological events occur simultaneously, but we are aware of only a few of them. These are the events we associate with sexual arousal, such as increasing heartbeat and tensing muscles. Others, such as curling toes, may not filter through to our consciousness.

Finally, internal scripts provide a sequence of body movements by acting as mechanisms that activate biological events and release tension. We learn, for example, that we may create an orgasm by manipulating the penis or clitoris during masturbation.

Interpersonal Scripting

The interpersonal level is the area of shared conventions, which make sexual activities possible. Very little of our public life is sexual. Yet there are signs and gestures—verbal and nonverbal—that define encounters as sexual. We make our sexual motives clear by the way we look at each other, the tone of our voices, the movements of our bodies, and other culturally shared phenomena. A bedroom or a motel room, for example, is a potentially erotic location, while a classroom, office, or factory is not. The movements we use in arousing ourselves or others are erotic activators. Within a culture, there are normative scripts leading to sexual intercourse. People with little experience, especially young adolescents, are often unfamiliar with sexual scripts. What do they do after kissing? Do they embrace? Caress above the waist? Below? Eventually, they learn a comfortable sequence based on cultural inputs and personal and partner preferences. For gay men and lesbians, learning the sexual script is more difficult because it is socially stigmatized. The sexual script is also related to age. Older children and young adolescents often limit their scripts to kissing, holding hands, and embracing, and they feel completely satisfied. Kissing for them may be as exciting as intercourse for more experienced people. When the range of their scripts increases, the earlier stages lose some of their sexual intensity.

AUTOEROTICISM

autoeroticism Sexual self-stimulation or behavior involving only the self; includes masturbation, sexual fantasies, and erotic dreams.

Autoeroticism consists of sexual activities that involve only the self. Autoeroticism is an *intrapersonal* activity rather than an *interpersonal* one. It includes sexual fantasies, erotic dreams, and masturbation. A universal phenomenon in one form or another (Ford & Beach, 1951), autoeroticism is one of our earliest expressions of sexual stirrings. It is also one that traditionally has been condemned in our society. By condemning it, however, our culture sets the stage for the development of deeply negative and inhibitory attitudes toward sexuality.

Sexual Fantasies

"A fantasy is a map of desire, mastery, escape, and obscuration," wrote Nancy Friday (1980), "the navigational path we invent to steer ourselves between the reefs and shoals of anxiety, guilt, and inhibition." Erotic fantasy is probably the most universal of all sexual behaviors. Nearly everyone has experienced such fantasies, but because they touch on feelings or desires considered personally or socially unacceptable, they are not widely discussed.

Occurring spontaneously or as a result of outside stimuli, fantasies are part of the body's regular healthy functioning. A study of 120 men and women found that the average number of sexual fantasies was eight a day

(Schwartz & Masters, 1984). Research indicates that sexual fantasies are related to sexual drives: The higher the sexual drive, the higher the frequency of sexual fantasies (Wilson, 1978). Fantasies help create an equilibrium between our environment and our inner selves, seeking a balance between the two (Wilson, 1978). They usually accompany our masturbatory experiences to enhance them, as well as oral-genital sex, sexual intercourse, and other interpersonal experiences. Our erotic fantasies develop with our experiences, although there are distinct gender differences.

The Function of Sexual Fantasies Sexual fantasies have a number of important functions. First, fantasies help direct and define our erotic goals. They take our generalized sexual drives and give them concrete images and specific content. We fantasize about certain types of men or women, and reinforce our attraction through fantasy involvement. Unfortunately, our fantasy model may be unreasonable or unattainable, which is one of the pitfalls of fantasy; we can imagine perfection, but we can rarely find it in the real world.

Second, sexual fantasies allow us to plan or anticipate situations that may arise. Fantasies provide a form of rehearsal, allowing us to practice in our minds how to act in various situations. Our fantasies of what *might* take place on a date, after a party, or in bed with our partner give us a certain amount of preparation.

Third, erotic fantasies provide escape from a dull or oppressive environment. Routine or repetitive labor often gives rise to fantasies as a way of coping with boredom. Fourth, even if our sexual lives are satisfactory, we may indulge in sexual fantasies to bring novelty and excitement into the relationship. Many people fantasize things they would not actually do in real life. Fantasy offers a safe outlet for sexual curiosity. One researcher (Wilson, 1978) notes:

> We all have a need for adventure, but set limits on how far we permit curiosity to determine our actual behavior. This limit varies according to our personality and stage of development. Imagining an experience is less radical than doing it, so our criterion of what is socially and personally acceptable often falls between the two. The nice thing about fantasy is that it allows us to explore, yet at the same time retain our physical safety and avoid hurting other people.

One study found that fantasies appear to help many married women become sexually aroused and experience orgasm during sexual intercourse (Davidson & Hoffman, 1986).

Fifth, sexual fantasies have an expressive function in somewhat the same manner as dreams do. Our sexual fantasies may offer a clue to our current interests, pleasures, anxieties, fears, or problems. Because fantasies use only a few details from the stream of reality, what we select is significant, expressing feelings that often lie beneath the surface of our consciousness (Sue, 1979). Fantasies of extramarital relationships, for example, may signify deep dissatisfaction with a marriage, whereas fantasies centering around impotence may represent fears about sexuality or a particular relationship.

Fantasies During Intercourse A sizable number of people fantasize during sex. The fantasies are usually a continuation of daydreams or masturbation fantasies, transforming one's partner into a Luke Perry or Janet

Jackson. Various studies report that 60–90% of the respondents fantasize during sex, depending on gender and ethnicity (Knafo & Jaffe, 1984; Price & Miller, 1984; Sue, 1979). In one of these studies, 38% of males and 46% of females fantasized in order to sexually arouse themselves; 30% of males and 22% of females fantasized to increase their partner's sexual attractiveness (Sue, 1979). The only significant difference between men and women in this study was that twice as many men as women fantasized from the beginning of a sexual relationship. Another study found that during sexual intercourse, some women fantasized about forced sex, group sex, and sex with an imaginary lover (Hariton & Singer, 1974). Their feelings of guilt were related to the degree to which they believed their fantasies were deviant or abnormal.

Erotic Dreams

Almost all of the men and two-thirds of the women in Kinsey's studies reported having had overtly sexual dreams (Kinsey et al., 1948, 1953). Sexual images in dreams are frequently very intense. Although people tend to feel responsible for fantasies, which occur when awake, they are usually less troubled by sexual dreams.

Overtly sexual dreams are not necessarily exciting, although dreams that are apparently nonsexual may cause arousal. It is not unusual for individuals to awaken in the middle of the night to find their bodies moving as if they were making love. They may also experience nocturnal orgasm. About 2–3% of a woman's orgasms may be nocturnal, while for men the number may be around 8% of their total orgasms (Kinsey et al., 1948, 1953). About 50% of the men interviewed by Kinsey had more than five nocturnal orgasms a year, but less than 10% of the women experienced them that frequently.

Dreams almost always accompany nocturnal orgasm. The dreamer may awaken, and men usually ejaculate. Although the dream content may not be overtly sexual, it is always accompanied by sensual sensations. Erotic dreams run the gamut of sexual possibilities: heterosexual, homosexual, or autoerotic; incestuous, dominance and submission, bestial, fetishistic. Women seem to feel less guilt or fear about nocturnal orgasms than men do, accepting them more easily as pleasurable experiences.

Masturbation

masturbation Stimulation of the genitals for pleasure.

People **masturbate** by rubbing, caressing, or otherwise stimulating their genitals to give themselves sexual pleasure or to release sexual tension (Figures 9.1 and 9.2). They may masturbate during particular periods or throughout their entire lives. Kinsey (1953) reported that 92% of the men and 58% of the women he interviewed said they had masturbated. Today, there appears to be a slight increase in both incidence and frequency. Nevertheless, gender differences continue to be significant (Atwood & Gagnon, 1987; Leitenberg, Detzer, & Srebnik, 1993).

Attitudes toward masturbation and masturbatory behaviors vary along ethnic lines. Whites are the most accepting of masturbation, for example, while African Americans are less so. The differences can be explained culturally. Because whites tend to begin coital activities later than blacks,

FIGURE 9.1 Masturbation is an important form of sexual behavior in which individuals explore their erotic capacities and bring pleasure to themselves.

FIGURE 9.2 Many people "discover" their sexual potential through masturbation. Sometimes women learn to be orgasmic through masturbation, then carry this knowledge over into their relationships.

whites regard masturbation as an acceptable alternative to sexual intercourse. Black culture, by contrast, accepts sexual activity at an earlier age. In this context, blacks may view masturbation as a sign of personal and sexual inadequacy. As a result, many blacks tend to view sexual intercourse as normal and masturbation as deviant (Cortese, 1989; Kinsey et al., 1948; Wilson, 1986). Recently, however, masturbation is becoming more accepted within the African American community as a legitimate sexual activity (Wilson, 1986).

Latinos, like African Americans, are more conservative than Anglos in their attitudes about masturbation (Cortese, 1989; Padilla & O'Grady, 1987). In Latino culture, masturbation is not considered an acceptable sexual option for either men or women (Guerrero Pavich, 1986). In part, this is because of the cultural emphasis on sexual intercourse and the influence of Catholicism, which regards masturbation as sinful. As with other forms of sexual behavior, however, acceptance becomes more likely as Latinos become more assimilated. A study of Mexican American college students found their attitudes toward masturbation more liberal than the Mexican American community as a whole (Padilla & O'Grady, 1987).

In general, going to college appears to make masturbation more acceptable (Atwood & Gagnon, 1987). Among college women, masturbation becomes increasingly accepted as a healthy sexual activity as they progress in their education; this is especially true if they have studied sexuality (Adams, 1986; Davidson & Darling, 1986). Despite these changes among women, another study of college students found that twice as many men as women had ever masturbated. Furthermore, the men masturbated about three times as often as the women. Researchers point out that their results suggest that "young women in our society simply do not find masturbation as pleasurable or acceptable as do young men." They point out that women, more than men, have been socialized to associate sex with romance, relationships, and emotional intimacy. Their results, they note, suggest that "the recent effort to encourage women to take more responsibility for their own sexuality and the explicit suggestion to masturbate more has not altered this socialization process" (Leitenberg, Detzer, & Srebnik, 1993).

Masturbation is an important means of learning about our bodies (Atwood & Gagnon, 1987). Through masturbation, children and adolescents learn what is sexually pleasing, how to move their bodies, and what their natural rhythms are. The activity has no harmful physical effects. Although masturbation often decreases significantly when individuals make love regularly, it is not necessarily a temporary substitute for sexual intercourse but a legitimate form of sexual activity in its own right. Sex therapists may encourage clients to masturbate as a means of overcoming specific sexual problems and discovering their personal sexual potential. Masturbation, whether practiced alone or mutually with a partner, is also a form of safer sex, because ordinarily there is no exchange of semen, vaginal secretions, or blood, which could transmit HIV or other organisms that cause STDs (see Chapters 15 and 16).

We are capable of experiencing genital pleasure from birth through old age. Male infants have been observed with erect penises a few hours after birth. A baby boy may laugh in his crib while playing with his erect penis (although he does not ejaculate). Baby girls sometimes move their bodies rhythmically, almost violently, appearing to experience orgasm. And men as old as 102 have reported masturbating. In fact, for the aged, because of the loss of partners, masturbation regains much of the primacy it lost after adolescence as a means of sexual pleasure.

Childhood Children often accidentally discover that playing with their genitals is pleasurable and continue this activity until reprimanded by an adult (see Chapter 6). By the time they are 4 or 5, children have usually been taught that adults consider this form of behavior "nasty." Parents generally react overwhelmingly negatively to masturbation, regardless of the age and gender of the child (Gagnon, 1985). Later, this negative attitude becomes generalized to include the sexual pleasure that accompanies the behavior. Children thus learn to conceal their masturbatory play.

Adolescence When boys and girls reach adolescence, they no longer regard masturbation as ambiguous play, but know that it is sexual. As discussed in Chapter 6, this is a period of intense change emotionally and biologically. Complex emotions are often involved in adolescent masturbation. Teenagers may feel guilt and shame for engaging in a practice that their parents and other adults indicate is wrong or bad, and they may be fearful of discovery. A girl who feels vaginal lubrication or finds stains on her underpants for the first time may be frightened, as may a boy who sees the semen of his first ejaculation. Although open discussion could alleviate fears, frank talk is not always possible in a setting that involves shame.

According to one survey, teenage boys masturbate about five times a week (LoPresto, Sherman, & Sherman, 1985). By the end of adolescence, virtually all males and about three-quarters of females have masturbated to orgasm. These gender differences may be the result of social conditioning and communication. Most boys discuss masturbatory experiences openly, relating different methods and recalling "near misses" when they were almost caught by their parents. Among boys, masturbation is a subject for camaraderie. In contrast, girls usually learn to masturbate through self-discovery. Because "nice girls" are not supposed to be sexual, they seldom talk about their own sexuality but hide it, repress it, or try to forget it. Although white males are most likely to have their first ejaculation during masturbation, African American males more often experience their first ejaculation during sexual intercourse (Staples & Johnson, 1993). Comparable information is not available for female black adolescents and young adults.

Adulthood Masturbation continues after adolescence, although the frequency often declines among men and increases among women. A study found that 60% of women between ages 18 and 24 masturbated; they masturbated an average of 37 times a year (Hunt, 1974). About 80% of women reported masturbating by their late twenties or early thirties. Their masturbatory experiences remained stable through middle age and then slowly decreased.

Women who masturbate appear to hold more positive sexual attitudes and are more likely to be orgasmic than women who don't masturbate (Kelly, Strassberg, & Kircher, 1990). Among women who experience multiple orgasms, 26% experience them through masturbation (Darling, Davidson, & Jennings, 1991). Although the majority of women feel that orgasms experienced through masturbation differ from those experienced in sexual intercourse, they felt the same levels of sexual satisfaction (Davidson & Darling, 1986).

Most people continue to masturbate after they marry, although the rate is significantly smaller. Hunt reported that among married men in their late twenties or early thirties, about 72% masturbated, with a median frequency of 24 times a year (Hunt, 1974). Sixty-eight percent of the married women of this age group masturbated according to the median frequency. A *Redbook* survey of 100,000 women indicated that almost 75% masturbated during marriage—20% occasionally, and 20% often (Tavris & Sadd, 1977). The frequency was significantly higher among women who rated their marriages as unsatisfactory, suggesting that they masturbated because their personal and sexual relationships were unfulfilling.

There are many reasons for continuing the activity during marriage: Masturbation is a pleasurable form of sexual excitement, a spouse is away or unwilling, sexual intercourse is not satisfying, the partner(s) fear(s) sexual inadequacy, the individual acts out fantasies, or he or she seeks to release tension. During times of marital conflict, masturbation may act as a distancing device, with the masturbating spouse choosing masturbation over sexual intercourse as a means of emotional protection (Betchen, 1991).

Masturbation becomes an increasingly important means of sexual expression as men and women enter old age. Among older men and women, one researcher (Brecher, 1984) found in a nonrepresentative sample that among 60- to 69-year-old subjects, 50% of the men and 37% of the women reported masturbating; among those older than 70, 43% of the men and 33% of the women reported masturbating. As men aged, the frequency of masturbation increased while that of sexual intercourse declined (Weizman & Hart, 1987). By the time married men and women reached their eighties, the most common overt genital activity was masturbation. Masturbatory rates remained more or less constant between ages 80 and 90.

INTERPERSONAL SEXUALITY

We often think that sex is sexual intercourse and that sexual interactions end with orgasm (usually the male's). But sex is not limited to sexual intercourse. Heterosexuals engage in a wide variety of sexual activities, which may include erotic touching, kissing, and oral and anal sex. Except for sexual intercourse, gay and lesbian couples engage in basically the same sexual activities as do heterosexuals.

Touching

Where does sex begin for you? Whether it begins with the heart or the genitals, touch is the fire that melds the two into one. Touching is both a sign of caring and a signal for arousal.

Touching does not need to be directed toward genitals or erogenous zones. The entire body is responsive to a touch or a caress. Although women appear to be especially responsive to touch, traditional male sex roles give little significance to touching. Some men regard touching as simply a prelude to intercourse. When this occurs, touch is transformed into a demand for intercourse rather than an expression of intimacy or erotic play. The man's partner may become inhibited from touching or showing affection for fear her gestures will be misinterpreted as a sexual invitation (Barbach, 1982).

Pleasuring is the giving and receiving of erotic pleasure for its own sake.

Masters and Johnson suggest a form of touching they call "pleasuring." **Pleasuring** is nongenital touching and caressing. Neither partner tries to sexually stimulate the other; they simply explore, discovering how their bodies respond to touching. The man guides the woman's hand over his body, telling her what feels good; she then takes his hand and moves it over her body, telling him what she likes.

Such sharing gives each a sense of his or her own responses; it also allows each to discover what the other likes and dislikes. We can't assume we know what a particular person likes, for there is too much variation between people. Pleasuring opens the door to communication; couples discover that the entire body, not just the genitals, is erogenous.

Nude or clothed massages, back rubs, foot rubs, scalp massages—all are soothing and loving forms of touch. The sensuousness of touching may be enhanced by the use of lubricating oils. Such erotic touching is a form of safer sex.

Other forms of touching are more directly sexual, such as caressing, fondling, or rubbing our own or our partner's genitals or breasts. Sucking or licking earlobes, the neck, toes, or the insides of thighs, palms, or arms, can be highly stimulating. Oral stimulation of a woman's or man's breasts or nipples is often exciting. Moving one's genitals or breasts over a partner's face, chest, breasts, or genitals is very erotic for some people.

pleasuring   Erotic nongenital touching.

Stimulating your partner's clitoris or penis with your hand or fingers can increase excitement or lead to orgasm. Inserting a finger or fingers into your partner's wet vagina and rhythmically moving it at the pace your partner likes may be pleasing. Some women like to have their clitoris licked or stimulated with one hand while their vagina is being penetrated with the other. Men like having their penises lubricated so that their partner's hand glides smoothly over the shaft and glans penis. (Be sure to use a water-based lubricant if you plan to use a condom later, because oil-based lubricants may cause the condom to deteriorate.) Masturbating while your partner is holding you can be highly erotic for both people. Mutual masturbation can also be intensely sexual. Some people use sex toys, such as dildos, vibrators, or ben-wah balls to enhance sexual touching. (These are discussed in Chapter 14.)

As we enter old age, touching becomes increasingly significant as a primary form of erotic expression. Touching in all its myriad forms, ranging from holding hands to caressing, massaging to hugging, walking with arms around each other to fondling, becomes the touchstone of eroticism for the elderly (Weg, 1983b). One study found touching to be the primary form of erotic expression for married couples over age 80 (Bretschneider & McCoy, 1988).

Kissing

Kissing is usually our earliest interpersonal sexual experience, and its primal intensity may be traced back to our suckling as infants. Kissing is probably the most acceptable of all premarital sexual activities (Jurich & Polson, 1985). The tender lover's kiss symbolizes love, and the erotic lover's kiss, of course, simultaneously represents and *is* passion. Both men and women regard kissing as a romantic act, a symbol of affection as well as desire (Tucker, 1992; Tucker, Marvin, & Vivian, 1991).

The lips and mouth are highly sensitive to touch and are exquisitely erotic parts of our bodies. Kisses discover, explore, and excite the body. They also involve the senses of taste and smell, which are especially important because they activate unconscious memories and associations.

Although kissing may appear innocent, it is in many ways the height of intimacy. The adolescent's first kiss is often regarded as a milestone, a rite of passage, the beginning of adult sexuality (Alapack, 1991). It is an important developmental step, marking the beginning of a young person's sexuality. Blumstein and Schwartz (1983) report that many of their respondents found it unimaginable to engage in sexual intercourse without kissing. In fact, they found that those who have a minimal (or nonexistent) amount of kissing feel distant from their partners but may have intercourse anyway as a physical release. (Interestingly, both female and male prostitutes are more willing to engage in oral sex, sexual intercourse, or other sexual activities than to kiss their clients, specifically *because* kissing symbolizes intimacy.)

The amount of kissing differs according to sexual orientation. Lesbian couples tend to engage in kissing more than heterosexual couples, while gay male couples kiss less than heterosexual couples (Blumstein & Schwartz, 1983).

Ordinary kissing is considered safer sex. French kissing is probably safe, unless the kiss is hard and draws blood, or either partner has sores or cuts in or around the mouth. (See Chapter 16 for further discussion of kissing and HIV.)

Oral-Genital Sex

In recent years, oral sex has become a part of our sexual scripts (Gagnon, 1986). The two types of oral-genital sex are cunnilingus and fellatio. **Cunnilingus** is the erotic stimulation of a woman's vulva by her partner's mouth and tongue. The word is derived from the Latin *cunnus*, vulva, and *lingere*, to lick. **Fellatio** is the oral stimulation of a man's penis by his partner's sucking and licking. It is from the Latin *fellare*, to suck. Cunnilingus and fellatio may be performed singly or simultaneously. When two people orally stimulate each other simultaneously, their activity is sometimes called "sixty-nine." The term comes from the configuration "69," which visually suggests the activity.

For people of every orientation (especially among high school and college students), oral sex is an increasingly important and healthy aspect of their sexual selves (Wilson & Medora, 1990). Psychologist Lilian Rubin reports that young women today express pleasure about oral sex, in contrast to twenty years ago; a minority of middle-aged women, who earlier believed oral sex was "dirty" or immoral, continue to feel some ambivalence (Rubin, 1990). Of the men and women in various studies, 60–90% report that they have engaged in oral sex (Delamater & MacCorquodale, 1979; Peterson, Kretchmer, Nellis, Lever, & Hertz, 1983). Blumstein and Schwartz (1983) found that 50% of gay couples, 39% of lesbian couples, and 30% of heterosexual couples usually or always had oral sex as part of their lovemaking routine.

Although oral-genital sex is increasingly accepted by white middle-class Americans, it remains less permissible among some ethnic groups. African Americans, for example, have lower rates of oral-genital sex than whites, because many blacks consider it immoral (Wilson, 1986). A recent large-scale national study found that 79% of white men had performed oral sex, compared with 43% of African American men and 74.8% of Latino men. Eighty-one percent of white men had received oral sex, compared to 61% of African American men, and 79.3% of Latinos. The higher the education level, the greater the likelihood of having been involved in oral sexual activities (Billy, Tanfer, Grady, & Klepinger, 1993). Oral sex is becoming increasingly accepted, however, among black women (Wyatt, Peters, & Gutherie, 1988). This is especially true if they have a good relationship and communicate well with their partners (Wyatt & Lyons-Rowe, 1990). Among married Latinos, oral sex is relatively uncommon. When oral sex occurs, it is usually at the male's instigation, as women are not expected to be interested in erotic variety (Guerrero Pavich, 1986). Although little is known about older Asian Americans and Asian immigrants, college-age Asian Americans appear to accept oral-genital sex to the same degree as middle-class whites (Cochran, Mays, & Leung, 1991).

Cunnilingus In cunnilingus, a woman's genitals are stimulated by her partner's tongue and mouth, which gently and rhythmically caress and lick her clitoris and the surrounding area (Figure 9.3). During arousal, the mouth and lips can nibble, lick, and kiss the inner thighs, the stomach, the mons pubis, and then move to the sensitive labia minora. Orgasm may be brought on by rhythmically stimulating the clitoris. Many women find

cunnilingus Oral stimulation of the female genitals.

fellatio Oral stimulation of the penis.

FIGURE 9.3 Cunnilingus.

cunnilingus one of the most arousing activities. Hite (1976) reported that 42% of the women in her study had orgasms regularly from cunnilingus. One woman wrote: "A tongue offers gentleness and precision and wetness and is the perfect organ for contact. And, besides, it produces sensational orgasms!"

Among lesbians, cunnilingus is a common activity for experiencing orgasm. In contrast to heterosexual couples, lesbian couples may be more inventive, less restrained, and more involved (Califia, 1979). This may be partly because, as women, each partner can identify with what the other may enjoy. But as many as 25% of the lesbians in Blumstein and Schwartz's study (1983) engaged in cunnilingus rarely or never. Instead, they relied on holding, kissing, manual stimulation, and pressing themselves erotically against each other. Nevertheless, the more often lesbians in the study had oral sex, the more likely they were to be satisfied with their sex lives and partners.

Some women, however, have concerns regarding cunnilingus. The most common worries revolve around whether the other person is enjoying it and, especially, whether the vulva has an unpleasant odor (Hite, 1976). Concerns about vaginal odors may be eased by washing. Undeodorized white soap will wash away unpleasant smells without disturbing the vagina's natural erotic scent. If an unpleasant odor arises from the genitals, it may be because the woman has a vaginal infection.

A woman may also worry that her partner is not enjoying the experience because the partner is giving pleasure rather than receiving it. What she may not recognize is that such sexual excitement is often mutual. Because our mouths and tongues are erotically sensitive, the giver finds erotic excitement in arousing his or her partner.

FIGURE 9.4 Fellatio.

Fellatio In fellatio, a man's penis is taken into his partner's mouth. The partner licks the glans penis and gently stimulates the shaft (Figure 9.4). If the penis is not erect, it usually will become erect within a few minutes. The partner sucks more vigorously as excitement increases, down toward the base of the penis and then back up, in a rhythmical motion, being careful not to bite hard or scrape the penis with the teeth. While the man is being stimulated by mouth, his partner can also stroke the shaft of the penis by hand. Gently playing with the testicles is also arousing as long as they are not held too tightly. As in cunnilingus, the couple should experiment to discover what is most stimulating and exciting. The man should be careful not to thrust his penis too deeply into his partner's throat, for that may cause a gagging reflex. He should let his partner control how deeply the penis goes into the mouth. The gag reflex can also be reconditioned by slowly inserting the penis into the mouth at increasing depth over a number of times. Some women feel that fellatio is more intimate than sexual intercourse, whereas others feel that it is less intimate (Petersen et al., 1983). It is the most common form of sexual activity performed on men by prostitutes (Freund, Lee, & Leonard, 1991).

Although men are generally enthusiastic about fellatio, women may have mixed feelings about it (Blumstein & Schwartz, 1983). Some find it highly arousing, while others feel it is a form of submissiveness, especially if they sense that their partner demands it. If the woman's partner is too demanding or directing, she may feel he is controlling or selfish. If she accedes to his wishes, she may feel psychologically coerced. This sense of coercion may block the pleasure she may otherwise have enjoyed by engaging in fellatio.

For gay men, fellatio is an important component of their sexuality. As with sexual intercourse for heterosexual men, however, fellatio is only one activity in their sexual repertoire. Generally speaking, the more often gay couples engage in giving and receiving oral sex, the more satisfied they are (Blumstein & Schwartz, 1983). Because oral sex often involves power symbolism, reciprocity is important. If one partner always performs oral sex, he may feel he is subordinate to the other. The most satisfied gay couples alternate between giving and receiving oral sex.

A common concern about fellatio centers around ejaculation. Should the male ejaculate into his partner's mouth? It is simply a matter of personal preference, and the man who is receiving fellatio should accept his partner's feelings about it and avoid equating a dislike for swallowing with a personal rejection.

Some partners worry, as they should, about the transmission of HIV through fellatio (see Chapter 16). It is possible to orally contract HIV if there are sores or openings within the mouth. Excessive toothbrushing, flossing, biting on the side of the mouth, and/or abrasions (from orthodontia or dental work) can cause small cuts in the mouth that, if exposed to HIV, allow the virus to enter into the bloodstream. To be safe, a condom should be worn during fellatio.

Sexual Intercourse

Sexual intercourse has intense personal meaning (Cate, Long, Angera, & Draper, 1993; Schwartz, 1993). It is a source of pleasure, communication, and love. If forced, however, it becomes an instrument of aggression and pain. Its meaning changes depending on the context in which we engage in it (Sprecher & McKinney, 1993). How we feel about it may depend as much (or more) on the feelings and motives we bring to it as on the techniques we use or the orgasms we experience.

Although sexual intercourse is important for most sexually involved couples, the significance of it differs between men and women (Blumstein & Schwartz, 1983; Sprecher & McKinney, 1993). For men, sexual intercourse is only one of several activities that they enjoy. For many heterosexual women, however, intercourse is central to their sexual satisfaction. More than any other heterosexual sexual activity, sexual intercourse involves equal participation by both partners. Both partners equally and simultaneously give and receive. As a result, women feel a greater shared intimacy than they do in other activities.

There are two basic positions in sexual intercourse—face-to-face and rear-entry—although the playfulness of the couple, their movement from one bodily configuration to another, and their ingenuity can provide an infinite variety. The same positions played out in different settings can cause an intensity that transforms the ordinary into the extraordinary.

The most common position is face-to-face with the man above (Figure 9.5). Many people prefer this position, for several reasons. First, it is the traditional, correct, or "official" position in our culture, which many people find reassuring and validating of their sexuality. (The man-above position is commonly known as the missionary position because it was the position missionaries encouraged people to use.) Second, it can allow the man maximum activity, movement, and control of coitus, validating the

AMERICANS AND SEX: NEW INFORMATION IS IN

Just how do Americans behave in their bedrooms? Results of various surveys have been reported throughout this text, with their flaws and limitations noted. Now, new figures have been published, and they show us to be in a different place from when Kinsey did his research 40 years ago. Researchers from the University of Chicago have released the results of a comprehensive, scientific survey that tells us who is doing what with whom, under what circumstances, and, of course, how often. The results have surprised many of us.

A random sample of 3500 Americans, ages 18 to 59, in face-to-face interviews, have shown Americans to be far more conventional than previous studies indicated. The 700 pages of findings provide new information on a broad range of topics, from fidelity to sexual satisfaction, from sexual practices to contraception. (For full survey results, see *The Social Organization of Sexuality*, by Laumann, Gagnon, Michael, & Michaels, published by University of Chicago, 1994).

Among the key findings are the following:

- When frequency of sex is considered, adults fall roughly into three groups: nearly 30% have sex with a partner only a few times a year or not at all, 35% have sex once or several times a month, and about 35% have sex at least two or more times a week. On average, Americans have sex about once a week.

- Americans are largely monogamous. The median number of sex partners since age 18 for men is six and for women is two.

- Adultery is the exception, not the rule, in America. Among those who are married, 75% of men and 85% of women said they had been faithful to their spouses.

- Most Americans are fairly traditional in the bedroom. When respondents were asked to name their preferences from a long list of sexual practices, vaginal intercourse was considered "very appealing" by most of those interviewed. Ranking second, but far behind, was watching a partner undress. Oral sex ranked third.

- According to this survey, homosexuality is not as prevalent as was originally believed. The study found that 2.8% of men and 1.4% of women describe themselves as homosexual or bisexual. But when asked whether they ever had a sexual experience with someone of the same gender, more than 9% of men and more than 4% of women said yes. This leads researchers to warn that it is impossible to define the prevalence of homosexuality. When compared to other studies, it makes researchers question how random this sample was.

- Orgasms appear to be the rule for men, the exception for women. When asked if they always had an orgasm when having sex with their primary partner, three-quarters of the men answered yes, compared with 29% of the women. Married women were most likely to report that they always or usually had orgasms.

- Religious affiliation seemed to be associated with orgasm, with conservative Protestant women—Baptists, Pentecostals, and members of other fundamentalist denominations—most likely to report that they always had an orgasm.

- Forced sex and the misperception of it remains a critical problem in our society. Twenty-two percent of women said they have been forced to do sexual things they didn't want to do, usually by a loved one. But only 3% of men admitted to ever forcing themselves on women.

- Three percent of adult Americans have never had sex.

The results of the survey have surprised and shocked many who had very different ideas about Americans and sex. They have also offended and upset groups, such as right-to-life activists, some AIDS educators, and interracial couples, who see the results undermining or dampening their cause or beliefs. Most scientists have praised the study but have noted its weaknesses, such as limited sample size, omission of people over age 59, and the absence of certain subgroups (e.g., gay Hispanics).

Surprising and noteworthy is the finding that marriage is still a powerful institution in this country, with faithfulness holding as a value for both partners.

FIGURE 9.5 Face-to-Face, Man Above.

FIGURE 9.6 Face-to-Face, Woman Above.

traditional gender roles, in which the man controls and the woman responds. Third, it allows the woman freedom to stimulate her clitoris to assist in her orgasm. The primary disadvantages are that it limits the woman's movement and that she may feel too much weight on her if her partner does not raise himself with his arms or elbows.

FIGURE 9.7 Rear-Entry.

Another common position is face-to-face with the woman above (Figure 9.6). The woman either lies above her partner or sits astride him. This position allows the woman maximum activity, movement, and control. She can control the depth to which the penis penetrates. Additionally, when the woman sits astride her partner, either of them can caress or stimulate her vulva and clitoris. A disadvantage is that some men or women may feel uneasy about the woman assuming a position that signifies an active role in coitus.

Intercourse can also be performed with the man positioned behind the woman. There are several variations on the rear-entry position. The woman may kneel supported on her arms and receive the penis in her vagina from behind. The couple may lie on their sides, with the woman's back to her partner (Figure 9.7). This position offers variety and may be particularly suitable during pregnancy. Clitoral stimulation by the woman is facilitated in this position. Generally, it is also possible for the man to stimulate her during intercourse. Some people object to the rear-entry position as being "animal-like." Or they may feel it inhibits intimacy or resembles anal intercourse.

In the face-to-face side position, both partners lie on their sides facing each other (Figure 9.8). Each partner has greater freedom to caress and stimulate the other. The major drawback is that some may find it difficult to keep the penis inside the vagina.

Anal Eroticism

Anal eroticism refers to sexual activities involving the anus, whose delicate membranes (as well as tabooed nature) make it erotically sensitive for many

FIGURE 9.8 Face-to-Face on Side.

analingus The licking of the anal region.

anal intercourse The insertion of the erect penis into the partner's anus.

people. These activities include **analingus,** the licking of the anal region (colloquially known as "rimming" or "tossing salad"). Anal-manual contact consists of stimulating the anal region with the fingers; sometimes an entire fist may be inserted (known as "fisting" among gay white males and "fingering" by gay African Americans). Many couples engage in this activity along with fellatio or sexual intercourse.

Anal intercourse refers to the male's inserting his erect penis into his partner's anus. Both heterosexuals and gay men participate in this activity (colloquially known as "butt fucking" by heterosexuals, "Greek" by gay white males, and "georging" by gay African Americans [Mays, Cochran, Bellinger, & Smith, 1992]). Anal intercourse is a major mode of sexual interaction for gay men. In fact, there are more colloquial terms for anal eroticism among gay men than any other form of sexual activity (Mays et al., 1992; Mays, Cochran, Smith, & Daniels, 1993). For heterosexual couples, anal intercourse is generally an experiment or occasional activity rather than a common mode of sexual expression. A national study of anal sex practices by American men (orientation not stated) found considerable variation by ethnicity (Billy, Tanfer, Grady, & Klepinger, 1993). Among men age 20–39, about 21% of whites, 13.6% of African Americans, and 24% of Latinos have experienced anal intercourse. A review of recent studies found that about 10% of heterosexual couples regularly engage in anal sex (Voeller, 1991).

Among gay men, anal intercourse is less common than oral sex, but it is, nevertheless, an important ingredient to the sexual satisfaction of many gays (Berger, 1991; Blumstein & Schwartz, 1983). Although heterosexual imagery portrays the person who penetrates as "masculine" and the pene-

CHAPTER 9 SEXUAL EXPRESSION

trated person as "feminine," this imagery does not generally reflect gay reality. For both partners, anal intercourse is regarded as masculine.

Although anal sex may heighten eroticism for those who engage in it, from a health perspective it is riskier than most other forms of sexual interaction. The rectum is particularly susceptible to sexually transmitted diseases (Agnew, 1986). Because of HIV, anal intercourse is potentially the most dangerous form of sexual interaction. Anal intercourse is the most prevalent mode of transmitting HIV sexually, among both gay men and heterosexuals (Voeller, 1991). Because the delicate rectal tissues are easily lacerated, the tissues allow the AIDS virus (carried within semen) to enter the bloodstream. If a couple practices anal intercourse, they should engage in it *only* if both are certain that they are free from HIV *and* if they use a condom. As a result of health concerns, the rate of unprotected anal sex between gay men is diminishing (McKusick, Coates, Morin, & Pollack, 1990).

If the penis or a foreign object is inserted in the anus, it must be washed before insertion into the vagina because it may cause a bacterial infection. Other health hazards associated with anal erotic practices include rupturing the rectum with foreign objects, and laceration of the anus or rectal wall through the use of enemas. Licking the anus puts individuals at risk of acquiring HIV, hepatitis, or other sexually transmitted diseases (see Chapter 15).

As we have seen, sexual behaviors cannot be separated from attraction and desire. Although the sexual behaviors we examined in this chapter are the most common in our society, there are other, less typical activities in which many of us engage. These include transvestism and fetishism, as well as such consensual activities as dominance and submission. Still others include nonconsensual behaviors ranging from exhibitionism and voyeurism to child molestation. We discuss these atypical behaviors in Chapter 10.

SUMMARY

Sexual Attraction

• What constitutes sexual attractiveness varies across cultures. Our culture prefers slender women with large breasts and men with well-defined arm and pectoral muscles. Both men and women are attracted to the buttocks of the other sex. Gay men and heterosexual women share many of the same ideals regarding body shape for men; bisexuals may be attracted to others on the basis of particular physical characteristics rather than on the basis of gender.

• Because of the halo effect, attractive people are assumed to be more sexual and permissive than unattractive people. Attractive college women may be more likely to have engaged in sexual intercourse and oral sex than unattractive women.

• Sexual desire is affected by erotophilia, a positive emotional response to sex, and by erotophobia, a negative response to sex.

Sexual Scripts

• Sexual scripts organize our sexual impulses. They have three major components: cultural, intrapersonal, and interpersonal. The cultural script provides the general patterns sexual behaviors are expected to take in a particular society. The intrapersonal script interprets our physiological responses as sexual or not. The interpersonal script is the shared conventions and signals that make sexual activities between two people possible.

Autoeroticism

• Autoeroticism refers to sexual activities that involve only the self. These activities include sexual fantasies, erotic dreams, and masturbation, or stimulation of the genitals for pleasure.

• Sexual fantasies are probably the most universal of all sexual behaviors; they are normal aspects of our sexuality. Erotic fantasies have several functions: they take our generalized sexual drives and help define and direct them, they allow us to plan or anticipate erotic situations, they provide pleasurable escape from routine, they introduce novelty, and they offer clues to our unconscious.

• Most men and women masturbate. Masturbation may begin as early as infancy and continue throughout old age. Attitudes toward masturbation vary by ethnicity.

Interpersonal Sexuality

• The erotic potential of touching has been undervalued because our culture tends to be orgasm-oriented, especially among males. Pleasuring is a means by which couples get to know each other erotically through touching and caressing.

• Erotic kissing is usually our earliest interpersonal sexual experience and is regarded as a rite of passage into adult sexuality.

• Oral-genital sex is becoming increasingly accepted, especially among young adults. Cunnilingus is the stimulation of the vulva with the tongue; it is engaged in by both heterosexuals and lesbians. Fellatio is the stimulation of the penis with the mouth; it is engaged in by both heterosexuals and gay men.

• Sexual intercourse is a complex interaction between two people. It is both a means of reproduction and a form of communication.

• Anal eroticism refers to sexual activities involving the anus. It is engaged in by heterosexuals, gay men, and lesbians. Analingus, the licking of the anal region, and anal intercourse, or insertion of an erect penis into a partner's anus, are examples of anal eroticism.

SUGGESTED READINGS

Barbach, Lonnie. *For Each Other: Sharing Sexual Intimacy*. New York: Bantam, 1984. A best-selling book describing women's sexual activities, attitudes, and feelings.

Comfort, Alex. *The Joy of Sex: A Gourmet Guide to Love-making*, 2nd ed. New York: Crown Publishers, 1986. A revised version of the contemporary classic on sex and sexuality.

Dodson, Betty. *Sex for One*. New York: Harmony Publications, 1987. Self-discovery techniques through masturbation for women and men; includes sensitive illustrations.

Friday, Nancy. *Women on Top: How Real Life Has Changed Women's Sexual Fantasies*. New York: Simon & Schuster, 1991. A proactive book about how women's fantasies have reflected societal change.

Kennedy, Adele, and Susan Dean. *Touching for Pleasure*. Chatsworth, CA: Chatsworth Press, 1986. An exploration of the varieties of sensual and sexual touch, with soft charcoal drawings.

Kroll, Ken, and Erica Levy Klein. *Enabling Romance: A Guide to Love, Sex, and Relationships for the Disabled*. New York: Harmony Books, 1992. Hundreds of men and women with disabilities discuss stereotypes, different ways of being sexual, the use of sex toys, and strengthening relationships.

Loulan, JoAnn. *Lesbian Sex*. San Francisco: Spinsters Books, 1984. One of the most popular books on lesbian sexuality and sexual enhancement.

Silverstein, Charles, and Felice Picano. *The New Joy of Gay Sex*. New York: HarperCollins, 1992. An illustrated guide to gay male sexuality.

Zilbergeld, Bernie. *The New Male Sexuality Book*. Boston: Little, Brown, 1992. An updated version of the classic work on male sexuality, describing sexual myths, communication, and sexual expression.

Chapter Ten

ATYPICAL AND PARAPHILIC SEXUAL BEHAVIOR

PREVIEW: SELF-QUIZ

1. Domination and submission activities are generally more secret among heterosexuals than among gay men and lesbians. True or false?

2. Sadomasochism is clinically described as a sexual perversion. True or false?

3. Exhibitionists are usually old men who expose their genitals to children. True or false?

4. According to Kinsey, 17% of men reared on farms report sexual contact with animals. True or false?

5. In most cases, the best response to receiving an obscene phone call is to say nothing and hang up. True or false?

6. Men who molest boys may identify themselves as gay, bisexual, or heterosexual in their adult sexual relationships. True or false?

7. Voyeurs are often also exhibitionists or obscene phone callers. True or false?

8. The story of Sleeping Beauty contains elements of necrophilia. True or false?

9. As many as 1000 males accidentally hang or asphyxiate themselves each year while engaging in unusual masturbatory activities. True or false?

10. Unusual or bizarre sexual fantasies are experienced at times by most people. True or false?

ANSWERS 1. T, 2. F, 3. F, 4. T, 5. T, 6. T, 7. T, 8. T, 9. T, 10. T

Chapter Outline

In a particularly vicious election campaign, the late Florida senator Claude Pepper was accused of being a "shameless extrovert," whose sister was known to be a New York "thespian." His opponent claimed that the senator "practiced celibacy" prior to marriage and later engaged in "nepotism" with his sister-in-law (Catchpole, 1992). These "accusations," which Pepper's opponent hoped would imply some kind of unnatural or perverted activity, refer simply to the senator's being outgoing (an extrovert), having an actress sister (a thespian), being sexually abstinent prior to marriage (celibacy), and giving his sister-in-law preferential treatment because of their relationship (nepotism). But the use of clinical- or moral-sounding terms points to the power of labeling. Sometimes, labels help us understand behavior; at other times, they interfere. This is especially true as we examine unusual or atypical sexual activities.

In this chapter, we examine atypical sexual behaviors, such as cross-dressing and domination and submission, which are not within the range of sexual behaviors in which people typically engage. Then we turn to sexual behaviors that are classified by the American Psychiatric Association (1994) as paraphilias (defined below). The noncoercive paraphilias include fetishism, transvestism, and zoophilia. The coercive paraphilias include pedophilia, sexual sadism, sexual masochism, and necrophilia, among others. Finally, we examine treatment for paraphilias.

ATYPICAL VERSUS PARAPHILIC BEHAVIOR

The range of human sexual behavior is almost infinite. Yet most of our activities and fantasies, such as coitus, oral-genital sex, masturbation, and our orientation as heterosexual, gay, lesbian, or bisexual, cluster within a general range of behaviors and desires. Those behaviors and fantasies that do not fall in this general range are considered atypical. In this chapter, we use the term **atypical sexual behavior** to refer to those consensual behaviors that are not *statistically* typical of American sexual behaviors. It is important to remember, however, that atypical does not necessarily mean abnormal; it simply means that the majority of people do not engage in that particular behavior. Sexual behaviors that are classified as mental disorders are known as paraphilias. Atypical sexual behaviors tend to differ from paraphilic ones in that paraphilic behaviors tend to be compulsive, long-standing, and distressing to the individual.

atypical sexual behavior Consensual sexual activity that is not statistically typical of American sexual behavior.

According to the American Psychiatric Association's *Diagnostic and Statistical Manual of Mental Disorders IV (DSM-IV)* (1994), a **paraphilia** is a mental disorder characterized by "recurrent intense sexual urges and sexually arousing fantasies" lasting at least 6 months and involving (1) nonhuman objects, (2) the suffering or humiliation of oneself or one's partner (not merely simulated), or (3) children or other nonconsenting people. In addition, "the person has acted upon these urges or is markedly distressed by them" (American Psychiatric Association, 1994).

paraphilia A mental disorder characterized by sexual behaviors that are compulsive, long-standing and distressing to the individual.

The distinction between atypical and paraphilic behavior is sometimes more a difference of degree than kind. For example, many men find that certain objects, such as black lingerie, intensify their sexual arousal, while for others, it is a necessity for arousal. In the first case, there is nothing particularly unusual. In fact, a study of almost 200 students found that 16% of the women and 7% of the men had recently worn erotic garments (Person, Terestman, Myers, & Goldberg, 1989). But if a man were unable to become excited without the lingerie and the purpose of sex was to bring him in contact with the panties, the behavior would be considered paraphilic.

It is also important to recognize that seemingly scientific or clinical terms may not be scientific at all. Instead, they may be pseudoscientific terms hiding moral judgments, as in the case of the terms *nymphomania* and *satyriasis*. **Nymphomania** is a pejorative term, usually referring to "abnormal or excessive" sexual desire in a woman. It is usually applied to sexually active single women. What is "abnormal" or "excessive" is often defined moralistically rather than scientifically. Nymphomania is not recognized as a clinical condition by the *DSM-IV* (American Psychiatric Association, 1994). Although the term "nymphomania" dates back to the seventeenth century, it was popularized in the nineteenth century by Krafft-Ebing and others. Physicians and psychiatrists used the term to pathologize women's sexual

nymphomania A pseudoscientific term referring to "abnormal" or "excessive" sexual desire in a woman.

Think About It

BODY PLAY: TATTOOING AND PIERCING

It's nearly impossible to watch MTV, televised sports, or fashion events these days without seeing someone with a small tattoo or ring discreetly displayed on his or her body. As the latest expression of individuality, piercing and tattooing have attracted a diverse set of enthusiasts.

Like hairstyles, tattooing and piercing have been around forever. A pierced navel was considered a sign of royalty among the ancient Egyptians, and the Crusaders of the Middle Ages were tattooed with crucifixes to ensure a Christian burial. Every culture and time has had its own standards of beauty and sexual attractiveness, and piercing and tattooing have been used to enhance both.

Although tattooing in our culture was once reserved for the biker and sailor crowds, it has now become much more widespread and nearly routine, with tattoo "studios" presenting their services as art. The tattooing procedure involves injecting dye into the skin, resulting in a permanent marking. Potential problems associated with the painful procedure include the risk of infection, including infection with hepatitis or HIV. Between 12 and 20 million Americans have tattoos; studies indicate that nearly half these people want them removed, most often because of psychological discomfort and/or job discrimination (Marin, Hannah, Colin, Annin, & Gegax, 1995). Although the removal procedure is also painful, new technology and lower costs have allowed many individuals to have their tattoos removed. Using the flickering beam of a laser, physicians can explode the indelible ink into minute particles, which are absorbed and discarded by the body.

Like tattooing, body piercing has become increasingly popular as a personal statement. The motivation can be either decorative or erotic, depending on where the pierce is made. What keeps piercing exotic, in part, is the pain factor. Unlike plastic surgeons, piercers are not licensed to offer any kind of anesthetic, and even if they were, a shot of novocaine would probably be as painful as the piercing (Betts, 1994).

Piercing capitalizes on a fascination with the look of deviance, with its sadomasochistic undertones. If placed strategically, rings and studs provide both physical stimulation and psychological titillation. The most common site for piercing, besides the earlobe, is the nipple, followed by the navel. Other sites include the tongue, lips, labia, frenum and scrotum. Each type of pierce involves a specific method of puncturing and a prescribed course of healing. Some plastic surgeons report a doubling of business involving stitching together body parts damaged by piercing.

A third practice is branding. A hazing rite of passage in many black fraternities, hot-iron branding leaves a scar that may be treated with steroid injections but that can never be totally removed.

Because all these markings are considered permanent and potentially dangerous, the procedures should be performed only by professionals. Keys to safety and satisfaction include awareness of anatomy and knowledge of proper healing procedures on the part of the person providing the services, proper placement of the marks or piercings, and the use of sterile tools.

---

satyriasis A pseudoscientific term referring to "abnormal" or "uncontrollable" sexual desire in a man.

behavior if it deviated from nineteenth-century moral standards. Even today, "nymphomania," "nymphomaniac," and "nympho" retain pathological connotations.

Satyriasis, referring to "abnormal" or "uncontrollable" sexual desire in men, is less commonly used than nymphomania because men are expected

Bondage and discipline, or B&D, often involves leather, handcuffs, and other restraints as part of its scripting.

to be more sexual than women. For this reason, definitions of satyriasis infrequently include the adjective "excessive." Instead, reflecting ideas of male sexuality as a powerful drive, "uncontrollable" becomes the significant adjective. Satyriasis is not recognized by the American Psychiatric Association (1994).

As you continue this chapter, remember to distinguish clearly between the use of the various terms clinically, judgmentally, or casually. It can be tempting to define a behavior you don't like or approve of as paraphilic. But unless you are clinically trained, you cannot diagnose someone (including yourself) as having a mental disorder.

ATYPICAL SEXUAL BEHAVIORS

Atypical sexual behaviors are not rare. Although the majority of people do not engage in these activities, they are not necessarily uncommon. A study of recent sexual behaviors and fantasies among 193 college and graduate students found that 23% of the women and 38% of the men had recently watched their partner masturbate (Person et al., 1989). Fourteen percent of the women and 6% of the men had used sex toys. Eleven percent of the women and 18% of the men had performed sexual acts in front of mirrors. And 5% of the women and 4% of the men had watched others engage in sexual intercourse. In terms of fantasies, 10% of men and of women had imagined themselves members of the other gender. Ten percent of the women and 5% of the men fantasized themselves as prostitutes. One film critic suggests that the popularity of vampire movies and novels may reflect our fascination with forbidden impulses or obsessions about which we may fantasize but never act out (James, 1992).

In this section we discuss one of the more controversial and widespread forms of atypical sexual behavior—domination and submission.

Domination and Submission

domination and submission (D/S) Sexual activities involving the consensual acting out of fantasy scenes in which one person dominates and the other submits.

sadomasochism (S&M) A popular, nonclinical term for domination and submission.

Domination and submission (D/S) refers to sexual arousal derived from the *consensual* acting out of sexual scenes in which one person dominates and the other submits. The term **sadomasochism (S&M)** is also used by the general public to describe domination and submission, but it is no longer used as a clinical term in psychiatry and psychology to describe consensual domination and submission (Breslow, 1989).

Domination and submission are forms of fantasy sex. The critical element is not pain, but power. The dominant partner is all-powerful and the submissive partner is all-powerless. Significantly, the amount or degree of "pain," which is usually feigned or slight, is controlled by the submissive partner. As such, fantasy plays a central role, especially for the submissive person (Arndt, 1991).

A large-scale study of a nonclinical population found that the majority involved in domination and submission did so as "a form of sexual enhancement which they voluntarily and mutually choose to explore" (Weinberg, Williams & Moser, 1984). As such, domination and submission is not paraphilic. To be considered paraphilic, such behavior requires the suffering or humiliation of oneself or one's partner to be real, not merely simulated (American Psychiatric Association, 1994). (Sexual sadism and sexual masochism, which are considered paraphilias, are discussed later in the chapter.)

bondage and discipline (B&D) Sexual activities in which one person is bound while another simulates or engages in light or moderate "discipline" activities, such as spanking and whipping.

dominatrix In bondage and discipline, a woman who specializes in "disciplining" a submissive partner.

Domination and submission take many forms. The participants generally assume both dominant and submissive roles at different times; few are interested only in being "top" or "bottom" (Moser, 1988). Probably the most widely known form is bondage and discipline. **Bondage and discipline (B&D)** refers to activities in which a person is bound with scarves, leather straps, underwear, handcuffs, chains, or other such devices while another simulates or engages in light to moderate discipline activities, such as spanking, whipping, and so on. The bound person may be blindfolded or gagged. A woman specializing in disciplining a person is known as a **dominatrix,** and her submissive partner is called a slave.

Bondage and discipline may take place in specialized settings called "dungeons" furnished with restraints, body-suspension devices, racks, whips, and chains (Stoller, 1991). Eleven percent of both men and women have had experience with bondage, according to a recent study (Janus & Janus, 1993).

Another common form of domination and submission is *humiliation,* in which the person is debased or degraded (Arndt, 1991). Five percent of the men and 7% of the women in the Janus study had engaged in verbal humiliation (Janus & Janus, 1993). One-third of the submission respondents in

Betty Page, who has become a cult figure among those interested in domination and submission, was one of the most photographed women in the 1950s.

another study received enemas ("water treatment"), were urinated on ("golden showers"), or defecated on ("scat") (Breslow, Evans, & Langley, 1985). In the Janus study, 6% of the men and 4% of the women had participated in golden showers (Janus & Janus, 1993). Humiliation activities may include servilism, babyism, kennelism, and tongue lashing. In *servilism*, the person desires to be treated as a servant or slave. In *babyism*, the person acts in an infantile manner—using baby talk, wearing diapers, being pampered, scolded, or spanked by his or her "mommy" or "daddy." *Kennelism* refers to being treated like a dog, wearing a studded dog collar, and being tied to a leash, or ridden like a horse, while the dominant partner applies whip or spurs. *Tongue lashing* is verbal abuse by a dominant partner who uses language that humiliates and degrades the other.

People engage in D/S in private or as part of an organized subculture complete with clubs and businesses catering to the acting out of D/S fantasies (Stoller, 1991). This subculture is sometimes known as "the velvet underground." There are scores of noncommercial D/S clubs throughout the

United States (Arndt, 1991). The clubs are often specialized: lesbian S&M, dominant men/submissive women, submissive men/dominant women, gay men's S&M, and transvestite S&M. Leather sex bars are meeting places for gay men who are interested in D/S. The D/S subculture includes D/S videos, books, and magazines (Houlberg, 1991; Murray, 1989).

The world of D/S is secretive, but the degree of secrecy depends on the different groups involved and the types of activities they undertake. The world of heterosexual D/S is more hidden; their contacts are limited to private, small networks (Weinberg & Kamel, 1983). One study of heterosexual D/S participants found that most of their friends and families did not know of their involvement (Spengler, 1983).

THE PARAPHILIAS

We have no reliable estimates as to how many individuals are paraphiliacs. But recent work suggests that many of the activities of convicted sex offenders, such as exhibitionism, voyeurism, and pedophilia, may also be present in the general population (Crepault & Couture, 1980; Finkelhor, Hotaling, Lewis, & Smith, 1990; Koss, 1988; Templeman & Stinnett, 1991). A study of 60 college men attempted to find out what percentage of the young male nonoffender, nonclinical population engaged in coercive atypical sexual behaviors (Templeman & Stinnett, 1991). By collecting life histories of the men, the researchers found that 65% had engaged in some form of sexual misconduct, such as voyeurism, obscene phone calling, or sexually rubbing themselves against a woman. The study concluded that young men were easily aroused to diverse stimuli, blurring the distinction between typical and atypical behavior.

The overwhelming majority of paraphilias occur among men. Paraphilias occur among heterosexuals, gay men, male bisexuals, and transsexuals. It is important to realize that sexual orientation is not related to paraphilia. A gay exhibitionist, for example, is considered paraphilic not because of his attraction to other men but because he exposes his genitals (Levine, Risen, & Althof, 1990).

NONCOERCIVE PARAPHILIAS

An important aspect of paraphilias is whether they involve coercion. Noncoercive paraphilias are regarded as relatively benign or harmless because they are victimless. Noncoercive paraphilias include fetishism, transvestism, and zoophilia.

Fetishism

We attribute special or magical powers to many things: a lucky number, a saint's relic, an heirloom, a lock of hair, or an automobile. These objects possess a kind of symbolic magic (Belk, 1991). We will carry our boyfriend's or girlfriend's photograph (and sometimes talk to it or kiss it), ask for a keepsake if we part, become nostalgic for an old love when we hear a particular song. All these are normal, but point to the symbolic power of objects, or fetishes.

Think About It

CROSS-DRESSING: WHAT'S IN A NAME?

Each year vast numbers of ordinary men dress as women during Halloween, Mardi Gras, and Carnival. **Cross-dressing** is a staple of television shows, such as "Martin," "Saturday Night Live," and "In Living Color." It has been the focus of many movies, including *Tootsie* and *Mrs. Doubtfire.* Rock culture includes cross-dressed performances by Little Richard, Alice Cooper, Mick Jagger, David Bowie, and Madonna. In the gay subculture, cross-dressing (or **drag**) is a source of humor and parody. In all these cases, cross-dressing represents a loosening of traditional boundaries. Behind masks and costumes, men and women play out fantasies that are forbidden to them in their daily lives.

As can readily be seen, people cross-dress for a wide variety of reasons. Some people cross-dress to relieve the pressure associated with traditional gender roles. Others are satirizing or parodying social conventions. Still others want to challenge what they see as narrow views of gender and sexuality.

Given the humor, playfulness, and sense of relaxation apparent in many cases of cross-dressing, how do we distinguish this phenomenon from fetishistic transvestism, which is considered a paraphilia? If those who cross-dress are labeled paraphiliacs, what effect does it have on them? Does labeling ever create mental distress in an otherwise relatively well-adjusted person?

Questions like these lead us to consider the effect of labeling in general and to ask, What's in a name? Although clinical labels and definitions help professionals to diagnose illnesses and create treatment plans, labeling can also cause problems. Consider the difference between a seven-year-old boy who is called "active" and one who is labeled "hyperactive." Or between a person described as "compassionate" and one labeled "co-dependent." Or between someone said to have a lot of libido and someone labeled a "sex addict." In each case, the label adds a clinical dimension to the person's behavior. Labeling can have a profound effect both on the individual's self-concept and on the perceptions and behaviors of those involved with the person.

Among those who cross-dress, being labeled a paraphiliac can contribute to maladaptation by fostering unnecessary shame and guilt. It can even become a self-fulfilling prophecy if the person begins to experience significant distress and impairment as a result of being labeled. Although cross-dressing is atypical, the majority of cross-dressers are not maladapted or mentally disordered, nor is their behavior pathological. To label all those who cross-dress as paraphiliacs is incorrect and potentially harmful.

Fetishism is sexual attraction to objects, which become for the fetishist sexual symbols. Instead of relating to another person, a fetishist gains sexual gratification from kissing a shoe, caressing a glove, drawing a lock of hair against his or her cheek, or masturbating with a piece of underwear. But the person does not necessarily focus on an inanimate object; he may be attracted to a woman's feet, ears, breasts, legs, elbows, or any other part of her body (Cautela, 1986). (According to the *DSM-IV*, exclusive attraction to body parts is known as **partialism.**) Some researchers consider *Playboy*'s centerfold to be fetishistic in its focus on female breasts and genitalia (Rosegrant, 1986). Reports of types of fetishes even include arousal from sneezes (King, 1990). According to a recent study, 11% of the men and 6% of the women had engaged in fetishistic behaviors (Janus & Janus, 1993).

Paul Gebhard views fetishistic behavior as existing on a continuum, moving from a slight preference for an object to a strong preference, to the necessity of the object for arousal, and finally to the object as a substitute

cross-dressing Wearing the clothing of a member of the other sex.

drag Cross-dressing, often with comic intent.

fetishism A paraphilia in which a person is sexually attracted to an object, which has become a sexual symbol.

partialism A paraphilia in which a person is sexually attracted to a part of the body.

for a sexual partner (Gebhard, 1976). Most people have slight fetishistic traits: Men describe themselves as leg men or breast men; they prefer dark-haired or light-haired women. Some women are attracted to muscular men, others to hairy chests, and still others to shapely buttocks. It is only when a person develops a strong preference for an object that his or her attachment moves outside the range of statistical normality.

Transvestism

transvestism The wearing of clothing of the other sex, usually for purposes of sexual arousal.

Transvestism is the wearing of clothing of a member of the other sex, usually for purposes of sexual arousal. The term is derived from the Latin *trans*, cross, and *vestire*, to dress. One study found that 6% of men and 3% of women reported cross-dressing (Janus & Janus, 1993). Although the literature indicates that cross-dressing occurs almost exclusively in males, there are studies of women who have erotic attachment to men's garments (Stoller, 1982; Bullough & Bullough, 1993).

People cross-dress for many reasons. Some who cross-dress are considered psychologically disordered, as in **fetishistic transvestism.** According to the American Psychiatric Association, these are heterosexual men who, over a period of at least six months, act upon intense, usually distressful, sexual urges and fantasies involving the wearing of women's clothes. Because many transvestites contend they are not abnormal, but merely revealing a legitimate source of sexual expression and arousal, they resist and shun this diagnosis (see the box: Cross-Dressing: What's in a Name?).

fetishistic transvestite A man who cross-dresses for the purpose of sexual arousal.

Transvestites are usually quite conventional in their masculine dress and attitudes. Dressed as women or wearing only one women's garment, they may become sexually aroused and masturbate or make love with a woman. As time passes, however, the erotic element of the female garment may decrease and their comfort level increase. The majority of transvestites have no desire to undertake a sex-change operation. If they do, there may be an accompanying diagnosis of gender dysphoria. Transvestites are rarely attracted to other men (Wise & Meyer, 1980). They believe they have both masculine and feminine personalities within them. Their feminine personality appears when they cross-dress; sometimes they give their feminine personality a name (Brierly, 1979). Transvestites may even walk around town as women and not be recognized.

Over two-thirds of transvestites are or have been married. In fact, a number of them marry in hopes of "curing" their desire to cross-dress. Of those married, about two-thirds have children. Some voluntarily reveal their cross-dressing after marriage, but the majority have it discovered. Invariably, the transvestites' partners are distressed and blame themselves for somehow "emasculating" their partners. Many transvestites and their wives and families are able to adjust to the cross-dressing. Wives sometimes accompany their cross-dressed husbands in public (Brown & Collier, 1989). Many women have sex with male partners when the men are wearing undergarments, nightgowns, or other feminine attire (Bullough & Weinberg, 1988). But often the stress is too great, and separation follows soon after the transvestism is discovered.

As transvestism is neither dangerous nor reversible, the preferred clinical treatment is to help the transvestite and those close to him accept his cross-dressing. He needs to cope, for example, with feelings of guilt and shame (Peo, 1988).

Why does our culture seem disproportionately preoccupied with cross-dressing? Our interest, writes Marjorie Garber (1992), reflects a "crisis in categories." She asserts that the categories of male/female and heterosexual/homosexual are inadequate for describing the full range of human experience. Just as bisexuality challenges the heterosexuality/homosexuality dichotomy, cross-dressing challenges the traditional masculine/feminine dichotomy. Can a man wearing a dress really be a man? Can a heterosexual male wearing a dress really be heterosexual? Cross-dressing destroys our usual either/or ways of categorizing people (Garber, 1992).

Zoophilia

Zoophilia, sometimes referred to as "bestiality," involves sexual excitement derived from animals (American Psychiatric Association, 1994). Kinsey reported that about 8% of the men and 3% of the women he surveyed had experienced at least one sexual contact with animals. Seventeen percent of the men who had been reared on farms had had such contact, but these activities accounted for less than 1% of their total sexual outlet (Kinsey et al., 1948, 1953). Sexual contact with animals usually takes place among adolescents and is a transitory phenomenon. Among adults, such contact usually occurs when human partners are not available.

Ru-Paul is a well-known cross-dresser who appears on MTV. Cross-dressing has been an important part of popular culture, especially comedy, since Shakespeare's time.

COERCIVE PARAPHILIAS

Few noncoercive paraphilias are brought to public attention because of their private, victimless nature. But coercive paraphilias, which involve victimization, are the subject of concern by society because of the harm they cause others. The majority of adult women have been victimized by some kind or another of these coercive paraphilias.

All of these paraphilias involve some kind of coercive or nonconsensual relationship with another person. A study of over 400 outpatient sex offenders found that they attempted over 239,000 sex crimes, of which the majority were exhibitionism, voyeurism, obscene phone calls, and frotteurism (sexually rubbing against another person). These disorders also appear to be linked to child sexual abuse and rape. As many as 80% of rapists begin their assaultive behavior with "hands-off" sexual behavior, such as exhibitionism, voyeurism, obscene phone calls, and so on. Of exhibitionists, 29.7% were involved in child sexual abuse, and 29.2% were involved in rape. Of voyeurs, 13.8% were involved in child sexual abuse and 20.2% in rape (Knopp, 1984).

zoophilia A paraphila involving recurrent, intense urges to engage in sexual activities with animals.

Voyeurism

Viewing sexual activities is a commonplace activity. As we saw earlier, relatively large percentages of individuals have used mirrors to view themselves in sex acts, watched their partners masturbate, or watched others having intercourse (Person et al., 1989). Americans' interest in viewing sexual activities has spawned a multibillion-dollar sex industry devoted to fulfilling visual desires. Erotic magazines, books, and X-rated videos are available in almost every city, town, and hamlet in America. Topless bars, strip and peep shows, and erotic dancing attest to the attraction of visual erotica.

As Arndt (1991) notes, "Since looking at erotic scenes is so pervasive among males, it is difficult to determine when these acts are pathological." It is generally agreed, however, that the critical difference between casual, consensual viewing and voyeurism is consent.

Voyeurism involves recurring, intense sexual urges and fantasies to secretly observe another person who is nude, disrobing, or engaging in sexual activity (American Psychiatric Association, 1994). In order to become aroused, the man must hide and remain unseen, and the woman or couple must be unaware of his presence. The excitement is intensified by the possibility of being discovered. Sometimes the voyeur will masturbate while he is peering through the window or keyhole.

Very little study has been done of voyeurs, nine out of ten of whom are men. Voyeurs do not seek random females to watch undress or engage in sexual activities; instead, they seek out females they find sexually attractive. What voyeurs consider arousing differs from one voyeur to another. Some require viewing nude bodies, breasts, or vulvas; others desire watching sexual intercourse or lesbian sex. Voyeurism appears to appeal primarily to heterosexual men (Arndt, 1991).

Exhibitionism

Also known as "indecent exposure," **exhibitionism** is the recurring, intense urge or fantasy to display one's genitals to an unsuspecting stranger (American Psychiatric Association, 1994). The individual has acted on these urges or is greatly disturbed by them. Although exhibitionists derive sexual gratification from the exposure of their genitals, the exposure is not a prelude or invitation to intercourse. Instead, it is an escape from intercourse, for the man never exposes himself to a willing woman—only to strangers or near strangers. Exhibitionists generally expose themselves to children, adolescents, and young women; they rarely expose themselves to older women. In those few instances in which a woman shows interest, the exhibitionist immediately flees (Stoller, 1977). Usually, there is no physical contact.

Exhibitionism is a fairly common paraphilia; over one-third of all males arrested for sexual offenses are arrested for exhibitionism. Many of the men arrested for exhibitionism also had engaged in voyeurism, frotteurism, obscene phone calling, and attempted rape (Lang, Checkley, & Pugh, 1987). Seven percent of college men in one study expressed interest in exhibiting themselves; 2% actually had (Templeman & Stinnett, 1991). Another study found that exhibitionistic offenders became slightly more aroused by descriptions of exposure than nonoffending men (Marshall, Eccles, & Barabee, 1991). Because of the widespread incidence of exhibitionism, at least half of adult women may have witnessed indecent exposure at least once in their lives (Arndt, 1991).

The stereotype of the exhibitionist as a dirty old man, lurking in parks or building entryways, dressed only in a raincoat and sneakers, is erroneous. (Fewer than 10% of exhibitionists are over 50 years old, although a few may be as old as in their eighties when they first begin [Arndt, 1991; Kenyon, 1989].)

Exhibitionists appear to find fully clothed women more erotic than nude

voyeurism A paraphilia involving recurrent, intense urges to view nonconsenting others while they are engaged in sexual activities.

exhibitionism A paraphilia involving recurrent, intense urges to expose the genitals to another, nonconsenting person.

Some people like to exhibit their bodies within public settings that are "legitimized," as in this wet T-shirt party. Such displays may be exhibitionistic, but they are not considered exhibitionism in the clinical sense.

or partially nude women. For some reason, they misinterpret neutral or nonerotic signals from women as erotic (Fedora, Reddon, & Yeudall, 1986). Most reportedly hope that the women will enjoy the experience (Lang et al., 1987).

Exhibitionists are generally introverted, insecure, or sexually inadequate men (Arndt, 1991; Marshall, Eccles, & Barabee, 1991). They feel impotent as men, and their sexual relations with their wives are usually poor. This sense of impotence gives rise to anger and hostility, which they direct toward other women by exhibiting themselves.

Telephone Scatalogia

Telephone scatalogia, the making of obscene phone calls, is a paraphilia because the acts are compulsive and repetitive or because the associated fantasies cause distress to the individual.

Sixty-one percent of the women in one study reported receiving at least one obscene phone call; 45% had received two or more calls (Herold, Mantel, & Zemitis, 1979). Eight percent of the college students in another study reported making such calls at least once (Templeman & Stinnett, 1991). Obscene phone calls are generally made randomly, by chance dialing or phone book listings.

The overwhelming majority of callers are male, but there are some female obscene callers as well (Saunders & Awad, 1991). Male callers frequently make their female victims annoyed, frightened, anxious, upset, or angry. Their victims often feel violated. But female callers have a different effect on male recipients, who generally do not feel violated or who may enjoy the call as titillation (Matek, 1988).

telephone scatalogia A paraphilia involving recurrent, intense urges to make obscene telephone calls.

You and Your Sexual Well-Being

IF YOU RECEIVE AN OBSCENE PHONE CALL . . .

An obscene phone call can be shocking or even traumatizing. A person who receives such a call may feel attacked, singled out, or victimized. If you have had this experience, it may be helpful to know that the obscene phone caller very often picks his victim randomly from a phone book or just by dialing and is merely trying to elicit a response. Horror, anger, and shock are the reactions he anticipates and finds arousing; thus, your initial response is critical.

If you receive an obscene phone call, the best thing to do is to quietly hang up the telephone. Banging down the receiver or trying to retaliate by screaming or scolding only gives the caller the response he desires. The telephone company claims that tactics such as pretending to be hard of hearing, blowing a whistle into the telephone, pretending to go to another phone, and letting the phone remain off the hook simply are not necessary. If the phone immediately rings again, don't answer it. If obscene calls are repeated, the telephone company suggests changing your number (many companies will do this at no charge) or, in more serious cases, working with law enforcement departments to trace the calls. Some states permit the individual to purchase and use caller identification technology, which enables you to identify the telephone number of incoming calls.

Fortunately, the obscene phone caller rarely follows up his verbal intrusion with a physical attack on his victim.

Frotteurism

frotteurism A paraphilia involving recurrent, intense urges to touch or rub against a nonconsenting person for the purpose of sexual arousal.

Frotteurism (also known as "frottage") involves recurrent, intense urges or fantasies—lasting at least 6 months—to touch or rub against a nonconsenting person for the purpose of sexual arousal and gratification (American Psychiatric Association, 1994). It is not known how many people practice frotteurism, but one study of normal college males found that 21% had engaged in at least one frotteuristic act (Templeman & Stinnett, 1991).

The frotteur usually carries out his touching or rubbing in crowded subways, buses, or large sporting events or rock concerts. When he enters a crowd, his initial rubbing can be disguised by the crush of people. He usually rubs against his victim's buttocks or thighs with his erect penis inside his pants. At other times, he may use his hands to rub a woman's buttocks, pubic region, thighs, or breasts. Generally, he rubs against the woman for 60–90 seconds. If he ejaculates, he stops. If not, he usually moves on to find another victim (Abel, 1989).

Frotteurism often occurs with other paraphilias, especially exhibitionism, voyeurism, pedophilia, and sadism, the sexually arousing infliction of pain. It is also associated with rape.

Necrophilia

necrophilia A paraphilia involving recurrent, intense urges to engage in sexual activities with a corpse.

Necrophilia is sexual activity with a corpse. It is regarded as nonconsensual because a corpse is obviously unable to give consent. There are relatively few instances of necrophilia, yet it retains a fascination in horror literature, especially vampire stories and legends, and in gothic novels. It is also associated with ritual cannibalism in other cultures. Within our own culture, *Sleeping Beauty* features a necrophilic theme, as does the crypt scene in Shakespeare's *Romeo and Juliet*. Some heavy metal music deals with necrophilia (Rosman & Resnick, 1989).

A review of 122 cases of supposed necrophilia or necrophilic fantasies found only 54 instances of true necrophilia (Rosman & Resnick, 1989). The study found that neither sadism, psychosis, nor mental impairment was inherent in necrophilia. Instead, the most common motive for necrophilia was the possession of a partner who neither resisted nor rejected. In order to find such "partners," necrophiliacs often choose occupations giving them access to corpses, such as mortician or morgue attendant. Yet even some who have access to bodies nevertheless commit murder as part of their necrophilic behavior.

Pedophilia

Pedophilia refers to "recurrent intense sexual urges and sexually arousing fantasies involving sexual activity with a prepubescent child or children" that the individual, referred to as a **pedophile,** has acted upon or finds distressing (American Psychiatric Association, 1994). The children are age 13 or younger. A pedophile must be at least 16 and at least 5 years older than the child. (A late adolescent is not considered pedophilic if he or she is involved in an ongoing sexual relationship with a 12-year-old or older child.) A large number of arrested pedophiles currently are or previously have been involved in exhibitionism, voyeurism, or rape. In this section, we discuss only pedophilia. Nonpedophilic child sexual abuse and incest, their impact on the victim, and prevention of child sexual abuse are discussed in Chapter 17. Child sexual abuse is illegal in every state.

Sexual attraction to children is fairly widespread in the nonoffending population. A study of child-focused thoughts and fantasies among 193 male college students found that 21% reported sexual attraction to children, 9% had sexual fantasies of children, and 5% had masturbated to such fantasies (Briere & Runtz, 1989). These individuals tended to have had negative early sexual experiences; they reported dominance attitudes toward women, as well as a likelihood of raping them.

For most adult men and women, whether they are heterosexual, gay, or lesbian, the gender of their partner is important. But heterosexual/homosexual orientation is less important to pedophiles. For pedophiles, it is more important that the child *is* a child (Freund & Watson, 1993; Freund, Watson, Dickey, & Rienzo, 1991). As a consequence, many heterosexually identified men may molest boys or boys and girls. Homosexually identified men may molest both boys and girls, although they are less likely to molest girls (Arndt, 1991; Freund et al., 1991).

Cross-Sex Pedophilia Some male pedophiles seek to sexually molest female children, the majority of whom are between ages 8 and 9. Adolescent pedophiles, averaging 15 years of age, sexually misuse girls around age 7 (Arndt, 1991). About half the pedophiles report stressful events, such as marital or work conflict, personal loss, or rejection, preceding the act of

pedophilia A paraphilia characterized by recurrent, intense urges to engage in sexual activities with a prepubescent child.

pedophile A person who is sexually attracted to children.

molestation. Many are fearful that their sexual abilities are decreasing or that they are impotent. Alcohol consumption, resulting in disinhibition, is involved in 30–50% of the offenses. One-third claim that viewing explicit child pornography led, at least occasionally, to their committing the offense (Marshall, 1988).

Seduction and enticement were used in about one-third of the cases reported (Groth & Birnbaum, 1978). In these instances, the pedophile is known to the girl. The pedophile befriends the girl, talking to her, giving her candy, taking her to the store, going for walks with her, letting her watch TV at his house. Gradually, he initiates tactile contact with her, such as having her sit on his lap, rough-housing with her, or giving her a back rub. Eventually, he will attempt to fondle her (Lang & Frenzel, 1988). If she resists, he will stop and try later. He will try added inducements or pressure but will rarely use force (Groth, Hobson, & Gary, 1982).

Pedophilic acts rarely involve sexual intercourse. The pedophile usually seeks to fondle or touch the child, usually on her genitals, legs, and buttocks. Sometimes the pedophile exposes himself and has the child touch his penis. Occasionally, oral or anal stimulation is involved (Arndt, 1991).

Although a pedophile may have sexual relationships with women, they are not necessarily his preferred partners. About half of pedophiles are or have been married. Most married pedophiles claim their marriages are happy, although they describe their wives as controlling and sexually distant. Their frequency of marital intercourse does not differ from nonoffenders, but many report a low sex drive and erectile difficulties. Few have serious mental disorders, such as psychosis (Arndt, 1991).

Same-Sex Pedophilia

Same-sex pedophilia is a complicated phenomenon. It does not appear to be as closely linked to homosexuality as cross-sex pedophilia is to heterosexuality. A different kind of psychosexual dynamic seems to be at work for a large number of same-sex pedophiles. While most same-sex pedophiles have little interest in heterosexual relationships, a significant number do not identify themselves as gay. One study of imprisoned offenders, for example, found that over half identified themselves as heterosexual or bisexual. Many reject a gay identity or are homophobic. Although some people believe that pedophilia is the means by which the gay community "recruits" boys into homosexuality, pedophiles are soundly rejected by the gay subculture (Peters, 1992).

The mean age of the molested boy is between 10 and 12. A large number of pedophiles describe feelings of love, friendship, or caring for the boy. Others blatantly entice or exploit their victims. Force is rarely used. Voluntary interviews with 27 same-sex pedophiles reveal four themes to explain their involvement with children: (1) Their pedophilic desire feels "natural" to them, (2) children are appealing because they are gentle and truthful, (3) adult-child sexual involvement can be positive for the child, and (4) the relationship is characterized by romantic love, not casual sex (Li, 1990). Such views are generally regarded as cognitive distortions or rationalizations. Adult-child sexual relationships are by definition exploitive. The majority of children report feelings of victimization (Finkelhor, 1990).

The most common activities are fondling and masturbation, usually the man masturbating the boy. Other acts include oral-genital sex, with the adult fellating the boy, and anal sex, with the adult assuming the active role.

Female Pedophilia   Although there are relatively few reports of female pedophiles, there appears to be a small percentage (Arndt, 1991; Rowan, 1988). Female pedophilia appears to be underreported for two reasons (Rowan, 1988). First, male/female stereotypes disguise female sexual contact with children. Men are viewed as aggressive and sexual, while women are viewed as maternal and nurturing. Because of these stereotypes, women are given greater freedom than men in touching children and expressing feelings for them. As a consequence, when a pedophilic female embraces, kisses, or pets a child, her behavior is viewed as nurturing rather than sexual. But when a nonpedophilic male does the same thing, his behavior may be misinterpreted as sexual.

Second, the majority of male children who have sexual contact with adult women generally view the experience positively rather than negatively (Condy, Templer, Brown, & Veaco, 1987). As a consequence, they do not report the contact. The media also reinforce a belief in the essentially benign nature of female pedophilia in such films as *Rambling Rose*, in which a central comic scene depicts a sexually curious 13-year-old boy petting with Rose, a nonpedophilic but sex-loving young woman. Because of our feelings about female and same-sex molestation, it is impossible to imagine a comparable scene with a 13-year-old girl with a sex-loving young man, or an adult male with a young boy being depicted comically.

Adult female sexual contact with young boys is fairly common. A study of almost 1600 male and female college students and prison inmates found that 16% of male college students and 46% of male prison inmates had sexual contacts with women when they were 12 years old or younger and the women were in their early twenties (Condy, Templer, Brown, & Veaco, 1987). Over half of the men in the study reported having sexual intercourse with the women. The majority of the women were friends, neighbors, babysitters, or strangers. Among the women in the study reporting sexual contact with boys, 0.5% were college students, and 7.5% were prisoners.

Over half the college males and two-thirds of the prisoners in the study reported that at the time, they felt their childhood experiences with adult females were positive. Twenty-five percent of the college males and 6% of the male prisoners regarded it as negative. And 12% of the college males and 25% of the prisoners regarded the experience as mixed. The critical factor affecting how they evaluated the experience was whether force was used. Those forced into sex generally regarded the experience as negative.

Female sexual abuse of male children differs from male sexual abuse of female children in several significant ways (Condy, Templer, Brown, & Veaco, 1987; Cooper, Swaminath, Baxter, & Poulin, 1990; Fritz, Stoll, & Wagner, 1981; Okami, 1991). First, half the female sexual abusers had sexual intercourse with the male children, while relatively few male sexual abusers had sexual intercourse with female children. Second, female abusers forced male children to engage in sexual activities significantly less frequently than male abusers forced female children. Third, male children tend not to be as traumatized by female abusers as female children are by male abusers.

Sexual Sadism and Sexual Masochism

Although we tend to think of sadism and masochism as different aspects of a single phenomenon, sadomasochism, sadists are not necessarily masochists, nor are masochists necessarily sadists. Sadism and masochism are separate but sometimes related phenomena. In order to make this distinction clear, the American Psychiatric Association (1994) has created separate categories: sexual sadism and sexual masochism.

There is no clear dividing line between sexual sadism and sexual masochism, and domination and submission. In the case of sadism, coercion separates sexual sadism from domination. But in consensual behaviors, there is no clear distinction. A rule of thumb separating consensual sexual sadism and masochism from domination and submission may be that the activities are extreme, compulsive, and dangerous.

According to the *DSM-IV*, a person may be diagnosed with **sexual sadism** if, over a period of at least 6 months, he or she experiences intense, recurring sexual urges or fantasies involving real (not simulated) acts in which physical or psychological harm (including humiliation) is inflicted upon a victim for purposes of sexual arousal. The individual has acted on these urges or finds them extremely distressful (American Psychiatric Association, 1994). Characteristic symptoms include obsessive, compelling sexual thoughts and fantasies involving acts centering on a victim's physical suffering. The victim may be a consenting masochist or someone abducted by the sadist. The victim may be tortured, raped, mutilated, or killed; often the victim is physically restrained and blindfolded or gagged (Money, 1990).

Most rapes are not committed by sexual sadists, but sadistic rapes do account for about 5% of all stranger rapes (Groth, 1979). Sadistic rapes are the most brutal. The rapist finds "intentional maltreatment gratifying and takes pleasure in torment, anguish, distress, helplessness, and suffering" (Groth, 1979). There is often bondage and a ritualistic quality to such rapes.

For a diagnosis of **sexual masochism** to be made, a person must experience for a period of at least 6 months intense, recurring sexual urges or fantasies involving real (not simulated) acts of being "humiliated, beaten, bound, or otherwise made to suffer." The individual has acted on these urges or is highly distressed by them (American Psychiatric Association, 1994).

Treating Paraphiliacs

Paraphiliacs generally come into treatment as the result of arrest. When their exhibitionism, child molestation, or other paraphilic behavior is made public, the stress and humiliation lead to a sudden and dramatic decrease of their previously secret activities. They often believe they are cured. The reduction of paraphilic desire, however, is only temporary. Once the intense crisis stage passes, the desires often return. But the paraphiliac believes that he has conquered his deviancy. This belief feeds into the paraphiliac's denial. Once again, he believes he does not need treatment. In fact, one of the first tasks clinicians must undertake is to make their clients recognize that they *do* need treatment. The principal approaches to treatment involve decreasing the paraphilic behavior, sometimes through drug or aversion therapy, and teaching social skills and stress management techniques.

Studying atypical and paraphilic sexual behaviors reveals the variety and complexity of sexual behavior. It also underlines the limits of tolerance. Some unconventional sexual behaviors, undertaken in private between consenting adults as the source of erotic pleasure, are of concern only to the people involved. As long as physical or psychological harm is not done to the self or others, it is no one's place to judge.

sexual sadism A paraphilia characterized by recurrent, intense urges to engage in real (not fantasy) sexual acts in which the person inflicts physical or psychological harm on a victim.

sexual masochism A paraphilia characterized by recurrent, intense urges to engage in real (not fantasy) sexual acts in which the person is humiliated, harmed, or otherwise made to suffer.

AUTOEROTIC ASPHYXIA

What would you do to achieve or enhance an orgasm? Would you buy pornographic magazines? Cross-dress? Use illegal drugs? Risk death?

It is estimated that as many as 1000 individuals die annually as a result of inadvertently strangling themselves while masturbating. This type of death is known as **autoerotic asphyxia,** or sexual asphyxia. The goal of its victims appears to be the heightening of sexual sensation by cutting off the oxygen supply to the brain, with death occurring accidentally.

Because of the secrecy and shame that accompanies this and other masturbatory activities, it is difficult to estimate the number of individuals who find this practice arousing. Reports by survivors are extremely rare. It is known that most of the victims are adolescent, heterosexual male Caucasians (Rosenblum & Faber, 1979). Why this is true still remains unexplained.

The practice involves a variety of techniques, all of which cut off oxygen to the brain and can cause death. It is suggested that the interference with the blood supply to the brain causes cerebral anoxia (lack of oxygen), which is experienced as giddiness, lightheadedness, and exhilaration, thereby heightening and reinforcing the masturbatory sensation (Resnick, 1972).

Individuals often use ropes, cords, or chains along with padding around the neck to prevent telltale signs (Coe, 1974). Others may place bags or blankets over their heads. Still others inhale asphyxiating gases such as aerosol sprays or nitrous oxide. The corpses are usually found either naked or partially clothed, often in women's clothing. Various forms of bondage have also been observed (Blanchard & Hucker, 1991).

The characteristic features that rule out the possibility of suicide are the presence of pornographic materials, the use of a mirror or video camera, evidence of penile engorgement and/or ejaculation, and the absence of a suicide note (Sheehan & Garfinkel, 1988).

The origins of the syndrome are obscure but are believed to date back to the seventeenth century (Rosenblum & Faber, 1979). During that time period, some people in England experimented with self-hanging as a possible cure for impotence (Resnik, 1972). Anthropologists have reported observing similar practices among Eskimo children, some Indian tribes in North and South America, and some Asian societies (Rosenblum & Faber, 1979).

Several theories about who participates in this activity and why have been put forward. Many victims seem to have had strict, punitive parents, in particular, dominant mothers and rejecting and/or abusive or ill fathers. For some, childhood conflicts somehow lead to a fascination with ropes, cords, or chains, which are soon incorporated into sexual activities at the adolescent stage of development (Rosenblum & Faber, 1979). Other factors may include severe guilt, castration anxiety, and a fascination with masochism (Resnick, 1972: Saunders, 1989).

Regardless of the origins, it is important that medical personnel, parents, and other adults be aware of this practice so they can recognize signs of it and respond with strategies commensurate with its seriousness. Those who engage in such sexual practices rarely realize the potential consequences of their behavior; therefore, parents and others must be alert to physical and other telltale signs. An unusual neck bruise; bloodshot eyes; disoriented behavior, especially after the person has been alone for awhile; and an unexplained possession of or fascination with ropes or chains are the key signs (Saunders, 1989). Until we as a society can educate, recognize, and respond to autoerotic asphyxia assertively and with compassion, we can expect to see more deaths occur as a result of this practice.

autoerotic asphyxia Accidental asphyxiation as a result of attempting to heighten sexual sensation by strangling oneself during masturbation, usually with a rope or chain.

SUMMARY

Atypical Versus Paraphilic Behavior

• Atypical sexual behavior is consensual behavior in which less than the majority of individuals engage. Atypical sexual behavior is not abnormal behavior, the definition of which varies from culture to culture and from one historical period to another.

• Today, sexual behaviors that are classified as mental disorders are known as paraphilias. Paraphilias tend to be either coercive or injurious, compulsive, and long-standing. A paraphilia is characterized by recurring, intense sexual urges and sexual fantasies involving nonhuman objects, the suffering or humiliation of oneself or one's partner, or children or other nonconsenting individuals.

Atypical Sexual Behaviors

• Domination and submission (D/S), also known as sadomasochism (S&M), is a form of fantasy sex with power the central element.

The Paraphilias

• Although there are no reliable statistics on the number of individuals involved, paraphilic activities are widespread in the nonoffender population.

Noncoercive Paraphilias

• Fetishism is sexual attraction to objects. Transvestism is the wearing of clothes of a member of the other sex, usually for purposes of sexual arousal. Zoophilia involves sexual excitement derived from animals.

Coercive Paraphilias

• Voyeurism is the nonconsensual and secret observation of others for the purpose of sexual arousal.

• Exhibitionism is the exposure of the genitals to a nonconsenting stranger.

• Telephone scatalogia is the nonconsensual telephoning of strangers and using obscene language.

• Frotteurism involves touching or rubbing against a nonconsenting person for the purpose of sexual arousal.

• Necrophilia is sexual activity with a corpse.

• Pedophilia refers to sexual arousal and contact with children age 13 or younger by adults, or with children age 11 or younger by adolescents older than age 16. Child sexual abuse is illegal in every state. Heterosexuals and gay men may both be pedophilically attracted to boys, while gay pedophiles are less attracted to girls.

• The majority of pedophiles know their victim. About half of pedophiles have been married. The most common activities are fondling and masturbation.

• There are relatively few reported cases of female pedophilia, but it may be underreported for two reasons. Because of stereotypes of female nurturance, pedophilic activities may not be recognized; and the majority of male children apparently view the event positively or neutrally.

• Sexual sadism refers to sexual urges or fantasies of intentionally inflicting real physical or psychological pain or suffering on a partner. About 5% of all rapes are sadistic.

• Sexual masochism is the recurring sexual urge or fantasy of being humiliated or caused to suffer through real acts, not simulated ones. Autoerotic asphyxia is death occurring as a result of masturbatory activities linked with hanging or suffocation.

• Most paraphiliacs come into treatment as a result of arrest. Principal approaches to treatment involve decreasing the behavior and teaching social skills and stress management techniques.

SUGGESTED READINGS

Arndt, William B., Jr. *Gender Disorders and the Paraphilias*. Madison, CT: International Universities Press, 1991. A comprehensive look at transvestism, transsexuality, and the paraphilias.

Dailey, Dennis, ed. *The Sexually Unusual: A Guide to Understanding and Helping*. New York: Harrington Park Press, 1988. A thoughtful and often compassionate examination of what are usually considered paraphilias.

Garber, Marjorie. *Vested Interests: Cross-Dressing and Cultural Anxiety*. New York: Routledge, 1992. A provocative study of the role of cross-dressing in contemporary culture. Cross-dressers, the author argues, call attention to cultural inconsistencies about being male and female in our society.

Maletsky, Barry M. *Treating the Sexual Offender*. Newbury Park, CA: Sage Publications, 1991. An extensive and detailed examination of sex offenders, most of whom were offenders against children.

Chapter Eleven

CONTRACEPTION AND BIRTH CONTROL

P R E V I E W : S E L F - Q U I Z

1. Recent studies show that most couples use some form of birth control the first time they have intercourse. True or false?

2. The most common forms of birth control in the United States are surgical sterilization and the pill. True or false?

3. Birth control pills do *not* help protect against sexually transmitted diseases. True or false?

4. A condom that is worn by women is currently available. True or false?

5. Spermicides (chemicals toxic to sperm) may also be toxic to organisms that cause sexually transmitted diseases. True or false?

6. It is clearly understood how the IUD works to prevent pregnancy. True or false?

7. The hormonal implant Norplant can remain in place over a period of up to 5 years. True or false?

8. A woman can get pregnant up to 72 hours following ovulation. True or false?

9. The rate of abortions performed in the United States has declined to a rate similar to that of 1979. True or false?

10. Women in over 80 countries take injections of the hormone DMPA (Depo-Provera) every 3 or 6 months as their method of birth control, but the drug is not available in this country. True or false?

ANSWERS 1. F, 2. T, 3. T, 4. T, 5. T, 6. F, 7. T, 8. F, 9. T, 10. F

Chapter Outline

To humankind both ancient and modern, the management of fertility has been a primary pursuit. The fertility of people and of the land that sustains them is essential for survival itself. Abundant crops—of grains, produce, animals, and children—are a great boon. In addition, historically and today, people have used fertility as a measure of individual worth. Because of their failure to produce offspring, women in some societies have been abandoned or even killed.

And yet, though greatly desired, animal and human fertility must be controlled. Too many cattle will eat all the grain; too many dogs will roam the streets, half-starved. As for the children, even they can become too much of a good thing when there isn't enough food in the community to sustain

Planning contraception requires us to acknowledge our sexuality. One way a responsible couple can reduce the risk of pregnancy is by visiting a family planning clinic—together.

them. Fertility is a double-edged sword. It is the object of great struggle and fervent prayer. Yet it often must be suppressed in order to preserve life itself.

Those of us who wish to take charge of our reproductive destinies need to be informed about the methods we have to choose from. But information is only part of the picture. We also need to understand our own personal dynamics so that we can choose methods we will use consistently. In this way, we avoid taking risks. In this chapter, we begin by examining the psychology of risk taking and the role of individual responsibility in contraception. We then describe in detail the numerous contraceptive devices and techniques (including abstinence) that are used today: methods of use, effectiveness rate, advantages, and possible problems. We also take a look at the future of contraceptive research. Finally, we look at the process of abortion and its effect on individuals and society.

RISK AND RESPONSIBILITY

A woman has about a 2–4% chance of becoming pregnant during intercourse without contraception. If intercourse occurs the day before ovulation, the chance of pregnancy is about 30%; if it occurs on the day of ovulation, the chance is about 15% (Hatcher et al., 1990). Over a period of a year, a couple that does not use contraception has a 90% chance of pregnancy. More than half of these pregnancies are unplanned (Ingrassia, Springen, & Rosenberg, 1995).

Because the possibility of pregnancy is so high for a sexually active couple, it seems reasonable that sexually active men and women would use contraception to avoid unintended pregnancy. Unfortunately, all too often this is not the case. One major study found that during their first intercourse,

THE PSYCHOLOGY OF RISK TAKING

Most people know they are taking a chance when they don't use contraception. But, as demonstrated in Kristin Luker's classic study (1975) of contraceptive risk taking, the more frequently a person takes chances with unprotected intercourse without resultant pregnancy, the more likely he or she is to take chances again. A subtle psychology develops: Somehow, apparently by will power, "good vibes," or the gods' kindly intervention, the woman will not get pregnant. Eventually, the woman or couple will feel almost magically invulnerable to pregnancy. Each time they are lucky, their risk taking is reinforced.

The consequences of an unintended pregnancy—economic hardships, adoption, or abortion—may be overwhelming. So why do people take chances in the first place? Part of the reason is faulty knowledge. People often underestimate how easy it is to get pregnant. Or, they may not know how to use a contraceptive method correctly. Some people become pregnant because they deny their sexuality. Others subconsciously desire a child.

Let's examine some of the perceived costs of contraceptive planning versus the anticipated benefits of pregnancy.

Perceived Costs of Contraceptive Planning

One reason people avoid taking steps to prevent pregnancy is that they don't want to acknowledge their own sexuality. On the surface, it may seem fairly simple to acknowledge that we are sexual beings, especially if we have conscious sexual desires and engage in sexual intercourse. Yet acknowledging our sexuality is not necessarily easy, for it may be accompanied by feelings of guilt, conflict, and shame. The younger or less experienced we are, the more difficult it is to acknowledge our sexuality.

Planning contraception requires us to admit not only that we are sexual but also that we plan to be sexually active. Without such planning, men and women can pretend that their sexual intercourse "just happens"—in a moment of passion, when they have been drinking, or when the moon is full—even though it happens frequently.

Another reason people don't use contraception is difficulty in obtaining it. It is often embarrassing for sexually inexperienced people to be seen in contexts that identify them as sexual beings. The person who sits behind you in your chemistry class may be sitting next to you in the waiting room of the family planning clinic. If you go to the drugstore to buy condoms, who knows if your mother, teacher, or minister might be down the aisle buying toothpaste (or contraceptives, for that matter) and might see you?

Many people also have trouble planning and continuing contraception. Contraceptive developments in the last few decades (especially the pill) shifted responsibility from the man to the woman. Required to more consciously define themselves as sexual, women have had to abandon traditional, passive sexual roles. Some women, however, are reluctant to plan contraceptive use because they fear they will be regarded as sexually aggressive or promiscuous.

Because it is women who get pregnant, men tend to be unaware of their responsibility or to downplay their role in conception and pregnancy, although with the reemerging popularity of the condom, responsibility may become more balanced (especially if women insist on it). Nevertheless, males, especially adolescents, of-

fewer than half the couples used contraception (Zelnick & Shaw, 1983). In recent years, there has been a slight increase in contraceptive use. Jacqueline Forrest and Susheela Singh (1990) found that nearly two-thirds of the adolescent girls they surveyed used contraception. Moreover, as men and ten lack the awareness that supports contraceptive planning (Freeman, 1980). Yet males are more fertile than females. The average male is fertile 24 hours a day for 50 years or more. Females, in contrast, are fertile only a day or two out of the month for 35 or so years.

Many people, especially women using pills, practice birth control consistently and effectively within a steady relationship but give up their contraceptive practices if the relationship breaks up. They define themselves as sexual only within the context of a relationship. When men or women begin a new relationship, they may not use contraception because the relationship has not yet become established. They do not expect to have sexual intercourse or to have it often, so they are willing to take chances.

Using contraceptive devices such as a condom or diaphragm may destroy the feeling of "spontaneity" in sex. For those who justify their sexual behavior by romantic impulsiveness, using these devices seems cold and mechanical. Others do not use them because they feel it would interrupt the passion of the moment.

Anticipated Benefits of Pregnancy

Many men and women fantasize that even an "accidental" pregnancy might be beneficial. Ambivalence about pregnancy is a powerful incentive *not* to use contraception (Demb, 1991). What are some of the perceived benefits of pregnancy?

First, for many, being pregnant proves that a woman is indeed feminine on the most fundamental biological level. Getting a woman pregnant provides similar proof of masculinity for a man. Being a mother is one of the most basic definitions of traditional womanhood. In an era in which there is considerable confusion about women's roles, pregnancy helps, even forces, a woman to define herself in a traditional manner. Adolescent and young men may also find the idea of fatherhood compelling. They may feel that fathering a child will give them a sense of accomplishment and an aura of maturity.

Pregnancy also proves beyond any doubt that a person is fertile. Many men and women have lingering doubts about whether they can have children. This is especially true for couples who have used contraception for a long time, but it is also true for those who constantly take chances. If they have taken chances many times without pregnancy resulting, they may begin to have doubts about their fertility.

Another anticipated benefit of pregnancy is that it requires a couple to define their relationship and commitment to each other. It is a form of testing, albeit often an unconscious one. It raises many questions that must be answered. How will the partner react? Will it lead to marriage or a breakup? Will it solidify a marriage or a relationship? Will the partner be loving and understanding, or will he or she be angry and rejecting? What is the real nature of the commitment? Many men and women unconsciously expect their partners to be pleased; frequently, however, this is not the case.

Finally, pregnancy involves not only the couple but their parents as well (especially the woman's). Pregnancy forces a young person's parents to pay attention and deal with him or her as an adult. Being pregnant puts a female on the very verge of adulthood, for in most cultures, marriage and motherhood are major rites of passage. Similarly, fatherhood is an adult status for a male, transforming him from a boy into a man. Pregnancy may mean many things in regard to the parent-child relationship. It may be a sign of rebellion, a form of punishment for a parental lack of caring, a plea for help and understanding, or an insistence on autonomy, independence, or adulthood.

women age, they become more consistent contraceptive users. One national study found that twice as many married women as single women (whether never married, separated, or divorced) used contraception (Bachrach, 1984).

Numerous studies have indicated that the most consistent users of contraception are men and women who explicitly communicate about the subject. Those at greatest risk are those in casual dating relationships and those who infrequently discuss contraception with their partners or others. A review of the literature on the interpersonal factors in contraceptive use concluded: "Individuals in stable, serious relationships of long duration who had frequent, predictable patterns of sexual activity were most likely to use contraception" (Milan & Kilmann, 1987).

Who should be responsible for birth control? Because women bear children and have most of the responsibility for raising them, they may have a greater interest than their partners in controlling their fertility. Women "want to know they are in charge," says Roberta Synal of Planned Parenthood (cited in Perkins, 1991). Also, it has generally been easier to keep one egg from being fertilized once a month than to stop millions of sperm during each act of intercourse. Nevertheless, it is unfair to assume, as people generally do in our society, that the total responsibility for birth control should lie with women. In some countries, such as Italy and Japan, male methods of contraception (such as withdrawal or condoms) are used more than female methods. Although withdrawal is not considered a reliable method of birth control, the condom is quite effective when used properly, especially in combination with a spermicide.

In addition to using a condom, a man can help take contraceptive responsibility by (1) exploring ways of making love without intercourse; (2) helping pay doctor or clinic bills and sharing the cost of pills, implants, or other birth control supplies; (3) checking on supplies, helping keep track of the woman's menstrual cycle, and helping his partner with her part in the birth control routine; and (4) in a long-term relationship, if no (or no more) children are wanted, having a vasectomy.

METHODS OF CONTRACEPTION AND BIRTH CONTROL

The methods we use to prevent pregnancy or to keep it from progressing vary widely according to our personal beliefs, tastes, health, and other life circumstances. For many people, especially women, the search for an "ideal" method of birth control is one of ongoing frustration. Some methods pose health risks to certain women, others run counter to religious or moral beliefs, and others are inconvenient or aesthetically displeasing. There are a number of methods and techniques to choose from, however, and scientific research is increasing our options for safe and effective contraception. Most individuals and couples can find a method that they can use with comfort and, most important, with regularity.

Birth Control and Contraception

Although the terms "birth control" and "contraception" are often used interchangeably, there is actually a subtle difference in meaning. **Birth control** is any means of preventing a birth from taking place. Thus, methods that prevent a fertilized egg from implanting in the uterine wall (such as the IUD in some instances) and methods that remove the **conceptus**—the fertilized egg, embryo, or fetus—from the uterus (such as "morning-after" pills and surgical abortions) are forms of birth control. These are not, how-

birth control Any means of preventing a birth from taking place, including contraception and abortion.

conceptus In medical terminology, the developing human offspring from fertilization through birth.

ever, true contraceptive methods. **Contraception,** the prevention of conception altogether, is the category of birth control in which the sperm and egg are prevented from uniting. This is done in a variety of ways, including barrier methods, such as condoms and diaphragms, which place a physical barrier between sperm and egg; spermicides, which kill the sperm before they can get to the egg; and hormonal methods, such as the pill and implants, which inhibit the release of the oocyte from the ovary.

contraception The prevention of conception.

Choosing a Method

In order to be fully responsible in using birth control, a person must know what options he or she has available, how reliable these methods are, and the advantages and disadvantages (including possible side effects) of each method. How to choose the best form of birth control for yourself and your partner, especially if you have not been practicing contraception, is not easy. But knowing the facts about the methods gives you a solid basis from which to make decisions, and more security once a decision is reached. If you need to choose a birth control method for yourself, remember that *the best method is the one you will use consistently.* When you are having intercourse, a condom left in a purse or wallet, a diaphragm in the bedside drawer, or a forgotten pill in its packet on the other side of town is *not* an effective means of birth control.

In the following discussion of method effectiveness, "theoretical effectiveness" implies perfectly consistent and correct use; "user effectiveness" refers to *actual* use (and misuse) based on studies by health-care organizations, medical practitioners, academic researchers, and pharmaceutical companies. User effectiveness is sometimes significantly lower than theoretical effectiveness because of factors that keep people from using a method properly or consistently. These factors may be inherent in the method or may be the result of a variety of influences on the user.

Sexual Abstinence

Before we begin our discussion of devices and techniques for preventing conception, we must acknowledge the oldest and most reliable birth control method of all. **Abstinence**—refraining from sexual intercourse—should be regarded as a legitimate personal choice, yet those who choose not to express their sensuality or sexuality through genital contact risk being stigmatized as uptight, frigid, or weird. The term "celibacy" is sometimes used interchangeably with "abstinence." We use the word "abstinence" because "celibacy" often implies the avoidance of *all* forms of sexual activity and, often, the religious commitment to not marry or to maintain a nonsexual lifestyle.

abstinence Refraining from sexual intercourse.

Individuals who choose not to have intercourse are still free to express affection (and give and receive sexual satisfaction if they so desire) in a variety of ways. Ways to show love without making babies include talking, hugging, massaging, kissing, petting, and manual stimulation of the genitals. Those who choose sexual abstinence as their method of birth control need to communicate this clearly to their dates or partners. They should also be informed about other forms of contraception. And, in the event that either partner experiences a change of mind, it can't hurt to have a

You and Your Sexual Well-Being

CHOOSING A BIRTH CONTROL METHOD

It is important to choose a method of birth control that works. All the methods offered at a family planning clinic will work well—if you use them properly.

It is also important to choose a method you will like! In order to make an informed decision, ask yourself these questions: What type of birth control are you thinking about? Have you ever used it before? If yes, how long did you use it?

	Circle Your Answers		
Are you afraid of using this method?	Yes	No	Don't know
Would you rather not use this method?	Yes	No	Don't know
Will you have trouble remembering to use this method?	Yes	No	Don't know
Have you every become pregnant while using this method?	Yes	No	Don't know
Will you have trouble using this method carefully?	Yes	No	Don't know
Do you have unanswered questions about this method?	Yes	No	Don't know
Does this method make menstrual periods longer or more painful?	Yes	No	Don't know
Does this method cost more than you can afford?	Yes	No	Don't know
Does this method ever cause serious health problems?	Yes	No	Don't know
Do you object to this method because of religious beliefs?	Yes	No	Don't know
Have you already had problems using this method?	Yes	No	Don't know
Is your partner opposed to this method?	Yes	No	Don't know
Are you using this method without your partner's knowledge?	Yes	No	Don't know
Will using this method embarrass you?	Yes	No	Don't know
Will using this method embarrass your partner?	Yes	No	Don't know
Will you enjoy intercourse less because of this method?	Yes	No	Don't know
Will this method interrupt lovemaking?	Yes	No	Don't know
Has a nurse or doctor ever told you not to use this method?	Yes	No	Don't know

Do you have any "Don't know" answers? If so, ask your clinic counselor, college's health staff, or physician to help you with more information.

Do you have any "Yes" answers? "Yes" answers mean you may not like this method. Ask a medical person to talk this over with you. You may need to think about another method.

Source: Adapted from Hatcher, Robert, et al. *Contraceptive Technology.* New York: Irvington Publishers, 1990.

condom handy. An advantage of abstinence is that refraining from sexual activity allows a couple to get to know and trust each other gradually before facing the emotions and stresses brought about by high degrees of intimacy.

Hormonal Methods: The Pill and Implants

In addition to the tried-and-true birth control pill, a number of new forms of hormonal contraception are or soon will be available. These include capsules that are implanted under a woman's skin and injectable hormones for both women and men.

Oral Contraceptives.

The Pill Oral contraceptives, popularly called "the pill," are used by approximately 13.8 million women in the United States today (Hatcher et al., 1990), making it the most popular method among women ("Sterilization," 1990). The pill is actually a series of pills (20, 21, or 28 to a package) containing synthetic estrogen and/or progesterone that regulates egg production and the menstrual cycle. When taken for birth control, they accomplish some or all of the following:

- Inhibit ovulation.
- Thicken cervical mucus (preventing sperm entry).
- Inhibit implantation of the fertilized ovum.
- Promote early spontaneous abortion of the fertilized ovum.

The pill produces basically the same chemical conditions that would exist in a woman's body if she were pregnant.

Oral contraceptives must be prescribed by a physician or family planning clinic. A number of brands are available, containing various amounts of hormones. Most commonly prescribed are the combination pills, which contain a fairly standard amount of estrogen and different doses of progestin according to the pill type. In the triphasic pill, the amount of progestin is altered during the cycle, purportedly to approximate the normal hormonal pattern. (The various manufacturers of the triphasic pills seem to disagree with one another, however, as to what constitutes a normal hormonal pattern [Hatcher et al., 1990].) There is also a "minipill" containing progestin only, but it is generally prescribed only in cases when the woman should not take estrogen. It is considered slightly less effective than the combined pill, and it must be taken with precise, unfailing regularity to be effective.

The pill is considered the most effective birth control method available (except for sterilization) when used correctly. (When adequate time has passed to study the effects of the hormonal implant, it will likely also be highly rated.) It is not effective when used carelessly. The pill must be taken every day, as close as possible to the same time each day. If one is missed, it should be taken as soon as the woman remembers, and the next one taken on schedule. If two are missed, the method cannot be relied on, and an additional form of contraception should be used for the rest of the cycle. It should be remembered that the pill in no way protects against sexually transmitted diseases. Women on the pill should consider the additional use of a condom to reduce the risk of STDs. A year's supply of birth control pills costs between $180 and $240.

oral contraceptive A series of pills containing synthetic estrogen and/or progesterone that regulates egg production and the menstrual cycle. Commonly known as "the pill."

Effectiveness The combined pill is more than 99.5% effective theoretically. User effectiveness (the rate shown by actual studies) is between 95% and 98%. Progestin-only pills are somewhat less effective, especially among younger, presumably more fertile, women (Trussell & Kost, 1987; Vessey, Lawless, Yeates, & McPherson, 1985).

Advantages Pills are easy to take. They are dependable. No applications or interruptions are necessary before or during intercourse. Some women experience side effects that please them, such as more regular or reduced menstrual flow, enlarged breasts, or less acne.

Possible Problems There are many possible side effects, which may or may not bother the user, from taking the pill. Those most often reported are:

- Change (usually a decrease) in menstrual flow
- Breast tenderness
- Nausea or vomiting
- Weight gain or loss

Some of the other side effects are:

- Spotty darkening of the skin
- Nervousness, dizziness
- Loss of scalp hair
- Change in appetite
- Change (most commonly, a decrease) in sex drive
- Mood changes
- Increase in body hair
- Increase in vaginal discharges and yeast infections

These side effects can sometimes be eliminated by changing the prescription, but not always. Certain women react unfavorably to the pill because of existing health factors or extra sensitivity to female hormones. Women with heart or kidney diseases, asthma, high blood pressure, diabetes, epilepsy, gall bladder disease, sickle-cell anemia, or those prone to migraine headaches or depression are usually considered poor candidates for the pill. Certain medications may react differently or unfavorably with the pill.

The pill also creates certain health risks, but to what extent is a matter of controversy. Women taking the pill stand a greater chance of problems with circulatory diseases, blood clotting, heart attack, and certain kinds of liver tumors. There is also an increased risk of contracting chlamydia. The health risks are low for the young (about half the number of risks encountered at childbirth), but they increase with age. The risk for smokers, women over 35, and those with certain other health disorders is about four times as great as childbirth. For women over 40, the risks are considered high. Current literature on the pill especially emphasizes the risks for women who smoke. Definite risks of cardiovascular complications and various forms of cancer exist because of the synergistic action of the ingredients of cigarettes and oral contraceptives.

A number of studies have linked pill use with certain types of cancer, but they are not conclusive. The risk of some types of cancer, such as ovarian and endometrial, appears to be significantly *reduced* by pill use (Hankinson, Colditz, Hunter, Spencer, Rosner, & Stampflau, 1992). On the other hand, a link between cervical cancer and long-term pill use has been suggested by several studies (Vessey et al., 1983; World Health Organization, 1992).

Findings regarding the pill and breast cancer are conflicting. The largest study, however, involving more than 9300 women, found no increased risk of breast cancer among pill users (Centers for Disease Control, 1986b; Schlesselman, 1990).

Certain other factors may need to be taken into account in determining if oral contraceptives are appropriate. Young girls who have not matured physically may have their development slowed by early pill use. Nursing mothers cannot use pills containing estrogen because the hormone inhibits milk production. Some lactating women use the minipill successfully (Hatcher et al., 1990).

Millions of women use the pill with moderate to high degrees of satisfaction. For many women, if personal health or family history does not contraindicate it, the pill is both effective and safe.

Implants In December 1990, the FDA approved the contraceptive **implant,** thin, matchstick-sized capsules containing levonorgestrel (a progestin) that are implanted under a woman's skin. Over a period of up to 5 years, the hormone is slowly released. When the implants are removed, which may be done at any time, fertility is restored. A set of soft tubes is surgically implanted under the skin of the upper arm in a simple office procedure with a local anesthetic. Once implanted, the capsules are not visible (or are barely visible) but may be felt under the skin. The implants, under the trade name **Norplant,** are currently on the market in more than 14 countries. The cost of the implant, including the insertion and removal, is between $500 and $750, depending on where it is obtained. It may seem high, but it is probably less expensive than a 5-year supply of birth control pills.

implant A contraceptive method of using thin, matchstick-sized capsules inserted under the skin of a woman's arm.

Norplant The trade name of a contraceptive implant that is inserted under the skin of a woman's arm.

Effectiveness Although Norplant has not been observed or tested to the degree that other contraceptives have, initial reports indicate an effectiveness rate of 99.96%. The implants should be removed after 5 years, as their effectiveness drops sharply in the sixth year. New implants may be inserted at that time. Removable progestin implants such as Norplant may be the most effective reversible contraceptive ever marketed (Hatcher et al., 1990).

Advantages Effectiveness and convenience are clearly big advantages of the implant. Once the implant is in, there's nothing to remember, buy, do, or take care of. Because implants contain no estrogen, users generally experience fewer side effects than with the pill. Many users report light to nonexistent menstrual flow and a reduction of menstrual cramps and pain. The risk of endometrial cancer may be reduced (Hatcher et al., 1990).

Contraceptive implants are inserted under the skin of a woman's arm in a 10-minute office procedure. One set of implants prevents pregnancy for 5 years.

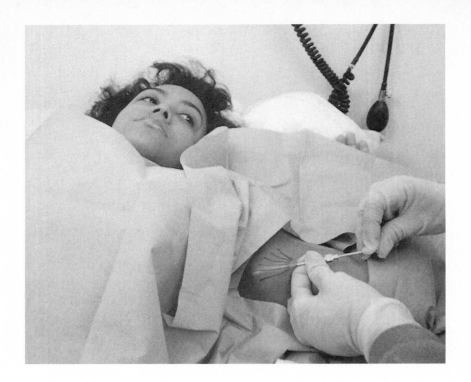

Depo-Provera (DMPA) An injectable contraceptive containing medroxyprogesterone acetate (DMPA).

coitus interruptus The removal of the penis from the vagina prior to ejaculation.

Possible Problems Side effects of contraceptive implants may be similar to those of oral contraceptives. The chief negative side effect, experienced by about half of implant users, is a change in the pattern of menstrual bleeding, such as lengthened periods or spotting between periods. Progestin implants should not be used by women with acute liver disease, breast cancer, blood clots, or unexplained vaginal bleeding, nor should they be used by women who are breast-feeding or those who may possibly be pregnant. Implant users are advised not to smoke. Difficult and painful removal of the device has also been reported. Possible long-term negative effects are not known at this time.

Depo-Provera (DMPA) The injectable contraceptive medroxyprogesterone acetate, **Depo-Provera,** or **DMPA,** which provides protection from pregnancy for 3–6 months, is used in over 80 countries throughout the world and has recently been approved for use in the United States. Generally speaking, DMPA has been considered to be remarkably free of serious side effects and complications, though it is still somewhat controversial. There are some less serious side effects and complications associated with its use, including weight gain, hair loss, cessation of menstruation, emotional reactions, and delayed fertility (by up to 1 year). There is still some debate about whether the drug may be associated with increased risk of breast cancer in some women (Stone, 1992). A year's protection with DMPA (given in four injections at 3-month intervals) costs about $120.

Think About It

UNRELIABLE AND MYTHICAL METHODS OF CONTRACEPTION

Humans are a very inventive species. In the area of birth control, however, some of our inventions do not deserve to be patented. "Traditional" birth control techniques such as withdrawal and lactation have some merit in that they work some of the time for some people. Other methods, such as Coca Cola douches or plastic bag condoms, are worse than useless; they may be harmful.

Coitus Interruptus (Withdrawal)

The oldest contraceptive technique known is **coitus interruptus** (also known as *withdrawal*, or "pulling out"), which involves removing the penis from the vagina before ejaculation. This method is widely used throughout the world and can be considered somewhat successful for *some* people. Success may depend on technique, combination with calendar methods, or on the physical characteristics of the partners (such as the tendency toward infertility in one or both partners).

A problem with this method is its riskiness. Secretions from the man's Cowper's glands, urethra, or prostrate, which sometimes seep into the vagina before ejaculation, can carry thousands of healthy sperm. Also, the first few drops of ejaculate carry most of the sperm. If the man is slow to withdraw or allows any ejaculate to spill into (or near the opening of) the vagina, the woman may get pregnant. A man using this method should wipe off any fluid at the tip of the penis before insertion into the vagina. If he has difficulty determining when he is about to ejaculate, he should *not* rely on withdrawal for contraception. The theoretical effectiveness rate using coitus interruptus is 84%. The actual user effectiveness rate is 77%. Although it is generally considered an unreliable method of birth control, coitus interruptus is certainly better than nothing.

Douching

Douching involves flushing the vagina with water or a medicated liquid. As a contraceptive method it is faulty, because after ejaculation, douching is already too late. By the time a woman can douche, the sperm may already be swimming through the cervix into the uterus. The douche liquid may even push the sperm into the cervix. Douching with any liquid, especially if done often, tends to upset the normal chemical balance in the vagina and may cause irritation or infection. There is also evidence that frequent douching can result in ectopic pregnancy (Chow et al., 1985).

Lactation

When a woman breast-feeds her child after giving birth, she may not begin to ovulate as long as she continues to nourish her child exclusively by breast-feeding. However, although some women do not ovulate while lactating, others do. Cycles may begin immediately after delivery or in a few months. The woman never knows when she will begin to be fertile. Lactation is considered a contraceptive method in some countries, but the success rate is extremely low.

Mythical Methods

There are many myths among young and old about contraception. Widely known methods that are *totally* useless include:

- Standing up during or after intercourse (sperm have no problem swimming "upstream").

- Taking a friend's pill the day of, or the day after, intercourse (doesn't work, and may even be dangerous).

- Only having intercourse occasionally (it is when, not how often, that makes a difference; once is enough, if the woman is fertile at that time).

- Using plastic wrap or plastic bags as condoms (too loose, undependable, and unsanitary).

FIGURE 11.1 Using a Condom.
(a) Place the rolled condom on the erect penis, leaving about a half-inch of space at the tip (first, squeeze any air out of the condom tip). (b) Roll the condom down, smoothing out any air bubbles. (c) Roll the condom to the base of the penis. (d) After ejaculation, hold the condom base while withdrawing the penis.

(a) (b) (c) (d)

Condoms.

Barrier Methods: The Condom, Diaphragm, Cervical Cap, and Female Condom

Barrier methods are designed to keep sperm and egg from getting together. The barrier device worn by men is the condom. Barrier methods available to women are the diaphragm, the cervical cap, and the female condom. The effectiveness of all barrier methods is increased by use with spermicides, which are discussed later in this chapter.

The Condom A **condom** is a thin sheath of latex rubber (or processed animal tissue) that fits over the erect penis and thus prevents semen from being transmitted (Figure 11.1). Condoms are available in a variety of sizes, shapes, and colors. Some are lubricated, and some are treated with spermicides. They are easily obtainable from drugstores and family planning clinics, and most kinds are relatively inexpensive. Condoms are the third most widely used form of birth control in the United States (after sterilization

condom A thin sheath of latex rubber (or processed animal tissue) that fits over the erect penis to prevent semen from being transmitted and to help protect against sexually transmitted diseases.

WOMEN AND CONDOM USE

Today, 40–70% of condoms are purchased by women, and condom advertising and packaging increasingly reflect this trend (Barron, 1987; Hatcher et al., 1990). Four key points are relevant to the issue of women and condom use (Hatcher et al., 1990):

- Women have more to lose than men when it comes to sexually transmitted diseases; they can suffer permanent infertility, for example.

- Men infected with STDs infect two out of three of their female partners, whereas women with STDs transmit the illness to one out of three male partners.

- Condoms help protect women against unplanned pregnancy, ectopic pregnancy, bacterial infec-

tions such as vaginitis and PID, viral infections such as herpes and HIV, cervical cancer, and infections that may harm a fetus or an infant during delivery.

- A woman has the right to insist on condom use. Even if a woman regularly uses another form of birth control, such as the pill or an IUD, she may want to have the added protection provided by a condom, especially if it has been treated with spermicide (which provides further protection against disease organisms). Contraceptive aerosol foam and contraceptive film (a thin, translucent square of tissue that dissolves into a gel) are the most convenient spermicidal preparations to use with condoms.

and the pill). Their use has increased significantly since the late 1980s, due in large part to their effectiveness in helping prevent the spread of STDs. A condom costs anywhere from about thirty cents (for "plain") to $1.50 (for "fancy"). They are often available free from college health services, family planning clinics, and AIDS education programs.

Condoms provide effective contraception when properly used. *Latex* condoms (but not those made of animal tissue) also help guard against the transmission of a number of sexually transmitted diseases such as chlamydia, gonorrhea, genital herpes, and HIV infection. Due to increased publicity regarding the transmissibility of HIV, both heterosexuals and gay men are increasingly using condoms as prophylactic devices. Condom use does not guarantee *total* safety from STDs, however, because sexual partners may also transmit certain diseases by hand, mouth, and genital areas other than the penis or vagina. Condoms may also occasionally tear or leak. As mentioned above, animal tissue (or "lambskin") condoms can be permeated by viruses such as HIV. Therefore, they should be used only for contraceptive purposes by monogamous couples who understand that such condoms do not protect against STDs. The first polyurethane condom will be marketed soon, under the trade name, Avanti. Its manufacturer states that it will be thinner and more sensitive than the standard latex condom (Ingrassia, Springen, & Rosenberg, 1995).

"Hear me, and hear me good, kid. Unroll the condom all the way to the base of the erect penis, taking care to expel the air from the reservoir at the tip by squeezing between the forefinger and thumb . . ." (Reproduced by Special Permission of PLAYBOY Magazine. Copyright © 1989 by PLAYBOY.)

Effectiveness Condoms are 98–99% effective theoretically. User effectiveness is about 88%. Failures sometimes occur from mishandling the condom, but they are usually the result of not putting it on until after some semen has leaked into the vagina, or simply not putting it on at all.

Advantages Condoms are easy to obtain. They are easy to carry in a wallet or purse. Latex rubber condoms help protect against STDs, including herpes and AIDS. They are inexpensive or can be free.

Possible Problems The chief drawback of a condom is that it must be put on after the man has been aroused but before penetration. This interruption is the major reason for users to neglect or "forget" to put them on. Some men complain that sensation is dulled, and (very rarely) cases of allergy to rubber are reported. Men who experience significant loss of feeling with a condom are advised to try other kinds. Many of the newer condoms are very thin (but also strong); they conduct heat well and allow quite a bit of sensation to be experienced. The condom user (or his partner) must take care to hold the sheath at the base of his penis when he withdraws, in order to avoid leakage. Condoms should be used with water-based lubricants only, as oil-based lubricants such as Vaseline can weaken the rubber. Vaginally applied medications such as Monistat (for yeast infections) and Premarin (an estrogen cream) may also cause condom breakage.

HINTS FOR EFFECTIVE CONDOM USE

- Use condoms every time you have sexual intercourse; this is the key to successful contraception and disease prevention.

- Use a spermicide with the condom. Foam and film are both easy to apply. Spermicide helps protect against pregnancy and STDs, including chlamydia, gonorrhea, genital herpes, and HIV infection.

- Always put the condom on before the penis touches the vagina. Even if the man has great "control," there is always the possibility of leakage prior to ejaculation.

- Leave about a half-inch of space at the condom tip, and roll the condom all the way down to the base of the penis.

- Soon after ejaculation, the penis should be withdrawn. Make sure someone holds the base of the condom firmly against the penis as it is withdrawn.

- After use, check the condom for possible torn spots. If you are not using a spermicide and you find a tear or hole, immediately insert foam or jelly into the vagina. This may reduce the chance of pregnancy. If torn condoms are a persistent problem, use a water-based lubricant, such as K-Y jelly, or a spermicide to reduce friction.

- Do not reuse a condom.

- Keep condoms in a cool, dry, and convenient place.

- To help protect against HIV and other organisms, always use a latex rubber condom, *not* one made of animal tissue.

If you or your partner are uncomfortable with condom use, consider the following:

- *Stand your ground.* (This is mainly for women, as it is generally men who object to condoms.) Unless you want to be pregnant and are sure your partner is free of STDs, you need protection during sex. If he says no to condoms, you can say no to him. If he cares about you, he will work with you to find birth control and safer sex methods that suit you both.

- Communication is crucial. It may seem "unromantic," but planning your contraception strategy before you are sexually entangled is essential. Giving or getting a disease or worrying about pregnancy is about as unromantic as you can get. Consider visiting a family planning clinic for counseling—together. Neither partner should be forced to use a form of birth control he or she is truly unhappy with. But the issue of protection must be dealt with—by both of you.

- Don't forget your sense of humor and playfulness. Condoms can actually provide lots of laughs, and laughter and sex go well together. Fancy condoms—colored, ribbed, glow-in-the-dark, etc.—are popular for their entertainment value.

The Diaphragm A **diaphragm,** a rubber cup with a flexible rim, is placed deep inside the vagina, blocking the cervix, to prevent sperm from entering the uterus and fallopian tubes. Different women require different sizes, and a woman may change size, especially after a pregnancy; the size must be determined by an experienced practitioner. Diaphragms are available by prescription from doctors and family planning clinics. Somewhat

diaphragm A rubber cup with a flexible rim that is placed deeply inside the vagina, blocking the cervix, to prevent sperm from entering the uterus.

The Diaphragm.

effective by itself, the diaphragm is highly effective when used with a spermicidal cream or jelly. (Creams and jellies are considered more effective than foam for use with a diaphragm.) Diaphragm users should be sure to use an adequate amount of spermicide and to follow their practitioner's instructions with care. Diaphragms cost between $15 and $125 plus the cost of spermicide and the initial exam and fitting.

The diaphragm can be put in place up to 2 hours before intercourse. It should be left in place 6 to 8 hours afterward. A woman should not dislodge it or douche before it is time to remove it. If intercourse is repeated within 6 hours, the diaphragm should be left in place but more spermicide should be inserted with an applicator. However, a diaphragm should not be left in place for more than 24 hours.

A diaphragm should be replaced about once a year; the rubber may deteriorate and lose elasticity, thus increasing the chance of splitting. Any change in the way the diaphragm feels, as well as any dramatic gain or loss of weight, calls for a visit to a doctor or clinic to check the fit.

Effectiveness Numerous studies of diaphragm effectiveness have yielded varying results. Typical user effectiveness (actual statistical effectiveness) is in the 81–83% range. Consistent, correct use is essential to achieve maximum effectiveness. For this reason, the risk of diaphragm failure is approximately double for women who are under 30 (and therefore more fertile than older women) or who have intercourse four times weekly or more (Hatcher et al., 1990).

Advantages The diaphragm can be put in place well before the time of intercourse. For most women, there are few health problems associated with its use. It helps protect against diseases of the cervix and PID (see Chapter 15).

Possible Problems Some women dislike handling or placing diaphragms, or the mess or smell of the chemical contraceptives used with them. Some men complain of rubbing or other discomfort caused by the diaphragm. Occasionally, a woman will be allergic to rubber. Some women become more prone to urinary tract infections (see Chapter 15). As there is a small risk of toxic shock syndrome (TSS) associated with its use, a woman should not use a diaphragm under the following conditions:

- During menstruation or other vaginal bleeding
- Following childbirth (for several months)
- During abnormal vaginal discharge
- If she has had TSS or if *Staphylococcus aureus* bacteria are present

She should also:

- Never wear the diaphragm for more than 24 hours
- Learn to watch for the warning signs of TSS (see Chapter 13)

cervical cap A small, rubber, contraceptive barrier device that fits snugly over the cervix.

The Cervical Cap The **cervical cap** is a small rubber barrier device that fits snugly over the cervix; it is held in place by suction and can be filled with spermicidal cream or jelly. Cervical caps come in different sizes and shapes. Proper fit is extremely important, and not everyone can be fitted. Fitting must be done by a physician or a health-care practitioner.

Effectiveness There is a limited amount of research data in this country regarding the cervical cap's effectiveness. Reported user effectiveness ranges from 73% to 92%.

Advantages The cervical cap may be more comfortable and convenient than the diaphragm for some women. Much less spermicide is used than with the diaphragm; spermicide need not be reapplied if intercourse is repeated. The cervical cap does not interfere with the body physically or hormonally.

Possible Problems Some users are bothered by an odor that develops from the interaction of the cap's rubber with either vaginal secretions or the spermicide. There is some concern that the cap may contribute to erosion of the cervix. If a partner's penis touches the rim of the cap, it can become displaced during intercourse. Theoretically the same risk of TSS exists for the cervical cap as for the diaphragm. The precautions listed in the section on diaphragms also apply.

The Female Condom Two types of condoms are designed for women to wear. One is a disposable, soft, loose-fitting polyurethane sheath with a diaphragmlike ring at each end. One ring, which is sealed shut, is inside the sheath and is used to insert and anchor the condom against the cervix. The larger outer ring remains outside the vagina and acts as a barrier, protecting the vulva and the base of the penis (Figure 11.2). The other type of female condom, made of latex, is secured by a G-string. A condom pouch in the crotch of the G-string unfolds as the penis pushes it into the vagina. Female condoms cost approximately $2.50 each at drugstores, less at family

The Cervical Cap.

The Female Condom.

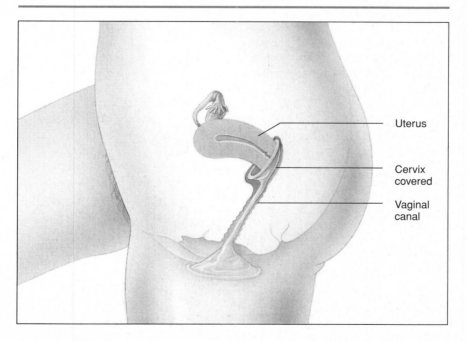

Uterus

Cervix covered

Vaginal canal

FIGURE 11.2 The Female Condom in Position. The female condom, a sheath of soft polyurethane, is anchored around the cervix with a flexible ring (much like a diaphragm). A larger ring secures the sheath outside the vagina and also helps protect the vulva.

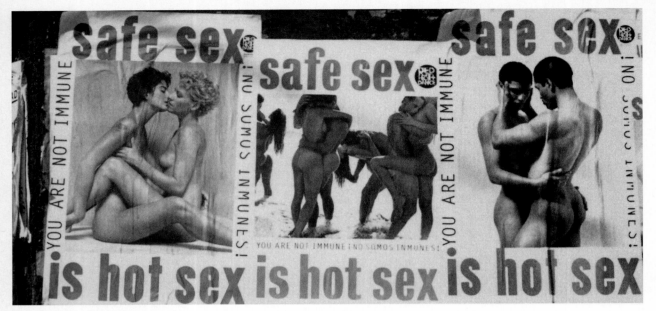

What is the message of these posters? What myths or stereotypes do they challenge?

planning clinics. With both types, using extra lubricant during intercourse helps to reduce the awareness of the presence of the device (Curtis, 1993).

Because polyurethane is stronger than latex, the device is less likely than the male condom to break. Nevertheless, during testing, the failure rates have ranged up to 26% making it considerably less effective than male condoms. Evidently, the outer edges of the condom can push into the vagina, thereby permitting the semen to leak (Baker, 1993; Leary, 1993). In laboratory tests, this condom was not permeated by HIV, indicating that it may be a promising alternative for both contraception and the control of STDs. Female condoms may prove advantageous for women whose partners are reluctant to use a male condom. They give women an additional way to control their fertility.

The Contraceptive Sponge   The Today Sponge, once welcomed as an effective alternative in the lineup of barrier methods, is no longer available. The decision to stop production was made in January 1995 by the Food and Drug Administration, which found unacceptably high levels of bacteria in the water and air of the New Jersey plant where the sponges were made (*San Jose Mercury News*, 1995). As of now, there are no plans to continue manufacturing the device.

Spermicides

spermicide   A substance that is toxic to sperm.

nonoxynol-9   The sperm-killing chemical in spermicide.

A **spermicide** is a substance that is toxic to sperm. The most commonly used spermicide in products sold in the United States is the chemical **nonoxynol-9.** Spermicidal preparations are available in a variety of forms: foam, film, jelly, cream, tablets, and suppositories. Some condoms are also treated with spermicides. Spermicidal preparations are considered most effective when used in combination with a barrier method. Spermicidal preparations are sold in tubes, packets, or other containers that hold about 12–20 applications. The cost per use is about forty cents to one dollar.

Considerable circumstantial evidence has suggested that nonoxynol-9 provides women with some protection against HIV infection, but there is also evidence that it causes mucosal inflammation and micro-ulcerations, or sores, when used in high doses or with high frequency (that is, twice a day or more) (Elias & Heise, 1993). Such sores could actually increase the possibility of HIV infection if exposure occurred. In the face of these contradictory findings, most health officials are remaining silent about the issue. (See Chapter 15 for further information on STD prevention.)

Contraceptive Foam

Contraceptive foam is a chemical spermicide sold in aerosol containers. It is a practical form of spermicide for use with a condom. Methods of application vary with each brand, but foam is usually released deep in the vagina either directly from the container or with an applicator. The foam forms a physical barrier to the uterus, and its chemicals inactivate sperm in the vagina. It is most effective if inserted no more than half an hour before intercourse. Shaking the container before applying the foam increases its foaminess so that it spreads further. The foam begins to go flat after about half an hour. It must be reapplied when intercourse is repeated.

contraceptive foam A chemical spermicide dispensed in an aerosol container.

Effectiveness Foam has a theoretical effectiveness rate of 98.5%. User failure brings its effectiveness down to as low as 71%. Failure tends to result from not applying the foam every single time the couple has intercourse, from relying on foam inserted hours before intercourse, from relying on foam placed hurriedly or not placed in deeply enough, or from foam whose expiration date has passed. If used properly and consistently, however, it is quite reliable. Used with a condom, foam is highly effective.

Advantages Almost no medical problems are associated with the use of foam. Foam may help provide protection against sexually transmitted diseases.

contraceptive film A small, translucent tissue that contains spermicide and dissolves into a sticky gel when inserted into the vagina.

Possible Problems Some women dislike applying foam. Some complain of messiness, leakage, odor, or stinging sensations. Occasionally, a woman or man may have an allergic reaction to it.

Contraceptive Film

Contraceptive film (also called vaginal contraceptive film, or VCF) is a relatively new spermicidal preparation. It is sold in packets of small (2-inch square), translucent tissues. This paper-thin tissue contains the spermicide nonoxynol-9, which dissolves into a sticky gel when inserted into the vagina. It is placed directly over the cervix, not less than 5 minutes or more than 1.5 hours before intercourse. It remains effective for 2 hours after insertion. Contraceptive film works effectively in conjunction with the condom.

Contraceptive Film.

Effectiveness Extensive research has not been done on the effectiveness of film because of its relative newness on the market. The highest effectiveness rates reported are 82–90%. Of course, proper and consistent use with a condom will greatly increase the effectiveness.

Advantages Many women find film easy to use. It is easily obtained from a drugstore and is easy to carry in a purse, wallet, or pocket.

Possible Problems Some women may not like inserting the film into the vagina. Some women may be allergic to it. Increased vaginal discharge and temporary pain while urinating after using contraceptive film have been reported. Some couples have difficulty with the timing necessary for its proper use.

Creams and Jellies Creams and jellies come in tubes and are inserted with applicators or placed inside diaphragms or cervical caps. These chemical spermicides can be bought without prescription at most drugstores. They work in a manner similar to foams, but are considered less effective when used alone. Like foam, jellies and creams may provide some protection against STDs. This factor makes their use with a diaphragm even more attractive.

Suppositories and Tablets These chemical spermicides are inserted into the vagina before intercourse. Body heat and fluids dissolve the ingredients, which will inactivate sperm in the vagina after ejaculation. They must be inserted early enough to dissolve completely before intercourse.

Effectiveness of Creams, Jellies, Suppositories, and Tablets Reports on these methods vary widely. It is suspected that the variations are connected with each user's technique of application. Directions for use that come with these contraceptives are not always clear. Jellies, creams, vaginal tablets, and suppositories should be used in conjunction with a barrier method for maximum effectiveness.

Advantages The methods are simple and easily obtainable, with virtually no medical problems. They may help protect against STDs, including chlamydia, trichomonas, gonorrhea, genital herpes, and HIV.

Possible Problems Some people have allergic reactions to spermicides. Some women dislike the messiness, odor, or necessity of touching their own genitals. Others experience irritation or inflammation, especially if they use any of the methods frequently. A few women lack the vaginal lubrication to dissolve the tablets in a reasonable amount of time. And a few women complain of having anxiety about the effectiveness of any of the methods during intercourse.

A 1981 study linked spermicide use with congenital birth defects in children born to women who were spermicide users (Jick, Hannon, Stergachis, Heidrich, Perera, & Rothman, 1981). A clear link, however, has not been proven to the satisfaction of a number of experts. Some clinicians recommend that spermicides not be used when a possible pregnancy exists (Hatcher et al., 1990).

The IUD (Intrauterine Device)

The **intrauterine device,** or **IUD,** is a tiny plastic or metal device that is inserted into the uterus through the cervical os (opening) (Figure 11.3).

intrauterine device (IUD) A T-shaped device inserted into the uterus through the cervical os to prevent contraception or implantation of the fertilized egg.

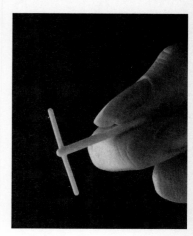

The IUD.

FIGURE 11.3 An IUD (Progestasert) in Position.

The particular type of device determines how long it may be left in place; the range is one year to indefinitely.

Although most IUDs have been withdrawn from the U.S. market because of the proliferation of lawsuits against their manufacturers in recent years, they are still considered a major birth control method. The two IUDs currently available in the United States are the Copper T-380A, marketed as the ParaGard, and the progesterone T device, marketed as the Progestasert IUD. The Copper T-380A is made of polyethylene; the stem of the T is wrapped with fine copper wire. It is approved for 4 years of use. More than 8 million Copper T-380As have been distributed worldwide. The Progestasert is also in the form of a T. It is made of a polymer plastic with a hollow stem containing progesterone, which is continually released. The Progestasert is effective for 1 year. At the time an IUD is removed, a new one may be inserted. The cost of an IUD, including insertion, starts at about $200 at family planning clinics.

The IUD apparently works in a number of ways, some of which are not yet clearly understood. Its mechanisms of action are thought to include the following (Alvarez et al., 1988; Ortiz & Croxatto, 1987; Treiman & Liskin, 1988):

- Immobilization of sperm and interference with their migration to the fallopian tubes
- Speeded transport of the oocyte through the fallopian tube
- Inhibition of fertilization
- Inhibition of implantation

IUDs must be inserted and removed by a trained practitioner.

Effectiveness IUDs are 97–99% effective theoretically. User effectiveness is 90–96%. The Copper T-380A has the lowest failure rate of any IUD developed to date.

Advantages Once inserted, IUDs require little care. They don't interfere with spontaneity during intercourse. If used over a period of years, they are also relatively inexpensive.

Possible Problems Insertion may be painful. Heavy cramping usually follows and sometimes persists. Menstrual flow usually increases, often significantly. Up to one-third of users, especially women who have never been pregnant, expel the device within the first year. This usually happens during menstruation. The IUD can be reinserted, however, and many women retain it the second time.

The IUD is associated with increased risk of pelvic inflammatory disease (see Chapter 15). Because of the risk of sterility induced by PID, many physicians recommend that women planning to have children use alternative methods. Women who have had PID or who have multiple sex partners should be aware that an IUD will place them at significantly greater risk of PID, STDs, and other infections.

The IUD cannot be inserted in some women because of unusual uterine shape or position. Until recently, it was considered difficult to insert and less effective for teenage girls. But newer, smaller IUDs have been found to provide good protection even for young teenagers. Occasionally, the device perforates the cervix. This usually happens at the time of insertion, if it happens at all. Removal sometimes requires surgery.

Sometimes pregnancy or ectopic pregnancy (implantation within the fallopian tube) occurs and is complicated by the presence of the IUD. If the IUD is not removed, there is about a 50% chance of spontaneous abortion; if it is removed, the chance is around 25%. Furthermore, spontaneous abortions that occur when an IUD is left in place are likely to be septic (infection-bearing) and possibly life-threatening. Ectopic pregnancies have been found to occur six to ten times more frequently in users of Progestasert than in users of the Copper T-380A (Hatcher et al., 1990).

Fertility Awareness Methods

fertility awareness method
One of several contraceptive methods based on a woman's knowledge of her body's reproductive cycle, including calendar (rhythm), basal body temperature (BBT), mucus, and sympto-thermal methods.

Fertility awareness methods of contraception require substantial education, training, and planning. They are based on a woman's knowledge of her body's reproductive cycle. Requiring a high degree of motivation and self-control, these methods are not for everyone. Fertility awareness is also referred to as "natural family planning." Some people make the following distinction between the two. With fertility awareness, the couple may use an alternate method (such as a diaphragm with jelly or a condom with foam) during the fertile part of the woman's cycle. Natural family planning does not include the use of any contraceptive device and is thus considered to be more natural; it is approved by the Catholic church.

Fertility awareness methods include the calendar (rhythm) method, the basal body temperature (BBT) method, the mucus (also called the Billings or ovulation) method, and the sympto-thermal method, which combines the latter two. These methods are not recommended for women who have irregular menstrual cycles, including postpartum and lactating mothers.

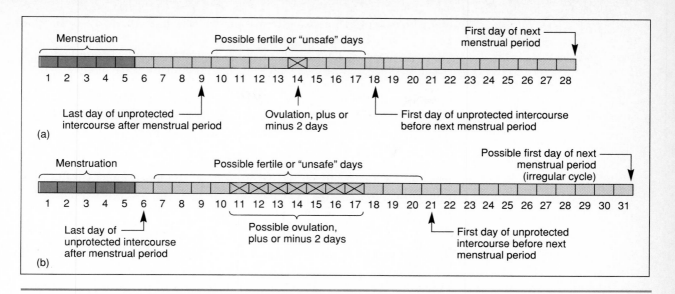

FIGURE 11.4 Fertility Awareness Calendar. To use the calendar method or other fertility awareness methods, a woman must keep track of her menstrual cycles. (a) The top chart shows probable safe and unsafe days for a woman with a regular 28-day cycle. (b) The bottom chart shows safe and unsafe days for a woman whose cycles range from 25 to 31 days. Note that the woman with an irregular cycle has significantly more unsafe days. The calendar method is most effective when combined with the basal body temperature (BBT) and mucus methods.

All women can benefit from learning to recognize their fertility signs. It is useful to know when the time of greatest likelihood of pregnancy occurs, both for women who wish to avoid pregnancy and for those who want to become pregnant.

The Calendar (Rhythm) Method

The **calendar (rhythm) method** is based on calculating "safe" days, which depends on the range of a woman's longest and shortest menstrual cycles. It may not be practical or safe for women with irregular cycles. For women with regular cycles, the calendar method is reasonably effective because the period of time when an oocyte is receptive to fertilization is only about 24 hours. As sperm generally live 2–4 days, the maximum period of time in which fertilization could be expected to occur may be calculated with the assistance of a calendar.

Ovulation generally occurs 14 (plus or minus 2) days before a woman's menstrual period. (However, ovulation *can* occur anytime during the cycle, including during the menstrual period.) Taking this into account, and charting her menstrual cycles for a minimum of 8 months to determine the longest and shortest cycles, a woman can determine her expected fertile period. Figure 11.4 shows the interval of fertility calculated in this way. During the fertile period, a woman must abstain from sexual intercourse or use an alternative method of contraception. A woman using this method must be meticulous in her calculations, keep her calendar up to date, and be able to maintain an awareness of what day it is. Statistically, only about one-third of all women have cycles regular enough to use this method satisfactorily.

The Basal Body Temperature (BBT) Method

A woman's temperature tends to be slightly lower during menstruation and for about a week afterward. Just before ovulation, it dips; it then rises sharply (one-half to

calendar (rhythm) method A contraceptive method based on calculating "safe" days depending on the range of a woman's longest and shortest menstrual cycles.

one whole degree) following ovulation. It stays high until just before the next menstrual period.

basal body temperature (BBT) method A contraceptive method based on a woman's temperature in the morning upon waking; when the temperature rises, the woman is fertile.

A woman practicing the **basal body temperature (BBT) method** must record her temperature every morning upon waking for 6–12 months to have an accurate idea of her temperature pattern. This change can best be noted using a basal body temperature thermometer and taking the temperature in the morning, before getting out of bed. When she is quite sure she recognizes the rise in temperature and can predict about when in her cycle it will happen, she can begin using the method. She will abstain from intercourse or use an alternate contraceptive method for 3–4 days before the expected rise, and for 4 days after it has taken place. If she limits intercourse to only the "safe" time after her temperature has risen, the method is more effective. The method requires high motivation and control. For greater accuracy, it may be combined with the mucus method described next.

The Mucus Method (Billings or Ovulation Method) Women who use the **mucus method** determine their point in the menstrual cycle by examining the mucous secretions of the cervix. In many women, there is a noticeable change in the appearance and character of cervical mucus prior to ovulation. After menstruation, most women experience a moderate discharge of cloudy, yellowish, or white mucus. Then, for a day or two, a clear, slippery mucus is secreted. Ovulation occurs immediately after the clear, slippery mucous secretions appear. The preovulatory mucus is elastic in consistency, rather like raw egg white, and a drop can be stretched between two fingers into a thin strand. Following ovulation, the amount of discharge decreases markedly. The 4 days before and the 4 days after these secretions are considered the unsafe days. An alternative contraception method may be used during this time. The method requires training and a high degree of motivation to be successful. This method may be combined with the BBT method for greater effectiveness.

mucus method A contraceptive method using a woman's cervical mucus to determine ovulation.

The Sympto-Thermal Method When the BBT and mucus methods are used together, it is called the **sympto-thermal method.** Additional signs that may be useful in determining ovulation are midcycle pain in the lower abdomen on either side (*mittelschmerz*) and a very slight discharge of blood from the cervix ("spotting"); however, neither of these signs may be apparent.

sympto-thermal method A fertility awareness method combining the BBT and mucus methods.

Effectiveness of Fertility Awareness Methods It is problematic to calculate the effectiveness of fertility awareness methods. With this type of contraception, in a sense, the user *is* the method: The method's success or failure rests largely on her diligence. Women who wish to rely on fertility awareness methods of contraception should enroll in a class at a clinic. Learning to read one's own unique fertility signs is a complex process requiring one-on-one counseling and close monitoring. Many studies show fairly high failure rates with these methods. Some researchers believe this is due to risk taking during the fertile phase. Additionally, there is always some difficulty in predicting ovulation with pinpoint accuracy; thus, there is a greater chance of pregnancy as a result of intercourse prior to ovulation than as a result of intercourse following it. All fertility awareness methods increase in effectiveness if intercourse is unprotected only during the safe period following ovulation.

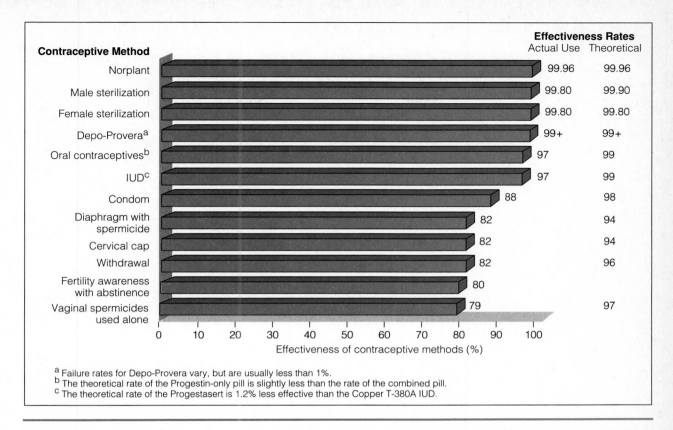

Contraceptive Method	Effectiveness Rates	
	Actual Use	Theoretical
Norplant	99.96	99.96
Male sterilization	99.80	99.90
Female sterilization	99.80	99.80
Depo-Provera[a]	99+	99+
Oral contraceptives[b]	97	99
IUD[c]	97	99
Condom	88	98
Diaphragm with spermicide	82	94
Cervical cap	82	94
Withdrawal	82	96
Fertility awareness with abstinence	80	
Vaginal spermicides used alone	79	97

Effectiveness of contraceptive methods (%)

[a] Failure rates for Depo-Provera vary, but are usually less than 1%.
[b] The theoretical rate of the Progestin-only pill is slightly less than the rate of the combined pill.
[c] The theoretical rate of the Progestasert is 1.2% less effective than the Copper T-380A IUD.

FIGURE 11.5 Theoretical Versus Actual Use Failure Rates. This chart compares the effectiveness rates of various methods during the first year of their use. SOURCE: Adapted from Hatcher, Robert, et al. *Contraceptive Technology*. New York: Irvington, 1990, p. 134.

Advantages Fertility awareness (or natural family planning) methods are acceptable to most religious groups. They are free and pose no health risks. If a woman wishes to become pregnant, awareness of her own fertility cycles is very useful.

Possible Problems These methods are not suitable for women with irregular menstrual cycles or couples who are not highly motivated to use them. Some couples who practice abstinence during fertile periods may begin to take risks out of frustration. These couples may benefit by exploring other forms of sexual expression, and counseling can help.

See Figure 11.5 for a comparison of the effectiveness of various contraceptive methods.

Sterilization

Among married couples in the United States, sterilization (of one or both partners) is the most popular form of birth control. **Sterilization** involves surgical intervention that makes the reproductive organs incapable of producing or delivering viable gametes (sperm and eggs). Annually, about 1 million Americans choose this method of family planning, which is also known as **voluntary surgical contraception** (Hatcher et al., 1990). Before

sterilization or **voluntary surgical contraception** A surgical procedure that makes the reproductive organs incapable of producing or "delivering" viable gametes (sperm and eggs).

FIGURE 11.6 Tubal Ligation.

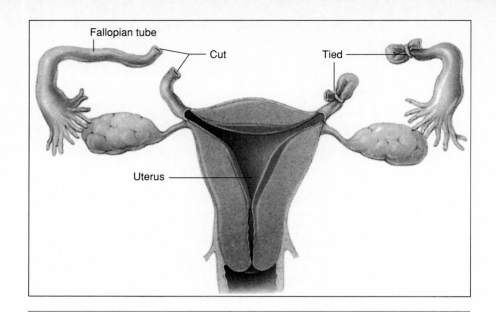

Fallopian tube

Cut

Tied

Uterus

1975, most sterilizations in this country were performed on men, but currently, women choose to be sterilized at twice the rate of men. By 1984, 137 million people had been sterilized worldwide (Population Crisis Committee, 1985).

Sterilization for Women For the first time, more women are opting for sterilization over any other form of birth control. Of all American women using contraception in 1990, 29.5% had **tubal ligations,** or "tying the tubes" (Ingrassia, Springen, and Rosenberg, 1995). (See Figure 11.6.) The two most common operations are laparoscopy and minilaparotomy. Less commonly performed types of sterilization for women are culpotomy, culdoscopy, and hysterectomy. Generally, this surgery is not reversible; only women who are completely certain that they want no (or no more) children should choose this method.

Sterilization for women is quite expensive. Surgeon, anesthesiologist, and hospital fees are substantial. The newer procedures, in which the woman returns home on the same day, have the advantage of being one-half to one-third as expensive as abdominal surgery, but they still may cost one to several thousand dollars. Many health insurance policies will cover all or part of the cost of sterilization for both men and women. In some states, Medicaid pays for certain patients.

Methods Used Sterilization by **laparoscopy** usually requires a day or less in the hospital or clinic. General anesthesia is usually recommended. The woman's abdomen is inflated with gas to make the organs more visible. The surgeon inserts a rodlike instrument with a viewing lens (the laparoscope) through a small incision at the edge of the navel and locates the fallopian tubes. Through this incision or a second one, the surgeon inserts another

tubal ligation The cutting and tying off (or other method of closure) of the fallopian tubes so that ova cannot be fertilized.

laparoscopy A form of tubal ligation using a viewing lens (the laparoscope) to locate the fallopian tubes and another instrument to cut or block and close them.

instrument that closes the tubes, usually by electrocauterization (burning). Special small forceps that carry an electric current clamp the tubes and cauterize them. The tubes may also be closed off or blocked with tiny rings, clips, or plugs. There is a recovery period of several days to a week. During this time, the woman will experience some tenderness and some vaginal bleeding. Rest is important. Local or general anesthesia is used with **minilaparotomy.** A small incision is made in the lower abdomen, through which the fallopian tubes are brought into view. They are then tied off or sealed with electric current, clips, or rings. Recovery is the same as with laparoscopy. Sometimes the incision is made through the back of the vaginal wall and is called a culpotomy.

minilaparotomy A form of tubal ligation in which a small incision is made in the lower abdomen.

Hysterectomy Hysterectomy (surgical removal of the uterus) is not performed for sterilization except under special circumstances. Because it involves the removal of the entire uterus, it is both riskier and more costly than other methods. It involves greater recovery time and, for some women, is potentially more difficult psychologically. It may be appropriate for women who have a uterine disease or other problem that is likely to require a future hysterectomy anyway. (Hysterectomy is discussed at greater length in Chapter 13.)

Effectiveness Surgical contraception is essentially 100% effective. In *extremely* rare instances (less than one-quarter of 1%), probably because of improperly performed surgery, a tube may reopen or grow back together, allowing an egg to pass through.

Once sterilization has been done, no other method of birth control will ever be necessary. (A woman who risks exposure to STDs, however, may wish to protect herself with a condom.)

Sterilization does not reduce or change a woman's feminine characteristics. It is not the same as menopause and does not hasten the approach of menopause, as some people believe. A woman still has her menstrual periods until whatever age menopause naturally occurs for her. Her ovaries, uterus (except in the case of hysterectomy), and hormonal system have not been changed. The only difference is that sperm cannot now reach her eggs. (The eggs, which are released every month as before, are reabsorbed by the body.) Sexual enjoyment is not diminished. In fact, a high percentage of women report that they feel more relaxed during intercourse because anxiety about pregnancy has been eliminated. There seem to be no harmful side effects associated with female sterilization.

Sterilization should be considered irreversible. Only 15–25% percent of women who attempt to have their tubal ligations reversed succeed in conceiving.

The tubal ligation itself is a relatively safe procedure. With electrocauterization, there is a chance that other tissues in the abdomen may be damaged or that infection will occur, especially if the surgeon is not highly skilled. There may also be complications from anesthesia.

Sterilization for Men A **vasectomy** is a minor surgical procedure that can be performed in a doctor's office under a local anesthetic. It takes approximately half an hour. In this procedure, the physician makes a small incision (or two incisions) in the skin of the scrotum. Through the incision,

vasectomy A form of surgical sterilization in which each vas deferens is severed, thereby preventing sperm from entering the seminal fluid.

FIGURE 11.7 Vasectomy.

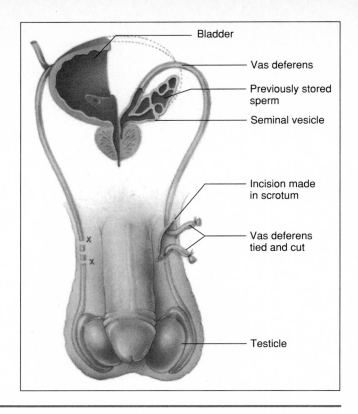

- Bladder
- Vas deferens
- Previously stored sperm
- Seminal vesicle
- Incision made in scrotum
- Vas deferens tied and cut
- Testicle

each vas deferens (sperm-carrying tube) is lifted, cut, tied, and often cauterized with electricity (Figure 11.7). After a brief rest, the man is able to walk out of the office; complete recuperation takes only a few days.

A man may retain some viable sperm in his system for days or weeks following a vasectomy. He should use other birth control until his semen has been checked, about 8 weeks following the operation.

Effectiveness Vasectomies are 99.85% effective. In very rare cases, the ends of a vas deferens may rejoin. But this is virtually impossible if the operation is correctly performed.

Advantages No birth control method will ever be needed again. But the man may still wish to use a condom to prevent getting or spreading an STD. Sexual enjoyment will not be diminished; he will still have erections and orgasms and ejaculate semen. Vasectomy is relatively inexpensive.

Possible Problems Compared to other birth control methods, the complication rates for vasectomy are very low. Most problems occur when proper antiseptic measures are not taken during the operation, or when the man exercises too strenuously in the few days after it. Hematomas (bleeding under the skin) and granulomas (clumps of sperm) can be treated with ice packs and rest. Epididymitis (inflammation of the tiny tubes that connect the testicle and vas deferens) can be treated with heat and scrotal support.

One-half to two-thirds of men develop sperm antibodies following vasectomy. The body produces these antibodies in response to the presence of sperm that have been absorbed by body tissues. There is no evidence that this poses any threat to a man's health.

Tests on monkeys have shown some increased risks of heart disease with vasectomy, but recent studies on humans have not produced similar findings. One large study of more than 10,000 men with vasectomies found *less* cardiovascular disease than in other men (Massey et al., 1984).

A few men, those who equate fertility with virility and potency, may experience psychological problems following vasectomy. However, according to the authors of *Contraceptive Technology* (Hatcher et al., 1985), "Most well-adjusted males will experience no adverse psychological changes following their sterilization, if they understand what to expect . . . and are given an opportunity to express their fears and have their questions answered."

Among men who attempt to have their vasectomies reversed, about 50% experience success. The cost is high and not covered by insurance in many cases. Vasectomy should be considered permanent.

Informed Consent   Because sterilization is irreversible, it is of paramount importance that a person who contemplates it be informed about the procedure and be sure about his or her own needs and wishes. About 10% of sterilized people later decide they want children (Cushner, 1986). Federal law requires that recipients of sterilization give informed consent prior to undergoing surgery. Requirements vary from state to state, but their intent is to protect people from making hasty or ill-informed decisions or being coerced into an act that has serious, lifelong consequences.

Postcoital Birth Control

Postcoital birth control (also called "morning-after birth control") is a controversial issue. **Postcoital birth control** involves the expulsion of an ovum that may have been fertilized; it can be viewed as a type of early abortion. Postcoital birth control is administered by many physicians and family planning clinics.

postcoital birth control   A form of birth control involving the early expulsion of an ovum that may have been fertilized. Also known as morning-after birth control.

The Morning-After Pill and Menstrual Extraction   The principal form of this type of birth control is the morning-after pill or the emergency contraceptive pill (ECP). It is generally a combined estrogen-progestin birth control pill, given in a larger-than-normal dose under medical supervision, within 72 hours after unprotected intercourse (Trussell, Stewart, Guest, & Hatcher, 1992). (Information regarding the use of birth control pills for postcoital birth control is available at many family planning clinics.)

Another method of after-the-fact birth control is **menstrual extraction,** which involves the removal of the endometrial contents by suction through a small tube attached to a vacuum pump. This procedure may be performed until an expected menstrual period is 2 weeks late. It can be done with or without a positive diagnosis of pregnancy. Another form of postcoital birth control is to have an IUD inserted within 5–7 days after unprotected inter-

menstrual extraction   The removal of the endometrial contents by suction; sometimes used as a form of postcoital birth control.

RECONSIDERING BIRTH CONTROL AFTER 30

After age 30, and certainly by 40, most women who are sexually active have reexamined their birth control options and most likely have chosen a method of contraception that better suits their physiology and lifestyle. With the possibility of conception occurring into the early or middle 50s for some women, safety often replaces effectiveness as a major consideration during this decision-making time.

The 1992 Ortho Birth Control Study of 7000 women found that 40% of fertile married women between 15 and 44 have themselves sterilized, or their partners opt to get sterilized. With virtually no systematic side effects and high reliability, sterilization is seen by many as the most satisfying and liberating method available.

For those who do not want a permanent procedure, reversible forms of contraception—the pill and the IUD—have been thoroughly studied and greatly refined; they are both options for many women.

Low estrogen or progestin-only oral contraceptives are considered safe for most healthy, nonsmoking women. Those with high blood pressure, a high cho-

lesterol level, or diabetes should consult with a physician. Women over 40 are also at higher risk.

Barrier methods—condoms, diaphragms, and cervical caps—offer protection against both pregnancy and sexually transmittable disease, though their failure rate is higher than that of the pill. They have the advantage of having few, if any, side effects.

The IUD appears to be regaining popularity among physicians and many women as a viable, reversible alternative to sterilization. Of the two types available in the United States, one, the Copper T-380A, is effective for 4 years after insertion. The other, the Progestasert, is effective for 1 year. Because of the increased risk of pelvic inflammatory disease (PID) associated with the IUD, it is appropriate only for women in mutually monogamous relationships. Other reversible yet long-lasting methods are Norplant implants and Depo-Provera injections, though the latter has a somewhat checkered past.

Article adapted from "Reconsidering Birth Control After 30." *San Francisco Chronicle*, July 25, 1994.

course. This method is not recommended for women who have not had children, have multiple sex partners, or have a history of PID.

RU-486 An oral, postcoital birth control method containing mifepristone.

RU-486 In 1986, a study of a new drug, mifepristone, known as **RU-486,** concluded that it is "an effective and safe method for termination of very early pregnancy but that it should be used only under close medical supervision" (Couzinet, LeStrat, Ulmann, Boulieu, & Schaison, 1986). RU-486 is an antiprogesterone steroid (or progesterone antagonist) developed by a French physician. It prevents the cells of the uterine lining from getting the progesterone they need to support a blastocyst (fertilized ovum). This "tricks" the body into thinking it's at the end of a menstrual cycle; it sheds the lining of the uterus in what appears to be "an abundant painless menstrual period" (Couzinet et al., 1986). The blastocyst or embryo is expelled, too.

RU-486 has the potential to be used in three ways. One use is as a morning-after pill, taken within a few days of unprotected intercourse. In this

TABLE 11.1 How RU-486 Compares to Surgery

	RU-486
When it can be done	First seven weeks of pregnancy.
Minimum office visits	Three.
Medical requirements	Not recommended for women with heart problems, smokers or those under age 18 or over 35.
Procedure	First visits to confirm pregnancy. Second visit, the first pill is given, no waiting required. If the woman has not aborted, a second drug is given and the woman stays at the office for four hours during which time she usually aborts.
Side effects	Cramping, bleeding, abdominal pain, nausea.
Price	The price of the drug has not been determined. In France, it is the same as first-term surgical abortion.
Who can perform/administer it	All doctors who are licensed to evaluate and perform abortions.
Availability	Pending tests and federal approval.
	Standard surgery
When it can be done	Until end of second trimester; third trimester only to save woman's life.
Minimum office visits	Two. In states with mandatory 24-hour waiting period, minimum of three.
Medical requirements	Given with local or general anesthesia. Recommended no eating or drinking starting midnight before procedure.
Procedure	Methods vary. In first trimester, fetus is usually removed by suction, followed by scraping of the uterus.
Side effects	Cramping, bleeding, abdominal pain, nausea.
Price	$260–390 (for first-term abortions).
Who can perform/administer it	Varies state to state, but usually performed by an obstetrician/gynecologist.
Availability	Every state has at least one abortion clinic.

SOURCES: Planned Parenthood, L.A.; Feminist Majority; Population Council. Researched by D'Jamila Salem. *Los Angeles Times*, 23 June 1994.

case, the oocyte, if present, will be expelled before fertilization or, if it has been fertilized, before implantation (Glasier, Thong, Dewar, Mackie, & Baird, 1992). Another use is as an agent to induce a very early abortion—within the first 5 or 6 weeks of pregnancy. (For a comparison of RU-486 and surgical abortion, see Table 11.1.) The final use would be as a once-a-month birth control pill, taken a few days before an expected menstrual period.

Clinical trials of RU-486 have been conducted over a 5-year period in 15 countries to date. With the exception of heavy bleeding and cramping in some women, no serious side effects have been noted (Couzinet et al., 1986; Nieman et al., 1987). The effectiveness rate for terminating pregnancy has been about 85%. The safety of the drug taken over a longer period of time is not known.

RU-486 is used in several countries, including China, Britain, France, Sweden, and Germany. Currently, RU-486 may be imported to the U.S. for individual use. As of this writing, it has been approved by the FDA for manufacture. It is expected to be available to the public soon.

ABORTION

abortion The expulsion of the conceptus, either spontaneously or by induction.

When most people hear the word "abortion," they think of a medical procedure. But **abortion,** or expulsion of the conceptus, can happen naturally, or can be made to happen in one of several ways. Many abortions happen spontaneously—because a woman suffers a physical trauma, because the conceptus is not properly developed, or, more commonly, because physical conditions within the uterus break down and end the development of the conceptus. Approximately one-third of all abortions reported in a year in the U.S. are **spontaneous abortions;** these are commonly referred to as miscarriages (see Chapter 12). In this section, however, we examine *induced abortion*, the intentional termination of a pregnancy. Unless otherwise noted, when we refer to abortion, we mean induced abortion.

spontaneous abortion The natural expulsion of the conceptus, commonly referred to as miscarriage.

Under safe, clean, and legal conditions, abortion is a very safe medical procedure. Obstetrical residents must now be trained in how to perform abortions according to a new policy adopted by the Accreditation Council for Graduate Medical Education ("New Policy," 1995). Self-administered or under illegal, clandestine conditions, abortion can be very dangerous. The continued availability of legal abortion is considered by most physicians, psychologists, and public health professionals to be critical to the public's physical and mental well-being (Stephenson, Wagner, Badea, & Serbanescu, 1992; Susser, 1992).

Methods of Abortion

An abortion can be induced in several ways. Surgical methods are most common, but the use of medications is also possible. Methods for early abortions (those performed in the first 3 months of pregnancy) differ from those for late abortions (those performed after the third month). RU-486, a medical (nonsurgical) method of early abortion, was discussed earlier in the chapter.

laminaria A small stick of seaweed placed into the cervical opening about 6 hours prior to an abortion to dilate the cervix.

Surgical Methods Surgical methods include vacuum aspiration, dilation and curettage (D & C), dilation and evacuation (D & E), hysterotomy, and several other methods. To facilitate the dilation of the cervix prior to abortion, the health-care practitioner may insert a **laminaria,** a small stick of sterilized, compressed seaweed, into the cervical opening. The laminaria expands gradually, dilating the cervix gently in the process. It must be placed at least 6 hours prior to the abortion.

(a)

Uterus

Amniotic sac

Vaginal canal

Attaches to suction curettage unit

(b) Speculum

(c) Suction curette

FIGURE 11.8 Vacuum Aspiration. (a) The vagina is opened with a speculum, and a thin vacuum tube is inserted. (b) The uterus is gently vacuumed. (c) The curette end of the vacuum tube may be used to gently scrape the uterine wall; the conceptus and other contents of the uterus are suctioned out.

Vacuum Aspiration (First-Trimester Method) **Vacuum aspiration** is performed under local anesthesia. The cervix is dilated with a series of graduated rods (a laminaria may have been used to begin dilation). Then, a small tube attached to a vacuum is inserted through the cervix. The uterus is gently vacuumed, removing the conceptus, placenta, and endometrial tissue (Figure 11.8).

Curettage may follow. The patient returns home the same day. She will experience cramping, bleeding, and, possibly, emotional reactions over the following days. Serious complications are unusual for a legal, properly performed abortion.

Dilation and Curettage (D & C) (First-Trimester Method) In **dilation and curettage,** the cervix is dilated under general anesthesia, and the uterine wall is scraped with a small spoon-shaped instrument (a curette). This method is generally considered less desirable than vacuum aspiration because it causes more bleeding, is more painful, and is sometimes less effective.

Dilation and Evacuation (D & E) (Second-Trimester Method) **Dilation and evacuation (D & E)** is usually performed between the 13th and 20th weeks of pregnancy. Local or general anesthesia is used. The cervix is slowly dilated, and the fetus is removed by alternating curettage and solution. The patient is given an intravenous solution of the hormone oxytocin to encourage contractions and limit blood loss. Because it is a second-trimester procedure, a D & E is somewhat riskier and often more traumatic than a first-trimester abortion.

Hysterotomy (Second-Trimester Method) In **hysterotomy,** the fetus is removed through an incision made in the woman's abdomen. This is essentially a caesarean section—major surgery requiring several days in the hospital. Its use is limited.

vacuum aspiration A first-trimester form of abortion using vacuum suction to remove the conceptus and other tissue from the uterus.

dilation and curettage (D & C) A first-trimester abortion method using a small spoon-shaped instrument (curette) to remove the conceptus.

dilation and evacuation (D & E) A second-trimester abortion method in which the cervix is slowly dilated and the fetus removed by alternating solution and curettage.

hysterotomy A later abortion method in which the fetus is removed through an incision made in the woman's abdomen; used only in emergencies.

Other Methods of Abortion Abortion can also be induced medically with injections or suppositories. These abortions are performed during the second trimester and generally require hospitalization. Prostaglandins, saline solutions, and urea are used in this way, alone or in various combinations.

As discussed in Chapter 3, many cells of the body contain prostaglandins, fatty-acid-based hormones that are active in many body processes including reproduction. Prostaglandins are injected into the amniotic sac (which contains the fetus within the uterus) or administered as vaginal suppositories to stimulate uterine contractions and induce abortion. Some of the side effects associated with their use are gastrointestinal symptoms, cervical lacerations, and temperature elevation. Saline solutions and solutions of urea are toxic to the fetus and can be injected amniotically. These solutions are relatively inexpensive; they are generally considered more effective when used in combination with prostaglandins.

Another type of second-trimester abortion uses amniocentesis and amnioinfusion. This procedure involves the removal of amniotic fluid surrounding the fetus with a long needle—amniocentesis—followed by the replacement of that fluid with some type of medication—amnioinfusion. Solutions containing prostaglandins or urea, saline solution, or a combination may be used.

A Decline in the Prevalence of Abortion

The latest data on abortions in the United States indicate that the number performed in 1992 was a 13-year low (Alan Guttmacher Institute, 1994). The 1,529,000 abortions that were performed in 1992 were 80,000 fewer than the 1,608,600 reported in 1992 and the fewest since 1979, when the number was just under 1.5 million. Furthermore, the abortion rate (number of abortions per 1000 women aged 15–44) and the abortion ratio (the percentage of pregnancies ending in abortion) were the lowest since 1976.

Researchers offer several possible reasons for this lower rate:

- Reduced access to the procedure, especially in rural areas. Currently, 84% of U.S. counties have no doctor or facility providing abortions.
- Baby boomers getting older.
- Greater use of condoms because of fear of AIDS.
- More single women keeping their babies.
- The influence of anti-abortion activists, along with pressure on hospitals to perform fewer abortions.
- Changing attitudes toward abortion or toward childbirth.

Although some may oppose abortion and contraception, all would agree that these figures translate into fewer unwanted babies.

Women and Abortion

A key research issue is one concerning the psychological effects of legal abortion on women who obtain them. A report released by the American

Psychological Association reviewing the scientific literature on the psychological effects of legal abortion concluded that most women felt the most distress immediately *preceding* an abortion, and felt relief following it (Adler et al., 1990). Only a small minority of women report adverse psychological effects (Major & Cozzarelli, 1992).

There are many stereotypes about women who have an abortion: They are selfish, promiscuous, single, unwilling to accept family responsibilities, childless, nonmaternal, depressed, sinful, and immoral (Gordon, 1990; Petchesky, 1990). Furthermore, national public opinion surveys depict a "simplistic image" of women's reasons for abortion (Adler et al., 1992). Because few women openly discuss their abortion experiences, stereotypical views of abortion continue unchallenged.

Women generally have multiple reasons for wanting an abortion (Torres & Forrest, 1988; Adler et al., 1992). An important study by Aida Torres and Jacqueline Forrest (1988) came to the following conclusions:

1. *The abortion decision is complex, with several reasons at play.* It is not undertaken lightly. The multiple reasons most commonly cited by women include concern about how a child would change her life, not being able to afford a child, problems in the relationship, or wanting to avoid being a single parent.

2. *The woman's developmental life stage is important.* Eleven percent of the women stated they were "too immature" or "too young" to have a child; 21% said they were "unready for responsibility."

3. *Many reasons have to do with women's relationships with other people or educational or economic circumstances.* Decisions reflect not just the woman's personal qualities. Twenty-three percent said their husband or partner didn't want a child. Over two-thirds said they couldn't afford a child. These reasons point to women's ongoing sense of responsibility to others or outside circumstances.

Torres and Forrest (1988) found that being white, African American, or Latina had little influence in abortion decision making. Latinas were only slightly less likely than non-Latinas to say they did not want additional children.

Making an abortion decision, regardless of the ultimate outcome, raises many emotional issues for women. There is no painless way of dealing with an unwanted pregnancy. For many, such a decision requires a reevaluation of their relationships, an examination of their childbearing plans, a search to understand the role of sexuality in their lives, and an attempt to clarify their life goals.

Men and Abortion

In the decision-making process, the man is often forgotten. Attention is usually focused on the woman, who is undergoing personal agony in making the decision. If the man is thought of, it is often with hostility and blame. And yet the man, like the woman, may be undergoing his own private travail, experiencing guilt and anxiety, feeling ambiguous about the possibility of parenthood.

A common feeling men experience is powerlessness. They may try to remain cool and rational, believing that if they reveal their confused feelings, they will be unable to give their partners emotional support (Wade, 1978). Because the drama is within the woman and her body, a man may feel he must not influence her decision.

There is the lure of fatherhood, all the same. A pregnancy forces a man to confront his own feelings about parenting. Parenthood for males, as for females, is a profound passage into adulthood. For young men, there is a mixture of pride and fear about the potential for being a father and an adult.

After an abortion, many men feel residual guilt, sadness, and remorse. It is not uncommon for some men to temporarily experience erectile or ejaculatory difficulties. It is fairly common for couples to split up after an abortion; the stress, conflict, and guilt can be overwhelming. Many abortion clinics now provide counseling for men, as well as women, involved in an abortion.

Control over our fertility helps us control our lives. It also allows the human race to survive and, at least in parts of the world, to prosper. The topic of birth control provokes much emotional controversy. Individuals and institutions alike are inclined to believe in the moral rightness of their particular stance on the subject, whatever that stance may be. As each of us tries to find his or her own path through the quagmire of controversy, we can be guided by what we learn. We need to arm ourselves with knowledge—not only about the methods and mechanics of contraception and birth control but also about our own motivations, needs, weaknesses, and strengths.

SUMMARY

Risk and Responsibility

• Over the period of 1 year, a couple that does not use contraception has a 90% chance of pregnancy. Most couples do not use contraception during their first intercourse. As people become older, they tend to become more consistent users of contraceptive methods.

• Many people knowingly risk pregnancy by having unprotected intercourse. The more "successful" they are at risk taking, the more likely they are to take chances again. People also take risks because of faulty knowledge, denial of their sexuality, or a subconscious desire for a child.

• Because women are the ones who get pregnant, they may have greater interest than men in controlling their fertility. But it is important for men to share the responsibility.

Methods of Contraception and Birth Control

• Birth control is any means of preventing a birth from taking place. Contraception is birth control that works specifically by preventing the union of sperm and egg.

• The most reliable method of birth control is abstinence—refraining from sexual intercourse.

• Oral contraceptives are the most widely used form of reversible birth control in the U.S. Birth control pills contain synthetic hormones: progestin and (usually) estrogen. The pill is highly effective if taken regularly. There are side effects and possible problems that affect some users. The greatest risks are to smokers, women over 35, and women with certain health disorders, such as cardiovascular problems.

• Thin capsules containing progestin that are implanted under the skin of a woman's arm protect against pregnancy for five years. When they are removed, fertility is restored. These implants (marketed as Norplant) may be the most effective reversible contraceptive ever marketed. Recently, the injectable hormone Depo-Provera (DMPA) became available in the U.S. Its effects last 3–6 months.

• A condom is a thin sheath of latex rubber (or processed animal tissue) that fits over the erect penis and prevents semen from being transmitted. It is the third most widely used birth control method in the U.S. Condoms are very effective for contraception when used correctly, especially in combination with spermicidal foam or film. Latex condoms also help provide protection against STDs.

• The diaphragm, cervical cap, and female condom are barrier methods used by women. The diaphragm and cervical cap cover the cervical opening. They are used with spermicidal jelly or cream. The diaphragm is effective if used properly. The effectiveness of cervical caps is not yet well established. Female condoms have not yet been widely tested. In addition to lining the vagina, they cover much of the vulva, providing more protection against disease organisms. The contraceptive sponge is no longer available.

• Spermicides are chemicals that are toxic to sperm. Nonoxynol-9 is the most common ingredient. Contraceptive foam provides fairly good protection when used alone, but other preparations are more effective if combined with a barrier method. Other spermicidal products are film, cream, jelly, suppositories, and tablets.

• Many types of IUDs (intrauterine devices) have been taken off the market in the U.S. because of the threat of lawsuits. An IUD is a tiny plastic or metal device that is inserted through the cervical os into the uterus. It disrupts the fertilization and implantation processes. The most serious problem associated with the IUD is increased risk of pelvic inflammatory disease; therefore, IUDs are not recommended for women who have multiple sex partners or who plan to have children in the future.

• Fertility awareness methods (or natural family planning) involve a woman's awareness of her body's reproductive cycles. These include the calendar (rhythm), basal body temperature (BBT), mucus, and symptothermal methods. These methods are suitable only for women with regular menstrual cycles and high motivation.

• Surgical sterilization (or voluntary surgical contraception) is the most popular form of birth control among married couples and women in this country. The most common form for women is tubal ligation, closing off the fallopian tubes. The surgical procedure that sterilizes men is a vasectomy, in which each vas deferens (sperm-carrying tube) is closed off. These methods of birth control are close to 100% effective.

• Postcoital ("morning-after") birth control is a controversial issue. Some doctors give high doses of birth control pills to induce the shedding of the uterine lining. A new drug known as RU-486 should soon be available in the U.S. It can be used as a morning-after pill, a once-a-month pill, or to induce an early abortion.

• Unreliable methods of contraception include withdrawal, douching, relying on lactation, and using plastic bags as condoms.

Abortion

• Abortion, the expulsion of the conceptus from the uterus, can be spontaneous or induced. Surgical methods of abortion are vacuum aspiration, dilation and curettage (D & C), dilation and evacuation (D & E), and hysterotomy. Nonsurgical methods utilize injections of prostaglandins, saline solution, or urea solution. Abortion is generally safe if done in the first trimester. Second-trimester abortions are significantly riskier.

• A decline to 1979 rates in the incidence of abortion has been reported. Possible causes include reduced access, an aging population, and greater use of condoms.

• For women, the abortion decision is complex; their developmental/life stage is important, and their reasons for choosing abortion have to do with relationships or educational or economic circumstances. Men often feel powerless and ambivalent; many men feel residual guilt and sadness following an abortion.

SUGGESTED READINGS

Chesler, Ellen. *A Woman of Valor: Margaret Sanger and the Birth Control Movement in America*. New York: Simon & Schuster, 1992. The biography of Margaret Sanger who, in the early decades of this century, fought for women's contraceptive rights, an idea as divisive then as abortion rights are today.

Greer, Germaine. *Sex and Destiny*. New York: Harper & Row, 1984. A critique of the politics of fertility that is brilliant, controversial, opinionated, passionate, and refreshing; covers a wide range of topics, including contraception, abortion, infanticide, eugenics, and population control.

Hatcher, Robert, F. Stewart, J. Trussel, D. Kowal, F. Guest, G. Stewart, and W. Cates. *Contraceptive Technology: Special Sections: AIDS and Abnormal Pap Smears*. New York: Irvington Publishers, 1994. The most comprehensive and technically reliable book on developments in contraceptive technology; updated regularly.

Luker, Kristin. *Taking Chances*. Berkeley, CA: University of California Press, 1975. A major work on contraceptive risk taking; one of the most influential books in the field.

Tribe, Laurence. *Abortion: The Clash of Absolutes*. New York: W. W. Norton, 1992. An incisive, balanced book on the social, medical, political, legal, religious, and moral aspects of the abortion debate.

Chapter Twelve

CONCEPTION, PREGNANCY, AND CHILDBIRTH

PREVIEW: SELF-QUIZ

1. The greatest increase in infertility is found among couples in the 20–24-year-old range. True or false?

2. Miscarriage and stillbirth are major life events for parents. True or false?

3. The primary cause of infertility in women is an untreated sexually transmitted disease. True or false?

4. Fertilization generally takes place within the uterus. True or false?

5. Home pregnancy tests are about 95% accurate. True or false?

6. Even a moderate amount of alcohol consumption affects the fetus. True or false?

7. The United States ranks 24th among developed countries for low infant mortality. True or false?

8. About one-fourth of all U.S. births involve cesarean sections. True or false?

9. Circumcision, the surgical removal of the foreskin of the penis, is performed mainly for health reasons. True or false?

10. Breast-feeding is recommended by the American Academy of Pediatricians because it provides better nutrition and protection from disease than formula. True or false?

ANSWERS 1. T, 2. T, 3. T, 4. F, 5. T, 6. T, 7. T, 8. T, 9. F, 10. T

Chapter Outline

The birth of a wanted child is considered by many parents to be the happiest event of their lives. Today, however, pain and controversy surround many aspects of this completely natural process. As we struggle to balance the rights of the mother, the father, the fetus, and soci-

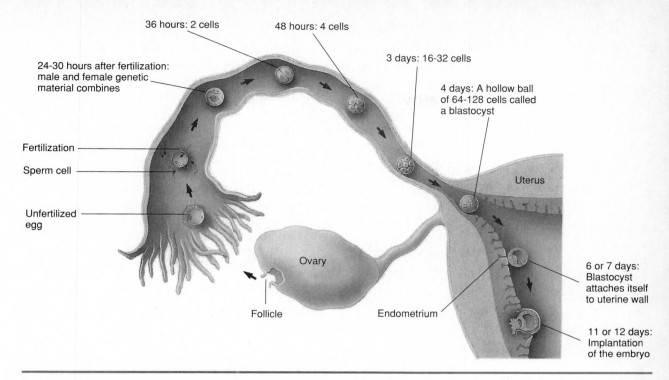

36 hours: 2 cells

48 hours: 4 cells

3 days: 16-32 cells

24-30 hours after fertilization: male and female genetic material combines

4 days: A hollow ball of 64-128 cells called a blastocyst

Fertilization

Sperm cell

Unfertilized egg

Uterus

Ovary

Follicle

Endometrium

6 or 7 days: Blastocyst attaches itself to uterine wall

11 or 12 days: Implantation of the embryo

FIGURE 12.1 Ovulation, Fertilization, and Development of the Blastocyst. This drawing charts the progress of the ovulated oocyte (unfertilized egg) through fertilization and pre-embryonic development.

ety itself in these matters, we find ourselves considering the quality of life as well as life's mere existence.

For most American women, pregnancy will be relatively comfortable and the outcome predictably joyful. Yet for increasing numbers of others, especially among the poor, the prospect of having children raises the specters of drugs, disease, malnutrition, and familial chaos. And there are those couples who have dreamed of and planned for families for years, only to find that they are unable to conceive.

In this chapter, we view pregnancy and childbirth from biological, social, and psychological perspectives. We consider pregnancy loss, infertility, and reproductive techniques. And we look at the challenges of the transition to parenthood.

FERTILIZATION AND FETAL DEVELOPMENT

As you will recall from Chapter 3, once the secondary oocyte has been released from the ovary, it drifts into the fallopian tube, where it may be fertilized if live sperm are present (Figure 12.1). If the pregnancy proceeds without interruption, the birth will occur in approximately 266 days. (Traditionally, physicians count the first day of the pregnancy as the day on which the woman would have begun her menstrual period; they calculate the due date to be 280 days, which is also 10 lunar months, from that day.)

The Fertilization Process

The oocyte remains viable for 12–24 hours after ovulation; most sperm are viable in the female reproductive tract for 12–48 hours, although some "super sperm" may be viable for up to 72 hours (Marieb, 1992). Therefore, for fertilization to occur, intercourse must take place within a period of 3 days before and 1 day after ovulation.

Of the millions of sperm ejaculated into the vagina, only a few thousand (or even just a few hundred) actually reach the fallopian tubes. The others leak from the vagina or are destroyed within its acidic environment. Those that make it into the cervix (which is easier during ovulation, when the cervical mucus becomes more fluid) may still be destroyed by white blood cells within the uterus. Furthermore, the sperm that actually reach the oocyte within a few minutes of ejaculation are not yet capable of getting through its outer layers. They must first undergo **capacitation,** the process by which their membranes become fragile enough to release the enzymes from their acrosomes (the helmetlike coverings of the sperm's nuclei). It takes 6–8 hours for this acrosomal reaction to occur. Enzymes from hundreds of sperm must be released in order for the oocyte's outer layers (the corona radiata and the zona pellucida) to soften sufficiently to allow a sperm to be absorbed.

Once a single sperm is inside the oocyte cytoplasm, an electrical reaction occurs that prevents any other sperm from entering the oocyte. Immediately, the oocyte begins to swell, detaching the sperm that still cling to its outer layer. Then it completes the final stage of cell division and becomes a mature ovum by forming the ovum nucleus. The nuclei of sperm and ovum then release their chromosomes, which combine to form the diploid zygote, containing 23 pairs of chromosomes. (Each parent contributes one chromosome to each of the pairs.) Fertilization is now complete, and pre-embryonic development begins. Within 9 months, this single cell, the zygote, may become the 6000 billion cells that constitute a human being.

Development of the Conceptus

Following fertilization, the zygote undergoes a series of divisions, during which the cells replicate themselves. After 4 or 5 days, there are about 100 cells, now called a **blastocyst.** On about the fifth day, the blastocyst arrives in the uterine cavity, where it floats for a day or two before implanting in the soft, blood-rich uterine lining (endometrium), which has spent the past 3 weeks preparing for its arrival. The process of **implantation** takes about 1 week. Human chorionic gonadotropin (HCG) secreted by the blastocyst maintains the uterine environment in an "embryo-friendly" condition and prevents the shedding of the endometrium, which would normally occur during menstruation.

The blastocyst, or pre-embryo, rapidly grows into an **embryo,** which will, in turn, be referred to as a **fetus** around the eighth week of **gestation** (pregnancy). During the first 2 or 3 weeks of development, the **embryonic membranes** are formed. These include the **amnion** (amniotic sac), a membranous sac that will contain the embryo and **amniotic fluid;** the **yolk sac,** producer of the embryo's first blood cells and the germ cells that will develop into gonads; and the **chorion,** the embryo's outermost membrane (Figure 12.2).

capacitation The process by which a sperm's membranes become fragile enough to release the enzymes from its acrosomes.

blastocyst A collection of about 100 human cells that develops from the zygote.

implantation The process by which a blastocyst becomes embedded in the uterine wall.

embryo The early form of life in the uterus between the stages of blastocyst and fetus.

fetus The stage of life from 8 weeks of gestation to birth.

gestation Pregnancy.

embryonic membrane One of the embryo's membranes, including the amnion, yolk sac, chorion, and allantois.

amnion An embryonic membranous sac containing the embryo and amniotic fluid.

amniotic fluid The fluid within the amniotic sac that surrounds the embryo or fetus.

yolk sac The producer of the embryo's first blood cells and germ cells, which will develop into gonads.

chorion The embryo's outermost membrane.

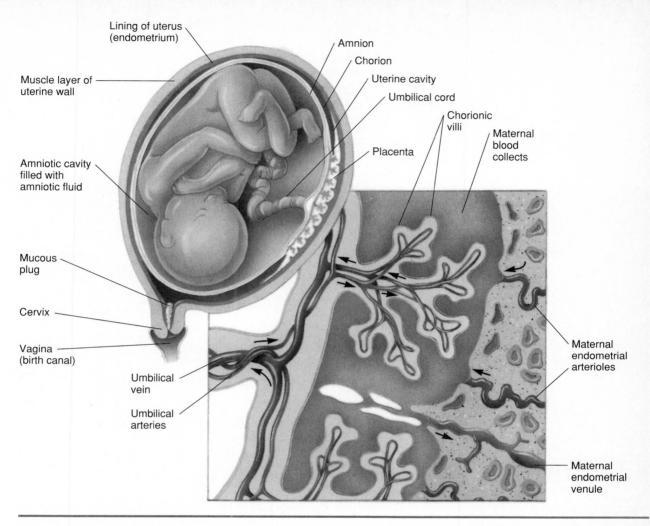

Lining of uterus
(endometrium)

Muscle layer of
uterine wall

Amniotic cavity
filled with
amniotic fluid

Mucous
plug

Cervix

Vagina
(birth canal)

Umbilical
vein

Umbilical
arteries

Amnion

Chorion

Uterine cavity

Umbilical cord

Chorionic
villi

Maternal
blood
collects

Placenta

Maternal
endometrial
arterioles

Maternal
endometrial
venule

FIGURE 12.2 The Fetus in the Uterus and a Cross Section of the Placenta. The placenta is the organ of exchange between mother and fetus. Nutrients and oxygen pass from the mother to the fetus, and waste products pass from the fetus to the mother via blood vessels within the umbilical cord.

During the 3rd week, extensive cell migration occurs, and the stage is set for the development of the organs. The first body segments and the brain begin to form. The digestive and circulatory systems begin to develop in the 4th week, and the heart begins to pump blood. By the end of the first month, the spinal cord and nervous system have also begun to develop. The 5th week sees the formation of arms and legs. In the 6th week, the eyes and ears form. At 7 weeks, the reproductive organs begin to differentiate in males; female reproductive organs continue to develop. At 8 weeks, the fetus is about the size of a thumb, although the head is nearly as large as the body. The brain begins to function to coordinate the development of the internal organs. Facial features begin to form, and bones begin to develop. Arms, hands, fingers, legs, feet, toes, and eyes are almost fully developed at 12 weeks. At 15 weeks, the fetus has a strong heartbeat, some digestion, and active muscles. Most bones are developed by then, and the

lanugo The fine, downy hair covering the fetus.

placenta The organ of exchange between the mother and the fetus.

umbilical cord The cord connecting the placenta and fetus, through which nutrients pass.

eyebrows appear. At this stage, the fetus is covered with a fine, downy hair called **lanugo.**

Throughout its development, the fetus is nourished through the **placenta.** The placenta begins to develop from part of the blastocyst following implantation. It grows larger as the fetus does, passing nutrients from the mother's bloodstream to the fetus, to which it is attached by the **umbilical cord.** The placenta serves as a biochemical barrier; it allows dissolved substances to pass to the fetus but blocks blood cells and large molecules.

a

b

c

d

e

(a) After ejaculation, several million sperm move through the cervical mucus toward the fallopian tubes; an ovum has moved into one of the tubes. On their way to the ovum, millions of sperm are destroyed in the vagina, uterus, or fallopian tubes. Some go the wrong direction in the vagina, and others swim into the wrong tube. (b) The mother's and father's chromosomes have united, and the fertilized ovum has divided for the first time. After about 1 week, the blastocyst will implant itself in the uterine lining. (c) The embryo is 5 weeks old and is ⅖ of an inch long. It floats in the embryonic sac. The major divisions of the brain can be seen, as well as an eye, hands, arms, and a long tail. (d) The embryo is now 7 weeks old and is almost 1 inch long. Its external and internal organs are developing It has eyes, nose, mouth, lips, and tongue. (e) At 12 weeks, the fetus is over 3 inches long and weighs almost 1 ounce. (f) At 16 weeks, the fetus is more than 6 inches long and weighs about 7 ounces. All its organs have been formed. The time that follows is now one of simple growth.

f

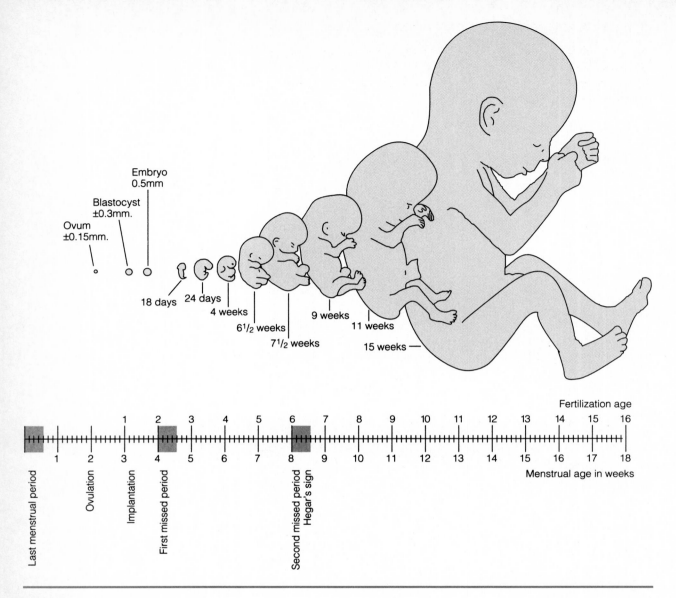

FIGURE 12.3 Growth of the Embryo and Fetus. In this drawing, the actual sizes of the developing embryo and fetus are shown, from conception through the first 15 weeks.

By 5 months, the fetus is 10–12 inches long and weighs between ½ and 1 lb. The internal organs are well developed, although the lungs cannot function well outside the uterus. At 6 months, the fetus is 11–14 inches long and weighs more than 1 lb. At 7 months, it is 13–17 inches long and weighs about 3 lb. At this point, most healthy fetuses are viable—that is, capable of surviving outside the womb. (Although some fetuses are viable at 5 or 6 months, they require specialized care to survive.) The fetus spends the final 2 months of gestation growing rapidly. At term (9 months), it will be about 20 inches long and will weigh about 7 lb (Figure 12.3).

BEING PREGNANT

Pregnancy is an important life event for both women and their partners. From the moment it is discovered, a pregnancy affects people's feelings about themselves, their relationships with their partners, and the interrelationships of other family members as well.

Pregnancy Tests

Chemical tests designed to detect the presence of **human chorionic gonadotropin (HCG),** secreted by the developing placenta, usually determine pregnancy approximately two weeks following a missed (or spotty) menstrual period. In the **agglutination test,** a drop of the woman's urine causes a test solution to coagulate if she is not pregnant; if she is pregnant, the solution will become smooth and milky in consistency. Home pregnancy tests to detect HCG may be purchased in most drugstores. The directions must be followed closely. Blood analysis can also be used to determine if a pregnancy exists. Although such tests diagnose pregnancy with better than 95% accuracy, no absolute certainty exists until a fetal heartbeat and movements can be detected or ultrasound is performed.

The first reliable physical sign of pregnancy can be distinguished about 4 weeks after a woman misses her period. By this time, changes in her cervix and pelvis are apparent during a pelvic examination. At this time the woman would be considered to be 8 weeks pregnant, according to medical terminology; physicians calculate pregnancy as beginning at the time of the woman's last menstrual period rather than at the time of actual fertilization (because that date is often difficult to determine). Another signal of pregnancy, called **Hegar's sign,** is a softening of the uterus just above the cervix, which can be felt during a vaginal examination. Additionally, a slight purple hue colors the labia minora; the vagina and cervix also take on a purplish color rather than the usual pink.

Changes That Occur During Pregnancy

A woman's feelings during pregnancy will vary dramatically according to who she is, how she feels about pregnancy and motherhood, whether the pregnancy was planned, whether she has a secure home situation, and many other factors. Her feelings may be ambivalent; they will probably change over the course of the pregnancy.

A woman's first pregnancy is especially important because it has traditionally symbolized her transition to maturity. Even as social norms change and it becomes more common and "acceptable" for women to defer childbirth until they've established a career or for them to choose not to have children, the significance of first pregnancy should not be underestimated. It is a major developmental milestone in the lives of mothers—and of fathers as well (Notman & Lester, 1988; Snarey et al., 1987; for male procreative consciousness, see Marsiglio & Donnelley, 1991).

A couple's relationship is likely to undergo changes during pregnancy. It can be a stressful time, especially if the pregnancy was unanticipated. Communication is especially important during this period, because each partner may have preconceived ideas about what the other is feeling. Both partners

human chorionic gonadotropin (HCG) A hormone secreted by the developing placenta and needed to support a pregnancy.

agglutination test A pregnancy test using the woman's urine.

Hegar's sign The softening of the uterus above the cervix, indicating pregnancy.

Think About It

SEXUALITY DURING PREGNANCY

It is not unusual for a woman's sexual feelings and actions to change during pregnancy, although there is great variation among women in these expressions of sexuality. Some women feel beautiful, energetic, sensual, and interested in sex, whereas others feel awkward and decidedly unsexy. Some studies indicate a lessening of women's sexual interest during pregnancy and a corresponding decline in coital frequency, while others show a shift in the type of activities preferred. It is also quite possible that a woman's sexual feelings will fluctuate during this time. Men may also feel confusion or conflicts about sexual activity. They, like many women, may have been conditioned to find the pregnant body unerotic. Or they may feel deep sexual attraction to their pregnant partners, yet fear their feelings are "strange" or unusual. They may also worry about hurting their partner or the baby.

Although there are no "rules" governing sexual behavior during pregnancy, a few basic precautions should be observed:

- If the woman has had a prior miscarriage, she should check with her health practitioner before having intercourse, masturbating, or engaging in other activities that might lead to orgasm. Powerful uterine contractions could induce a spontaneous abortion in some women, especially during the first trimester.

- If there is bleeding from the vagina, the woman should refrain from sexual activity and consult her physician or midwife at once.

- If the insertion of the penis into the vagina causes pain that is not easily remedied by a change of position, the couple should refrain from intercourse.

- Pressure on the woman's abdomen should be avoided, especially during the final months of pregnancy.

- Late in pregnancy, an orgasm is likely to induce uterine contractions. Generally, this is not considered harmful, but the pregnant woman may want to discuss it with her practitioner. (Occasionally, labor is begun when the waters break as the result of orgasmic contractions.)

A couple, especially if it is their first pregnancy, may be uncertain as to how to express their sexual feelings. The following guidelines may be helpful:

- Even during a normal pregnancy, sexual intercourse may be uncomfortable. The couple may want to try such positions as side-by-side or rear-entry, to avoid pressure on the woman's abdomen and to facilitate more shallow penetration. (See illustrations of different sexual positions in Chapter 9.)

- Even if intercourse is not comfortable for the woman, orgasm may still be intensely pleasurable. She may wish to consider the possibilities of masturbation (alone or with her partner) or of cunnilingus. It is important to note that air should *not* be blown into the vagina during cunnilingus.

- Both partners should remember that there are no "rules" about sexuality during pregnancy. This is a time for relaxing, enjoying the woman's changing body, talking a lot, touching each other, and experimenting with new ways—both sexual and nonsexual—of expressing affection.

may have fears about the baby's well-being, the approaching birth, their ability to parent, and the ways in which the baby will interfere with their own relationship. All of these concerns are normal. Sharing them, perhaps in the setting of a prenatal group, can deepen and strengthen the relationship (Kitzinger, 1989). If the pregnant woman's partner is not supportive or if she does not have a partner, it is important that she find other sources of support—family, friends, women's groups—and that she not be reluctant to ask for help.

A pregnant woman's relationship with her own mother may also undergo changes. In a certain sense, becoming a mother makes a woman the equal of her own mother. She can now lay claim to being treated as an adult. Women who have depended on their mothers tend to become more independent and assertive as their pregnancy progresses. Women who have been distant, hostile, or alienated from their own mothers may begin to identify with their mothers' experience of pregnancy. Even women who have delayed childbearing until their thirties may be surprised to find their relationships with their mothers changing and becoming more "adult." Working through these changing relationships is a kind of "psychological gestation" that accompanies the physiological gestation of the fetus (Silver & Campbell, 1988).

The first trimester (3 months) of pregnancy may be difficult physically for the expectant mother. She may experience nausea, fatigue, and painful swelling of the breasts. She may also have fears that she may miscarry or that the child will not be normal. Her sexuality may undergo changes, resulting in unfamiliar needs (for more, less, or differently expressed sexual love), which may in turn cause anxiety. (Sexuality during pregnancy is discussed further earlier in this section.) Education about the birth process and her own body's functioning, as well as support from partner, friends, relatives, and health-care professionals, are the best antidotes to fear.

During the second trimester, most of the nausea and fatigue disappear, and the pregnant woman can feel the fetus move within her. Worries about miscarriage will probably begin to diminish, too, for the riskiest part of fetal development has passed. The pregnant woman may look and feel radiantly happy. She will very likely feel proud of her accomplishment and be delighted as her pregnancy begins to show. She may feel in harmony with life's natural rhythms. Some women, however, may be concerned about their increasing size. They may fear that they are becoming unattractive. A partner's attention and reassurance will ease these fears.

The third trimester may be the time of the greatest difficulties in daily living. The uterus, originally about the size of the woman's fist, has now enlarged to fill the pelvic cavity and pushes up into the abdominal cavity, exerting increasing pressure on the other internal organs (Figure 12.4). Water retention (edema) is a fairly common problem during late pregnancy. Edema may cause swelling in the face, hands, ankles, and feet, but it can often be controlled by cutting down on salt and carbohydrates. If dietary changes do not help this condition, a pregnant woman should consult her physician. Her physical abilities are limited by her size. She may be required by her employer to stop working (many public schools, for example, do not allow women to teach after their 6th month). A family dependent on the pregnant woman's income may suffer a severe financial crunch.

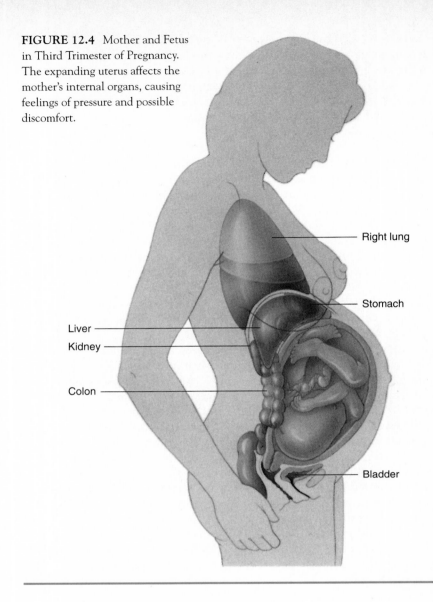

FIGURE 12.4 Mother and Fetus in Third Trimester of Pregnancy. The expanding uterus affects the mother's internal organs, causing feelings of pressure and possible discomfort.

Right lung

Stomach

Liver

Kidney

Colon

Bladder

The woman and her partner may become increasingly concerned about the upcoming birth. Some women experience periods of depression in the month preceding their delivery; they may feel physically awkward and sexually unattractive. Many feel an exhilarating sense of excitement and anticipation marked by energetic bursts of industriousness. They feel that the fetus is a member of the family (Stanton, 1985). Both parents may begin talking to the fetus and "playing" with it by patting and rubbing the mother's belly.

The principal developmental tasks for the expectant mother and father may be summarized as follows (Valentine, 1982; also see Notman & Lester, 1988; Silver & Campbell, 1988; Snarey et al., 1987):

Tasks of an Expectant Mother

- Development of an emotional attachment to the fetus
- Differentiation of the self from the fetus
- Acceptance and resolution of the relationship with the woman's own mother
- Resolution of dependency issues (generally involving parents or husband/partner)
- Evaluation of practical and financial responsibilities.

Tasks of an Expectant Father

- Acceptance of the pregnancy and attachment to the fetus
- Evaluation of practical and financial responsibilities
- Resolution of dependency issues (involving wife/partner)
- Acceptance and resolution of the relationship with the man's own father

Complications of Pregnancy and Dangers to the Fetus

Usually, pregnancy proceeds without major complications. Good nutrition is one of the most important factors in having a complication-free pregnancy. However, some women experience minor to serious complications.

Effects of Teratogens Substances other than nutrients may reach the developing embryo or fetus through the placenta. Although few extensive studies have been done on the subject, toxic substances in the environment can also affect the health of the fetus. Whatever a woman breathes, eats, or drinks is eventually received by the conceptus in some proportion. A fetus's blood-alcohol level, for example, is equal to that of the mother (Rosenthal, 1990). **Teratogens,** substances that cause defects (such as brain damage or physical deformities) in developing embryos or fetuses, are directly traceable in only about 2–3% of cases of birth defects. They are thought to be linked to 25–30% of such cases; the causes of the remaining cases remain unknown (Healy, 1988).

teratogen A toxic substance that causes birth defects.

   Chemicals and environmental pollutants are also potentially threatening. Continuous exposure to lead, most commonly in paint products or water from lead pipes, has been implicated in a variety of learning disorders. Mercury, from fish contaminated by industrial wastes, is a known cause of physical deformities. Solvents, pesticides, and certain chemical fertilizers should be avoided or used with extreme caution both at home and in the workplace.

Infectious Diseases Infectious diseases can also damage the fetus. If a woman contracts German measles (rubella) during the first 3 months of pregnancy, her child may be born with physical or mental disabilities. Immunization against rubella is available, but it must be done before the woman is pregnant; otherwise, the injection will be as harmful to the fetus as the disease itself. Group B streptococcus, a bacterium carried by 15–40% of pregnant women, is harmless to adults but can be fatal to newborns. Each year, about 12,000 infants are infected; 1600–2000 of them die.

PREGNANCY AND DRUGS DON'T MIX

Among the lessons most of us learned from our parents was to be good to our children. This lesson is crucial during pregnancy, when the unborn child is most vulnerable. But many people are not putting this lesson into action: Between 1979 and 1990, there was a 456% increase in the number of drug-affected newborns discharged from hospitals (Dicker & Leighton, 1994).

Because there is no built-in barrier or filter between mother and fetus blocking out all substances, it is safe to assume that there is no safe drug. With the exception of a handful of prescription and over-the-counter medications, all drugs—including alcohol, tobacco, street drugs, and many legal drugs—have the capacity to cause physical damage, malformation, or miscarriage. The most devastating outcomes occur for pregnant women who lack information about drugs and whose judgment is impaired because they are under the influence of uncontrolled street drugs.

The following is a partial list of drugs and their effects on the fetus. Not well understood or studied are the effects of the father's drug use on the health of the fetus. Regardless, it is prudent for both partners to assume healthy lifestyles before considering pregnancy.

Alcohol Studies have linked chronic ingestion of alcohol during pregnancy to fetal alcohol syndrome (FAS), which can include unusual facial characteristics, small head and body size, congenital heart defects, defective joints, poor mental capabilities, and abnormal behavior patterns. Lesser amounts of alcohol may result in fetal alcohol effect (FAE), the most common problem of which is growth retardation (Waterson & Murray-Lyon, 1990). The Centers for Disease Control (CDC) estimate that more than 8000 alcohol-affected babies are born every year in this country (2.7 babies out of every 1000). Some studies place the figure higher—as high as 50,000 alcohol-affected births per year (Getlin, 1989). The CDC also reports that FAS is six times more common in African Americans than in whites and thirty times more common in Native Americans (Rosenthal, 1990a). Most experts counsel pregnant women to abstain entirely

Sexually Transmitted Diseases Sexually transmitted diseases may also damage the fetus. In 1988, the CDC recommended that all pregnant women be screened for hepatitis B, a virus that can be passed to the infant at birth. If the mother tests positive, her child can be immunized immediately following birth (Moore, 1988). A woman with gonorrhea may expose her child to blindness from contact with the infected vagina; the baby will need immediate antibiotic treatment. A woman with HIV or AIDS has a 25–40% chance of passing the virus to the fetus via the placenta (Cowley, 1991; Fischl, Dickinson, Segal, Flannagan, & Rodriguez, 1987). The number of infants with HIV or AIDS is increasing as more women become infected with the virus either before or during pregnancy.

The increasingly widespread incidence of genital herpes may present some hazards for newborns. The herpes simplex virus may cause brain damage and is potentially life-threatening for these infants. Careful monitoring by a physician can determine whether or not a vaginal delivery should take place. Charles Prober (1987) and colleagues at the Stanford Medical School have extensively studied births to mothers with herpes. They found that a from alcohol because there is no safe dosage known at this time.

Opiates and Cocaine   Mothers who regularly use opiates (heroin, morphine, codeine, and opium) are likely to have infants who are addicted at birth. Cocaine—especially in the smokable "crack" form—may be associated with devastating birth defects (Chasnoff, 1988). A study in New York of drug-exposed infants revealed that the opiate-exposed babies showed more neurological damage than the cocaine-exposed babies, and that those infants exposed to polydrug abuse (both opiates and cocaine) were worse off than those exposed to any single drug in terms of gestational age at birth, birth weight, and length of hospital stay (Kaye, Elkind, Goldberg, & Tytun, 1989). It should be noted that many drug-exposed infants have been exposed to alcohol as well.

Tobacco   Cigarette smoking affects the unborn child. Babies born to women who smoke during pregnancy are an average of one-fourth to one-half pound lighter at birth than babies born to nonsmokers. Secondhand smoke is also considered dangerous to the developing fetus (Healy, 1988; Martinez et al., 1994). Smoking has been implicated in sudden infant death syndrome (SIDS), respiratory disorders in children, and various adverse pregnancy outcomes. Maternal smoking during pregnancy may also create a serious risk for smoking dependence in female offspring (Kandel, Wu, & Davies, 1994).

Prescription and Over-the-Counter Drugs   Prescription drugs should be used only under careful medical supervision, as some may cause serious harm to the fetus. Isotretinoin (Acutane), a popular antiacne drug, has been implicated in over 1000 cases of severe birth defects over the past several years (Kolata, 1988). Vitamins, aspirin, and other over-the-counter drugs, as well as large quantities of caffeine-containing food and drink (coffee, tea, cola, chocolate) should be avoided or used only under medical supervision. Vitamin A in large doses can cause serious birth defects.

number of infants born to infected mothers had herpes antibodies in their blood; these infants did not contract herpes during vaginal delivery. Although the harmful potential of neonatal herpes should not be underestimated, if the appropriate procedures are followed by the infected mother and her physician or midwife, the chance of infection from genital lesions is minimal (Dr. Margaret Yonekura in "Neonatal Herpes," 1984).

Testing for genital herpes is recommended for both expectant parents. Once the baby is born, a mother who is experiencing an outbreak of either oral or genital herpes should wash her hands often and carefully and not permit contact between her hands, contaminated objects, and the baby's mucous membranes (inside of eyes, mouth, nose, penis, vagina, vulva, and rectum). If the father is infected, he should do likewise until the lesions have subsided.

Ectopic Pregnancy   In **ectopic pregnancy** (tubal pregnancy), the incidence of which has more than quadrupled in the last 20 years, the fertilized egg implants itself in the fallopian tube. Generally, this occurs because

ectopic pregnancy   A pregnancy in which the fertilized egg implants in a fallopian tube instead of in the uterus. Also known as tubal pregnancy.

the tube is obstructed, most often as a result of pelvic inflammatory disease (Hilts, 1991). The pregnancy will never come to term. The embryo may spontaneously abort, or the embryo and placenta will continue to expand until they rupture the fallopian tube. Salpingectomy (removal of the tube) and abortion of the conceptus may be necessary to save the mother's life.

toxemia High blood pressure and edema that may occur between the 20th and 24th weeks of pregnancy.

preeclampsia A condition in pregnancy characterized by increasingly high blood pressure.

Toxemia and Preeclampsia **Toxemia,** which may appear in the 20th to 24th week of pregnancy, is characterized by high blood pressure and edema. It can generally be treated through nutritional means. If untreated, toxemia can develop into preeclampsia after the 24th week.

Preeclampsia is characterized by increasingly high blood pressure. Toxemia and preeclampsia are also known as gestational edema-proteinuria-hypertension complex. If untreated, they can lead to eclampsia, maternal convulsions that pose a serious threat to mother and child. Eclampsia is not common; it is prevented by keeping the blood pressure down through diet, rest, and sometimes medication. It is important for a pregnant woman to have her blood pressure checked regularly.

low birth weight (LBW) Prematurity; a condition in which the newborn weighs less than 5.5 lb; a major complication in the third trimester of pregnancy.

Low Birth Weight Prematurity, or **low birth weight (LBW),** is a major complication in the third trimester of pregnancy, affecting about 7% of newborns yearly (over 284,391 in 1989) in the United States (Pear, 1992). The most fundamental problem of prematurity is that many of the infant's vital organs are insufficiently developed. An LBW baby usually weighs less than 5.5 lb at birth. Most premature infants will grow normally, but many will experience disabilities. LBW infants are subject to various respiratory problems as well as infections. Feeding, too, is a problem because the infants may be too small to suck a breast or bottle, and their swallowing mechanisms may be too underdeveloped to permit them to drink. As premature infants get older, problems such as low intelligence, learning difficulties, poor hearing and vision, and physical awkwardness may become apparent.

Premature delivery is one of the greatest problems confronting obstetrics today. About half the cases are related to teenage pregnancy, smoking, poor nutrition, and poor health in the mother (Pear, 1992; Schneck, Sideras, Fox, & Dupuis, 1990); the causes of the other half are unknown.

Prenatal care is extremely important as a means of preventing prematurity (Rush et al., 1988). One-third of all LBW births could be averted with adequate prenatal care (Scott, 1990a). We need to understand that if children's needs are not met today, we will all face the consequences of their deprivation tomorrow. The social and economic costs are bound to be very high.

Diagnosing Abnormalities of the Fetus

In addition to the desire to bear children, the desire to bear healthy children has encouraged the development of new diagnostic technologies. In cases where serious problems are suspected, these technologies may be quite helpful, but sometimes it seems that they are used "simply because they're there."

ultrasound The use of high-frequency sound waves to create a visual image of the fetus in utero.

Ultrasound examinations use high-frequency sound waves to create a picture of the fetus in the uterus. The sound waves are transmitted through a quartz crystal; when they detect a change in the density, the sound waves

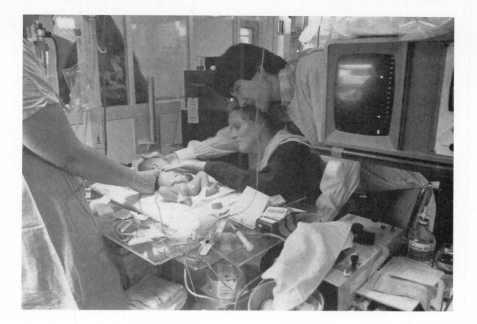

Low birth weight (prematurity) affects about 7% of newborns in the United States. Adequate prenatal care significantly reduces the risk of low birth weight.

The pictures produced by ultrasound are called sonograms. They are used to determine fetal age, position of the fetus and placenta, and possible developmental problems.

bounce back to the crystal. The results are interpreted on a televisionlike screen; the picture is called a **sonogram.** Sonograms are used to determine fetal age and the location of the placenta; when used with amniocentesis, they help determine the fetus's position so that the needle may be inserted safely. Often, it is possible to determine the fetus's sex. More extensive ultra-

sonogram A visual image created by ultrasound.

sound techniques can be used to gain further information if there is the possibility of a problem with fetal development.

In **amniocentesis,** amniotic fluid is withdrawn from the uterus with a long, thin needle inserted through the abdominal wall (the position of the fetus is determined by ultrasound) (Figure 12.5). The fluid is then examined for evidence of possible birth defects such as Down syndrome, cystic fibrosis, Tay-Sachs disease, spina bifida, and conditions that are caused by chromosomal abnormalities. The sex of the fetus can also be determined. About 80–90% of amniocentesis tests are performed in cases of "advanced" maternal age, usually when the mother is over 35. The test is performed at about 16 weeks of pregnancy. Amniocentesis carries a slight risk (a 0.5–2% chance of fetal death, depending on how early in pregnancy the test is performed (Brandenburg, Jahoda, Pijpers, Reuss, Kleyer, & Wladmiroff, 1990; Hanson, Happ, Tennant, Hune, & Peterson, 1990).

An alternative to amniocentesis recently introduced in the United States is **chorionic villus sampling (CVS)** (see Figure 12.5). This procedure involves removal through the abdomen (by needle) or through the cervix (by catheter) of tiny pieces of the membrane that encases the embryo; it can be performed between 9 and 11 weeks of pregnancy. There may be a somewhat greater-than-normal chance of miscarriage with CVS due to the possible introduction of infectious microorganisms at the time of the procedure (Baumann, Jovanovic, Gellert, & Rauskolb, 1991).

Alpha-feto protein (AFP) screening is a test (or series of tests) performed on the mother's blood after 16 weeks of pregnancy. It reveals defects of the spine, spinal cord, skull, and brain, such as anencephaly and spina bifida. It is much simpler than amniocentesis but sometimes yields false positive results (Samuels & Samuels, 1986). If the results are positive, other tests, such as amniocentesis and ultrasound, will be performed to confirm or negate the AFP screening findings.

For approximately 95% of women who undergo prenatal testing, the results are negative. The results of amniocentesis and AFP screening can't be determined, however, until approximately 20 weeks of pregnancy; consequently, if the pregnancy is terminated through abortion at this stage, the process is likely to be physically and emotionally difficult. If a fetus is found to be defective, it may be carried to term, aborted, or, in rare but increasing instances, surgically treated while still in the womb (Kolata, 1990).

Pregnancy Loss

The loss of a child through **miscarriage,** (or spontaneous loss of a fetus before it can survive on its own), stillbirth, or death during early infancy is often a devastating experience that has been largely ignored in our society. The statement, "You can always have another one," may be meant as consolation, but it is particularly chilling to the ears of a grieving mother. In the past few years, however, the medical community has begun to respond to the emotional needs of parents who have lost a pregnancy or an infant.

Spontaneous Abortion Spontaneous abortion, or miscarriage, is a powerful natural selective force toward bringing healthy babies into the world. About one out of four women is aware she has miscarried at least once

amniocentesis A process in which amniotic fluid is withdrawn by needle from the uterus and then examined for evidence of possible birth defects.

chorionic villus sampling (CVS) A procedure in which tiny pieces of the membrane that encases the embryo are removed and examined for evidence of possible birth defects.

alpha-feto protein (AFP) screening A blood test of a pregnant woman's blood to determine the existence of neural tube defects.

miscarriage The spontaneous expulsion of the fetus from the uterus; also called spontaneous abortion.

Amniocentesis

Ultrasound scanner

Amniotic fluid

Placenta

Fetus

Uterus

(a)

FIGURE 12.5 (a) Amniocentesis and (b) Chorionic Villus Sampling.

Chorionic villus sampling

Ultrasound scanner

Uterus

Embryo

Chorion

Catheter

(b)

(Beck, 1988). Studies indicate that at least 60% of all miscarriages are due to chromosomal abnormalities in the fetus (Adler, 1986). The first sign that a pregnant woman may miscarry is vaginal bleeding (spotting). If a woman's symptoms of pregnancy disappear and she develops pelvic cramps, she may be miscarrying; the fetus is usually expelled by uterine contractions. Most miscarriages occur between the 6th and 8th week of pregnancy (Welch & Herman, 1980). Evidence is increasing that certain occupations involving exposure to chemicals increase the likelihood of spontaneous abortions (Hemminki et al., 1983).

Infant Mortality The U.S. infant mortality rate, while at its lowest point ever, remains far higher than that of most of the developed world. The U.S. Public Health Service reported 8.9 deaths for every 1000 live births in 1991. Nevertheless, among developed nations, our country ranks 24th for low infant mortality (Pear, 1992). This means that 23 countries have *lower* infant mortality rates than the United States. In some inner-city areas, such as Detroit, Washington, DC, and parts of Oakland (California), the infant mortality rate approaches that of nonindustrialized countries, with more than 20 deaths per 1000 births (Petit, 1990). Of the more than 35,000 American babies less than 1 year old who die each year, most are victims of the poverty that often results from racial or ethnic discrimination. Up to one-third of these deaths could be prevented if mothers were given adequate health care (Scott, 1990b).

The infant mortality rate for African Americans is more than twice that for whites. Native Americans are also at high risk; for example, about one out of every 67 Navajo infants dies each year (Wilkerson, 1987).

Although many infants die of poverty-related conditions, others die from congenital problems (conditions appearing at birth) or from infectious diseases, accidents, or other causes. Sometimes the causes of death are not apparent; in 1985, one out of every 378 infant deaths was attributed to **sudden infant death syndrome (SIDS),** a perplexing phenomenon wherein an apparently healthy infant dies suddenly while sleeping. Sleeping position may be one variable contributing to SIDS in vulnerable infants. The American Academy of Pediatrics recommends that infants be placed on their backs for sleeping. No one knows what all the factors are that contribute to this unpredictable and unpreventable event (Brazelton, 1995).

Coping with Loss The depth of shock and grief felt by many who lose an infant before or during birth is sometimes difficult to understand for those who have not had a similar experience. What they may not realize is that most women form a deep attachment to their children even before birth. At first, the attachment may be a "fantasy image of [the] future child" (Friedman & Gradstein, 1982). During the course of the pregnancy, the mother forms an actual acquaintance with her infant through the physical sensations she feels within her. Thus, the death of the fetus can also represent the death of a dream and of a hope for the future. This loss must be acknowledged and felt before psychological healing can take place (Panuthos & Romeo, 1984).

The healing process takes time—months, a year, perhaps more for some. Support groups or counseling are often helpful, especially if healing does not seem to be progressing—if, for example, depression and physical symptoms don't appear to be diminishing.

INFERTILITY

Some couples experience the pain of loss when they plan to have a child and then discover that they cannot get pregnant. **Infertility** is broadly defined as the inability to conceive a child after trying for a year or more. Until recently, the problem of infertility attracted little public attention. In the last few years, however, approximately one in six couples or over 1 million Americans, many of whom have deferred pregnancy because of career plans or later marriages, have experienced fertility problems and sought treatment each year (Pearson, 1992). Still, a study by the National Center for Health Statistics showed that overall, the fertility rate for American women is not declining (Cimons, 1990; Faludi, 1991). Because approxi-

sudden infant death syndrome (SIDS) A phenomenon in which an apparently healthy infant dies suddenly while sleeping.

infertility The inability to conceive a child after trying for a year or more.

mately 40–50% of the factors contributing to infertility are male (Grunfeld, 1989) and because in 15% of couples, both partners have problems (Hudson, Pepperell, & Wood, 1987), it is important that each individual be evaluated. The greatest increase in infertility is found among young couples in the 20- to 24-year-old bracket. Infertility among young African American couples has risen even more dramatically; it is almost twice that of white couples (Faludi, 1991).

Female Infertility

Most cases of infertility among women are due to physical factors. Hormones, stress, immunological factors, and environmental factors may also be involved.

Physical Causes The leading cause of female infertility is blocked fallopian tubes, generally the result of pelvic inflammatory disease (PID), an infection of the fallopian tubes or uterus that is usually the result of a sexually transmitted disease. It can be caused by *gonococcus, chlamydia,* or several other organisms. About 1.7 million cases of PID were treated in 1986; doctors estimate that about half of the cases go untreated because PID is often symptomless, especially in the early stages (Hilts, 1991; Mueller, Luz-Jimenez, Daling, Moore, McKnight, & Weiss, 1992). Generally, only the woman with PID seeks treatment, and the man from whom she contracted the STD that caused it may continue to pass it on (Hilts, 1991). Surgery, including laser surgery, may restore fertility if the damage has not progressed too far.

The second leading cause of infertility in women is endometriosis; it is sometimes called the "career woman's disease" because it is most prevalent in women age 30 and over, many of whom have postponed childbirth. In this disease, uterine tissue grows outside the uterus, often appearing on the ovaries, in the fallopian tubes (where it may also block the tubes), and in the abdominal cavity. In its most severe form it may cause painful menstruation and intercourse, but most women with endometriosis are unaware that they have it. Hormone therapy and sometimes surgery are used for treatment.

A below-normal percentage of body fat, due to excessive dieting or exercise, may inhibit ovulation and delay pregnancy. In addition, benign growths such as fibroids and polyps on the uterus, ovaries, or fallopian tubes may also affect a woman's fertility. Surgery can restore fertility in many of these cases.

Hormonal and Psychological Causes In addition to physical causes, there may be hormonal reasons for infertility. The pituitary gland may fail to produce sufficient hormones (follicle-stimulating hormone, or FSH, and luteinizing hormone, or LH) to stimulate ovulation, or it may release them at the wrong time. Stress, which may be increased by the anxiety of trying to achieve a pregnancy, may also contribute to lowered fertility (Menning, 1988). Occasionally, immunological causes may be present, the most important of which is the production of sperm antibodies by the woman. For an unknown reason, a woman may be allergic to her partner's sperm, and her immune system will produce antibodies to destroy them.

Environmental Factors Toxic chemicals or exposure to radiation therapy threaten a woman's reproductive capacity. Smoking appears to reduce fertility in women (Baird & Wilcox, 1985; Laurent, Thompson, Addy, Garrison, & Moore, 1992). Evidence indicates that the daughters of mothers who took diethylstilbestrol (DES), a drug once thought to increase fertility and reduce the risk of miscarriage, have a significantly higher infertility rate, although studies remain somewhat contradictory (Berger & Goldstein, 1984).

Nature also plays a part. Beginning around age 30, a woman's fertility naturally begins to decline. By age 35, about one-fourth of women are infertile (Carroll, 1990).

Male Infertility

The primary causes of male infertility are low sperm count, lack of sperm motility, and blocked passageways. Some studies show that men's sperm counts have dropped by as much as 50% over the last 30 years (Andrews, 1984; Faludi, 1991).

As with women, environmental factors may contribute to men's infertility. Increasing evidence suggests that toxic substances, such as lead or chemicals found in some solvents and herbicides, are responsible for decreased sperm counts (Andrews, 1984). Smoking may produce reduced sperm counts or abnormal sperm (Evans et al., 1981). Prescription drugs such as cimetidine (Tagamet, for ulcers), prednisone (a corticosteroid that reduces tissue inflammation), or some medications for urinary tract infections have also been shown to affect the number of sperm that a man produces (Andrews, 1984).

Large doses of marijuana cause decreased sperm counts and suppression of certain reproductive hormones. These effects are apparently reversed when marijuana smoking stops (Ehrenkranz & Hembree, 1986). Men are more at risk than women from environmental factors because they are constantly producing new sperm cells; for the same reason, men may also recover faster once the affecting factor has been removed (Menning, 1988).

Sons of mothers who took DES may have increased sperm abnormalities and fertility problems (Retik & Bauer, 1984). Too much heat may temporarily reduce a man's sperm count (the male half of a couple trying to conceive may want to stay out of the hot tub for a while). A fairly common problem is the presence of a varicose vein called a **varicocele** above the testicle. Because it impairs circulation to the testicle, the varicocele causes an elevated scrotal temperature and thus interferes in sperm development. The varicocele may be surgically removed, but unless the man has a fairly good sperm count to begin with, his fertility may not improve.

varicocele A varicose vein above the testicle that may cause lowered fertility in men.

Emotional Responses to Infertility

By the time a couple seeks medical advice about their fertility problems, they may have already experienced a crisis in confronting the possibility of not being able to become biological parents. Many such couples feel they have lost control over a major area of their lives (Golombok, 1992; Olshansky, 1992). A number of studies suggest that women generally are more intensely affected than men (Andrews, Abbey, & Halman, 1991; Brand,

1989; McEwan, Costello, & Taylor, 1987; Wright, Duchesne, Sabourin, Bissonnette, Benoit, & Girard, 1991).

Infertility Treatment

Almost without exception, fertility problems are physical, not emotional, despite myths to the contrary, which often prevent infertile couples from seeking medical treatment. The two most popular myths are that anxiety over becoming pregnant leads to infertility, and that if an infertile couple adopts a child, the couple will then be able to conceive on their own (Kolata, 1979). Neither has any basis in medical fact, although it is true that some presumably infertile couples have conceived following an adoption. (This does not mean, however, that one should adopt a child to remedy infertility.) Approximately 10% of infertility cases are unexplained. In some of these cases, fertility is restored for no discernible reason; in others, the infertility remains a mystery (Jones, 1989). About 60% of couples with serious infertility problems will eventually achieve a pregnancy (Lord et al., 1987).

The techniques and technologies developed to achieve conception include fertility drugs, intrauterine insemination, and the establishment of sperm banks, in vitro fertilization (including embryo freezing), surrogate motherhood, and embryo transplants.

Medical Intervention In cases where infertility is a result of impaired ovulatory function in women, it may be remedied with medication. Treatment may include hormones that stimulate the ovarian follicles or regulate the menstrual cycle (Toback, 1992). Hormone therapy may be used alone or in combination with the techniques discussed below. About 10–20% of the pregnancies achieved with the help of "fertility drugs" result in multiple births as the result of more than one egg being released by the ovary (Rosenthal, 1992). Multiple births pose higher risks to both mothers and infants. Twins are about ten times more likely than babies born alone to have very low birth weights (3.3 lb or less); triplets are over 30 times more likely to have very low birth weights and three times more likely to have severe disabilities than infants born alone (Dr. Barbara Luke, cited in Rosenthal, 1992).

Current medical research is focusing increasingly on "male factor infertility." Approaches for treating men include new methods of sperm evaluation and processing, and the use of medication to improve sperm velocity (Go, 1992; Meacham & Lipshultz, 1991; Ohninger & Alexander, 1991).

Intrauterine Insemination When childlessness is the result of male infertility (or low fertility) or a genetically transmitted disorder carried by the male, couples may try **intrauterine insemination (IUI),** also known as **artificial insemination (AI).** Single women who want children but who have not found an appropriate partner or who wish to avoid emotional entanglements have used this technique, as have lesbian couples. The American Fertility Society estimates that there are about 30,000 births a year from intrauterine insemination (Kantrowitz & Kaplan, 1990).

During ovulation, semen is deposited by syringe near the cervical opening. The semen may come from the partner; if he has a low sperm count,

intrauterine insemination (IUI) or artificial insemination (AI) A means of achieving pregnancy by depositing semen by syringe near the cervical opening during ovulation.

therapeutic donor insemination (TDI) Intrauterine insemination in which the semen is from a donor rather than from the woman's husband.

several collections of semen may be taken and frozen, then collectively deposited in the woman's vagina, improving the odds of conception. If the partner had a vasectomy earlier, he may have had the semen frozen and stored in a sperm bank. If the man is sterile or has a genetically transferable disorder, **therapeutic donor insemination (TDI),** also known as artificial insemination by donor (AID), may be used. Anonymous donors—often medical students—are paid nominal amounts for their deposits of semen. Intrauterine insemination tends to produce males rather than females; in the general population, about 51% of the children born are male, but this figure reaches about 60% when conception is achieved artificially. Intrauterine insemination has a success rate of about 60% for infertile couples.

Some lesbians, especially those in committed relationships, are choosing to create families through artificial insemination. To date, there are no reliable data on the number of such births, but anecdotal information indicates that it is in the thousands. There are many questions raised when a lesbian couple contemplates having a baby in this way: Who will be the birth mother? What will the relationship of the other mother be? Will the donor be known or unknown? If known, will the child have a relationship with him? Will the child have a relationship with the donor's parents? Which, if any, of the child's grandparents will have a relationship with him or her? Will there be a legal contract between the parenting parties? There are few precedents to learn from or role models to follow in these cases (Pies, 1987). Another issue that such couples have to face is that the nonbiological parent generally has no legal tie to the child (de la Madrid, 1991). Furthermore, society may not recognize her as a "real" parent, because children are expected to have only one real mother and one real father.

in vitro fertilization (IVF) A means of achieving pregnancy by combining sperm and oocyte in a laboratory dish and implanting the blastocyst in the mother's uterus.

In Vitro Fertilization and Embryo Transfer
In vitro fertilization (IVF) entails combining sperm and oocyte in a laboratory dish and subsequently implanting the blastocyst, or pre-embryo, into the uterus of the mother or a surrogate. To help increase the chances of pregnancy, several oocytes are generally collected, fertilized, and implanted. The mother takes hormones to regulate her menstrual cycle so that the uterus will be prepared for the fertilized ovum. Sometimes the blastocysts are frozen and stored, to be implanted at a later date. The egg can come from the mother or from a donor. If it is a donor oocyte, the donor may be artificially inseminated with the father's sperm and the embryo removed from the donor and transplanted in the mother-to-be's uterus. More commonly, donor oocytes are "harvested" from the donor's ovary, which has been hormonally stimulated to produce 12–18 eggs instead of the usual one. This procedure is done by inserting a 16-inch needle into the donor's ovary by way of the vagina and drawing out the egg cells, which are then mixed with the father's sperm. In two days, three or four blastocysts are implanted in the mother's uterus. Women who give their oocytes in "donor egg programs" may receive up to $2500, according to guidelines set by the American Fertility Society (Rafferty, 1992a, 1992b).

These procedures are all quite costly (a single attempt typically costs $8000) and must usually be repeated a number of times before a viable pregnancy results. The average cost of an in vitro delivery is $72,000. Varying success rates—from 12% to about 20%—have been reported (Cowan,

1992; Jones, 1989; Yulsman, 1990). The number of IVF births is increasing yearly. In 1990, there were 2345 live deliveries as a result of IVF (American Fertility Society, 1992). This figure does not represent the actual number of babies, as there is a high rate of multiple births (twins or triplets) with IVF.

GIFT and ZIFT   Another fertilization technique, **gamete intrafallopian transfer (GIFT),** may be recommended for couples who have no known reason for their infertility. In this process, sperm and eggs are collected from the parents and deposited together in the fallopian tube. In 1988, 892 live GIFT babies were delivered in the United States, including 159 sets of twins, 34 sets of triplets, 3 sets of quadruplets, and 1 set of quintuplets (Perlman, 1990).

In **zygote intrafallopian transfer (ZIFT),** eggs and sperm are united in a petri dish and then transferred immediately to the fallopian tube to begin cell division. In 1988, there were 98 ZIFT babies, representing a success rate of about 20% (Perlman, 1990). As with IVF, both GIFT and ZIFT carry an increased risk of multiple pregnancy (Bollen et al., 1991).

Direct Sperm Injection   A revolutionary new method of fertilization, developed by a Belgian physician, involves the direct injection of a single sperm into an oocyte in a laboratory dish (Kolata, 1993). As in IVF, the

gamete intrafallopian transfer (GIFT)   A means of achieving pregnancy by collecting oocyte and sperm and depositing them in the fallopian tube.

zygote intrafallopian transfer (ZIFT)   A means of achieving pregnancy in which oocyte and sperm are combined in a laboratory dish and immediately transferred to the fallopian tube.

You and Your Sexual Well-Being

THE ETHICS OF REPRODUCTIVE TECHNOLOGY

The desire to have healthy, happy, beautiful children is understandable, basic, and human. But in the face of today's reproductive technology, many of us may have to search our souls for the answers to a number of ethical questions. When faced with infertility, the possibility of birth defects, or the likelihood of a difficult labor, we need to weigh the possible benefits of a given technique against the costs and risks involved. What are your feelings about the following reproductive issues?

- *Fetal diagnosis.* If you (or your partner) were pregnant, would you choose to have ultrasound? Should ultrasound be used routinely in all pregnancies or only in selected cases, such as when the mother is over 35 or there is a suspected problem? When would you consider amniocentesis appropriate? Should all fetuses be electronically monitored during birth (entailing the attachment of electrodes to the infant's scalp in the uterus), or should this technique be reserved for problem births? Would you want your child to be routinely monitored in this way?

- *Cesarean section.* How would you determine that C-section was necessary for yourself or your partner? Should vaginal delivery be attempted first? What if it was a breech birth? What if you (or your partner) had had a previous C-section?

- *Artificial insemination and in vitro fertilization.* Should these techniques be available to anyone who wants them? Under what circumstances, if any, would you use these techniques? What are the rights of all the parties involved: parents, donors, physicians, child? What are the embryo's or fetus's rights? For example, does a frozen embryo have the "right to life" if its parents die before it is implanted in a surrogate? Can you envision a situation in which you would want to donate ova or sperm? What if your partner wanted to?

- *Surrogate motherhood.* Should a woman be allowed to "carry" a pregnancy for a couple using father-donated sperm? Does it matter if profit is involved? Should a contract involving surrogate motherhood be legally

---

blastocyst is then implanted in the mother. It was previously believed that such a technique would not work because it bypasses both the capacitation of the sperm and the softening of the oocyte's outer layers (which requires the presence of several hundred sperm). However, hundreds of pregnancies have been produced by this method and over 100 babies have been born. Direct sperm injection holds great promise for many men who have low sperm counts or large numbers of abnormal sperm.

Surrogate Motherhood

surrogate motherhood An approach to infertility in which one woman bears a child for another.

The idea of **surrogate motherhood,** in which one woman bears a child for another, is not new. In the Old Testament (Genesis 16:1–15), Abraham's wife Sarah, finding herself unable to conceive, arranged for her husband to impregnate the servant Hagar. These days, the procedures are considerably more complex, and the issues are definitely cloudier. Some people question the motives of surrogate mothers. There have been cases of women having binding? Whose rights should take precedence, those of the surrogate (who is the biological mother) or of the couple (which includes the biological father)? What are the child's rights? Who decides? Can you think of a circumstance when you might wish to have the services of a surrogate mother? Could you be a surrogate or accept your partner's being one?

For all the preceding techniques, consider the following questions: Who is profiting (scientists, physicians, business people, donors, parents, children)? Who is bearing the greatest risks? How great are the costs—monetary and psychological—and who is paying them? What are the long-range goals of this technology? Are we "playing God"? How might this technology be abused? Are there certain techniques you think should be outlawed?

- *Abortion.* When do you think human life begins? Do we ever have the right to take human life? Under what conditions, if any, should abortion be permitted? Whenever the pregnant woman requests it? If there is a serious birth defect? If there is a minor birth defect (such as a shortened limb)? If the fetus is the "wrong" sex? If rape or incest led to the pregnancy? Under what conditions, if any, would you have an abortion or want your partner to have one? If you had an unmarried pregnant teenage daughter, would you encourage her to have one?

- *Tissue donation.* Is it appropriate to use the tissues or organs of human corpses for medical purposes? Is it appropriate to use aborted fetuses for tissue donation? For research?

- *Life and death.* Is prolonging the life of an infant always the most humane choice? What if it also prolongs suffering? Should life be prolonged whenever possible, at all costs? Who decides?

- *Fertility and fulfillment.* Do you think your reproductive values and feelings about your own fertility (or lack of it) are congruent with reality, given the world's population problems? For you, are there viable alternatives to conceiving or bearing a child? What are they? Would adoption be one alternative? Why?

babies for their friends or even for their relatives. In 1991, a South Dakota woman became the first American "surrogate granny" when she was implanted with the fertilized ova of her daughter, who had been born without a uterus (Plummer & Nelson, 1991). Some women simply extend this kind of altruism to women they don't know. A study of 125 surrogate candidates found their major motivations to be money (they are usually paid $10,000–$25,000 or more), enjoying being pregnant, and unreconciled birth traumas, such as abortion or relinquishing a child for adoption (Parker, 1983).

In the United States, there are thought to be several hundred births to surrogate mothers each year (Andrews, 1984; Woodward, 1987). A number of new, privately run agencies have been created to match surrogates and couples, highlighting the commercial potential of surrogate motherhood. Although new technologies to assist human reproduction have brought hope and joy to many couples, they have also raised new ethical issues. The commercial aspect of surrogate motherhood is just one of these difficult issues.

During labor, uterine contractions cause the opening and thinning of the cervix. The length of labor varies from woman to woman and birth to birth; it is usually between 4 and 16 hours. During transition, the end of first-stage labor, contractions are the most intense.

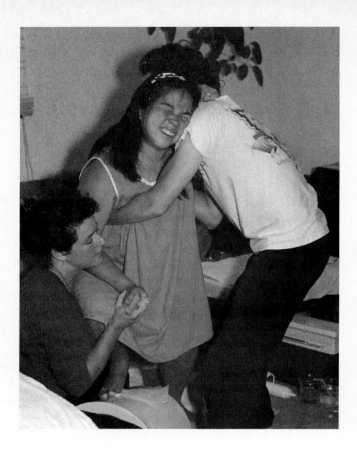

GIVING BIRTH

Throughout pregnancy, numerous physiological changes occur in order to prepare the woman's body for childbirth. Hormones secreted by the placenta regulate the growth of the fetus, stimulate maturation of the breasts for lactation, and ready the uterus and other parts of the body for labor. During the later months of pregnancy, the placenta produces the hormone **relaxin,** which increases flexibility in the ligaments and joints of the pelvic area. In the last trimester, most women occasionally feel uterine contractions that are strong but generally not painful. These are called **Braxton Hicks contractions.** They exercise the uterus, preparing it for labor.

Labor and Delivery

During labor, contractions begin the **effacement** (thinning) and **dilation** (opening up) of the cervix. It is difficult to say exactly when labor starts, which helps explain the great differences reported in lengths of labor for different women. When the uterine contractions become regular, true labor begins. During these contractions, the lengthwise muscles of the uterus involuntarily pull open the circular muscles around the cervix. This process generally takes 2–36 hours. Its duration depends on the size of the baby,

relaxin A hormone produced by the placenta in the later months of pregnancy that increases flexibility in the ligaments and joints of the pelvic area. In men, relaxin is contained in semen, where it assists in sperm motility.

Braxton Hicks contractions Uterine contractions during the last trimester of pregnancy that exercise the uterus, preparing it for labor.

effacement Thinning of the cervix during labor.

dilation Opening up of the cervix during labor.

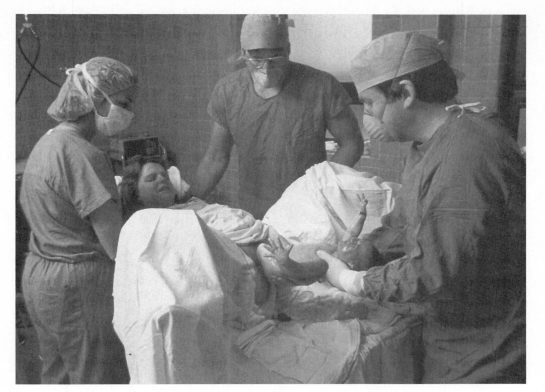

The second stage of labor is the delivery of the infant. In this photograph, the newborn exhibits the "startle reflex" at the unexpected sensations of the world outside the womb.

Mother and baby rest together following delivery. The umbilical cord will be cut and tied off when it stops pulsating.

the baby's position in the uterus, the size of the mother's pelvis, and the condition of the uterus. The length of labor tends to shorten after the first birth experience.

Labor can generally be divided into three stages. The first stage is usually the longest, lasting 4–16 hours. An early sign of first-stage labor is the expulsion of a plug of slightly bloody mucus that has blocked the opening of the cervix during pregnancy. At the same time or later on, there is a second fluid discharge from the vagina. This discharge, referred to as the "breaking of the waters," is the amniotic fluid, which comes from the ruptured amnion. (Because the baby is subject to infection after the protective membrane breaks, the woman should receive medical attention soon thereafter, if she has not already.)

oxytocin A hormone produced by the fetus that stimulates strong uterine contractions.

transition The end of the first stage of labor, when the infant's head enters the birth canal.

The hormone **oxytocin** produced by the fetus, along with prostaglandins from the placenta, stimulates strong uterine contractions. At the end of the first stage of labor, which is called **transition,** the contractions come more quickly and are much more intense than in the early stages of labor. Many women report time as the most difficult part of labor. During the last part of first-stage labor, the baby's head enters the birth canal. This marks the shift from dilation of the cervix to expulsion of the infant. The cervical opening is now almost fully dilated (about 10 cm [4 in.] in diameter), but the baby is not yet completely in position to be pushed out. Some women feel despair, isolation, and anger at this point. Many appear to lose faith in those assisting in the birth. A woman may find that management of the contractions seems beyond her control; she may be afraid that something is wrong. At this time, she needs the full support and understanding of her helpers. Transition is usually, though not always, brief (half an hour to one hour).

Second-stage labor begins when the baby's head moves into the birth canal and ends when the baby is born. During this time, many women experience a great force in their bodies. Some women find this the most difficult part of labor. Others find that the contractions and bearing down bring a sense of euphoria.

The baby is usually born gradually. With each of the final few contractions, a new part of the infant emerges (Figure 12.6). The baby may even cry before he or she is completely born, especially if the mother did not have medication.

vernix The milky substance that sometimes covers an infant at birth.

The baby will still be attached to the umbilical cord connected to the mother, which is not cut until it stops pulsating. He or she will appear wet, often covered by a milky substance called **vernix.** The head may look oddly shaped at first, from the molding of the soft plates of bone during birth. This shape is temporary, and the baby's head usually achieves a normal appearance within 24 hours.

neonate A newborn.

Apgar score The cumulative rating of the newborn's heart rate, respiration, color, reflexes, and muscle tone.

After the baby has been delivered, the uterus will continue to contract, expelling the placenta, also called the afterbirth, and completing the third and final stage of labor. The doctor or midwife will examine the placenta to make sure it is whole. If the practitioner has any doubt that the entire placenta has been expelled, he or she may examine the uterus to make sure no parts of the placenta remain to cause adhesions or hemorrhage. Immediately following birth, the attendants assess the physical condition of the **neonate,** or newborn. Heart rate, respiration, color, reflexes, and muscle tone are individually rated with a score of 0 to 2. The total, called an **Apgar**

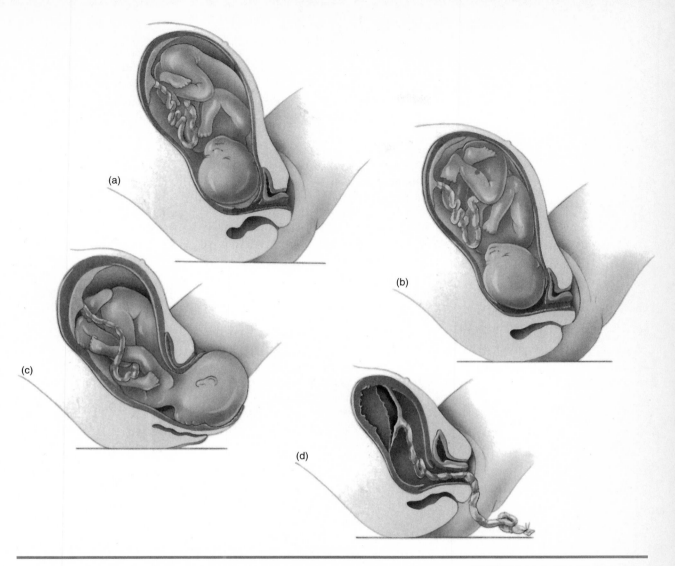

FIGURE 12.6 The Birth Process: Labor and Delivery. (a) First stage: cervix beginning to dilate. (b) Transition: cervix dilated. (c) Second stage: delivery of the infant. (d) Third stage: delivery of the placenta.

score, will be at least 8 if the child is healthy. For a few days following labor (especially if it is a second or subsequent birth), the mother will probably feel strong contractions as the uterus begins to return to its prebirth size and shape. This process takes about 6 weeks. She will also have a bloody discharge called **lochia,** which continues for several weeks.

Following birth, if the baby has not been drugged by anesthetics administered to the mother, he or she will probably be alert and ready to nurse. Breast-feeding (discussed later) provides benefits for both mother and child. If the infant is a boy, the parents will need to decide about circumcision, the surgical removal of the foreskin of the penis (also discussed later).

lochia A bloody vaginal discharge following childbirth.

Choices in Childbirth

Women and couples planning the birth of a child have decisions to make in a variety of areas: place of birth, birth attendant(s), medications, preparedness classes, circumcision, breast-feeding—to name just a few. The "childbirth market" is beginning to respond to consumer concerns, so it's important for prospective consumers to fully understand their options.

Hospital Birth   Because of impersonal, routine care at some facilities, some hospitals are responding to the need for a family-centered childbirth. Fathers and other relatives or close friends often participate today. Some hospitals permit rooming-in, in which the baby stays with the mother rather than in the nursery, or a modified form of rooming-in. Regulations vary as to when the father and other family members and friends are allowed to visit.

Some form of anesthetic is administered during most hospital deliveries, as well as various hormones (to intensify the contractions and to shrink the uterus after delivery). The mother isn't the only recipient of the drugs, however; they go directly through the placenta to the baby, in whom they may reduce heart and respiration rates.

During delivery, the mother will probably be given an **episiotomy,** a cut that enlarges the vaginal opening by cutting through the perineum toward the anus. Although an episiotomy may be helpful if the infant is in distress, it is usually performed routinely in order to prevent possible tearing of the perineum. Recent studies show that episiotomies are performed in about 80% of first vaginal births in hospitals (Hetherington, 1990; Klein et al., 1992); yet one midwife who has assisted at over 1200 births reports a rate of less than 1% (Armstrong & Feldman, 1990). A Canadian study of 703 uncomplicated births found no advantage to routine episiotomies; the disadvantages were pain and bleeding (Klein et al., 1992). The authors recommended that "liberal or routine use of episiotomy be abandoned."

The baby is usually delivered on a table. If such factors as medication or exhaustion slows labor, he or she may be pulled from the womb with a vacuum extractor (which has a small suction cup that fits onto the baby's head) or forceps. (In some cases of acute fetal distress, these instruments may be crucial in order to save the infant's life, but they are sometimes used by physicians as a substitute for patience and skill.)

Cesarean Section   **Cesarean section,** or **C-section,** is the removal of the fetus by an incision in the mother's abdominal and uterine walls. In 1970, 5.5% of American births were done by cesarean section. Today, cesarean births account for about 24% of all births; more than 900,000 women have C-sections each year (U.S. Bureau of the Census, 1990). This represents more than a 400% increase in 20 years.

Although there is a decreased mortality rate for infants born by C-section, the mothers' mortality rate is higher. As with all major surgeries, there are possible complications, and recovery can be slow and difficult.

Hoping to reduce the number of C-sections, the National Institutes of Health (NIH) have issued the following guidelines:

1.   Because a woman has had a previous cesarean delivery does not mean

---

episiotomy   A surgical procedure during childbirth that enlarges the vaginal opening by cutting through the perineum toward the anus.

cesarean section (C-section)   Removal of the fetus by an incision in the mother's abdominal and uterine walls.

MAKING A BIRTH PLAN

Prospective parents must make many important decisions. The more informed they are, however, the better able they will be to decide what is right for them. If you were planning a birth, how would you answer the following questions?

- Who will be the birth attendant—a physician, a nurse-midwife? Do you already have someone in mind? If not, what criteria are important to you in choosing a birth attendant? Have you considered hiring a labor assistant, or *doula*, a professional childbirth companion employed to guide the mother during labor?

- Who will be present at the birth—the husband or partner? Other relatives or friends? Children? How will these people participate? Will they provide emotional support and encouragement? Will they provide practical help, such as "coaching" the mother, giving massages, fetching supplies, taking photographs or videos? Can these people be sensitive to the needs of the mother?

- Where will the birth take place—in a hospital, a birth center, at home? If in a hospital, is there a choice of rooms?

- What kind of environment will you create in terms of lighting, room furnishings, and sounds? Is there special music you would like to hear?

- What kinds of medication, if any, do you feel comfortable with? Do you know what the options are for pain-reducing medications? What about hormones to speed up or slow down labor? How do you feel about having an IV inserted as a precaution, even if medication is not planned? If you should change your mind about medication part of the way through labor, how will you communicate this to your attendants?

- What about fetal monitoring? Will there be machines attached to you or the baby? What types and degree of monitoring do you feel comfortable with?

- What is your attendant's policy regarding food and drink during labor? What kinds of foods or drinks, such as ice cream, fruit, juices, or ice chips, do you think you (or your partner) might want to have?

- What about freedom of movement during labor? Will you (or your partner) want the option of walking around during labor? Will there be a shower or bath available? Will the baby be delivered with the mother lying on her back with her feet in stirrups, or will she be free to choose her position, such as squatting or lying on her side?

- Do you want a routine episiotomy? Under what conditions would it be acceptable?

- What do you wish the role of instruments or other interventions, such as forceps or vacuum extraction, to be? Who will determine if and when they are necessary?

- Under what conditions is a cesarean section acceptable? Who will decide?

- Who will "catch" the baby as she or he is born? Who is going to cut the umbilical cord, and at what point will it be cut?

- What will be done with the baby immediately after birth? Will he or she be with the mother or the father? Who will bathe and dress the baby? What kinds of tests will be done on the baby, and when? What other kinds of procedures, such as shots and medicated eye drops, will be given, and when?

- Will the baby stay in the nursery, or is there rooming-in? Is there a visiting schedule?

- How will the baby be fed—by breast or bottle? Will feeding be on a schedule or "on demand"? Is there someone with breast-feeding experience available to answer questions if necessary? Will the baby have a pacifier between feedings?

- If the baby is a boy, will he be circumcised? When?

that subsequent deliveries must be C-sections; whenever possible, women should be given the option of a vaginal birth.

2. Abnormal labor does not mean that a C-section is necessary. Sleep or medication may resolve the problems. Only after other measures have been tried should a physician perform a cesarean, unless the infant is clearly in danger.

3. Breech babies—those who enter the birth canal buttocks-first or feet-first—do not necessarily require C-sections. A physician's experience using his or her hands to deliver the baby vaginally is crucial.

If a woman does not want a C-section unless it is absolutely necessary, she should learn about her physician's attitude about and record on performing cesareans. It is noteworthy that the greatest number of cesareans are performed in the socioeconomic group of women with the lowest medical risk (Hurst & Summey, 1984). In a study of 245,854 births, the C-section rate for middle- and upper-income women was 22.9%, whereas for lower-income women it was 3.2% (Gould, Davey, & Stafford, 1989). Therefore, it is assumed that cesareans are often performed for reasons other than medical risk. Some of the reasons offered include threat of malpractice (although such suits are apparently rare for vaginal deliveries), lack of physician training in vaginal births, and "economic incentives" for the hospital and the physician (Cohen & Estner, 1983).

Prepared Childbirth Increasingly, Americans are choosing among such childbirth alternatives as prepared childbirth, rooming-in, birthing centers, home births, and midwives.

Prepared childbirth (or natural childbirth) was popularized by Grantly Dick-Read (1972), who observed that fear causes muscles to tense, which in turn increases pain and stress during childbirth. He taught both partners about childbirth and gave them physical exercises to ease muscle tension. Encouraged by Dick-Read's ideas, women began to reject anesthetics during labor and delivery, and were consequently able to take a more active role in childbirth, as well as be more aware of the whole process.

In the 1950s, Fernand Lamaze (1956, 1970) developed a method of prepared childbirth based on knowledge of conditioned reflexes. Women learn to mentally separate the physical stimulus of uterine contractions from the conditioned response of pain. With the help of a partner, women use breathing and other exercises throughout labor and delivery. Although Lamaze did much to advance the cause of prepared childbirth, he has been criticized by other childbirth educators as too controlling or even "repressive," according to Armstrong and Feldman (1990). A woman does not give birth, they write, "by direction, as if it were a flight plan."

Prepared childbirth, then, is not so much a matter of controlling the birth process as of understanding it and having confidence in nature's plan. Clinical studies consistently show better birth outcomes for mothers who have had prepared childbirth classes (Conway, 1980). Prepared mothers (who usually attend classes with the father or other partner) handle pain more successfully, use less medication and anesthesia, express greater satisfaction with the childbirth process, and experience less postpartum depression than women undergoing routine hospital births (Hetherington, 1990).

prepared childbirth An approach to childbirth that encourages the mother's understanding of the process and teaches exercises to reduce tension; also known as natural childbirth.

Childbirth classes enable both partners to understand and share the birth process.

Birthing Rooms and Centers Birth (or maternity) centers, institutions of long standing in England and other European countries (see Odent, 1984), now are being developed in the United States. Although they vary in size, organization, and orientation, birth centers share the view that childbirth is a normal, healthy process that can be assisted by skilled practitioners (midwives or physicians) in a homelike setting. The mother (or couple) has considerable autonomy in deciding the conditions of birth: lighting, sounds, visitors, delivery position, and so on. Some of these centers can provide some kinds of emergency care; all have procedures for transfer to a hospital if necessary.

An extensive survey of 11,814 births in birth centers in 1988 concluded that "birth centers offer a safe and acceptable alternative to hospital confinement for selected pregnant women, particularly those who have previously had children, and that such care leads to relatively few cesarean sections" (Rooks, Weatherby, Ernst, Stapleton, Rosen, & Rosenfield, 1989).

Home Birth Home births have increased during the last two decades, although they still constitute a small fraction of total births, amounting to not quite 2%, according to available data. Careful medical screening and planning that eliminate all but the lowest-risk pregnancies can make this a viable alternative for some couples. A couple can create their own birth environment at home, and home births cost considerably less, usually at least one-third less, than hospital delivery. With the supervision of an experienced practitioner, parents have little to worry about. But if a woman is at risk, she is wiser to give birth in a hospital where medical equipment is readily available.

THE QUESTION OF CIRCUMCISION

In 1975, when about 93% of newborn boys were circumcised, the American Academy of Pediatrics and the American College of Obstetricians and Gynecologists issued a statement declaring that there is "no absolute medical indication" for routine **circumcision.** This procedure, which involves slicing and removing the sleeve of skin (foreskin) that covers the glans penis, has been performed routinely on newborn boys in the United States since the 1930s (Romberg, 1985). Although it is obviously painful, circumcision is often done without anesthesia. Parents should discuss with their pediatrician the use of an anesthetic cream or medication. Circumcision carries medical risks in 4–28% of the cases (Samuels & Samuels, 1986). The principal risks are excessive bleeding, infection, and faulty surgery.

In 1989, the American Academy of Pediatrics modified its stance on circumcision, stating that "newborn circumcision has potential medical benefits and advantages as well as disadvantages and risks." They recommended that "the benefits and risks should be explained to the parents and informed consent obtained." This change was at least partially in response to several studies that indicate a possible connection between lack of circumcision and urinary tract infections, penile cancer, and sexually transmitted diseases (Wiswell, 1990). Studies also indicate that more extensive research is necessary before conclusions can be drawn (Maden et al., 1993). Factors such as hygiene and number of sexual partners must also be taken into consideration. Education can go a

long way in preventing both of these problems by teaching boys to clean under their foreskin and, if they become sexually active, to use a condom.

Almost 60% of newborn boys were circumcised in 1985, according to the National Center for Health Statistics. Although this represents a substantial drop from 93% in 1975, it still places the United States far ahead of other Western countries, which circumcise less than 1% of their newborn boys. The exception is Israel. In Judaism, the ritual circumcision, the *bris*, is an important religious event. Circumcision has religious significance for Muslims as well (Bullough, 1976).

Aside from religious reasons, the other reasons given by parents for circumcising their infants are "cleanliness" and "so he'll look like his dad." A circumcised penis is not necessarily any cleaner than an uncircumcised one. Infants do not require cleaning under their foreskins (Brody, 1985); adults do. If reasonable cleanliness is observed, an intact penis poses no more threat of disease to a man's sexual partner than a circumcised one would. As for "looking like dad," there is no evidence to suggest that little boys are seriously traumatized if dad's penis doesn't look exactly like theirs.

A recent analysis of the potential financial costs and health benefits of circumcision concluded that "there is no medical indication for or against circumcision" and that decisions "may be most reasonably made on [the basis of] nonmedical factors such as parent preference or religious convictions" (Lawler, Bisonni, & Holtgrave, 1991).

circumcision The surgical removal of the foreskin that covers the glans penis.

Midwifery The United States has an increasing number of certified nurse-midwives who are registered nurses trained in obstetrical techniques. They are well qualified for routine deliveries and minor medical emergencies. They also often operate as part of a total medical team that includes a backup physician, if needed. Their fees are generally considerably less than a doctor's. Nurse-midwives usually participate in both hospital and home births, although this may vary according to hospital policy, state law, and the midwife's preference.

If a woman decides she wants to give birth with the aid of a midwife outside a hospital setting, she should have a thorough medical screening to make sure she or her infant will not be at risk during delivery. She should learn about the midwife's training and experience, what type of backup services the midwife has in the event of complications or emergencies, and how the midwife will handle a transfer to a hospital if necessary.

Breast-Feeding

About three days after childbirth, **lactation**—the production of milk—begins. Before lactation, sometimes as early as the second trimester, a yellowish liquid called **colostrum** is secreted by the nipples. It is what nourishes the newborn infant before the mother's milk comes in. Colostrum is high in protein and contains antibodies that help protect a baby from infectious diseases. Hormonal changes during labor begin the changeover from colostrum to milk, but unless a mother nurses her child, her breasts will

lactation The production of milk in the breasts (mammary glands).

colostrum A yellowish substance containing nutrients and antibodies that is secreted by the breast 2 or 3 days prior to actual milk production.

BREAST VERSUS BOTTLE: WHICH IS BEST FOR YOU AND YOUR CHILD?

If you are a woman who plans to have children, you will have to decide whether to breast- or bottle-feed your child. Perhaps you already have an idea that breast-feeding is healthier for the baby but are not sure why.

The following list of benefits and advantages should help you understand why breast-feeding is recommended (assuming that the mother is healthy and has a good diet).

Physical Benefits of Breast-Feeding

- Breast milk contains antibodies that protect the baby from infectious diseases for at least six months.
- It forms softer curds in the infant's stomach, making digestion and elimination easier.
- It puts less stress on the infant's immature liver and kidneys because its total protein is lower than that of mammalian milk.
- It is high in cholesterol, which is needed for proper development of the nervous tissue.
- It causes fewer allergic reactions because of its concentration and type of protein.
- It is a better source of nutrition for low birth weight babies because "nature adapts mother's milk to meet infant's needs" (Johnson & Goldfinger, 1981).
- Babies who have been breast-fed have fewer problems with tooth decay.
- Breast-feeding is thought to encourage the development of the dental arch, preventing the need for orthodontia later on.
- For mothers, hormonal changes stimulated by breast-feeding cause the uterus to contract and return to its normal size.

soon stop producing milk. If she chooses not to breast-feed, she is usually given an injection of estrogen soon after delivery to stop lactation. It is not certain, however, whether estrogen is actually effective; furthermore, it may cause an increased risk of blood clotting.

BECOMING A PARENT

Men and women who become parents enter a new phase of their lives. Even more than marriage, parenthood signifies adulthood—the final, irreversible end of youthful roles. A person can become an ex-spouse but never an ex-parent. The irrevocable nature of parenthood may make the first-time parent doubtful and apprehensive, especially during the pregnancy. Yet, for the most part, parenthood has to be learned experientially, although ideas can modify practices. A person may receive assistance from more experienced parents, but, ultimately, each new parent has to learn on his or her own.

Many of the stresses felt by new parents closely reflect gender roles (Cowan & Cowan, 1988; Scott & Alwin, 1989). Overall, mothers seem to

Psychological Benefits of Breast-Feeding

- The close physical contact of breast-feeding provides a sense of emotional well-being for mother and baby.
- Sustaining the life of another through her milk may affirm a woman's sense of self and ability to give.
- It is natural and pleasurable.

Health and Logistical Advantages of Breast-Feeding

- It requires no buying, mixing, or preparation of formulas.
- It is not subject to incorrect mixing or spoilage.
- Breast milk is clean, not easily contaminated.
- Breast-feeding provides some protection against pregnancy (if the woman is breast-feeding exclusively).
- It is always available and can be adapted to the infant's needs.

Because there are almost no disadvantages to breast-feeding, it is impossible to compile a list to match the advantages. For those women whose work schedules, health problems, or other demands prohibit them from breast-feeding, holding and cuddling the baby while bottle feeding can contribute to the sense of emotional well-being that comes from a close parent-baby relationship. Bottle-feeding affords a greater opportunity for fathers to become involved in the feeding of the baby. Working women and mothers whose lifestyles or choices do not include breast-feeding often find bottles more convenient.

Regardless of the choices that parents make regarding their infants' feeding, it may well be the care and love with which it is done that are most important to the growth and development of a healthy child.

experience greater stress than fathers (Harriman, 1983). When we speak of "mothering" a child, everyone knows what we mean: nurturing, caring for, diapering, soothing, loving. Mothers generally "mother" their children almost every day of the year for at least 18 consecutive years. The meaning of "fathering" is quite different. Nurturant behavior by a father toward his child has not typically been referred to as "fathering." Because the lines between roles are becoming increasingly blurred as fathers take a more active role in the raising of their children, the verb "to parent" has been used to describe the child-tending behaviors of both mothers and fathers (Verzaro-Lawrence, 1981).

The time immediately following birth is a critical period for family adjustment. No amount of reading, classes, and expert advice can prepare expectant parents for the real thing. The 3 months or so following childbirth (the "fourth trimester") constitute the **postpartum period.** This time is one of physical stabilization and emotional adjustment. The abrupt transition from being a nonparent to being a parent may create considerable stress. Parents take on parental roles literally overnight, and the job goes on without relief around the clock. Many parents express concern about

postpartum period The period (about 3 months) following childbirth, characterized by physical stabilization and emotional adjustment.

Think About It

GAY AND LESBIAN PARENTS

There may be as many as 1.5 million lesbian mothers rearing their children in the United States (Hoeffer, 1981). The number of gay fathers is estimated at 1–3 million (Bozett, 1987b). Most of these parents are or have been married; consequently, many children of lesbians and gay men begin their lives in "traditional" families, even though separation or divorce may occur later on. Adoption, insemination, surrogacy, and foster parenting are also options being used increasingly by both singles and couples who are lesbian or gay (Goldman, 1992; Ricketts & Achtenberg, 1989). Because of the nontraditional nature of these families, it is difficult to determine the number of gays and lesbians who choose these alternatives.

Studies of gay fathers indicate that "being gay is compatible with effective parenting" (Bozett, 1987c; Goldman, 1992; Harris & Turner, 1985). Furthermore, it appears that gays who disclose their orientation to their children and who have a stable gay relationship tend to provide better-quality parenting than those who remain married and keep their sexual orientation hidden (Barret & Robinson, 1990).

Heterosexual fears about gays and lesbians as parents center around concerns about parenting abilities, fears of sexual abuse, and worries that the children will "catch" the homosexual orientation. All of these fears are unwarranted. A review of the literature on children of gay men and lesbians found virtually no documented cases of sexual abuse by gay parents or their lovers; such exploitation appears to be disproportionately committed by heterosexuals (Barret & Robinson, 1990; Cramer, 1986).

Fears that gay and lesbian parents may reject children of the other sex also appear unfounded. Such fears reflect two common misconceptions: that being gay or lesbian is a rejection of members of the other sex, and that people are able to choose their sexual orientation. A review of about three dozen studies of children of lesbians and gays found the parents' orientation to have no impact on the children's sexual orientation or their feelings about their gender (Patterson, 1992). According to Dr. Michael Lamb, chief of the Section on Social and Emotional Development at the National Institute of Child Health and Human Development, "What evidence there is suggests there are no particular developmental or emotional deficits for children raised by gay or lesbian parents. . . . These kids look OK" (quoted in Goldman, 1992).

Despite the abundance of research and millions of case scenarios to support the above conclusion, gays and lesbians still fight for the legal rights and protections they deserve. Because they cannot legally marry and because of pervasive anti-gay prejudices, such issues as custody, visitation, and adoption remain legal dilemmas or obstacles for many contemplating or trying to become parents.

A number of services and programs have been established to assist prospective gay and lesbian parents in sorting through the myriad questions and issues they face. In the end, it is the welfare of the child that society aims to support. This can best be achieved with loving, caring, responsible parents, regardless of sexual orientation.

their ability to meet all the responsibilities of child rearing (Klinman & Vukelich, 1985).

New mothers, who may well have lost most of their interest in sexual activity during the last weeks of pregnancy, will probably find themselves returning to prepregnancy levels of desire and coital frequency. Some women, however, may have difficulty reestablishing their sexual lives

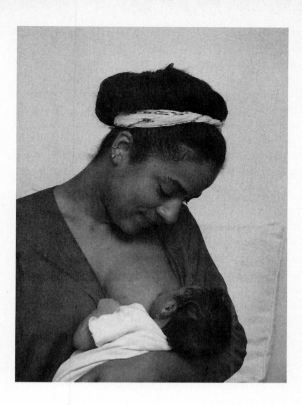

Breast-feeding provides the best nutrition for infants. It also helps protect against many infectious diseases and gives both mother and child a sense of well-being.

because of fatigue, physiological problems such as continued vaginal bleeding, and worries about the infant (Reamy & White, 1987).

The postpartum period also may be a time of significant emotional upheaval. Even women who had easy and uneventful deliveries may experience a period of "postpartum blues," characterized by alternating periods of crying, unpredictable mood changes, fatigue, irritability, and occasionally mild confusion or lapses of memory. A woman has irregular sleep patterns because of the needs of her newborn, the discomfort of childbirth, or the strangeness of the hospital environment. Some mothers may feel lonely, isolated from their familiar world.

Biological, psychological, and social factors are all involved in postpartum depression. Biologically, during the first several days following delivery, there is an abrupt fall in certain hormone levels. The physiological stress accompanying labor, as well as dehydration, blood loss, and other physical factors, contribute to lowering the woman's stamina. Psychologically, conflicts about her ability to mother and communication problems with the infant or partner may contribute to the new mother's feelings of depression and helplessness. Finally, the social setting into which the child is born is important, especially if the infant represents a financial or emotional burden for the family. Postpartum counseling prior to discharge from the hospital can help couples gain perspective on their situation so that they know what to expect and can evaluate their resources (Reamy & White, 1987).

Although the postpartum blues are felt by many women, they usually don't last more than a couple of weeks. Interestingly, men seem to get a form of postpartum blues as well. Dr. Martha Zaslow and colleagues (1981) at the National Institute of Child Health observed, "It looks increasingly as if a number of the things we assumed about mothers and motherhood are really typical of parenthood."

For many, the arrival of a child is one of life's most important events. It fills parents with a deep sense of accomplishment. The experience itself is profound and totally involving. A father describes his wife (Kate) giving birth to their daughter (Colleen) (Armstrong and Feldman, 1990):

> Toward the end, Kate had her arms around my neck. I was soothing her, stroking her, and holding her. I felt so close. I even whispered to her that I wanted to make love to her—It wasn't that I would have or meant to—it's just that I felt that bound up with her. Colleen was born while Kate was hanging from my neck. . . . I looked down and saw Mimi's [the midwife's] hands appearing and then, it seemed like all at once, the baby was in them. I had tears streaming down my face. I was laughing and crying at the same time. . . . Mimi handed her to me with all the goop on her and I never even thought about it. She was so pink. She opened her eyes for the first time in her life right there in my arms. I thought she was the most beautiful thing I had ever seen. There was something about that, holding her just the way she was. . . . I never felt anything like that in my life.

SUMMARY

Fertilization and Fetal Development

• Fertilization of the oocyte by a sperm usually takes place in the fallopian tube. The chromosomes of the ovum combine with those of the sperm to form the diploid zygote; it divides many times to form a blastocyst, which implants itself in the uterine wall.

• The blastocyst becomes an embryo, then a fetus, which is nourished through the placenta, via the umbilical cord.

Being Pregnant

• The first reliable pregnancy test can be made two to four weeks after a woman misses her menstrual period by the agglutination test. Hegar's sign can be detected by a trained examiner. Pregnancy is confirmed by the detection of the fetal heartbeat and movements, or examination by ultrasound.

• A woman's feelings vary greatly during pregnancy. It is important for her to share her fears and to have support from her partner, friends, relatives, and health-care workers. Her feelings about sexuality are likely to change during pregnancy. Men may also have conflicting feelings. Sexual activity is generally safe unless there is pain, bleeding, or history of miscarriage.

• Harmful substances may be passed to the embryo or fetus through the placenta. Substances that cause birth defects are called teratogens; these include alcohol, tobacco, certain drugs, and environmental pollutants. Infectious diseases, such as rubella, may damage the fetus. Sexually transmitted diseases may be passed to the infant through the placenta or the birth canal during childbirth.

• Ectopic pregnancy, toxemia, preeclampsia, and low birth weight (prematurity) are the most common complications of pregnancy.

- Abnormalities of the fetus may be diagnosed using ultrasound, amniocentesis, chorionic villus sampling (CVS), or alpha-feto protein (AFP) screening.

- Some pregnancies end in spontaneous abortion (miscarriage); about 1 in 4 women is aware she has miscarried at least once. Infant mortality rates in the U.S. are extremely high compared to those in other industrialized nations. Loss of pregnancy or death of a young infant is recognized as a serious life event.

Infertility

- Infertility is the inability to conceive a child after trying for a year or more. The primary causes of female infertility are blocked fallopian tubes (often the result of pelvic inflammatory disease), endometriosis, and hormonal abnormalities. The primary causes of male infertility are low sperm count, blocked passageways, and lack of sperm motility. Couples with fertility problems often feel they have lost control over an important area of their lives.

- Techniques for combating infertility include hormonal treatments, intrauterine insemination, in vitro fertilization, GIFT, ZIFT, and direct sperm injection. Surrogate motherhood is also an option for childless couples, but it raises many legal and ethical issues.

Giving Birth

- Throughout pregnancy, a woman feels Braxton Hicks contractions. These contractions also begin the effacement and dilation of the cervix to permit delivery.

- Labor can be divided into three stages. First-stage labor begins when uterine contractions become regular. When the cervix has dilated approximately 10 cm, the baby's head enters the birth canal; this is called transition. In second-stage labor, the baby emerges from the birth canal. In third-stage labor, the placenta (afterbirth) is expelled.

- Cesarean section is the removal of the fetus by an incision through the mother's abdomen into her uterus. A dramatic increase in C-sections in recent years has led to criticism that the procedure is used more often than necessary.

- Prepared childbirth encompasses a variety of methods that stress the importance of understanding the birth process and of relaxation and emotional support of the mother during childbirth.

- Birth centers and birthing rooms in hospitals are providing attractive alternatives to hospital birth settings for normal births. Instead of standard medical care, many women are now choosing midwives.

- Circumcision has been performed routinely in this country for many years. Debate in the medical community still exists regarding its usefulness. Circumcision holds religious meaning for Jews and Muslims.

- A little over 50% of American women breast-feed their babies today. Mother's milk is more nutritious than formula or cow's milk and provides immunity to many diseases. Nursing offers emotional rewards to mother and infant.

Becoming a Parent

- Because the roles involving "mothering" and "fathering" are becoming blurred, the term "to parent" has been used to describe child-tending behaviors.

- A critical adjustment period follows the birth of a child. The mother may experience feelings of depression (sometimes called "postpartum blues") that are a result of biological, psychological, and social factors.

- Lesbian and gay parents often face additional challenges because society tends to view them with suspicion. Gay and lesbian parenting, however, appears to differ very little from heterosexual parenting.

SUGGESTED READINGS

For the most current research findings in obstetrics, see Obstetrics and Gynecology, The New England Journal of Medicine, *and* Journal of the American Medical Association (JAMA).

Dorris, Michael. *The Broken Cord.* New York: Harper & Row, 1990. A moving account of the author's experience with his adopted son, who was affected by fetal alcohol syndrome.

Dunham, Carrell (The Body Shop Staff). *Mamatoto: A Celebration of Birth.* New York: Viking Penguin, 1992. Childbirth in many cultures, joyously explored through words and pictures.

Eisenberg, Arlene, Sandy Hathaway, and Heidi E. Merkoff. *What to Expect While You're Expecting,* rev. ed. New York: Workman Publishing, 1991. A thorough and thoroughly readable "encyclopedia" for expectant and new parents.

Menning, Barbara Eck. *Infertility: A Guide for the Childless Couple*, 2nd ed. New York: Prentice-Hall Press, 1988. Useful information for couples facing infertility.

Nilsson, Lennart, and Lars Hamberger. *A Child Is Born*. New York: Delacourt/Seymour Lawrence, 1990. The story of birth, beginning with fertilization, told in stunning photographs with text.

Chapter Thirteen

THE SEXUAL BODY IN HEALTH AND ILLNESS

PREVIEW: SELF-QUIZ

1. People with eating disorders often have histories of abuse, including sexual abuse. True or false?

2. Sexual enjoyment tends to decline as people age because of physiological changes. True or false?

3. About half of all men over 50 experience some enlargement of the prostate gland. True or false?

4. A woman can eliminate the "hot flashes" that often accompany menopause by taking estrogen. True or false?

5. People with spinal cord injuries generally cannot have sexual relations. True or false?

6. Breast cancer affects about 1 out of 9 American women by age 85. True or false?

7. Most women over 30 should have an annual mammogram (breast X ray) to screen for cancer. True or false?

8. Cervical cancer is the most common reproductive cancer among women. True or false?

9. Hysterectomy (removal of the uterus) is not performed unless it is an absolute medical necessity. True or false?

10. Prostate cancer is the most common cancer among men. True or false?

ANSWERS 1. T, 2. F, 3. T, 4. F, 5. F, 6. T, 7. F, 8. F, 9. F, 10. T

Chapter Outline

Health is more than the absence of disease, and sexual health is more than healthy sex organs. According to the World Health Organization (1992), "sexual health is the integration of the physical, emotional, intellectual, and social aspects of sexual being, in ways that are positively enriching and that enhance personality, communication, and love."

Sexual health has to do with how we function biologically, but it is also a function of our behavior and our awareness and acceptance of our bodies. In terms of sexuality, health requires us to know and understand our bodies, to feel comfortable with them. It requires women and men to feel at ease with the sight, feeling, and smell of their genitals, to accept their bodies, and acknowledge changes and problems. It asks each gender to abandon stereotyped behaviors and attitudes and encourages each individual to express his or her uniqueness.

In this chapter, we look at our attitudes and feelings about our bodies in addition to looking at specific health issues. We begin with a discussion of body image and eating disorders. We next discuss aging and its effects on the sexual lives of both women and men. Then we turn to issues of sexuality and disability. We discuss the physical and emotional effects of specific diseases such as arthritis, diabetes, heart disease, and cancer as they influence our sexual functioning. Other issues specific to women or men are then addressed. Finally, we look at the effects of alcohol and other drugs on our sexuality.

As we grow emotionally as well as physically, we may also develop new perceptions of what it means to be healthy. We may discover new dimensions in ourselves to lead us to a more fulfilled and healthier sexuality.

LIVING IN OUR BODIES: THE QUEST FOR PHYSICAL PERFECTION

Our general health affects our sexual functioning. Fatigue, stress, and minor ailments all affect our sexual interactions. If we ignore these aspects of our health, we are likely to experience a decline in our sexual drive, as well as suffer physical and psychological distress. A person who always feels tired or is constantly ill or debilitated is likely to feel less sexual than a healthy person. Health and sexuality are gifts we must take care of.

Eating Disorders

Our culture worships physical perfection and religiously pursues it (Wolf, 1991). Our deities are slim, sexy, perfectly muscled actors, actresses, models, and athletes. Their images are everywhere: on billboards, magazine covers, movie screens. We spend hours every week in front of our televisions, mesmerized by their glory. As for scripture, we have volumes upon volumes of holy words: sermons and testimonies on the subjects of fitness, exercise, weight loss, diet, nutrition, health, and beauty.

Many of us are willing to pay high costs—physically, emotionally, and financially—in order to meet the expectations of our culture and to feel worthy, lovable, and sexually attractive. Although having these desires is clearly a normal human characteristic, the means by which we try to fulfill them can be extreme and even self-destructive. Many American women and some men try to control their weight by dieting at some time in their lives, but some people's fear and loathing of fat (often combined with fear or disgust regarding sexual functions) impels them to extreme forms of eating behavior. Compulsive overeating (also called binge eating) and compulsive

PREVENTION AND TREATMENT OF EATING DISORDERS

Parents, teachers, counselors, and even friends can help prevent eating disorders in young people. The first task in prevention may be the most difficult because it involves combating the contradicting major cultural images and expectations having to do with weight. The basic message should be: Thinness is not an appropriate measure of the value of a human being. Goodness, desirability, and success do not increase in inverse proportion to one's waistline.

In addition, it is important to recognize the role of low self-esteem in the development of eating disorders. People who feel they are worthy of love and respect are not likely to develop self-destructive behaviors. The causes of low self-esteem and rejection of the body may be rooted in childhood psychological or sexual abuse (Beckman & Burns, 1990; Young, 1992; Zerbe, 1992). These issues need to be dealt with in supportive therapeutic situations before healing can begin.

Dieting should not be undertaken unless one understands the motivations behind it. Feelings of inadequacy need to be dealt with in some type of therapy (counseling, or a self-help group). Once undertaken, a diet should be supervised by a qualified medical practitioner.

As discussed in Chapter 9, studies show that most of us think attractive (which includes slim) people are more healthy, lovable, sexual, poised, and generally "better" than unattractive (which includes fat) people (Dion, Berscheid, & Walster, 1972; Hatfield & Sprecher, 1986). Before we can be of assistance to someone with an eating disorder, we need to look at ourselves to see what kind of messages we are sending (consciously or unconsciously) about our own emotional responses to fat.

Treatment strategies for eating disorders take a variety of forms. Behaviorist approaches may utilize group therapy, drug therapy, reality imaging, or hypnotherapy. Sex therapy, including the woman's partner if she has one, may be recommended. Humanistic and existential approaches focus on each anorexic's unique experience (Dittmar & Bates, 1987). As is true with many other kinds of psychiatric disorders, the role of family dynamics is significant in the development and treatment of eating disorders.

Although early intervention with psychotherapy can sometimes forestall hospitalization, many girls and women with anorexia do need to be hospitalized, especially if their body functioning has reached starvation levels.

---

overdieting (purging)—and combinations thereof—are the behaviors classified as eating disorders. The eating disorders we will discuss are known as anorexia nervosa, bulimia, and binge eating disorder. As many as 7 million American women may suffer from these disorders (Shute, 1992).

Michael P. Levine (1987; 1993) defines **eating disorders** as eating and weight management practices that have the following characteristics:

eating disorder Eating and weight-management practices that endanger a person's physical and emotional health.

1. They reduce a person's health and vigor and threaten his or her life.

2. They are carried out in secrecy, reducing the person's ability to fulfill obligations to self and others.

3. The person suffers from obsessions, anxiety, irritability, depression, and guilt.

4. The person becomes increasingly self-absorbed as well as emotionally unstable.

5. The person is out of control.

Anorexia Nervosa "Anorexia" is the medical term for loss of appetite. The term "anorexia nervosa" is a misnomer for the condition it purports to describe. Those with anorexia are, in fact, obsessively preoccupied with food; they live in a perpetual struggle with the pangs of hunger. Dr. Hilde Bruch (1978), a pioneer in the study of eating disorders, defined **anorexia nervosa** as the "relentless pursuit of excessive thinness." About 90–96% of *anorexics*, people with anorexia, are female (Levine, 1993). Most anorexia begins during the teenage years; only 10–30% of cases develop after age 20–25 (Eckert, 1985). Between 1 and 6 out of every 200 young women are estimated to be affected by anorexia (Levine, 1993).

Most anorexics share a number of characteristics. Basically, they are ruled by a desire for thinness, the conviction that their bodies are too large (even in the face of evidence to the contrary), and the "grim determination" to sustain weight loss (Levine, 1987). Typically, the anorexic loses a significant amount of weight, becomes debilitated and ill as a result, refuses help, and continues in a potentially life-threatening downward spiral. Like other eating disorders, anorexia is often the "tip of the iceberg," a symptom of an underlying psychological disturbance or set of disturbances (Zerbe, 1992).

Physiologically, anorexics suffer from amenorrhea (delay of menarche or cessation of menstrual periods); they may also suffer from hypothermia, the body's inability to maintain heat. Other symptoms include the growth of lanugo (fine body hair), insomnia, constipation, dry skin and hair, and problems with teeth and gums.

Behaviorally, anorexics often exhibit hyperactivity, social withdrawal, binge eating, and purging with self-induced vomiting, laxatives, or diuretics. The accumulated physical and psychological effects of anorexia are profound. The mortality rate is higher than that for any other psychiatric illness (Bayer & Baker, 1985).

Bulimia The word "bulimia" is derived from Greek roots meaning "ox hunger." **Bulimia** is characterized by episodes of uncontrolled overeating (binge eating), which the person then tries to counteract by purging—vomiting, exercising or dieting excessively, or using laxatives or diuretics. Psychologically, bulimics experience chronic depression, anxiety, and guilt. Other characteristics associated with bulimia are dramatic weight fluctuation, emotional instability, and a high need for approval. Bulimia is more prevalent than anorexia; it may occur in as many as 1 out of every 5 college women (Bayer & Baker, 1985).

Binge Eating Disorder A newly recognized eating disorder, **binge eating disorder,** is similar to bulimia except that there is no purging behavior. Loss of control may be accompanied by a variety of symptoms, including rapid eating, eating to the point of discomfort or beyond, continual eating throughout the day, and eating large amounts when not hungry. Obsessive thinking, embarrassment, and feelings of guilt and disgust often accompany the overeating. A person with binge eating disorder is often overweight;

Fashion doll   "Happy To Be Me" doll

The Barbie doll (left) represents an unattainable ideal for American girls. In 1991, a rival, the Happy to Be Me doll, appeared on the scene. Happy's creator wanted to present a more realistic image to young, impressionable minds. Do you think the American public is ready for Happy?

anorexia nervosa An eating disorder characterized by the pursuit of excessive thinness.

bulimia An eating disorder characterized by episodes of uncontrolled overeating followed by purging (vomiting).

binge eating disorder An eating disorder characterized by rapid eating, eating to the point of discomfort or beyond, continual eating, and eating when not hungry.

many are dieters. Evidence indicates that between 25% and 45% of obese dieters, most of whom are women, may have binge eating disorder.

Eating Disorders as a Retreat from Sexual Identity

Clinicians who work with eating-disordered patients often find that they have histories of abuse, including incest or other sexual abuse (Simpson & Ramberg, 1992). They may also have been raised to be fearful of sex and to view the body as dirty or sinful. Sexual dysfunctions and inhibitions are common among those with severe eating disorders (Rothschild, Fagan, Woodall, & Andersen, 1991; Zerbe, 1992).

Eating disorders, especially anorexia, often develop during adolescence. A feminist analysis views eating disorders among teenage girls as a way of retreating from sexuality (Orbach, 1982). It is not unusual for adolescents to experience fear and feelings of powerlessness as their bodies and roles change. For some young women, manipulation of their own bodies may be the only area of life over which they feel control. The refusal of food, in spite of the intense demands of hunger, may be equated with strength. It may also be perceived as a tool that results in decreased attractiveness which, in turn, reduces frequency of potential sexual encounters (Jones & Emerson, 1994).

Sexual abuse may also be involved in rejection of the body (Young, 1992). Through self-starvation, a young woman may demonstrate her wish to simply disappear. Others may express their rejection of sexuality by insulating themselves in a protective layer of fat. Both anorexia and bulimia "express the tension about acceptance and rejection of the constraints of femininity" (Orbach, 1982).

SEXUALITY AND AGING

Men and women tend to view aging differently. As men approach their fifties, they generally fear the loss of their sexual capacity but not their attractiveness; in contrast, women generally fear the loss of their attractiveness but not their sexuality.

Most older studies on aging and sexuality indicated a decline in sexual desire or interest as people age. Several recent studies seem to indicate, however, that although physiological functions such as lubrication and erection may be slowed, sexual interest, enjoyment, and satisfaction often remain strong (Garrison, 1989; Mulligan, Retchin, Chinchilli, & Bettinger, 1988; Mulligan & Moss, 1991; Schiavi, Schreiner-Engel, Mandel, Schanzer, & Cohen, 1990). In a recent longitudinal study, almost 700 middle-aged women were interviewed twice, at a 6-year interval (Hällstrom & Samuelsson, 1990). Almost two-thirds of the women studied experienced no significant change in their levels of desire after 6 years. Although 27% experienced a decline, 10% actually experienced an increase. What is most notable about this study is that it shows the impact of marital satisfaction and mental health on sexual desire. Not surprisingly, many of the women whose desire decreased over 6 years felt that their marriages lacked intimacy, had spouses who were alcoholic, and were themselves depressed. Such

Marital satisfaction and emotional health foster the desire for sexual intimacy in lasting relationships.

an unhappy combination is a sure antidote to desire. Those whose desire increased had initially experienced weaker desire, had troubled marriages, and had been depressed. Six years later, as their marriages improved and their mental health improved, their desire increased, moving them closer to the average.

For older lesbian and gay couples, as well as heterosexuals, the happiest are those with a strong commitment to the relationship. The need for intimacy, companionship, and purpose transcends issues of sexual orientation (Lipman, 1986).

Because our society tends to desexualize the old, aging people may interpret their slower responses as signaling the end of their sexuality. Education programs for older people, in which they learn about anatomy, physiology, and sexual response, have been shown to be helpful in dispelling myths, building confidence, and giving permission to be sexual (Fazio, 1987; Goldman & Carroll, 1990; Kellett, 1991).

Women's Issues

Beginning sometime in their forties, most women begin to experience a decline in fertility. The ovaries produce less and less estrogen, and ovulation becomes less regular. Over a few year's time, menstrual periods become irregular and eventually stop, usually between the ages of 45 and 55. This period of time is referred to as the **climacteric.** The average age of **menopause,** the complete cessation of menstruation, is 52, although about 10% of women complete it before age 40 (Beck, 1992). Most women experience some physiological or psychological symptoms during menopause, but for only about 5–15% of women are the effects severe enough to cause them to seek medical assistance (Brody, 1992).

climacteric The time during which a woman's menstrual periods become increasingly irregular prior to menopause. It also refers to the normal diminishing sexual activity that occurs among men as they age.

menopause The complete cessation of menstruation.

Physical Effects of Menopause The most common physical effects of menopause are hot flashes and vaginal symptoms, such as dryness, thinning of the vaginal walls, and pain or bleeding during intercourse. These effects may begin while a woman is still menstruating and may continue after menstruation has ceased. As many as 75% of women experience some degree of hot flashes, which usually diminish within 2 years following the end of menopause. A **hot flash** is a period of intense warmth, flushing, and (often) perspiration, typically lasting for a minute or two (but ranging anywhere from 15 seconds to 1 hour in length). Some women perspire so heavily that they soak through their clothing or bedclothes. A hot flash occurs when falling estrogen levels cause the body's "thermostat" in the brain to trigger dilation (expansion) of blood vessels near the skin's surface, producing a sensation of heat. Some women who are going through menopause experience insomnia (which can be related to hot flashes), mood changes, changes in sexual interest (more commonly a decrease), urinary incontinence, weakening of pelvic floor muscles, headaches, or weight gain.

hot flash An effect of menopause consisting of a period of intense warmth, flushing, and perspiration, typically lasting 1–2 minutes.

Long-term effects related to lowered estrogen levels may be experienced by some women. **Osteoporosis,** the loss of bone mass, leads to problems such as wrist and hip fractures in about 25% of white and Asian women and Latinas; African American women are less susceptible to osteoporosis (Greenwood, 1992). Women who are fair-skinned, thin, or who smoke are at increased risk for osteoporosis. Lowered estrogen can also contribute to diseases of the heart and arteries related to rising levels of LDL cholesterol and falling levels of HDL cholesterol. Hereditary factors also play a part in cardiovascular disease.

osteoporosis The loss of bone mass.

For many women, menopause is not viewed as a medical condition and does not require any special treatment. Others may be bothered enough by attendant symptoms to seek medical advice or assistance. Some women may be concerned about the possibility of future problems, such as osteoporosis. Others may be concerned about changes in their sexual feelings or patterns, or about the implications of fertility loss, aging, and changing standards of attractiveness. Because physicians may have a tendency to treat menopause as a medical "problem," women may find themselves subjected to treatments they don't understand or would not choose if they were better informed. It's important for women seek out practitioners who will work with them to meet their needs in the ways that are most appropriate for each individual.

Different approaches may be appropriate for treating the physical effects of menopause, depending on the individual's experience and her feelings about the alternatives. A common medical treatment for symptoms of menopause is hormone replacement therapy, which is discussed below. Other approaches include exercise and calcium supplements to reduce bone loss, low-cholesterol diets, exercise and nutritional supplements to lower cholesterol, topical lubricants to counteract vaginal dryness, and Kegel exercises to strengthen pelvic floor muscles. Frequent sexual stimulation (by self or partner) may help maintain vaginal moistness. For women who smoke, quitting smoking provides benefits in many areas, including reducing the risk of osteoporosis, less intense hot flashes, and an improved sense of well-being (Greenwood, 1992).

Hormone Replacement Therapy

Hormone replacement therapy (HRT) is the administration of estrogen—often combined with progestin—in the form of pills, vaginal cream, or a small adhesive patch. The pills are generally taken daily; progestin pills may be added for part of the cycle. The woman will often take pills for part of a month and then stop taking them, to allow the uterine lining to be shed. Some women prefer to apply estrogen directly to the vagina in the form of a cream; this may be done either daily or less frequently. The estrogen patch, worn on the back or abdomen, must be changed every few days. Additional progestin may also be prescribed.

HRT has both benefits and risks. A woman should investigate before beginning treatment. The principal benefits of HRT are that it greatly reduces the risks of osteoporosis, heart attack, and stroke; it virtually eliminates hot flashes; and it allows the vaginal walls to remain supple and moist (Sarrel, 1988). This latter effect can have a positive impact on the sexual interactions of those women who would otherwise experience pain or bleeding with intercourse (Walling, Andersen, & Johnson, 1990). The possible risks of HRT include increased chance of cancers of the uterine lining and breast; there is also the possibility of PMS-like symptoms. Adding progestin to part of the cycle is thought to prevent endometrial cancer, but it may have unpleasant side effects for some women. The inconvenience of a menstrual-type flow at the end of the monthly HRT cycle may also discourage some women from taking progestin. The risk of breast cancer may be higher in women with a family history of the disease. Women who take HRT for less than 5 years do not appear to be at increased risk of breast cancer. Furthermore, among older women in general, the risk of heart diseases are considerably greater than the risk of breast cancer. For example, a white woman age 50–94 has a 31% chance of dying of heart disease but only a 2.8% chance of dying of breast cancer (Brody, 1992). About 15–18% of postmenopausal women use HRT (Brody, 1992).

Psychological Aspects

Many women find they feel relieved when they no longer have to worry about getting pregnant. Not having to worry about birth control may be very liberating. Most women are pleased when they no longer have to deal with a monthly menstrual flow. Some women may be bothered by the physical effects of menopause, while for others, the psychological effects are greater. Even though most women close to their fifties no longer wish to bear children, the knowledge that she is no longer capable of reproduction may be painful for a woman. In addition to grieving for the loss of her fertility, she may also feel that she is losing her sexual attrac-

hormone replacement therapy (HRT) The administration of estrogen, often with progestin, in the form of pills, vaginal cream, or a small adhesive patch.

tiveness. Because women in our society are often judged on the basis of their appearance and youthfulness, those who have "used their glamour and sexiness to attract men and enhance their self-esteem" may find aging particularly painful (Greenwood, 1992).

Men's Issues

Changes in male sexual responsiveness begin to become apparent when men are in their forties and fifties, a period of change sometimes referred to as the male climacteric. For about 5% of men, these physical changes are accompanied by experiences such as fatigue, an inability to concentrate, depression, loss of appetite, and a decreased interest in sex (Kolodny, Masters, & Johnson, 1979). As a man ages, his frequency of sexual activity declines; achieving erection requires more stimulation and time, and the erection may not be as firm (Mulligan & Moss, 1991). Ejaculation takes longer and may not occur every time the penis is stimulated; the force of the ejaculation is less than before, as is the amount of ejaculate (Zilbergeld, 1992). The refractory period is extended (up to 24 hours or longer in older men). Sexual interest and enjoyment generally do not decrease (Schiavi et al., 1990). Although some of the changes are related directly to age and a normal decrease in testosterone production, others may be the result of diseases associated with aging (Mulligan et al., 1988; Whitbourne, 1990). Poor general health, diabetes, atherosclerosis, urinary incontinence, and some medications can contribute to sexual dysfunction.

It is important for older men to understand that slower responses are a normal function of aging and are unrelated to the ability to give or receive sexual pleasure. "The senior penis," writes Bernie Zilbergeld (1992), "can still give and take pleasure, even though it's not the same as it was decades ago."

About half of men over age 50 are affected to some degree by **benign prostatic hypertrophy,** an enlargement of the prostate gland. The enlarged prostate may put pressure on the urethra, resulting in the frequent and urgent need to urinate. It does not affect sexual functioning. If the blockage of the urethra is too severe, surgery can correct the problem. The surgery may lead to **retrograde ejaculation,** in which the ejaculate is released into the bladder instead of the urethra upon orgasm. Retrograde ejaculation is not dangerous, and the sensations of orgasm are generally unchanged (Thompson, 1990).

benign prostatic hypertrophy Enlargement of the prostate gland, affecting over half of men over age 50.

retrograde ejaculation The backward expulsion of semen into the bladder rather than out of the urethral opening.

SEXUALITY AND DISABILITY

A wide range of disabilities and physically limiting conditions affect human sexuality, yet the sexual needs and desires of those with disabilities have been generally overlooked and ignored. One physician was amazed to learn from a panel of people with paraplegia (paralysis of the lower body) that "if they had their choice between getting back their walking or their normal sexual function, they'd choose sex." He went on to say, "In the hospital we put all our effort toward walking—we were doing nothing about this other problem" (*Medical World News*, 1972).

Physical Limitations

Many people are subject to sexually limiting conditions for some or all of their lives. These conditions may be congenital, appearing at birth, such as cerebral palsy (a neuromuscular disorder) and Down syndrome (a developmentally disabling condition). They may be caused by a disease such as arthritis or cancer, or be the result of an accident, as in the case of spinal cord injuries.

Changing Expectations Educating people with physical limitations as to their sexual potential, and providing counseling to build self-esteem and combat negative stereotypes, are increasingly being recognized as crucial issues by the medical community (Beckmann, Gittler, Barzansky, & Beckmann, 1989; Bullard & Knight, 1981; Rieve, 1989).

To establish sexual health, the person must overcome previous sexual performance expectations and realign them with his or her actual sexual capacities. In cases where the spinal cord is completely severed, for example, there is no feeling in the genitals, but that does not eliminate sexual desires or put a stop to other possible sexual behaviors. Many men with spinal cord damage are able to have erections or partial erections; some may ejaculate, although the orgasmic feelings accompanying ejaculation are generally absent. Those who are not capable of ejaculation may be able to father a child through electroejaculation sperm retrieval and intrauterine insemination of the man's partner. In this procedure, the prostate gland is electrically stimulated through the rectum, causing erection and ejaculation. It is successful in about 45% of cases but carries some risk of internal burns (Bennett et al., 1988).

Women with spinal cord injuries generally do not experience orgasm, although they are able to experience sensuous feelings in other parts of their bodies. People with spinal cord injuries (and anyone else, for that matter) may engage in oral or manual sex—anything, in fact, they and their partners find pleasurable and acceptable. They may discover new erogenous areas of their bodies, such as their thighs, necks, ears, or underarms. Spinal cord injuries do not usually affect fertility. Many women with such injuries are able to have painless childbirth, although forceps delivery, vacuum extraction, or cesarean section may be necessary.

Overcoming Guilt A major problem for many of those with disabilities is overcoming the guilt they feel because their bodies don't meet the cultural "ideal." They often live in dread of rejection, which may or may not be realistic, depending on whom they seek as partners. Many people with disabilities have rich fantasy lives. This is fortuitous, because imagination is a key ingredient to developing a full sexual life. Robert Lenz, a consultant in the field of sexuality and disability, received a quadriplegic (paralyzed from the neck down) spinal cord injury when he was 16 (Lenz & Chaves, 1981). In the film *Active Partners*, he says:

> One thing I do know is that I'm a much better lover now than I ever was before. There are a lot of reasons for that, but one of the biggest is that I'm more relaxed. I don't have a list of do's and don'ts, a timetable or a proper sequence of moves

THE SEXUAL RIGHTS OF PEOPLE WITH DISABILITIES

Although many of the concerns of people with disabilities are becoming more visible through the courageous efforts of certain groups and individuals, much of their lives still remains hidden. There is a marked tendency on the part of the rest of humanity to put its collective head in the sand, believing that what it doesn't see does not exist. But none of us is immune to accidents or to numerous debilitating diseases and conditions. By refusing to recognize the existence and concerns of those with physical and developmental limitations, the rest of us do a profound disservice to our fellow human beings—and, ultimately, to ourselves.

The sexual rights of those with disabilities include:

1. The right to sexual expression
2. The right to privacy
3. The right to be informed and to have access to needed services, such as contraceptive counseling, medical care, genetic counseling, and sex counseling
4. The right to choose one's marital status
5. The right to have or not have children
6. The right to make one's own decisions and develop to one's fullest potential

Children with physical or developmental disabilities may have special needs when it comes to sexuality education. Here, students with visual impairments take a hands-on approach to learning about pregnancy and childbirth with the help of lifelike models.

to follow, or the need to "give" my partner an orgasm every time we make love. Sex isn't just orgasm for me; it's pleasuring, playing, laughing, and sharing.

A major function of therapists working with disabilities is to give their clients "permission" to engage in sexual activities that are appropriate to their capacities, and to suggest new activities or techniques (Kolodny, Masters, & Johnson, 1979). Clients should also be advised about the use of vibrators and artificial penises and vaginas; these devices "should be available in surgical supply stores as freely as the porno supply shops, where they are presently sold" (Diamond, 1974).

Impairment of Sight and Hearing

Loss of sight or hearing, especially if it is total and has existed from infancy, presents many difficulties in both the theoretical and the practical understanding of sexuality. A young person who has been blind from birth is unlikely to know what a person of the other sex actually "looks" (or feels) like. Children who are deaf often do not have parents who communicate well in sign language; as a result, they may not receive much instruction about sex at home, nor are they likely to understand abstract concepts such as "intimacy" (Cornelius, Chipouras, Makas, & Daniels, 1982; FitzGerald & FitzGerald, 1977). Older individuals who experience significant losses of sight or hearing may become depressed, develop low self-esteem, and withdraw from contact with others. Because they don't receive visual or auditory cues that most of us take for granted, the hearing-impaired or sight-impaired may have communication difficulties within their sexual relationships. These difficulties can often be overcome with education or counseling, depending on the circumstances. Schools and programs for visually and hearing-impaired children offer specially designed curricula for teaching about sexuality.

Chronic Illness

Diabetes, cardiovascular disease, and arthritis are three of the most prevalent diseases in America. Although these conditions are not always described as disabilities, they may require considerable adjustments in a person's sexuality because they (or the medications or treatments given to control them) may affect libido, sexual capability or responsiveness, and body image. Many older couples find themselves dealing with issues of disease and disability in addition to aging (Power-Smith, 1991). Other disabling conditions, too numerous to discuss here, may also affect our lives or those of people we know. Some of the information presented here may be applicable to conditions not specifically dealt with, such as multiple sclerosis or postpolio syndrome. We encourage readers with specific questions regarding sexuality and chronic diseases to seek out networks, organizations, and self-help groups that specialize in those issues.

Diabetes **Diabetes mellitus,** commonly referred to simply as diabetes, is a chronic disease characterized by an excess of sugar in the blood and urine, due to a deficiency of insulin, a protein hormone. Men with diabetes are more affected sexually by their disease than are women. Almost half of men with diabetes experience erectile dysfunctions, although there is apparently little or no relationship between the severity of the diabetes and the dysfunction.

Women who have diabetes generally experience little or no decline in libido and are able to lubricate during sexual activity (Ellenberg, 1980). There is conflicting opinion, however, about the effects of diabetes on women's orgasmic response (Ellenberg, 1980; Kolodny, 1971).

Cardiovascular Disease A heart attack or stroke is a major event in a person's life, affecting important aspects of daily living. Following an attack, a person often enters a period of depression in which the appetite declines, sleep habits change, and there is fatigue and a loss of libido. There is often an overwhelming fear of sex from the belief that sexual activity might provoke another heart attack or stroke. The wives of male heart attack patients also expressed great concern about sexuality. They were fearful of the risks, concerned over their husbands' sexual difficulties, apprehensive during intercourse of possible symptoms of another attack. Usually, sexual activity is safe 2 to 3 weeks after the heart attack patient returns home from the hospital, but it depends on the individual's physical and psychological well-being. He or she should consult with a physician.

Arthritis Whereas more men suffer from cardiovascular disease, the majority of people with arthritis are women. About 20 million people have symptoms of arthritis, most of them older women, but the disease may afflict and disable children and adolescents as well. Arthritis is a painful inflam-

diabetes mellitus A chronic disease characterized by excess sugar in the blood and urine due to a deficiency of insulin.

mation and swelling of the joints, usually of the knees, hips, and lower back, which may lead to deformity of the limbs. Sometimes the joints can be moved only with great difficulty and pain; sometimes they cannot be moved at all. The cause of arthritis is not known.

Sexual intercourse may be painful or impossible for arthritic women because they are not able to rotate their hip joints or spread their legs sufficiently for their partners to enter in the male-above position. Simply the pressure of their partners' bodies can cause excruciating pain. A woman with this type of arthritis may experiment to find a position that is comfortable for her. For men with arthritis, the best position is the male-above position. Oral sex, as well as the pleasuring of the body, has definite advantages for those with arthritis.

Developmental Disabilities

About 6 million Americans have varying degrees of developmental disabilities (sometimes referred to as "mental retardation"). The sexuality of these people has only recently been widely acknowledged by those who work with them. Their sexual rights are just beginning to be recognized, although there is a great deal of debate about these issues. The capabilities of the developmentally disabled vary widely. Mildly or moderately disabled people may be able to learn to behave appropriately, protect themselves from abuse, and understand the basics of reproduction. Some may manage to marry, work, and raise families with little assistance (Monat-Haller, 1982; Pincus, 1988).

Sex education is of great importance for adolescents who have developmental disabilities. Some parents may fear that this will "put ideas into their heads," but it is more likely, given the combination of explicit media presentations and the effects of increased hormonal output, that the ideas are already there. It may be difficult or impossible to teach more severely affected people how to engage in safe sexual behaviors. There is ongoing debate about the ethics of mandatory birth control devices—such as IUDs or implants—or sterilization for these people. These issues are especially salient in cases where there is the chance of passing the disability genetically to a child.

SEXUALITY AND CANCER

In ancient Greece, physicians examining the invasive tissues extending from malignant breast tumors thought these tissues looked like the jutting claws of a crab. From the Greek word for crab, *karkinos*, we have derived our word, "cancer." Cancer, however, is not a single disease; it is more than 300 distinct illnesses that can affect any organ of the body. These various cancers grow at different speeds and have different treatment success and failure rates. Most cancers, but not all (leukemia, for example), form solid tumors.

All cancers have one thing in common: They are the result of the aberrant behavior of cells. Cancer-causing agents (carcinogens) are believed to jumble up the DNA's messages, causing the cell to abandon its normal functions. Tumors are either benign or malignant. **Benign tumors** usually are nonmalignant, slow growing, and remain localized. **Malignant tumors,** how-

benign tumor A nonmalignant tumor that is slow growing and remains localized.

ever, are cancerous. Instead of remaining localized, they invade nearby tissues and disrupt the normal functioning of vital organs. The process in which the disease spreads from one part of the body to another unrelated part is called **metastasis.** This metastatic process, not the original tumor, accounts for 80% of cancer deaths.

Women and Cancer

Cancers of the breasts and reproductive organs are feared by many women. Because of these fears, some women avoid having regular breast examinations or Pap tests. If a woman feels a breast lump or her doctor tells her she has a growth in her uterus, she may plunge into despair or panic. These reactions are understandable, but they are also counterproductive. Most lumps and bumps are benign conditions, such as uterine fibroids, ovarian cysts, and fibroadenomas of the breast.

Breast Cancer   Breast cancer is the second most prevalent form of cancer among women, following lung cancer. Each year, it strikes 183,000 American women, and each year, almost 46,000 die from it (Ubell, 1994). An estimated 1 out of every 9 American women will contract it by age 85 (Kaplan, 1992). Those who survive the cancer may suffer psychologically because mastectomy (the removal of the breast and surrounding tissue) leaves them feeling sexually unattractive or deformed, and wondering if the cancer will recur in another 5, 10, or 20 years.

On a more hopeful note, the survival rate for cancer is constantly improving, especially with early detection. The 5-year survival rate is 93% for localized breast cancer and 72% for cancer that has spread regionally (Ubell, 1994). "Five-year survival rate" refers to the percentage of patients who are living 5 years after cancer diagnosis. Because of increased success in treating cancer, more emphasis is being put on the quality of the patient's life after diagnosis.

Breast cancer is a catch-all term for at least 15 different types of tumors. Each type has a different rate of growth and tendency to metastasize in different organs. By the time a breast tumor is large enough to be felt, it is usually at least 2 years old. A slow-growing tumor can take as long as 9 years to develop to the size of a pea. During this time, in approximately half the cases, there has already been some micrometastasis—microscopic spreading of malignant cells—to other organs. Some cancerous cells are destroyed by the body's own immune system; others continue to grow slowly.

The principal risk factors connected with breast cancer are a family history of cancer, a history of breast cancer (principally mother or sister), and previous cancer (breast or other). Other possible factors include being childless or late childbearing (starting after age 30), early menstruation, late menopause, and a history of fibrocystic disease. Diet may also play a part; a high consumption of animal fat is associated with increased risk (Boston Women's Health Book Collective, 1992). Alcohol consumption and smoking have also been implicated in the development of breast cancer, according to recent studies. Women with high levels of natural estrogen are two to four times more likely to develop breast cancer as those with lower levels of the hormone ("Study Relates," 1995). A sedentary lifestyle may be a risk factor for breast cancer as well. New research from the University of

malignant tumor   A cancerous tumor that invades nearby tissues and disrupts the normal functioning of vital organs.

metastasis   The process in which cancer spreads from one part of the body to another unrelated part via the bloodstream or lymphatic system.

BREAST SELF-EXAMINATION

Follow the steps below to examine your breasts regularly once a month. This examination is best done after your menstrual period. If you find something you consider abnormal, contact your doctor for an examination. Most breast lumps are not serious, but all should come to the doctor's attention for an expert opinion after appropriate examination. You may have a condition that will require treatment or further study. If necessary, your doctor may recommend laboratory tests or X rays as part of a more detailed examination. Follow your doctor's advice. Your early recognition of a change in your breast and the doctor's thoughtful investigation will determine the safest course. Keep up this important health habit even during pregnancy and after menopause.

Stand in front of a mirror. Examine your breasts with your arms raised. Look for changes in contour and shape of the breasts, color and texture of the skin and nipple, and evidence of discharge from the nipple.

While lying on your back, use your left hand to palpate the right breast, while holding your right arm at a right angle to the rib cage, with your elbows bent. Repeat the procedure on the other side. Use the pads of three or four fingers to examine every inch of your breast tissue. Move your fingers in circles about the size of a dime. Do not lift your fingers from your breast between palpations. You can use powder or lotion to help your fingers glide from one spot to the next.

Use varying levels of pressure for each palpation, from light to deep, to examine the full thickness of your breast tissue. Using pressure will not injure the breast.

Use one of the following search patterns to examine all of your breast tissue. Examine all of the shaded areas.

a. Start in the armpit and proceed downward to the lower boundary. Move a finger's width toward the middle and continue palpating upward until you reach the collarbone. Repeat this until you have covered all breast tissue.

b. Examine each "wedge" of your breast, moving from the outside boundary toward the nipple.

c. Imagine your breasts as the face of a clock. Start at 12 o'clock and palpate along the boundary of each circle until you return to your starting point. Then move down a finger's width and continue palpating in ever smaller circles until you reach the nipple. Depending on the size of your breast, you may need 8 to 10 circles.

Once you have completed the pattern, perform two additional exams: (1) squeeze your nipples to check for discharge (some women have a normal discharge), and (2) examine the breast tissue that extends into your armpit while your arm is relaxed at your side.

Southern California has found that women who exercise four or more hours per week during their reproductive years can reduce their risk of breast cancer by as much as 60% (Koga, 1994). In spite of the number of risk factors that have been identified, however, 70% of all new cases of breast cancer are diagnosed in women who have no known risk factors for the disease.

Detection There is considerable debate about the effectiveness of various methods in detecting breast cancer. Experts agree, however, that the key to effective treatment is early detection. The American Cancer Society (ACS) recommended in 1980 that all women over 20 perform a breast self-examination once a month, that women between 20 and 40 have a breast examination by a physician every 3 years, and that women over 40 have an examination by a physician every year. After the age of 50, a woman should have an annual **mammogram** (low-dose X-ray screening); a woman between 40 and 50 should have an annual mammogram if her physician recommends it, especially if her mother or sister has had breast cancer. Due to the cost of mammograms (about $60–$250) and doctor's visits, many women have problems affording preventive breast care.

mammogram A low-dose X ray of the breast.

Recent research suggests that mammography may not be helpful in detecting tumors in women under age 50 because the breast tissue is usually too dense for a tumor to be discerned (Lavecchia, Negri, Bruzzi, & Franceschi, 1993). Women under 50 should be especially diligent in examining their own breasts, especially if they are at above-average risk for breast cancer. Mammography screening reduces the chance of death from breast cancer among women over 50 by 30–50% (Boston Women's Health Book Collective, 1992).

It is important to recognize that most breast lumps—75–80%—are *not* cancerous. Many disappear on their own. Of lumps that are surgically removed for diagnostic purposes (biopsied), 80% prove to be benign. Most are related to **fibrocystic disease** (a common and generally harmless breast condition, not really a disease at all), or they are fibroadenomas (round, movable growths, also harmless, that occur in young women).

fibrocystic disease A common and generally harmless breast condition.

Treatment Surgical removal of the breast is called **mastectomy.** The leading treatments for breast cancer are modified radical mastectomy and simple (or total) mastectomy. In modified radical mastectomy, the entire breast is removed, along with the lining of the underlying chest muscles and some or all of the nearby lymph nodes. Less drastic is simple mastectomy, which involves the removal of only the breast and a few lymph nodes if necessary. Another approach, increasingly popular, is known as **lumpectomy.** It involves removal of only the tumor and lymph nodes, thus sparing the breast and underlying muscle. Lumpectomy is generally followed by radiation treatments to halt the further spread of cancerous cells.

mastectomy The surgical removal of the breast.

lumpectomy Breast surgery that removes only the malignant tumor and surrounding lymph nodes.

Because many women fear the loss of a breast as much as they fear the cancer itself (Kaplan, 1992), they delay seeking diagnosis for breast lumps. The possibility of being able to keep her breast even if a tumor is discovered may inspire a woman to seek early diagnosis, according to Dr. Bernard Fisher, a pioneer developer of lumpectomy (Kotulak, 1979). In 1985, a study of more than 1800 women indicated that the survival rate for lumpectomy combined with radiation is the same as for mastectomy (Fisher et al., 1985).

A woman who undergoes a mastectomy is confronted with the loss of one or several visible parts of her body. First, she has lost her breast. Sec-

Surviving cancer can deepen one's appreciation of life. Notice the tattoo along this woman's mastectomy scar.

ond (in the case of radical surgery), the removal of chest muscles and auxiliary lymph tissues leaves not only visible scars but also may restrict the movement and strength of her arm. Psychologically, the loss of her breast may symbolize for her the loss of sexuality; she may feel scarred and be fearful of rejection, because breasts in American culture are such primary sexual symbols (Kaplan, 1992). She also may experience a definite decrease in her sexual excitability. Because the breasts play an important role in sexual arousal and foreplay for many women, their loss may prevent some women from becoming fully aroused sexually (Woods, 1984).

Much of the emotional adjustment after a mastectomy depends on how the woman's partner reacts. She is often fearful that he will reject her; the two may find themselves unable to discuss their sexuality. Some men are initially shocked and feel repulsion and confusion. Other men may be fearful of resuming intercourse lest they hurt their partners. If the relationship prior to the mastectomy was good and the couple were sexually happy, the postmastectomy adjustment will be less difficult (Woods, 1984).

Lesbians and Breast Cancer In 1993, an epidemiologist with the National Cancer Institute reported that lesbians have a hypothetical risk of developing breast cancer that is two to three times higher than that of heterosexual women ("Lesbians' Cancer Risk," 1993). Cancer researcher Suzanne Haynes estimated that lesbians have a one-in-three lifetime chance of breast cancer based on known risk factors and information from a 1987 survey of lesbian health. Smoking, alcohol use, lack of childbearing, and poor access to health care are all factors that contribute to breast cancer risk; these are all apparently more common among lesbians (due in part to psychological and social pressures resulting from discrimination) than among heterosexual women.

Cervical Cancer and Cervical Dysplasia

Cervical dysplasia, also called **cervical intraepithelial neoplasia (CIN),** is a condition of the cervical epithelium (covering membrane) that *may* lead to cancer if it is not treated. It is more common than cancer of the breast or uterus. Cervical dysplasia, however, is almost 100% curable; for this reason, cervical cancer is generally not even included in cancer statistics (Salsbury & Johnson, 1981).

Some health researchers consider cervical dysplasia to be a sexually transmitted disease (Hatcher et al., 1990). Sexually active women do appear to be at higher risk than others. The greatest risks are posed for women who begin sexual intercourse before age 20, women who have more than three sex partners before age 35, or women whose partners have had more than three partners (Richart, 1983).

cervical dysplasia or **cervical intraepithelial neoplasia (CIN)** A condition of the cervical epithelium (covering membrane) that may lead to cancer if not treated.

Detection: The Pap Test The most reliable means of making an early detection of cervical cancer is the **Pap test** (or Pap smear). This is a simple procedure that not only can detect cancer but also can reveal changes in cells that make them precancerous. A Pap test can warn against cancer even before it begins.

The Pap test is usually done during a pelvic exam and takes about a minute or so. Cell samples are gently and usually painlessly scraped from the cervix and examined under a microscope. If any are suspicious, the physician will make further exams. Women should have a Pap test yearly unless their physician recommends differently. Unfortunately, the test is not as effective in detecting cancer in the body of the uterus, which occurs in women most frequently during or after menopause.

Pap test A method of testing for cervical cancer by scraping cell samples from the cervix and examining them under a microscope.

Treatment Cervical dysplasia is very responsive to treatment in its early stages. With an irregular Pap smear, a **biopsy**—surgical removal for diagnosis—may be performed. As some abnormalities clear up on their own, the physician may wait several months and do a follow-up smear. There may be some risk in delaying treatment, however. If the cervix shows visible signs of abnormality, a biopsy should be performed at once. Cervical biopsies are done with the aid of a colposcope, an instrument that contains a magnifying lens. Sometimes conization, the removal of a cone of tissue from the center of the cervix, is performed. This procedure is time-consuming and requires hospitalization. Depending on the extent and severity of the dysplasia and whether it has progressed to cancer, other treatment options range from electric cauterization, or cryosurgery, to laser surgery, radiotherapy, or hysterectomy.

biopsy The surgical removal of tissue for diagnosis.

Ovarian Cancer

Cancers of the ovaries are relatively rare. They make up only about 5% of all gynecological cancers, yet they are among the most deadly. Ovarian cancer is hard to diagnose because there are no symptoms

You and Your Sexual Well-Being

GYNECOLOGICAL SELF-EXAMINATION

In a space that is comfortable for you, take time to look at your outer genitals, using a mirror and a good light. The name given to female outer genitals is the vulva. The large, soft folds of skin with hair on them are the outer lips, or labia majora. The color, texture, and pattern of this hair vary widely among women. Inside the outer lips are the inner lips, or labia minora. These have no hair and vary in size from small to large and protruding. They extend from below the vagina up toward the pubic bone, where they form a hood over the clitoris. If you pull back the hood you will be able to see your clitoris. The size and shape of the clitoris, as well as the hood, vary widely among women. These variations have nothing to do with a woman's ability to respond sexually. You may also find some cheesy white matter under the hood. This is called smegma and is normal.

Below the clitoris is a smooth area and then a small hole. This is the urinary opening, or meatus. Below the urinary opening is the vaginal opening, which is surrounded by rings of tissue. One of these, which you may or may not be able to see, is the hymen. Just inside the vagina, on both sides, are the Bartholin's glands. They may secrete a small amount of mucus during sexual excitement but little else of their function is known; if they are infected, they will be swollen, but otherwise you won't notice them. The smooth area between your vagina and anus is called the perineum.

Once you're familiar with the normal appearance of your outer genitals, you can check for unusual rashes, soreness, warts, or parasites, such as crabs.

You can also examine your inner genitals, using a speculum, flashlight, and mirror. A speculum is an instrument used to hold the vaginal walls apart, allowing a clear view of the vagina and cervix. You should be able to obtain a speculum and information about doing an internal exam from a clinic that specializes in women's health or family planning.

It is a good idea to observe and become aware of what the normal vaginal discharges look and feel like (refer back to Chapter 3 for more information). Colors vary from white to gray and change in consistency from thick to thin and clear (similar to egg white that is stretched between the fingers) over the course of the menstrual cycle. Distinct changes or odors, along with burning, bleeding between menstrual cycles, pain in the pelvic region, itching, or rashes, should be reported to a physician.

In doing a vaginal self-exam, you may initially experience some fear or uneasiness about touching your body. In the long run, however, your patience and persistence will pay off in increased body awareness and a heightened sense of personal health.

in the early stages; it is not usually detectable by a Pap smear. Diagnosis is done by pelvic examination and needle aspiration (removal of fluid) or biopsy. Treatment involves surgical removal of the tumor and ovary, often followed by radiation or chemotherapy. Follow-up care is especially important (Madaras & Patterson, 1984).

Uterine Cancer More than 99% of cancers of the uterus involve the endometrium, the lining of the uterus. Certain women appear more at risk of developing endometrial cancer than others. White women contract endometrial cancer at almost twice the rate of black women. The risk factors include extreme obesity, childlessness, late menopause, diabetes, hypertension, certain ovarian disorders, breast and ovarian cancer, radiation exposure, menstrual irregularity, and inherited characteristics. Estrogen is associated with endometrial cancer. The safety of hormone replacement therapy continues to be controversial; HRT may increase the risk of endometrial cancer at least four to seven times, although the administration of progestin with the estrogen is thought to greatly reduce the risk (Madaras & Patterson, 1984).

Hysterectomy **Hysterectomy** is the surgical removal of the uterus. It may consist of a simple hysterectomy (removing the uterus and a portion of the vagina) or a radical hysterectomy, which involves the additional removal of ovaries, tubes, vagina, and adjacent tissues. Approximately 650,000 hysterectomies are performed each year, many of which are unnecessary (Boston Women's Health Book Collective, 1992). Certain conditions, however, make a hysterectomy necessary: (1) when a cancerous or precancerous growth cannot be treated otherwise; (2) when noncancerous growths on the uterus become so large that they interfere with other organs (such as when they hinder bladder or bowel functions), or cause pain or pressure; (3) when bleeding is so heavy that it cannot be controlled, or when it leads to anemia; (4) when severe infection cannot be controlled in any other way.

hysterectomy The surgical removal of the uterus.

The hysterectomy is performed by removing the uterus surgically through the vagina or through an abdominal incision. At the same time, there may be an oophorectomy, removal of one or both ovaries, because of endometriosis, cysts, or tumors. If both ovaries are removed from a premenopausal woman, she may begin hormone therapy to control the symptoms caused by the lack of estrogen. But because estrogen therapy may be linked to increased cancer risk, such therapy should be undertaken with caution.

For many couples, a hysterectomy may cause a major crisis. For others, it brings well-founded fears. From 33% to 46% of women report difficulties with arousal and orgasm following hysterectomy, especially if oophorectomy was also performed (Zussman et al., 1981). The absence of the cervix and uterus deprives a woman of certain sensations that may have been important for both arousal and orgasm. Removal of the ovaries can result in lowered libido because testosterone (the sex-drive hormone) is mainly produced there. Furthermore, the absence of ovarian estrogen can cause menopausal symptoms such as vaginal dryness and thinning of the vaginal walls. Therapy and self-help groups for posthysterectomy patients can be very useful for women who wish to increase sexual desire and pleasure. **Androgen replacement therapy**—testosterone administered orally, by injection, or by a slow-release pellet placed under the skin—may be helpful to some women (Boston Women's Health Book Collective, 1992).

androgen replacement therapy The administration of testosterone to increase sex drive.

Men and Cancer

Generally speaking, men are less likely than women to get regular checkups and to seek help at the onset of symptoms. This tendency can have unfortunate consequences where reproductive cancers are concerned, because early detection can often mean the difference between life and death. Prostate and testicular cancer both appear to be increasing dramatically, so it is of paramount importance that men pay attention to what goes on in their genital and urinary organs. Just as women should regularly examine their breasts, men should regularly examine their testicles. Men over 40 should have an annual rectal examination of the prostate gland.

Prostate Cancer Prostate cancer is the most common form of cancer among men; it is second only to lung cancer as a fatal disease in men. Since 1973, the rate of prostate cancer has increased by more than 50%. Prostate cancer strikes 1 out of every 9 men, most frequently after the age of 65. Around 200,000 new cases are diagnosed each year; approximately 38,000 men die from it annually ("Blood Test," 1994). As a man gets older, his chances of developing prostate cancer increase. One recent study reports a gentic link between brothers (Narod, 1995). Prostate cancer appears to be more common in African Americans than whites, but it is suggested that this may be the result of later detection among those with limited access to health care (Centers for Disease Control, 1992b).

Detection Various signs may point to prostate cancer, a slow-growing disease. Although these signs are more likely to indicate prostatic enlargement or benign tumors than cancer, they should never be ignored. They include:

- Weak or interrupted flow of urine
- Inability to urinate or difficulty in beginning to urinate
- Frequent need to urinate, especially at night; bed-wetting
- Urine flow that is not easily stopped
- Painful or burning urination
- Continuing pain in lower back, pelvis, or upper thighs

The first step in diagnosing prostate cancer is to have a physician conduct a digital exam. By inserting a finger into the rectum, the physician can usually feel an irregular or unusually firm area on the prostate that may indicate a tumor. If the physician discovers a suspicious area, he or she will then make a battery of tests including X rays, urine and blood analysis, and biopsy.

Many men are reluctant to get rectal examinations. Urologist William Catalona asserts that "85% of men will not submit to a rectal exam unless they're already having problems" (quoted in Angier, 1991). A blood test, called the prostate-specific antigen (PSA) test and costing between $50 and $75, is also helpful in diagnosing prostate cancer. When used in conjunction with a digital rectal exam, the test can sharpen early detection of the disease. Early detection is crucial and often makes the difference between life and death.

Treatment If detected early, prostate cancer has a high cure rate. Depending on the stage of the cancer, treatment may include surgery, hormone treatment, radiation therapy, or chemotherapy. If the cancer has not spread beyond the prostate gland, all or part of the gland is removed by surgery. Modern surgical techniques can usually ensure that the man's sexual functioning remains unimpaired (Angier, 1991). Men who had prostate surgery prior to the development of these techniques, or whose tumors have spread beyond the prostate gland itself, may experience sexual difficulties following surgery resulting from damage to nearby nerves. In a study conducted by the Veterans Administration and the University of California at Los

TESTICULAR SELF-EXAMINATION

Just as women practice breast self-examination each month, men should practice preventive medicine by doing testicular self-examination regularly.

The best time to discover any small lumps is right after a hot shower or bath, when the skin of the scrotum is most relaxed. Each testicle should be gently examined with the fingers of both hands, slowly and carefully. Learn what the collecting structure at the back of the testicle (the epididymis) feels like so that you won't mistake it for an abnormality. If you find any lump or growth, it most often will be on the front side of the testicle.

Any lumps or suspicious areas should be promptly reported to your urologist or another health-care practitioner.

Roll each testicle between the thumb and fingers; the testicles should feel smooth, except for the epididymis at the back of each. A hard lump, enlargement, or contour changes should be reported to your health-care practitioner.

Angeles, 72% of prostate cancer patients reported sexual dysfunctions following surgery. Thirty-one percent reported diminished sexual interest (Parachini, 1987).

Some men choose to have penile implants following prostate surgery so that intercourse will again be possible. In any event, sensitive sex counseling should be an integral part of treatment. Some men who retain the ability to become erect experience retrograde ejaculation and are infertile because semen does not pass out of the urethra.

Testicular Cancer Cancer of the testes was once one of the rarest cancers among men, but for unknown reasons, its rates have tripled since 1972. There is some evidence linking it to a man's mother's having taken DES (a drug formerly prescribed to prevent miscarriage) while pregnant (Kolodny et al., 1979). Testicular cancer is highest among young white men between ages 20 and 35. These men tend to be middle and upper class; young professionals have four times the incidence as unskilled laborers. This cancer is rare among African Americans. Approximately 3000 cases are diagnosed each year, but the actual incidence may be significantly higher. Malignancies that start in the testes spread to the lymph nodes or lungs and then are reported at the latter sites. If testicular cancer is caught early, it is curable; if it is found late, it is often deadly. Except for the rarest form of testicular cancer, the cure rate is about 95%.

Detection The first sign of testicular cancer is usually a painless lump or slight enlargement and a change in the consistency of the testicle; the right testicle is more often involved than the left. Although the tumors that grow on the testes are often painless, there is often a dull ache in the lower abdomen and groin, accompanied by a sensation of dragging and heaviness. If the tumor is growing rapidly, there may be severe pain in the testicles.

Because of the lack of symptoms and pain in the early stage, patients often do not go to a doctor for several months after discovering a slightly enlarged testicle. This delay accounts for the fact that in 88% of patients with testicular cancer, it has already metastasized by the time it is diagnosed.

A self-examination is the best line of defense against metastasis of testicular cancer. It only takes a couple of minutes and should be performed once a month. Suspicious findings should be reported to a physician at once.

Treatment After the affected testicle is removed, an artificial one may be inserted in the scrotal sac. Radiation treatment or chemotherapy may follow. Although the cure rate for all testicular cancer is over 95% (provided the disease has not widely metastasized), the aftermath of treatment is problematic for some men. Sperm-banking and support groups may be helpful resources for some men and their partners.

OTHER SEXUAL HEALTH ISSUES

There are a number of other disorders of the female reproductive system. Those that are generally sexually transmitted are discussed in Chapter 15.

Toxic Shock Syndrome

toxic shock syndrome (TSS) A potentially life-threatening condition caused by the *Staphylococcus aureus* bacterium and linked to the use of superabsorbent tampons.

Toxic shock syndrome (TSS) is caused by the *Staphylococcus aureus* bacterium, a common agent of infection. Although approximately 17% of menstruating women have these bacteria in their vaginas, they do not pose a threat under normal circumstances. Tampons, especially the superabsorbent type, or other devices that block the vagina or cervix during menstruation apparently lead to the creation of an ideal culture medium for staph bacteria. Once TSS is diagnosed, it is easily treated with antibiotics. It is important to stop the infection early before it does significant damage.

The risk of developing TSS is actually quite low—about 3 out of 100,000 women develop it. The group at highest risk is 15- to 19-year-old women. According to one study, the incidence rate for this group was almost 5 out of 100,000 (Markowitz et al., 1987). The FDA advises all women who use tampons to reduce the already low risk by using sanitary napkins during part of their menstrual periods (at night, for example). Tampons should also be changed frequently.

TSS *can* be treated effectively if it is detected. The warning signs are fever (101°F or higher), diarrhea, vomiting, muscle aches, and/or a sunburnlike rash (Hatcher et al., 1990).

Endometriosis

endometriosis A disease caused by endometrial tissue (uterine lining) spreading and growing in other parts of the body; a major cause of infertility.

Sometimes called the "career woman's disease," **endometriosis** may affect as many as 10 million American women. Its nickname derives from its apparent prevalence among women who have delayed childbearing, although recent studies suggest that, as Dr. Donald Chatman observed, endometriosis is "an equal-opportunity disease," available to women of all socioeconomic groups (quoted in Wallis, 1986). Endometriosis is caused by bits of endometrial tissue (uterine lining) that spread to and grow in other parts of the body. It is a major cause of infertility.

It is not known for certain how endometriosis begins. Although endometriosis generally occurs in the pelvic cavity, it may also affect other parts of the body, including the kidneys, intestines, lungs, and even the nasal passages (Wallis, 1986). Symptoms of endometriosis include pain (usually pelvic pain, which can be very intense) and abnormal menstrual bleeding. It is usually diagnosed by palpation (feeling) and laparoscopic examination.

Treatment is a complex issue. The woman's age, her childbearing plans, and the extent of the disease are all significant factors. Hormone therapies to interfere with ovulation can help. Sometimes birth control pills are prescribed. A synthetic male hormone, danazol, stops ovulation and thus causes shrinkage of endometrial tissues. It does have masculinizing side effects, however, and it is very expensive (Madaras & Patterson, 1984). Pregnancy can help if it is feasible for a woman to arrange her childbearing plans accordingly. Surgery is also a possibility, and it may be the only choice if the endometriosis is severe.

Prompt treatment is crucial if endometriosis is suspected. It is also important for the woman who has endometriosis to inform herself about the disease and thoroughly investigate the options, because treatment for this condition is very much an individual matter.

Lesbian Health Issues

In addition to many of the medical concerns shared among all women, lesbians face additional difficulties. Several studies have found that lesbians encounter prejudice and discrimination when seeking health care (Robertson, 1992; Stevens, 1992). First, it may be assumed that they are heterosexual, leading to the inclusion of inappropriate questions, comments, or procedures and the exclusion of appropriate measures. Second, if they do disclose their orientation, they are likely to be treated with hostility. As a result of these experiences, lesbians are less likely than heterosexuals to seek health care. Thus, they may put themselves at higher risk for diseases that should be detected early on. Older lesbians are especially vulnerable because they are not generally as willing to disclose their sexual orientation; they often feel "invisible" (Tully, 1989). Surveys of lesbians regarding health-care choices have found preferences for female practitioners, holistic approaches, preventive care and education, and woman-managed clinics (Lucas, 1992; Trippet & Bain, 1992).

Men's Health: Prostatitis

Many of men's sexual health problems are related to sexually transmitted diseases. One condition affecting men that is not sexually transmitted is **prostatitis,** the inflammation of the prostate gland. It affects as many as 30–40% of American men between 20 and 40 years of age. There are two

prostatitis Inflammation of the prostate gland.

types: infectious prostatitis and congestive prostatitis. Infectious prostatitis is generally caused by *E. coli* bacteria. Congestive prostatitis usually results from abstention from ejaculation or infrequent ejaculation. It is sometimes called the "priest's disease."

The prostate secretes most of the fluid portion of a man's ejaculate (semen). If a man does not ejaculate, this fluid begins to decompose, and the prostate becomes congested, causing congestive prostatitis (Roen, 1974). Congestive prostatitis can also be caused by dramatic changes in a man's sexual behavior patterns. The prostate develops its own production pattern based on the man's sexual activity; therefore, if a highly active man cuts back his sexual routine, his prostate will continue its high production and become congested with too much fluid over a period of time. Similarly, if the man goes from no orgasms a day to several, he may develop congestive prostatitis (Rowan & Gillette, 1973).

Symptoms of prostatitis include swelling in the genital area, a feeling of heat, and pain. Frequently, there is pain in the lower back. When there is infection, there may be a thin mucous discharge from the penis that may be visible in the morning before urination. Acute prostatitis often results in a loss of libido and painful ejaculations; chronic prostatitis is often associated with sexual dysfunctions (Davis & Mininberg, 1976). Infectious prostatitis is treated with antibiotics.

DES Daughters and Sons

diethylstilbestrol (DES) A synthetic estrogen once used to prevent miscarriages; associated with a possible increased cancer risk among the women who took it and their children.

Between 1941 and 1971, an estimated 6 million women used **diethylstilbestrol,** or **DES,** a synthetic estrogen, to prevent miscarriages, particularly if they had a previous history of miscarriage or bleeding during pregnancy or were diabetic (Burger, 1981). About 3 million women whose mothers took DES were born during these years. They range in age now from early adulthood to middle age. Approximately 50–85% of these daughters have developed immature glandular cells in the cervix and wall of the vagina, or adenosis. The effects of DES on reproductive abilities are unclear (Barnes et al., 1980; Herbst et al., 1980), although new research from Columbia University has revealed that women who took DES when pregnant were more likely to have daughters with bisexual or homosexual tendencies. No such link was made with DES sons (Fagin, 1995).

What is well established is that DES daughters run a significantly higher risk of developing cancer of the vagina. Vaginal cancer is extremely rare and usually strikes women in their late fifties and older. Among DES daughters, the peak years for developing the cancer are ages 19–22 (Adess, 1980). The earlier it is found, the more successfully it can be treated.

About 1 in 4 DES sons has some problem with his reproductive system, including low sperm count, abnormal sperm, epididymal cysts, and, in some cases, genitals that do not mature during puberty (Adess, 1980).

ALCOHOL, DRUGS, AND SEXUALITY

In the minds of many Americans, sex and alcohol (or sex and "recreational" drugs) go together like hamburger and fries. Although experience shows us that sexual performance and enjoyment generally go down as alcohol or

Among college students, the use of alcohol is associated with increased risk of unwanted intercourse, sexual violence, pregnancy, and sexually transmitted diseases.

drug levels go up, many people persist in believing the age-old myths. One study of 125 women age 15–31 found that 65% had combined alcohol use with sex in the preceding month, and that 43% had used alcohol at the time of their first sexual experience (Flanigan, 1990). In a survey of 243 single college students, only 19% of those over 21 had never had sex as a result of intoxication (Butcher, Manning, & O'Neal, 1991).

Alcohol Use and Sexuality

Because of the ambivalence we often have about sex ("It's good but it's bad"), many people feel more comfortable about initiating or participating in sexual activities if they have had a drink or two. This phenomenon of activating behaviors that would normally be suppressed is known as **disinhibition** (Woods & Mansfield, 1981). Although a small amount of alcohol may have a small disinhibiting, or relaxing, effect, greater quantities can result in aggression, loss of judgment, poor coordination, and loss of consciousness. Alcohol is also generally detrimental to sexual performance and enjoyment. Furthermore, large amounts of alcohol ingested by both men and women can contribute to infertility and birth defects.

Alcohol affects the ability of both men and women to become sexually aroused. Men may have difficulty achieving or maintaining an erection, and

disinhibition The phenomenon of activating behaviors that would normally be suppressed.

women may not experience vaginal lubrication. Physical sensations are likely to be dulled. Chronic users of alcohol typically experience desire and arousal difficulties (O'Farrell, Choquette, & Birchler, 1991; Schiavi et al., 1990). This may be due in part to poor general health and also to lowered production of reproductive hormones. Alcohol has been demonstrated to affect RNA in male rats, suppressing its function in testosterone and sperm production (Emanuele, Tentler, Emanuele, & Kelley, 1991). Researchers have determined that drinking a six-pack of beer in less than 2 hours can halt a man's RNA activity for up to 12 hours. (This does not mean, however, that no sperm are present; production is slowed, but most men will remain fertile.)

Alcohol use also puts people at high risk for numerous unwanted or dangerous consequences. These include unwanted intercourse, sexual violence, pregnancy, and sexually transmitted diseases. A study of 243 college students found that 47% of the men and 57% of the women had had intercourse from one to five times *primarily* because they were intoxicated (Butcher et al., 1991). Nineteen percent of the men and 33% of the women said they had had intercourse because they felt awkward about refusing.

The disinhibiting effect of alcohol allows some men to justify acts of sexual violence they would not otherwise commit (Abbey, 1991; Roenrich & Kinder, 1991). Men may expect that alcohol will make them sexually aggressive and act accordingly; they may believe that if a woman drinks, she is consenting to have sex. Additionally, a woman who has been drinking may have difficulty in sending and receiving cues about expected behavior and in resisting assault (Abbey, 1991). Alcohol use is often a significant factor in sexual violence of all types (Benson, Charlton, & Goodhart, 1992).

Drug Use and Sexuality

Human beings have always been interested in the effects of drugs and other concoctions on sexual interest and performance. Substances that supposedly increase sexual desire or improve sexual performance are called aphrodisiacs. Painstaking research, both personal and professional, inevitably leads to the same conclusion: one's inner fantasy life, coupled with an interested and responsive partner, is the most powerful and effective aphrodisiac available. Nevertheless, the search continues for the magic potion.

Most recreational drugs, although they may be perceived as increasing sexual enjoyment (Bills & Duncan, 1991), actually have the opposite effect. Marijuana and alcohol continue to be the most widely used and abused drugs among people anxious to increase libido and performance. But drugs, although they may reduce inhibitions and appear to enhance the sexual experience, have the capacity to interfere with sexual functioning and even cause impotence and infertility. Marijuana may give the illusion of prolonged arousal and orgasm because it acts to distort time. But its use can decrease sexual desire and testosterone levels, thereby reducing sperm production (Nelson, 1988).

The substance amyl nitrate is reputed to intensify orgasmic pleasure. It is a fast-acting smooth muscle relaxant and coronary vasodilator, expanding blood vessels around the heart. Medically, it is used to relieve attacks of angina. Some people attempt to intensify their orgasms by "popping" an

ANABOLIC STEROIDS: NOT ALL THEY'RE PUMPED UP TO BE

What would you be willing to do to obtain the "perfect body"? Exercise 3 hours a day at the gym? Spend hundreds of dollars each month on exercise equipment and gym fees? Take anabolic steroids? For many, this last alternative offers the quickest and most dramatic route to a toned and muscular body. Unfortunately for the many thousands who choose this alternative, it is also the most dangerous.

Anabolic steroids are synthetic derivatives of testosterone, the male hormone that helps the body to build muscle and synthesize protein. Beyond this function, the mechanism of action of steroids is unclear. Though anabolic steroids are legitimately prescribed to combat some diseases, athletes may often take ten times the recommended dosage to increase muscle mass, improve strength, and promote tissue growth. Abuse can have serious and long-lasting negative effects on the health of the user.

Acne, baldness, and changes in sexual desire are the most common side effects of anabolic steroids. In men, steroids can cause a decrease in sperm production as well as infertility if the drug is used over a prolonged period. The size of the testicles may decrease, and men may have a difficult time achieving and maintaining an erection. In women, steroids usually have a masculinizing effect; they may cause the growth facial hair, a deepening of the voice, menstrual irregularities, an enlargement of the clitoris, and, if the woman is genetically predisposed, male-patterned baldness.

When first starting to use steroids, before any negative effects appear, users often report an increase in libido, a heightened sense of sexuality, and euphoria. But these feelings are offset by the depression that occurs if the athlete goes off the drug. As use continues, larger doses must be taken to achieve the highs that were experienced early on. Psychological and physical dependence follows, accompanied by dramatic emotional highs and lows. The user may experience personality changes, becoming hostile, paranoid, or violent.

Steroid abuse may also have significant effects on the cardiovascular system, leading to atherosclerosis. Increased water retention combined with atherosclerosis causes high blood pressure, another problem experienced by abusers. Liver structure and function are disrupted, but this process stops when steroid use is discontinued. Because steroids are often injected, users are at risk for HIV infection from sharing unclean needles.

Anabolic steroids sold on the "black market" include a wide range of drugs, many approved only for animals. Because there is little or no quality control, users are at extreme risk. Although we know many of the dangers associated with these drugs, it may be years before their full effects on athletes using them now begin to surface.

Adapted from *Health Tips*, a publication of the California Medical Education and Research Foundation, February 1992.

---

amyl nitrate vial and inhaling the vapor. The drug causes engorgement of the blood vessels in the pelvis. It also causes a drop in blood pressure, which may result in feelings of dizziness and giddiness. The most common side effects are severe headaches, fainting, and, because it is flammable, risk of burns.

Another drug widely considered to be an aphrodisiac is cantharides, or "Spanish fly." Derived from a specific beetle, this substance is produced by drying and heating the insects' bodies until they disintegrate into a powder. Taken internally, the substance causes acute irritation and inflammation of the genitourinary tract, including the bladder and urethra. It can result in permanent tissue damage and death.

LSD and other psychedelic drugs (including mescaline and psilocybin) have no positive effects on sexual ability. They may actually cause constant and painful erections, a condition called priapism.

Cocaine, a central nervous system stimulant, reduces inhibitions and enhances feelings of well-being. But regular use nearly always leads to sexual dysfunction, as well as an inability to achieve erection or orgasm (Washton, 1989). The same levels of sexual impairment were found among those who sniffed the drug and those who smoked it as "freebase." Those who injected cocaine experienced the greatest dysfunction.

Yohimbine, a substance derived from the sap of the yohimbre tree of West Africa, is the only substance that has been shown to have a genuine aphrodisiac effect on laboratory animals. It may also enhance sexual desire or performance in some humans, though research is still inconclusive (Morales, Condra, Owen, Surridge, Fenemore, & Harris, 1987; Sondra, Mazo, & Chancellor, 1990).

Aside from the adverse physical effects of drugs themselves, a major negative consequence of substance abuse is that it puts many people at significant risk of acquiring sexually transmitted diseases, including HIV infection (Cottler, Helzer, & Tipp, 1990). Addiction to cocaine, especially in the smokable form known as "crack," has led to the widespread practice of bartering sex for cocaine (Fullilove, Fullilove, Bowser, & Gross, 1990). This practice, as well as the practice of injecting cocaine or heroin, combined with the low rate of condom usage, has led to epidemics of STDs, including AIDS, in some urban areas.

We've explored issues of self-image and sexual well-being as they affect our feelings about beauty, weight, aging, and physical limitations or disabilities. We've covered territory from menopause to cancer, and looked at the effects of alcohol and certain drugs on our sexuality. Our intent is to give you information to assist you in personal health issues and to stimulate thinking about how society deals with certain aspects of sexual health. We encourage you to learn more about your own body and your own sexual functioning. If things don't seem to work right, if you don't feel well, if you have questions, see your physician or other health-care practitioner. If you're not satisfied, get a second opinion. Read about health issues that apply to you and the people you're close to. Because we live in our bodies, we need to appreciate and respect them. By taking care of ourselves physically, we can maximize our pleasures in sexuality and in life.

SUMMARY

Living in Our Bodies: The Quest for Physical Perfection

• Our society is preoccupied with bodily perfection. As a result, eating disorders have become common, especially among young women. Eating disorders reduce a person's health and vigor; are carried out in secrecy; are accompanied by obsessions, depression, anxiety, and guilt; lead to self-absorption and emotional instability; and are characterized by a lack of control. Those with eating disorders may have a history of psychological or sexual abuse in childhood.

• Anorexia nervosa is characterized by an all-controlling desire for thinness. Anorexics, usually female teenagers, are convinced that their bodies are too large, no matter how thin they actually are. Sexual dysfunction often accompanies anorexia. Anorexics diet (and often exercise) obsessively. Anorexia is potentially fatal.

• Bulimia is characterized by episodes of uncontrolled overeating (binge eating), counteracted by purging—vomiting, dieting, exercising excessively, or taking laxatives or diuretics.

• Binge eating disorder is similar to bulimia except that the purging does not occur.

Sexuality and Aging

• Although some physical functions may be slowed by aging, sexual interest, enjoyment, and satisfaction remain high for many older people. Women tend to be more concerned about the loss of attractiveness, whereas men tend to worry about their sexual capacity.

• In their forties, women's fertility begins to decline. Generally, between ages 45 and 55, menopause, the cessation of menstrual periods, occurs. Other physical changes occur, which may or may not present problems. The most common are hot flashes, changes in the vagina, and a gradual loss of bone mass. Hormone replacement therapy (HRT) is sometimes used to treat these symptoms. Women need to weigh the risks and benefits of HRT.

• Men need to understand that slower sexual responses are a normal part of aging and are not related to the ability to give or receive sexual pleasure. About half of men experience some degree of prostate enlargement after age 50. If it is severe, surgery can be performed.

Sexuality and Disability

• A wide range of disabilities and physical limitations can affect sexuality. People with these limitations need support and education so they may enjoy their full sexual potential. Society as a whole needs to be aware of the concerns of the disabled and to allow them the same sexual rights as others.

• Chronic illnesses, such as diabetes, cardiovascular disease, and arthritis, pose special problems for a sexual life. People with these diseases (and their partners) can learn what to expect of themselves sexually and how to best cope with their particular conditions.

Sexuality and Cancer

• Cancer (in its many forms) occurs when cells begin to grow aberrantly. Most cancers form tumors. Benign tumors grow slowly and remain localized. Malignant tumors can spread throughout the body. When malignant cells are released into the blood or lymph system, they begin to grow away from the original tumor; this process is called metastasis.

• Breast cancer strikes 1 in 9 American women by age 85. Although the survival rate is improving, those who survive it may still suffer psychologically. Breast self-examination and mammograms (low-dose X-ray screenings) are the principal methods of detection. Surgical removal of the breast is called mastectomy. Radiation and chemotherapy are also used to fight breast cancer.

• Cervical dysplasia, or cervical intraepithelial neoplasia (CIN), the appearance of certain abnormal cells on the cervix, can be diagnosed by a Pap test. It may then be treated by biopsy, cauterization, cryosurgery, or other surgery. If untreated, it may lead to cervical cancer.

• The most common gynecological cancer that poses a serious threat is uterine cancer; over 99% of these cancers affect the endometrium, the uterine lining. It is treated with surgery (hysterectomy), radiation, or both.

• Hysterectomy is the surgical removal of the uterus. Conditions requiring hysterectomy are (1) when cancerous or precancerous growth cannot be treated otherwise, (2) when noncancerous growths interfere with other organs, (3) when heavy bleeding cannot be otherwise controlled, and (4) when severe infection cannot be otherwise controlled. Other problems may sometimes require hysterectomy. The removal of the ovaries will precipitate menopausal symptoms because the estrogen supply stops.

- Prostate cancer is the most common form of cancer among men. If detected early, it has a high cure rate. Surgery, radiation, hormone therapy, and chemotherapy are possible treatments. If the entire prostate is removed, sterility results, and erectile difficulties may occur.

- Testicular cancer rates are increasing. If caught early, it is curable; if not, it may be deadly. Self-examination is the key to detection; even slight symptoms should be reported at once. Because of lowered fertility following the removal of a testicle, some men experience psychological distress and feelings of inadequacy.

Other Sexual Health Issues

- Toxic shock syndrome (TSS) is a potentially fatal disease caused by Staphylococcus aureus bacteria. Tampons, especially "superabsorbent" ones, can lead to TSS by creating ideal conditions for staph germs to multiply in a menstruating woman's vagina. TSS is easily cured with antibiotics if caught early.

- Endometriosis is the growth of endometrial tissue outside the uterus. It is a major cause of infertility. Symptoms include intense pelvic pain and abnormal menstrual bleeding. Treatment depends on a number of factors. Various hormone treatments and types of surgery are employed.

- Lesbians tend to have poorer health care than heterosexual women, partly because they face hostility from health-care practitioners. Fear of discrimination may keep them from getting early diagnosis of serious diseases, such as breast cancer.

- Prostatitis is the inflammation of the prostate gland. Congestive prostatitis is usually the result of abstention from ejaculation or infrequent ejaculation. Infectious prostatitis is difficult to treat, although antibiotics are prescribed for it; chronic prostatitis is painful and can lead to sexual dysfunctions.

- DES (diethylstilbestrol) is a synthetic estrogen that was widely prescribed between 1941 and 1971 to prevent miscarriages. Women who took DES, and their children,

are subject to various cancers and other problems at a far higher rate than the general population. DES sons and daughters need to be aware of their special health risks and seek treatment accordingly.

Alcohol, Drugs, and Sexuality

- Drugs and alcohol are commonly perceived as enhancers of sexuality, although in reality this is rarely the case. These substances have the effect of disinhibition, activating behaviors that would otherwise be suppressed.

- Some people use alcohol to give themselves permission to be sexual. Some men may use alcohol to justify sexual violence. People under the influence of alcohol or drugs tend to place themselves in risky sexual situations, such as exposing themselves to sexually transmitted diseases.

SUGGESTED READINGS

Journals with articles relevant to sexual health include Journal of the American Medical Association (JAMA), The New England Journal of Medicine, Women and Health, *and the British journal* Lancet.

Greenwood, Sadja. *Menopause, Naturally: Preparing for the Second Half of Life*. Volcano, CA: Volcano Press, 1992. A compassionate and comprehensive guide through menopause by a female physician.

Hepburn, Cuca, and Bonnie Gutierrez. *Alive and Well: A Lesbian Health Guide*. Freedom, CA: Crossing Press, 1988. A comprehensive guide addressing the health needs of lesbians, who are often excluded from sensitive medical care.

Love, Susan. *Dr. Susan Love's Breast Book*. Reading, MA: Addison-Wesley, 1990. Breast care and information on cancer from a leading authority.

Schover, Leslie, and Soren Jensen. *Sexuality and Chronic Illness*. New York: Guilford Press, 1988. How people living with chronic disease can have a healthy sex life.

White, Evelyn C., ed. *The Black Women's Health Book: Speaking for Ourselves*. Seattle, WA: Seal Press, 1990. Addresses issues typically faced by African American women in seeking competent and compassionate health care.

Chapter Fourteen

SEXUAL ENHANCEMENT AND THERAPY

PREVIEW: SELF-QUIZ

1. Normal men and women do not experience erectile or orgasmic difficulties. True or false?

2. Communication and intimacy are important to maintaining sexual functioning in relationships. True or false?

3. Ethnicity affects the definition of what is a sexual problem. True or false?

4. Most sexual difficulties originate from physical problems. True or false?

5. Premature ejaculation is the most difficult sexual problem to treat. True or false?

6. Conflict between partners may lead to the disappearance of sexual desire. True or false?

7. Some sexual problems experienced by gay men and lesbians are the result of psychological conflicts they feel about their homosexuality. True or false?

8. Sexual problems are considered signs of neurosis by most sex therapists. True or false?

9. Evaluating one's performance during sexual activities often leads to improvement. True or false?

10. Smaller proportions of women than men experience arousal difficulties. True or false?

ANSWERS 1. F, 2. T, 3. T, 4. F, 5. F, 6. T, 7. T, 8. F, 9. F, 10. T

Chapter Outline

The quality of our sexuality is intimately connected to the quality of our lives and relationships. Because our sexuality is an integral part of ourselves, it reflects our excitement and boredom, intimacy and distance, emotional well-being and distress, health and illness. As a consequence, our sexual desires and activities ebb and flow. Sometimes they are highly erotic; at other times, they may be boring. Furthermore, many of us who are sexually active may sometimes experience sexual difficulties or problems. A review of 23 studies on sexual problems found that nearly half the men and women reported occasional or frequent lack of desire, problems in arousal or orgasm, and painful intercourse (Spector & Carey, 1990).

The widespread variability in our sexual functioning, however, suggests how "normal" at least occasional sexual difficulties are. Bernie Zilbergeld (1992) writes:

> Sex problems are normal and typical. I know, I know, all of your buddies are functioning perfectly and never have a problem. If you really believe that, I have a nice piece of oceanfront property in Kansas I'd like to talk to you about.

In this chapter, we examine some ways to enhance your sexuality to bring you greater pleasure and intimacy. Then we look at several common sexual problems and their causes. Finally, we see how those problems are treated.

SEXUAL ENHANCEMENT

Sexual enhancement refers to improving the quality of one's sexual relationship. There are a number of sexual-enhancement programs for people who function well sexually, but who nevertheless feel they can improve the quality of their sexual interactions and relationships. The programs generally aim at providing accurate information about sexuality, developing communication skills, fostering positive attitudes, and increasing self-awareness (Cooper, 1985). In some ways, your study of human sexuality examines many of the same cognitive, attitudinal, and communication themes explored in sexual-enrichment programs.

Zilbergeld (1992) suggests that there are six requirements for what he calls "great sex." They form the basis of many sexual-enhancement programs:

1. Accurate information about sexuality, especially your own and your partner's

2. An orientation toward sex based on pleasure, such as arousal, fun, love, and lust, rather than performance and orgasm

3. Being involved in a relationship that allows each person's sexuality to flourish

4. An ability to communicate verbally and nonverbally about sex, feelings, and relationships

5. Being equally assertive and sensitive about your own sexual needs and those of your partner

6. Accepting, understanding, and appreciating differences between partners

Self-Awareness

Being aware of your own sexual needs is often critical to enhancing your sexuality. Because of gender-role stereotypes and negative learning about sexuality, we often lose sight of our own sexual needs.

Sexual stereotypes present us with images of how we are supposed to behave sexually. Images of the "sexually in charge" man and the "sexual, but not too sexual" woman may interfere with our ability to express our own individual sexual feelings, needs, and desires. We follow the scripts and stereotypes we have been socialized to accept, rather than our own unique

sexual enhancement Improvement of the quality of one's sexual relationship.

Good sex involves the ability to communicate nonverbally— through laughter and good times— as well as verbally.

responses. Following these cultural images may impede our ability to have what therapist Carol Ellison calls "good sex." In an essay about intimacy-based sex therapy, Ellison (1985) writes that you will know you are having good sex if you feel good about yourself, your partner, your relationship, and what you're doing. It's good sex if, after a while, you still feel good about yourself, your partner, your relationship, and what you did. Good sex does not necessarily include orgasm or intercourse. It can be kissing, holding, masturbating, oral sex, anal sex, and so on. It can be heterosexual, gay, lesbian, or bisexual.

Zilbergeld (1992) suggests that to fully enjoy our sexuality, we need to explore our "conditions for good sex." There is nothing unusual about requiring conditions for any activity. For a good night's sleep, for example, each of us has certain conditions. We may need absolute quiet, no light, a feather pillow, an open window. Others, however, can sleep during a loud dormitory party, curled up in the corner of a stuffy room. Of conditions for good sex, Zilbergeld writes:

> In a sexual situation, a condition is anything that makes you more relaxed, more comfortable, more confident, more excited, more open to your experience. Put

DISCOVERING YOUR CONDITIONS FOR GOOD SEX

Different individuals report different conditions for good sex. Some common conditions, according to Zilbergeld (1992), include:

- *Feeling intimate with your partner.* This is often important for both men and women, despite stereotypes of men wanting only sex. If the partners are feeling distant from each other, they may need to talk about their feelings before becoming sexual. Emotional distance can take the heart out of sex.

- *Feeling sexually capable.* Generally, this relates to an absence of anxieties about sexual performance. For men, these include anxiety about becoming erect or ejaculating too soon. For women, it includes worry about painful intercourse or lack of orgasm. For both men and women, it includes worry about whether one is a good lover.

- *Feeling trust.* Both men and women may need to know they are emotionally safe with their partner. They need to feel confident that they will not be judged, ridiculed, or talked about.

- *Feeling aroused.* A person does not need to be sexual unless he or she is sexually aroused or excited. Simply because your partner wants to be sexual does not mean that you have to be.

- *Feeling physically and mentally alert.* This condition requires a person not to feel particularly tired, ill, stressed, or preoccupied. It requires one not to be under the influence of excessive alcohol or drugs.

- *Feeling positive about the environment and situation.* A person may need privacy, to be in a place where he or she feels protected from intrusion. Each needs to feel that the other is sexually interested and wants to be sexually involved.

Each individual has his or her own unique conditions for good sex. If you are or have been sexually active, to discover your conditions for good sex, think about the last few times you were sexual and were highly aroused. Compare those times to other times when you were much less aroused (Zilbergeld, 1992). Make a list of the factors that were different between the two.

Put the list away for a few days, then see if there is anything you want to add or change. Reword the list so that each of the conditions is specific. For example, if you wrote "Felt pressured to have sex," rewrite as "Need to feel unpressured." When you rewrite these conditions, you can get a clearer sense of what your conditions for good sex are. If you feel comfortable, you should communicate your needs with your partner.

differently, a condition is something that clears your nervous system of unnecessary clutter, leaving it open to receive and transmit sexual messages in ways that will result in a good time for you.

Intensifying Erotic Pleasure

One of the most significant elements in enhancing one's physical experience of sex is intensifying arousal. Intensifying arousal centers sexual experience on erotic pleasure rather than on sexual performance. This can be done in many ways, some of which are described in this chapter.

You and Your Sexual Well-Being

HOMEWORK EXERCISES

We are often unaware of our body and our erotic responses. Sexual-enhancement programs often give us specific exercises to undertake in privacy. Such "homework" exercises require individuals to make a time commitment to themselves or their partner to carry out homework assignments. Typical assignments include the exercises below. If you feel comfortable with any of the assignments, you might want to try one or more. (For additional exercises for men, see Zilbergeld, 1992; for exercises for women, see Barbach, 1982).

- *Mirror examination*. Use a full-length mirror to examine your body while nude. Use a hand mirror to view your genitals. Look at all your features in an uncritical manner; view yourself with a feeling of acceptance.

- *Body relaxation and exploration*. Take 30 minutes to an hour to fully relax. Begin with a leisurely shower or bath; then, remaining nude, find a comfortable place to touch and explore your body and genitals.

- *Masturbation*. In a relaxed situation, with body oils or lotions to enhance your sensations, explore ways of touching your body and genitals that bring you pleasure. Do this exercise for several sessions without having an orgasm; experience erotic pleasure without orgasm as its goal. If you are about to have an orgasm, decrease stimulation. After several sessions without having an orgasm, continue pleasuring yourself until you have an orgasm.

- *Erotic aids*. **Erotic aids** are devices, such as vibrators and dildos, or oils and lotions, designed to enhance erotic responsiveness. Erotic devices are also called **sex toys,** emphasizing their playfulness. You may wish to try using a sex toy or shower massage as you masturbate, with your partner or by yourself. You may also want to view videos at home or read erotic poetry or stories to yourself or partner (Neidigh & Kinder, 1987).

Many of these exercises can be also done with a partner; each takes turn in erotically exploring the other.

erotic aid or **sex toy**   A device, such as a vibrator or dildo, or a product, such as oils or lotions, designed to enhance erotic responsiveness.

Sexual Arousal   Sexual arousal refers to the physiological responses, fantasies, and desires associated with sexual anticipation and sexual activity. We have different levels of arousal. The first element in increasing sexual arousal is having your conditions for good sex met. A second element in increasing arousal is focusing on the sensations you are experiencing. Once you begin an erotic activity, such as massaging or kissing, do not let yourself be distracted.

Alternatives to Intercourse   Waiting, delays, and obstacles may intensify arousal. This is one of the pleasures of sexual abstinence that may get lost soon after one begins coitus. Lonnie Barbach (1982) suggests that sexually active people may intensify arousal by placing a ban on sexual intercourse for a period of time. If you are gay or lesbian, you may place a comparable ban on your preferred activity. During this time, you may explore other ways of being erotic or sexual. Barbach (1982), JoAnn Loulan (1984), and Zilbergeld (1992) suggest the following activities, among others:

Some individuals and couples use erotic aids such as vibrators, dildos, oils, and lotions to enhance their sexual responsiveness.

- Sit or lie down close to each other. Gaze into each other's eyes to establish an intimate connection. Gently caress each other's face and hair as you continue gazing. Tell each other what fantasies you have about the other.

- Bathe or shower with your partner, soaping his or her body slowly and sensually but not touching the genitals. At another time, you may want to include genital stimulation.

- Give and receive a sensual, erotic massage. Do not touch the genitals, but massage around them teasingly. Use body oils and lotions to increase tactile sensitivity. Later, you may want to include genital stimulation.

- Use your lips, tongue, and mouth to explore your partner's body, especially the neck, ears, nipples, inner thighs, palms, fingers, feet, and toes. Take your time.

- "Dirty dance" together, feeling the curves and textures of your partner's body; put your hands under your partner's clothes, and caress him or her. Kiss and caress each other as you slowly remove each other's clothing. Then hold each other close, kiss and massage each other, explore each other's body with your mouth, tongue, and lips.

SEXUAL DISORDERS AND DYSFUNCTIONS

Sexual disorders and dysfunctions refer to difficulties individuals experience in their sexual functioning. Heterosexuals, gay men, and lesbians experience similar kinds of sexual problems (Margolies, Becher, & Jackson-Brewer, 1988; Nichols, 1987; Reece, 1988).

sexual dysfunction An impaired physiological response that prevents an individual from functioning sexually, such as erectile difficulties or absence of orgasm.

Sexual dysfunctions are generally defined as impaired physiological responses that prevent individuals from functioning sexually, such as erectile difficulties or absence of orgasm. Common sexual dysfunctions among men include erectile dysfunction, the inability to have or maintain erection; premature ejaculation, the inability to delay ejaculation; inhibited ejaculation, the inability to ejaculate; and delayed ejaculation, prolonged delay in ejaculating. Common dysfunctions among women include anorgasmia, the absence of orgasm; vaginismus, the tightening of the vaginal muscles, prohibiting penetration; and dyspareunia, painful intercourse.

Recently, researchers and therapists have become interested in defining and treating sexual disorders as well as dysfunctions. **Sexual disorders** include such problems as hypoactive sexual desire, low or absent sexual desire, and sexual aversion, a consistently phobic response to sexual activities or the idea of such activities. Disorders are similar to sexual dysfunctions insofar as they limit an individual's ability to be sexual. But properly speaking, disorders affect the brain's arousal capabilities rather than physiological responses. Individuals with sexual disorders retain their ability to respond physically; the problem is that they have no desire to be sexual. They have shut down their brains' erotic centers.

sexual disorder An impairment of an individual's sexual responsiveness caused by interference with the brain's arousal capacity.

Sexual Disorders

Hypoactive sexual desire and sexual aversion may be deeply rooted psychological problems; they are difficult to treat (Hawton, Catalan, & Fagg, 1991; Kaplan, 1987; Levine, 1987).

hypoactive sexual desire (HSD) or **inhibited sexual desire** A sexual disorder characterized by low or absent sexual desire.

Hypoactive Sexual Desire **Hypoactive sexual desire (HSD),** or low or absent sexual desire, is a widespread problem. Kaplan (1979) described the characteristics of a person experiencing hypoactive sexual desire, also known as **inhibited sexual desire:**

> [He] behaves as though his sexual circuits have been "shut down." He loses interest in sexual matters, will not pursue sexual gratification, and if a sexual situation presents itself, is not moved to avail himself of the opportunity.

HSD is fairly common to both men and women (Spector & Carey, 1990). One study found that a third of 365 couples ceased having sexual intercourse for long periods; the median time of abstinence was 8 weeks (Edwards & Booth, 1977). Some therapists and psychiatrists state that HSD is the primary complaint of men in therapy (Botwin, 1979).

Hypoactive sexual desire is related to other sexual dysfunctions insofar as it is rooted in anxieties. Sometimes, however, HSD is a means of coping with other sexual dysfunctions that precede it. Kolodny, Masters, and Johnson (1979) observe: "By developing a low interest in sexual activity, the person avoids the unpleasant consequences of sexual failure such as embarrassment, loss of self-esteem, and frustration."

There appear to be a number of causes of HSD (Hawton et al., 1991; Kaplan, 1979). Depression is probably the most common cause. Anger toward the partner also may be significant. Over a period of time, if anger is not resolved, it may develop into resentment or hatred that colors every aspect of the relationship. Most people cannot experience sexual desire for someone with whom they are angry or deeply resentful.

In addition, stress, traumatic marital separation or divorce, loss of work, or forced retirement are frequently associated with HSD. When a person is under stress, energies and resources are directed toward dealing with emotional problems. When the stress ends, the person usually reexperiences his or her sexual desires. Drugs, hormone deficiency, and illness also decrease desire.

Gay men and lesbians may experience hypoactive sexual desire if they are unable to accept their sexual orientation (Margolies et al., 1988; Reece, 1988). Because of HIV and AIDS, some gay men have become especially depressed and have lost their sexual desire (Reece, 1988; Shannon & Woods, 1991).

The treatment for most sexual dysfunctions involves some form of behavior modification, but such therapies do not work well for HSD (Kaplan, 1979; Kolodny, Masters, & Johnson, 1979). Treatment requires psychosexual therapy to gain insight into the underlying motives that inhibit sexual desire.

Sexual Aversion

Sexual aversion is a consistently phobic response to sexual activities or the idea of such activities (Kaplan, 1987). It is often confused with hypoactive desire because avoidance often manifests itself as a lack of interest in sexual matters. Closer examination, however, may show that the lack of desire is a defense against anxiety-causing situations, such as intimacy or touch (Ponticas, 1992).

In cases of sexual aversion, the frequency of intercourse typically falls to once or twice a year (or less). Although it is not uncommon for some people to be uninterested or to dislike various forms of noncoital sexual activity, they nevertheless enjoy (or tolerate) sexual intercourse. A person experiencing sexual aversion, however, feels overwhelming anxieties about *any* kind of sexual contact. A mere kiss, touch, or caress may cause a phobic response out of fear that it might lead to something sexual. Sometimes these responses are internalized, but at other times, they can lead to physical responses such as sweating, nausea, vomiting, or diarrhea. Anticipating sex often provokes greater anxiety than the sexual activity itself.

Sexual aversion often results from severely negative parental attitudes during childhood; sexual trauma, such as rape or sexual abuse; consistent sexual pressure from a long-term partner; and gender identity confusion (Masters et al., 1990). Many cases of sexual aversion appear to be linked to adolescent difficulty with body image or self-esteem. Adolescent boys with gynecomastia (transitory breast enlargement), girls with excessive body or facial hair, and adolescents of both sexes with acne or obesity problems often avoid the sexual experimentation and activity typical for their age.

As with heterosexuals, gay men and lesbians may enjoy certain activities, such as kissing or mutual masturbation, but feel aversive to other activities. For gay men, sexual aversion often focuses on issues of anal eroticism (Reece, 1988). For lesbians, aversion frequently focuses on cunnilingus (Nichols, 1988). Although cunnilingus is often the preferred activity among lesbians for reaching orgasm, as many as 25% rarely or never engage in it (Blumstein & Schwartz, 1983).

sexual aversion A sexual disorder characterized by a consistently phobic response to sexual activities or the idea of such activities.

Male Sexual Dysfunctions

Both males and females may experience desire disorders. They may also experience dyspareunia, painful intercourse, but it is relatively uncommon among men (Lazarus, 1989). Most specifically, male sexual problems focus on the excitement stages of the response cycle: the ability to have or maintain an erection, and premature or delayed ejaculation.

Erectile Dysfunctions

erectile dysfunction A sexual dysfunction characterized by the inability to have or maintain an erection during intercourse. Commonly referred to as impotence.

Erectile dysfunction is the inability to have or maintain an erection during intercourse. (Erectile dysfunctions were previously known as "impotence.") Such dysfunctions are common; it is estimated that nearly half of all adult men have occasional episodes (Sharlip, 1984) and that the percentage increases after age 50 (Tiefger & Melman, 1989). Erectile dysfunctions are divided into primary and secondary dysfunctions. Those men with primary erectile dysfunction have never had an erection, and those with secondary erectile dysfunction have had erections in the past. Secondary erectile dysfunctions are more common than primary dysfunctions and are easier to treat, because they are often situational in origin.

Erectile difficulties may occur because of fatigue, too much alcohol, certain medical conditions, depression, conflict, or a host of other transitory reasons. Despite their common and usually transitory occurrence, erectile difficulties deeply affect a man's masculine self-concept.

Premature Ejaculation

premature ejaculation A sexual dysfunction characterized by the inability to control or delay ejaculation as long as desired, causing distress.

In **premature ejaculation,** a man, with minimal stimulation, is unable to control or delay his ejaculation as long as he wishes, resulting in personal or interpersonal distress. It is estimated that 36–38% of American men experience premature ejaculation (Spector & Carey, 1990). Although it is one of the most common sexual dysfunctions of heterosexual men in sex therapy, women more than men complain of it (Masters & Johnson, 1970). Often, couples are confused, bewildered, and unhappy when the man consistently ejaculates too early. The woman may be sexually dissatisfied, while her partner may feel that she is too demanding. He may also feel considerable guilt and anxiety. They may begin to avoid sexual contact with each other. The man may experience erectile problems because of his anxieties over premature ejaculation; he may withdraw from sex completely.

Inhibited and Delayed Ejaculation

inhibited ejaculation A sexual dysfunction characterized by the male's inability to ejaculate despite an erection and stimulation.

delayed ejaculation A sexual dysfunction characterized by the male's inability to ejaculate easily during intercourse.

In **inhibited ejaculation,** the penis is erect, but the man is unable to ejaculate. Because ejaculation and orgasm are separate phenomena, the man may nevertheless be able to have an orgasm. In mild forms, it occurs with some frequency. About 4–9% of men have experienced this difficulty (Spector & Carey, 1990). In **delayed ejaculation,** the man is not able to ejaculate easily in intercourse; it may take 40 minutes of concentrated thrusting before ejaculation occurs.

Anxiety-provoking situations can interfere with a man's ejaculatory reflex. He may not be able to have an orgasm in certain situations in which he feels guilt or conflict. He may experience orgasm only from masturbation. Often this inhibition is overcome when the situation or partner changes or when the man engages in a fantasy, receives additional stimulation, or is distracted.

Female Sexual Dysfunctions

Most female sexual difficulties center on the orgasmic phase, although occasionally women experience vaginismus during the excitement phase.

Vaginismus In **vaginismus,** the muscles around the vaginal entrance go into involuntary spasmodic contractions, preventing the insertion of the penis. During the nineteenth century, vaginismus was one of the most common complaints among women, who were taught to dread intercourse or to perform it perfunctorily. Today, about 2% of women are estimated to experience vaginismus (Renshaw, 1988). Vaginismus is essentially a conditioned response that reflects fear, anxiety, or pain. It may result from negative attitudes about sexuality, harsh early sexual experiences, sexual abuse or rape, or painful pelvic examinations (Vandeweil, Jaspers, Schultz, & Gal, 1990).

vaginismus   A sexual dysfunction characterized by muscle spasms around the vaginal entrance, preventing the insertion of a penis.

Dyspareunia **Dyspareunia,** painful intercourse, often occurs because a woman is not entirely aroused before her partner attempts intercourse (Lazarus, 1989). About 8–23% of women have reported dyspareunia (Spector & Carey, 1990). Men may attempt intercourse too early, either because they are in a rush or because they mistake lubrication alone as a sign that their partner is ready for intercourse. Sexual inhibitions, a poor relationship with her partner, or hormonal imbalances may contribute to dyspareunia. Women past menopause have decreased vaginal lubrication and lose much of the elasticity of the vagina from a decrease in estrogen production. The use of lubricating jelly or estrogen therapy may help. Vaginitis, endometriosis, or pelvic inflammatory disease may make intercourse painful. If longer stimulation or the use of lubricants does not relieve the dyspareunia, a woman should consult her physician or health-care practitioner to determine the cause.

dyspareunia   A female sexual dysfunction characterized by painful intercourse.

Anorgasmia **Anorgasmia** is the condition of not being orgasmic. (Anorgasmia is also known as orgasmic dysfunction, inorgasmia, and preorgasmia.) It is the most common female dysfunction seen by sex therapists; 18–76% of women in therapy are anorgasmic (Spector & Carey, 1990). (Previously, anorgasmia was known as "frigidity," a pejorative term connoting emotional coldness.) There are several types of anorgasmia.

anorgasmia   A sexual dysfunction characterized by the absence of orgasm.

In *primary anorgasmia,* a woman has never experienced an orgasm. Various studies suggest that approximately 5–10% of American women have never experienced orgasm (Spector & Carey, 1990). In *secondary anorgasmia,* a woman has previously experienced orgasm in sexual intercourse but no longer does so. In *situational anorgasmia,* a woman has had orgasms in certain situations, such as when masturbating, but not when being sexually stimulated by her partner.

Absence of orgasm may occur for any number of reasons, such as lack of effective penile stimulation during intercourse, insufficient manual stimulation of the clitoris by the woman or her partner, or insufficient duration of intercourse. Not being orgasmic, however, does not mean a woman is not sexual; many anorgasmic women rate their sexual experiences positively (Raboch & Raboch, 1992).

PHYSICAL CAUSES OF SEXUAL DYSFUNCTIONS

Most sexual dysfunctions are psychological in origin, but some may have physical or hormonal causes. It is generally believed that 10–20% of sexual dysfunctions are organic (structural) in nature. Organic causes may partially contribute to another 10–15% (Kaplan, 1983; LoPiccolo, 1991). Even individuals whose disorders are organic in origin, however, may develop psychological problems as they try to cope with their difficulties (Krauss et al., 1990).

Our vascular, neurological, and endocrine systems are sensitive to changes and disruptions. As a result, various illnesses may have an adverse effect on our sexuality (Wise, Epstein, & Ross, 1992). Some prescription drugs, such as medication for hypertension or for depression, may affect sexual responsiveness (Buffum, 1992; "Drugs That Cause Sexual Dysfunction," 1992). Chemotherapy and radiation treatment for cancer affect sexual desire and responsiveness (Ofman & Auchincloss, 1992).

Physical Causes in Men

Diabetes and alcoholism are the two leading causes of erectile dysfunctions; together they account for several million cases. Alcoholism is widely associated with sexual dysfunctions (Schiavi, Schreiner-Engle, Mandeli, Schanzer, & Cohen, 1990). Diabetes, which causes impotence in as many as 1 million men, damages blood vessels and nerves, including those within the penis. Other causes of sexual difficulties include lumbar-disc disease and multiple sclerosis, which interfere with the nerve impulses regulating erection (J. Weiss, 1992). Atherosclerosis is another major physical problem causing blockage of the arteries, including the blood flow necessary for erection. Spinal cord injuries may affect erectile abilities (Stein, 1992). Smoking may also contribute to sexual difficulties (Rosen et al., 1991).

Although sexual dysfunctions often reflect or cause disruptions in relationships, if the dysfunction is due to cancer, paraplegia, or diabetes, there may be less relationship strain. If the relationship was stable before the onset of the illness, a couple may have a satisfactory relationship without sexual intercourse. Other forms of sexual interaction may also provide sexual intimacy and pleasure. "When the bond between the mates is love and intimacy," observes Peter Martin (1981), "the loss of sex due to physical illness does not make the marriage an unhappy one." In part this is true because sexual dysfunctions often reflect conflict and discord within a relationship.

Physical Causes in Women

Organic causes are linked to about 5% of anorgasmia cases in women. These include medical conditions such as diabetes and heart disease, hormone deficiencies, and neurological disorders, as well as drug use and alcoholism. Spinal cord injuries may affect sexual responsiveness (Stein, 1992). Multiple sclerosis can decrease vaginal lubrication and sexual response (J. Weiss, 1992).

Dyspareunia may result from an obstructed or thick hymen, clitoral adhesions, a constrictive clitoral hood, or a weak **pubococcygeus,** the pelvic

pubococcygeus A part of the muscular sling stretching from the pubic bone in front to the tailbone in back.

floor muscle surrounding the urethra and, in women, the vagina. Antihistamines used to treat colds and allergies, as well as marijuana, may reduce vaginal lubrication. Endometriosis and ovarian and uterine tumors and cysts may affect a woman's sexual response.

The skin covering the clitoris can become infected. Women who masturbate too vigorously can irritate their clitoris, making intercourse painful. Men can stimulate their partners too roughly, causing soreness in the vagina, urethra, or clitoral area. If their hands are dirty, they may cause a vaginal or urinary tract infection.

Treatment of Physical Problems

Sexual dysfunctions are often a combination of physical and psychological problems (LoPiccolo, 1991). Even people whose disorders are physical may develop psychological or relationship problems as they try to cope with their difficulties (Krauss et al., 1990). Thus, treatment for organically based dysfunctions may need to include psychological counseling.

Coital pain caused by inadequate lubrication and thinning vaginal walls often occurs as a result of decreased estrogen associated with menopause. Lubricants or hormone replacement therapy, discussed in Chapter 13, often resolve the difficulties. There are no other widely used medical treatments for organic female sexual difficulties.

Most medical and surgical treatment for men centers on erectile dysfunctions. Often these problems are due to illnesses or injuries that impair the vascular system, affecting penile vasocongestion. Microsurgery may correct the blood-flow problem, but it is not always successful (Mohr & Beutler, 1990; Puech-Leao, 1992; Weidner, Weiske, Rudnick, Becker, Schroeder-Printzen, & Brahler, 1992).

Medications may also be injected into the penis to dilate the blood vessels (Althof & Turner, 1992). Once the vessels are enlarged, the penis can become engorged with blood, allowing an erection. The man may inject the medication himself a few minutes prior to intercourse. The resulting erection may last as long as 4 hours.

Suction devices may also be used to induce and maintain an erection. A vacuum chamber is placed over the flaccid penis and the air suctioned out, causing blood to be drawn into the penis. When the penis is erect, an elastic ring is placed around the base of the penis to prevent the blood from exiting. The chamber is removed, and the penis stays erect as long as the band is intact.

Erections may also be assisted by implanting a penile prosthesis in the penis and testicles (Gregoire, 1992). There are two types of penile implants. One type consists of a pair of semirigid rods imbedded in the cavernous bodies of the penis. They are relatively easy to implant, but the penis remains permanently semierect. The second type is an inflatable implant that permits the penis to be either erect or flaccid. A pair of inflatable tubes is implanted in the penis' cavernous bodies, a fluid-filled reservoir is inserted near the bladder, and a pump is placed in the scrotum (Figure 14.1). To get an erection, the man or his partner squeezes the scrotal pump, and fluid fills the empty tubes, causing an erection. A release valve is triggered to empty the fluid from the tubes back into the reservoir.

FIGURE 14.1 An inflatable penile prosthesis enables men with physical difficulties to have and maintain erections.

Reservoir

Cylinder

Pump

PSYCHOLOGICAL CAUSES OF SEXUAL DYSFUNCTIONS

Sexual dysfunctions may have their origin in any number of psychological causes. Some dysfunctions originate from immediate causes, others from conflict within the self, and still others from a particular sexual relationship. Gay men and lesbians often have unique issues affecting their sexual functioning.

Immediate Causes

The immediate causes of sexual dysfunctions lie in the current situation, including fatigue, stress, ineffective sexual behavior, and sexual anxieties.

Fatigue and Stress Many dysfunctions have fairly simple causes. Men and women may find themselves physically exhausted from the demands of work or child rearing. They may bring their fatigue into the bedroom in the form of sexual apathy or disinterest. "I'm too tired to make love tonight" may be a truthful description of a person's feelings. What these couples may need is not therapy or counseling but a vacation, relief from their daily routines.

Long-term stress can also contribute to lowered sexual drive and less responsiveness. A man or woman preoccupied with making ends meet, with an unruly child, or with prolonged illness can temporarily lose his or her sexual desire.

Ineffective Sexual Behavior Kaplan (1974) found that a surprising amount of ignorance and misinformation prevents couples from being effectively sexual with each other. Ineffective sexual behavior appears to be especially relevant in explaining why many women do not experience orgasm in sexual interactions. The couple may not be aware of the significance of the clitoris or the necessity for direct stimulation.

Some gay men and lesbians have not learned effective sexual behaviors because they are inexperienced. They have grown up without easily accessible sexual information or positive role models (Reece, 1988).

Sexual Anxieties A number of anxieties, such as performance anxiety, can lead to sexual problems. If a man fails to experience an erection or a woman is not orgasmic, he or she may feel anxious and fearful. The anxiety may block the very response the man or woman desires.

Performance anxieties may give rise to **spectatoring,** the process in which a person becomes a spectator of his or her sexual performance (Masters & Johnson, 1970). When people become spectators of their sexual activities, they critically evaluate and judge whether they are "performing" well or whether they are doing everything "right" for having orgasms. Kaplan (1983) believes spectatoring is involved in most orgasmic dysfunctions.

Performance anxiety may be even more widespread among gay men. Rex Reece (1988) writes: "Many gay men move in a social, sexual milieu where sexual arousal is expected immediately or soon after meeting someone. If response is not rapidly forthcoming, rejection is very likely."

spectatoring The process in which a person becomes a spectator of his or her sexual activities, thereby causing sexual dysfunctions or disorders.

Excessive Need to Please a Partner Another source of anxiety is an excessive need to please a partner (Kaplan, 1974). A man who experiences this anxiety may want a speedy erection to please (or impress) his partner. He may feel he must always delay his orgasm until after his partner's. A woman who experiences this anxiety may want to have an orgasm quickly to please her partner. She may worry that she is not sufficiently attractive to her partner.

Conflict Within the Self

Our religious traditions tend to view sex as inherently dangerous, as lust and fornication. Sexual intercourse within marriage is the only sexual behavior and context endorsed by *all* Christian and Jewish denominations. Premarital intercourse, oral sex, cohabitation, and gay and lesbian relationships are condemned to various degrees. As a consequence, religious background may contribute to sexual problems (Simpson & Ramberg, 1992). And among gay men and lesbians, internalized homophobia, self-hatred because of one's homosexuality, is a major source of conflict traced to a conservative religious upbringing (Nichols, 1988; Reece, 1988).

Guilt and conflict do not usually eliminate a partner's sexual drive; rather, they inhibit the drive and alienate a person from his or her sexuality. A person may come to see sexuality as something bad or "dirty," rather than a force to happily affirm. Sexual expression is forced, Kaplan (1974) writes, "to assume an infinite variety of distorted, inhibited, diverted, sublimated, alienated and variable forms to accommodate the conflict."

Relationship Causes

Sexual problems do not exist in a vacuum, but usually within the context of a relationship. Most frequently, married couples go into therapy because they have a greater investment in the relationship than couples who are dating or living together. Sexual difficulties in a dating or cohabiting relationship often do not rise to the surface. It is often easier for unmarried couples to break up than to change the patterns that contribute to their sexual problems.

If left unresolved, rage, anger, disappointment, and hostility often become a permanent part of couple interaction. Desire discrepancies become sources of conflict rather than acceptance. Underlying fears of rejection or abandonment may help form the relationship structure. But these factors vastly influence the nature and quality of the relationship between partners.

TREATING SEXUAL PROBLEMS

There are several approaches to sex therapy, the most important ones being behavior modification and psychosexual therapy. William Masters and Virginia Johnson were the pioneers in the cognitive-behavioral approach, while the most influential psychosexual therapist is Helen Singer Kaplan. The cognitive-behavioral approach works well with sexual dysfunctions, such as erectile and orgasmic problems. Psychosexual therapy is more effective in treating sexual disorders, such as hypoactive desire and sexual aversion (Atwood & Dershowitz, 1992).

Masters and Johnson: A Cognitive-Behavioral Approach

In this section, we examine the program developed by Masters and Johnson in the treatment of sexual dysfunctions. Their work has been the starting point for contemporary sex therapy. First, not only did they reject the Freudian model of tracing sexual problems to childhood, they relabeled sexual problems as sexual dysfunctions rather than aspects of neuroses. Masters and Johnson (1970) argued that the majority of sexual dysfunctions are the result of sexual ignorance, faulty techniques, or relationship problems. Second, they treated dysfunctions using a combination of cognitive and behavioral techniques. Third, they treated couples rather than individuals. In cases where a partner was unavailable, Masters and Johnson used, as part of their therapeutic team, **sex surrogates,** whose role it was to have sexual interactions with a client.

sex surrogates Sexual partners who assist sexually dysfunctional clients in sex therapy without spouses or other partners.

Dysfunctional Couples Cognitive-behavioral therapists approach the problems of erectile and orgasmic difficulties by dealing with the couple rather than the individual. They regard sexuality as an interpersonal phenomenon rather than an individual one. In fact, they tell their clients that there are no dysfunctional individuals, only dysfunctional couples, and that faulty sexual interaction is at the root of sexual problems. Neither individual is to blame; rather, it is their mutual interaction that sustains a dysfunction.

Treatment lasts 12 days on the average. During this time, couples are seen daily by the therapists. The couple is told not to attempt sexual intercourse until they are given permission by their therapist team, a man and a woman. In this way, each partner is immediately relieved of any pressure to perform, thus easing anxieties and allowing the development of a more relaxed attitude toward sex.

Case Histories The first morning, each individual is interviewed separately by the therapist of the same sex; in the afternoon, the interview is repeated by the therapist of the other sex. The therapists are careful not to assign blame to either partner, for it is the couple, rather than the individual, that is being treated.

After the interviews and the case histories have been taken, the couple meets with both therapists to discuss what has been learned so far. The therapists explain what they have learned about the couple's personal and sexual interaction, encouraging the man and woman to expand or correct what they are saying. Then the therapists discuss the sexual myths and fallacies that the couple holds that may interfere with their sexual interaction.

Sensate Focus At the end of the third day, the therapists introduce **sensate focus,** focusing on touch and the giving and receiving of pleasure. The other senses—smell, sight, hearing, and taste—are worked on indirectly as a means of reinforcing the touch experience. To increase their sensate focus, the couple is given "homework" assignments. In the privacy of their own room, they are to take off their clothes so that nothing will restrict their sensations. One partner must give pleasure and the other receive it. The giver touches, caresses, massages, strokes his or her partner's body everywhere except the genitals and the breasts. The purpose is not sexual arousal but simply sense awareness.

Through the fourth day, therapy is basically the same for any type of sexual dysfunction. Thereafter, the therapists begin to focus on the particular dysfunction affecting the couple.

Treating Male Dysfunctions The therapists use different techniques for treating the specific dysfunction.

Erectile Dysfunctions When dealing with erectile difficulties, the couple is taught that fears and anxieties are largely responsible, and that the removal of these fears is the first step in therapy. Once the fear is removed, the man is less likely to be an observer of his sexuality; he can become an actor rather than a spectator or judge.

After the sensate focus exercises have been integrated into the couple's behavior, they are told to play with each other's genitals, but not to attempt an erection. Often, erections may occur because there is no demand on the man; but he is encouraged to let his penis become soft again, then erect, then soft, as reassurance that he can successfully have erections. This builds his confidence and his partner's by letting her know that she can excite him. During this time, the couple is counseled on other aspects of their relationship that contribute to their sexual difficulties. Then, about the tenth day, the couple attempts their first intercourse, if the man has had erections with some success. Eventually, in the final session, the man will have an orgasm.

sensate focus The focusing on touch and the giving and receiving of pleasure as part of the treatment of sexual difficulties.

CULTURAL/ETHNIC DIFFERENCES AND SEX THERAPY

Sex therapy assumes a Western middle-class model of sexuality. Although this model may be effective in explaining and treating sexual difficulties among white middle-class Americans, it may be ineffective in treating members of other cultures and ethnic groups. As Yoav Lavee (1991) notes, the dominant Western model makes four assumptions about sexuality:

- Sex is primarily a means of exchanging pleasure.
- Both partners are equally involved.
- People need and want information about sex.
- Communication is important for good sexual relationships.

These assumptions about sexuality, however, are not universal. Among non-Western clients, the issues focus on men's obtaining sexual pleasure; there is little concern about women's pleasure. In treating Arab, North African, and Asian Jews in Israel, Lavee (1991) found that his clients were primarily men who complained about erectile difficulties. Premature ejaculation was problematical only when it interfered with the man's pleasure. When both husband and wife were invited to attend therapy, usually only the man attended. Finally, individuals and couples alike resisted suggestions of sensate focus exercises. Even if they did agree to do them, most did not follow through; many dropped out of therapy.

Many issues must be considered when treating members of diverse cultural and ethnic groups. First, there are differing cultural definitions of what is a problem. If the purpose of sex is male pleasure or reproduction, then most female "problems" disappear as long as they do not interfere with sexual intercourse. Low sexual desire and lack of orgasm in women are deemed irrelevant. Vaginismus or painful intercourse are perceived as problems only if they prevent sexual intercourse. These beliefs are consistent with cultural beliefs that women are not supposed to seek or experience sexual pleasure. Female sexual problems in male-centered cultures are usually viewed as reproductive ones, especially infertility.

We do not know whether women's perceptions

Premature Ejaculation Cognitive-behavioral therapists treat premature ejaculation by using initially the same pattern they use in treating erectile dysfunctions. They concentrate especially on reducing fears and anxieties and increasing sensate focus and communication. Then they use a simple exercise called the **squeeze technique** (Figure 14.2). (This technique was developed in the 1950s and remains the most effective treatment to date [St. Lawrence & Madakasira, 1992].) The man is brought manually to a full erection. Just before he is about to ejaculate, his partner squeezes his penis with her thumb and forefinger just below the corona. After 30 seconds of inactivity, she arouses him again and, just before he ejaculates, she squeezes again.

squeeze technique A technique for the treatment of premature ejaculation in which the partner squeezes the man's erect penis below the glans immediately prior to ejaculation.

Inhibited Ejaculation Inhibited ejaculation is treated by having the man's partner manipulate his penis. The partner asks for verbal and physical direction to bring him the most pleasure possible. It may take a few sessions before the man reaches his first orgasm. The idea is to identify his partner with sexual pleasure and desire. He is encouraged to feel stimulated not necessarily support some or all of these cultural views. In male-centered societies, it is difficult for women to speak out. Furthermore, tradition and socialization, as well as the fear of being labeled immoral, lead many women to accept and embrace beliefs that appear highly alien to us.

Another issue that must be considered in treating members of cultural and ethnic groups is that there are different "explanations" about what causes sexual problems. In many rural areas in the world, erectile and infertility problems are blamed on sorcery or supernatural causes, and most cultures have folk remedies to deal with them. Although treatments vary from culture to culture, many have stood the test of time and may be quite effective among those for whom they were formulated.

There are also cultural differences concerning *whom* to consult for problems. If the problem is thought to be caused by supernatural forces, *curanderos*, curers, are called in Latin America to furnish the victim with charms or medicines to ward off the evil. Sometimes priests are called in to pray for deliverance (Lavee, 1991).

Even within American society there is considerable variation about whom to call for treatment. Among individualistic, white, working-class and middle-class American men, no one is called. The man is supposed to solve the problem by himself; talking to others is a sign of weakness (Rubin, 1976). African Americans tend to use the extended family network, although women are more willing than males to initiate therapy (Hines & Boyd-Franklin, 1982). Among Asian Americans, sexual problems are expected to be worked out within the family, especially between the spouses. Traditional Irish Americans and Latinos are more likely to turn to priests (Espín, 1984; McGoldrick, 1982).

Because there is considerable cultural and ethnic variation, Lavee (1991) writes:

> If the client's sexual values are different, we ought to remember that a well-integrated life philosophy, that has proven effective for many generations, stands behind them. It may therefore be easier and wiser to fit the treatment to the client's values than to attempt to "teach" them what healthy sex is.

only by his partner, but also by her erotic responses to him. After the man has reached orgasm through manual stimulation, he then proceeds to vaginal intercourse. With further instruction and feedback, the man is able to function sexually without fear of ejaculatory inhibition.

Treating Female Dysfunctions   Each female dysfunction is treated differently in behavior modification therapy.

Anorgasmia   After the sensate focus sessions, the woman's partner begins to touch and caress her vulva; she guides his hand to show him what she likes. The man is told, however, not to stimulate the clitoris directly because it may be extremely sensitive, and that may cause pain instead of pleasure. Instead, he caresses and stimulates the area around the clitoris, the labia, and the upper thighs. During this time, the couple is told not to attempt orgasm because it would place undue performance pressure on the woman. They are simply to explore the woman's erotic potential and discover what brings her the greatest pleasure.

Vaginismus Vaginismus is one of the easiest sexual dysfunctions to eliminate, using vaginal dilators, plastic penile-shaped rods. The woman uses a set of dilators graduated in diameter. She inserts one before going to bed at night, taking it out in the morning. As soon as the woman is able to receive a dilator of one size without having vaginal spasms, a larger one is used. In most cases, the vaginismus disappears.

Helen Singer Kaplan: Psychosexual Therapy

Helen Singer Kaplan (1974, 1979, 1983) modified Masters and Johnson's behavioral treatment program to include psychosexual therapy. The cognitive-behavioral approach works well for excitement and orgasmic dysfunctions resulting from mild to mid-level sexual anxieties. But if the individual experiences severe anxieties resulting from intense relationship or psychic conflicts, or from childhood sexual abuse or rape, a behavioral approach alone frequently does not work. Such severe anxieties usually manifest themselves in sexual aversion or hypoactive sexual desire.

The role of the therapist in such instances is to provide clients with insight into the origins of the dysfunction. Individuals with desire disorders, for example, often resist behavioral exercises such as sensate focus and pleasuring. They may respond to these exercises with boredom, anxiety, or discomfort; they resist experiencing pleasure. The therapist can intervene by pointing out that they are actively (consciously or unconsciously) creating inhibitions by focusing on negative feelings ("She makes strange sounds"; "His arms are too hairy"), by distracting themselves with thoughts of work or household matters, or by calling up performance fears ("I won't be able to come").

The therapist creates a crisis by confronting individuals with their resistances, then pointing out that they are in control of their resistances and that they can change if they want to. Some individuals will improve as a result of the crisis. Others, however, feel powerless to change. They require

KEGEL EXERCISES

Kegel exercises were originally developed by Dr. Arnold Kegel *(KAY-gul)* to help women with problems controlling urination. They are designed to strengthen and give you voluntary control of a muscle called pubococcygeus *(pew-bo-kawk-SEE-gee-us)*, or P.C. for short. The P.C. muscle is part of the sling of muscle stretching from your pubic bone in front to your tailbone in back. Because the muscle encircles not only the urinary opening but also the outside of the vagina, some of Dr. Kegel's patients discovered a pleasant side effect—increased sexual awareness. (Men may also benefit from doing Kegels!)

Why Do Kegel Exercises?
Learning Kegel exercises:

- Can help you be more aware of feelings in your genital area
- Can increase circulation in the genital area
- May help increase sexual arousal started by other kinds of stimulation
- Can be useful during childbirth to help control the strength and duration of pushing
- Can be helpful after childbirth to restore muscle tone in the vagina

Identifying the P.C. Muscle Sit on the toilet. Spread your legs apart. See if you can stop and start the flow of urine without moving your legs. That's your P.C. muscle, the one that turns the flow on and off. If you don't find it the first time, don't give up; try again the next time you have to urinate.

The Exercises
Slow Kegels Tighten the P.C. muscle as you did to stop the urine. Hold it for a slow count of three. Relax it.

Quick Kegels Tighten and relax the P.C. muscle as rapidly as you can.

Pull in—Push out Pull up the entire pelvic floor as though trying to suck water into your vagina. Then push or bear down as if trying to push the imaginary water out. (This exercise will use a number of "stomach" or "abdominal" muscles as well as the P.C. muscle.)

At first, do ten of each of these exercises (one "set") five times every day. Each week, increase the number of times you do each exercise by five (15, 20, 25, etc.). Keep doing five "sets" each day.

- You can do these exercises any time during daily activities that don't require a lot of moving around: driving your car, watching television, doing dishes, sitting in school or at your desk or lying in bed.
- When you start, you will probably notice that the muscle doesn't want to stay "contracted" during "Slow Kegels" and that you can't do "Quick Kegels" very fast or evenly. Keep at it. In a week or two you will probably notice that you can control it quite well.
- Sometimes the muscle will start to feel a little tired. Not surprising. You probably haven't used it very much before. Take a few seconds' rest and start again.
- A good way to check on how you are doing is to insert one or two lubricated fingers into your vagina.
- Remember to keep breathing naturally and evenly while doing your Kegels!

Kegel exercises A set of exercises designed to strengthen and give voluntary control over the pubococcygeus and to increase sexual pleasure and awareness.

additional psychosexual therapy to gain insight into their disorders. They need to discover and resolve the unconscious roots of their disorders, in order to permit themselves to experience desire once again for their partners.

Other Therapeutic Approaches

Both cognitive-behavioral and psychosexual therapy are expensive and take a considerable amount of time. In response to these limitations, brief sex therapy, self-help, and group therapy have developed.

PLISSIT model A model for sexual therapy consisting of four progressive levels: Permission, Limited Information, Specific Suggestions, and Intensive Therapy.

PLISSIT Model of Therapy

One of the most widespread models used by sex therapists is the **PLISSIT model** (Annon, 1974, 1976). PLISSIT is an acronym for the four progressive levels of sex therapy: Permission, Limited Information, Specific Suggestions, and Intensive Therapy.

The first level in the PLISSIT model is *permission giving*. At one time or another, most sexual behaviors were prohibited by important figures in our lives.

Because desires and activities such as fantasies or masturbation were not validated, we often questioned their "normality" or "morality." We shrouded them in secrecy or covered them with shame. Without permission to be sexual, we may experience sexual disorders and dysfunctions.

Sex therapists act as "permission givers" for us to be sexual. They become authority figures who validate our sexuality by helping us accept our sexual feelings and behaviors. They reassure us and help us clarify our sexual values. They also validate our ability to say no to activities in which we are uncomfortable.

The second level is giving *limited information*. This information is limited to the specific area of difficulties. If a woman is anorgasmic in intercourse, for example, the therapist might explain that not all women are orgasmic in coitus without additional manual stimulation before, during, or after penetration. The therapist might discuss the effects of drugs such as alcohol, marijuana, and cocaine on sexual responsiveness.

The third level is *specific suggestions*. If permission giving and limited information are not sufficient, the therapist next suggests specific "homework" exercises. If a man experiences premature ejaculation, the therapist may suggest that he and his partner try the squeeze technique. An anorgasmic woman might be instructed to masturbate with or without her partner to discover the best way for her partner to assist her to experience orgasm.

The fourth level is *intensive therapy*. If the individual still continues to experience a sexual problem, he or she will need to enter intensive therapy, such as psychosexual therapy.

Self-Help and Group Therapy

Perhaps the first step in dealing with a sexual problem is to turn to your own immediate resources. Begin by discussing the problem with your partner; find out what he or she thinks. Discuss specific strategies that might be useful. Sometimes simply communicating your feelings and thoughts will resolve the difficulty. Seek out friends with whom you can share your feelings and anxieties. Find out what they think. Ask them whether they have had similar experiences, and how they handled them. Try to keep your perspective—and your sense of humor.

SEEKING PROFESSIONAL ASSISTANCE

Because something is not "functioning" according to a therapist's model does not necessarily mean that something is wrong. You need to evaulate your sexuality in terms of your own and your partner's satisfaction and the meanings you give to your sexuality. If, after doing this, you are unable to resolve your sexual difficulties yourself, seek professional assistance. It is important to realize that seeking such assistance is not a sign of personal weakness or failure. Rather, it is a sign of strength, for it demonstrates an ability to reach out and a willingness to change. It is a sign that you care for your partner, your relationship, and yourself. As you think about therapy, consider the following points:

- What are your goals in therapy? Are you willing to make changes in your relationship to achieve your goals?

- Do you want individual, couple, or group therapy? If you are in a relationship, is your partner willing to attend therapy?

- What characteristics are important for you in a therapist? Do you prefer a female or male therapist? Is the therapist's age, religion, or ethnic background important to you?

- What are the therapist's professional qualifications? There are few certified sex therapy programs; most therapists who treat sexual difficulties come from various professional backgrounds, such as psychiatry, clinical psychology, psychoanalysis, marriage and family counseling, and social work. Because there is no licensing in the field of sex therapy, it is important to seek out those trained therapists who have licenses in their generalized field. This way, the patient has recourse if questionable practices arise. It is worth noting that professionals view sexual contact between themselves and the client as unethical and unlawful.

- What is the therapist's approach? Is it behavioral, psychosexual, psychoanalytic, religious, spiritual, feminist, or something else? What is the therapist's attitude toward gender roles? Do you feel comfortable with the approach?

- If necessary, does the therapist offer a sliding scale fee, based on your level of income?

- If you are lesbian or gay, does the therapist affirm your sexual orientation? Does the therapist understand the special problems gays and lesbians face?

- After a session or two with the therapist, do you have confidence in him or her? If not, discuss your feelings with the therapist. If you believe your dissatisfaction is not a defense mechanism, change therapists.

Just how successful is sex therapy? Nobody really knows. Though Masters and Johnson have reported higher success rates than other therapists, some of their methods of evaluating patients have come under attack. What constitutes success or failure is subjective and open to interpretation. Much of therapy's success depends on a person's willingness to confront painful feelings and to change. This entails time, effort, and often considerable amounts of money. But, ultimately, the difficult work may reward you with greater satisfaction and a deeper relationship.

Group therapy may be particularly valuable for providing us with an open, safe forum in which we can discuss our sexual feelings. It is an opportunity to experience and discover that many of our sexual behaviors, fantasies, and problems are very common. The presence of a therapist in these sessions can provide valuable insight and direction. Another benefit of group therapy is that it is often less expensive than most other types of therapy.

It is important for gay men and lesbians with sexual difficulties to choose a therapist who affirms their orientation and understands the special issues confronting them.

Gay and Lesbian Sex Therapy

Until recently, sex therapy treated sexual dysfunctions and disorders as implicitly heterosexual. The model for sexual functioning, in fact, is generally orgasmic heterosexual intercourse. There was virtually no mention of gay or lesbian sexual concerns (Margolies et al., 1988; Reece, 1988).

For gay men and lesbians, sexual issues differ from those of heterosexuals in several ways. First, although gay men and lesbians may have desire, erectile, or orgasmic difficulties, the context in which they occur may differ significantly from that of heterosexuals. Problems among heterosexuals most often focus on sexual intercourse, while gay and lesbian sexual difficulties focus on other behaviors. Gay men in sex therapy, for example, most often experience aversion toward anal eroticism (Reece, 1988). Lesbians in sex therapy frequently complain about aversive feelings toward cunnilingus. Anorgasmia, however, is not frequently viewed as a problem (Margolies et al., 1988). Heterosexual women, by contrast, frequently complain about lack of orgasm.

Second, lesbians and gay men must deal with both societal homophobia and internalized homophobia (Friedman, 1991; Margolies et al., 1988). Fear of violence makes it difficult for gay men and lesbians to openly express their affection in the same manner as heterosexuals. As a consequence, lesbians and gay men learn to repress their expressions of feelings in public; this repression may carry over into private as well. Internalized homophobia may result in diminished sexual desire, creating sexual aversion, and fostering guilt and negative feelings about sexual activity.

Third, gay men must deal with the association between sex and HIV infection that has cut a deadly swath through the gay community. Grieving over the death of friends, lovers, and partners has left many depressed. In turn, this affects their sexual desire and creates high levels of sexual anxiety. Many are fearful of contracting HIV even if they practice safer sex.

And HIV-positive men, even if they are practicing safer sex, are often afraid of transmitting the infection to their loved ones (Friedman, 1991; Rudolph, 1989b; Shannon & Woods, 1991).

These unique lesbian and gay concerns require that sex therapists expand their understanding and treatment of sexual problems. If the therapist is not gay or lesbian, he or she needs to have a thorough knowledge of homosexuality and the gay and lesbian world. Therapists further need to be aware of their own assumptions and feelings about homosexuality. Some therapists continue to believe that homosexuality is morally wrong and convey their beliefs to their clients under the guise of therapy (Coleman, Rosser, & Strapko, 1992). Therapists working with gay or lesbian clients need to develop inclusive models of sexual treatment that are "gay-positive."

As we consider our sexuality, it is important to realize that sexual difficulties and problems are commonplace. But sex is more than orgasms or certain kinds of activities. Even if we have difficulties in some areas, there are other areas in which we may be fully sexual. If we have erectile or orgasmic problems, we can use our imagination to expand our repertoire of erotic activities. We can touch each other sensually, masturbate alone or with our partner, caress, kiss, eroticize and explore our bodies with fingers and tongues. We can enhance our sexuality if we look at sex as the mutual giving and receiving of erotic pleasure, rather than a command performance. By paying attention to our conditions for good sex, maintaining intimacy, and focusing on our erotic sensations and those of our partner, we can transform our sexual relationships.

SUMMARY

Sexual Enhancement

• Many people experience sexual difficulties or problems at one time or another. Nearly half of the men and women in various surveys report occasional or frequent lack of desire, problems in arousal or orgasm, and painful intercourse. The widespread variability of sexual functioning suggests the "normality" of at least occasional sexual difficulties.

• Sexual enhancement refers to improving the quality of one's sexual relationship. Sexual-enhancement programs generally aim at providing accurate information about sexuality, developing communication skills, fostering positive attitudes, and increasing self-awareness. Awareness of your own sexual needs is often critical to enhancing your sexuality. Enhancing sex includes the intensification of arousal.

Sexual Disorders and Dysfunctions

• Sexual dysfunctions are impaired physiological responses. Sexual disorders are problems affecting the brain's arousal capabilities.

• Hypoactive sexual desire (HSD) is low sexual desire. Depression is probably the most common cause. Anger toward the partner, stress, traumatic marital separation or divorce, loss of work, anxiety, and guilt are frequently associated with HSD. Sexual aversion is a consistently phobic response to sexual activities or the idea of such activities.

• Male sexual problems focus on the excitement stage. Erectile dysfunction is the inability to have or maintain an erection during intercourse. Erectile difficulties may occur because of fatigue, too much alcohol, depression, conflict, certain medical conditions, or a host of other transitory reasons.

• Premature ejaculation is the inability to control or delay ejaculation as long as desired, causing personal or interpersonal distress. In inhibited ejaculation, the penis is erect but the man is unable to ejaculate. In delayed ejaculation, the man is not able to ejaculate easily in intercourse.

• In vaginismus, the muscles around the vaginal entrance go into spasmodic contractions. Vaginismus is essentially a conditioned response that reflects fear, anxiety, or pain. Dyspareunia, painful intercourse, often occurs because a woman is not entirely aroused before her partner attempts intercourse. Sexual inhibitions, a poor relationship with her partner, or hormonal imbalances may contribute to dyspareunia.

• Anorgasmia refers to the condition of not being orgasmic. Absence of orgasm may occur from a lack of effective penile stimulation during intercourse, insufficient manual stimulation of the clitoris by the woman or her partner, or insufficient duration of intercourse. Not being orgasmic, however, does not mean a woman is not sexual; many anorgasmic women rate their sexual experiences positively.

Physical Causes of Sexual Dysfunctions

• About 10–20% of sexual dysfunctions are organic (structural); organic problems may contribute to an additional 10–15% of dysfunctions. Diabetes and alcoholism are the two leading causes of erectile dysfunctions. Some prescription drugs affect sexual responsiveness.

• Coital pain caused by inadequate lubrication and thinning vaginal walls often occurs as a result of decreased estrogen associated with menopause. Lubricants or hormone replacement therapy often resolve the difficulties.

• Illnesses or injuries may impair the vascular system, affecting penile vasocongestion. Microsurgery may correct the blood-flow problem, but it is not always successful. Medications may be injected into the penis to dilate the blood vessels. Suction devices may be used to induce and maintain an erection. Erections may also be assisted by implanting a penile prosthesis.

Psychological Causes of Sexual Dysfunctions

• Sexual dysfunctions may have their origin in any number of psychological causes. The immediate causes of sexual dysfunctions lie in the current situation, including fatigue and stress, ineffective sexual behavior, sexual anxieties, and an excessive need to please one's partner. Conflict within the self, including religious teachings, guilt, negative learning, and internalized homophobia can contribute to dysfunctions, as can relationship conflicts.

Treating Sexual Problems

• Masters and Johnson developed a cognitive-behavioral approach to sexual difficulties. They relabeled sexual problems as dysfunctions rather than neuroses or diseases, used direct behavior modification practices, and treated couples rather than individuals. Treatment includes sensate focus exercises without intercourse, different "homework" exercises, and finally, "permission" to engage in sexual intercourse. Kaplan's psychosexual therapy program combines behavioral exercises with insight therapy.

• The PLISSIT model of sex therapy refers to four progressive levels: Permission, Limited Information, Specific Suggestions, and Intensive Therapy. Individuals and couples can often resolve their difficulties by talking over their problems with their partners or friends, reading self-help books, and attending sex therapy groups. If they are unable to resolve their difficulties in these ways, they should consider intensive sex therapy.

• There are three significant concerns for gay men and lesbians in sex therapy. (1) The context in which problems occur may differ significantly from that of heterosexuals, such as issues revolving around anal eroticism and cunnilingus. (2) They must deal with both societal homophobia and internalized homophobia. (3) Gay men must deal with the association between sex and HIV/AIDS.

SUGGESTED READINGS

Barbach, Lonnie. *For Each Other: Sharing Sexual Intimacy.* New York: Doubleday, 1982. A thoughtful book for exploring women's sexuality; includes exercises.

Heiman, Julia, and Joseph LoPiccolo. *Becoming Orgasmic: A Sexual Growth Program for Women.* Englewood Cliffs, NJ: Prentice-Hall, 1988. Suggestions on how to develop one's orgasmic responsiveness.

Leiblum, Sandra, and Raymond Rosen, eds. *Principles and Practice of Sex Therapy: Update for the 1990s.* New York: Guilford Press, 1989. A collection of essays on various aspects of sex therapy designed for professionals.

Zilbergeld, Bernie. *The New Male Sexuality.* New York: Bantam Books, 1992. The most widely recommended book by therapists for men on enhancing sexual relationships. Women can equally profit from it, not only for themselves but also for understanding male sexuality.

Chapter Fifteen

SEXUALLY TRANSMITTED DISEASES

PREVIEW: SELF-QUIZ

1. A person can have a sexually transmitted disease (STD) and not even know it. True or false?

2. By law, physicians must report all cases of sexually transmitted diseases to the Public Health Service. True or false?

3. The most common STD in the United States today is chlamydia. True or false?

4. Because of penicillin, syphilis is no longer considered a major health problem. True or false?

5. About 1 out of every 6 or 7 Americans carries the herpes virus. True or false?

6. A vaccination against hepatitis B is widely available. True or false?

7. In general, men experience more severe consequences of STDs than women do. True or false?

8. You can often tell by looking at someone whether or not he or she is the type to have an STD. True or false?

9. Condoms have been demonstrated to help protect against many STDs, including chlamydia, gonorrhea, syphilis, and HIV/AIDS. True or false?

10. The only foolproof method of preventing STDs is abstinence. True or false?

ANSWERS 1. T, 2. F, 3. T, 4. F, 5. T, 6. T, 7. F, 8. F, 9. T, 10. T

Chapter Outline

The consequences of sexually transmitted diseases (STDs) are felt on both personal and societal levels. Personal costs range from inconvenience and discomfort to severe pain, serious illness, infertility, and even death. STDs, primarily syphilis, gonorrhea, and chlamydia, cause almost one-third of all reproductive deaths of mothers or infants (Grimes, 1986). Society as a whole pays for the damage caused by STDs.

In this chapter and the next one, we discuss the factors that contribute to the "STD epidemic" in this country. We explore the particular issues affecting women and the urban poor. This chapter contains an overview of the incidence, symptoms, and treatment of the principal STDs that affect Americans, with the exception of HIV/AIDS, which is the subject of Chapter 16. Much of this chapter is devoted to the prevention of STDs, including positive health behaviors and safer sex practices.

X-RATED DISEASES: THE PSYCHOLOGICAL IMPACT OF STDS

If you missed school or work because of strep throat or chickenpox, you probably wouldn't mind telling people why you were gone. But if you were absent because of chlamydia or gonorrhea, chances are you would hesitate to reveal the actual nature of your illness. You would probably also think carefully about what and how to tell your girlfriend, boyfriend, wife, or husband.

What accounts for the different emotions we have about an STD versus strep throat? Where do all the fear, hesitation, denial, embarrassment, guilt, shame, and humiliation come from? Why are STDs the only class of illnesses we categorize by their *mode of transmission* rather than by the type of organism that causes them? All these questions stem from a common source: Americans are so ambivalent and anxious about sex that we don't deal with STDs rationally. We pretend we won't get them and ignore them when we do. We lie to ourselves and our partners. And even if we feel *we* wouldn't put someone down or think badly of him or her for having an STD, if we get one ourselves, we feel embarrassed, ashamed, and guilty. We may even feel (or others may tell us) we are being punished by God or fate for being sinful or bad. Meanwhile, our culture continues to extol the attractions of uninhibited sexual activity (during which no one ever uses a condom or contracts a sexually transmitted disease) through movies, music, television programs, and advertising. The great gap between our behavior and our ideals is clearly demonstrated by the widespread occurrence of STDs (Brandt, 1987; Nilsson Schonnesson, 1990).

THE STD EPIDEMIC

Since the late 1950s, STDs have increased dramatically in the United States. In addition to the ambivalence about being sexual that leads to risk taking, there are a number of other reasons for this increase. These factors include changes in society, the particular biological characteristics of the disease organism, and the way in which diseases are spread within groups of people.

Social Factors

The following social trends and cultural factors have all contributed to the spread of STDs:

You and Your Sexual Well-Being

STD ATTITUDE SCALE

This scale was developed by William Yarber, Mohammad Torabi, and C. Harold Veenker to measure the attitudes of young adults in terms of high or low risk for sexually transmitted diseases. Follow the directions, and mark your responses to the statements below. Then calculate your risk as indicated.

Read each statement carefully. Indicate your first reaction by writing the letter that corresponds to your answer.

Key

SA = Strongly Agree	D = Disagree
A = Agree	SD = Strongly Disagree
U = Undecided	

1. How one uses his/her sexuality has nothing to do with STDs.

2. It is easy to use the prevention methods that reduce one's chances of getting an STD.

3. Responsible sex is one of the best ways of reducing the risk of STDs.

4. Getting early medical care is the main key to preventing the harmful effects of STDs.

5. Choosing the right sex partner is important in reducing the risk of getting an STD.

6. A high frequency of STDs should be a concern for all people.

7. People with an STD have a duty to get their sex partners to seek medical treatment.

8. The best way to get a sex partner to STD treatment is to take him/her to the doctor with you.

9. Changing one's sex habits is necessary once the presence of an STD is known.

10. I would dislike having to follow the medical steps for treating an STD.

11. If I were sexually active, I would feel uneasy doing things before and after sex to prevent getting an STD.

12. If I were sexually active, it would be insulting if a sex partner suggested we use a condom to avoid getting an STD.

13. I dislike talking about STDs with my peers.

---

prophylaxis Protection from disease.

- Changes in sexual mores have led to the widespread acceptance of sexual activity outside of marriage, for both women and men.

- Beginning in the 1960s with the advent of the pill and IUD, condom use declined dramatically, removing a very effective method of **prophylaxis,** or protection, from mainstream use. Condom use began to increase, however, in recent years because of the serious nature of AIDS. Still, it is obvious from the prevalence of STDs today that a large portion of the population remains unconvinced about the efficacy of condoms in STD prevention (Cates & Stone, 1992).

- Educational efforts regarding STDs (and sexuality in general) are often

14. I would be uncertain about going to the doctor unless I was sure I really had an STD.

15. I would feel that I should take my sex partner with me to a clinic if I thought I had an STD.

16. It would be embarrassing to discuss STD with one's partner if one were sexually active.

17. If I were to have sex, the chance of getting an STD makes me uneasy about having sex with more than one partner.

18. I like the idea of sexual abstinence (not having sex) as the best way of avoiding STDs.

19. If I had an STD, I would cooperate with public-health people to find the source of my infection.

20. If I had an STD, I would avoid exposing others while I was being treated.

21. I would have regular STD checkups if I were having sex with more than one partner.

22. I intend to look for STD signs before deciding to have sex with anyone.

23. I will limit my sexual activity to just one partner because of the chances of getting an STD.

24. I will avoid sexual contact anytime I think there is even a slight chance of getting an STD.

25. The chance of getting an STD would not stop me from having sex.

26. If I had a chance, I would support community efforts toward controlling STDs.

27. I would be willing to work with others to make people aware of STD problems in my town.

Scoring
Calculate points as follows: Items 1, 10–14, 16, and 25: Strongly Agree = 5, Agree = 4, Undecided = 3, Disagree = 2, Strongly Disagree = 1. Items 2–9, 15, 17–24, 26, and 27: Strongly Agree = 1, Agree = 2, Undecided = 3, Disagree = 4, Strongly Disagree = 5.

The higher the score, the stronger the attitude that predisposes a person toward risky sexual behaviors. You may also calculate your points within three subscales: items 1–9 represent the "belief subscale," items 10–18 the "feeling subscale," and items 19–27 the "intention to act" subscale.

Source: Adapted from Yarber, Torabi, & Veenker, 1989.

hampered by vocal minorities who feel that knowledge about sex is what causes people to engage in it.

- The confusion of moral and medical issues also hampers funding for research and treatment of illnesses that are seen as somehow "deserved." For example, significant funding for AIDS research did not begin until it was clear that heterosexuals as well as gay men were threatened (Altman, 1985; Shilts, 1987).

- The health-care system cannot meet our needs. STDs are rampant in low-income urban areas where health services are limited and health-care workers may not be responsive to the community's needs. Racism,

THE HEALTH BELIEF MODEL

Although we are aware of STDs and their consequences, many of us do not take steps to prevent them unless we perceive the disease as a specific threat to ourselves. The **health belief model** helps explain the psychology behind our sexual health behaviors (Darrow & Siegel, 1990; Rosenstock, 1974). According to this model, four factors must be present in order for an individual to take action to avoid a disease:

1. The person must believe that he or she is personally susceptible to it.

2. The individual must believe that the disease would have at least a moderately severe effect on his or her life.

3. He or she must believe that taking a particular action will reduce the susceptibility to or the severity of the disease.

4. He or she must believe that the costs of prevention (or treatment) are worth the benefits.

Let's take a closer look at each of these factors.

Susceptibility

People tend to underestimate their risk of getting STDs. They may not understand that the risk of STD infection goes up exponentially with each new sex partner. This is because when we have sex with someone, we are potentially in contact with all the sexually transmittable organisms of every person our partner has ever had sex with, which include (potentially) all the organisms of those with whom each of our partner's former partners have had sex, and so on. Furthermore, people persist in believing that they can distinguish a person who has an STD simply by looking at her or him (Balshem, Oxman, Van Rooven, & Girod, 1992).

Severity

In the "Age of AIDS," we can hardly afford to be blasé about the consequences of getting an STD. Moreover, the consequences (especially for women) of STDs such as chlamydia, gonorrhea, and genital warts may be painful, expensive, and heartbreaking, even if they are not usually life-threatening.

Appropriate Action

Knowledge about ways to prevent, recognize, and treat STDs enables us to act in ways that benefit our health. For example, we are more likely to use a condom if we believe it will actually help us avoid getting an STD. If we don't understand how condoms work or if we are unaware of their proven effectiveness, we may not use them or may use them only grudgingly at our partner's insistence.

Benefits Versus Costs

People may not act to prevent STDs because they perceive the costs as being too high. The costs could include the embarrassment of talking to a partner about STDs, the actual monetary expense of treatment, the inconvenience of buying or putting on a condom, or the change of lifestyle from many partners to a single, monogamous relationship. A person has to determine if these kinds of costs are worth the benefits of preventive action or treatment, such as feeling healthy, being pain-free, not having to worry about getting infected, and not passing an STD to a partner.

---

health belief model A health behavior model arguing that four factors must be present for an individual to take action to avoid a disease: belief in personal susceptibility, belief that the disease would have at least a moderately severe effect on one's life, belief that taking a particular action will reduce the susceptibility to or the severity of the disease, and belief that the costs of prevention or treatment are worth the benefits.

Social factors contributing to the spread of STDs include acceptance of sexual activity outside of marriage and the excessive consumption of alcohol.

or at least an insensitivity to ethnic issues, may be partly responsible. Funds for public-health programs—to provide education, diagnosis, treatment, partner tracing, and follow-up—are limited, to say the least. Health-care agencies often find themselves vying with one another for funding.

- Alcohol and drug abuse contribute indirectly to the spread of STDs by impairing people's ability to make rational decisions about sexual conduct (Hibbs & Gunn, 1991; Romanowski & Piper, 1988).

Biological Factors

The characteristics of certain organisms and the diseases they produce also contribute to STD transmission (Alexander, 1992).

- Many STDs are **asymptomatic;** they produce no symptoms, especially in the first stages. A person may have an STD and infect others without knowing that he or she is affected.

- Because resistant strains of viruses, bacteria, and other pathogens are continuously developing, antibiotics that have worked in the past may no longer be effective. Infected people may continue to transmit the disease, either because they believe they have been cured or because they were asymptomatic to begin with. The clinician or the patient may underrate the value of a follow-up examination to ensure that the initial treatment has worked, or to try an alternative medication if necessary.

- Some STDs, such as herpes, genital warts, and HIV, cannot be cured. A person who carries any of these viruses is always theoretically able to transmit them to others.

asymptomatic Without symptoms.

FIGURE 15.1 Estimated number of new cases of the principal STDs occurring in the United States, 1993. These numbers are complicated by several issues, including substantial underreporting of diseases and the fact that viral infections are incurable and therefore ongoing. If all cases (not just new cases) of genital warts, herpes, and hepatitis B were included here, the graph would change substantially. Trichomonas is not considered a primary STD by some health officials since it may be transmitted without sexual contact. It is included here to demonstrate its impact in this country and because its primary mode of transmission is through sexual contact. Trichomonas affects up to 8 million Americans per year.

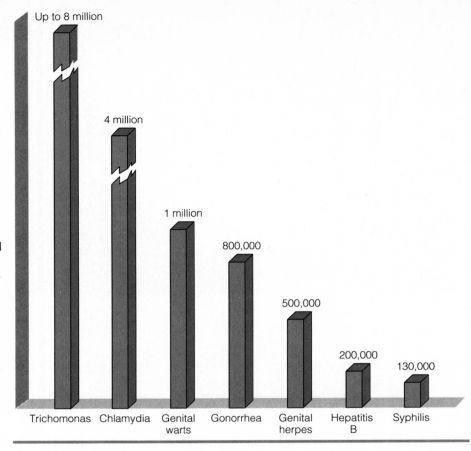

STD Incidence and Prevalence

incidence   Number of new cases of a disease within a specified time, usually 1 year.

The **incidence,** or number of new cases, of STDs occurring each year in this country is estimated to be between 12 and 13 million. Three million of these cases occur among teenagers (CDC, 1994a) (Figure 15.1). Two-thirds of STD cases occur in persons under 25 years of age (CDC, 1994a). Based on reports of publicly funded clinics and private practitioners, public-health officials can only estimate the number of STD cases. Reporting regulations vary. For example, reports of syphilis are thought to be the most accurate because of the strict laws regarding both screening (testing) and reporting. Gonorrhea reporting, however, is less complete. Although public clinics are required to report gonorrhea cases, private physicians are not, and many, in fact, do not (Moran, Aral, Jenkins, Peterman, & Alexander, 1989). Therefore, officials must calculate the numbers as best they can. The same is true for other STDs. Furthermore, a large number of STD cases may go entirely undiagnosed because there are no symptoms or symptoms are ignored and untreated, especially among people with limited access to health care. It is quite likely that the **prevalence,** or total number of cases, of STDs is greater rather than smaller than the current estimates. This can be seen when the incidence of new cases is added to those that have already been diagnosed but cannot be cured, as is the case with the viral STDs.

prevalence   Overall occurrence; the total number of cases of a disease.

A MESSAGE TO THE YOUNG AND SEXUALLY ACTIVE

If you are between the ages of 15 and 25 and are sexually active, you are the potential victim of a sexually transmitted disease. Some sobering statistics underscore this fact (CDC, 1994a):

- Teenage girls have the highest rates of gonorrhea in the nation (10% of sexually active girls have it). Teenage boys rank second.

- The rate of gonorrhea is 20 times higher in adolescent girls than in women over 30.

- Nationwide, 1 in 4 sexually active adolescents will become infected with an STD by the age of 19.

- STD infections boost the risk of contracting HIV, becoming infertile, or giving birth to babies with health problems.

- About 1 in 5 reported AIDS cases is diagnosed among people in their 20s. Because the virus has a long incubation period—about 10 years—most people were adolescents when they were infected.

- Many STDs act together with HIV to enhance the transmission of both. Having an STD increases the chance of contracting HIV from an infected partner by as much as 100 times.

Because young people are generally more promiscuous, less likely to use condoms, less likely to see a physician, and, among females, more biologically prone to an STD, they stand to suffer the greatest consequences.

The above statistics are not only startling, they are disturbing in light of the vast number and variety of AIDS and safer sex programs and materials that are currently available.

What can we as individuals do? Protect ourselves, arm ourselves with education, share the message with others, and support legislation and policy that protect the population from sexually transmitted diseases.

The stakes are too high to do anything less.

Adapted from "Young, Active and Infected," *SF Chronicle*, October 31, 1994.

PRINCIPAL STDS

The following STDs are discussed in order of their estimated prevalence, although the actual numbers may be higher because of unreported or untreated cases. This is particularly true for the viruses that cannot be cured.

Chlamydia

The most common STD in the United States, affecting up to 4 million people each year, is caused by an organism called *Chlamydia trachomatis*, commonly known as **chlamydia,** which has properties of both a bacterium and a virus (CDC, 1994a). It affects the urinary tract and reproductive organs of both women and men. Chlamydia has been responsible for hundreds of thousands of cases of pelvic inflammatory disease (PID), a leading cause of infertility and ectopic pregnancy (Washington, Cates, & Zaidi, 1984). (PID is discussed later in this chapter.) Also, untreated chlamydia can be quite painful and can lead to conditions requiring hospitalization, including acute arthritis. Infants of mothers infected with chlamydia may develop dangerous eye, ear, and lung infections.

chlamydia An STD caused by the *Chlamydia trachomatis* organism. Also known as chlamydial infection.

About 80% of women with chlamydia show no symptoms until serious complications have arisen (Ault & Faro, 1993; Keim, Woodard, & Anderson, 1992). When early symptoms do occur, they are likely to include:

- Unusual vaginal discharge
- Burning sensation when urinating and frequent urination
- Unexplained vaginal bleeding between menstrual periods (Krettek, Arkin, Chaisilwattana, & Monif, 1993)

Later symptoms, occurring up to several months after exposure, are:

- Low abdominal pain
- Bleeding between menstrual periods
- Low-grade fever

One-third to one-half of men are asymptomatic when first infected. Men's symptoms may include:

- Unusual discharge from the penis
- Burning sensation when urinating
- Itching and burning around the urethral opening (urethritis)
- Pain and swelling of the testicles
- Low-grade fever

epididymitis Inflammation of the epididymis.

The last two symptoms may indicate the presence of chlamydia-related **epididymitis,** inflammation of the epididymis. Untreated epididymitis can lead to infertility. For both women and men, early symptoms will appear 7–21 days after exposure, if they appear at all. Chlamydia responds well to antibiotic therapy, generally with doxycycline.

In many instances, chlamydia is not detected unless the affected person is tested for it in the process of being treated for something else, or unless he or she has been named as a partner, or "contact," of someone diagnosed with chlamydial infection (Zimmerman et al., 1990). Because so many people with chlamydial infections are asymptomatic, it is a sound health practice for those who are sexually active—especially if they have numerous partners—to be checked for it regularly (every 3–6 months).

Genital Warts

genital warts An STD caused by the human papilloma virus (HPV).

human papilloma virus (HPV) The virus that causes genital warts.

About one-half to 1 million Americans develop **genital warts** every year (CDC, 1994a). One study conducted at a university revealed that nearly half of the women students had contracted **human papilloma virus (HPV),** the virus responsible for those warts (Blakeslee, 1992). The virus is transmitted through direct contact with the warts, which are highly contagious. Many cases may be passed along by people who are asymptomatic or haven't noticed the warts. Studies of people with genital warts show that HPV is correlated with earlier onset of sexual activity, more sexual partners, and less regular contraceptive use than among controls (Schneider, Sawada, Gissman, & Shaw, 1987). HPV has been shown to be linked with cervical dysplasia and cervical cancer in a number of studies (Crum et al., 1984;

Reeves et al., 1989). Therefore, any woman with a history of genital warts should have an annual Pap smear. The virus has also been found in cancers of other organs, including the penis and anus (Rando, 1988; Amschler, 1991).

Genital warts usually appear within 3 months of exposure. They generally range in size from a pencil point to a quarter of an inch in diameter. They may be flat, bumpy, round, or smooth; white, gray, pink, or brown. Some look like miniature cauliflowers, others like tiny fingers. In men, genital warts usually develop on the shaft or glans of the penis or around the anus. In women, they are found on the cervix, vaginal wall, vulva, or anus. Warts inside the cervix, vagina, or rectum are difficult to detect without examination. The virus can be transmitted from an infected pregnant mother to her baby during vaginal delivery if warts are present on the cervix or in the vagina. For reasons that are not yet understood, genital warts proliferate during pregnancy and regress after delivery. The warts are removed by freezing (cryosurgery), laser therapy, cutting, or a chemical solution such as podophyllin. Removal of the warts is done for cosmetic reasons or for comfort; it does not eliminate HPV from the person's system. The extent to which a person can still transmit HPV after the visible warts have been removed is unknown. In 80% of cases, the warts eventually reappear (Hatcher et al., 1990). If symptoms are present, a condom may help to prevent transmission.

Gonorrhea

Affecting approximately 800,000 Americans yearly (CDC, 1994a) is **gonorrhea,** popularly referred to as "the clap" or "drip." It is caused by the *Neisseria gonorrhoeae* bacterium, which thrives in the warm, moist environment provided by the mucous membranes lining the mouth, throat, vagina, cervix, urethra, and rectum. Symptoms of gonorrhea, if they occur, appear within 2–21 days after exposure. Men tend to experience the symptoms of gonorrhea more readily than women, notably as a watery discharge ("drip") from the penis, the first sign of urethritis. ("Gonorrhea" is from the Greek, meaning "flow of seed.") Other symptoms in men may include:

- Itching or burning at the urethral opening
- Pain when urinating

If untreated, the disease soon produces these other symptoms:

- Thick yellow or greenish discharge
- Increasing discomfort or pain with urination

Although most men seek treatment by this stage, some do not. Even if the symptoms diminish, the bacteria are still present. Those who do not get treatment can still infect their partners and may develop serious complications, such as abscesses of the prostate gland and epididymitis.

About 50–80% of women with gonorrhea show no symptoms or very mild symptoms, which many tend to ignore (Hook & Holmes, 1985). Because untreated gonorrhea, like untreated chlamydia, can lead to PID, it is important for a woman to be on guard for symptoms and to be treated if

Genital warts appear in a variety of forms. In women, genital warts may appear on the vaginal wall.

gonorrhea An STD caused by the *Neisseria gonorrhoeae* bacterium.

Gonorrhea infection in men is often characterized by a discharge from the penis.

she thinks she may have been exposed to gonorrhea (if she has had multiple sex partners, for example). Symptoms a woman may experience include:

- Thick yellow or white vaginal discharge
- Burning sensation when urinating
- Unusual pain during menstruation
- Severe lower abdominal pain

Gonorrhea may be passed to an infant during childbirth, causing conjunctivitis (an eye infection) and even blindness if not treated. (Most states require that all newborn infants have their eyes treated with antibiotics in the event that they may have been exposed to gonorrhea in the birth canal.) Penicillin and related antibiotics are effective against most strains of gonorrhea; tetracycline may be used in the case of allergy to penicillin. Because *N. gonorrhoeae* can evolve rapidly into penicillin-resistant strains, a variety of antibiotics may need to be tried before the infection is eliminated. It is not uncommon for a person to have gonorrhea and chlamydia at the same time. Like chlamydia, once it is treated, it can recur if a person is reexposed to it.

Genital Herpes

genital herpes An STD caused by the herpes simplex virus (HSV).

herpes simplex virus (HSV) The virus that causes genital herpes.

Genital herpes, caused by the **herpes simplex virus (HSV),** is carried by an estimated 31 million Americans. The number of cases are increasing by approximately 200,000–500,000 each year (CDC, 1994a). HSV exists in two strains: HSV type 1, which is usually responsible for cold sores and fever blisters around the mouth; and HSV type 2, which is usually associated with genital lesions. Both types of HSV, however, can and do develop equally well on the mouth or genitals (Buchman et al., 1980). Serious complications from HSV are rare in adults but may result if the individual's general health is not good or the immune system is depressed. In women there appears to be some association between HSV and CIN or cervical cancer (Hatcher et al., 1990), although the nature of the connection is debated (Franco, 1991). Newborns may contract HSV if they come into contact with active lesions during birth. This may result in infections of the eyes, skin, or mucous membranes; infections of the central nervous system; or even death.

For many people with HSV, the initial infection is the most severe. Sometimes it is the only outbreak a person experiences. Within 3–20 days after exposure, small bumps called vesicles or papules appear on the genitals: penis, anus, perineum, vulva, or within the vagina. The papules may itch at first; they then form blisters or pustules that rupture, forming small, often painful, ulcers. These sores may be further irritated by tight clothing, moisture, or urine. In addition, an affected person may experience:

- Swollen lymph nodes in the groin
- Flulike symptoms

Women may develop herpes lesions on the vulva, perineum, anus, or within the vagina.

The first outbreak lasts an average of 12 days. Subsequent outbreaks last an average of 5 days. They may begin with feelings of itchiness or tingling at the site where the lesions will appear. Just prior to the outbreak is a period of a few days known as the **prodrome.** During this time, and while there are actual lesions, the virus is active; live viruses are shed from the affected areas and are spread upon contact. Some people with HSV may shed the virus without experiencing symptoms (Maccato & Kaufman, 1992; Mertz, Benedetti, Ashley, Selke, & Corey, 1992). People who experience recurrent herpes outbreaks note they are often preceded by stress, fatigue, overexposure to cold or sun, or certain foods, such as nuts or citrus fruits.

Managing HSV The antiviral drug acyclovir (brand name Zovirax) is often helpful in reducing or suppressing HSV symptoms (Goldberg, Kaufman, Kurtz, Conant, & Eron, 1993). It can be administered either orally (as a pill) or topically (as an ointment). Acyclovir is especially effective during initial infections, but some people with recurrent episodes find taking the oral medication helpful, either at a low "maintenance" dosage to ward off outbreaks, or at a higher dosage when they feel an outbreak coming on (American Social Health Association, 1992). Other methods reported to be useful in preventing, shortening, or lessening the severity of recurrent outbreaks are:

- *Plenty of rest.* This allows the immune system to work at its best capacity
- *A balanced diet.* This also fosters a healthy immune system. Observing foods that appear to trigger outbreaks may be helpful.
- *L-lysine.* The amino acid L-lysine, taken orally, is reportedly helpful to a number of people.
- *No tight clothes.* Tight jeans, tight or nylon underwear, and nylon pantyhose create an ideal, warm, moist environment for HSV. Loose-fitting, cotton clothing is preferable.
- *Keeping the area cool and dry.* If lesions do appear, an icepack may provide temporary relief. Baby powder or cornstarch may be used to absorb moisture.
- *Aspirin or other pain relievers.* These may be helpful to relieve the discomfort that is associated with an outbreak.

Reasonable Precautions HSV can be spread by hand—to another person, or even to a different location on one's own body. A person experiencing an outbreak should wash his or her hands frequently with soap. Caution should also be taken not to touch one's eyes (or another's) if one has touched a lesion. Serious eye infection may result. Pregnant women or their partners who have HSV should be sure to discuss precautionary procedures with their medical practitioners. Use of a condom reduces the chance of infection.

Hepatitis

Hepatitis is a viral disease affecting the liver. The most common types of the virus that can be sexually transmitted are hepatitis A and hepatitis B. A third type, hepatitis C, is a common virus passed via the bloodstream, but may also be transmitted by sexual contact with an infected person. Hepatitis A is most often contracted through unsanitary conditions, in contaminated food or water. It is believed to be transmitted sexually mainly via infected fecal matter—for example, during oral-anal sex ("rimming") or anal intercourse. Immune serum globulin injections provide some immunity to hepatitis A. Although the symptoms of hepatitis A are similar to those of hepatitis B, the disease is not considered as dangerous. Affected individuals usually recover within 6 weeks and develop immunity against reinfection. Hepatitis B is commonly spread through sexual contact, in blood, semen, saliva, vaginal secretions, and urine. It can also be contracted by using contaminated needles and syringes, including those used in ear piercing, acupuncture, and tattooing, or by sharing the toothbrush or razor of an infected person. It affects an estimated 200,000 Americans annually (CDC, 1994a). Though most are unaware of its presence, an estimated 1.5 million people in the United States are chronic carriers of the virus. The incidence of hepatitis B is declining among gay men (probably due to safer sex practices) and increasing among heterosexuals.

The symptoms of hepatitis include:

- Fatigue

- Diarrhea

- Nausea

- Abdominal pain

- Jaundice, or yellowing of the whites of the eyes or skin (caused by accumulating blood pigments not destroyed by the liver)

- Darkened urine

- Enlarged liver

There is no medical treatment for hepatitis. Rest and fluids are recommended until the disease runs its course, generally in a few weeks. Occasionally, serious liver damage or death results.

Hepatitis B can be prevented by a simple, widely available vaccination. Many health authorities recommend routine vaccination for those most at risk, including people with more than one sexual partner, teenagers, gay men, IV drug users, and health-care workers who come into contact with blood. Relatively few people, however, take advantage of the hepatitis B vaccine. Screening for hepatitis B is also recommended for pregnant women so that their newborns can be immediately vaccinated if necessary.

Syphilis

syphilis An STD caused by the *Treponema pallidum* bacterium.

When **syphilis** first appeared in Europe in the late 1490s, its early manifestations were considerably more horrible than they appear today. Whether syphilis was introduced to Europe from the New World by Spanish explorers or from Africa by those who plied the slave trade is debated by historians. Its legacy of suffering, however, is debated by no one.

spirochete A spiral-shaped bacterium.

T. pallidum is a spiral-shaped bacterium (a **spirochete**) that requires a warm, moist environment, such as the genitals or the mucous membranes inside the mouth, to survive. It is spread through vaginal, anal, and oral sexual contact. A mother infected with syphilis can pass it to the fetus through the placenta. Because neonatal syphilis can lead to brain damage and death, it is imperative for pregnant women to be screened for it within the first trimester. If they are treated during this period, the newborn will not be affected. Untreated syphilis in adults may lead to brain damage, heart disease, blindness, or death.

Beginning in the 1980s, the number of cases of syphilis began increasing dramatically, especially within inner cities. In 1990, the syphilis rate was the highest it had been since 1953; it has continued to climb an estimated 100,000–110,000 cases annually (CDC, 1994a). The current epidemic appears to be concentrated mainly in young, heterosexual, minority populations.

The course of syphilis as it appears today progresses through four discrete stages, although it is most often treated during the first two. The earliest stage is referred to as primary syphilis. The first symptom appears 1–12 weeks after contact with an infected partner. It is a small, red, pea-sized bump that soon develops into a round, painless sore called a **chancre** (*SHANK-er*). The chancre may be covered by a crusty scab; it may be hard around the edges and ringed by a pink border. It appears at the site where the bacteria initially entered the body, usually within the vagina or on the cervix in women, or on the glans of the penis in men. The chancre may also appear on the labia, the shaft of the penis, the testicles, rectum, within the mouth, or on the lips. Unless it is in a visible area, it may not be noticed. Without treatment, it will disappear in 1–5 weeks, but the bacteria remain in the body, and the person is still highly contagious.

Untreated primary syphilis develops into secondary syphilis about 6 weeks after the chancre has disappeared. The principal symptom at this stage is a skin rash that neither itches nor hurts. The rash is likely to occur on the palms of the hands and the soles of the feet, as well as on other areas of the body. The individual may also experience flulike symptoms. The rash or other symptoms may be very mild or may pass unnoticed. The skin rash is swarming with spirochetes and the person is highly contagious.

If secondary syphilis is not treated, the symptoms disappear within 2–6 weeks, beginning the latent stage. The infected person may feel no further symptoms for years, or perhaps will never experience any. Or he or she may have symptoms that are vague or difficult to diagnose without a blood test to screen for *T. pallidum*. After about a year, the bacteria can no longer be spread to sexual partners, although a pregnant women can still transmit the disease to the fetus.

In the United States, syphilis is rarely seen in its tertiary stage because treatment usually prevents the disease from progressing that far. The symptoms of tertiary syphilis may appear years after the initial infection. Because the bacterium travels in the bloodstream, it can potentially affect every organ in the body. Possible effects include:

- Gummas (large ulcers) within the muscles, liver, lungs, eyes, or endocrine glands

- Heart disease

- Neurosyphilis (leading to "general paralysis" or "paresis") involving the brain and spinal cord, and leading to muscular paralysis, psychosis, and death

In the primary, secondary, and early latent stages, syphilis is easily treated with penicillin (Goldmeier & Hay, 1993). Later stages may require additional injections. Other antibiotics can be used if the infected person is allergic to penicillin.

The first symptom of syphilis is a red, pea-sized bump called a chancre at the site where the bacteria originally entered the body.

chancre   A round, pea-sized, painless sore symptomatic of the first stage of syphilis.

Urinary Tract Infections (NGU/NSU)

Both women and men are subject to sexually transmitted infections of the urinary tract. Most of these infections are caused by either C. *trachomatis* (chlamydia) or N. *gonorrhoeae* (gonorrhea), but others are caused by different organisms, such as *Ureaplasma urealyticum*. These urinary tract infections are sometimes referred to as **nongonococcal urethritis (NGU)** or **nonspecific urethritis (NSU).** In men **urethritis,** inflammation of the urethra, produces:

- Painful urination
- Urinary frequency
- White or yellowish discharge from the penis

Women are likely to be asymptomatic. They may not realize they are infected until a male partner is diagnosed. If a woman does have symptoms, they are likely to include:

- Itching or burning while urinating
- Unusual vaginal discharge

It is important to have a laboratory test for an unusual discharge from the penis or vagina so that the appropriate antibiotic can be prescribed. Tetracycline and erythromycin are usually effective against NGU. Untreated NGU may result in the consequences described for chlamydia. The most common urinary tract infection among women, cystitis, is discussed later in this chapter.

Vaginal Infections

Vaginal infections, or **vaginitis,** affect 3 out of 4 women at least once in their lives. These infections are often, although not always, sexually transmitted. They may also be induced by an upset in the normal balance of vaginal organisms by such things as stress, birth control pills, antibiotics, nylon underwear, and douching. The three principal types of vaginitis are bacterial vaginosis, candidiasis, and trichomonal infection.

Bacterial Vaginosis Bacterial vaginal infections, referred to as **bacterial vaginosis,** may be caused by a number of different organisms, most commonly *Gardnerella vaginalis,* often a normal inhabitant of the healthy vagina. An overabundance of *Gardnerella,* however, produces:

- Vaginal itching
- Whitish discharge, with a fishy odor that is more pronounced when the discharge is combined with semen

Most men who carry *Gardnerella* are asymptomatic; some may experience inflammation of the urethra or glans. Bacterial vaginosis in women is commonly treated with metronidazole (Flagyl), unless the woman is pregnant or breast-feeding; then clindamycin may be prescribed. Some people experience unpleasant side effects, such as nausea, with metronidazole. There is disagreement as to the usefulness of treating men unless they actually have symptoms (Hatcher et al., 1990; Mengel, 1989). However, if a man has

---

nongonococcal urethritis (NGU) Urethral inflammation caused by something other than the gonococcus bacterium.

nonspecific urethritis (NSU) Inflammation of the urethra with an unspecified, nongonococcal cause.

urethritis Inflammation of the urethra.

vaginitis Any of several kinds of vaginal infection.

bacterial vaginosis A vaginal infection commonly caused by the bacterium *Gardnerella vaginalis.*

You and Your Sexual Well-Being

MAINTAINING VAGINAL HEALTH

Here are some simple guidelines that may help a woman avoid getting vaginitis:

- Do not use vaginal deodorants, especially deodorant suppositories or tampons. They upset the natural chemical balance of the vagina. Despite what pharmaceutical companies may advertise, the healthy vagina does not have a bad odor. If the vagina does have an unpleasant smell, then something is wrong, and you should check with your doctor or clinic.

- For the same reason, do not use douches, except medicated douches that have been recommended by a clinician, or vinegar solutions for yeast infections.

- Maintain good genital hygiene by washing regularly (about once a day is fine) with mild soap. Bubble baths and strongly perfumed soaps may cause irritation to the vulva.

- After a bowel movement, wipe the anus from front to back, away from the vagina, to prevent contamination with fecal bacteria.

- Wear cotton underpants and pantyhose with a cotton crotch. Nylon does not "breathe," and it allows heat and moisture to build up and create an ideal environment for infectious organisms to reproduce.

- If you use a vaginal lubricant, be sure it is water-soluble. Oil-based lubricants such as Vaseline encourage bacterial growth.

- If you have candidiasis (yeast infection), try douching every 2 or 3 days with a mild vinegar solution (2 tablespoons of vinegar to 1 quart of warm water). You can also try applying plain yogurt twice a day to the vulva and vagina. (It must be plain yogurt that contains live lactobacillus culture.) Adding yogurt to your diet and avoiding foods with a high sugar content may also help.

- If you are diagnosed with a vaginal infection, particularly trichomoniasis, be sure to have your male partner treated also, to avoid being reinfected.

symptoms, then treating him is necessary to prevent infection or reinfection of his partner.

Candidiasis The fungus *Candida albicans* is normally present in the healthy vagina of many women. Various conditions may cause *C. albicans* to multiply rapidly, producing the condition known as **candidiasis** (*can-di-DYE-a-sis*), moniliasis, or, more commonly, yeast infection. Symptoms include:

- Intense itching of the vagina and vulva
- A lumpy, cottage cheese-like discharge

C. albicans may be transmitted sexually, although this does not necessarily lead to symptoms. Conditions that may induce candidiasis include dietary imbalances, antibiotics, birth control pills, and pregnancy. Clotrimazole (Gyne-Lotrimin) and miconazole (Monostat) are available over the

candidiasis A yeast infection caused by the fungus *Candida albicans*. Also known as moniliasis.

counter as vaginal creams or suppositories for the treatment of yeast infections. A woman who is uncertain about the symptoms should be diagnosed by a clinic or physician.

Trichomoniasis

trichomoniasis A vaginal infection caused by *Trichomonas vaginalis.* Also known as trich.

Trichomoniasis, commonly referred to as trichomonas or "trich" (pronounced "trick"), is caused primarily by the single-cell protozoan *Trichomonas vaginalis.* It is one of the most common causes of vaginal infection, with up to 8 million cases occurring annually among women in the United States (Martens & Faro, 1989). It is a hardy parasite that may survive for several hours on damp items such as towels and toilet seats. Its principal mode of transmission, however, is sexual intercourse. Even though they are often asymptomatic, men may carry *Trichomonas.* If men do exhibit symptoms, they tend to be those associated with urethritis (Krieger et al., 1993). The symptoms of trichomoniasis can be very unpleasant for women. They include:

- Intense itching of the vagina and vulva
- A frothy, unpleasant-smelling vaginal discharge
- Painful intercourse

Metronidazole (Flagyl) is effective in treating trichomoniasis. To prevent reinfection, both partners must be treated.

Parasites

Although they are not diseases per se, parasites such as scabies and pubic lice can be spread by sexual contact.

scabies A red, intensely itchy rash appearing on the genitals, buttocks, feet, wrists, knuckles, abdomen, armpits, or scalp, caused by the barely visible mite *Sarcoptes scabiei.*

Scabies

The red, intensely itchy rash caused by the barely visible mite *Sarcoptes scabiei* is called **scabies.** It usually appears on the genitals, buttocks, feet, wrists, knuckles, abdomen, armpits, or scalp as a result of the mites' tunneling beneath the skin to lay their eggs and the baby mites' making their way back to the surface. It is highly contagious and spreads quickly among people who have close contact, both sexual and nonsexual. The mites can also be transferred on clothes, towels, and bedding. Scabies is usually treated with a prescribed lotion containing lindane, applied at bedtime and washed off in the morning. Young children and pregnant or nursing women should obtain an alternate prescription to lindane, because it can be toxic to infants and young children. Clothing, towels, and bedding of people who have scabies should be disinfected by washing in hot water and drying in high heat, or dry cleaning.

pubic lice *Phthirus pubis,* colloquially known as crabs; tiny lice that infest the pubic hair.

Pubic Lice

The tiny *Phthirus pubis,* commonly known as a "crab," moves easily from the pubic hair of one person to that of another (probably along with several of its relatives). When **pubic lice** mate, the male and female each grasp an adjacent hair; the female soon begins producing eggs (nits), which she attaches to the hairs at the rate of about three eggs a day for 7–10 days. The nits hatch within 7–9 days and begin reproducing in about 2 weeks, creating a very ticklish (or itchy) situation. Pubic lice can be transmitted nonsexually. They may fall into underwear, sheets, or towels, where they can survive up to a day *and* lay eggs that hatch in about a week. Thus, it is possible to get crabs simply by sleeping in someone else's bed, wearing his or her clothes, or sharing a towel.

A person can usually tell when he or she has pubic lice. There is intense itching, and upon inspection, one discovers a tiny, pale, crablike louse or its minuscule, pearly nits attached near the base of a pubic hair. There are both prescription and over-the-counter treatments for pubic lice. A Gamma-benzene solution sold as Kwell may be prescribed. Other preparations such as Nix (permethrin) and RID (A-200 pyrinate) do not require a prescription. In addition to killing all the lice and nits on the body, the person must wash all infected linen and clothing in hot water and dry it on high heat, or the crabs may survive.

See Table 15.1 for the symptoms and treatments of the principal STDs.

Pubic lice, or "crabs," are easily spread during intimate contact; they may also be transmitted on bedclothes, towels, or underwear.

Other STDs

A number of other sexually transmitted diseases appear in the United States but with less frequency than they do in some developing countries.

- *Chancroid* is a painful sore or group of sores on the penis, caused by the bacterium *Hemophilus ducreyi*. Women may carry the bacteria but are generally asymptomatic for chancroid.

- *Cytomegalovirus (CMV)* is a virus of the herpes group that affects people with depressed immune systems. A fetus may be infected with CMV in the uterus.

- *Enteric infections* are intestinal infections caused by bacteria, viruses, protozoans, or other organisms that are normally carried in the intestinal tract. Amebiasis, giardiasis, and shigellosis are typical enteric infections. They often result from anal sex or oral-anal contact.

- *Granuloma inguinale* appears as single or multiple nodules, usually on the genitals, that become lumpy but painless ulcers that bleed on contact.

- *Lymphogranuloma venereum (LGV)* begins as a small, painless lesion at the site of infection, then develops into a painful abscess, accompanied by pain and swelling in the groin.

- *Molluscum contagiosum*, caused by a relatively large virus, is characterized by smooth, rounded, shiny lesions, appearing on the trunk, the genitals, or around the anus.

STDS AND WOMEN

STDs affect men and women similarly in some ways and differently in others. Overall, the consequences for women appear to be more serious than those for men. Generally speaking, heterosexual women contract STDs more readily than men and risk greater damage to their health and reproductive functioning. As a group, lesbians are at the lowest risk for STDs; they are not immune, however, and can still benefit by observing safer sex guidelines and basic hygiene to avoid transmitting organisms such as HSV by hand.

TABLE 15.1 Principal Sexually Transmitted Diseases

STD and Infecting Organism	Symptoms	Time from Exposure to Occurrence	Medical Treatment	Comments
Chlamydia (*Chlamydia trachomatis*)	Women: 80% asymptomatic; others may have vaginal discharge or pain with urination. Men: 30–50% asymptomatic; others may have discharge from penis, burning urination, pain and swelling in testicles, or persitent low fever.	7–21 days	Doxycycline, tetracycline, erythromycin	If untreated, may lead to pelvic inflammatory disease (PID) and subsequent infertility in women.
Genial warts (Human papilloma virus)	Variously appearing bumps (smooth, flat, round, clustered, fingerlike, white, pink, brown, etc.) on genitals, usually penis, anus, vulva, vagina, or cervix.	1–6 months (usually within 3 months)	Surgical removal by feezing, cutting, or laser therapy. Chemical treatment with podophyllin (80% of warts eventually reappear).	Virus remains in the body after warts are removed.
Gonorrhea (*Neisseria gonorrhoeae*)	Women: 50–80% asymptomatic; others may have symptoms similar to chlamydia. Men: ithching, burning or pain with urination, discharge from penis ("drip").	2–21 days	Penicillin, tetracycline, or other antibiotics	If untreated, may lead to pelvic inflammarory disease (PID) and subsequent infertility in women.
Genital herpes (Herpes simplex virus)	Small, itchy bumps on genitals, becoming blisters that may rupture, forming painful sores; possibly swollen lymph nodes; flulike symptoms with first outbreak.	3–20 days	No cure although acyclovir may relieve symptoms. Nonmedical treatments may help relieve symptoms.	Virus remains in the body, and outbreaks of contagious sores may recur. Many people have no symptoms after the first outbreak.
Syphilis (*Treponema pallidum*)	Stage 1: Red, painless sore (chancre) at bacteria"s point of entry. Stage 2: Skin rash over body, including palms of hands and soles of feet.	Stage 1: 1–12 weeks Stage 2: 6 weeks to 6 months after chancre appears	Penicillin or other antibiotics	Easily cured, but untreated syphilis can lead to ulcers of internal organs and eyes, heart disease, neurological disorders, and insanity.

STD and Infecting Organism	Symptoms	Time from Exposure to Occurrence	Medical Treatment	Comments
Hepatitis (Hepatitis A or B virus)	Fatigue, diarrhea, nausea, abdominal pain, jaundice, darkened urine due to impaired liver function.	1–4 months	No medical treatment available; rest and fluids are prescribed until the disease runs its course.	Hepatitis B more commonly spread through sexual contact; can be prevented by vaccination.
Urethritis (various organisma)	Painful and/or frequent urination; discharge from penis; women may be asymptomatic.	1–3 weeks	Penicillin, tetracycline, or erythromycin, depending on organism	Laboratory testing is important to determine appropriate treatment.
Vaginitis (*Gardnerella vaginalis*, *Trichomonas vaginalis*, or *Candida albicans*)	Intense itching of vagina and/or vulva, unusual discharge with foul or fishy odor, painful intercourse. Men who carry organisms may be asymptomatic.	2–21 days	Depends on organism; oral medications include metronidazole and clindamycin. Vaginal medications include clotrimazole and miconazole.	Not always acquired sexually. Other causes include contact with an infected toilet seat, stress, oral contraceptives, pregnancy, tight pants or underwear, antibiotics, douching, and dietary imbalance.
HIV infection and AIDS (Human immunodeficiency virus)	Possible flulike symptoms but often no symptoms during early phase. Variety of later symptoms including weight loss, persitent fever, night sweats, diarrhea, swollen lymph nodes, bruiselike rash, persitent cough.	Several months to several years	No cure available, although many symptoms and opportunistic infections can be treated with a variety of medications. Good general health practices can delay or reduce the severity of symptoms.	Cannot be self-diagnosed; a blood test must be performed to determine the presence of the virus.
Pelvic inflammory disease (PID) (women only)	Low abdominal pain, bleeding between menstrual periods, persistent low fever.	Several weeks or months after exposure to chlamydia or gonorrhea (if untreated)	Penicillin or other antibiotics; surgery	Caused by untreated chlamydia or gonorrhea; may lead to chronic problems such as arthritis and infertility.

Biological Sexism

Where STDs are concerned, there is a kind of "biological sexism" working to the disadvantage of women. According to Robert Hatcher and colleagues (1990), this is partly a result of the "fluid dynamics of intercourse," wherein "women are apparently more likely than men to acquire a sexually transmitted infection from any single sexual encounter." For example, the risk of acquiring gonorrhea from a single "coital event" when one partner is infectious is approximately 25% for men and 50% for women. Long-term effects of STDs for women include pelvic inflammatory disease, ectopic pregnancy, infertility, and cervical cancer.

A woman's anatomy may increase her susceptibility to STDs. The warm, moist interiors of the vagina and uterus are ideal environments for many organisms. The thin, sensitive skin inside the labia and the mucous membranes lining the vagina may also be more permeable to infecting organisms than the skin covering a man's genitals. Additionally, menstruation may cause a woman to be more vulnerable. As the endometrium sloughs off the uterine walls, tiny blood vessels rupture, causing bleeding and incidentally providing a pathway for infecting organisms directly into the woman's bloodstream. (If a woman has a bloodborne disease such as hepatitis, or HIV/AIDS, it may also be passed to her partner in menstrual blood.)

Women who use barrier methods of contraception, such as the diaphragm or female condom, tend to be better protected against STDs than women who rely on men to use a condom (Rosenberg, Davidson, Chen, Judson, & Douglas, 1992).

Pelvic Inflammatory Disease (PID)

pelvic inflammatory disease (PID) An infection of the fallopian tube (or tubes) caused by an organism, such as C. trachomatis or N. gonorroehae, in which scar tissue may form within the tubes and block the passage of eggs or cause an ectopic pregnancy; a leading cause of female infertility.

Pelvic inflammatory disease (PID), also known as salpingitis, is one of the leading causes of female infertility. Over 750,000 cases of PID occur annually, resulting in about 165,000 hospitalizations of women aged 15–44 (CDC, 1994a). PID begins with an initial infection of the fallopian tube (or tubes) by an organism such as C. trachomatis or N. gonorrhoeae, which makes it possible for bacteria to invade and develop (Ault & Faro, 1993). As the infection spreads, the tubes swell and fester, often causing acute pain. Scar tissue begins to form within the tubes and may block the passage of eggs en route to the uterus, or cause a fertilized egg to implant within the tube itself—an ectopic pregnancy. PID occurs more commonly in women who have had a number of sex partners, women with a previous history of PID, and very young women. Adolescent females run a 1-in-8 risk of contracting PID, whereas women 24 years or older run a 1-in-80 risk (Sweet, 1986). A woman may be more susceptible to PID during the first few days of her period, or if she uses an IUD.

Symptoms of PID include:

- Lower abdominal pain
- Cervical discharge
- Cervical tenderness
- Fever

Because definitive diagnosis of PID usually requires laparoscopy (an expensive examination involving minor surgery to insert the viewing instrument), physicians may go ahead and prescribe antibiotics once such conditions as appendicitis and ectopic pregnancy have been ruled out. Untreated PID can lead to life-threatening conditions such as pelvic abscesses and ectopic pregnancy. Once the infection is under control, further examination and treatment may be necessary to prevent infertility, ectopic pregnancy, or chronic abdominal pain, all of which may result from scar tissue buildup. To prevent reinfection, women with PID should be sure their partners are examined and treated for STDs.

Cystitis

Cystitis, a bladder infection that affects mainly women, is often related to sexual activity, although it is not transmitted from one partner to another. Cystitis is characterized by:

- Painful, burning urination
- A nearly constant need to urinate

It occurs when bacteria such as *Escherichia coli,* normally present in the lower intestine and in fecal material, are introduced into the urinary tract. This can occur when continuous friction (from intercourse or manual stimulation) in the area of the urethra traumatizes the tissue and allows nearby bacteria to easily enter the urinary tract. It often occurs at the beginning of a sexual relationship, when sexual activity is high (hence the nickname "honeymoon cystitis"). If cystitis is not treated promptly, more serious symptoms will occur:

- Lower abdominal pain
- Fever
- Kidney pain

Damage to the kidneys may occur.

cystitis A bladder infection affecting mainly women that is often related to sexual activity, although it is not transmitted from one partner to another.

PREVENTING STDS

It seems that STDs should be easy to prevent, at least in theory. But in reality, STD prevention involves a subtle interplay of knowledge, psychological factors, and behaviors. In other words, STD prevention *is* easy, *if* you know the facts, *if* you believe in it, and *if* you act in accordance with your knowledge and belief. In the earlier part of this chapter, you read the facts. Now let's think about the psychological and behavioral components of preventing STDs.

Risk Taking

The psychology of risk taking where STDs are concerned is similar in many ways to the psychology of contraceptive risk taking. Our ambivalence about sexuality may cause us to deny that we are sexual creatures at the same time that we are engaging in sexual behaviors that put us at risk. Thus, we may

You and Your Sexual Well-Being

PREVENTING AND TREATING CYSTITIS

The following precautions may help a woman avoid cystitis:

- Urinate frequently, to avoid the buildup of highly acidic urine.

- Urinate before sexual activity and immediately afterward, to flush bacteria from the urethra.

- Drink plenty of fluids (water is best), especially just before and just after intercourse.

- Eat a well-balanced diet and get plenty of rest, especially if your resistance is low.

- If you use a diaphragm and are troubled by cystitis, have it checked for proper fit. You may need a smaller size, or you may need to consider another form of contraception.

If you have cystitis:

- Drink copious amounts of water (at least 16 glasses a day). It won't hurt you, as long as you urinate frequently. A pinch of baking soda in a glass of water may help neutralize the urine's acidity. Some women find that drinking cranberry juice provides relief. Coffee, tea, colas, and alcohol are not advisable as they may irritate the urinary tract.

- Pain and itching may be relieved by spraying or sponging water on the urethral opening. If urination is very painful, try urinating while sitting in a few inches of warm water (in the bathtub or a large pan).

- If symptoms persist or in the case of fever, see your doctor or clinic. Sulfa drugs or other antibiotics will usually clear up the symptoms within a few days. (A caution about sulfa drugs: 10–14% of African Americans have an inherited deficiency of a blood enzyme called glucose-6-phosphate-dehydrogenase [G6PD]; sulfa drugs may cause a serious anemic reaction in these people.)

---

not use a condom because our partner "doesn't look like the type to have an STD," or we may be monogamous "except for once in a while." Denying our sexuality in this way is not just psychologically unhealthy—it is physically dangerous.

Abstinence

The most absolutely foolproof method of STD prevention is to abstain from intimate sexual contact, specifically penile-vaginal intercourse, anal intercourse, and oral sex. Hugging, massaging, kissing, petting, and mutual masturbation are all ways of sharing intimacy that are extremely unlikely to transmit STDs. (But watch out for colds!)

Abstinence is the only reliable course of action for a person who has an STD or whose partner has an STD (or a suspected STD). Freely chosen abstinence is a legitimate personal choice regarding sexuality. People who wish to be abstinent need to communicate their preferences clearly and unambiguously to their dates or partners. They also need to learn to avoid high-pressure sexual situations and to stay away from alcohol and drugs, which can impair their judgment.

SAFER AND UNSAFE SEXUAL PRACTICES

Safer sex practices are an integral part of good health practices. (Many people prefer the term "safer sex" to "safe sex," because all sexual contact carries at least a slight risk—a condom slipping off, perhaps—no matter how careful we try to be.)

Safer Practices

- Hugging
- Kissing (but possibly not deep, French kissing)
- Massaging
- Petting
- Masturbation (solo or mutual, unless there are sores or abrasions on the genitals or hands)
- Erotic videos, books, etc.

Possibly Safe Practices

- Deep, French kissing, unless there are sores in the mouth
- Vaginal intercourse with a latex condom and spermicide
- Fellatio with a latex condom
- Cunnilingus, if the woman does not have her period or a vaginal infection (a latex dental dam or a square of plastic wrap provides extra protection)
- Anal intercourse with a latex condom and spermicide (authorities disagree as to whether this should be considered "safer" even with a condom, because it is the riskiest sexual behavior without one)

Unsafe Practices

- Vaginal or anal intercourse without a latex condom
- Fellatio without a latex condom
- Cunnilingus, if the woman has her period or a vaginal infection and a dental dam is not used
- Oral-anal contact
- Contact with blood, including menstrual blood
- Semen in the mouth
- Sharing vibrators, dildos, etc., without washing them between uses

Good Health, Safer Sex

When we value ourselves, our bodies, and our lives, we are likely to practice good health behaviors, such as eating well, exercising, getting enough rest, and seeking medical care when we need it. When we become sexual, we need to develop particular habits and patterns to promote our continuing good health. Specific health behaviors that help protect us from STDs include:

- Consistent use of a latex condom
- Practicing safer sex
- Knowing the signs and symptoms of STDs
- Talking to a partner about past and current exposure, or possible exposure, to an STD
- Examining self and partner for genital sores or unusual discharge

You and Your Sexual Well-Being

A VISIT TO AN STD CLINIC

Let's say you think you may have an STD. Perhaps you've noticed a peculiar discharge from your vagina or penis, and it hurts when you urinate. Or maybe you noticed some unusual little bumps on your partner's genitals—*after* you'd made love. So you decide that a visit to your local STD clinic or your college health clinic is in order. You call first to see if you need an appointment. (Check the yellow pages of your telephone directory under Clinics, Family Planning, or Health Services if you don't know the number.)

After an uncomfortable, semisleepless night, you find yourself at the clinic at 10:00 the next morning. Here's a version of what might happen next:

- The receptionist gives you a clipboard with a bunch of papers to fill out. The most important of these is a medical/sexual history. Take your time filling it out, and include any information you think might be helpful to the clinician who will see you and recommend treatment. You return the papers to the receptionist.

- You wait. Most clinics are working within a limited budget. They may have a small staff and a large clientele. Bring your patience (and a book).

- Your name or number is called. You go into another room and sit down to talk with a counselor or social worker. (This may happen after your medical exam, or be combined with it.) She or he is there to give you information and to answer your questions, in addition to getting more specific details about the reason for your visit. The more honest and straightforward you are about your sexual activities, the more help you will be able to receive. Health-care workers are not interested in passing judgment on you; they are there to help you get well. Your records will be kept confidential.

- Depending on your symptoms, you may next be asked for a urine sample or a blood sample. The health-care worker should explain the reasons for any test or procedure.

- Next, you go to an examination room. If you are a woman, you will probably be instructed to remove your clothes from the waist down and cover yourself with a paper gown or drape. You will probably lie down on an examining table with your feet in stirrups so that the clinician can have a clear view of your genital area and give you a vaginal examination. If you are a man, you will probably be asked to remove your pants or simply to lower them. The clinician who examines you may be a physician, intern, public-health nurse, nurse practitioner, or other medically trained person. Depending on your symptoms, the clinician may use a cotton swab to take a small sample of the affected tissue or discharge for microscopic evaluation or culturing. For men, this may involve squeezing the glans to produce the discharge. For women, it may involve the insertion of a speculum to open the vagina and then a gentle swabbing of the cervix. (A note for women: If you are examined by a man, the law requires that a female assistant be present.) Be sure to tell the clinician about any discomfort or pain you experience during the exam. After the examination, you dress and go back to the waiting room or to a conference room.

- The clinician, counselor, or another health-care worker discusses your diagnosis with you. In some cases, treatment will be started right away. In others, you may have to wait several days for lab results. In any event, it is imperative to follow the clinic's instructions exactly. If you have questions, be sure to ask.

- You get your medication from the clinic or pharmacy, and begin taking it.

- You inform your partner (or partners) of your diagnosis and insist that he or she (or they) seek immediate treatment. This is crucially important for halting the spread of an STD and preventing your own possible reinfection.

- You refrain from sexual activity until the clinician tells you it is safe. You return for a follow-up visit if required.

- You decide that next time, you'll use a condom.

(continued from page 449)

- Good genital hygiene (simply washing with mild soap and warm water, especially under the foreskin for uncircumcised males, before and after sex)
- Seeking medical care at the onset of symptoms and/or getting tested regularly if you have multiple sex partners
- Following treatment instructions

People who are sexually active with more than one partner should have a medical examination to screen for STDs every 3–6 months (Hatcher et al., 1990). This is especially important for women because they are often asymptomatic.

Acquiring an STD requires that we get intimately close to another person. Avoiding an STD demands even more intimacy because very often it means having to talk. Putting aside embarrassment or learning to communicate isn't always easy—but it's a lot simpler than dealing with herpes, gonorrhea, or AIDS.

As individuals, we have the knowledge and means to protect ourselves from STDs. As a society, we should have a larger goal. In the words of King Holmes and the other editors of *Sexually Transmitted Diseases* (1990), "We must acknowledge and correct the failure of society and of politicians to support the basic needs for public health in general and for STD control in particular."

SUMMARY

X-Rated Diseases: The Psychological Impact of STDs

- Although the media and popular culture encourage us to express ourselves sexually, Americans continue to experience a great deal of embarrassment, guilt, and shame over their sexuality. This deep ambivalence discourages us from dealing realistically with sexually transmitted disease (STDs).

The STD Epidemic

- The incidence of STDs has increased dramatically since the 1950s for a number of reasons. Social factors include changes in sexual mores, decreased condom use due to the advent of the pill and IUD, obstruction of educational efforts and research by vocal minorities who confuse medical issues with moral ones, inadequate health-care facilities, and the misuse of alcohol and drugs. Biological factors include the fact that many STDs are *asymptomatic*, and the evolution of strains of viruses and bacteria that are resistant to prescribed antibiotics.

- The health belief model is used to help explain the psychology behind our sexual health behaviors. In order to take action to avoid a disease, according to this model, a person must believe that he or she is personally susceptible to it, the disease would have at least a moderately severe effect on his or her life, taking a particular action would reduce the susceptibility to or severity of the disease, and the costs are worth the benefits.

Principal STDs

- The principal STDs affecting Americans are chlamydia, genital warts, gonorrhea, genital herpes, syphilis, hepatitis, urinary tract infections (NGU or NSU), vaginitis, and HIV/AIDS. Parasites that may be sexually transmitted include scabies and pubic lice.

STDs and Women

- There is a kind of "biological sexism" where STDs are concerned. Women tend to be more susceptible to STDs than men and to experience graver consequences, such as pelvic inflammatory disease (PID), an infection of the fallopian tubes that can lead to infertility, and ectopic pregnancy. Intense stimulation of the vulva can irritate the urethra, leading to cystitis (bladder infection).

Preventing STDs

• STD prevention involves the interaction of knowledge, psychological factors, and behaviors to avoid taking risks. Abstinence is a legitimate personal strategy for avoiding STDs. Good health behaviors, including safer sex, are very effective in protecting against STDs. Consistent condom use is an important component of safer sex.

SUGGESTED READINGS

Brandt, Allan M. *No Magic Bullet: A Social History of Venereal Disease in the United States Since 1880*. New York: Oxford University Press, 1985. An informative and very readable history of the social and political aspects of STDs.

Hatcher, Robert. *Safely Sexual*. New York: Irvington Publishers, 1991. A practical and sensitive guide to safer sex and pregnancy prevention.

Holmes, King K., et al., eds. *Sexually Transmitted Diseases*, 2nd ed. New York: McGraw-Hill, 1990. The definitive collection of recent research by leading authorities on STDs in the U.S. and Europe (95 chapters, over 1000 pages).

Jones, James. *Bad Blood: The Tuskegee Syphilis Experiment—A Tragedy of Race and Medicine*. Rev. ed. New York: Free Press, 1981, 1993. A fascinating—and chilling—account of a 40-year experiment by the Public Health Service, using African Americans in the rural South as human guinea pigs. Discusses the experiment's impact on current HIV/AIDS prevention efforts in the black community.

Chapter Sixteen

HIV AND AIDS

PREVIEW: SELF-QUIZ

1. Acquired immune deficiency syndrome (AIDS) is caused by the human immunodeficiency virus (HIV). True or false?

2. The virus that causes AIDS can get through microscopic holes that naturally occur in latex condoms. True or false?

3. Scientists have not actually seen a human immunodeficiency virus. True or false?

4. Women are more likely than men to acquire HIV during sexual intercourse with an infected partner. True or false?

5. Viruses can "crawl" from one surface to another. True or false?

6. Today the chance of being exposed to HIV during a blood transfusion is between 1 in 40,000 and 1 in 225,000. True or false?

7. It is expected that in the U.S. by the year 2000, the number of men and women affected by HIV will be equal. True or false?

8. If a pregnant woman has HIV, her child is sure to have it also. True or false?

9. If you receive an HIV-positive blood test, it means you definitely have AIDS. True or false?

10. HIV is *not* transmitted through normal household or social activities. True or false?

ANSWERS 1. T, 2. F, 3. F, 4. T, 5. F, 6. T, 7. T, 8. F, 9. F, 10. T

Chapter Outline

human immunodeficiency virus (HIV) The virus that causes AIDS.

I n the past 15 years, no single phenomenon has changed the face of sexuality so much as the appearance of the minuscule virus known as **HIV, or human immunodeficiency virus.** Although researchers know a great deal about the virus and the way it works, among the general public, misinformation abounds. By now most of us know how HIV is spread. And yet, for a variety of reasons, people continue engaging in behaviors that put them at risk. Our goal in this chapter is to give a solid grounding in the biological, psychological, and sociological aspects of the disease. Because it is not likely that a cure for AIDS will be found in the near future, we must develop the attitudes and behaviors that will stop its deadly progression.

AIDS *is* preventable. We hope that the material in this chapter will assist you in making healthy, informed choices for yourself and in becoming a force for education and positive change in the community.

We begin this chapter by exploding some common myths about AIDS, then go on to describe the disease, the virus itself, and the workings of the immune system. We next discuss modes of transmission, the effects of HIV and AIDS on certain groups of people, current treatments, prevention, and HIV testing. Then we deal with the demographic aspects of the epidemic— its effect on various communities and groups: the gay community, women, children, and teenagers. The final section of the chapter is about living with HIV or AIDS. We offer practical advice for those who have the virus or whose friends or loved ones do.

WHAT IS AIDS?

AIDS is an acronym for **acquired immune deficiency syndrome.** This condition is so named for the following reasons:

A   Acquired, because it is not inherited

I   Immune, because it affects the immune system, which protects the body against foreign organisms

D   Deficiency, because the body lacks immunity

S   Syndrome, because the symptoms occur as a group

To receive an AIDS diagnosis according to the Centers for Disease Control (CDC) classification system (and thus be eligible for treatments, programs, and insurance funds that would not otherwise be available), a person must, in most cases, have a positive blood test indicating the presence of HIV antibodies and a T-cell count (discussed later) below 200 (CDC, 1994b). If the T-cell count is higher, the person must have one or more of the diseases or conditions listed in the following section. This is a broader definition than was in effect prior to 1993, and its institution had led to a dramatic increase in the number of people diagnosed with AIDS. This increase reflects the change in definition rather than a sudden leap in number of cases (CDC, 1994b). If a person has HIV antibodies but does not meet the other criteria, he or she is said to "have HIV" or be "living with HIV."

Conditions Associated with AIDS

The CDC currently lists 27 clinical conditions to be used in diagnosing AIDS along with HIV-positive status (CDC, 1994b). These conditions fall into several categories: opportunistic infections, cancers, conditions associated specifically with AIDS, and conditions that *may* be diagnostic for AIDS under certain circumstances. The most commonly occurring diseases and conditions within these categories are listed in this chapter.

Opportunistic Infections **Opportunistic infections (OIs)** are diseases that take advantage of a weakened immune system; normally they do not develop in healthy people or are not life-threatening. Common OIs associated with HIV are:

acquired immune deficiency syndrome (AIDS) A usually fatal disease caused by the human immunodeficiency virus (HIV), in which the immune system is weakened and unable to fight opportunistic infections, such as pneumocystitis carinii pneumonia (PCP) and Kaposi's sarcoma.

opportunistic infection (OI) An infection that normally does not occur or is not life threatening, that takes advantage of a weakened immune system.

Think About It

AIDS MYTHS, AIDS FACTS

Myths and rumors about HIV and AIDS abound. Many are kept alive by the media, especially the tabloid newspapers, read by millions, and certain talk-show hosts and newspaper columnists. Some politicians and religious leaders, especially those with "anti-sex" agendas, are also responsible for the spread of misinformation. We briefly discuss some common myths below. As you read the chapter, you will understand more about the issues that are raised.

- *Myth:* If you're not in a high-risk group, you don't have to worry about AIDS. In other words, "low risk means no risk."

  Fact: This is one of the most deadly myths about AIDS. Statistics don't seem very relevant when the "1 out of 100" (or whatever the number) happens to be you. Protecting ourselves or our children from potentially deadly diseases such as diphtheria or whooping cough is something most of us take for granted. We get the vaccinations even if we are not in a high-risk area or group. But it is precisely because virtually everyone takes these precautions that these diseases no longer threaten the general public. Admittedly, it is easier to get a shot than to use a condom each time you have sex, but that doesn't change the principle: If everyone assumes responsibility, together we can stop the transmission of most diseases, including AIDS.

- *Myth:* Scientists have not actually seen an AIDS virus.

- *Fact:* Researchers have seen countless AIDS viruses (through a microscope, of course) and understand a great deal about them. Because the presence of the virus is determined by testing for the antibodies that the immune system develops to fight HIV, people may erroneously assume that the virus itself cannot be found. It can be, but the tests would be prohibitively expensive and involve unnecessary pain and risk.

- *Myth:* HIV was developed in the laboratory as germ warfare against gays or blacks, or it was spread through contaminated vaccines, such as that for polio.

- *Fact:* There have been many theories as to the origin of HIV. Some are grounded in science, whereas others have sprung solely from fear or paranoia. The pattern of HIV's spread does not ultimately support any of these theories. There is not a shred of evidence that the virus was made in a laboratory, nor have any traces of it been found in samples of frozen early vaccines. The most promising work in the search for HIV's origin is based on the obvious—but not yet well-understood—relationship of HIV (especially HIV-2) to SIV (simian immunodeficiency virus) (Essex & Kanki, 1988). SIV is widely prevalent among African green monkeys, but it is not deadly to them. Scientists hope that by studying SIV they will discover mechanisms by which HIV can be weakened or disabled.

- *Myth:* The AIDS virus is easy to "catch."

---

pneumocystis carinii pneumonia (PCP) An opportunistic lung infection caused by a common, usually harmless organism; the most common opportunistic infection among people with AIDS.

- **Pneumocystis carinii pneumonia (PCP).** The most common opportunistic infection of people with AIDS; a lung disease caused by a common organism (probably a protozoan or fungus) that is not usually harmful. The organisms multiply, resulting in the accumulation of a fluid in the lungs (pneumonia).

- *Mycobacterium avium intracellulare (MAI).* An atypical tuberculosis, usu-

Fact: The virus is only easy to catch in intimate situations when infected blood, semen, vaginal secretions, or breast milk have a direct pathway into the bloodstream of an uninfected person. The virus is delicate and dies quickly when exposed to spermicide, bleach, and a variety of other disinfectants. It can't survive in the open air. It is not spread by handshakes, hugs, or kisses where blood is not present.

- *Myth:* Latex condoms have naturally occurring holes that are 50 times bigger than the human immunodeficiency virus, so condoms do not really provide protection.
- *Fact:* Good quality latex condoms do not have such holes. Laboratory tests have shown that virus-sized particles do not normally leak from the better brands (Voeller et al., 1988). Although poorer brands have been shown to leak minute amounts of virus-sized particles, in laboratory studies, researchers nevertheless conclude that "worst-case condom barrier effectiveness" is "at least 10,000 times better than not using a condom at all" (Carey, Herman, Retta, Rinaldi, Herman, & Athey, 1992). Numerous studies of couples in which one person is HIV-positive and one is not have shown extremely low rates of transmission when condoms are consistently used (CDC, 1993; De Vincenzi et al., 1992; Fischl et al., 1987; Padian, 1990).
- *Myth:* HIV doesn't cause AIDS.
  Fact: Although the exact way (or ways) in which HIV destroys the immune system is still under investigation, there is no reason to doubt that it is the "first cause" of AIDS (Delaney, 1992). It has been estimated that 20–50% of HIV-infected people will progress to AIDS within 5 years of infection. At 10 years, 50–70% will have developed AIDS. After that, another 25% will develop AIDS. It is most unlikely that 100% of those who are infected will develop AIDS (Stine, 1993).
- *Myth:* You can have AIDS without HIV.
  Fact: Some people are discouraged from being tested for HIV because they believe they can have AIDS without having the virus. Although it is true that "false negative" results occasionally appear in HIV testing, retesting at a later date (recommended for those who think they may be at risk) should determine if the virus is present. Numerous other well-known diseases and conditions affect the immune system, but these are generally not infectious.
- *Myth:* If you are HIV-positive, it means you have AIDS.
  Fact: Although it currently appears that 95–99% of people who test positive for HIV will go on to develop AIDS eventually, having the virus is not the same as having AIDS. Many people who are HIV-positive feel perfectly normal and healthy. If they maintain a healthful lifestyle, their immune system may continue to function well for a number of years. It is important to remember, though, that anyone who is HIV-positive can transmit the virus regardless of how healthy he or she may look or feel.

ally affecting the lungs. MAI is the most common form of TB among people with AIDS.

- *Mycobacterium tuberculosis (TB).* An infection that generally occurs in the lungs and may appear in other sites such as the lymph nodes.
- *Bacterial pneumonia.* Accumulation of fluid in the lungs due to the presence of any of several common bacteria.

Kaposi's sarcoma is a cancer of the blood vessels commonly associated with AIDS. It causes red or purple blotches to appear under the skin's surface.

Kaposi's sarcoma A rare cancer of the blood vessels that is common among people with AIDS.

wasting syndrome Severe weight loss, usually accompanied by weakness and persistent diarrhea.

- *Toxoplasmosis.* A disease of the brain and central nervous system caused by a parasite frequently present in cat feces.

Cancers Certain types of cancer are commonly associated with AIDS, including the following:

- **Kaposi's sarcoma.** A cancer of the blood vessels, causing red or purple blotches to appear under the skin. Before AIDS, it was rare except in older men of central African or Mediterranean descent.
- *Lymphomas.* Cancers of the lymphatic system.
- *Invasive cervical cancer.* Cancer or cervical dysplasia that can lead to cancer. Cervical cancer and dysplasia are more common in women who are HIV-positive than in other women.

Clinical Conditions Associated with AIDS Conditions that are specifically linked to AIDS include:

- **Wasting syndrome.** Severe weight loss, usually accompanied by weakness and persistent diarrhea.
- *HIV encephalopathy (AIDS dementia).* Impairment of mental functioning, changes in mood or behavior, or impaired movement caused by direct infection of the brain with HIV.

Other Infections Infections listed by the CDC that may lead to an AIDS diagnosis under certain circumstances include:

- *Candidiasis (thrush).* A fungal (yeast) infection affecting the mouth, throat, esophagus, trachea, lungs, or vagina.
- *Herpes simplex.* A common viral STD. Persistent lesions (lasting a month or more) or lesions on the lungs or esophagus may be diagnostic for AIDS.
- *Cytomegalovirus (CMV).* A virus of the herpes family, often sexually transmitted. In people with AIDS, it can lead to encephalitis (a brain infection), retinitis (infection of the retina that can lead to blindness), pneumonia, or hepatitis.

Because the immune systems of people with HIV may not be functioning well (and those of people with advanced AIDS certainly are not), they may be subject to numerous other infections that would not normally be much of a problem, such as colds, flus, and intestinal infections. Health precautions for people living with HIV are discussed later in the chapter.

Symptoms of HIV Infection and AIDS A person with HIV may feel fine, or he or she may experience one or more of the symptoms that follow. A person who has received an AIDS diagnosis is more likely to experience at least some of them. It is important to remember, however, that all of these are also common symptoms of conditions that are not related to HIV or AIDS. *AIDS cannot be self-diagnosed.* A person who is experiencing persistent discomfort or illness should be checked out by a medical practitioner. Symptoms that may be associated with HIV or AIDS include:

- Unexplained persistent fatigue

- Unexplained fever, chills, or night sweats for a period of several weeks or more
- Unexplained weight loss greater than 10 lb or 10% of body weight in less than 2 months
- Swollen lymph nodes in the neck, armpits, or groin that are unexplained and last more than 2 months. This condition is called *lymphadenopathy.*
- Pink, purple, or brown blotches on or under the skin, inside the mouth, nose, eyelids, or rectum that do not disappear
- Persistent, fuzzy, white spots or other sores in the mouth (indicative of either *hairy leukoplakia* or candidiasis)
- Persistent dry cough and shortness of breath
- Persistent diarrhea

In addition, women may experience the following:

- Abnormal Pap smears
- Persistent vaginal candidiasis
- Abdominal cramping (due to PID)

The Immune System

The principal ingredients in blood are plasma (the fluid base), red blood cells, white blood cells, and platelets.

Leukocytes White blood cells, or **leukocytes,** are distributed throughout the body in the lymph nodes (located mainly in the neck, face, armpits, and groin), spleen, and other lymphatic tissues (within connective tissue, throughout the small intestine, in the tonsils). There are several kinds of leukocytes, all of which play major roles in defending the body against invading organisms or mutant (cancerous) cells. Because HIV invades and eventually kills some kinds of leukocytes, it impairs the body's ability to ward off infections and other harmful conditions that ordinarily would not be threatening. The principal type of leukocyte we will be discussing is the lymphocyte.

leukocyte White blood cell.

Macrophages, Antigens, and Antibodies **Macrophages,** literally "big eaters," are formed from monocytes (another type of leukocyte) within the bone marrow. Although some circulate in the blood, most migrate to lymph nodes or lymphatic tissues, where they wait for foreign particles to be brought to them. The macrophage engulfs the foreign particle and displays the invader's antigen (*antibody generator*) like a signal flag on its own surface. **Antigens** are large molecules that are capable of stimulating the immune system and then reacting with the antibodies that are released to fight them. **Antibodies** bind to antigens, inactivate them, and mark them for destruction by killer cells. If the body has been previously exposed to the organism (by fighting it off or being vaccinated), the response is much quicker because memory cells are already biochemically programmed to respond.

macrophage A type of white blood cell that destroys foreign cells.

antigen A molecular structure on the wall of a cell capable of stimulating the immune system and then reacting with the antibodies that are released to fight it.

antibody A cell that binds to the antigen of an invading cell, inactivating it and marking it for destruction by killer cells.

*A T cell infected with HIV begins
to replicate the viruses, which bud
from the cell wall, eventually
killing the host cell.*

B Cells and T Cells The **lymphocytes** crucial to the immune system's functioning are **B cells** and several types of **T cells.** Like macrophages, **helper T cells** are programmed to "read" the antigens and then begin directing the immune system's response. They send chemical signals to B cells, which begin making antibodies specific to the presented antigen. Helper T cells also stimulate the proliferation of B cells and T cells (which are genetically programmed to replicate, or make copies of themselves) and activate both macrophages and **killer T cells,** transforming them into Ramboesque agents of destruction whose only purpose is to attack and obliterate the enemy. Suppressor T cells are activated when an antigen has been successfully destroyed. They slow and finally stop the immune response. T cells are also identified by the type of protein receptor (called CD4 or CD8) they display on their surface. The number of helper T cells in an individual's body is an important indicator of how well the immune system is functioning, as we will discuss later.

The Virus

In some ways, viruses are really very primitive entities. They have no life on their own. They can't propel themselves independently, and they can't reproduce unless they are inside a host cell. It would take 16,000 human immunodeficiency viruses to cover the head of a pin in a single layer. Under strong magnification, HIV resembles a spherical pincushion, bristling with tiny pinheadlike knobs. These knobs are the antigens; the CD4 receptors on a helper T cell are attracted (fatally, as it turns out) to a protein in the antigen (Redfield & Burke, 1988). Within the virus's protein is an enzyme and the genetic material (RNA) that carries the information the virus needs to replicate itself. When a cell is functioning normally, its DNA (genetic material) manufactures RNA, programming it to run the cell's "machinery." Viruses with the ability to reverse the normal genetic writing process are known as **retroviruses.** Numerous variant strains of HIV-1 result from mutations (Jean-Claude Chermann, cited in Challice, 1992). The tendency to mutate is one factor that makes HIV difficult to destroy.

T-Cell Destruction When HIV enters the bloodstream, helper T cells rush to the invading viruses, as if they were specifically designed for them. Normally at this stage, a T cell reads the antigen, stimulating antibody production in the B cells and beginning the process of eliminating the invading organism. Although antibody production does begin, the immune process starts to break down almost at once. The virus injects its contents into the host T cell and copies its own genetic code into the cell's genetic material (DNA). As a result, when the immune system is activated, the T cell begins producing HIV instead of replicating itself. The T cell is killed in the process.

HIV-1 and HIV-2 Almost all cases of HIV in the U.S. involve the subtype of the virus known as HIV-1. Another subtype, HIV-2, has been found to exist mainly in West Africa (Essex & Kanki, 1988). Overall, it appears that HIV-2 takes longer than HIV-1 to damage the immune system; it may not always develop into AIDS (Essex & Kanki, 1988).

AIDS Pathogenesis: How the Disease Progresses

As discussed earlier, when viruses are introduced into the body, they are immediately snatched up by helper T cells and whisked off to the lymph nodes. Although HIV begins replication right away within the host cells, the virus itself may not be detectable in the blood for some time. HIV antibodies, however, are generally detectable in the blood within 2–6 months (the testing process is discussed later). The process in which a person develops antibodies is called **seroconversion.** A person's **serostatus** is HIV-negative if antibodies are not detected and HIV-positive if antibodies are detected.

T-Cell (CD4) Count   T-cell count or CD4 count refers to the number of helper T cells that are present in a cubic milliliter of blood. A healthy person's T-cell count averages about 1000, but it can range from 500 to 1600, depending on a person's general health and whether he or she is fighting off an illness.

Early Phase of Infection   When a person is first infected with HIV, he or she may experience severe flulike symptoms as the immune system goes into high gear to fight off the invader. The person's T-cell count may temporarily plunge as the virus begins rapid replication. During this period, the virus is dispersed throughout the lymph nodes, where it replicates, a process called "seeding" (Kolata, 1992). HIV may also be trapped within certain leukocytes and stay localized, but it continues to replicate and destroy T cells. Most researchers agree that it does not have an actual "dormant" period, as previously believed (Kolata, 1992).

Intermediate Phase   As time goes by, the T cells gradually diminish in number, destroyed by newly created HIV. During this phase, as the number of infected cells goes up, the number of T cells goes down, generally to between 200 and 500 per milliliter of blood.

Advanced Phase   When AIDS is in the advanced phase, the lymph nodes appear "burned out" (Israelski, 1992). The T cells and other fighter cells of the immune system are no longer able to trap foreign invaders. Infected cells continue to increase, and the T-cell count drops to under 200. The virus is detectable in the blood. At this point, the person is fairly ill to very ill. The T-cell count may continue to plummet to zero. Figure 16.1 diagrams the general pattern of HIV infections.

EPIDEMIOLOGY AND TRANSMISSION OF HIV

An *epidemic* is the rapid and wide spreading of a contagious disease. In this country over about the past 15 years, the number of people known to have HIV or AIDS has grown from a few dozen to well over 1 million (about 1 in 250). Worldwide, over 16+ million people are infected with HIV (Figure 16.2). Rates of infection are rising in Latin America, the Caribbean, Sub-Saharan Africa, the Middle East, eastern Europe, and southeast Asia.

seroconversion   The process by which a person develops antibodies.

serostatus   The absence or presence of antibodies for a particular antigen.

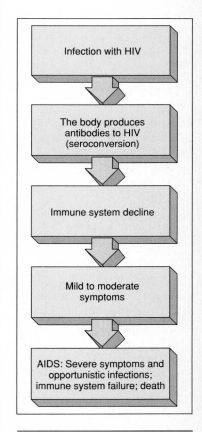

FIGURE 16.1 The General Pattern of HIV Infection.

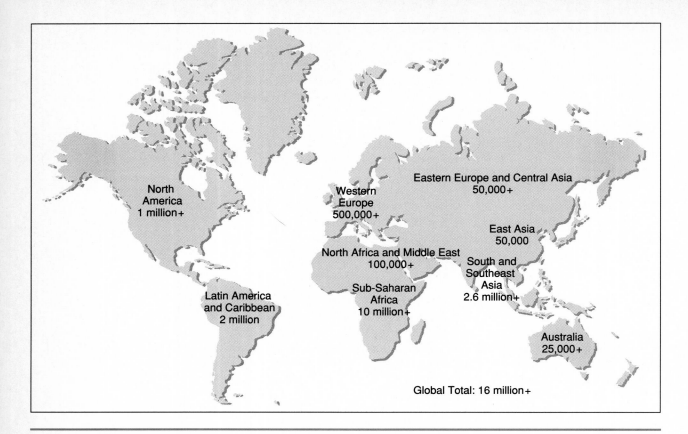

North
America
1 million+

Western
Europe
500,000+

Eastern Europe and Central Asia
50,000+

East Asia
50,000

North Africa and Middle East
100,000+

South and
Southeast
Asia
2.6 million+

Latin America
and Caribbean
2 million

Sub-Saharan
Africa
10 million+

Australia
25,000+

Global Total: 16 million+

FIGURE 16.2 Estimated World-wide Adult HIV Distribution, 1994. (SOURCE: Data from WHO.)

The steepest rises are occurring in southern Asia and Southeast Asia (Merson, 1993). These numbers suggest it is not unreasonable to refer to HIV/AIDS as an epidemic.

A great deal has been discovered about AIDS since it first perplexed physicians and scientists in 1981. Much of what we now know regarding HIV transmission is due to the work of epidemiologists who track the progress of the disease in the U.S. and throughout the world.

Epidemiology of HIV/AIDS

At this book's publication, the latest figures from the CDC indicated that, since 1981, 441,528 people have been diagnosed with AIDS in the United States, with 18% of those cases reported during 1994 (CDC, 1994b). Of the total 80,691 new AIDS cases reported in 1994, 54% fell under the expanded definition adopted at the beginning of 1993. Total deaths attributed to AIDS through 1994 were 270,870. Approximately 1 million people, or 1 out of every 250, were estimated to be infected with HIV. About 43% of the total reported U.S. AIDS cases involved gay or bisexual men. Women, blacks, and Hispanics, and persons with heterosexually acquired HIV infections account for the greatest growth in the epidemic. Injection drug use and sex with at-risk partners, especially among heterosexuals and young homosexual/bisexual men, also continue to challenge HIV prevention programs (CDC, 1994b). AIDS-related complications are the leading cause of death among American men between the ages of 25 and 44. Currently, the face of HIV/AIDS is changing, as gays have tended to modify their sexual behaviors, whereas heterosexuals have not. As we discussed earlier, heterosexual transmission is becoming more common, increasing from 1.9% in 1985 to 10.3% in 1994, and the increase is expected to continue (CDC, 1994b). The role of IV and injection drug use in the spread of HIV is also increasing as HIV-infected drug users pass the virus to each other in blood and to female partners during sexual activity (Koziol & Henderson, 1992). Pregnant women may also infect the fetus in utero. One model epidemiologists use to understand the spread of HIV views the infection as a "traveling wave" that moves at a fixed rate outward from core areas of infection, such as middle-class gay communities and inner-city ghettoes (Wallace, 1991). The role of education in changing behaviors has been demonstrated in some populations, notably the gay community, which has slowed the rate of new infection markedly (Koziol & Henderson, 1992).

YOU CAN'T LIVE ON HOPE.

NO SE PUEDE VIVIR DE ESPERANZAS.

Myths and Modes of Transmission

Before we discuss further the ways in which HIV has been shown to be transmitted, we should mention some of the ways in which it is *not* transmitted. You *cannot* get HIV from:

- *Casual contact.* Normal household or social contact does not transmit HIV. Shaking hands, hugging, kissing, playing, and providing personal care such as bathing, feeding, and dressing are extremely unlikely to transmit HIV. Extensive studies of households with an HIV-infected member have shown no evidence of transmission through casual contact (Fischl, Dickinson, Segal, Flanagan, & Rodriguez, 1987; Friedland, 1986; Mann et al., 1986; Rogers et al., 1990).

- *Inanimate objects.* HIV cannot live outside the body fluids in which it is normally found. It cannot survive on countertops, toilet seats, drinking fountains, telephones, eating utensils, and so on. If a surface or object is contaminated by infected blood or semen, it can be disinfected with bleach, alcohol, hydrogen peroxide, Lysol, or other household cleaners (Martin, Gresenguet, Massanga, Georges, & Testa, 1992).

- *Blood donation.* In the U.S., it is not possible to get HIV from donating blood. Sterilized needles are used to draw the blood; they are disposed of afterward; they are never reused.

- *Animals.* Household pets and farm animals can neither get HIV nor pass it on. Laboratory chimpanzees may be intentionally infected with HIV, but there are no known cases of transmission from chimps to humans.

- *Insect bites.* Extensive research has shown that HIV is not transmitted by biting insects such as mosquitoes. The virus has been demonstrated not to replicate in flies, ticks, and mosquitoes.

- *Saliva.* About 1% of people with HIV have detectable virus in their saliva (Ho et al., 1985). The amounts are very small, and enzymes in the saliva are hostile to the virus (Levy, 1988). There are no known cases of transmission from saliva, although theoretically there could be a slight risk if the saliva from a person with advanced AIDS were to enter another's bloodstream or if a person with HIV had blood in the mouth.

- *Tears or sweat.* HIV exists in minute quantities in the tears of some infected people, but researchers have found no evidence of transmission via tears (Tsoukas et al., 1986). Researchers have been unable to find the virus in the sweat of HIV-infected people (Wormser et al., 1992).

- *Vaccines.* The processes by which vaccines are manufactured effectively remove or inactivate HIV (CDC, 1984, 1987). In the U.S., sterile, fresh needles are used to give the vaccinations, and they are destroyed afterward.

- *Water.* HIV cannot live or replicate in water. It is not transmitted in drinking water, nor in hot tubs or swimming pools.

In order for HIV to replicate in the body, it must have a path of entry into the bloodstream. The most common modes of transmission involve HIV-infected semen, blood, or vaginal secretions. Activities or situations that may promote transmission include:

- Vaginal or anal intercourse without a latex condom, fellatio without a latex condom, cunnilingus without latex or other barrier

- Sharing needles contaminated with HIV-infected blood during IV drug use, tattooing, home injections of medications, or self-administered steroid injections

- Passing the virus from mother to fetus in the uterus (20–50% chance) or in blood during delivery

- Breast-feeding, if the mother is HIV-positive

- Sharing sex toys such as dildos or vibrators without disinfecting them

- Accidental contamination with infected blood entering the body through the mucous membranes of the eyes or mouth, or through cuts, abrasions, or punctures in the skin

- Before April 1, 1985, from contaminated blood (transfusions) or organs (transplants)

The first three modes are the most common. We discuss each of these in greater detail in the following sections.

Sexual Transmission

Semen and vaginal secretions of people with HIV may contain infected cells, especially in the later phases of AIDS. Latex barriers, condoms, dental dams, and surgical gloves can provide good protection against the transmission of HIV if used properly.

Anal Intercourse The riskiest form of sexual interaction for both men and women is receiving anal sex (de Vincenzi et al., 1992; Voeller, 1991). The membrane lining the rectum is delicate and ruptures easily, exposing tiny blood vessels to infection from virus-carrying semen. Infected blood from the rectum may also enter the penis through the mucous membrane at the urethral opening. Heterosexual anal intercourse is more common than many people realize; studies show that at least 10% of heterosexual couples regularly practice it (Voeller, 1991). Some couples rely on it as a way to avoid pregnancy.

Vaginal Intercourse Vaginal sex is also quite risky, especially for women. Women are at higher risk if they already have a vaginal infection because HIV will attract white blood cells that are present and infect them (Anderson, 1989). Women with cervical ectopy are also at higher risk because the epithelium (covering tissue of the cervix) is unusually thin (Moss et al., 1991). Men contract HIV during intercourse at 1/10–1/20 the rate that women contract it from men. Menstrual blood in which there is HIV can facilitate transmission of the virus to a sex partner (de Vincenzi et al., 1992), as can infected vaginal secretions containing abundant leuko- cytes.

Oral Sex HIV may be transmitted through oral sex between heterosex- uals, gay men, or lesbians (Lifson et al., 1990; UCSF, 1991). Infection can occur when semen or vaginal secretions from a person with HIV gets into an uninfected person's body via sores or cuts in or around a person's mouth, such as cold sores (herpes) or lesions from gum disease or excessive dental hygiene.

Sex Toys HIV can be transmitted in vaginal secretions on such objects as dildos and vibrators; therefore, it is very important that these objects not be shared or be washed thoroughly before use.

Male and Female Transmission Rates As discussed in Chapter 15, women are more likely than men to contract an STD when exposed to it during intercourse. HIV provides no exception to this rule. In a study of 379 heterosexual couples in which only one person of each pair was infected, researchers found that the rate of transmission from man to woman (in unprotected intercourse) was 20 times greater than from woman to man (Padian, Shiboski, & Jewell, 1991). In spite of this, heterosexual couples often do not use condoms during sex, even when one partner is known to be infected with the AIDS virus (de Vincenzi, 1994).

IV and Other Drug Use

Sharing needles or other paraphernalia (including cotton pieces) used to inject drugs provides an ideal pathway for HIV (Celentano, Vlahov, Cohn, Anthony, Solomon, & Nelson, 1991; National Commission, 1991). Infec- tion via the bloodstream is called **parenteral transmission.** An intravenous drug user (IVDU) or injection drug user (IDU) may already have an immune system weakened by poor health, poor nutrition, or an STD. Nearly three-quarters of the 40,000 injections that occurred in 1994 were among addicts.

An increasing number of affected individuals are crack addicts who con- tract the AIDS virus through unprotected sex, often with multiple partners.

parenteral transmisssion Infec- tion via the bloodstream.

Sharing needles and other injection-drug paraphernalia is a common mode of HIV transmission via infected blood. In this photograph, Jon Stuen Parker of the National AIDS Brigade distributes clean needles and alcohol (for sterilization) to IV drug users.

Men and women often go on binges, exchanging sex for crack or for the money to buy it. The crack addicts who become infected are mostly young men and women who live in inner cities and are members of minority groups. They often also have other sexually transmitted diseases, which is believed to make them more vulnerable to the AIDS virus (Kolata, 1995). Using drugs, including alcohol, also makes a person less inclined to think about safe sex.

When we think of injection drug use, we usually think in terms of psychotropic (mind-affecting) drugs such as heroin or cocaine. We may conjure up images of run-down tenement rooms or "shooting galleries," where needles are passed around. But these are not the only settings for sharing drugs. HIV transmission in connection with the recreational use of injection drugs also occurs among people who are of middle or upper socioeconomic status (Glaser, Strange, & Rosati, 1989). Moreover, injection drug use exists among athletes who may share needles for steroids to increase muscle mass. HIV can be transmitted just as easily in a brightly lit locker room or upscale living room as in a dark alley.

Mother-to-Child Transmission

The Geneva-based World Health Organization estimates that nearly 200,000 infants were born with HIV infection in 1994. Passing a disease from mother to child in the womb is known as **perinatal transmission.** The virus can also be transmitted as the infant moves through the birth canal.

perinatal transmission The passing of a disease from mother to fetus.

Infants whose mothers are HIV-positive will have HIV antibodies at birth. This does not necessarily mean they will become infected with the virus, though there is a 1 in 4 chance that the baby will be born with AIDS. Of those not born with AIDS, some will develop the disease within the first six months of life, while others will not develop it for 10 years or longer. Why this is true is still a scientific mystery.

It is not known exactly how HIV is passed from mother to fetus, although it is generally accepted that HIV manages to cross the placental barrier (Minkoff, 1989). In addition, it has recently been found that the likelihood of infecting the offspring rises with the amount of the virus in a pregnant woman's blood ("AIDS Test," 1995). The CDC now recommends that all pregnant women be tested for HIV and, if infected, be given the antiviral drug AZT during and immediately after delivering their infant. That dosage reduces by two-thirds the chance a mother will infect her unborn child ("AIDS Test," 1995).

Uncommon Modes of Transmission

Although the great majority of HIV infections are acquired in the ways just discussed, many people still worry about getting the virus through casual (nonsexual) contact or accidents. There is also concern about transmission through blood transfusions, although this mode is very unlikely today in countries that routinely test donated blood for HIV.

Nonsexual Contact As mentioned earlier in this chapter, nonsexual, casual contact that typically occurs with health-care workers, family members, and in school and day-care settings is highly unlikely to transmit HIV under ordinary circumstances. Many studies have shown the risk of transmission within families (excluding sexual partners) to be extremely low (Fischl et al., 1987; Friedland, 1986; Mann et al., 1986).

Much media attention has been focused on the possibility of transmission in health-care situations, either from infected providers (doctors, dentists, nurses, and so on) to their patients or from infected patients to their care providers. All studies of these situations show that the risk of transmission is very low, especially if standard infection control precautions and common sense are observed (Figure 16.3) (Klein et al., 1988; Koziol & Henderson, 1992).

Accidents People sometimes express concern about the possibility of accidental blood exchange—during children's play, or contact sports, for example. Although it is theoretically possible for blood to be passed in this way, it is highly unlikely that the blood of one person could spill into another person's open wound and from there into the bloodstream. (It was this kind of fear, expressed by professional basketball players, that led HIV-positive basketball superstar Magic Johnson to retire once and for all.)

Medical and dental accidents are also feared, although the chance of transmission in these situations is slight. A CDC surveillance project of 870 health-care workers who had been accidentally injected with HIV-positive blood found a very small incidence of transmission: less than 1% (CDC, 1988).

FIGURE 16.3 Relative Risks. Although people may worry about contracting HIV in health-care settings, the actual risks are very low. This graph compares various medical risks: the chance of contracting HIV from a surgeon of unknown HIV status and from an HIV-infected surgeon, and chances of death from several other sources including car accidents and childbirth. There are no known cases of HIV transmission by a surgeon; however, by the time you finish this chapter, at least three people in the U.S. will be killed in car accidents. (SOURCE: Data from *Health* Magazine, Sept. 1992.)

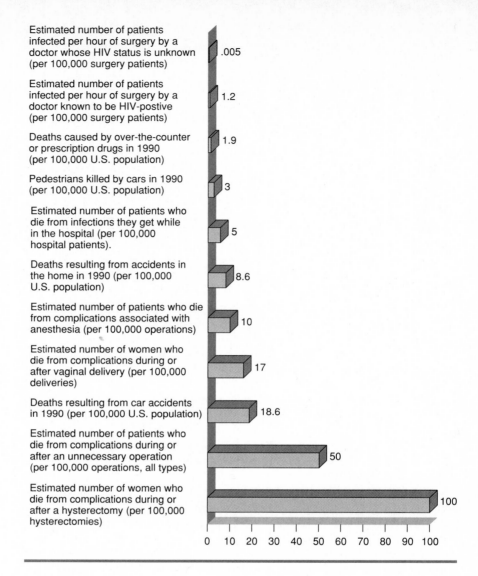

Estimated number of patients infected per hour of surgery by a doctor whose HIV status is unknown (per 100,000 surgery patients) .005

Estimated number of patients infected per hour of surgery by a doctor known to be HIV-postive (per 100,000 surgery patients) 1.2

Deaths caused by over-the-counter or prescription drugs in 1990 (per 100,000 U.S. population) 1.9

Pedestrians killed by cars in 1990 (per 100,000 U.S. population) 3

Estimated number of patients who die from infections they get while in the hospital (per 100,000 hospital patients). 5

Deaths resulting from accidents in the home in 1990 (per 100,000 U.S. population) 8.6

Estimated number of patients who die from complications associated with anesthesia (per 100,000 operations) 10

Estimated number of women who die from complications during or after vaginal delivery (per 100,000 deliveries) 17

Deaths resulting from car accidents in 1990 (per 100,000 U.S. population) 18.6

Estimated number of patients who die from complications during or after an unnecessary operation (per 100,000 operations, all types) 50

Estimated number of women who die from complications during or after a hysterectomy (per 100,000 hysterectomies) 100

0 10 20 30 40 50 60 70 80 90 100

Blood Transfusions and Organ Donations Theoretically, donated blood, plasma, body organs, and semen are all capable of sustaining HIV. Because of this, today these medical procedures include either screening out HIV or destroying it. Since April 1, 1985, blood has been screened for HIV. Plasma is treated to inactivate any virus that may be present. The chance of being infected with HIV via blood transfusion is estimated at 1 per 40,000–225,000 units (Dodd, 1992). Donated organs must be screened for HIV, and there are guidelines regarding semen donation for artificial insemination (discussed in Chapter 12).

Members of Act Up focus public attention on issues affecting people with HIV and AIDS.

AIDS DEMOGRAPHICS

The statistical characteristics of populations are called **demographics.** Public-health researchers often look at groups of people in terms of age, socioeconomic status, living area, ethnicity, or sex in order to understand the dynamics of disease transmission and prevention. In instances where sexually transmitted diseases are involved, they also look at sexual behaviors. This may entail studying groups based on sexual orientation as well as other characteristics that may be considered risk markers. No one is exempt from HIV exposure by virtue of belonging or not belonging to a specific group. Certain groups, however, appear *as a whole* to be at greater risk than others, or to face special difficulties where HIV is concerned. Many individuals within these groups may not be at risk, however, because they do not engage in risky behaviors.

demographics The statistical characteristics of human populations.

The Gay Community

"AIDS has given a human face to an invisible minority," says Robert Bray of the National Gay and Lesbian Task Force. As of 1994, 211,779 gay and bisexual men had been diagnosed with AIDS (CDC, 1994b). Over 100,000 had died. Another several hundred thousand are estimated to be infected with HIV. Although epidemiologists do not know for certain how HIV first arrived in the gay community, they do know that it spread like wildfire mainly because anal sex is such an efficient mode of transmission. Furthermore, initial research, education, and prevention efforts were severely hampered by a lack of government and public interest in what was perceived to be a "gay disease" (Shilts, 1987). Now, more than 15 years after the virus first appeared, the gay community continues to reel under the repeated

The Names Project has created a giant quilt, each square of which has been lovingly created by friends and families of people who have died of AIDS. The quilt now contains over 24,000 squares.

blows dealt by AIDS. Overall, sexual practices have become much safer, and the rate of new infection has fallen dramatically. But men who were infected years ago continue to sicken and die.

Many members of the gay community have lost dozens of their friends. They may be coping with multiple-loss syndrome, a psychological condition that may be characterized by depression, hypochondria, feelings of guilt, sexual dysfunction, or self-destructive behavior.

In spite of the initial lack of public support for the fight against AIDS, or perhaps at least partly because of it, the gay and lesbian communities rallied together in a variety of ways to support each other, educate themselves and the public, and influence government policies. Grass-roots projects such as clinics, self-help groups, and information clearinghouses were created by people from both the gay and the straight communities whose lives were affected by HIV. The role of volunteers remains a crucial component of many AIDS organizations. Many people have devoted themselves to supporting the HIV/AIDS community or educating the public.

Women and Children

Over 58,000 women are currently diagnosed with AIDS in this country; several hundred thousand are estimated to be infected with HIV (CDC, 1994b). AIDS among women represented 18% of all cases reported in 1994. Most were infected through injection drug use (41%) or heterosexual contact with an infected partner (38%). Public health officials expect that by the year 2000, the numbers of men and women with HIV will be equal (NIAID/CDC, 1991). Although women as a group are not at special risk for HIV, the activities which put them at risk include IV or injection drug use, being a sex partner of an IV drug user or gay or bisexual man, or having multiple sex partners.

Women are often diagnosed at a later stage than men. They are also one-third more likely to die without an AIDS-defining condition than are HIV infected men (The Nation's Health, 1995). There are several probable reasons that contribute to these sobering facts. First, women are not generally perceived to be at risk for HIV, so neither they nor their physicians will be alert to signs of HIV infection. Secondly, women with HIV often have poorer access to use of health care resources, as compared to men. Third, because they are often caretakers and may be breadwinners, they are less likely to seek care for themselves until they are quite ill. In addition, domestic violence and lack of social support for women inhibit their efforts to care for themselves.

As of December 30, 1994, 3400 deaths of children under 13 had been attributed to AIDS (CDC, 1994b). At this time, about 6200 children have been diagnosed with AIDS and thousands more with HIV. The epidemic in children is closely associated with the epidemic in women. In 1994, 1017 pediatric AIDS cases were reported, an 18% increase from the number reported in 1993. Of these, 92% were acquired perinatally; the mothers of these children were exposed to HIV through injection drug use (30%) and heterosexual contact with an infected man (36%) (CDC, 1994b). As these numbers rise, so does the burden on families and society, which must care for hundreds (or possibly thousands) of orphans, many of whom have HIV or AIDS (Chu, Buehler, Oxtoby, & Kolbourne, 1991).

The incidence of AIDS among children has been affected by recommendations by the Public Health Service, which suggests routine counseling and voluntary prenatal HIV testing for women, and the use of AZT to prevent perinatal transmission (CDC, 1994b).

Teenagers

HIV cases are increasing rapidly among young people (Mangasarian, 1993). Between 1990 and 1992, the number of AIDS cases among 13- to 24-year-olds rose by 77% to nearly 17,000. (Select Committee, 1992). (We should bear in mind that most of those in their twenties were probably infected in their teens.) Young gays, blacks, Latinos, and runaways are among those most affected, but others are also at increasing risk, including whites, heterosexuals, and rural teens.

Adolescence and risk taking often seem to go together like peanut butter and jelly. Because teenagers often have a sense of invulnerability, they may put themselves at great risk without really understanding what it means.

PREVENTION AND TREATMENT

As a whole, our society remains in denial about the realities of HIV risk. A sample of 574 clients attending an STD clinic found that among heterosexuals who reported having sex with people other than their regular partner, 79% did not consider themselves at risk for HIV (James, Gillies, & Bignell, 1991). Studies of college students generally indicate inconsis-

The Faces of HIV: Krista, who contracted HIV as a teenager.

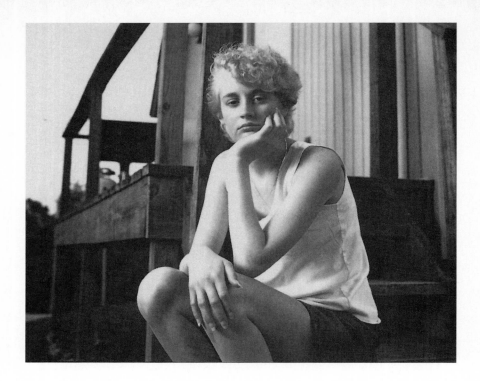

tent condom use as well as frequent high-risk behaviors, such as alcohol intoxication (Bruce, Shrum, Trefethen, & Slovik, 1990; Butcher, Manning, & O'Neal, 1991).

Protecting Ourselves

In order to protect ourselves and those we care about from HIV, there are some things we should know in addition to the basic facts about transmission and prevention.

What We Need to Know First, we should be aware that alcohol and drug use significantly increase risky behaviors. If we are serious about protecting ourselves, we need to assess our risks when we are clearheaded and act to protect ourselves. Second, we need to develop our communication skills so that we can discuss risks and prevention with our partner or potential partner. If we want our partner to disclose information about past high-risk behavior, we have to be willing to do the same (Shtarkshall & Awerbuch, 1992). Third, we may need to have information on HIV testing. If we have engaged in high-risk behavior, we may want to be tested for our own peace of mind and that of our partner. If we test positive for HIV, we need to make important decisions regarding our health, sexual behavior, and lifestyle. Fourth, if we are sexually active with more than one long-term, monogamous partner, we need to become very familiar with condoms.

HIV PREVENTION ATTITUDE SCALE

Read each statement carefully. Record your immediate reaction to each statement by writing the letter that corresponds to your answer. There is no right or wrong answer for each statement, so mark your own response.

Key

A = Strongly agree   D = Disagree
B = Agree   E = Strongly disagree
C = Undecided

1. I am certain that I could be supportive of a friend with HIV.
2. I feel that people with HIV got what they deserve.
3. I am comfortable with the idea of using condoms for sex.
4. I would dislike the idea of limiting sex to just one partner to avoid HIV infection.
5. It would be embarrassing to get the HIV antibody test.
6. It is meant for some people to get HIV.
7. Using condoms to avoid HIV is too much trouble.
8. I believe that AIDS is a preventable disease.
9. The chance of getting HIV makes using IV drugs stupid.
10. People can influence their friends to practice safe behavior.
11. I would shake hands with a person having HIV.
12. I will avoid sex if there is a slight chance that the partner might have HIV.
13. If I were to have sex, I would insist that a condom be used.
14. If I used IV drugs, I would not share the needles.
15. I intend to share HIV facts with my friends.

Scoring
Calculate the total points for each form using the following point values.
Items 1, 3, 8–15: Strongly agree = 5, Agree = 4, Undecided = 3, Disagree = 2, Strongly disagree = 1. For the remaining items: Strongly agree = 1, Agree = 2, Undecided = 3, Disagree = 4, Strongly disagree = 5.

The higher the score, the more positive the prevention attitude.

Source: William L. Yarber, Professor of Health Education, Indiana University, Bloomington; Mohammad Torabi, Professor of Health Education, Indiana University, Bloomington; L. Harold Veenker, Professor Emeritus of Health Education, Purdue University, Lafayette, IN.

Condoms Although America has responded to the threat of AIDS by increased purchasing of condoms, condom use remains low among many segments of the population (Catania et al., 1992; CDC, 1992a). Following Surgeon General Koop's 1987 report endorsing condoms for safer sex, there

LEARNING TO LOVE LATEX

"It's like taking a shower in a raincoat!" goes the old (male) complaint about wearing a condom. Many of the complainers, however, have not actually tried using condoms or have only tried one or two kinds. Becoming a virtuoso of safer sex requires becoming experienced with different varieties of condoms and other latex products. Although the idea of using a piece of rubber as part of normal sexual activity may appear clinical to the uninitiated, experienced safer-sex practitioners have found ways to turn latex protective devices into sexual enhancers.

Latex Care

Latex products that are used in safer sex include condoms, dental dams, gloves (for sex and cleanup), and finger covers. Proper care of these products helps assure their effectiveness as barriers to disease-causing organisms. Here are some guidelines for latex care:

- Check the expiration date on the package of your latex product. Latex deteriorates with age; its shelf life averages $2^1/_2$–5 years.

- Keep your latex away from heat. For example, don't leave condom packets in the sun or in your glove compartment. It's all right to carry condoms in your wallet, but don't leave them there for more than 2 weeks or so.

- Handle latex with care. Be especially careful not to tear your latex product when you open the package. Be careful with long fingernails.

- Keep all oil-based products away from your latex. These include oil-based lubricants (such as Vaseline), massage oils, cocoa butter, and vaginal medications such as estrogen preparations and antifungal creams. To see what oil does to latex, try this experiment: Rub a little massage oil, cooking oil, or Vaseline into a condom. Wait a minute or so, then stretch the latex and see what happens.

Dental Dams

Because HIV and other STDs can be transmitted in vaginal fluids (including menstrual blood), it's important to know how to practice cunnilingus safely. Organisms from genital sores or lesions, such as herpes, also can be spread during oral or manual sexual contact. There are several products that can provide barrier protection during these activities.

Dental dams are squares of latex used by dentists to isolate a particular tooth during dental procedures. They can usually be obtained at family planning clinics, women's clinics, or AIDS organizations. During sex, dams can be used over the vulva or anus while it is being orally or manually stimulated.

was a 50% increase in condom sales (*U.S. News and World Report,* 1994). Although increased sales imply increased use, it is clear that many people remain unconvinced regarding either their own vulnerability to HIV or the usefulness of condoms in preventing its spread.

Although any sexual activity involving semen, vaginal fluid, or blood carries some degree of risk, condoms have repeatedly been demonstrated to effectively reduce risk (CDC, 1993; Conant, Hardy, Sernatinger, Spicer, &

Some people have found an alternative to dental dams that is more comfortable for them—plastic wrap! Although no tests have been performed on the efficacy of plastic wrap as a barrier against disease organisms, it is thought to provide protection equivalent to that of latex dams when used according to similar guidelines. You can cut it to any size (the more area it covers, the better). Don't expose it to heat (including hot water), however, and don't reuse it. An additional caveat is to be aware of the risk of inhalation during use.

Another alternative for cunnilingus is a condom that has been cut open and flattened. You can snip the condom on one side before unrolling it. Use sharp scissors, and cut from the rolled edge to the center of the tip, then simply unroll it. You'll find the thin latex to be an excellent transmitter of heat and touch. A condom can also be slipped over the fingers for clitoral, vaginal, or anal stimulation. Latex gloves and finger covers (cots) also provide protection during manual sexual activities where there are sores, cuts, or abrasions.

Condom Sense

Basic guidelines for condom use are given in Chapter 11. Here are a few additional suggestions to help you use condoms safely and pleasurably.

- Some brands are more highly rated for safety than others. A study funded by the NIH rated Ramses Non-Lube, Ramses Sensitol, Gold Circle Coin, Gold Circle, and Sheik Elite the highest (Nakamura et al., 1988, Voeller et al., 1988). A *Consumer Reports* study found the most effective condoms to be Gold Circle Coin, LifeStyles Extra-Strength Lubricated, Saxon Wet Lube, Ramses Non-Lube, and Sheik Non-Lube ("Can You Rely on Condoms?" 1989). The best-selling brand, Trojan, was generally rated low by both studies. Many Japanese condoms are also considered to be of high quality because they are individually tested, rather than randomly tested, as American condoms are. For up-to-date studies, check your library, family planning clinic, or AIDS resource center.

- To maximize your pleasure, try different kinds of condoms. Some brands and styles may fit more comfortably than others. Some, including the Japanese brands, are quite thin and allow a lot of sensitivity. Some brands of thinner condoms may be more prone to tearing than others. In cases of tears or slippage, apply spermicide or lubricant with nonoxynol-9 to reduce the chance of infection. If one brand consistently tears, try a different one.

- If breakage is a problem no matter what kind of condom you use (some people are just friskier than others), consider "double bagging"—using two condoms! Some folks swear by this.

There is no product or practice (except abstinence) that can guarantee 100% safety from HIV and other STDs, but with a little latex and common sense, we can provide a lot of protection for ourselves and those we care about.

Levy, 1986; Fischl et al., 1987; Van-de-Perre, Jacobs, & Sprecher-Goldberger, 1987). As we have stressed before, condoms do not guarantee 100% safety from HIV. Even if used properly, there is a 1 in 50 chance that a latex condom will break (*U.S. News and World Report*, 1994). Abstinence is safer. But if we choose to have sex, using a condom significantly reduces the risk (just as putting on a seat belt improves your safety when riding in a car).

IF YOU ARE HIV-POSITIVE OR HAVE AIDS

People with AIDS, sometimes referred to as **PWAs,** and people with HIV, **PWHs,** have the same needs as everyone else—and a few more. Although a diagnosis may be a cause for sadness and grieving, it may also be a time for reevaluation and growth.

Early detection of HIV can greatly enhance both the quality and quantity of life. It is important to find a physician who is experienced and sensitive to the health and psychological needs of people with HIV and AIDS. In addition to appropriate medical treatment, factors that can help to promote your continuing good health include good nutrition, plenty of rest, appropriate exercise, limited (or no) alcohol use, and stress reduction. People with HIV or AIDS should stop smoking tabacco because it increases susceptibility to PCP. This doesn't mean shutting yourself up in a room and never coming out. It simply means you need to take a little more than ordinary care not to expose yourself to infectious organisms, such as any spoiled or improperly cooked foods, unwashed glasses or utensils used by sick households members, or certain kinds of pets. Your physician or nearest HIV/AIDS resource group should have more information about these measures.

In addition, if you have decided to have sexual relations, it means practicing safer sex, even if your partner is also HIV-positive. Researchers caution that one can become reinfected with different HIV strains—definitely not a pleasant thought (Chermann in Challice, 1992). Moreover, STDs of all kinds can be much worse for people with an impaired immune system. HIV doesn't mean an end to being sexual, but it does mean that different ways of expressing love and lust may be explored.

It is recommended that women who are HIV-positive have Pap tests every 6 months to a year. Cervical biopsies may also be necessary to determine if cervical dysplasia or cancer is present.,

Besides taking care of one's physical health, a person who is living with HIV needs to take care of his or her psychological and emotional needs. The stigma and fear surrounding HIV and AIDS often make it difficult to just get on with the business of living. People who live with HIV and AIDS say that it's important not to feel ioslated. If you are HIV-positive, we encourage you to seek support from AIDS organizations in your area.

PWA A person with AIDS.

PWH A person with HIV.

HIV Testing

Free or low-cost and anonymous or confidential HIV testing is available in many areas, although in some places, people are turned away from test sites because of a lack of funding.

Types of Tests Almost everyone who has the HIV virus will develop antibodies within 2–6 months after exposure. The most common tests look for these antibodies. Occasionally, a person with HIV will not have discernible antibodies when tested; if there is reason to suspect HIV, other tests can be performed that will be definitive (Pan, Sheppard, Winkelstein, & Levy, 1991).

ELISA A simple blood test that screens for HIV antibodies; the most common test for HIV.

The most common test for HIV is called the **ELISA,** an acronym for enzyme-linked immunosorbent assay. This simple blood test screens for the antibodies to HIV that are usually present 2 months after infection with

The Faces of HIV: Kevin and Cyndi. Kevin and Cyndi are a couple living with HIV.

the virus. A negative test result—meaning no antibodies are found—is considered highly (99.7%) accurate if received 6 months after the date of last possible exposure (Damon Clinical Laboratories, 1990). In the event of a positive or inconclusive test result, a person should be retested; in ELISA tests on the general population, only about 20–30% of seropositive results will be true positives indicating HIV infection. The test used to recheck positive ELISA results is called the **Western blot.** In the Western blot procedure, the antibodies are tested to determine whether they are specific to HIV or not. Usually, Western blot results are clearly either positive or negative; if there is an inconclusive result, the person should be tested again in 6 months.

Western blot A test to determine whether antibodies are specific to HIV.

Getting Tested Most people who go for an HIV test are anxious. Even though the vast majority of test results are negative, there is still the understandable fear that one has drawn the short straw. For many people, there are probably also feelings of ambivalence or guilt about the risky behaviors that led them to the test site.

Counseling is vitally important for those who are HIV-positive. Early treatment and positive health behaviors are essential to retaining good health and prolonging life. AIDS counselors and health-care practitioners currently encourage those with HIV to make all possible efforts to contact past and current partners. In some cases, counselors try to make such contacts, with their clients' permission.

Existing Treatments

There are three basic types of medical treatment for HIV and AIDS. One type consists of therapies to treat the symptoms and infections; these

IF YOU ARE CARING FOR SOMEONE WITH HIV INFECTION OR AIDS

When someone you know is diagnosed with HIV or AIDS, you, as a support person, should be aware of the unchartered territory ahead in terms of discrimination, experimental drug treatments, the unpredictable and dreadful course of the disease, new and strong emotions, and always the hope that accompanies each treatment. Added to all this is a changing sense of time and increasing feelings of urgency, which intensify all of the above.

Caring for someone with HIV or AIDS also means dealing with your own profound emotions. This includes confronting your fears about death and dying, accepting your changing relationship with your partner, and addressing your anger, depression, loneliness, guilt, and/or sense of abandonment.

To help your friend or partner, you may need to actively seek information and support from legal, medical, and psychological resources. National, state, and city hotlines, referral agencies, texts, professionals with experience and compassion, and support groups can be found by searching through telephone directories and/or libraries in your region. Reaching out and sharing empower you to meet the challenges you face today and will undoubtedly continue to face in the future.

include antibiotics, pain medications, and so on. Another type consists of drugs that affect the virus in some way. This category includes newly formulated antiretroviral drugs that act directly on the virus to change or delay the way in which it progresses. A third category includes treatments designed to bolster the immune system's natural responses. Most physicians agree that early detection of HIV is essential for deriving optimum benefits from medical care and healthy lifestyle choices. Those who seek testing and early treatment tend to be white, educated, middle-class gay men with good health insurance and access to doctors who work with HIV (Lambert, 1990). Most of the medicines used to treat HIV are very costly.

AZT (zidovudine or azidothymidine) has been used to increase CD4+ T cells or prevent their decrease. It does this by slowing the production of reverse transcriptase, the enzyme HIV uses to replicate. During treatment, HIV quickly becomes resistant to AZT, and there can be negative side effects such as nausea, headaches, and anemia. A number of researchers believe AZT therapy should begin in the early (asymptomatic) phase of HIV infection (Graham et al., 1992; Gruters et al., 1991). Other antiretroviral drugs, however, can be used if resistance develops. These include ddI (didanosine) and ddC (dideoxycytidine).

Like AZT, ddI interferes with HIV replication and slows the onset of AIDS symptoms. It has proved most useful for people with resistance to AZT and generally has fewer negative side effects. There is recent evidence that the combination of AZT and ddI is more effective than either drug used alone, but the long-term effectiveness is still unknown (Project Inform, 1990b).

Among the most common drugs used to treat the opportunistic infections associated with AIDS are preventive antibiotics such as Septra and

Bactrim, dapsone, and aerosolized pentamidine, all of which can be very effective against pneumocystis (PCP).

"Education is going to be the vaccine for AIDS," says June Osborn, Dean of the University of Michigan's School of Public Health and former chair of the National Commission on AIDS. As we have seen, there are many public misperceptions concerning HIV and AIDS, and the denial of risk appears to be epidemic in many areas. But AIDS can be prevented. We hope that this chapter has provided you with information that will serve as your vaccine.

SUMMARY

What Is AIDS?

- AIDS is an acronym for acquired immune deficiency syndrome. In order for a person to receive an AIDS diagnosis, he or she must have a positive blood test indicating the presence of HIV (human immunodeficiency virus) antibodies and have a T-cell count below 200; if the T-cell count is higher, the person must have one or more of the 27 diseases or conditions associated with AIDS. These include opportunistic infections, such as Pneumocystis carinii pneumonia and tuberculosis; cancers, such as Kaposi's sarcoma, lymphomas, and cervical cancer; and conditions associated with AIDS, such as wasting syndrome and AIDS dementia. Other conditions may lead to an AIDS diagnosis, including persistent candidiasis and outbreaks of herpes.

- A host of symptoms are associated with HIV/AIDS. Because these symptoms may be indicative of many other diseases and conditions, HIV and AIDS cannot be self-diagnosed; testing by a clinician or physician is necessary.

- Leukocytes, or white blood cells, play major roles in defending the body against invading organisms and cancerous cells. One type, the macrophage, engulfs foreign particles and displays the invader's antigen on its own surface. Antibodies bind to antigens, inactivate them, and mark them for destruction by killer cells. Other white blood cells called lymphocytes include helper T cells, which are programmed to "read" the antigens and then begin directing the immune system's response. The number of helper T cells in an individual's body is an important indicator of how well the immune system is functioning.

- Viruses are primitive entities; they can't propel themselves independently, and they can't reproduce unless they are inside a host cell. Within the human immuno-deficiency virus's protein core is the genetic material (RNA) that carries the information the virus needs to replicate itself. A retrovirus can "write" its RNA (the genetic program) into a host cell's DNA.

- Although HIV begins replication right away within the host cells, it is not detectable in the blood for some time—often years. HIV antibodies, however, are generally detectable in the blood within 2–6 months. A person's serostatus is HIV-negative if antibodies are not present and HIV-positive if antibodies are detected. "T-cell count" or "CD4 count" refers to the number of helper T cells that are present in a cubic milliliter of blood. A healthy person has a T-cell count in the range of 500–1600.

- When a person is first infected with HIV, he or she may experience severe flulike symptoms. During this period, the virus is dispersed throughout the lymph nodes and other tissues. The virus may stay localized in these areas for years, but it continues to replicate and to destroy T cells. As the number of infected cells goes up, the number of T cells goes down. In advanced AIDS, the T-cell count drops to under 200, and the virus itself is detectable in the blood.

Epidemiology and Transmission of HIV

- Over 440,000 people are currently diagnosed with AIDS in the U.S. Another 1 million are estimated to be infected with HIV; worldwide, over 16 million people are infected with HIV. Heterosexual transmission is becoming more common and is expected to continue to increase. The role of IV drug use in the spread of HIV is increasing as HIV-infected drug users pass the virus to each other in blood and to women partners during sexual activity. Women may then infect their children in utero, as they pass through the birth canal, or through breast-feeding.

- HIV is not transmitted by casual contact. Saliva is unlikely to transmit HIV.

- Activities or situations that may promote transmission include sexual transmission through vaginal or anal intercourse without a condom; fellatio without a condom; cunnilingus without a latex or other barrier; sharing needles contaminated with infected blood; in utero infection from mother to fetus, from blood during delivery, or in breast milk; sharing sex toys without disinfecting them; accidental contamination with infected blood entering the body through mucous membranes (eyes or mouth) or cuts, abrasions, or punctures in the skin (relatively rare); or blood transfusions administered prior to April 1, 1985.

AIDS Demographics

- Certain groups appear as a whole to be a greater risk than others, or to face special difficulties where HIV is concerned, including gay men, women, teenagers, and young inner-city African Americans.

- The gay and lesbian communities, along with other concerned individuals, have rallied together in a variety of ways to support people with HIV and AIDS, to educate themselves and the public, and to influence government policies.

- It is expected that by the year 2000, the numbers of women and men with HIV will be equal. Women face unique issues where HIV is concerned. As the number of infected women rises, the number of infected children is also expected to rise. Because teenagers often have a sense of invulnerability, they may put themselves at great risk without really understanding what it means.

Prevention and Treatment

- To protect ourselves and those we care about from HIV, we need to be aware that alcohol and drug use significantly increases risky behaviors, develop communication skills so that we can talk with our partner, and get information on HIV testing. If we are sexually active with more than one long-term, monogamous partner, we need to use condoms consistently.

- Free or low-cost, anonymous or confidential HIV testing is available in many areas, although in some places people are turned away from test sites because of a lack of funding. The most common test, ELISA, looks for antibodies for the virus.

- There are three basic types of medical treatments for HIV and AIDS: therapies to treat the symptoms and infections, such as antibodies and pain medications; drugs that affect the virus in some way, such as AZT; and therapies that boost the immune system.

- An HIV or AIDS diagnosis may be a cause for sadness and grieving, but it also may be a time for reevaluation and growth. Those whose friends or family members are living with HIV, or who are themselves HIV-positive, need information, practical support, and emotional support. People with HIV or AIDS often face discrimination in society.

- Early detection of HIV can greatly enhance both the quality and quantity of life. Appropriate medical treatment and a healthy lifestyle are important. People with HIV or AIDS also need to practice safer sex and consider seeking support from AIDS organizations. AIDS caregivers need support, too.

SUGGESTED READINGS

Arno, Peter S., and Karyn L. Feiden. *Against the Odds: The Story of AIDS Drug Development, Politics and Profits.* New York: HarperCollins, 1992. A fascinating and frustrating story of what can occur when human medical needs conflict with those of business and government.

DiClemente, Ralph J. *Adolescents and AIDS.* Newbury Park, CA: Sage Publications, 1992. A well-researched and sobering report on the risks teenagers face (and take) today.

Huber, Jeffrey T. *How to Find Information About AIDS.* New York: Haworth Press, 1992. An important resource guide.

Pizzi, Michael. *Productive Living Strategies for People with AIDS.* New York: Haworth Press, 1990. Practical advice for people with HIV and AIDS.

Shilts, Randy. *And the Band Played On: People, Politics and the AIDS Epidemic.* New York: St. Martin's Press, 1987. The fascinating story behind the "discovery" of AIDS, complete with real heroes and, unfortunately, real villains.

Stine, Gerald J. *Acquired Immune Deficiency Syndrome: Biological, Medical, Social, and Legal Issues.* Englewood Cliffs, NJ: Prentice-Hall, 1993. A factual study of the AIDS epidemic.

Chapter Seventeen

SEXUAL COERCION: HARASSMENT, AGGRESSION, AND ABUSE

PREVIEW: SELF-QUIZ

1. Most rapes are committed by acquaintances or dates. True or false?

2. Sexual harassment is considered illegal only when a superior requests sexual favors from a subordinate in exchange for keeping his or her job. True or false?

3. Men and women often have differing perceptions of what constitutes sexual harassment. True or false?

4. Men are more likely than women to report their rape to authorities. True or false?

5. Evidence indicates that relatively few gay men and lesbians have been physically attacked because of their sexual orientation. True or false?

6. Prejudices based on race and on sexual orientation share many characteristics. True or false?

7. Women often cry rape for revenge. True or false?

8. The majority of sexually victimized children are prepubescent girls. True or false?

9. Lack of sexual desire is common among rape survivors. True or false?

10. The least common form of sexual abuse within the family is uncle-niece abuse. True or false?

ANSWERS 1. T, 2. F, 3. T, 4. F, 5. F, 6. T, 7. F, 8. F, 9. T, 10. F

Chapter Outline

Although sexuality permits us to form and sustain deep bonds and intimate relationships, it may also have a darker side. For some people, sex is linked with coercion, degradation, aggression, and abuse. In these cases, sex becomes a weapon. Sex can be a means to exploit, humiliate, or harm others. In this chapter, we first examine the various aspects of sexual harassment, including the distinction between flirting and harassment and sexual harassment in schools, colleges, and the workplace. Next we look at harassment, prejudice, and discrimination directed against gay men and lesbians. Then we examine sexual aggression, including date rape and stranger rape, the motivations for rape, and the consequences of rape. Finally, we discuss child sexual abuse, examining the factors contributing to abuse, the types of sexual abuse and their consequences, and programs for preventing child sexual abuse.

SEXUAL HARASSMENT

Sexual harassment refers to two distinct types of behavior: the abuse of power for sexual ends, and the creation of a hostile environment. In abuse of power, sexual harassment consists of unwelcome sexual advances, requests for sexual favors, or other verbal or physical conduct of a sexual nature as a condition of instruction or employment. Only a person with power over another can commit the first kind of harassment. In a **hostile environment,** someone acts in sexual ways that interfere with a person's performance at school or in the workplace. Such harassment is illegal.

Sexual harassment is a mixture of sex and power; power may often be the dominant element. In school and in the workplace, men devalue women by calling attention to their sexuality. Sexual harassment may be a way to keep women "in their place" and make them feel vulnerable.

There are other forms of behavior that, although not illegal, are considered by many to be sexual harassment. These include unwelcomed whistles, taunts, and obscenities directed from a man or group of men to a woman walking past them. They also include a man "talking to" a woman's breasts or body during conversation, or persistently giving her "the once over" as she walks past him, sits down, or enters or leaves a room. Such incidents may make women feel uncomfortable and vulnerable. (They have been described, in fact, as "little rapes.") The cumulative effect of these behaviors is to lead women to limit their activities, to avoid walking past groups of men, and to stay away from beaches, concerts, parties, and sports events unless they are accompanied by others (Bowman, 1993).

Flirtation Versus Harassment

There is nothing wrong with flirtation per se. A certain smile, look, or compliment can give zest and pleasure to both people. But persistent and unwelcomed flirtation can be sexual harassment if the flirtatious person holds power over the other, or if the flirtation creates a hostile school or work environment. Whether flirtation is sexual harassment depends on three factors. These apply to male-female, male-male, and female-female interactions.

1. *Whether you have equal power.* A person's having power over you limits your ability to refuse, for fear of reprisal. For example, if a professor or teaching assistant in your class asks you for a date, you are placed in an awkward position. If you say no, will your grade suffer? Will you be ignored in class? What other consequences might occur? If your boss at work asks for dates, you may be similarly concerned about losing your job, being demoted, or having your work environment become hostile.

2. *Whether you are approached appropriately.* "Hi babe, nice tits, wanna screw?" or "Hey stud, love your buns, wanna do it?" are patently offensive. But approaches that are complimentary ("You look really nice today"), indirect ("What do you think of the course?"), or direct ("Would you like to have some coffee?") are acceptable because they do not pressure you. You have the opportunity to let the overture pass, respond positively, or politely decline.

sexual harassment The abuse of power for sexual ends; the creation of a hostile work or educational environment because of unwelcomed conduct or conditions of a sexual nature.

hostile environment As related to sexuality, a work or educational atmosphere that interferes with a person's performance because of sexual harassment.

3. *Whether you wish to continue contact.* If you find the other person appealing, you may want to continue the flirtation. You can express interest or flirt back. But if you don't, you may want to stop the interaction by not responding or by responding in a neutral or discouraging manner.

The issue is complicated by several factors related to culture and gender. Differing cultural expectations may lead to misinterpretation. For example, when a Latino, whose culture encourages mutual flirting, says *"muy guapa"* (good looking) to a Latina woman walking by, the words may be meant *and* received as a compliment. But when a Latino says the same to a non-Latina woman, he may be dismayed to find the woman insulted.

Three significant gender differences may contribute to sexual harassment. First, men are generally less likely to perceive activities as harassing than are women (Jones & Remland, 1992; Popovich et al., 1992). Second, men tend to misperceive women's friendliness as sexual interest (Johnson, Stockdale, & Saal, 1991; Stockdale, 1993). Third, men are more likely than women to perceive male-female relationships as adversarial (Reilly, Lott, Caldwell, & Deluca, 1992).

Power differences also affect perception (Popovich et al., 1986). Personal questions asked by an instructor or supervisor, for example, are more likely to be perceived as sexual harassment than they would be if a student or co-worker asked them. What needs to be clear is that the relationship has an educational, business, or professional basis rather than a romantic or sexual one. Flirtatious or sexual ways of relating are inappropriate in these contexts.

Harassment in School and College

Sexual harassment in various forms is widespread. It does not necessarily begin in adulthood; it may begin as early as middle childhood.

Elementary and High School Harassment

It's a "time-honored" practice for boys to "tease" girls: flipping up their skirts, calling them names, touching their breasts, spreading sexual gossip, and so on. If such behavior is defined as teasing, its impact is discounted; it is just "fun." But if the behavior is thought of as sexual harassment, then the acts may be evaluated in a new light. Such behavior, researcher Carrie Herbert (1989) found, leads girls to "become more subordinated, less autonomous, and less capable of resisting. This behavior controls the girls through intimidation, embarrassment, or humiliation."

Among students, sexual harassment occurs most often when boys are in groups. Their motives may often be homosocial—heightening their group status by denigrating girls rather than any specific animosity toward a particular girl (Carr, 1992). Harassment is usually either ignored by adults or regarded as normal or typical behavior among boys. Girls are frequently blamed for the harassment because they do not "stand up for themselves," or else they take the incidents "too seriously" (Herbert, 1989).

Many parents and educators are becoming increasingly aware that the roots of sexual harassment are found in what children learn from their peers at school.

College Harassment   Sexual harassment on college and university campuses has become a major concern in recent years (Bursik, 1992; Paludi, 1990; for a review of the literature, see Hotelling, 1991). Various studies suggest that 15–35% of women college students have experienced some form of harassment from other students, faculty members, or administrators (Bursik, 1992; Kenig & Ryan, 1986; Paludi, 1990).

Two major problems in dealing with issues of sexual harassment are gender differences in levels of tolerance and attribution of blame. Women are often blamed for not taking a "compliment" and for provoking unwanted sexual attention by what they wear or how they look. These attitudes also seem to be widely held in college settings, especially among men.

As a consequence of sexual harassment, students may find it difficult to study; others worry about their grades. If the harasser is an instructor controlling grades, students fear reporting the harassment. They may use strategies such as avoiding courses taught by the harasser. In extreme cases, the emotional consequences may sometimes be as severe as for those who are raped (Paludi, 1990).

Most universities and colleges have developed sexual harassment policies. Such policies help make students aware of harassment issues, but their effectiveness depends on educating students about what constitutes harassment (Gressman et al., 1992; Williams, Lam, & Shively, 1992). Younger female students, in particular, are often unable to define clearly harassing situations as harassment, despite feelings of discomfort (Bremer, Moore, & Bildersee, 1991; Jaschick & Fretz, 1991). With the exception of coercive or highly intrusive behaviors, many students are uncertain about what behaviors constitute sexual harassment (Fitzgerald & Ormerod, 1991). Because reporting requires enormous amounts of energy and consumes much time, victims may be unwilling or unable to deal with consequences.

If a student finds himself or herself sexually harassed, the first step is to request the harasser to stop. The person may not be aware of the impact of his or her behavior. If he or she does not stop, the student should consult an advisor, resident assistant, counselor, or dean.

Harassment in the Workplace

Issues of sexual harassment are complicated in the workplace because work, like college, is one of the most important places where adults meet potential partners. As a consequence, sexual undercurrents or interactions often take place. Flirtations, romances, and affairs are common in the work environment. Drawing the line between flirtation and harassment can be filled with ambiguity—especially for men.

Furthermore, sexuality and power issues can become intertwined. Power can manifest itself in sexual coercion or harassment. Sexual harassment tends to be most pervasive in formerly all-male occupations. In these occupations, sexual harassment is a means of exerting control over women and asserting male dominance. Such male bastions as the building trades, the trucking industry, law enforcement, and the military have been especially resistant to women entering (Niebhuhr & Boyles, 1991; Schmitt, 1990). Sexual harassment can be perpetuated by fellow employees as well as by supervisors.

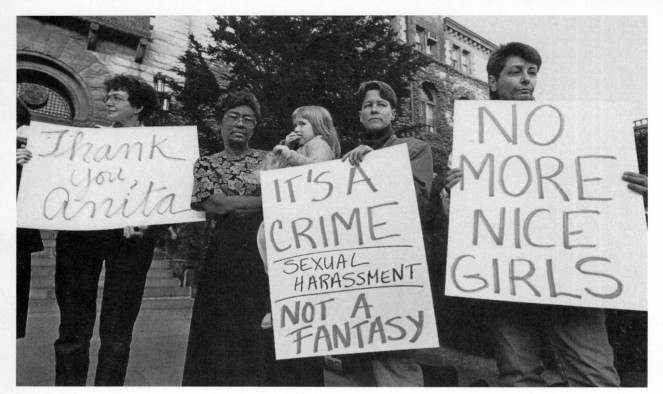

Sexual harassment has become an important but often divisive issue on many college campuses. Exactly what acts constitute sexual harassment is unclear to many.

Sexual harassment can have a variety of consequences. One study of the workplace found that about 9% of the women and 1% of the men quit their jobs because of harassment; almost 7% of the women and 2% of the men were dismissed from their jobs as part of the harassment (Gutek, 1985). Victims often report depression, anxiety, shame, humiliation, and anger (Paludi, 1990).

ANTI-GAY/LESBIAN HARASSMENT, PREJUDICE, AND DISCRIMINATION

Americans feel profoundly ambivalent about gay men and lesbians. A large-scale survey conducted by the *New York Times* in 1993 found that 55% believed sexual behavior between adult gay men or lesbians is morally wrong (Schmalz, 1993). At the same time, 78% believed gay men and lesbians should have equal job opportunities. Researchers have identified two forms of discrimination or bias against gay men and lesbians: heterosexual bias and anti-gay prejudice. **Heterosexual bias,** also known as **heterosexism,** is the tendency to see the world in heterosexual terms and to ignore or devalue homosexuality (Herek, Kimmel, Amaro, & Melton, 1991; Rich, 1983). Heterosexual bias may take numerous forms, including ignoring the existence of lesbians and gay men, segregating lesbians and gay men from heterosexuals, and submerging gay men and lesbians into a larger category.

heterosexual bias or **heterosexism** The tendency to see the world in heterosexual terms and to ignore or devalue homosexuality.

Anti-gay prejudice is a strong dislike, fear, or hatred of gay men and lesbians because of their homosexuality. *Homophobia* is an irrational or phobic fear of gay men and lesbians. Not all anti-gay feelings are phobic in the clinical sense of being excessive and irrational. They may be unreasonable or biased. (They may be, however, within the norms of a biased culture.) Because prejudice may not be clinically phobic, "homophobia" is being increasingly replaced by the nonclinical phrase "anti-gay prejudice" (Haaga, 1991).

Prejudice, Discrimination, and Violence

Anti-gay prejudice is acted out through offensive language, discrimination, and violence against gay men and lesbians. They are called "faggot," "dyke," "queer," and "homo." They are discriminated against in terms of housing, employment opportunities, adoption, parental rights, family acceptance, and so on. And they are the victims of violence, known as **gay-bashing** or **queer-bashing.**

Anti-gay prejudice adversely affects heterosexuals as well. First, it creates fear and hatred, negative emotions that cause distress and anxiety. Second, it alienates them from their gay family members, friends, neighbors, or co-workers (Holtzen & Agresti, 1990). Third, it limits their range of behaviors and feelings, such as hugging or being emotionally intimate with same-sex friends, for fear that such intimacy may be "homosexual" (Britton, 1990). Fourth, among men, it may lead to exaggerated displays of masculinity to prove that one is not gay, that is, effeminate (Mosher & Tompkins, 1988).

Discrimination and Antidiscrimination Laws As a result of anti-gay prejudice, gay men and lesbians are discriminated against in employment, insurance, housing, and parental rights. They face imprisonment for engaging in oral and anal sex, for which heterosexuals are seldom prosecuted. Medical and public-health efforts against HIV/AIDS were inhibited initially because AIDS was perceived as "the gay plague" and was considered "punishment" against gay men for their "unnatural" sexual practices (Altman, 1985). The fear of HIV/AIDS has contributed to increased anti-gay prejudice among some heterosexuals (Lewes, 1992). Anti-gay prejudice influences parental reactions to their gay and lesbian children, often leading to estrangement (Holtzen & Agresti, 1990). And in some cases, a gay man's advances toward a homophobic male have led to manslaughter.

Gay men and lesbians have been seeking legislation to protect themselves from discrimination based on sexual orientation. Such legislation guarantees lesbians and gay men equal protection under the law; it is not affirmative action or quota programs, as opponents often maintain. Public opinion supports equal employment opportunities for gay men and lesbians.

Violence Against Gay Men and Lesbians Violence against gay men and lesbians has a long history. At times, such violence has been sanctioned by religion. During the Renaissance, the Inquisition burned "sodomites." In the sixteenth century, England's King Henry VIII made sodomy punishable by death. In our own times, homosexuals were among the first victims of the Nazis, who killed 50,000 in concentration camps. Because of worldwide violence and persecution against lesbians and gay men, the Netherlands,

anti-gay prejudice A strong dislike, fear, or hatred of gay men and lesbians because of their homosexuality.

gay-bashing or **queer-bashing** Violence directed against gay men or lesbians because of their orientation.

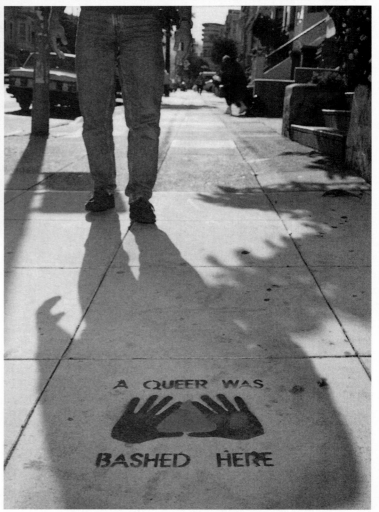

During the Middle Ages, gay men (called sodomites) were burned at the stake as heretics (above). In Germany in 1933, the Nazis burned Magnus Hirschfeld's library and forced him to flee the country (above, right). Gay men and lesbians were among the first Germans the Nazis forced into concentration camps, where over 50,000 people were killed. Today, violence against gay men and lesbians, known as gay-bashing, continues (right). The pink triangle recalls the symbol the Nazis required lesbians and gay men to wear, just as they required Jews to wear the star of David.

Germany, and Canada in 1992 granted asylum to men and women based on their homosexuality (Farnsworth, 1992).

Today, gay men and lesbians continue to be the targets of violence. Over 90% have been subjected to anti-gay verbal abuse or threats. Almost one-quarter reported they had been physically attacked (Herek, 1989).

Sources of Anti-Gay Prejudice   Anti-gay prejudice in people may be derived from several sources (Marmor, 1980b): (1) a deeply rooted insecurity concerning a person's own sexuality and gender identity, (2) a strong fundamentalist religious orientation, and (3) simple ignorance concerning homosexuality. The literature also indicates fairly consistent gender differences in attitudes toward lesbians and gay men (Herek, 1984). Heterosexuals tend to have more negative attitudes toward gays of their own sex than of the other sex. Heterosexual men tend to be less tolerant than heterosexual women.

In addition, much anti-gay prejudice is conveyed through some of our social institutions, especially conservative religious groups and the military. Christianity and Judaism have been particularly important in reinforcing negative views of homosexuality. According to researcher Bruce Voeller (1980): "Among societal institutions, the church is the primal source of intolerance of homosexuality. . . . This has created particularly severe problems for gays and lesbians who are religious." The spectrum of religious opinion runs from full equality for lesbians and gay men among Quakers and other groups that value tolerance to total rejection in Catholic and many fundamentalist teachings.

Despite hostility, many religious lesbians and gay men have formed their own churches and synagogues, such as the Metropolitan Community Church. Denominational caucuses, including the Catholic group Dignity, Affirmation, Lutherans Concerned, and Presbyterians for Lesbian and Gay Concerns, have emerged to advocate tolerance within the churches.

The U.S. military is another bastion of anti-gay prejudice. In Canada, Israel, Japan, Sweden, and several other European countries, gay men serve without restriction in the military. By contrast, when President Clinton announced his intention to end discrimination against gay men and lesbians in the U.S. military in 1993, a firestorm of protest ensued.

What accounts for the military's strong reaction to gay men *openly* serving in the armed forces? Writer Randy Shilts (1993) believes the official prohibition on gay men in the military has served to reinforce what he calls "the ideology of masculinity." The military's underlying logic, asserts Shilts, has been that gays must be banned so that the uniform is proof of heterosexuality. Although gay men and lesbians have served honorably for generations, anti-gay regulations "allow[ed] the military to say they ejected all gays." The regulations, he says, had "little to do with military goals and everything to do with a culture enforcing millennia-old taboos."

Ending Anti-Gay Prejudice

Although legislation to prohibit discrimination is important for ending prejudice, education and positive social interactions are also important vehicles for change. Negative attitudes about homosexuality may be reduced by arranging positive interactions between heterosexuals and gay men and lesbians (Herek, 1984). These interactions should be in settings of equal status, common goals, cooperation, and a moderate degree of intimacy. Such interactions may occur when family members or close friends come out. Other interactions should emphasize common group membership (such as religious, social, ethnic, or political) on a one-to-one basis (Herek, 1984). Religious volunteers working with people with HIV or AIDS often decrease their prejudice as they give care and comfort (Kayal, 1992).

SEXUAL AGGRESSION

rape Penile-vaginal penetration against a woman's will through the use or threat of force.

In recent years, we have increasingly expanded our knowledge about sexually aggressive acts and their consequences. We have expanded our focus beyond stranger rape and examined the consequences of sexually aggressive acts on survivors. Earlier, researchers had focused primarily on **rape,** penile-vaginal penetration performed against a *woman's* will through the use or threat of force. They assumed rape was committed by strangers for the purpose of sexual gratification. In their work, researchers generally examined the sexual psychopathology of male offenders and the characteristics of women that "precipitated" rapes, such as acting docile, living alone, and dressing in a certain way (White & Farmer, 1992).

sexual aggression Any kind of sexual activity against a person's will gained through the use of force, pressure, alcohol or drugs, or authority.

Contemporary research now views rape as a category of sexual aggression. **Sexual aggression** refers to sexual activity, including petting, oral-genital sex, anal intercourse, and sexual intercourse, performed against a person's will through the use of force, argument, pressure, alcohol or drugs, or authority (Cate & Lloyd, 1992; Muehlenhard, Ponch, Phelps, & Giusti, 1992). The principal motive is considered to be power rather than sex (Brownmiller, 1975). Unlike rape, which by definition excludes men as victims, sexual aggression includes both women *and* men as victims. It also includes gay men and lesbians, who have been excluded from such research because of rape's heterosexual definition (Muehlenhard et al., 1992). **Sexual coercion** is a broader term than rape or sexual aggression. It includes arguing, pleading, and cajoling, as well as force and the threat of force.

sexual coercion A broad term referring to any kind of sexual activity initiated with another person through the use of argument, pressure, pleading, or cajoling, as well as force, pressure, alcohol or drugs, or authority.

A recent large-scale survey revealed that 1.3% of men and nearly 22% or women have been forced to have sex by a man. On the other hand, 2.8% of the men in the survey report forcing a women to have sex (Laumann et al., 1994).

Rape

In rape, sex is a means of achieving power or releasing anger and hatred. Rape *forces* its victim into an intimate physical relationship with the rapist against her or his will. The victim does not experience pleasure; she or he experiences terror. In most cases, the victim is a woman; sometimes the victim is a man. In almost every case, however, the assailant is a man. The weapon in rape is the penis (which may be supplemented by a knife or a gun); the penis is used to attack, subordinate, and humiliate the victim.

Rape is not only an act but also a threat. As small girls, women are warned against taking candy from strangers, walking alone down dark streets, and leaving doors and windows unlocked. Men may fear assault, but women fear assault *and* rape. As a result, many women live with the possi-

Sexual assault peer educators at Brown University dramatize date rape to make students aware of its dynamics.

bility of being raped as a part of their consciousness. Rape, and the fear of rape, are facts of life for women; this is not true for men.

As many as 683,000 adult women were raped in 1990, according to a report sponsored by the Department of Health and Human Services (National Victim Center, 1992). The Department of Justice stated in 1994 that half of the rapes reported to the police involved girls who were under the age of 18.

Statistics often reveal discrepancies in rape estimates (George, Windfield, & Blazer, 1992; Koss, 1992; White & Farmer, 1992). This is due to several factors. First, definitions of rape may vary from one survey to another. Second, different sample sizes and methodologies may account for different estimates. Third, rape survivors are often reluctant to disclose their assault to interviewers. They fear being blamed or denigrated. As a result, figures may underestimate the actual number of rapes.

Forms of Rape

Rapists may be acquaintances, dates, husbands, fathers or other family members, as well as strangers.

Date Rape Unwanted sexual intercourse with a dating partner that occurs with force or the threat of force is known as **date rape** or **acquaintance rape.** It is the most common form of rape (Figure 17.1). (For an overview of current research, see Benson, Charlton, & Goodhart, 1992, and Berkowitz, 1992.)

Date rapes are usually not planned. Two researchers (Bechhofer & Parrot, 1991) describe a typical date rape:

> He plans the evening with the intent of sex, but if the date does not progress as planned and his date does not comply, he becomes angry and takes what he

date rape or **acquaintance rape**
Sexual intercourse with a dating partner that occurs against his or her will with force or the threat of force.

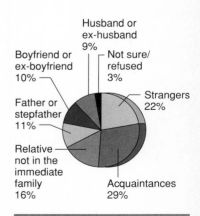

FIGURE 17.1 Types of Rape. (SOURCE: Data from National Victim Center, 1992.)

Think About It

RAPE MYTHS

Our society has a number of myths about rape, which serve to encourage rather than discourage rape (Burt, 1980). Such myths blame women for their own rapes as if they somehow "deserved" them or were responsible for them. In fact, in a large national sample, two-thirds of the women who were raped worried they might be blamed for their assaults (National Victim Center, 1992).

According to Martha Burt (1980), belief in rape myths is part of a larger belief structure that includes gender-role stereotypes, sexual conservatism, acceptance of interpersonal violence, and acceptance of a "battle of the sexes" philosophy of male-female relationships. Men are more likely than women to believe rape myths (Brady et al., 1991; Quackenbush, 1991; Reilly et al., 1992).

Myth #1: Women Want to Be Raped

It is popularly believed that women have an unconscious wish to be raped (Burt, 1980). The fact that many women have rape fantasies is cited as proof. But as Molly Haskell (1976) points out:

> The world of difference between "rape fantasy" and rape can be expressed in one word: control. The point of a fantasy is that a woman . . . orders the reality within it, ordains its terms, and censors it according to her needs; the point of rape is that a woman is violated against her will.

This myth supports the misconception that a woman enjoys being raped because she sexually "surrenders." The myth perpetuates the belief that rape is a sexual act rather than a violent one.

Myth #2: Women Ask for It

Many people believe that women "ask for it" by their behavior. One-quarter of the men believed this, according to one study (Holcomb, Holcomb, Sondag, & Williams, 1991). In another study, a woman going home with a man on their first date suggested to over half the respondents that she was inviting sex (Burt, 1980). Almost half believed that a woman wearing a short skirt or no bra was asking to be raped. Despite some attempts to reform rape laws, women continue to bear the brunt in proving their accusations (Goldberg-Ambrose, 1992).

Myth #3: Women Are Only Raped by Strangers

Women are warned to avoid or distrust strangers as a means of avoiding rape; such advice, however, isolates

feels is his right—sex. Afterward, the victim feels raped while the assailant believes that he has done nothing wrong. He may even ask the woman out on another date.

Alcohol and/or drugs are often involved. One study found that 79% of women who had been date raped had been drinking or taking drugs prior to the rape. Seventy-one percent said their assailant had been drinking or taking drugs (Copenhaver & Gauerholz, 1991). There are often high levels of alcohol and drug use among middle school and high school students who have unwanted sex (Rapkin & Rapkin, 1991).

Incidence Lifetime experience of date rape ranges from 15% to 28% for women, according to various studies. If the definition is expanded to include them from normal social interactions. Furthermore, studies indicate that half or more of all rapes are committed by nonstrangers such as acquaintances, friends, dates, husbands, or relatives (Russell, 1984).

Myth #4: Women Could Really Avoid Rape If They Wanted

This myth reinforces the stereotype that women "really" want to be raped or that they should curtail their activities. In one study, 25% of male students believed this myth (Holcomb et al., 1991). Women are often warned not to be out after dark alone, but few of the rapes in one study could have been avoided this way (Groth, 1979). Furthermore, a substantial number of rapes take place in the home or nearby, when a woman is going about her regular routine, according to one study of 320 victims of rape and attempted rape (McIntyre, 1980). Women are also approached at work, on their way to or from work, at church, or kidnapped from shopping centers or parking lots at midday. Restricting women's activities does not seem to have an appreciable impact on rape.

Myth #5: Women Cry Rape for Revenge

This myth suggests that women who are left by men accuse them of rape as a means of revenge. About 25% of the men in one study believed this (Holcomb et al., 1991). FBI crime statistics show that only about 2% of rape reports are false; this rate is lower than the rate for most other crimes. False reporting is unlikely because of the many obstacles that women face before an assailant is brought to trial and convicted.

Myth #6: Rapists Are Crazy or Psychotic

Very few men who rape are clinically psychotic. The vast majority are psychologically indistinguishable from other men, except that rapists appear to have more difficulty handling hostile feelings (Rodabaugh & Austin, 1981). In fact, studies on date rape find little psychological difference between rapists and nonrapists; they differ primarily in such ways as greater hostility toward women, acceptance of traditional gender roles, and greater willingness to use force (Cate & Lloyd, 1992).

Myth #7: Most Rapists Are Black Men

Most rapists and their victims are members of the same race or ethnic group. But the black rapist myth reinforces racism by calling up the sexual stereotype of the "oversexed" black man. It conjures images of African American men preying on white women. There is no evidence to suggest that black rapists prefer white women. Rapists appear to attack women on the basis of opportunity, not ethnicity (South & Felson, 1990).

attempted intercourse as a result of verbal pressure or the misuse of authority, then women's lifetime incidence increases significantly. When all types of unwanted sexual activity are included, ranging from kissing to sexual intercourse, 25–50% of college women report sexual aggression in dating (Cate & Lloyd, 1992). There is also considerable sexual coercion in gay male relationships. Coercion also exists in lesbian relationships, though less than in gay male and heterosexual ones (Waterman, Dawson, & Bologna, 1989).

When No Is No   There is considerable confusion and argument about consent. As we saw in Chapter 8, much sexual communication is nonverbal and ambiguous. The fact that we don't usually give verbal consent for sex indicates the significance of nonverbal clues. Nonverbal communication is imprecise. It can be misinterpreted easily if not reinforced verbally. For example, men frequently mistake a woman's friendliness for sexual interest (Johnson, Stockdale, & Saal, 1991; Stockdale, 1993). They often misinterpret a woman's cuddling, kissing, and fondling as interest in engaging in sexual intercourse (Muehlenhard, 1988; Muehlenhard & Linton, 1987). A woman needs to make her boundaries clear verbally, and men need to avoid misinterpreting clues. Because some women sometimes say "no" when they mean "coax me," male-female communication may be especially unclear regarding consent (Muehlenhard & Cook, 1988). A man may also feel he "should" persist because his role is to conquer, even if he's not interested in sex (Muehlenhard & Schrag, 1991; Muehlenhard & McCoy, 1991).

Stranger Rape The majority of rapes *reported* to the police are stranger rapes. A typical stranger rape scenario does not necessarily involve an unknown assailant hiding in the bushes or a stairwell on a dark night. Rather, it is likely to involve a chance meeting with a man who seems friendly and congenial. The woman relaxes her guard because the man seems nice, even protective. He casually maneuvers her to an isolated place—an alley, park, apartment, or house—where the rape occurs.

A study of women age 57–82 who were raped found that they were more likely to have been raped by strangers and to have been raped in their homes than younger rape victims (Muram, Miller, & Cutler, 1992). Stranger rapes are more likely to involve guns or knives than date rapes. Almost one-third of stranger rapes involve weapons (Harlow, 1991). A stranger rape is more likely to be taken seriously by the police because it reflects the rape stereotype better than date or marital rape (Russell, 1990).

Marital Rape Throughout the United States, a husband can be prosecuted for raping his wife, although 26 states limit the conditions, such as requiring extraordinary violence. Only 17 states offer full legal protection to wives (Muehlenhard et al., 1991). Laws against marital rape, however, have not been widely enforced. In the few cases in which husbands have been convicted of marital rape, they were separated and living apart from their wives.

Many people discount rape in marriage as a "marital tiff" that has little to do with "real" rape (Finkelhor & Yllo, 1985). When college students were asked to describe marital rape, they created "sanitized" images: "He wants to and she doesn't, so he does anyway." "They are separated but he really loves her, so when he comes back to visit, he forces her because he misses her." The realities are very different.

In Diana Russell's 1982 study on marital rape, 930 randomly selected women in San Francisco were interviewed. Eighty-seven out of the 644 women who had ever been married (about 13%) had been raped by their husbands. Russell found that force was used in 84% of the rapes and the threat of force in 9%. (The remaining victims were asleep, intoxicated, or surprised and not able to resist.) Of the wives who were raped, 31% reported their rapes as isolated events that occurred only once. But another 31% reported that they had been raped more than 20 times. Other studies of wives who had been raped by their husbands reported that 59–87% were raped multiple times (cited in Russell, 1990).

PREVENTING SEXUAL ASSAULT

There are no guaranteed ways to prevent sexual assault or coercion. Each situation, assailant, and targeted woman or man is different (Fischhoff, 1992). But rape education courses may be effective in reducing the rape myths that provide support for sexual aggression (Fonow, Richardson, & Wemmerus, 1992).

To reduce the risk of date rape, consider these guidelines:

- When dating someone for the first time, go to a public place, such as a restaurant, movie, or sports event.

- Share expenses. A common scenario is a date expecting you to exchange sex for his or her paying for dinner, the movie, drinks, and so on (Muehlenhard & Schrag, 1991; Muehlenhard et al., 1991).

- Avoid using drugs or alcohol if you do not want to be sexual with your date. Such use is associated with date rape (Abbey, 1991).

- Avoid ambiguous verbal or nonverbal behavior. Make sure your verbal and nonverbal messages are identical. If you only want to cuddle or kiss, for example, tell your partner that those are your limits. Tell him or her that if you say no, you mean no. If necessary, reinforce your statement emphatically, both verbally and physically (pushing him or her away) (Muehlenhard & Linton, 1987).

To reduce the risk of stranger rape, consider the guidelines below. But try to avoid becoming paranoid; use reasonable judgment. Do not let fear control your life.

- Do not identify yourself as a person living alone, especially if you are a woman. Use initials on the mailbox and in the telephone directory.

- Don't open your door to strangers; keep your house and car doors locked. Have your keys ready when you approach your car or house. Look in the back seat before getting into your car.

- Avoid dark and isolated areas. Carry a whistle or airhorn. Let people know where you are going.

- If someone approaches you threateningly, turn and run. If you can't run, resist. Studies indicate that resisting an attack by shouting, causing a scene, or fighting back can deter the assailant. Fighting and screaming may reduce the level of the abuse without increasing the level of physical injury. Most women who are injured during a rape appear to have been injured *prior* to resisting (Ullman & Knight, 1991). Trust your intuitions, whatever approach you take.

- Take self-defense training. It will raise your level of confidence and your fighting abilities. You may be able to scare off the assailant, or you may gain the opportunity to escape (Cummings, 1992). Many women take self-defense training following sexual aggression to reaffirm their sense of control.

If you are sexually assaulted (or the victim of an attempted assault), report the assault as soon as possible. You are probably not the assailant's first victim. As much as you might want to, do not change clothes or shower. Semen and hair or other materials on your body or clothing may be very important in arresting and convicting a rapist. You may also want to contact a rape crisis center; its staff members are knowledgeable about dealing with the police and the traumatic aftermath of rape. But most importantly, remember that you are not to blame for the rape. Don't blame yourself for doing something "stupid" or not doing something "right." If you survived the rape, you obviously took the most appropriate action. The rapist is the only one to blame.

Marital rape victims experience betrayal, anger, humiliation, and guilt (Finkelhor & Yllo, 1985). Following their rape, many wives feel intense anger toward their husbands. A minority feel guilt and blame themselves for not being better wives. Others develop negative self-images and view their lack of sexual desire as a reflection of their own inadequacies rather than as a consequence of abuse.

Gang Rape Gang rape may be perpetrated by strangers or acquaintances. It may be motivated not only by power but also by male-bonding factors (Sanday, 1990). It is a common form of adolescent rape, most often occurring with strangers (Holmes, 1991). Among adults, gang rape disproportionately occurs in tightly knit groups, such as fraternities, athletic teams, street gangs, or military units. When gang rape takes place on campus, the attackers may know the woman, who may have been invited to a party or apartment. Alcohol is often involved.

A recent study compared 44 college women who experienced gang sexual assault to 44 who were individually assaulted (Gidyez & Koss, 1990). In general, gang sexual assaults were more violent. Their victims offered greater resistance and were more likely to report the attack to the police. Gang assault victims were also more traumatized. As a result, they were more likely to contemplate suicide and seek psychotherapy.

People who would not rape alone may rape in groups for several reasons (O'Sullivan, 1991). Responsibility is diffused in a group; no single individual is to blame. A person may lose his sense of individuality and merge with the group's standards. He might model his behavior on the sexual aggressiveness of the others.

statutory rape Consensual sexual intercourse with a female under the age of consent.

age of consent The age at which a person is legally deemed capable of giving consent.

Statutory Rape **Statutory rape** is consensual sexual intercourse with a girl beneath a state's **age of consent,** the age at which a person is legally deemed capable of giving informed consent. It may not matter whether the male is the same age, older, or younger. If a female is younger than a certain age—varying from age 7 in Delaware to age 21 in Kansas—the court ignores her consent. The enforcement of statutory rape laws, however, is generally sporadic, accidental, or arbitrary.

Sexual Assault Against Males Sexual assault against males may be perpetrated by other men or by women. (For men we use the term "sexual assault" rather than rape because most rape definitions specify vaginal penetration by the penis.) Most sexual assaults on men are by other men. Female assaults on males are significantly less common. Although some gay men are sexually assaulted by other gays, we know very little about such assaults; crime statistics are not kept on such victimization (Duncan, 1990). But it is important to note that men who sexually assault other men are not necessarily gay. Because the motive in sexual assaults is power and domination, sexual orientation is often irrelevant (Gagnon, 1977).

Based on police reports, in 1991 about 1 man in 1000 was sexually assaulted; many were forced to perform fellatio or were anally penetrated (U.S. Department of Justice, 1991). In the aftermath of an assault, men attempt to restrain their emotions. They are significantly less likely than women to report specific emotional and behavioral reactions to their assault. Instead of saying they feel sad or feel their stomach muscles constricting, they are likely to say only that they are upset; they hesitate to go into detail (Sorenson & Siegel, 1992).

Sexual assault in prison is common. In 1990, the United States had the second largest prison incarceration rate in the world. Despite our immense prison population, we know very little about prison sex. What we do know, however, is that male-male prison sex is often devoid of affection. Rather, it is an important means by which domination is established. Most assailants and victims are heterosexual.

Although uncommon, there are some instances of women sexually assaulting men. Although threatened with knives and guns, the men were able to have erections (Sarrel & Masters, 1982). After the assaults, the men suffered rape trauma syndrome similar to that experienced by women (discussed later). They experienced sexual difficulties, depression, and anxiety. Most felt abnormal because they did respond sexually during the assault. Because they were sexually assaulted by women, they doubted their masculinity.

Motivations for Rape

Most stranger rapes and some acquaintance or marital rapes can be characterized as *anger rapes, power rapes,* or *sadistic rapes* (Groth, Burgess, & Holmstrom, 1977). This typology has been very influential, but it is based on interviews with incarcerated stranger rapists. As a result, it may not reflect the motivations of the majority of rapists, who are acquaintances, boyfriends, and husbands.

Anger rapists are physically brutal; the consequences of their extreme violence often require hospitalization of the victim. These rapes account for approximately 40% of stranger rapes (Groth & Birnbaum, 1978). Groth (1979) described anger rapes:

> The assault is characterized by physical brutality. Far more actual force is used . . . than would be necessary if the intent were simply to overpower the victim and achieve sexual penetration. . . . His aim is to hurt and debase his victim, and he expresses contempt for her through abusive and profane language. . . .

Power rapes, representing about 55% of stranger rapes in Nicholas Groth and Jean Birnbaum's study, are acts of dominance. Typically, the rapist does not want to hurt the woman but to dominate her sexually. The rape may be triggered by what the rapist regards as a slight to his masculinity. He attempts to restore his sense of power, control, and identity by raping. He uses sex to compensate for his sense of inadequacy. He uses only as much force as necessary to rape his victim.

Sadistic rapes, in which sex and aggression are violently fused, are by far the most brutal. A sadistic rapist finds "intentional maltreatment of his victim intensely gratifying and takes pleasure in her torment, anguish, distress, helplessness and suffering" (Groth & Birnbaum, 1978). There is often bondage and a ritualistic quality. The victim is often severely injured and may not survive the attack. Although sadistic rapes are overwhelmingly the most brutal, they are also the least frequent. About 5% of the stranger rapes in Groth and Birnbaum's study were sadistic.

You and Your Sexual Well-Being

HOW TO TELL IF YOU ARE IN AN ABUSIVE SITUATION

If you answer yes to one or more of the following questions, you may be experiencing domestic abuse:

- Does your partner constantly criticize you, blame you for things that are not your fault or verbally degrade you?
- Has he or she ever pushed, slapped, kicked, bitten, restrained, thrown objects at, spit at or used a weapon against you because he or she was angry or upset?
- Is he or she suspicious and jealous? Does he or she make it difficult for you to see friends and family, irrationally accuse you of having affairs or monitor your mail and phone calls?
- Does he or she prevent you from getting or maintaining a job, control your shared resources or restrict your access to money?
- Has he or she ever forced you to have sex or caused you pain sexually without your consent?
- Has he or she ever threatened to harm you, your family, friends, children, pets or property?
- Has he or she threatened to blackmail you if you leave?
- Does he or she have a history of violence against former partners?

Source: *San Francisco Chronicle*, 24 June 1994. Originally from Community United Against Violence.

The Aftermath of Rape

According to the National Victim Center (1992), more than two-thirds of the women who were raped in 1990 were not physically injured. Twenty percent received minor injuries, and 4% sustained serious injuries.

It is important that rape victims gain a sense of control over their lives to counteract the helplessness they experienced during their rape (Robertson, 1990). They need to cope with the depression and other symptoms resulting from their trauma.

rape trauma syndrome The emotional changes an individual undergoes as a result of rape.

post-traumatic stress disorder (PTSD) A characteristic group of symptoms, such as depression, that follows an intensely distressing event outside a person's normal life experience.

Rape Trauma Syndrome Rape is a traumatic event, to which a woman may have a number of responses. The emotional changes she undergoes as a result of rape are collectively known as **rape trauma syndrome.** Rape survivors are likely to experience depression, anxiety, restlessness, and guilt. These responses are consistent with **post-traumatic stress disorder (PTSD),** a group of characteristic symptoms that follow an intensely distressing event outside a person's normal life experience (Bownes, O'Gorman, & Sayers, 1991a, 1991b; Nadelson, 1990; Resnick, Kilpatrick, & Lipousky, 1991).

Rape trauma syndrome consists of two phases: an acute phase and a long-term reorganization phase. The acute phase begins immediately following the rape. It may last for several weeks or more. In the first few hours after a rape, the woman's responses are characterized by feelings of self-blame and fear. She may believe that she was somehow responsible for the rape: She was wearing something provocative, she should have kept her doors locked, she should have been suspicious of her attacker. Self-blame, however, leads to higher rates of depression (Frazier, 1991).

The woman is shaken by fears: that the attacker will return, that she may be killed, that others will react negatively. She may act out these feelings through expressive, controlled, or combined reactions. An expressive response leaves the woman crying, expressing signs and feelings of fear, anger, rage, anxiety, and tension. If she controls her responses, she hides her feelings and tries to appear calm. Nevertheless, there are often signs of tension: headaches, irritability, sleeplessness, restlessness, and jumpiness. Women may also feel humiliated, angry, embarrassed, vengeful, and fearful. Women are more likely than men to express these varied symptoms following rape (Sorenson & Siegel, 1992).

Following the acute phase, the rape survivor enters the long-term reorganization phase. The rape is a crisis in a woman's life and relationships (Nadelson, 1990). If the rape took place at home, she may move, fearing that the rapist will return. Some women develop fears of being indoors if the rape occurred indoors, while those raped outside sometimes fear being outdoors. About 3 months after their rapes, 60% of the women in one study reported depression. Forty percent rated their depressions as severe (Mackey et al., 1992).

Effect on Sexuality   Typically, women find that their sexuality is severely affected for a short time or longer after a rape (Nadelson, 1990). Some begin avoiding sexual interactions, because sex reminds them of the rape. Those who are less depressed, however, have fewer sexual difficulties (Mackey et al., 1992). The two most common sexual problems are fear of sex and a lack of sexual desire (Howard, 1980).

CHILD SEXUAL ABUSE

Child sexual abuse is a widespread occurrence, whether by relatives or non-relatives. **Child sexual abuse** is *any* sexual interaction (including fondling, sexual kissing, and oral sex, as well as vaginal or anal penetration) between an adult and a prepubertal child. It does not matter whether the child is perceived by the adult to be freely engaging in the sexual activity. Because of the child's age, he or she cannot give informed consent; the activity can only be considered as self-serving to the adult.

There is considerable variation in estimates of the prevalence of child abuse. A review of small-scale studies found prevalence estimates ranging from 6–62% for females and 3–31% for males (Peters et al., 1986). The first national survey found that 27% of the women and 16% of the men surveyed had experienced sexual abuse as children (Finkelhor, Hotaling, Lewis, & Smith, 1990). Different definitions of abuse, methodologies, samples, and interviewing techniques account for the varied estimates (Gelles & Conte, 1991).

Child sexual abuse is generally categorized in terms of kin relationship. **Extrafamilial abuse** is sexual abuse by unrelated people. **Intrafamilial abuse** is sexual abuse by biologically related people and step relatives. The abuse may be pedophilic or nonpedophilic. (As you recall from Chapter 10, pedophilia refers to an adult's sexual attraction to children.) **Nonpedophilic sexual abuse** refers to an adult's sexual interaction with a child that is not sexually motivated; the most important nonsexual motives are power and affection (Groth & Birnbaum, 1978).

child sexual abuse   Any sexual interaction (including fondling, erotic kissing, oral sex, and genital penetration) between an adult and a prepubertal child.

extrafamilial abuse   Child sexual abuse by unrelated individuals.

intrafamilial abuse   Child sexual abuse by biologically and step-related individuals.

nonpedophilic sexual abuse   An adult's sexual interaction with a child that is not motivated as much by sexual desire as by nonsexual motives, such as power or affection.

A therapist helps a child deal with her sexual abuse.

The victimization may include force or the threat of force, pressure, or the taking advantage of trust or innocence. The most serious or harmful forms of child sexual abuse include actual or attempted penile-vaginal penetration, fellatio, cunnilingus, and analingus, with or without the use of force. Other serious forms range from forced digital penetration of the vagina to fondling of the breasts (unclothed), or simulated intercourse without force. The least serious forms of sexual abuse range from kissing to intentional sexual touching of the clothed genitals or breasts or other body parts, with or without the use of force (Russell, 1984).

Most victimized children are between 8 and 12 years of age; the majority are girls (Finkelhor, 1984). We have only recently recognized the sexual abuse of boys; this neglect has been part of the more general neglect of all sexual victimization of males (Russell, 1984). A review of the literature shows that boys are estimated to be victims of about one-third of all pedophilic abuse committed by males (Groth, Hobson, & Gray, 1982). Finkelhor (1979) speculates that men tend to underreport sexual abuse because they experience greater shame; they feel their masculinity has been undermined. Boys tend to be blamed more than girls for their victimization, especially if they did not forcibly resist: "A real boy would never let someone do *that* without fighting back" (Rogers & Terry, 1984).

Forms of Intrafamilial Sexual Abuse

incest Sexual intercourse between individuals too closely related to legally marry, usually interpreted to mean father-daughter, mother-son, or brother-sister.

The incest taboo is nearly universal in human societies. **Incest** is generally defined as sexual intercourse between people too closely related to legally marry (usually interpreted to mean father-daughter, mother-son, or brother-sister). Sexual abuse in families can involve blood relatives, most commonly uncles and grandfathers, and step relatives, most often stepfathers and stepbrothers. In grandfather-granddaughter abuse, the grandfathers frequently have sexually abused their children as well.

It is not clear what type of familial sexual abuse is the most frequent

(Peters et al., 1986; Russell, 1986). Some researchers believe that father-daughter (including stepfather-daughter) abuse is the most common; others think that brother-sister abuse is most common. Still other researchers believe that incest committed by uncles is the most common (Russell, 1986). Mother-son sexual relations are considered to be rare (or are under-reported).

Father-Daughter Sexual Abuse   There is general agreement that the most traumatic form of sexual victimization is father-daughter abuse, including that committed by stepfathers. One study indicated that 54% of the girls sexually abused by their fathers were extremely upset (Russell, 1986). In contrast, 25% who were abused by other family members reported the same degree of emotional upset. Over twice as many abused daughters reported serious long-term consequences. Some factors contributing to the severity of father-daughter sexual relations include the following:

- Fathers were more likely to have engaged in penile-vaginal penetration than other relatives (18% versus 6%).

- Fathers sexually abused their daughters more frequently than other perpetrators abused their victims (38% of the fathers sexually abused their daughters 11 or more times, compared to a 12% abuse rate for other abusing relatives).

- Fathers were more likely to use force or violence than others (although the numbers for both fathers and others were extremely low).

In the past, many have discounted the seriousness of sexual abuse by a stepfather because there is no *biological* relationship. The emotional consequences are just as serious, however. Sexual abuse by a stepfather still represents a violation of the basic parent-child relationship.

Brother-Sister Sexual Abuse   There are contrasting views concerning the consequences of brother-sister incest. Researchers generally have expressed little interest in it. Most have intended to view it as harmless sex play, or sexual exploration between mutually involved siblings. The research, however, has generally failed to distinguish between exploitative and nonexploitative brother-sister sexual activity. One study found that brother-sister incest can be a devastating invasion of individual boundaries (Canavan, Myers, & Higgs, 1992). Russell (1986) suggests that the idea that brother-sister incest is usually harmless and mutual may be a myth. In her study, the average age difference between the brother (age 17.9 years) and sister (10.7 years) is so great that the siblings can hardly be considered peers. The age difference represents a significant power difference. Furthermore, not all brother-sister sexual activity is "consenting"; considerable physical force may be involved.

Uncle-Niece Sexual Abuse   Both Alfred Kinsey (Kinsey et al., 1953) and Diane Russell (1986) found the most common form of intrafamilial sexual abuse to involve uncles and nieces. Russell reported that almost 5% of the women in her study had been molested by their uncles, slightly more than the percentage abused by their fathers. The level of severity of the abuse was generally less in terms of the type of sexual act and the use of force. Although such abuse does not take place within the nuclear family, many victims found it quite upsetting. One-quarter of the respondents indicated long-term emotional effects (Russell, 1986).

Children at Risk

Not all children are equally at risk for sexual abuse. Although any child can be sexually abused, some groups of children are more likely to be victimized than others. A review (Finkelhor & Baron, 1986) of the literature indicates that those children at higher risk for sexual abuse are in the following groups:

- Female children
- Preadolescent children (particularly between the ages of 10 and 12)
- Children with absent or unavailable parents
- Children whose relationships with parents are poor
- Children whose parents are in conflict
- Children who live with a stepfather

Effects of Child Sexual Abuse

Until recently, much of the literature on child sexual abuse has been anecdotal, case studies, or small-scale surveys of nonrepresentative groups. Nevertheless, numerous well-documented consequences of child sexual abuse hold true for both intrafamilial and extrafamilial abuse (see Kendall-Tackett, Williams, & Finkelhor, 1993, for a review of the literature). These include both initial and long-term consequences. Many child sexual abuse survivors experience symptoms of post-traumatic stress disorder (McLeer, Deblinger, Henry, & Ovraschel, 1992).

Initial Effects The initial consequences of sexual abuse occur within the first 2 years. The proportion of victimized children who experience these disturbances ranges from one-quarter to almost two-thirds, depending on the study. Some of the typical effects are:

- *Emotional disturbances*, including fear, anger, hostility, guilt, and shame
- *Physical consequences*, including difficulty in sleeping, changes in eating patterns, and pregnancy
- *Sexual disturbances*, including significantly higher rates of open masturbation, sexual preoccupation, and exposure of the genitals (Hibbard & Hartman, 1992)
- *Social disturbances*, including difficulties at school, truancy, running away from home, and early marriages by abused adolescents. (A large proportion of homeless youth are fleeing parental sexual abuse [Athey, 1991].)

Long-Term Effects Although there can be some healing of the initial effects, child sexual abuse may leave lasting scars on the adult survivor (Beitchman et al., 1992). These adults often have significantly higher incidences of psychological, physical, and sexual problems than the general population. Abuse may predispose some women to sexually abusive dating relationships (Cate & Lloyd, 1992).

Long-term effects include the following (Beitchman et al., 1992; Browne & Finkelhor, 1986; Elliott & Briere, 1992; Wyatt, Gutherie, & Notgass, 1992):

- Depression, the most frequently reported symptom of adults sexually abused as children

- Self-destructive tendencies, including suicide attempts and thoughts of suicide (Jeffrey & Jeffrey, 1991)

- Somatic disturbances and dissociation, including anxiety and nervousness, eating disorders (anorexia and bulimia), feelings of "spaciness," out-of-body experiences, and feelings that things are "unreal" (De-Groot, Kennedy, Rodin, & McVey, 1992; Walker et al., 1992; Young, 1992)

- Negative self-concept, including feelings of low self-esteem, isolation, and alienation

- Interpersonal relationship difficulties, including difficulties in relating to both sexes, parental conflict, problems in responding to their own children, and difficulty in trusting others

- Revictimization, in which women abused as children are more vulnerable to rape and marital violence

- Sexual problems, in which survivors find it difficult to relax and enjoy sexual activities, or avoid sex and experience hypoactive (inhibited) sexual desire and lack of orgasm

Preventing Sexual Abuse

The idea of preventing sexual abuse is relatively new (Berrick & Barth, 1992). Prevention programs began about a decade ago, a few years after programs were started to identify and help child or adult survivors of sexual abuse. Such prevention programs have been hindered, however, by three factors (Finkelhor, 1986a, 1986b):

- Sexual abuse is complicated by differing concepts of what constitutes appropriate sexual behaviors and partners, which are not easily understood by children.

- Sexual abuse, especially incest, is a difficult topic for adults to discuss with children. Children who are frightened by their parents, however, may be less able to resist abuse than those who are given strategies of resistance.

- Sex education is controversial. Even where it is taught, instruction often does not go beyond physiology and reproduction. The topic of incest is especially opposed.

In confronting these problems, child abuse prevention (CAP) programs have been very creative. These programs typically aim at three audiences: children, parents, and professionals, especially teachers. CAP programs aimed at children include plays, puppet shows, filmstrips, videotapes, books, and comic books to teach children that they have rights. Children have the right to control their own bodies (including their genitals) and to feel "safe," and they have the right not to be touched in ways that feel confusing or wrong. The CAP programs stress that the child is not at fault when

Touch Talk!

What to do if someone touches you and you don't like it.

written and illustrated by Eric Berg

One objective of child-abuse prevention programs is to teach children the difference between "good" touching and "bad" touching.

DEALING WITH THE SEX OFFENDER

Few crimes elicit a more emotional response than those involving sexual abuse. Most of us respond with rage to the idea of our partners, mothers, sisters, daughters, or other innocent victims being the targets of sexual violence. The legal system too condemns the sex offender. Just how should perpetrators be dealt with?

As yet, no single method of treatment or intervention has proven to be a totally effective remedy. There are, however, a number of basic approaches (Groth, 1979), including the following:

- Chemotherapy, in particular Depo-Provera, an antiandrogen hormone, temporarily lowers testosterone levels and reduces the offender's interest in sexual activity. The offender reportedly experiences a release from his compulsive urges to commit sexual assault. Just how effective this is in controlling violence is controversial. Furthermore, there are ethical and legal questions about forcing a medical procedure on a person.

- Psychotherapy, a somewhat common technique, views assault as the result of psychological conflicts. It aims at helping the offender become aware of, understand, and ultimately control his undesirable behavior. As with chemotherapy, the effectiveness of this approach remains questionable. In addition, it is relatively expensive.

- Intense education to rehabilitate the offender may be combined with all treatment approaches. It usually consists of a combination of job training and human development courses.

- Behavior modification specifically addresses the offender's symptoms and sexual behaviors and attempts to alter them by instilling more appropriate responses. This may be combined with hyp-

notherapy, systematic desensitization, or shock treatment.

- Tracking, the monitoring of sex offenders' whereabouts, requires that they register with local police. Twenty-nine states have passed such laws in the past four years. Other states are examining the feasibility of requiring convicted sex criminals to register with police and mail their name and address to local newspapers and neighbors (*San Francisco Chronicle*, 8 August 1994). Many who are familiar with tracking point out the fine line between vigilance and vigilantism.

- Castration has been practiced in the past with mixed results. This approach raises legal, ethical, and moral questions. Currently, no states permit it.

- Imprisonment is the most common approach to handling the sex offender. Reducing the risk to the community and punishing the offender are the aims of such an approach. Just how long a person should be incarcerated, whether plea-bargaining should be allowed, and whether consideration should be given to the offender's age at the time of prosecution are issues that the legal system continues to wrestle with.

Ideally, a combination of approaches might be utilized to deal successfully with sex offenders. Practically, the options depend on support—financial, legal, and public opinion.

How would you deal with a sex offender? What variables would influence your decision? How many of your tax dollars would you be willing to invest in the offender's rehabilitation? How could you as a voter influence the system?

such abuse does occur. These programs generally teach three strategies (Gelles & Conte, 1991). First, children are taught to say "no." Second, they are told to get away from the assailant or situation. Third, they are instructed to tell a trusted adult about what happened (and to keep telling until they are believed). It is not known how well these strategies work, because assessment studies cannot ethically duplicate the various situations.

Other programs focus on educating parents who, it is hoped, will in turn educate their children. These programs aim at helping parents discover abuse or abusers by identifying warning signs. Such programs, however, need to be culturally sensitive, as Latinos and Asians may be reluctant to discuss these matters with their children (Ahn & Gilbert, 1992). Parents seem reluctant in general to deal with sexual abuse issues with their children, according to David Finkelhor (1986a). Many do not feel that their children are at risk, are fearful of unnecessarily frightening their children, and may also feel uncomfortable about talking with their children about sex in general, much less about such tabooed subjects as incest. In addition, parents may not believe their own children, or may feel uncomfortable confronting a suspected abuser, who may be a partner, an uncle, a friend, or a neighbor.

CAP programs also seek to educate professionals, especially teachers, physicians, mental-health professionals, and police officers. Because of their close contact with children and their role in teaching children about the world, teachers are especially important. Professionals are encouraged to be watchful for signs of sexual abuse and to investigate children's reports of such abuse.

Sexual harassment, anti-gay harassment and discrimination, sexual aggression, and sexual abuse of children represent the darker side of human sexuality. Their common thread is the humiliation, subordination, or victimization of others. But we need not be victims. We can educate ourselves and others about these activities; we can work toward changing attitudes and institutions that support these destructive and dehumanizing behaviors.

SUMMARY

Sexual Harassment

• Sexual harassment includes two distinct types of illegal harassment: the abuse of power for sexual ends and the creation of a hostile environment. Sexual harassment may begin as early as middle childhood. In college, 15–35% of women students have experienced some form of sexual harassment from other students, faculty members, or administrators.

• In the workplace, fellow employees as well as supervisors may engage in sexual harassment. In many instances, harassment may not represent sexual attraction as much as an exercise of power.

Anti-Gay/Lesbian Harassment, Prejudice, and Discrimination

• Researchers have identified two forms of discrimination or bias against gay men and lesbians: heterosexual bias and anti-gay prejudice. Heterosexual bias includes ignoring, segregating, and submerging gay men and lesbians into larger categories that make them invisible.

• Anti-gay prejudice is a strong dislike, fear, or hatred of gay men and lesbians. It is acted out through offensive language, discrimination, and violence. Anti-gay prejudice is derived from a deeply rooted insecurity, belief in dogma, or ignorance.

• Much anti-gay prejudice is conveyed and reinforced by conservative religious institutions and the military.

Sexual Aggression

• Rape is penile-vaginal penetration performed against a woman's will. Sexual aggression refers to any sexual activity against a person's will through the use of force, argument, pressure, use of alcohol/drugs, or authority. Sexual coercion, a broader term than rape or sexual aggression, includes arguing, pleading, and cajoling as well as force or the threat of force.

• Date rape is the most common form of rape. Date rapes are usually not planned. Alcohol or drugs are often involved. There is also considerable sexual coercion in gay male relationships; there is less coercion in lesbian relationships. There is considerable confusion and argument about consent, especially because much sexual communication is nonverbal and ambiguous.

• The majority of reported rapes are by strangers. Stranger rapes are more likely to involve guns or knives than date rapes.

• Rape myths serve to encourage rape by blaming women. Men are more likely than women to believe rape myths. Rape myths include beliefs that women want to be raped, women ask for it, women are only raped by strangers, women could really avoid rape if they wanted, women "cry rape" for revenge, rapists are crazy or psychotic, and most rapists are black.

• In most states, a husband can be prosecuted for raping his wife. Marital rape victims experience feelings of betrayal, anger, humiliation, and guilt.

• Gang rape may be perpetrated by strangers or acquaintances. It may be motivated by power and by male-bonding factors. Statutory rape is consensual sexual intercourse with a minor.

• Most sexual assaults on men are perpetrated by other men. Because the motive in sexual assaults is power and domination, sexual orientation is often irrelevant. In prison, sexual assault is common as a means of establishing dominance.

• Most stranger rapes (and some acquaintance or marital rapes) can be characterized as anger rapes, power rapes, or sadistic rapes. This typology, however, may not reflect the motivations of the majority of rapists who are acquaintances, boyfriends, and husbands.

• The emotional changes women undergo as a result of rape are collectively known as rape trauma syndrome. Women develop depression, anxiety, restlessness, and guilt. The symptoms following rape are consistent with post-traumatic stress disorder (PTSD). Women find their sexuality severely affected for a short time or for longer after rape.

Child Sexual Abuse

• Child sexual abuse is any sexual interaction between an adult and a prepubertal child. Incest is sexual intercourse between individuals too closely related to legally marry. The child's victimization may include force or the threat of force, pressure, or the taking advantage of trust or innocence.

• The most traumatic form of child sexual abuse is father-daughter incest. The most common form is probably uncle-niece.

• Initial consequences of abuse include physical consequences and emotional, social, and sexual disturbances. Child sexual abuse may leave lasting scars on the adult survivor.

• Child abuse prevention (CAP) programs have been hindered by different concepts of appropriate sexual behavior, adult fear of discussion, and controversy over sex education. Prevention programs generally teach children to say "no," to get away from the assailant or situation, and to tell a trusted adult about what happened.

SUGGESTED READINGS

Draucker, Claire Burke. *Counseling Survivors of Childhood Sexual Abuse.* Newbury Park, CA: Sage Publications, 1992. A comprehensive examination of treating adult survivors of childhood sexual abuse, using case studies.

Hasbany, Richard, ed. *Homosexuality and Religion.* New York: Haworth Press, 1990. A survey of recent Christian and Jewish positions on homosexuality, current biblical and theological scholarship, gay and lesbian ministers, priests, and rabbis, and pastoral counseling for gay men and lesbians.

Herek, Gregory, and Kevin Benl, eds. *Hate Crimes: Confronting Violence Against Lesbians and Gay Men.* Newbury Park, CA: Sage Publications, 1991. An overview of violence against gay men and lesbians: the context, the perpetrators, and responses.

Koss, Mary, and Mary Harvey. *The Rape Victim: Clinical and Community Intervention.* Newbury Park, CA: Sage Publications, 1991. A study of rape incidence, the impact on survivors, and societal attitudes; deals with rape crisis centers and ways of helping rape survivors cope.

Parrot, Andrea, and Laurie Bechhofer, eds. *Acquaintance Rape: The Hidden Crime.* New York: John Wiley, 1991. A collection of scholarly essays on date rape.

Chapter Eighteen

COMMERCIAL SEX: SEXUALLY ORIENTED MATERIAL AND PROSTITUTION

PREVIEW: SELF-QUIZ

1. Nonviolent, sexually explicit material does not appear to be linked with violence against women. True or false?

2. Sexually oriented material is obscene by definition. True or false?

3. Almost all adult Americans have read or viewed sexually explicit material. True or false?

4. Most Americans believe that sexually explicit material depicting consensual sexual activity between adults should be accessible to adults. True or false?

5. Criteria used to define obscenity are highly subjective. True or false?

6. The primary motivation for most prostitutes is to make money. True or false?

7. Prostitution is illegal everywhere in the United States. True or false?

8. Adolescents who enter prostitution often have a history of childhood sexual abuse. True or false?

9. Most women who work in prostitution are call girls. True or false?

10. With few exceptions, male prostitutes are gay. True or false?

ANSWERS 1. T, 2. F, 3. T, 4. T, 5. T, 6. T, 7. F, 8. T, 9. F, 10. F

Money and sex are bound together in the production and sale of sexually oriented material and in prostitution. Money is exchanged for sexual images or descriptions portrayed by videos, films, magazines, books, music, and photographs that depict people in explicit or suggestive sexual activities. Money is also exchanged for sexual services provided by streetwalkers, call girls, massage parlor workers, and other sex workers. The sex industry is a multibillion-dollar industry with countless millions of consumers and customers. As a nation, however, we feel profoundly ambivalent about sexually oriented material and prostitution. Many condemn it as immoral and exploitative and wish to censor or eliminate it. Others find it harmless, an erotic diversion, or an aspect of society that cannot (or should not) be regulated; they believe censorship and police action do greater harm than good.

In this chapter, we examine sexually oriented material, including depictions of sex in popular culture, the role of technology in developing new forms of sexually oriented material, the effects of sexually oriented material, and censorship issues. Then we examine prostitution, focusing on females and males working in prostitution and the legal issues involved.

SEXUALLY ORIENTED MATERIAL IN CONTEMPORARY AMERICA

Studying sexually oriented material objectively is difficult because it touches deep and often conflicting feelings we have about sexuality. Some enjoy it, others feel it is degrading, and still others believe it may lead to violence or moral chaos.

Is It Pornography or Erotica?

Much of the discussion about sexually oriented material concerns the question of whether such material is erotic or pornographic. Unfortunately, there is a lack of agreement about what constitutes erotica or pornography. Part of the problem is that erotica and pornography are subjective terms. **Erotica** describes a positive evaluation of sexually oriented material. (The word "erotica" is derived from the Greek *erotikos*, meaning a love poem.) **Pornography** represents a negative evaluation of sexually oriented material. ("Pornography" is a nineteenth-century word derived from the Greek *porne*, meaning prostitute, and *graphos*, meaning depicting.)

The same sexually oriented material may evoke a variety of responses in different people (Fisher, 1986; Reiss, 1990). Some people may enjoy the material, others may be repulsed, and still others may simultaneously feel aroused and guilty. "What I like is erotica, but what you like is pornography," may be a facetious statement, but one that's not entirely untrue. Judgments about sexually explicit material tend to be relative.

Because of the tendency to use "erotica" as a positive term and "pornography" as a negative term, we will use the neutral term "sexually oriented material" whenever possible. **Sexually oriented material** is material such as photographs, videos, films, magazines, or books whose primary themes, topics, or depictions involve sexuality or cause sexual arousal. **Sexually explicit material** is material that intimately depicts sexual activities, the vulva, the erect penis, or the anus. This material is also considered **hardcore.** Other sexually oriented material may be considered **softcore** if it is not explicit, such as the depiction of nudes in *Playboy.*

Technology and Sexually Oriented Material

In the nineteenth century, technology transformed the production of sexually oriented material. Cheap paper and large-scale printing, combined with mass literacy, created an enormous market for books and drawings. In the mid-nineteenth century, with the invention of photography, sexually oriented photographs began to be produced. (Nudes were among the earliest photographs made.) With the ability to reprint photographs on paper, photographic images were mass produced and mass distributed.

Today, technology is once again extending the forms in which sexually oriented material is conveyed. A New York cable TV program called "Voyeurvision" features a lingerie-clad woman on a bed who takes phone calls on the air (at $5 per minute) and acts out sexual fantasies as the caller (and hundreds of thousands of others) watches (M. Kaplan, 1992). Computer-directed "virtual reality" programs promise "simulated" sexual experiences, in which you can "experience" your fantasies.

Sex and Computers Hundreds of computer software programs, such as "Leisure Suit Larry," are animated and X-rated (Markoff, 1992). Computer bulletin boards may specialize in various sexual interests, ranging from "talking dirty" to dominance and submission. Some computer users change their age or assume cross-gender identities when they sign on.

Dial-a-Porn Millions of people have called 900-number telephone sex lines. One sex line in New York City receives over 500,000 calls daily (Matek, 1988). Advertisements for phone sex appear in most sexually oriented magazines; they depict nude or seminude women and men in sexually suggestive poses. The caller can either charge his or her call to a credit

erotica Sexually oriented material that is positively evaluated.

pornography Sexually oriented material that is negatively evaluated.

sexually oriented material Material such as photographs, videos, films, magazines, or books whose primary themes, topics, or depictions involve sexuality or sexual arousal.

sexually explicit material or **hardcore** Material that intimately depicts sexual activities, the vulva, the erect penis, or the anus.

softcore Nonexplicit sexually oriented material.

Dial-a-Porn is a multi-million dollar business. Despite attempts to censor or regulate it, it continues to flourish. Those favoring it argue that dial-a-porn is a form of safe sex and is protected by freedom of speech laws. Those opposed argue that it is obscene and easily accessible to people under 18 years of age, including young children.

card or call a 900-number, in which case the charges are billed to the person's telephone number. For fees generally ranging from $3 to $15 a minute, a person can have a woman or man "talk dirty" with him or her. Fantasy phone sex also caters to "specialty" interests, such as bondage and submission, transvestism, and transsexuality.

X-Rated Videocassettes
Videocassettes and VCRs have revolutionized both movies and television. The VCR revolution has been so great that bedrooms have supplanted adult theaters, or "porno" movie houses for the viewing of sexually oriented videos, which account for 15–25% of all videocassettes sold. Mainstream X-rated videos generally depict stereotypical gender roles, but sexual aggression is not typical. When it does occur, the victim is rarely depicted as enjoying it (Garcia & Milano, 1990).

Videocassettes have had a profound effect on *who* views erotic films. Adult movie houses were the domain of men; relatively few women entered them. But with erotic videos available in the privacy of the bedroom, women also have become consumers of sexually oriented films and videos. By 1986, video stores reported that they rented the majority of sexually oriented videos to women or couples.

The inclusion of women in the audience has led to **femme porn,** erotic films catering to women or couples. Femme porn avoids violence, is less male-centered, and is more sensitive to women's erotic fantasies.

femme porn Sexually oriented material catering to women and heterosexual couples.

The Effects of Sexually Oriented Material

There are a number of concerns about the effects of sexually oriented material. Does it cause people to engage in deviant acts? Is it a form of sex discrimination against women? And, finally, does it cause violence against women?

Sexual Expression
People who read or view sexually explicit material usually recognize it as fantasy; they use it as a release from their everyday world (Davis, 1983). Exposure to sexually oriented material temporarily encourages sexual expression and may activate a person's *typical* sexual behavior pattern.

Sexually oriented materials deal with fantasy sex, not sex as we know it in the context of human relationships. Sexually explicit sex usually takes place in a world in which people and situations are defined in exclusively sexual terms. People are stripped of their nonsexual connections.

People are interested in sexually oriented material for a number of reasons (Bryant & Brown, 1989). First, people enjoy the sexual sensations erotica arouses. It can be a source of pleasure. Masturbation or other sexual activities, pleasurable in themselves, may accompany the use of sexually oriented material or follow it. Second, since the nineteenth century, sexually oriented material has been a source of sexual information and knowledge (Marcus, 1964). Eroticism generally is hidden from view and discussion. When sexuality is discussed in the family, schools, or in public, it is discussed moralistically, rationally, or objectively. Most discussions are limited to sexual intercourse; other activities are avoided. Because the erotic aspects of sex are rarely talked about, sexually oriented material fills the void. In fact, several studies of college students have found that sexually oriented

The VCR revolution drove "porno" movie houses out of business as individuals became able to view X-rated videos in the privacy of their own homes. Over 200 million X-rated videos are rented annually.

material is an important source of sex information, especially concerning oral sex (Duncan, 1990; Duncan & Donnelly, 1991; Duncan & Nicholson, 1991). Third, sexually oriented material, like fantasy, may provide an opportunity for people to rehearse sexual activities. Fourth, reading or viewing sexually oriented material for pleasure or for enhancing one's fantasies or masturbatory experiences may be regarded as safe sex.

Sexually oriented material may perform an additional function for gay men by allowing safe sex and reaffirmation. Being HIV-positive or a person with AIDS creates anxieties about HIV transmission to others. But gay sexually oriented material permits those with HIV or AIDS to explore their own sexuality with masturbatory images and scenes while refraining from sexual relationships.

Men tend to react more positively to sexually explicit material than women (Thompson, Chaffe, & Oshagan, 1990). Men more than women believe sexually explicit material has positive effects, such as sexual release and a lowering of inhibitions. Both believe, however, that sexually explicit material may have negative effects, such as dehumanizing women and causing a loss of respect between men and women.

Sexually Oriented Material and Sexual Aggression: What Do We Know?
In 1970, the President's Commission on Pornography and Obscenity concluded that pornography did not cause harm or violence. It recommended that all legislation restricting adult access to it be repealed as inconsistent with the First Amendment.

In the 1980s, President Ronald Reagan established a new pornography commission under Attorney General Edwin Meese. In 1986, the Attorney General's Commission on Pornography stated that "the most prevalent forms of pornography" were violent; it offered no evidence, however, to substantiate its assertion (U.S. Attorney General's Commission on Pornography [AGCOP], 1986). There is no evidence, in fact, to indicate that the majority of sexually explicit material is violent.

In the 1970s, feminists and others who worked to increase rape awareness began to call attention to the violence against women portrayed in the media. They found rape themes in sexually explicit material especially disturbing. They believed these images reinforced rape myths. There is no evidence, however, that nonviolent sexually oriented material is associated with actual sexual aggression against women. Even the conservative Commission on Pornography agreed that nonviolent sexually oriented material had no such effect (AGCOP, 1986). But it did assert that "some forms of sexually explicit materials bear a causal relationship . . . to sexual violence." It presented no scientific evidence as proof, however.

The case concerning the relationship between violent sexually oriented material and sexual aggression against women has not been substantiated. The Society for the Scientific Study of Sex responded to the Meese Commission in a policy statement: "The evidence for a direct causal link between exposure to sexually explicit material, pornography, or violent pornography to consequences such as sexual violence, sexual coercion, or rape is incomplete and inadequate" (Board of Directors, 1987).

Child Pornography Child pornography is a form of child sexual exploitation. Children involved in pornography, who are usually between ages 8 and 16, are motivated by friendship, interest in sexuality, offers of money, or threats. Younger children may be unaware that their photographs are being used sexually. Many of these children are related to the photographer (Burgess, Hartman, McCausland, & Powers, 1984). Many children who have been exploited in this way exhibit distress and poor adjustment; they may suffer from depression, anxiety, and guilt. Many engage in destructive and antisocial behavior, according to Ann Burgess and colleagues (1984).

Although the courts have generally continued to oppose censoring sexually explicit material and to affirm the individual's right to possess such material, a major exception is child pornography. In 1990, the Supreme Court affirmed the right to prosecute individuals for the possession of child pornography (*Osborne v. Ohio*, No. 88-5986).

In 1977, the United States passed the Protection of Children Against Sexual Exploitation Act. (Unfortunately, this legislation does not address the widespread exploitation and victimization of adolescent prostitutes.) Since then, those involved in child pornography have been vigorously prosecuted. In 1993, for example, federal, state, and local law-enforcement officials served warrants on 30 individuals in 15 states involved in a Danish computer bulletin board that trafficked in obscene photographs of children (Foo, 1993). A problem with child pornography laws, however, is that they are often so broadly written that, in the words of Justice William Brennan, photographs of "teenagers in revealing dresses" or "toddlers romping unclothed" may lead to unjust arrests (*Osborne v. Ohio*, No. 88-5986). Such arrests of innocent parents or legitimate professional photographers have, in fact, occurred.

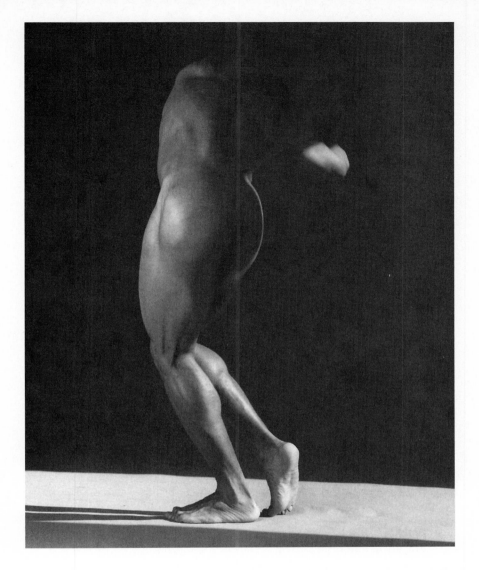

Fortunately, child pornography is not widespread, although it is commonly perceived as being so. Child pornography accounts for a tiny fraction of sexually explicit material, but it is often made to appear as representative of sexually explicit material in general.

Censorship, Sexually Oriented Material, and the Law

To censor means to examine in order to suppress or delete anything considered objectionable. **Censorship** occurs when the government, private groups, or individuals impose their moral or political values on others by suppressing words, ideas, or images they deem offensive.

Censorship and Obscenity

Obscenity is the state of being contrary to generally accepted moral standards. During the first half of this century,

censorship The suppression of words, ideas, or images by a government, private groups, or individuals based on their political or moral values.

obscenity That which is deemed offensive to "accepted" standards of decency or morality.

Two of the most heavily censored books in America are Leslea Newman's Heather Has Two Mommies, *about a lesbian family, and Michael Willhoite's* Daddy's Roommate, *about a child who visits his gay father and roommate. These books are opposed because they depict loving gay and lesbian families.*

under American obscenity laws, James Joyce's *Ulysses* and the works of D. H. Lawrence were prohibited, Havelock Ellis's *Studies in the Psychology of Sex* was banned, nude paintings were ripped from gallery and museum walls, and everything but tender kisses was banned from the movies for years.

U.S. Supreme Court decisions in the 1950s and 1960s eliminated much of the legal framework supporting literary censorship on the national level. But censorship continues to flourish on the state and local levels, especially among schools and libraries. The women's health book *Our Bodies, Ourselves* has been a frequent object of attack because of its feminist perspective and descriptions of lesbian sexuality. More recently, two children's books have been added to the list of most censored books: Leslea Newman's *Heather Has Two Mommies* and Michael Willhoite's *Daddy's Roommate*. Both books have come under attack because they describe children in healthy lesbian and gay families. Judy Blume's books for teenagers, J. D. Salinger's *The Catcher in the Rye,* and the *Sports Illustrated* swimsuit issue are regular items on banned-book lists. Exhibits of the photographs taken by the late Robert Mapplethorpe have been strenuously attacked for "promoting" homoeroticism, and contemporary music has been criticized for focusing on themes of sex, violence, suicide, incest, and sexism. Some retail stores have stopped carrying music having a "sexually explicit lyrics" label.

Obscenity Laws It is difficult to arrive at a legal definition of obscenity for determining whether a specific illustration, photograph, novel, or movie is obscene. Traditionally, American courts considered material obscene if it tended to corrupt or deprave its user. Over the years, the law has been debated in a number of court cases. This process has resulted in a set of guidelines for determining what is obscene:

1. The dominant theme of the work must appeal to prurient sexual interests and portray sexual conduct in a patently offensive way.
2. Taken as a whole, the work must be without serious literary, artistic, political, or scientific value.
3. A "reasonable" person must find the work, when taken as a whole, to possess no social value.

The problem with these criteria, as well as the earlier standards, is that they are highly subjective. Who is a reasonable person? You or I, the local minister, priest, or rabbi, Pat Robertson, Hugh Hefner, Gloria Steinem, Howard Stern, or Phyllis Schlafly? Moreover, there are many instances in which reasonable people disagree about whether material has social value. Most of us would probably find that a reasonable person has opinions regarding obscenity that closely resemble our own. (Otherwise, we would think that he or she was unreasonable.)

Our evaluation of sexually explicit material is closely related to how we feel about such material (Byrne, Fisher, Lambreth, & Mitchell, 1974). Our judgments are not based on reason but on emotion. Justice Potter Stewart's exasperation in *Jacobelis v. Ohio* (1965) reveals a reasonable person's frustration in trying to define pornography: "But I know it when I see it." Our inability to find criteria for objectively defining obscenity makes it potentially dangerous to censor such material. We may end up using our own *personal* standards for restricting freedom of speech guaranteed by the First Amendment. By enforcing our own biases, we endanger the freedom of others.

PROSTITUTION

Prostitution is the exchange of sexual acts, such as sexual intercourse, fellatio, anal intercourse, discipline and bondage, and obscene insults, for money. Both men and women, including transvestites and transsexuals, work as prostitutes.

Females Working in Prostitution

During the 1980s, an estimated 80,000 women worked in prostitution (Potterat, Woodhouse, Muth, & Muth, 1990). This estimate may be considerably smaller than the actual number because many women engage in it occasionally or drift in and out. Many women who accept money or drugs for sexual activities do not consider themselves prostitutes. According to Janus and Janus (1993), 4% of the women in their representative study reported exchanging sex for money.

Sex as Work Prostitutes often identify themselves as "working girls" or "sex workers," probably an accurate description of how they perceive themselves in relationship to sex. They are usually not prostitutes because they like anonymous sex and multiple partners per se, but because they perceive it as good-paying work. They generally do not expect to enjoy sex with their customers. They separate sex as a physical act for which they are paid from sex as an expression of intimacy and pleasure. One prostitute (quoted in Zausner, 1986) describes her feelings about sex:

I don't think about sex when I'm working. You have to be a good actress to make men think that you like it when you don't. I only enjoy sex if I'm with someone I care about.

Another study, however, found that many of the prostitutes interviewed enjoyed their sexual activities (Savitz & Rosen, 1988). Thirty-nine percent stated they enjoyed sexual intercourse with their clients most or all of the time. Fifty-seven percent reported they enjoyed fellatio most or all of the time; 70% said they enjoyed cunnilingus most or all of the time.

Although prostitutes may be willing to perform various sexual acts, many will not kiss; they regard kissing as a particular form of intimacy which they reserve for men they care about.

Entrance into Prostitution A major study of adolescent prostitution found that the majority of prostitutes under age 18 were less than 16 when they first began. The average age for the first act of prostitution was 14 (Weisberg, 1985).

Childhood sexual abuse is often a factor in adolescent girls' and boys' entrance into prostitution, for two reasons (Earls & David, 1990; Simons & Whitbeck, 1991). First, sexual abuse increases the likelihood that a preadolescent or adolescent will become involved in the deviant street culture and activities. Physically and sexually abused youths are more likely to be rejected by their conventional peers and become involved in delinquent activities. Second, one of their primary reasons for fleeing home is parental abuse—generally physical abuse for boys, sexual abuse for girls.

Girls are generally introduced into prostitution by pimps, men upon whom prostitutes are emotionally and financially dependent. Prostitutes give their pimps the money they earn. In turn, pimps provide housing, buy them clothes and jewelry, and offer them protection on the streets. Although girls meet their pimps in various ways, pimps most frequently initiate the contact. They use both psychological and physical coercion. Many girls and young women are "sweet-talked" into prostitution by promises of money, protection, and companionship. Adolescent prostitutes are more likely than adults to have pimps.

Once involved with pimps, women are frequently abused by them. The women also run the risk of abuse and violence from their customers. Streetwalkers are especially vulnerable.

Personal Background and Motivation Adult prostitutes are often women who were targets of early male sexual aggression, had extensive sexual experience in adolescence, were rejected by peers because of sexual activities, and were not given adequate emotional support by their parents. There are high rates of physical and sexual abuse (including intrafamilial abuse) in their childhoods (Silbert & Pines, 1981; Zausner, 1986). Their parents failed to provide their daughters with a model of affectionate interaction. As a result, as the girls grew up, they tended to be anxious, to feel lonely and isolated, and to be unsure of their own identity (Greenwald, 1970; Simon & Gagnon, 1973).

Adolescent prostitutes describe their general psychological state of mind as very negative, depressed, unhappy, or insecure at the time they first

Erotic dancing in bars, clubs, and peep shows led to the end of striptease in burlesque shows in the 1970s (left). Americans tend to romanticize prostitution on TV and in movies, as demonstrated by the movie "Pretty Woman" (above).

entered prostitution. There were high levels of drug use, including alcohol, marijuana, cocaine, and/or heroin (Weisberg, 1985). Their emotional state makes them particularly vulnerable to pimps.

No single motive seems to explain why a person becomes a prostitute. It is probably a combination of environmental, social, financial, and personal factors that lead a woman to this profession. When women describe the most attractive things about their lives in the prostitution subculture, they describe them in monetary and material terms. One prostitute notes (Weisberg, 1985), "I said to myself how can I do these horrible things and I said money, money, money." Compared to minimum-wage jobs, which may be the only alternative, prostitution appears to be an economically rational decision. But prostitutes also are aware of the psychological and physical costs. They fear the dangers of physical and sexual abuse, AIDS and other sexually transmitted diseases, harassment, jail, and legal expenses. They are also aware of the damage done to their self-esteem from stigmatization and rejection by family and society, negative feelings toward men and sex, bad working conditions, lack of a future, and control by pimps (Weisberg, 1985).

Prostitutes may justify their deviant behavior in terms of the cultural values accepted by the conventional world. They may take pride in financial success, their high earnings, easy life, beautiful clothes, expensive cars. Women who live two lives—mother and wife by day, prostitute by night—are likely to hold conventional middle-class values and to explain their prostitution in terms of family responsibilities: They need the money for their children, sick parents, unemployed husbands, or other reasons.

Prostitutes exhibit a range of feelings toward their customers. Some may project onto others their feelings of being deviant. If customers regard prostitutes as bad, the women feel that the so-called respectable people who come to them are worse—hypocrites, freaks, weirdos, and perverts who ask them to perform sexual acts which the women often consider degrading. Prostitutes frequently encounter such people, and may generalize from these experiences (Greenwald, 1970). Other prostitutes, however, are accepting and nonjudgmental of their customers. "My customers are people like everyone else," reports one prostitute (Zausner, 1986). "If they're nice to me and don't try to fuck with me, then I like them."

Forms of Female Prostitution   There are four major types of female prostitutes: those who work as streetwalkers, in brothels, in massage parlors, and as call girls.

Streetwalkers   Streetwalkers are by far the most numerous. Streetwalking is usually the first type of prostitution in which adolescents become involved; it is also the type they prefer (Weisberg, 1985). Women working as streetwalkers are often high school dropouts or runaways who fled abusive homes. Because streetwalkers make their contacts through public solicitation, they are more visible and more likely to be arrested. Without the ability to easily screen her customers, the streetwalker is more likely to be victimized, beaten, robbed, or raped. She is also more likely to have a pimp.

Streetwalkers in one study worked an average of 5 days a week and had 4 or 5 clients a day, half of whom were repeats (Freund et al., 1989). Fellatio was their most common activity; less than one-quarter of their contacts involved sexual intercourse.

Brothels   Brothels can be found in most large cities. They are legal in some counties in Nevada. A major attraction of brothels is their comfortable and personable atmosphere. In brothels, men can sit and have a cup of coffee or a drink, watch television, or casually converse with the women. Many customers are regulars. Sometimes they go to the brothel simply to talk or relax rather than to engage in sex (Perkins & Bennett, 1985).

Some brothels, such as B&D dungeons, which cater to bondage and discipline customers, specialize in different types of sex (Perkins & Bennett, 1985). These "dungeons" are equipped with whips, racks, leg irons; they replicate a gothic atmosphere. Women in such brothels adopt pseudonyms such as "Madam Lash" or add the prefix "Mistress" to their first names. They dress in black, studded leather and make themselves up as forbidding dominatrices (plural of dominatrix, a woman who dominates) (Delacoste & Alexander, 1987).

Masseuses   There are relatively few brothels any longer; most have been replaced by massage parlors. The major difference between brothels and massage parlors is that brothels present themselves as places of prostitution, while massage parlors try to disguise their intent. There are basically four types of massage parlors (Bryant & Palmer, 1975). First, genuine massage parlors actually provide exercise and physical therapy instead of sex. Second, "rip-off joints" entice customers with sexual advertising, women dressed as harem slaves, and brothel-like decor. The customers get a massage but no sex. Because most massage parlors depend on transient customers, they are not concerned that the customer will never return. A third type of massage parlor is little more than a brothel in disguise. The customer is able to get any type of sexual service he desires for a fee, which is negotiated with the masseuses. The fourth type is the "massage and masturbation only" parlor. These so-called M-and-M parlors are probably the most widespread; their primary service is the "local" or "relief" massage in which there is only masturbation. By limiting sex to masturbation, these parlors are able to avoid legal difficulties, because most criminal sex statutes require genital penetration, oral sex, discussion of fees, and explicit solicitation for criminal prosecution. Women who work M-and-M parlors are frequently referred to as "hand whores"; these women, however, often do not consider themselves prostitutes, although they may drift into prostitution later. Many masseuses run newspaper ads for their services and work on an out-call basis, meeting customers at their hotel rooms or homes.

Call Girls Call girls have the highest status among prostitutes. They are usually better educated than other prostitutes, often come from a middle-class background, dress fashionably, and live on "the right side of the tracks." A call girl is expensive; her fees may range from $50 to $75 an hour, or $500 to $1000 a night. She operates through contacts and referrals; instead of the street, she takes to the telephone and arranges to meet her customers. Call girls often work for escort services that advertise through newspapers.

Males Working in Prostitution

Although there is extensive research about prostitution, most of it concerns female prostitution. Most research on male prostitution focuses on street hustlers, the male equivalent of streetwalkers. There are other kinds of male prostitutes, such as call boys, masseurs, and prostitutes who work out of gay bars, who have not been extensively investigated. Few males who work as prostitutes are gigolos, heterosexual men providing sexual services for women in exchange for money. Gigolos are probably more the products of male fantasies—being paid for "having fun"—than reality. The overwhelming majority of male prostitutes sell their sexual services to other males.

Male prostitution is shaped by three subcultures: the peer delinquent subculture, the gay subculture, and the transvestite subculture. Young male prostitutes are called "chickens," and the customers who are attracted to them are known as "chickenhawks."

In female adolescent prostitution, the pimp plays a major role: He takes a girl's money and maintains her in the life. By contrast, there is usually no pimp role in male prostitution. Most males are introduced to prostitution through the influence of their peers. A typical male begins when a friend suggests he can make "easy money" on the streets. Hustlers usually live alone or with roommates, while female streetwalkers usually live with their pimps. Many of the psychological symptoms associated with hustling are as attributable to the delinquent environment as to the hustler's innate psychological condition (Simon et al., 1992).

The **peer delinquent subculture,** an antisocial youth culture, is part of

Hustlers, *who may or may not be gay, report that many of their clients are married males.*

peer delinquent subculture An antisocial youth subculture.

delinquent street life characterized by male and female prostitution, drug dealing, panhandling, theft, and violence. Young people in this culture sell sex like they sell drugs or stolen goods—as a means of making money. Teenage hustlers may not consider themselves gay because they are selling sex rather than seeking erotic gratification. Instead, they may identify themselves as bisexual or heterosexual. They may find their customers in urban "sex zones"—adult bookstores, topless bars, and X-rated movie houses—which cater to the sexual interests of people of all sexual orientations. They are more likely to work the street than bars.

In contrast to male delinquent prostitutes, gay male prostitutes engage in prostitution as a means of expressing their sexuality *and* making money (Weisberg, 1985). They identify themselves as gay and work primarily in gay neighborhoods or gay bars. Many are "pushed-away" children who fled their homes when their parents and peers rejected them because of their sexual orientation (Kruks, 1991). The three most important reasons they give for engaging in prostitution are money, sex, and fun/adventure.

Very little is known about male transvestite prostitutes. They are a diverse group and are distinct from other male and female prostitutes (Elifson, Boles, Posey, Sweat, Barrow, & Elsea, 1993). Their clients are both heterosexual and gay males. Many of their heterosexual clients believe the transvestites are women, but others are aware that the prostitutes are transvestites.

Prostitution and the Law

Arrests for prostitution and calls for cleanups seem to be a communal ritual practiced by influential segments of the population to reassert their moral, political, and economic dominance (Schur, 1980). The arrests are symbolic of community disapproval. They are not effective in ending prostitution.

Female prostitution is the only sexual offense for which women are extensively prosecuted; the male patron is seldom arrested. Prostitutes are subject to arrest for various activities, including vagrancy and loitering, but the most common charge is for solicitation. **Solicitation,** a word, gesture, or action that implies an offer of sex for sale, is defined vaguely enough that women who are not prostitutes occasionally are arrested on the charge because they act "suspiciously." It is usually difficult to witness a direct transaction in which money passes hands, and such arrests are also complicated by involving the patron. Laws may also include actions not ordinarily associated with prostitution; for example, some states define prostitution as offering oneself for promiscuous and indiscriminate intercourse without payment.

There are periodic attempts to repeal laws criminalizing prostitution because it is perceived as a victimless crime: Both the woman and her customer engage in it voluntarily. Others, especially feminists, want to repeal such laws because they view prostitutes as being victimized by their pimps, their customers, and the police and legal system (Basow & Campanile, 1990). Studies of prostitutes and their clients, as well as psychological and sociological studies, provide significant support for decriminalization (Rio, 1991).

solicitation In terms of prostitution, a word, gesture, or action that implies an offer of sex for sale.

HIV, AIDS, AND PROSTITUTION

Prostitution has received increased attention as a result of the HIV/AIDS epidemic. There are several reasons that female and male prostitutes are at higher risk than the general population. First, many prostitutes are IV drug users, and IV drug use is one of the primary ways of transmitting HIV infection (Morse et al., 1991; Quadagno et al., 1991). Among prostitutes using IV drugs, 25–50% have tested HIV-positive in some parts of the country (Des Jarlais et al., 1987; Turner et al., 1989). Second, prostitutes are at higher HIV risk because they have multiple partners. Third, prostitutes do not always require their customers to use condoms (Leonard, Freund, & Pratt, 1989). Male prostitutes are at even greater risk than female prostitutes because of their high-risk sexual practices, especially anal intercourse, and their high-risk gay/bisexual clientele.

Both female and male prostitutes are a major source for the heterosexual transmission of HIV. One study found that 17.5% of the hustlers tested HIV-positive (Morse et al., 1991). Many reported having girlfriends or wives, some of whom were also prostitutes. The hustlers indicated that they believed the majority of their clients were heterosexual or bisexual. They believed 39% of their clients were married. The study suggests that male prostitutes and their customers may serve as a bridge for HIV infection to the heterosexual population, which currently has a relatively low infection rate.

Supporters of continued criminalization of prostitution point to the prevalence of HIV/AIDS as an additional reason for arresting prostitutes. Prostitutes, they argue, are likely to contribute to the AIDS epidemic. Some suggest additional penalties for prostitutes who have AIDS or test positive for the virus. Those who wish to decriminalize prostitution point out that the current laws have not diminished prostitution. Further, they argue, if prostitution were regulated and prostitutes were made subject to routine STD/HIV testing, there would be a greater likelihood of preventing HIV transmission. In Nevada, for example, where brothel prostitution is legal, health officials require monthly mandatory HIV tests and the use of condoms.

Reformers propose that prostitution be either legalized or decriminalized. Those who support legalizing prostitution want to subject it to licensing and registration by police and health departments, as in Nevada and parts of Europe. Those who propose decriminalization want to remove criminal penalties for engaging in prostitution; prostitutes would be neither licensed nor registered.

The world of commercial sex is one our society approaches with confusion. Society simultaneously condemns sexually explicit material and prostitution, while it also provides their customers. Because of conflicting attitudes and behaviors, our society rarely approaches the issues surrounding sexually explicit material and prostitution with disinterested logic.

SUMMARY

Sexually Oriented Material in Contemporary America

• There is a lack of agreement about what constitutes erotica and pornography because they are subjective terms. The same sexually oriented material (or sexually explicit material) may evoke a variety of responses in different people.

• Today, technology is extending the forms in which sexually oriented material is conveyed, as with "virtual reality" programs, cable TV, X-rated computer software programs and bulletin boards, and dial-a-porn. X-rated videocassettes have increased the consumption of sexually oriented films by women. The inclusion of women in the audience has led to femme porn.

• People who read or view sexually explicit material usually recognize it as fantasy. They use it as a release from their everyday world. Pornography temporarily encourages sexual expression, activating a person's typical sexual behavior pattern. People are interested in sexually oriented material because they enjoy sexual sensations, it is a source of sexual information and knowledge, it enables people to rehearse sexual activities, and it is safer sex. For gay men, sexually oriented material offers safer sex and reaffirmation.

• In 1970, the President's Commission on Pornography and Obscenity concluded that pornography did not cause harm or violence. Over the years, there has been controversy and debate over the effects of pornography. There is no evidence, however, that nonviolent sexually oriented material is associated with sexual aggression against women.

• Child pornography is a form of sexual exploitation. Child pornography is not widespread; it appeals to a very limited audience.

• U.S. Supreme Court decisions in the 1950s and 1960s eliminated much of the legal framework supporting censorship on the national level. The guidelines for determining whether a work is obscene are somewhat vague and highly subjective. The inability to find criteria for objectively defining obscenity makes it potentially dangerous to censor such material.

Prostitution

• Prostitution is the exchange of sexual acts for money. Both men and women work as prostitutes. Prostitutes often identify themselves as "working girls" or "sex workers."

• Women are generally introduced into prostitution by pimps. Adolescent prostitutes describe their general psychological state of mind as very negative. The women, especially streetwalkers, also run the risk of abuse and violence from their customers. Prostitutes report various motives for entering prostitution, including earning quick and easy money, the prostitution subculture, and the excitement of "the life."

• Streetwalkers are the most numerous prostitutes. Streetwalking is usually the first type of prostitution in which adolescents become involved. Others work in brothels; a major attraction is their comfortable and personable atmosphere. Massage parlors are more widespread. Some masseuses have intercourse with clients, while others provide only masturbation. Call girls have the highest status among prostitutes.

• Most research on male prostitution focuses on street hustlers. Male prostitution is shaped by the peer delinquent, gay, and transvestite subcultures. The three most important reasons given for engaging in prostitution are money, sex, and fun/adventure.

• Arrests for prostitution are symbols of community disapproval; they are not effective in ending prostitution. Female prostitution is the only sexual offense for which women are extensively prosecuted; the male patron is seldom arrested.

• Prostitutes are at higher risk for HIV/AIDS than the general population because many are IV drug users, have multiple partners, and do not always require their customers to use condoms. Female and male prostitutes and their customers may provide a pathway for HIV into the general heterosexual community.

SUGGESTED READINGS

Davis, Murray S. *Smut: Erotic Reality/Obscene Ideology.* Chicago: University of Chicago Press, 1983. An excellent sociological analysis of the interrelatedness of sexuality, erotica/pornography, society, and religion.

Delacoste, Frédérique, and Priscilla Alexander, eds. *Sex Work: Writing by Women in the Sex Industry*. Pittsburgh, PA: Cleis Press, 1987. A collection of short, personal stories by women who work as prostitutes, masseuses, topless dancers, models, and actresses, many of who regard themselves as feminists.

Donnerstein, Edward, et al., eds. *The Question of Pornography*. New York: Free Press, 1987. A review of the scientific research on sexually oriented material, their effects, and the legal issues involved.

Steinberg, David, ed. *The Erotic Impulse: Honoring the Sensual Self*. New York: Jeremy Tarcher, 1992. A fascinating collection of essays and poems by writers, poets, teachers, and psychologists.

Steward, Samuel M. *Understanding the Male Hustler*. New York: Haworth Press, 1992. A look at the world of male prostitution from the hustler's point of view.

Weisberg, Kelly D. *Children of the Night: A Study of Adolescent Prostitution*. Lexington, MA: Lexington Books, 1984. An outstanding scholarly work on the world of adolescent prostitution.

Appendix

RESOURCE DIRECTORY

AIDS and HIV

CDC National AIDS Hotline
(800) 342-2437 (342-AIDS)
TTY/TDD Hotline
(800) 243-7889

The hotline gives general information on HIV and AIDS and referrals to doctors or services in your area. Free brochures in a number of languages are available.

Linea National de SIDA (Spanish)
(800) 344-7432 (344-SIDA)

A 24-hour service that provides information and referrals regarding HIV and AIDS.

CDC National AIDS Clearinghouse
(800) 458-5231

The clearinghouse provides information on services and educational resources. Also provides copies of Public Health Service publications.

Project Inform
347 Dolores Street, Suite 301
San Francisco, CA 94110
(415) 558-9051
(800) 822-7422

The project conducts research and collects data for educators, health-care practitioners, PWHs, and PWAs. Treatment information, newsletters, and other publications are available.

You can also contact your local state or county health departments, AIDS resource organization, or the American Red Cross for assistance in your area.

Alcohol and Drug Abuse

Alcoholics Anonymous (AA)
P.O. Box 459, Grand Central Station
New York, NY 10163
(212) 870-3400

AA is a voluntary worldwide fellowship of people who meet together to attain and maintain sobriety. Check your telephone directory for local chapters.

National Clearinghouse for Alcohol and Drug Information (NCADI)
P.O. Box 2345
Rockville, MD 20847
(800) 729-6686

NCADI provides a referral service, answering inquiries on alcohol- and drug-related subjects by telephone or mail. The clearinghouse also gathers and disseminates current information (including books, curriculum guides, directories, and posters) free of charge.

Breast-Feeding (See Infant Care)

Cancer

American Cancer Society and Reach for Recovery
1599 Clifton Road NE
Atlanta, GA 30329
(404) 320-3333

The organization provides information and support for people with cancer. Local chapters can be found by checking your telephone directory. Reach for Recovery is a group for breast cancer survivors.

Breast Cancer Action
P.O. Box 460185
San Francisco, CA 94146
(415) 922-8279

The group provides information and suggests political action for women with breast cancer.

National Cancer Institute
Cancer Information Service
Bldg. 31; Room 10-A07
31 Center Dr.
Bethesda, MD 20892-2580
(800) 4-CANCER (422-6237)

Calls are automatically directed to regional service centers. Counselors answer questions and give referrals to local doctors and support groups. Write or call for free brochures and other information.

Encore

Contact your local YWCA for information on Encore, a support organization for women with breast cancer.

Child Abuse

Child Help USA Child Abuse Hotline
(800) 422-4453

This 24-hour center provides general information and referrals for young people and adults in crisis. Related statistics and literature are also available.

Clearinghouse on Child Abuse and Neglect Information
P.O. Box 1182
Washington, DC 20013
(703) 385-7565
(703) 385-3206 (fax)

The clearinghouse provides information and publications for professionals and concerned citizens interested in child maltreatment issues. Write or call for a free catalog.

Parents Anonymous (PA)
7120 Franklin Ave.
Los Angeles, CA 90046
(213) 388-6685

This nationwide organization provides support for parents who abuse or fear they may abuse their children. Look for a local chapter in your telephone directory.

Chronic Illness

American Diabetes Association
1660 Duke Street
P.O. Box 25757
Alexandria, VA 22313
(703) 549-1500

The organization provides information and referrals concerning diabetes.

American Heart Association
7320 Greenville Avenue
Dallas, TX 75231
(214) 373-6300

The organization provides information and referrals concerning heart disease prevention and treatment.

Arthritis Information Clearinghouse
P.O. Box 34427
Bethesda, MD 20034
(301) 495-4484

Information and referrals concerning arthritis and other rheumatic diseases are available.

Drug Abuse (See Alcohol and Drug Abuse)

Eating Disorders

The American Anorexia-Bulimia Association
133 Cedar Lane
Teaneck, NJ 07666
(201) 836-1800

Information and referrals are available for people with eating disorders and their families.

Overeaters Anonymous
P.O. Box 92870
Los Angeles, CA 90009
(213) 542-8363

A support group for compulsive overeaters; listed in local telephone directories.

Family Planning (Also see Pregnancy, Infant Care)

Planned Parenthood Federation of America
810 Seventh Ave.
New York, NY 10019
(212) 541-7800

Planned Parenthood provides information, counseling, and medical services related to reproduction and sexual health to anyone who wants them, regardless of age, social group, or ability to pay. Most cities have a Planned Parenthood organization listed in the telephone directory.

Public Health Departments

Counties throughout the United States have county health clinics that will provide low-cost family planning services. Some cities also have public health clinics. Look in your telephone directory under headings such as these:
Department of Health
Family Planning
Family Services

Health
Public Health Department
(City or County's Name) Health (or Medical) Clinic

Zero Population Growth (ZPG)
1400 16th St. NW, Suite 320
Washington, DC 20036
(202) 332-2200

ZPG is a national, nonprofit, membership organization that works to achieve a sustainable balance between the earth's population and its environment and resources. Teaching materials, numerous publications, and a newsletter are available. (There is a charge for multiple copies.)

Fatherhood

The Fatherhood Project
Families and Work Institute
330 7th Ave., 14th Floor
New York, NY 10001
(212) 465-2044

A national research, demonstration, and dissemination project designed to encourage wider options for male involvement in childrearing. Pamphlets are available on various subjects related to families and work.

Gay and Lesbian Resources

National Federation of Parents and Friends of Lesbians and Gays (PFLAG)
P.O. Box 96519
Washington, DC 20009-6519
(202) 638-4200

PFLAG provides information and support for those who care about gay and lesbian individuals. Write or call for the number of a parent contact in your area, or check the telephone directory for regional offices. Publications are available.

National Gay and Lesbian Task Force
2320 17th St. NW
Washington, DC 20009-2702
(202) 332-6483
(202) 332-6219 (TTY)
(202) 332-0207 (fax)

The Task Force provides information and referrals on gay and lesbian issues and rights.

General Health Information

American Institute for Preventative Medicine (AIPM)
30445 Northwestern Hwy., Suite 350
Farmington Hills, MI 48334
(810) 539-1800

For $2.95, the AIPM will send you a directory of toll-free numbers to call for advice and referrals on numerous health-related issues, such as alcohol abuse and cancer.

Centers for Disease Control (CDC)
1600 Clifton Rd. NE
Atlanta, GA 30333
(404) 639-3534

Inquiries from the public on topics such as preventative medicine, health education, and STDs (including AIDS) can be directed to the Public Inquiries Office at the CDC. The office will also answer questions on family planning and public health problems. Inquiries are answered directly or referred to an appropriate resource.

CDC Voice/Fax Information Services
(404) 332-4565

A 24-hour service that offers prerecorded information or facsimile transmission of documents on a wide variety of health concerns, including HIV. Fax copies are sent free of charge.

National Health Information Center (NHIC)
P.O. Box 1133
Washington, DC 20013-1133
(301) 565-4167
(800) 336-4797 (referral database)

The NHIC is a central clearinghouse designed to refer consumers to health information resources. A variety of publications are available.

Infant Care

La Leche League International
1400 N. Meacham Rd.
Schaumberg, IL 60173-4840
(800) LA-LECHE
(708) 519-7730 (Counseling Hotline)

La Leche League provides advice and support for nursing mothers. Write for a brochure or catalog of its numerous publications. For local groups, check your local telephone directory or call its Counseling Hotline.

National Organization of Circumcision Information Resource Centers (NOCIRC)
P.O. Box 2512
San Anselmo, CA 94979
(415) 488-0883

NOCIRC is a nonprofit health resource center that provides medical and legal information on the subject of circumcision and female genital mutilation. The organization opposes routine hospital circumcision of newborns. Pamphlets, newsletters, and referrals to physicians and lawyers are available.

Infertility

The American Fertility Society
1209 Montgomery Hwy.
Burmington, AL 35216-2809
(205) 478-5000

The society provides up-to-date information on all aspects of infertility, reproductive endocrinology, conception control, and reproductive biology. Booklets, pamphlets, and related materials are provided. Write or call for further information.

The Center for Surrogate Parenting, Inc.
8383 Wilshire Blvd., Suite 750
Beverly Hills, CA 90211
(213) 655-1974 (collect calls accepted)
(800) 696-4664

The Center is a private organization that matches prospective parents and surrogates for a fee. Extensive screening is involved. Write or call for further information.

Resolve
1310 Broadway
Somerville, MA 02144-1731
(617) 623-0744
(617) 623-0252 (fax)

Resolve, a national nonprofit organization focusing on infertility, refers callers to chapters across the nation, provides fact sheets on male and female infertility, and publishes a newsletter and a directory of infertility resources. Phone counseling is also offered. There is a small charge for publications.

Pregnancy (Also see Family Planning, Infant Care)

American College of Nurse-Midwives
818 Connecticut Ave., NW, Suite 900

Washington, DC 20006
(202) 728-9860

Write or call for a directory of certified nurse-midwives in your area or to get information on accredited university-affiliated nurse-midwifery education programs.

California Teratogen Information Service
University of California at San Diego Medical Center
(800) 532-3749

The latest information about the effects of drugs and medications on unborn babies are available free of charge. Pregnant women who have been exposed to suspected teratogens (substances harmful to the fetus) can also participate in a free follow-up program after birth. Confidentiality is maintained.

National Life Center
686 N. Brond St.
Woodbury, NJ 08096
(800) 848-5683

The center is an assistance and counseling service for pregnant women. Services include telephone counseling in any aspect of pregnancy and referral to chapters and clinics throughout the United States and Canada. The center counsels against abortion and does not give out information on birth control.

National Abortion Rights Action League (NARAL)
1156 15th St. NW
Washington, DC 20005
(202) 823-9300

This political organization is concerned with family planning issues and is dedicated to making abortion "safe, legal, and accessible" for all women. It is affiliated with many state and local organizations. A newsletter and brochures are available.

Pregnancy Loss

National SHARE Office
St. Joseph's Health Center
300 First Capitol Dr.
St. Charles, MO 63301
(314) 947-6164

SHARE and its affiliate groups offer support for parents who have experienced miscarriage, stillbirth, or the death of a baby. Check your local directory for groups, which may also be listed under "Sharing Parents," "Hoping and Sharing," "HAND," or a similar heading.

Rape (Also see Sexual Abuse)

National Clearinghouse on Marital and Date Rape
2325 Oak St.
Berkeley, CA 94708
(510) 524-1582
24 hours (message tape)

The clearinghouse provides information, referrals, seminars, and speakers covering numerous aspects of marital and date rape. There is a nominal charge for publications and consultation services. Calls are returned, collect.

Check your telephone directory for Rape Crisis Center or a similar listing to find the local crisis center nearest you; the service is available in almost all cities.

Sex Education and Therapy

American Association of Sex Educators, Counselors, and Therapists (AASECT)
435 N. Michigan Ave., Suite 1717
Chicago, IL 60611-4067
(312) 644-0828
(312) 644-8557 (fax)

AASECT is an interdisciplinary professional organization devoted to the promotion of sexual health through the development and advancement of the fields of sex therapy, sex counseling, and sex education. It provides professional education and certification for sex educators, counselors, and therapists. It publishes a newsletter and the Journal of Sex Education and Therapy.

Sex Information and Education Council of the United States (SIECUS)
130 W. 42nd St., Suite 2500
New York, NY 10036
(212) 819-9770

SIECUS is a nonprofit educational organization that promotes "healthy sexuality as an integral part of human life." It provides information or referrals to anyone who requests them. It maintains an extensive library and computer database. Publications include sex education guides for parents (in English and Spanish) and a comprehensive bimonthly journal, SIECUS Report. Memberships are available.

Sexual Abuse

Parents United
232 E. Gish Rd.

San Jose, CA 95112
(408) 279-8228

Parents United and its related groups Daughters and Sons United and Adults Molested as Children United are self-help groups for all family members affected by incest and child sexual abuse. They provide referrals to treatment programs and self-help groups throughout the country. A number of informative publications are available, including a bimonthly newsletter. Write or call for a literature list.

Sexually Transmitted Diseases (Also see AIDS and HIV and General Health Information)

Herpes Resource Center
P.O. Box 13827
Research Triangle Park, NC 27709-9940
(919) 361-8488

The center provides referrals for people who are infected with the herpes virus or who think they may be. Services are confidential.

STD Hotline (American Social Health Association)
(800) 227-8922

The STD Hotline provides information on all aspects of sexually transmitted diseases. It will describe symptoms but cannot provide diagnosis. It provides referrals for testing and further information. Confidentiality is maintained.

U.S. Centers for Disease Control (CDC)
Division of STD/HIV Prevention
1600 Clifton Road NE
Atlanta, GA 30333
(404) 639-3286

The CDC conducts research and collects data from nationwide sources. Many publications, including the Morbidity and Mortality Weekly Report (MMWR), *which contains the latest STD information, are put out by the CDC.*

Single Parents

Parents Without Partners (PWP)
401 N. Michigan Ave.
Chicago, IL 60611
(312) 644-6610
(800) 637-7974

PWP is a mutual support group for single parents and their children. It has numerous local groups with more than 85,000 members. It offers educational programs and literature, including The Single Parent magazine. It also offers scholarships for PWP children.

Single Mothers by Choice (SMC)
P.O. Box 1642
Gracie Station
New York, NY 10028
(212) 988-0993

SMC is a national group that supports single women over 30 who are considering or have chosen motherhood. It offers workshops, support groups, a newsletter, and related information about donor insemination and adoption. Based in New York City, it has chapters throughout the United States.

Terminal Illness

National Hospice Organization (NHO)
1901 N. Moore St., Suite 901
Arlington, VA 22209
(703) 243-5900
(800) 658-8898 (referrals only)

Hospices provide support and care for people in the final phase of terminal disease. The hospice "team" provides personalized care to minister to the physical, spiritual, and emotional needs of the patient and family. Call or write for literature and referral information.

Women

National Organization for Women (NOW)
1000 16th St. NW, Suite 700
Washington, DC 20036
(202) 331-0066

NOW is an organization of women and men who support "full equality for women in truly equal partnerships with men." NOW promotes social change through research, litigation, and political pressure. A newspaper and other publications are available. Many cities have local chapters of NOW. Membership dues vary.

Miscellaneous

DES Action USA
1615 Broadway
Oakland, CA 94612
(415) 465-4011

The group provides information for those who believe they may have been exposed to DES in utero.

The Endometriosis Association
8585 N. 76th Place
Milwaukee, WI 53223
(800) 992-3636

The association provides information and referrals for women with endometriosis.

Bibliography

Abbey, A. (1991). Acquaintance Rape and Alcohol Consumption on College Campuses: How Are They Linked? *Journal of the American College Health, 39*(4), 165–169.

Abbey, A., Halman, L. J., & Andrews, F. M. (1992). "Psychosocial, Treatment, and Demographic Predictors of the Stress Associated with Infertility." *Fertility and Sterility, 57*(1), 122–128.

Abel, G. (1989). "Paraphilias." In H. I. Kaplan & B. Sadock (Eds.), *Comprehensive Textbook of Psychiatry, Vol. 1* (5th ed.), Baltimore, MD: Williams & Wilkins.

Aboukler, J. P., & Swart, A. M. (1993). "Preliminary Analysis of the Concorde Trial." *Lancet, 341*(8849), 889–890.

Ackerman, D. (1990). *A Natural History of the Senses.* New York: Random House.

Adams, D. (1986). "Instruction and Course Content in Sex Knowledge and Attitudes and Internal Locus of Control." *Psychological Reports, 58*(1), 91–94.

Adams, D. (1990). "Identifying the Assaultive Husband in Court: You Be the Judge." *Response to the Victimization of Women and Children, 13*(1), 13–16.

Adelman, M. B. (1992). "Sustaining Passion: Eroticism and Safe-Sex Talk." *Archives of Sexual Behavior, 21,* 481–494.

Adess, N. (1980). "DES Update." *Family Planning and Reproductive Health,* 11–12.

Adler, J. (1986, March 24). "Learning from the Loss." *Newsweek,* pp. 66–67.

Adler, J. (1992, October 19). "Must Boys Always Be Boys?" *Newsweek,* p. 7.

Adler, N. E. (1992). "Unwanted Pregnancy and Abortion: Definitional and Research Issues." *Journal of Social Issues, 48*(3), 19–35.

Adler, N. E., David, H. P., Major, B. N., Roth, S. H., Russo, N. F., & Wyatt, G. E. (1990). "Psychological Responses After Abortion." *Science, 246,* 41–44.

Adler, N. E., David, H. P., Major, B. N., Roth, S. H., Russo, N. F., & Wyatt, G. E. (1992). "Psychological Factors in Abortion: A Review." *American Psychologist, 47*(10), 1194–2204.

Adler, N., Hendrick, S., & Hendrick, C. (1989). "Male Sexual Preference and Attitudes Toward Love and Sexuality." *Journal of Sex Education and Therapy, 12*(2), 27–30.

Ageton, S. (1983). *Sexual Assault Among Adolescents.* Lexington, MA: Lexington Books.

Agnew, J. (1986). "Problems Associated with Anal Erotic Activity." *Archives of Sexual Behavior, 15*(4), 307–314.

Ahn, H. N., & Gilbert, N. (1992). "Cultural Diversity and Sexual Abuse Prevention." *Social Service Review, 66*(3), 410–428.

Ahrons, C., & Rogers, R. (1987). *Divorced Families.* New York: W. W. Norton.

"AIDS and Children: A Family Disease." (1989, November). *World AIDS Magazine,* pp. 12–14.

"AIDS Test for Pregnant Women." (1995, February 23). *San Francisco Chronicle.*

"AIDS Transmission from Mother to Baby; Risk Tied to Amount of Virus in Woman." (1994). *San Francisco Chronicle.*

Ainsworth, M., et al. (1978). *Patterns of Attachment: A Psychological Study of the Strange Situation.* Hillsdale, NJ: Erlbaum.

Alan Guttmacher Institute (1986). *Teenage Pregnancy in Developed Countries.* New Haven, CT: Yale University Press.

Alan Guttmacher Institute (1994). *Abortion Services in the United States, 1991 and 1992.* New Haven, CT: Yale University Press.

Alapack, R. (1991). "The Adolescent First Kiss." *Humanistic Psychologist, 19*(1), 48–67.

Alcott, W. (1868). *The Physiology of Marriage.* Boston: J. P. Jewett.

Alexander, L. L. (1992). "Sexually Transmitted Diseases: Perspectives on This Growing Epidemic." *Nurse Practitioner, 17*(10), 31 ff.

Alexander, W., & Judd, B. (1986). "Differences in Attitudes toward Nudity in Advertising." *Psychology: A Quarterly Journal of Human Behavior, 23*(1), 26–29.

Allgeier, A. R. (1982). "Sexuality and Gender Roles in Middle-Aged and Elderly Persons." In E. Allgeier & N. McCormick (Eds.), *Gender Roles and Sexual Behavior.* Mountain View, CA: Mayfield.

Allport, G. (1958). *The Nature of Prejudice.* Garden City, NY: Doubleday.

Aloni, R., Heller, L., Keren, O., Mendelson, E., & Davidoff, G. (1992). "Noninvasive Treatment for Erectile Dysfunction in the Neurologically Disabled Population." *Journal of Sex & Marital Therapy, 18*(3), 243–249.

Althof, S., & Turner, I. (1992). "Self-Injection Therapy and External Vacuum Devices in the Treatment of Erectile Dysfunction: Methods and Outcome." In R. Rosen & S. Leiblum (Eds.), *Erectile Disorders.* New York: Guilford Press.

Althof, S. E., Turner, L. A., Levine, S. B., Bodner, J., Kursh, E. D., & Resnick, M. I. (1992). "Through the Eyes of Women: The Sexual and Psychological Responses of Women to Their Partner's Treatment with Self-Injection or External Vacuum Therapy." *Journal of Urology, 147*(4), 1024–1027.

Altman, D. (1982). *The Homosexualization of America, the Americanization of the Homosexual.* New York: St. Martin's Press.

Altman, D. (1985). *AIDS in the Mind of America.* Garden City, NY: Doubleday.

Alvarez, F., et al. (1988). "New Insights on the Mode of Action of Intrauterine Devices in Women." *Fertility and Sterility, 49,* 768–773.

American Academy of Pediatrics. (1995). *Condom Availability for Youth.* Elkgrove, IL: author.

American Fertility Society. (1992). "In Vitro Fertilization–Embryo Transfer (IVF–ET) in the United States: 1990 Results from the IVF–ET Registry." *Fertility and Sterility, 57*(1), 15–24.

American Psychiatric Association. *Diagnostic and Statistical Manual of Mental Disorders* (4th ed.). Washington, DC: American Psychiatric Association, 1994.

Ames, M. A., & Houston, D. (1990). "Legal, Social, and Biological Definitions of Pedophilia." *Archives of Sexual Behavior, 19*(4), 333–342.

Amschler, D. H. (1991). "The Rising Incidence of HPV Infection and Its Implications for Reproductive Health." *Journal of Sex Education and Therapy, 17*(4), 244–250.

Andersen, D. A., Lustig, M. W., & Andersen, J. F. (1987). "Regional Patterns of Communication in the United States: A Theoretical Perspective." *Communication Monographs, 54,* 128–144.

Anderson, J. R. (1989). "Gynecologic Manifestations of AIDS and HIV Disease." *The Female Patient, 14,* 57ff.

Andrews, F. M., Abbey, A., & Halman, L. J. (1991). "Stress from Infertility, Marriage, Factors, and Subjective Well-Being of Wives and Husbands." *Journal of Health and Social Behavior, 32*(3), 238–253.

Andrews, L. (1984). *New Conceptions: A Consumer's Guide to the Newest Infertility Treatments.* New York: St. Martin's Press.

Andrews, S. (1992, November 2). "The Naked Truth." *San Jose Mercury News,* pp. 1, 4.

Aneshensel, C., Fielder, E., & Becerra, R. (1989). "Fertility and Fertility-Related Behavior Among Mexican-American and Non-Hispanic White Females." *Journal of Health and Social Behavior, 30*(1), 56–78.

Angier, N. (1991, November 13). "Prostate Cancer Gets Spotlight as Major Threat." *The New York Times*, p. B8.

Annon, J. (1974). *The Behavioral Treatment of Sexual Problems.* Honolulu, HI: Enabling Systems.

Annon, J. (1976). *Behavioral Treatment of Sexual Problems: Brief Therapy.* New York: Harper & Row.

Applebome, P. (1993, January 28). "Military People Split Over Ban on Homosexuals." *The New York Times*, p. A10.

Applebome, P. (1993, February 1). "Homosexual Issues Galvanizes Conservative Foes of Clinton." *The New York Times*, pp. A1, A8.

Aral, S., & Holmes, K. K. (1990). "Epidemiology of Sexual Behavior and Sexually Transmitted Diseases." In K. K. Holmes et al. (Eds.), *Sexually Transmitted Diseases* (2nd ed.). New York: McGraw-Hill.

Armstrong, P., & Feldman, S. (1990). *A Wise Birth.* New York: William Morrow.

Armsworth, M. W. (1991). "Psychological Responses to Abortion." *Journal of Counseling and Development, 69,* 377–379.

Arndt, W. B., Jr. (1991). *Gender Disorders and the Paraphilias.* Madison, CT: International Universities Press.

Arno, P. S., & Feiden, K. L. (1992). *Against the Odds: The Story of AIDS Drug Development.* New York: HarperCollins.

Aron, A., & Aron, E. (1991). "Love and Sexuality." In K. McKinney & S. Sprecher (Eds.), *Sexuality in Close Relationships.* Hillsdale, NJ: Erlbaum.

Aron, A., & Strong, B. "Prototypes of Love and Sexuality." Forthcoming.

Ash, M. (1980). "The Misnamed Female Sex Organ." In M. Kirkpatrick (Ed.), *Women's Sexual Development.* New York: Plenum Press.

Athey, J. L. (1991). "HIV Infection and Homeless Adolescents." *Child Welfare, 70*(5), 517–528.

Atwood, J. D., & Gagnon, J. (1987). "Masturbatory Behavior in College Youth." *Journal of Sex Education and Therapy, 13,* 35–42.

Atwood, J. D., & Dershowitz, S. (1992). "Constructing a Sex and Marital Therapy Frame: Ways to Help Couples Deconstruct Sexual Problems." *Journal of Sex and Marital Therapy, 18*(3), 196–218.

Auger, J., Kunstmann, J. M., Czyglik, F., & Jouannet, P. (1995). "Decline in Semen Quality Among Fertile Men in Paris During the Past 20 Years." *New England Journal of Medicine, 332*(5), 281–285.

Babouri, E. M. (1985). "Use of the Group Modality in the Prevention of Sexually Transmitted Diseases Among Adolescent Girls." *International Journal of Adolescent Medicine and Health,* July–December 1985 (1), 3–4.

Bachrach, C. (1984). "Contraceptive Practice Among American Women, 1973–1982." *Family Planning Perspectives, 16*(6), 253–258.

Bailey, J. M., & Pillard, R. C. (1991). "A Genetic Study of Male Sexual Orientation." *Archives of General Psychiatry, 48*(12), 1089–1096.

Bailey, J. M., Pillard, R. C., Neale, M. C., & Agyei, Y. (1993). "Heritable Factors Influence Sexual Orientation in Women." *Archives of General Psychiatry, 50*(3), 217–223.

Bailey, J. M., Willerman, L., & Parks, C. (1991). "A Test of the Maternal Stress Theory of Human Male Homosexuality." *Archives of Sexual Behavior, 20,* 277–293.

Baird, D. D., & Wilcox, A. J. (1985). "Cigarette Smoking Associated with Delayed Conception." *JAMA: Journal of the American Medical Association, 253*(20), 2979–2983.

Baker, B. (1993). "The Female Condom." *Ms., 3*(5), 80–81.

Baldwin, J. D., Whitely, S., & Baldwin, J. I. (1992). "The Effect of Ethnic Group on Sexual Activities Related to Contraception and STDs." *Journal of Sex Research, 29*(2), 189–206.

Balshem, N., Oxman, G., Van Rooven, D., & Girod, K. (1992). "Syphilis, Sex and Crack Cocaine: Images of Risk and Morality." *Social Science and Medicine, 35*(2), 147–160.

Bancroft, J. (1984). "Hormones and Human Sexual Behavior." *Journal of Sex and Marital Therapy, 10,* 3–21.

Barbach, L. (1982). *For Each Other: Sharing Sexual Intimacy.* Garden City, NY: Doubleday.

Barclay, A. (1980). "Changes in Sexual Fantasy with Age." *Medical Aspects of Human Sexuality,* 15ff.

Barkan, S., & Bracken, M. (1987). "Delayed Childbearing: No Evidence for Increased Low Risk of Low Birth Weight and Preterm Delivery." *American Journal of Epidemiology, 125*(1), 101–109.

Barker-Benfield, G. J. (1976). *The Horrors of the Half-Known Life: Male Attitudes toward Women and Sexuality in Nineteenth-Century America.* New York: Harper & Row.

Barnes, A. B., et al. (1980). "Fertility and Pregnancy Outcomes in Women Exposed in Utero to Diethylstilbestrol." *New England Journal of Medicine, 302*(11), 609–613.

Barnes-Kedar, I., Amiel, A., Maor, O., & Fejgin, M. (1993). "Elevated Human Chorionic Gonadotropin Levels in Pregnancies with Sex Chromosome Abnormalities." *American Journal of Medical Genetics, 45*(3), 356–357.

Barnett, W., Freudenberg, N., & Wille, R. (1992). "Partnership after Induced Abortion—A Prospective Controlled Study." *Archives of Sexual Behavior, 21*(5), 443–455.

Baron, L. (1983). "Sex Differences in Attitudes and Experiences of Romantic Love." *Dissertation Abstracts International, 43,* 372A.

Barret, R. L., & Robinson, B. E. (1990). *Gay Fathers.* Lexington, MA: Lexington Books.

Barron, J. (1987, June 3). "In Ads for Condoms a Focus on Women." *The New York Times*, p. 14.

Barrow, G., & Smith (1992). *Aging, Ageism, and Society.* St. Paul, MI: West.

Barrows, S. (1986). *Mayflower Madam.* New York: Arbor House.

Bartell, G. D. (1970). "Group Sex Among the Mid-Americans." *Journal of Sex Research, 6,* 113–130.

Barth, R., & Kinder, B. (1987). "The Mislabeling of Sexual Impulsivity." *Journal of Sex and Marital Therapy, 13*(1), 15–23.

Basow, S. A. (1986). *Gender Stereotypes: Traditions and Alternatives.* (2nd ed.) Pacific Grove, CA: Brooks/Cole.

Basow, S. A. (1992). *Gender: Stereotyping and Roles.* Pacific Grove, CA: Brooks/Cole.

Basow, S. A., & Campanile, F. (1990). "Attitudes Toward Prostitution as a Function of Attitudes Toward Feminism in College Students." *Psychology of Women, 14*(1), 135–141.

Baumann, P., Jovanovic, V., Gellert, G., & Rauskolb, R. (1991). "Risk of Miscarriage After Transcervical and Transabdominal CVS in Relation to Bacterial Colonization of the Cervix." *Prenatal Diagnosis, 11*(8), 551–557.

Baumeister, R. F. (1988a). "Gender Differences in Masochistic Scripts." *Journal of Sex Research, 25,* 478–499.

Baumeister, R. F. (1988b). "Masochism as an Escape from Self." *Journal of Sex Research, 25*(1), 28–59.

Bauserman, R. (1990). "Objectivity and Ideology: Criticism of Theo Sandfort's Research on Man-Boy Sexual Relations." *Journal of Homosexuality, 20*(1–2), 297–312.

Baxter, L. A. (1987). "Cognition and Communication in Relationship Process." In R. Burnett, P. McGhee, & D. Clarke (Eds.), *Accounting for Relationships: Explanation, Representation, and Knowledge.* London: Methuen.

Baxter, R. L., De Riemer, C., Landini, A., & Leslie, L. (1985). "A Content Analysis of Music Videos." *Journal of Broadcasting and Electronic Media, 29*(3), 333–340.

Bayer, A., & Baker, D. (1985). *Eating Disorders: Anorexia and Bulimia.* Santa Cruz, CA: Network Publications.

Bayer, R. (1981). *Homosexuality and American Psychiatry: The Politics of Diagnosis.* New York: Basic Books.

Bean, F., & Tienda, M. (1987). *The Hispanic Population of the United States.* New York: Russell Sage Foundation.

Becerra, R. (1988). "The Mexican American Family." In C. Mindel et al. (Eds.), *Ethnic Families in America: Patterns and Variations* (3rd ed.). New York: Elsevier North Holland.

Bechhofer, L., & Parrot, L. (1991). "What Is Acquaintance Rape?" In A. Parrot & L. Bechhofer (Eds.), *Acquaintance Rape: The Hidden Crime*. New York: John Wiley.

Beck, M. (1988, August 15). "Miscarriages." *Newsweek*, pp. 46–49.

Beck, M. (1992, May 25). "Menopause." *Newsweek*, pp. 71–79.

Beck, S. H., Cole, B. S., & Hammond, J. A. (1991). "Religious Heritage and Premarital Sex: Evidence from a National Sample of Young Adults." *Journal for the Scientific Study of Religion*, 30(2), 173–180.

Beckman, K. A., & Burns, G. L. (1990). "Relation of Sexual Abuse and Bulimia in College Women." *International Journal of Eating Disorders*, 9, 487–492.

Beckmann, C. R., Gittler, M., Barzansky, B. M., & Beckmann, C. A. (1989). "Gynecologic Health Care of Women with Disabilities." *Obstetrics and Gynecology*, 74(1), 75–79.

Beckstein, D. (1990). *AIDS Prevention in Public Sex Environments*. Santa Cruz, CA: Santa Cruz AIDS Project.

Begley, S. (1995, March 27). "Gray Matters." *Newsweek*, pp. 48–54.

Behar, R. (1989). "Sexual Witchcraft, Colonialism, and Women's Powers: Views from the Spanish Inquisition." In A. Lavrin (Ed.), *Sexuality and Marriage in Colonial Latin America*. Lincoln, NE: University of Nebraska Press.

Behr, A. (1986, July 21). "Gay Teens Often Turn to Suicide." *San Jose Mercury News*, pp. 1, 6.

Beier, E., & Sternberg, D. (1977). "Marital Communication." *Journal of Communication*, 27(3), 92–97.

Beitchman, J. H., et al. (1992). "A Review of the Long-Term Effects of Child Sexual Abuse." *Child Abuse and Neglect*, 16(1), 101–128.

Belcastro, P. (1985). "Sexual Behavior Differences Between Black and White Students." *Journal of Sex Research*, 21(1), 56–67.

Belk, R. (1991). "The Ineluctable Mysteries of Possessions." *Journal of Social Behavior and Personality*, 6(6), 17–55.

Belknap, J. (1989). "The Sexual Victimization of Unmarried Women by Non-Relative Acquaintances." In M. Pirog-Good & J. Stets (Eds.), *Violence in Dating Relationships*. New York: Praeger.

Bell, A. (1974). "Homosexualities: Their Range and Character." In J. K. Cole & R. Dienstbier (Eds.), *Nebraska Symposium on Motivation*. Lincoln, NE: University of Nebraska Press.

Bell, A., & Weinberg, M. (1978). *Homosexualities: A Study of Diversities Among Men*. New York: Simon & Schuster.

Bell, A., Weinberg, M., & Hammersmith, S. (1981). *Sexual Preference: Its Development in Men and Women*. Bloomington, IN: Indiana University Press.

Bello, D., Pitts, R., & Etzel, M. (1983). "The Communication Effects of Controversial Sexual Content in Television Programs and Commercials." *Journal of Advertising*, 12(3), 32–43.

Belsky, J., et al. (1984). *The Child in the Family*. Reading, MA: Addison-Wesley.

Belsky, J. (1986, September). "Transition to Parenthood." *Medical Aspects of Human Sexuality*, 20, 56–59.

Bem, S. L. (1974). "The Measurement of Psychological Androgyny." *Journal of Consulting and Clinical Psychology*, 42, 151–162.

Bem, S. L. (1975). "Androgyny vs. the Tight Little Lives of Fluffy Women and Chesty Men." *Psychology Today*, 9(4), 58–59ff.

Bem, S. L. (1981). "Gender Schema Theory: A Cognitive Account of Sex Typing." *Psychological Review*, 88, 354–364.

Bem, S. L. (1983). "Gender Schema Theory and Its Implications for Child Development: Raising Gender-Aschematic Children in a Gender Schematic Society." *Signs*, 8(4), 598–616.

Bem, S. L. (1989). "Genital Knowledge and Gender Constancy in Preschool Children." *Child Development*, 60(3), 649–662.

Bem, S. L., & Lewis, S. A. (1975). "Sex Role Adaptability: One Consequence of Psychological Androgyny." *Journal of Personality and Social Psychology*, 31(4), 634–643.

Bem, S. L., Martyna, W., & Watson, C. (1976). "Sex Typing and Androgyny: Further Explorations of the Expressive Domain." *Journal of Personality and Social Psychology*, 34, 1016–1023.

Bennett, C. J., et al. (1988). "Sexual Dysfunction and Electroejaculation in Men with Spinal Cord Injury." *Journal of Urology*, 139, 453–457.

Bennett, W. (1982). *The Dieter's Dilemma: Eating Less and Weighing More*. New York: Basic Books.

Benshoof, J. (1993). "Planned Parenthood v. Cases: The Impact of the Undue Burden Standard on Reproductive Health Care." *JAMA: Journal of the American Medical Association*, 269(17), 2249–2257.

Benson, D., Charlton, C., & Goodhart, F. (1992). "Acquaintance Rape on Campus: A Literature Review." *Journal of American College Health*, 40, 157–165.

Benson, D., & Thompson, G. (1982). "Sexual Harassment on a University Campus: The Confluence of Authority Relations, Sexual Interest, and Gender Stratification." *Social Problems*, 29, 236–251.

Benson, R. (1980). *Handbook of Obstetrics and Gynecology* (7th ed.). Los Altos, CA: Lane Medical Publications.

Bera, W., et al. (1991). *Male Adolescent Sexual Abuse*. Newbury Park, CA: Sage Publications.

Bergen, D. J., & Williams, J. E. (1991). "Sex Stereotypes in the United States Revisited: 1972–1988." *Sex Roles*, 24(7/8), 413–423.

Berger, A. A. (1991). "Of Mice and Men: An Introduction to Mouseology; or Anal Eroticism and Disney." *Journal of Homosexuality*, 21(1–2), 155–165.

Berger, M. J., & Goldstein, D. P. (1984). "Infertility Related to Exposure to DES in Utero: Reproductive Problems in the Female." In M. Mazor & H. Simons (Eds.), *Infertility: Medical, Emotional, and Social Considerations*. New York: Human Sciences Press.

Berger, R. M. (1982). "The Unseen Minority: Older Gays and Lesbians." *Social Work*, 27, 236–242.

Berkowitz, A. (1992). "College Men as Perpetrators of Acquaintance Rape and Sexual Assault: A Review of Recent Research." *Journal of American College Health*, 40(4), 175–181.

Bernard, J. (1982). *The Future of Marriage*. (2nd ed.). New York: Columbia University Press.

Bernstein, H. (1991, February 5). "Ruling May Curb Harassment." *Los Angeles Times*, p. 3.

Berrick, J. D., & Barth, R. P. (1992). "Child Sexual Abuse Prevention—Research Review and Recommendations." *Social Work Research and Abstracts*, 28, 6–15.

Berscheid, E. (1983). "Emotion." In H. H. Kelley et al. (Eds.), *Close Relationships*. New York: W. H. Freeman.

Berscheid, E., & Frei, J. (1977). "Romantic Love and Sexual Jealousy." In G. Clanton & L. Smith (Eds.), *Jealousy*. Englewood Cliffs, NJ: Prentice-Hall.

Berscheid, E., & Walster, E. H. (1974). "A Little Bit About Love." In T. L. Huston (Ed.), *Foundations of Interpersonal Attraction*. New York: Academic Press.

Bérubé, A. (1988, September). "Caught in the Storm: AIDS and the Meaning of Natural Disaster." *Out/Look*, 8–19.

Betchen, S. (1991). "Male Masturbation as a Vehicle for the Pursuer/Distancer Relationship in Marriage." *Journal of Sex and Marital Therapy*, 17(4), 269–278.

Betts, K. (1994, April). "Body Language." *Vogue*, 345–347.

Beyette, B. (1986, October 17). "Teen Sex-Education Campaign Launched." *Los Angeles Times*, pp. 20, 22.

Bieber, I. (1962). *Homosexuality: A Psychoanalytic Study*. New York: Basic Books.

Bills, S. A., & Duncan, D. F. (1991). "Drugs and Sex: A Survey of College Students' Beliefs." *Perceptual and Motor Skills, 72,* 1293–1294.

Billy, J. O., Tanfer, K., Grady, W. R., & Klepinger, D. H. (1993). "The Sexual Behavior of Men in the United States." *Family Planning Perspectives, 25*(2), 52–60.

Billy, J. O., & Udry, J. R. (1985). "The Influence of Male and Female Best Friends on Adolescent Sexual Behavior." *Adolescence, 20*(77), 21–32.

Binion, V. (1990). "Psychological Androgyny: A Black Female Perspective." *Sex Roles, 22*(7–8), 487–507.

Binsacca, B. D., et al. (1987). "Factors Associated with Low Birth Weight in an Inner-City Population." *American Journal of Public Health, 77*(4), 505–506.

Black, R. D. (1991). "Women's Voices After Pregnancy Loss: Couples' Patterns." *Social Work in Health Care, 16*(2), 19–36.

Blackwood, E. (1984). "Sexuality and Gender in Certain Native American Tribes: The Case of Cross-Gender Females." *Signs, 10,* 27–42.

Blakeslee, S. (1991, October 30). "Simplifying the Surgical Removal of Precancerous Cervical Lesions." *The New York Times,* p. B9.

Blakeslee, S. (1992a, January 21). "Wart Virus Tied to Cervix Cancer." *The New York Times,* p. B6.

Blakeslee, S. (1992b, January 22). "An Epidemic of Genital Warts Raises Concern but Not Alarm." *The New York Times,* p. C-12.

Blanchard, R., Steiner, B. W., Clemmensen, L. H., & Dickey, R. (1989). "Prediction of Regrets in Postoperative Transsexuals." *Canadian Journal of Psychiatry, 34*(1), 43–45.

Blanchard, R., Clemmensen, L., & Steiner, B. (1986). "Phallometric Detection of Fetishistic Arousal in Heterosexual Male Cross-Dressers." *Journal of Sex Research, 22*(4), 452–462.

Blanchard, R., & Hucker, S. (1991). "Age, Transvestism, Bondage, and Concurrent Paraphilic Activities in 117 Fatal Cases of Autoerotic Asphyxia." *British Journal of Psychiatry, 159,* 371–377.

Blatch, H. (Ed.). (1922). *Elizabeth Cady Stanton.* New York: Harper & Row.

Block, J. (1983). "Differential Premises Arising from Differential Socialization of the Sexes: Some Conjectures." *Child Development, 54,* 1335–1354.

"Blood Test for Prostate Cancer Okd." (1994, August 30). *San Francisco Chronicle,* p. A-2.

Blum, R., et al. (1992). "American Indian–Alaska Native Youth Health." *Journal of the American Medical Association, 267,* 1637.

Blumberg, M. L., & Lester, D. (1991). "High School and College Students' Attitude Toward Rape." *Adolescence, 26*(103), 727–729.

Blumenfeld, W., & Raymond, D. (1989). *Looking at Gay and Lesbian Life.* Boston: Beacon Press.

Blumstein, P., & Schwartz, P. (1983). *American Couples.* New York: McGraw-Hill.

Board of Directors of the Society for the Scientific Study of Sex. (1987). "SSSS Responds to the U.S. Attorney General's Commission on Pornography." *Journal of Sex Research, 23*(2), 284–285.

Boland, J., & Follingstad, D. (1987). "The Relationship Between Communication and Marital Satisfaction: A Review." *Journal of Sex and Marital Therapy, 13*(4), 286–313.

Boland, R. (1992). "Selected Legal Developments in Reproductive Health in 1991." *Family Planning Perspectives, 24*(4), 178–185.

Boles, A. J., & Curtis-Boles, H. (1986). "Black Couples and the Transition to Parenthood." *The American Journal of Social Psychiatry, 6*(1), 27–31.

Bollen, N., Camus, M., Staessen, C., Tournaye, H., Devroey, P., & VanSteirteghem, A. C. (1991). "The Incidence of Multiple Pregnancy After In Vitro Fertilization and Embryo Transfer, Gamete, or Zygote Intrafallopian Transfer." *Fertility and Sterility, 55*(2), 314–318.

Bonilla, L., & Porter, J. (1990). "A Comparison of Latino, Black, and Non-Hispanic White Attitudes Toward Homosexuality." *Hispanic Journal of Behavioral Sciences, 12,* 437–452.

Borhek, M. (1988). "Helping Gay and Lesbian Adolescents and Their Families: A Mother's Perspective." *Journal of Adolescent Health Care, 9*(2), 123–128.

Borneman, E. (1983). "Progress in Empirical Research on Children's Sexuality." *SIECUS Report,* 1–5.

Borrello, G., & Thompson, B. (1990). "A Note Regarding the Validity of Lee's Typology of Love." *Journal of Psychology, 124*(6), 639–644.

Boston Women's Health Book Collective. (1992). *The New Our Bodies, Ourselves.* New York: Simon and Schuster.

Boston Women's Health Collective (1978). *Our Bodies, Ourselves.* Boston: Little, Brown.

Bostwick, H. (1860). *A Treatise on the Nature and Treatment of Seminal Disease, Impotency, and Other Kindred Afflictions.* (12th ed.). New York: Burgess, Stringer.

Boswell, J. (1980). *Christianity, Social Tolerance, and Homosexuality.* Chicago: University of Chicago Press.

Botwin, C. (1979, September 16). "Is There Sex After Marriage?" *The New York Times Magazine,* pp. 108–112.

Boulton, M., Hart, G., & Fitzpatrick, R. (1992). "The Sexual Behavior of Bisexual Men in Relation to HIV Transmission." *AIDS Care, 4*(2), 165–175.

Bouman, P. G. (1988). "Sex Reassignment Surgery in Male-to-Female Transsexuals." *Annals of Plastic Surgery, 21*(6), 526–531.

Bowlby, J. (1969, 1973, 1980). *Attachment and Loss, Vols. I–III.* New York: Basic Books.

Bowman, C. G. (1993). "Street Harassment and the Informal Ghettoization of Women." *Harvard Law Review, 106*(3), 517–580.

Bownes, I. T., O'Gorman, E. C., & Sayers, A. (1991a). "Assault Characteristics and Post-Traumatic Stress Disorder in Rape Victims." *Acta Psychiatrica Scandinavica, 83,* 27–30.

Bownes, I. T., O'Gorman, E. C., & Sayers, A. (1991b). "Psychiatric Symptoms, Behaviorial Responses and Post-Traumatic Stress Disorder in Rape Victims." Division of Criminological and Legal Psychology First Annual Conference. *Issues in Criminological and Legal Psychology, 1,* 25–33.

Bowser, B. (1988). "Crack and AIDS: An Ethnographic Impression." *MIRA: Multicultural Inquiry and Research on AIDS, 2*(2), 1–3.

Bowser, B. P., Fullilove, M. T., & Fullilove, R. E. (1990). "African-American Youth and AIDS High-Risk Behavior: The Social Context and Barriers to Prevention." *Youth and Society, 22*(1), 54–66.

Bozett, F. W. (1987a). "Children of Gay Fathers." In F. W. Bozett (Ed.), *Gay and Lesbian Parents.* New York: Praeger.

Bozett, F. W. (1987b). "Gay Fathers." In F. W. Bozett (Ed.), *Gay and Lesbian Parents.* New York: Praeger.

Bozett, F. W. (Ed.). (1987c). *Gay and Lesbian Parents.* New York: Praeger.

Brady, E. C., et al. (1991). "Date Rape: Expectations, Avoidance, Strategies, and Attitudes Toward Victims." *Journal of Social Psychology, 131*(3), 427–429.

Brand, H. J. (1989). "The Influence of Sex Differences on the Acceptance of Infertility." *Journal of Reproductive and Infant Psychology, 7*(2), 129–131.

Brandenburg, H., et al. (1990). "Fetal Loss Rate After Chorionic Villus Sampling and Subsequent Amniocentesis." *American Journal of Medical Genetics, 35*(2), 178–180.

Brandt, A. M. (1987). *No Magic Bullet: A Social History of Venereal Disease in the United States Since 1880.* New York: Oxford University Press.

Brauer, A. P., Brauer, D., & Rhodes, R. (1991). *The ESO Ecstacy Program.* New York: Warner Books.

Braunthal, H. (1981). "Working with Transsexuals." *International Journal of Social Psychology, 27*(1), 3–12.

Brazelton, T. B. (1995, February 27). "Confusion Over Sleep Positions, SIDS." *San Francisco Chronicle*.

Brecher, E. (1984). *Love, Sex and Aging*. Boston: Little, Brown.

Bremer, B. A., et al. (1991). "Do You Have to Call It 'Sexual Harassment' to Feel Harassed?" *College Student Journal*, 25(3), 258–268.

Breslow, N. (1989). "Sources of Confusion in the Study and Treatment of Sadomasochism." *Journal of Social Behavior and Personality*, 4(3), 263–274.

Breslow, N., Evans, L., & Langley, J. (1985). "On the Prevalence and Roles of Females in the Sadomasochistic Subculture: Report on an Empirical Investigation." *Archives of Sexual Behavior*, 14, 303–317.

Bretschneider, J., & McCoy, N. (1988). "Sexual Interest and Behavior in Healthy 80- to 102-Year-Olds." *Archives of Sexual Behavior*, 17(2), 109–128.

Briere, J. (1992). "Methodological Issues in the Study of Sexual Abuse Effects." *Journal of Consulting and Clinical Psychology*, 60(2), 196–204.

Briere, J., & Runtz, M. (1989). "University Male's Sexual Interest in Children: Predicting Potential Indices of 'Pedophilia' in a Nonforensic Sample." *Child Abuse and Neglect*, 13(1), 65–75.

Brierly, H. (1979). *Transvestism*. New York: Pergamon Press.

Bringle, R., & Buunk, B. (1985). "Jealousy and Social Behavior: A Review of Personal, Relationship, and Situational Determinants." In P. Shaver (Ed.), *Review of Personality and Social Psychology*, Vol. 6: *Self, Situation, and Social Behavior*. Newbury Park, CA: Sage Publications.

Bringle, R., & Buunk, B. (1991). "Extradyadic Relationships and Sexual Jealousy." In K. McKinney & Susan Sprecher (Eds.), *Sexuality in Close Relationships*. Hillsdale, NJ: Erlbaum.

Brinton, L. A., et al. (1986). "Long-Term Use of Oral Contraceptives and Risk of Invasive Cervical Cancer." *International Journal of Cancer*, 38, 339ff.

Britton, D. M. (1990). "Homophobia and Homosociality: An Analysis of Boundary Maintenance." *Sociological Quarterly*, 31(3), 423–439.

Brody, E. (1985). "Parent Care as a Normative Family Stress." *Gerontologist*, 25, 19–29.

Brody, J. E. (1985, August 14). "Assessing the Question of Male Circumcision." *The New York Times*, p. 18.

Brody, J. E. (1986, July 6). "Teens and the Rush to Have Sex." *San Jose Mercury News*, p. 5.

Brody, J. E. (1992). "Estrogen Is Found to Improve Mood, Not Just Menopause Symptoms." *The New York Times*, p. 141.

Brody, J. E. (1993, February 24). "Don't Panic. Before Worrying About All the Medical Studies, Take a Close Look at the Evidence." *The New York Times*, p. B7.

Brotman, B. (1992, July 19). "Why Abortion Rights Is a White Fight." *San Jose Mercury News*, p. A4.

Brown, G. (1980). *The New Celibacy*. New York: McGraw-Hill.

Brown, G. R., & Collier, Z. (1989). "Transvestites' Women Revisted: A Nonpatient Sample." *Archives of Sexual Behavior*, 18, 73–83.

Brown, J. D., & Campbell, K. (1986). "Race and Gender in Music Videos: The Same Beat but a Different Drummer." *Journal of Communication*, 36(1), 94–106.

Brown, J. D., & Newcomer, S. F. (1991). "Television Viewing and Adolescents' Sexual Behavior." *Journal of Homosexuality*, 21(1-2), 77–91.

Brown, J. D., & Schulze, L. (1990). "The Effects of Race, Gender, and Fandom on Audience Interpretations of Madonna's Music Videos." *Journal of Communication*, 40, 88–102.

Brown, P. L. (1990, October 4). "Where to Put the TV Set?" *The New York Times*, p. 4.

Browne, A., & Finkelhor, D. (1986). "Initial and Long-Term Effects: A Review of the Research." In D. Finkelhor (Ed.), *Sourcebook on Child Sexual Abuse*. Beverly Hills, CA: Sage Publications.

Brownmiller, S. (1975). *Against Our Will: Men, Women, and Rape*. New York: Simon & Schuster.

Brozan, N. (1986, June 21). "Early Detection Is Key in Breast Cancer." *The New York Times*, pp. 19, 20.

Bruce, K. E., Shrum, J. C., Trefethen, C., & Slovik, L. F. (1990). "Students' Attitudes About AIDS, Homosexuality, and Condoms." *AIDS Education and Prevention*, 2(3), 220–234.

Bruch, H. (1978). *The Golden Cage: The Enigma of Anorexia Nervosa*. Cambridge, MA: Harvard University Press.

Bryant, C. (1982). *Social Deviancy and Social Proscription*. New York: Human Sciences Press.

Bryant, C., & Palmer, C. E. (1975). "Massage Parlors and 'Hand Whores'." *Journal of Sex Research*, 11, 227–241.

Bryant, J., & Brown, D. (1989). "Uses of Pornography." In Z. Dolf & B. Jennings (Eds.), *Pornography: Research Advances and Policy Considerations*. Hillsdale, NJ: Erlbaum.

Bryant, Z. L., & Coleman, M. (1988). "The Black Family as Portrayed in Introductory Marriage and Family Textbooks." *Family Relations*, 37(3), 255–259.

Buchanan, P. (1993, February 15). "Is the GOP Falling into Humpty Dumpty Country?" *San Jose Mercury News*, p. A12.

Buchholz, E., & Gol, B. (1986). "More Than Playing House: A Developmental Perspective on the Strengths in Teenage Motherhood." *American Journal of Orthopsychology*, 56(3), 347–359.

Buchman, T., et al. (1980). "The Structure of Herpes Simplex Virus DNA and Its Application to Molecular Epidemiology." *Annals of the New York Academy of Science*, 354, 279–290.

Budiansky, S. (1988, April 18). "The New Rules of Reproduction." *U.S. News and World Report*, pp. 66–69.

Buffum, J. (1992). "Prescription Drugs and Sexual Function." *Psychiatric Medicine*, 10(2), 181–198.

Bullard, D., & Knight, S. (Eds.). (1981). *Sexuality and Disability: Personal Perspectives*. St. Louis, MO: Mosby.

Bullough, V. (1976). *Sexual Variance in Society and History*. New York: John Wiley.

Bullough, V. (Ed.) (1979). *The Frontiers of Sex Research*. Buffalo, NY: Prometheus.

Bullough, V. (1991). "Transvestism: A Reexamination." *Journal of Psychology and Human Sexuality*, 4(2), 53–67.

Bullough, V. L., & Bullough, B. (1993). *Cross Dressing, Sex and Gender*. Philadelphia: University of Pennsylvania Press.

Bullough, V., & Weinberg, J. S. (1988). "Women Married to Transvestites: Problems and Adjustments." *Journal of Psychology and Human Sexuality*, 1, 83–104.

Bumpass, L. L., & Sweet, J. A. (1988, June 14). "University of Wisconsin Survey on Cohabitation." *Wall Street Journal*, p. 37.

Burch, B. (1987). "Barriers to Intimacy: Conflicts Over Power, Dependency, and Nurturing in Lesbian Relationships." In Boston Lesbian Psychologies Collective (Ed.), *Lesbian Psychology: Explorations and Challenges*. Urbana, IL: University of Chicago Press.

Burcky, W., Reuterman, N., & Kopsky, S. (1988). "Dating Violence Among High School Students." *School Counselor*, 35(5), 353–358.

Burger, E. (1981). "Radical Hysterectomy and Vaginectomy for Cancer." In D. Bullard & S. Knight (Eds.), *Sexuality and Disability: Personal Perspectives*. St. Louis, MO: Mosby.

Burgess, A., Harman, C., McCausland, M., & Powers, P. (1984). "Response Patterns in Children and Adolescents Exploited Through Sex Rings and Pornography." *American Journal of Psychiatry*, 141, 656–662.

Burnett, R., McGhee, P., & Clarke, D. (Eds.). *Accounting for Relationships: Explanation, Representation and Knowledge*. London: Methuen.

Burnham, M. (1992). "The Supreme Court Appointment Process and the Politics of Sex and Gender." In T. Morrison (Ed.), *Race-ing Justice, En-Gendering Power*. New York: Pantheon.

Burns, A., Farrell, M., & Christie-Brown, J. (1990). "Clinical Features of Patients Attending a Gender-Identity Clinic." *British Journal of Psychiatry, 157*, 265–268.

Bursik, K. (1992). "Perceptions of Sexual Harassment in an Academic Context." *Sex Roles, 27*(7–8), 401–412.

Burt, M. (1980). "Cultural Myths and Supports for Rape." *Journal of Personality and Social Psychology, 38*, 217–230.

Bush, C. R., Bush, J. P., & Jennings, J. (1988). "Effects of Jealousy Threats on Relationship Perceptions and Emotions." *Journal of Social and Personal Relationships, 5*(3), 285–303.

Butcher, A. H., Manning, D. T., & O'Neal, E. C. (1991). "HIV-Related Sexual Behaviors of College Students." *Journal of American College Health, 40*(3), 115–118.

Butter, I. H., & Kay, B. J. (1990). "Self-Certification in Law Midwives Organizations—A Vehicle for Professional Autonomy." *Social Science and Medicine, 30*(12), 1329–1339.

Butts, J. D. (1981). "Adolescent Sexuality and Teenage Pregnancy from a Black Perspective." In T. Ooms (Ed.), *Teenage Pregnancy in a Family Context*. Philadelphia: Temple University Press.

Buunk, B., & Hupka, R. (1987). "Cross-Cultural Differences in the Elicitation of Sexual Jealousy." *Journal of Sex Research, 23*(1), 12–22.

Buunk, B., & van Driel, B. (1989). *Variant Lifestyles and Relationships*. Newbury Park, CA: Sage Publications.

Buxton, R. (1991). "Dr. Ruth Westheimer: Upsetting the Normalcy of the Late-Night Talk Show." *Journal of Homosexuality, 21*(1-2), 139–153.

Byers, E. S., & Eno, R. J. (1991). "Predicting Men's Sexual Coercion and Aggression from Attitudes, Dating History, and Sexual Response." *Journal of Psychology and Human Sexuality, 4*(3), 55–70.

Byers, E. S., & Heinlein, L. (1989). "Predicting Initiations and Refusals of Sexual Activities in Married and Cohabiting Heterosexual Couples." *Journal of Sex Research, 26*, 210–231.

Bygdeman, M., Swahn, M. L., Gemzell-Danielsson, K., & Svalander, P. (1993). "Mode of Action of RU 486." *Annals of Medicine, 25*(1), 61–64.

Byrd, W., et al. (1990). "A Prospective Randomized Study of Pregnancy Rates Following Intrauterine and Intracervical Insemination Using Frozen Donor Sperm." *Fertility and Sterility, 53*(3), 521–527.

Byrne, D., et al. (1977). "Negative Sexual Attitudes and Contraception." In D. Byrne & L. A. Byrne (Eds.), *Exploring Human Sexuality*. New York: Harper & Row.

Byrne, D., Fisher, W. A., Lambreth, J., & Mitchell, H. E. (1974). "Evaluations of Erotica: Facts or Feelings." *Journal of Personality and Social Psychology, 29*, 111–116.

Byrne, D., & Murnen, K. (1988). "Maintaining Love Relationships." In R. Sternberg & M. Barnes (Eds.), *The Psychology of Love*. New Haven, CT: Yale University Press.

Cado, S., & Leitenberg, H. (1990). "Guilt Reactions to Sexual Fantasies During Intercourse." *Archives of Sexual Behavior, 19*(1), 49–63.

Calamidas, E. G. (1990). "AIDS and STD Education: What's Really Happening in Our Schools?" *Journal of Sex Education and Therapy, 16*(1), 54–63.

Calderone, M. (1983a). "Fetal Erection and Its Message to Us." *SIECUS Report, 11*(5-6), 9–10.

Calderone, M. S. (1983b). "Childhood Sexuality: Approaching the Prevention of Sexual Disease." In G. Albee et al. (Eds.), *Promoting Sexual Responsibility and Preventing Sexual Problems*. Hanover, NH: University Press of New England.

Calderone, M. S., & Johnson, E. W. (1989). *Family Book About Sexuality*. (Rev. ed.). New York: Harper & Row.

Califia, P. (1979). "Lesbian Sexuality." *Journal of Homosexuality, 4*, 255–266.

California Medical Education and Research Foundation. (1992, February). "Health Tips; Anabolic Steroids and Steroid Alternatives." San Francisco: California Medical Association Newsletter.

Callan, V. (1985). "Perceptions of Parents, the Voluntarily and Involuntarily Childless: A Multidimensional Scaling Analysis." *Journal of Marriage and the Family, 47*(4), 1045–1050.

Callendar, C., & Kochems, L. (1985). "Men and Not-Men: Male Gender-Mixing Statuses and Homosexuality." Special issue: Anthropology and Homosexual Behavior. *Journal of Homosexuality, 11*, 165–178.

Callendar, C., et al. (1983). "The North American Berdache." *Current Anthropology, 24*(4), 443–456.

"Can You Rely on Condoms?" (1989, March). *Consumer Reports*, p. 135.

Canavan, M. M., et al. (1992). "The Female Experience of Sibling Incest." *Journal of Marital and Family Therapy, 18*, 129–142.

Cantor, M. (1987). "Popular Culture and the Portrayal of Women: Content and Control." In M. Beth & M. M. Ferree (Eds.), *Analyzing Gender*. Newbury Park, CA: Sage Publications.

Cantor, M. (1991). "The American Family on Television: From Molly Goldberg to Bill Cosby." *Journal of Comparative Family Studies, 22*(2), 205–216.

Caplan, A. L. (1992). "Twenty Years After: The Legacy of the Tuskegee Syphilis Study. When Evil Intrudes." *Hastings Center Report, 22*(6), 29–32.

Carey, R. F., Herman, W. A., Retta, S. M., Rinaldi, J. E., Herman, B. A., & Athey, T. W. (1992). "Effectiveness of Latex Condoms as a Barrier to Human Immunodeficiency Virus-Sized Particles under Conditions of Simulated Use." *Sexually Transmitted Diseases, 19*(4), 230–234.

Cargan, L., & Melko, M. (1982). *Singles: Myths and Realities*. Beverly Hills, CA: Sage Publications.

Carl, D. (1986). "Acquired Immune Deficiency Syndrome: A Preliminary Examination of the Effects on Gay Couples and Coupling." *Journal of Marital and Family Therapy, 12*(3), 241–247.

Carlson, R. G., & Siegal, H. A. (1991). "The Crack Life: An Ethnographic Overview of Crack Use and Sexual Behavior Among African-Americans in a Midwest Metropolitan City." *Journal of Psychoactive Drugs, 23*(1), 11–20.

Carmen, A., & Moody, H. (1985). *Working Women: The Subterranean World of Street Prostitution*. New York: Harper & Row.

Carnes, P. (1983). *Out of Shadows*. Minneapolis, MN: CompCare Publications.

Carr, P. (1992, February 16). "Sexual Harassment Pushes Its Way into the Schoolyard." *San Jose Mercury News*, pp. 1L, 8L.

Carrera, M. (1980). "Sexual Learning in the Elementary School." In E. Roberts (Ed.), *Childhood Sexual Learning: The Unwritten Curriculum*. Cambridge, MA: Ballinger.

Carrera, M. (1981). *Sex: The Facts, the Acts, and Your Feelings*. New York: Crown.

Carrier, J. (1992). "Miguel: Sexual Life History of a Gay Mexican American." In G. Herdt (Ed.), *Gay Culture in America: Essays from the Field*. Boston: Beacon Press.

Carrier, J., Joseph, C., Nguyen, B., & Su, S. (1992). "Vietnamese American Sexual Behaviors and the HIV Infection." *Journal of Sex Research, 29*(4), 547–560.

Carroll, J. (1990, March 5). "Tracing the Causes of Infertility." *San Francisco Chronicle*, pp. 3ff.

Carroll, J., Volk, K. D., & Hyde, J. J. (1985). "Differences in Males and Females in Motives for Engaging in Sexual Intercourse." *Archives of Sexual Behavior, 14*, 131–139.

Carter, B., & McGoldrick, M. (Eds.). (1989). *The Changing Family Life Cycle* (2nd ed.). Boston: Allyn & Bacon.

Carter, D. B. (Ed.). (1987). *Current Conceptions of Sex Roles and Sex Typing*. New York: Praeger.

Cary, A. (1992, April 18). "Big Fans on Campus." *TV Guide*, pp. 26–31.

Cass, V. C. (1983). "Homosexual Identity: A Concept in Need of Definition." *Journal of Homosexuality*, 9(2-3), 105–126.

Cassell, C. (1984). *Swept Away*. New York: Simon & Schuster.

Catania, J. A., et al. (1992). "Prevalence of AIDS-Related Risk Factors and Condom Use in the United States." *Science*, 258(5085), 1101–1106.

Catchpole, T. (1992, November). "A Short History of Political Tricks." *Playboy*, pp. 86–87, 169.

Cate, R. M., & Lloyd, S. A. (1992). *Courtship*. Newbury Park, CA: Sage Publications.

Cates, W. J., & Stone, K. M. (1992). "Family Planning, Sexually Transmitted Diseases and Contraceptive Choices: A Literature Update. Part I." *Family Planning Perspectives*, 24(2), 75–84.

Cautela, J. E. (1986). "Behavioral Analysis of a Fetish: First Interview." *Journal of Behavior Therapy and Experimental Psychiatry*, 17(3), 161–165.

CDC. See Centers for Disease for Control or Centers for Disease Control and Prevention.

Celentano, D. D., Vlahov, D., Cohn, S., Anthony, J. C., Solomon, L., & Nelson, K. E. (1991). "Risk Factors for Shooting Gallery Use and Cessation Among Intravenous Drug Users." *American Journal of Public Health*, 81(10), 1291–1295.

Center for Population Options. (1992). *Teenage Pregnancy and Too-Early Childbearing: Public Costs, Personal Consequences*.

Centers for Disease Control. (1982). "Update on Acquired Immune Deficiency Syndrome (AIDS)—United States." *Morbidity and Mortality Weekly Report*, 31(37).

Centers for Disease Control. (1984). "Hepatitis B Vaccine Evidence Confirming the Lack of AIDS Transmission." *Morbidity and Mortality Weekly Report*, 33, 685–687.

Centers for Disease Control. (1985). "Recommendation for Assisting in the Prevention of Perinatal Transmission of Human T-lymphotrophic Virus Type III." *Morbidity and Mortality Weekly Report*, 34, 721–726, 731–732.

Centers for Disease Control. (1986a). "Acquired Immunodeficiency Syndrome in Western Palm Beach County, Florida." *Morbidity and Mortality Weekly Report*, 35, 609–613.

Centers for Disease Control. (1986b). "The Cancer and Steroid Hormone (CASH) Study of the Centers for Disease Control and the National Institute of Child Health and Human Development: Oral Contraceptive Use and the Risk of Breast Cancer." *New England Journal of Medicine*, 315, 405–411.

Centers for Disease Control. (1986c). "Positive HTLV-III/LAV Antibody Results for Sexually Active Members of Social/Sexual Clubs." *Morbidity and Mortality Weekly Report*, 1–2.

Centers for Disease Control. (1987). "Lack of Transmission of Human Immunodeficiency Virus Through RHo(D) Immune Globulin." *Morbidity and Mortality Weekly Report*, 36,728.

Centers for Disease Control. (1990). "Statewide Prevalence of Illicit Drug Use by Pregnant Women—Rhode Island." *Morbidity and Mortality Weekly Report*, 39(14), 225–227.

Centers for Disease Control. (1992a). "1993 Revised Classification System for HIV Infection and Expanded Surveillance Case Definition for AIDS Among Adolescents and Adults. *Morbidity and Mortality Weekly Report*, 41(RR-17), 1–19.

Centers for Disease Control. (1992b). "Update: CD4+ T-lymphocetopenia in Persons Without Evident Symptoms." *Morbidity and Mortality Weekly Report*, 41(31), 578–579.

Centers for Disease Control and Prevention. (1993a). "Update: Barrier Protection Against HIV Infection and Other Sexually Transmitted Diseases." *Morbidity and Mortality Weekly Report*, 42(30), 589–596.

Centers for Disease Control and Prevention. (1993b). Division of STD/HIV Prevention: *Annual Report, 1992*.

Centers for Disease Control and Prevention. (1993c). "Facts About Condoms and Their Use in Preventing HIV Infection and Other STDs." *HIV/AIDS Prevention*, 1–3.

Centers for Disease Control and Prevention. (1993d). "Surveillance Report: U.S. AIDS Cases Reported Through December 1992." *HIV/AIDS Surveillance Report*, 1–23.

Centers for Disease Control and Prevention. (1993e). "Surveillance Report: U.S. AIDS Cases Reported Through March 1993." *HIV/AIDS Surveillance Report*, 5(1), 1–19.

Centers for Disease Control and Prevention. (1993f). "Surveillance Report: U.S. AIDS Cases Reported through June 30, 1993." *HIV/AIDS Surveillance Report*, 5(2), 1–19.

Centers for Disease Control & Prevention. Division of STD/HIV Prevention. (1994a). "Sexually Transmitted Disease Surveillance, 1993." Author.

Centers for Disease Control and Prevention. (1994b). "Surveillance Report: U.S. AIDS Cases Reported Through December 1994." *HIV/Aids Surveillance Report*, 6(2).

Centers for Disease Control. (1995). *National Youth Risk Behavior Survey*. Washington, DC.

Challice, J. (1992, May). "AIDS Research." *PAACNotes*, 121–124.

Chapman, A. (1988). "Male-Female Relations: How the Past Affects the Present." In H. McAdoo (Ed.), *Black Families* (2nd ed.). Beverly Hills, CA: Sage Publications.

Chasnoff, I. J. (1988). "Drug Use in Pregnancy: Parameters of Risk." *Pediatric Clinics of North America*, 35(6), 1403–1412.

Chiasson, M. A., Stoneburner, R. L., & Joseph, S. C. (1990). "Human Immunodeficiency Virus Transmission Through Artificial Insemination." *Journal of Acquired Immune Deficiency Syndromes*, 3(1), 69–72.

Chirgwin, K., DeHovitz, J. A., D. S., & McCormack, W. M. (1991). "HIV Infection, Genital Ulcer Disease, and Crack Cocaine Use Among Patients Attending a Clinic for Sexually Transmitted Diseases." *American Journal of Public Health*, 81(12), 1576–1579.

Chong, J. M. (1990). "Social Assessment of Transsexuals Who Apply for Sex Reassignment Therapy." *Social Work in Health Care*, 14(3), 87–105.

Chow, W. H., et al. (1985). "Vaginal Douching as a Potential Risk Factor for Tubal Ectopic Pregnancy." *Family Planning Perspectives*, 153, 727ff.

Chrisman, R., & Allen, R. (Eds.). (1992). *Court of Appeal: The Black Community Speaks Out on the Racial and Sexual Politics of Clarence Thomas vs. Anita Hill*. New York: Ballantine.

Christian-Smith, L. K. (1990). *Becoming a Woman Through Romance*. New York: Routledge.

Christopher, F., & Cate, R. (1984). "Factors Involved in Premarital Decision-Making." *Journal of Sex Research*, 20, 363–376.

Christopher, F. S., & Frandsen, M. M. (1990). "Strategies of Influence in Sex and Dating." *Journal of Social and Personal Relationships*, 7, 89–105.

Chu, S. Y., Buehler, J. W., Oxtoby, M. J., & Kilbourne, B. W. (1991). "Impact of the Human Immunodeficiency Virus Epidemic on Mortality in Children, United States." *Pediatrics*, 87(6), 806–810.

Chu, S. Y., Peterman, T. A., Doll, L. S., Buehler, J. W., & Curran, J. W. (1992). "AIDS in Bisexual Men in the United States: Epidemiology and Transmission to Women." *American Journal of Public Health*, 82(2), 220–224.

Chung, W., & Choi, H. (1990). "Erotic Erection Versus Nocturnal Erection." *The Journal of Urology*, 143, 294–297.

Cimons, M. (1990, December 7). "American Infertility Rate Not Growing, Study Finds." *The New York Times*, p. 3.

Clanton, G., & Smith, L. (1977). *Jealousy*. Englewood Cliffs, NJ: Prentice-Hall.

Clapper, R. L., & Lipsitt, L. P. (1991). "A Retrospective Study of Risk-Taking and Alcohol-Mediated Unprotected Intercourse." *Journal of Substance Abuse, 3*(1), 91–96.

Clark, D. (1992). "Cagney & Lacey: Feminist Strategies of Detection." In M. E. Brown (Ed.), *Television and Women's Culture: The Politics of the Popular*. Newbury Park, CA: Sage Publications.

Clift, E. (1990, July 2). "The Right Wing's Cultural Warrior." *Newsweek*, p. 51.

Cochran, J. K., & Beeghley, L. (1991). "The Influence of Religion on Attitudes Toward Nonmarital Sexuality: A Preliminary Assessment of Reference Group Theory." *Journal of the Scientific Study of Religion, 30*(1), 45–63.

Cochran, S. D., Mays, V. M., & Leung, L. (1991). "Sexual Practices of Heterosexual Asian-American Young Adults: Implications for Risk of HIV Infection." *Archives of Sexual Behavior, 20*(4), 381–394.

Coe, J. (1974). "Sexual Asphyxias." *Life-Threatening Behavior, 4*, 171–175.

Cogen, R., & Steinman, W. (1990). "Sexual Function and Practice in Elderly Men of Lower Socioeconomic Status." *Journal of Family Practice, 31*(2), 162–166.

Cohen, B. (1992, September 14). "Discrimination: The Limits of the Law." *Newsweek*, pp. 35–40.

Cohen, J. (1993). "Early AZT Takes a Pounding in French-British 'Concorde' Trial." *Science, 260*(5105), 157.

Cohen, N. W., & Estner, L. J. (1983). "Silent Knife: Cesarean Section in the United States." *Society, 21*(1), 95–111.

Colditz, G. A., et al. (1993). "Family History, Age, and Risk of Breast Cancer—Prospective Data from the Nurses Health Study." *Journal of the American Medical Association, 270*(3), 338–343.

Cole, E., & Rothblum, E. (1990). "Commentary on 'Sexuality and the Midlife Woman'." Special Issue: Women at Midlife and Beyond. *Psychology of Women Quarterly, 14*(4), 509–512.

Cole, W. (1992). "Incest Perpetrators: Their Assessment and Treatment." *Psychiatric Clinics of North America, 15*(3), 689–701.

Coleman, E. (1986). "Sexual Compulsion vs. Sexual Addiction: The Debate Continues." *SIECUS Report, 14*, 7–10.

Coleman, E., Colgan, P., & Gooren, L. (1992). "Male Cross-Gender Behavior in Myanmar (Burma): A Description of the Acault." *Archives of Sexual Behavior, 21*(3), 313–321.

Coleman, E., Rosser, B. R., & Strapko, N. (1992). "Sexual and Intimacy Dysfunction Among Homosexual Men and Women." *Psychiatric Medicine, 10*(2), 257–271.

Coleman, M., & Ganong, L. (1991). "Remarriage and Stepfamily Research in the 1980s: Increased Interest in an Old Form." In A. Booth (Ed.), *Contemporary Families: Looking Forward, Looking Back*. Minneapolis, MN: National Council on Family Relations.

Collier, M. J. (1991). "Conflict Competence Within African, Mexican, and Anglo American Friendships." In S. Ting-Toomey & Felipe Korzenny (Eds.), *Cross-Cultural Interpersonal Communication*. Newbury Park, CA: Sage Publications.

Collins, P. H. (1991). "The Meaning of Motherhood in Black Culture." In R. Staples (Ed.), *The Black Family* (4th ed.). Belmont, CA: Wadsworth.

Conant, J., & Wingert, P. (1987, August 24). "You'd Better Sit Down, Kids." *Newsweek*, p. 58.

Conant, M., Hardy, D., Sernatinger, J., Spicer, D., & Levy, J. A. (1986). "Condoms Prevent Transmission of AIDS-Associated Retrovirus." *JAMA: Journal of the American Medical Association, 255*(13), 1702–1712.

Condry, J., & Condry, S. (1976). "The Development of Sex Differences: A Study of the Eye of the Beholder." *Child Development, 47*(4), 812–819.

Condy, S., Templer, D. E., Brown, R., & Veaco, L. (1987). "Parameters of Sexual Contact of Boys with Women." *Archives of Sexual Behavior, 16*(5), 379–394.

Connor, S. (1994, August 28). "Downward Spiral in Quality of Sperm." *San Francisco Chronicle*.

Conrad, P., & Schneider, J. (1980). *Deviance and Medicalization: From Badness to Sickness*. St. Louis, MO: Mosby.

Constantine, L., & Martinson, F. (Eds.). (1981). *Children and Sex*. Boston: Little, Brown.

Conway, C. (1980). "Psychophysical Preparations for Childbirth." In L. McNall (Ed.), *Contemporary Obstetric and Gynecological Nursing*. St. Louis, MO: Mosby.

Cook, A., et al. (1982). "Changes in Attitudes Toward Parenting Among College Women: 1972 and 1979 Samples." *Family Relations, 31*, 109–113.

Cooper, A. (1985). "Sexual Enhancement Programs: An Examination of Their Current Status and Directions for Future Research." *Archives of Sexual Behavior, 21*(4), 387–404.

Cooper, A., & Stoltenberg, C. D. (1987). "Comparison of a Sexual Enhancement and a Communication Training Program on Sexual and Marital Satisfaction." *Journal of Counseling Psychology, 34*, 309–314.

Cooper, A. J., Swaminath, S., Baxter, D., & Poulin, C. (1990). "A Female Sex Offender with Multiple Paraphilias." *Canadian Journal of Psychiatry, 35*(4), 334–337.

Copenhaver, S., & Gauerholz, E. (1991). "Sexual Victimization Among Sorority Women: Exploring the Link Between Sexual Violence and Institutional Practices." *Sex Roles, 24*, 31–41.

Corby, N., & Zarit, J. (1983). "Old and Alone: The Unmarried in Later Life." In R. Weg (Ed.), *Sexuality in the Later Years: Roles and Behavior*. New York: Academic Press.

Corby, N. H., Wolitski, R. J., Thornton-Johnson, S., & Tanner, W. M. (1991). "AIDS Knowledge, Perception of Risk, and Behaviors among Female Sex Partners of Injection Drug Users." *AIDS Education and Prevention, 3*(4), 353–366.

Corea, G. (1985). *The Mother Machine: Reproductive Technology from Artificial Insemination to Artificial Wombs*. New York: Harper & Row.

Cornelius, D., et al. (1982). *Who Cares? A Handbook on Sex Education and Counseling Services for Disabled People*. Baltimore, MD: University Park Press.

Cornett, C., & Hudson, R. (1985). "Psychoanalytic Theory and Affirmation of the Gay Lifestyle: Are They Necessarily Antithetical?" *Journal of Homosexuality, 12*(1), 97–108.

Cornog, M. (1986). "Naming Sexual Body Parts: Preliminary Patterns and Implications." *Journal of Sex Research, 22*(3), 399–408.

Cortese, A. (1989). "Subcultural Differences in Human Sexuality: Race, Ethnicity, and Social Class." In K. McKinney & S. Sprecher (Eds.), *Human Sexuality: The Societal and Interpersonal Context*. Norwood, NJ: Ablex.

Cosby, B. (1968, December). "The Regular Way." *Playboy*, pp. 288–289.

Cosgray, R. E., Hanna, V., Fawley, R., & Money, M. (1991). "Death from Auto-Erotic Asphyxiation in Long-Term Psychiatric Setting." *Perspectives in Psychiatric Care, 27*(1), 21–24.

Cottler, L. B., Helzer, J. E., & Tipp, J. E. (1990). "Lifetime Patterns of Substance Use Among General Population Subjects Engaging in High-Risk Sexual Behaviors; Implications for HIV Risk." *American Journal of Drug and Alcohol Abuse, 16*(3-4), 207–222.

Courtright, J., & Baran, S. (1980). "The Acquisition of Sexual Information by Young People." *Journalism Quarterly, 57*(1), 107–114.

Couzinet, B., et al. (1986, December 18). "Termination of Early Pregnancy by the Progesterone Antagonist RU 486 (Mifepristone)." *New England Journal of Medicine, 315*(25), 1565–1670.

Cowan, A. L. (1992, June 1). "Can a Baby-Making Venture Deliver?" *The New York Times*, pp. C1, C4.

Cowan, C. P., & Cowan, P. A. (1988). "Who Does What When Partners Become Parents: Implications for Men, Women, and Marriage." *Marriage and Family Review, 12*(3-4), 105–131.

Cowley, G. (1991, December 9). "Sleeping with the Enemy." *Newsweek*, pp. 58–59.

Cramer, D. (1986). "Gay Parents and Their Children: A Review of Research and Practical Implications." *Journal of Counseling and Development, 64*, 504–507.

Cramer, D., & Roach, A. (1987). "Coming Out to Mom and Dad: A Study of Gay Males and Their Relationships with Their Parents." *Journal of Homosexuality, 14*(1-2), 77–88.

Cramer, R. E., Dragna, M., Cupp, R. G., & Stewart, P. (1991). "Contrast Effects in the Evaluation of the Male Sex Role." *Sex Roles, 24*(3-4), 181–193.

Crepault, C., & Couture, M. (1980). "Men's Erotic Fantasies." *Archives of Sexual Behavior, 9*, 565–581.

Creti, L., & Libman, E. (1989). "Cognition and Sexual Expression in the Aging." *Journal of Sex and Marital Therapy, 15*(2), 83–101.

Crisp, Q. (1982). *The Naked Civil Servant*. New York: New American Library.

Crosby, J. (Ed.). (1985). *Reply to Myth: Perspectives on Intimacy*. New York: John Wiley.

Cruikshank, M. (1992). *The Gay and Lesbian Liberation Movement*. New York: Routledge.

Crum, C. P., et al. (1984). "Human Papillomavirus Type 16 and Early Cervical Neoplasm." *New England Journal of Medicine, 310*, 880–883.

Cuber, J. (1969). "Adultery: Reality vs. Stereotype." In G. Newbeck (Ed.), *Extramarital Relations*. Englewood Cliffs, NJ: Prentice-Hall.

Culp, R. E., Cook, A. S., & Housley, P. C. (1983). "A Comparison of Observed and Reported Adult-Infant Interactions: Effects of Perceived Sex." *Sex Roles, 9*, 475–479.

Cummings, J. (1987, June 8). "Disabled Model Defies Sexual Stereotypes." *The New York Times*, p. 17.

Cummings, N. (1992). "Self-Defense Training for College Women." *Journal of American College Health, 40*(4), 183–188.

Cupach, W. R., & Comstock, J. (1990). "Satisfaction with Sexual Communication in Marriage." *Journal of Social and Personal Relationships, 7*, 179–186.

Cupach, W. R., & Metts, S. (1991). "Sexuality and Communication in Close Relationships." In K. McKinney & Susan Sprecher (Eds.), *Sexuality in Close Relationships*. Hillsdale, NJ: Erlbaum.

Curie-Cohen, M., et al. (1979). "Current Practice of Artificial Insemination by Donor in the United States." *New England Journal of Medicine, 300*(11), 585–590.

Curtis, T. (1993, April). "The Female Condom." *Self*, 138–141; 176–179.

Cushner, I. M. (1986). "Reproductive Technologies: New Choices, New Hopes, New Dilemmas." *Family Planning Perspectives, 18*(3), 129–132.

Dailey, D. (Ed.). (1988). *The Sexually Unusual*. New York: Harrington Press.

Dalton, K. (1984). *The Premenstrual Syndrome and Progesterone Therapy*. London: William Heinemann Medical Books.

Damon Clinical Laboratories. (1990). *Clinical Insight: AIDS Profiles*. Needham Heights, MA: Damon Clinical Laboratories.

Dancey, C. (1992). "The Relationship of Instrumentality and Expressivity to Sexual Orientation in Women." *Journal of Homosexuality, 23*(4), 73–82.

Darling, C., Hicks, M. (1982). "Parental Influence on Adolescent Sexuality: Implications for Parents as Educators." *Journal of Youth and Adolescence, 11*, 231–245.

Darling, C. A., & Davidson, J. K. (1986). "Enhancing Relationships: Understanding the Feminine Mystique of Pretending Orgasm." *Journal of Sex and Marital Therapy, 12*, 182–196.

Darling, C. A., & Davidson, J. K., & Conway-Welch, C. (1990). "Female Ejaculation: Perceived Origins, The Grafenberg Spot/Area, and Sexual Responsiveness." *Archives of Sexual Behavior, 19*, 29–47.

Darling, C. A., Davidson, J. K., & Cox, R. P. (1991). "Female Sexual Response and the Timing of Partner Orgasm." *Journal of Sex and Marital Therapy, 17*(1), 3–21.

Darling, C. A., Davidson, J. K., & Jennings, D. A. (1991). "The Female Sexual Response Revisited: Understanding the Multiorgasmic Experience in Women." *Archives of Sexual Behavior, 20*, 527–540.

Darling-Fisher, C., & Tiedje, L. (1990). "The Impact of Maternal Employment Characteristics on Fathers' Participation in Child Care." *Family Relations, 39*(1), 20–26.

Darrow, W. W., & Siegel, K. (1990). "Preventive Health Behavior and STDs." In K. K. Holmes et al. (Eds.), *Sexually Transmitted Diseases*. (2nd ed.). New York: McGraw-Hill.

Davenport, W. (1987). "An Anthropological Approach." In James Geer & W. O'Donohue (Eds.), *Theories of Human Sexuality*. New York: Plenun Press.

Davidson, J. K., & Darling, C. A. (1986). "The Impact of College-Level Sex Education on Sexual Knowledge, Attitudes, and Practices: The Knowledge/Sexual Experimentation Myth Revisited." *Deviant Behavior, 7*, 13–30.

Davidson, J. K., Darling, C. A., & Conway-Welch, C. (1989). "The Role of the Grafenberg Spot and Female Ejaculation in the Female Orgasmic Response: An Empirical Analysis." *Journal of Sex and Marital Therapy, 15*(2), 102–120.

Davidson, J. K., & Hoffman, L. (1986). "Sexual Fantasies and Sexual Satisfaction: An Empirical Investigation of Erotic Thought." *Journal of Sex Research, 22*, 184–205.

Davis, J. E., & Mininberg, D. T. (1976, August). "Prostatitis and Sexual Function." *Medical Aspects of Human Sexuality, 10*, 32–40.

Davis, M. S. (1983). *Smut: Erotic Reality/Obscene Ideology*. Chicago: University of Chicago Press.

Davis, R. C., et al. (1991). "Supportive and Unsupportive Responses of Others to Rape Victims: Effects on Concurrent Victim Adjustment." *American Journal of Community Psychology, 19*(3), 443–451.

Davis, S. (1990). "Men as Success Objects and Women as Sex Objects: A Study of Personal Advertisements." *Sex Roles, 23*, 43–50.

Davis, S. M., & Harris, M. B. (1982). "Sexual Knowledge, Sexual Interest, and Sources of Sexual Information of Rural and Urban Adolescents from Three Cultures." *Adolescence, 17*(66), 471–492.

Davitz, J. R. (1969). *The Language of Emotion*. New York: Academic Press.

Dawson, D. (1986). "The Effects of Sex Education on Adolescent Behavior." *Family Planning Perspectives, 18*(4), 162ff.

De Armand, C. (1983). "Let's Listen to What the Kids Are Saying." *SIECUS Report*, 3–4.

"Death Rates for Minority Infants Were Underestimated, Study Says." (1992, January 8). *The New York Times*, p. A10.

Deaux, K. (1984). "From Individual Differences to Social Categories: Analysis of a Decade's Research on Gender." *American Psychologist, 39*(2), 105–116.

Deaux, K., & Lewis, L. L. (1983). "Components of Gender Role Stereotypes." *Psychological Documents, 13* (Ms. No. 2583), 25.

De Cecco, J. P. (Ed.). (1988). *Gay Relationships*. New York: Haworth Press.

De Cecco, J. P., & Elia, J. P. (1993). "A Critique and Synthesis of Biological Essentialism and Social Constructionist Views of Sexuality and Gender. Introduction." *Journal of Homosexuality, 24*(3-4), 1–26.

De Cecco, J. P., & Elia, J. P. (1993). "If You Seduce a Straight Person, Can You Make Them Gay—Issues in Biological Essentialism Versus Social Constructionism in Gay and Lesbian Identities. Preface." *Journal of Homosexuality, 24*(3-4), R23–R24.

De Cecco, J. P., & Shively, M. (1983). "From Sexual Identity to Sexual Relationships: A Conceptual Shift." *Journal of Homosexuality, 9*(2-3), 1–26.

Degler, C. (1980). *At Odds.* New York: Oxford University Press.

De Groot, J. M., et al. (1992). "Correlates of Sexual Abuse in Women with Anorexia Nervosa and Bulimia Nervosa." *Canadian Journal of Psychiatry, 37*(7), 516–581.

De La Chappelle, A. (1983). "Sex Chromosome Abnormalities." In A. F. Emery & D. L. Rimarin (Eds.), *Principles and Practices of Medical Genetics.* New York: Churchill Livingstone.

Delacoste, F., & Alexander, P. (Eds.). (1987). *Sex Work: Writings by Women in the Sex Industry.* Pittsburgh, PA: Cleis Press.

Delamater, J. D., & MacCorquodale, P. (1979). *Premarital Sexuality: Attitudes, Relationships, Behavior.* Madison, WI: University of Wisconsin Press.

Delaney, J., et al. (1976). *The Curse: A Cultural History of Menstruation.* New York: Dutton.

Delaney, M. (1992, September 4). "Evidence Does Not Back Duesberg's AIDS Views." *San Francisco Chronicle,* p. A14.

Del Carmen, R. (1990). "Assessment of Asian-Americans for Family Therapy." In F. Serafica et al. (Eds.), *Mental Health of Ethnic Minorities.* New York: Praeger.

de Mauro, D. (1990). "Sexuality Education 1990." *SIECUS Report, 18*(2), 1–9.

Demb, J. M. (1991). "Abortion in Inner-City Adolescents: What the Girls Say." *Family Systems Medicine, 9,* 93–102.

Demb, J. M. (1992). "Are Gay Men Artistic? A Review of the Literature." *Journal of Homosexuality, 23*(4), 83–92.

Demian, A. S. B. (1994). "Relationship Characteristics of American Gay and Lesbian Couples: Findings from a National Survey." *Journal of Gay and Lesbian Social Services, 1*(2), 101–117.

D'Emilio, J., & Freedman, E. (1988). *Intimate Matters: A History of Sexuality in America.* New York: Harper & Row.

Derlega, V. J., Metts, S., Petronio, S., & Margulis, S. (1993). *Self-Disclosure.* Newbury Park, CA: Sage Publications.

DES Action. (1980). *You May Be a DES Daughter.* San Francisco: DES Action/California.

De Salvo, S. (1985, December 22). "Teen Parents." *San Jose Mercury,* pp. 1, 2.

"Detailed U.S. AIDS Report Offers Hints, Warnings." (1993, June 11). *Baltimore Sun,* p. 3A.

de Vincenzi, I. (1994). "A Longitudinal Study of Human Immuno-Deficiency Virus Transmission by Heterosexual Partners." *New England Journal of Medicine, 331*(6), 341.

de Vincenzi, I., et al. (1992). "Comparison of Female to Male and Male to Female Transmission of HIV in 563 Stable Couples." *British Medical Journal, 304*(6830), 809–813.

Dewaraja, R., & Money, J. (1986). "Transcultural Sexology: Formicophilia, a Newly Named Paraphilia in a Young Buddhist Male." *Journal of Sex and Marital Therapy, 12*(2), 139–145.

De Young, M. (1988). "The Indignant Page: Techniques of Neutralization in the Publications of Pedophile Organizations." *Child Abuse and Neglect, 12*(4), 583–591.

De Young, M. (1989). "The World According to NAMBLA." *Journal of Sociology and Social Welfare, 16*(1), 111–126.

Diamond, M. (1974). "Sexuality and the Handicapped." *Rehabilitation Literature, 35,* 34–40.

Diamond, M., & Dannemiller, J. E. (1989). "Pornography and Community Standards in Hawaii: Comparisons with Other States." *Archives of Sexual Behavior, 18,* 6.

Diaz, E. (1990). "Public Policy, Women, and HIV Disease." *SIECUS Report, 19,* 4–5.

Di Blasio, F. A., & Benda, B. B. (1992). "Gender Differences in Theories of Adolescent Sexual Activity." *Sex Roles, 27*(5-6), 221–236.

Dick-Read, G. (1972). *Childbirth Without Fear.* (4th ed.). New York: Harper & Row.

Dimen, M. (1984). "Politically Correct? Politically Incorrect?" In C. S. Vance (Ed.), *Pleasure and Danger: Exploring Female Sexuality.* New York: Routledge & Kegan Paul.

Dion, K. K., Berscheid, E., & Walster, E. (1972). "What Is Beautiful Is Good." *Journal of Personality and Social Psychology, 24,* 285–290.

Diop, C. A. (1987). *Precolonial Black Africa.* Trenton, NJ: Africa World.

Dittmar, H., & Bates, B. (1987). "Humanistic Approaches to the Understanding and Treatment of Anorexia Nervosa." *Journal of Adolescence, 10,* 57–69.

Djerrasi, C. (1979). *The Politics of Contraception.* New York: Norton.

Dodd, R. Y. (1992). "The Risk of Transfusion-Transmitted Infection." *New England Journal of Medicine, 327*(6), 419–421.

Doll, L. S., et al. (1991). "Homosexual Men Who Engage in High-Risk Sexual Behavior. A Multicenter Comparison." *Sexually Transmitted Diseases, 18*(3), 170–175.

Donat, P. L., & D'Emilio, J. (1992). "A Feminist Redefinition of Rape and Sexual Assault: Historical Foundations and Change." *Journal of Social Issues, 48*(1), 9–22.

Donovan, P. (1986). "New Reproductive Technologies: Some Legal Dilemmas." *Family Planning Perspectives, 18,* 57ff.

Dowell, K. A., Lo Presto, C. T., & Sherman, M. F. (1991). "When Are AIDS Patients to Blame for Their Disease? Effects of Patients' Sexual Orientation and Mode of Transmission." *Psychological Reports, 69*(1), 211–219.

Downey, J., Elkin, E. J., Erhard, A. A., Meyer, B. H. F., Bell, J. J., & Morishima, K. J. (1991). "Cognitive Ability and Everyday Functioning in Women with Turner Syndrome." *Journal of Learning Disabilities, 24*(1), 32–39.

Drugger, K. (1988). "Social Location and Gender-Role Attitudes: A Comparison of Black and White Women." *Gender and Society, 2*(4), 425–448.

"Drugs That Cause Sexual Dysfunction: An Update." (1992, August 7). *Medical Letter on Drugs and Therapeutics, 34*(876), 73–74.

Dryfoos, J. (1985). "What the United States Can Learn About Prevention of Teenage Pregnancy from Other Developed Countries." *SIECUS Report, 14*(2), 1–7.

Duncan, D. F. (1990). "Prevalence of Sexual Assault Victimization Among Heterosexual and Gay/Lesbian University Students." *Psychological Reports, 66*(1), 65–67.

Duncan, D. F. (1991). "Who Does Have a Test for AIDS?" *Psychological Reports, 68*(1), 138.

Duncan, D. F., & Donnelly, J. W. (1991). "Pornography as a Source of Sex Information for Students at a Private Northeastern University." *Psychological Reports, 68*(3, Pt. 1), 782.

Duncan, D. F., & Nicholson, T. (1991). "Pornography as a Source of Sex Information for Students at a Southeastern State University." *Psychological Reports, 68*(3, Pt. 1), 802.

Dunkle, J. H., & Francis, P. L. (1990). "The Role of Facial Masculinity/Femininity in the Attribution of Homosexuality." *Sex Roles, 23*(3-4), 157–167.

Durant, R., Pendergast, R., & Seymore, C. (1990). "Contraceptive Behavior Among Sexually Active Hispanic Adolescents." *Journal of Adolescent Health, 11*(6), 490–496.

Dworkin, A. (1989). *Pornography: Men Possessing Women.* New York: Dutton.

Dwyer, S. M., & Myers, S. (1990). "Sex Offender Treatment: A Six-Month to Ten-Year Follow-Up Study." *Annals of Sex Research, 3*(3), 305–318.

Eagly, A. H. (1987). *Sex Differences in Social Behavior: A Social-Role Interpretation.* Hillsdale, NJ: Erlbaum.

Eakins, P. S. (1989). "Free-Standing Birth Centers in California." *Journal of Reproductive Medicine, 34*(12), 960–970.

Earls, C. M., & David, H. (1990). "Early Family and Sexual Experiences of Male and Female Prostitutes." *Canada's Mental Health, 38,* 7–11.

Eber, M., & Wetli, C. (1985). "A Case of Autoerotic Asphyxia." *Psychotherapy, 22*(3), 662–668.

Eckert, E. D. (1985). "Characteristics of Anorexia Nervosa." In J. E. Mitchell (Ed.), *Anorexia Nervosa and Bulimia: Diagnosis and Treatment.* Minneapolis, MN: University of Minnesota Press.

Edelman, R. (1986). "Adaptive Training for Existing Male Transsexual Gender Role: A Case History." *Journal of Sex Research, 22*(4), 514–519.

Edwards, J., & Booth, A. (1977). "The Cessation of Marital Intercourse." *American Journal of Psychiatry, 133,* 1333–1336.

Ehrenkranz, J. R., & Hembree, W. C. (1986). "Effects of Marijuana on Male Reproductive Function." *Psychiatric Annals, 16*(4), 243–248.

Eichler, M. (1989). "Reflections on Motherhood, Apple Pie, the New Reproductive Technologies and the Role of Sociologists in Society." *Society-Societe, 13*(1), 1–5.

Eldh, J. (1993). "Construction of a Neovagina with Preservation of the Glans Penis as a Clitoris in Male Transsexuals." *Plastic and Reconstructive Surgery, 91*(5), 895–903.

Elias, C., & Heise, L. (1993). "The Development of Microbicides: A New Method of HIV Prevention for Women." New York: The Population Council.

Elkind, D. (1984). *All Grown Up and No Place to Go.* Reading, MA: Addison-Wesley.

Ellenberg, M. (1980). "Vaginal Lubrication in Diabetic Women." *Medical Aspects of Human Sexuality, 14,* 66.

Elliott, D. M., & Briere, J. (1992). "Sexual Abuse Trauma Among Professional Women: Validating the Trauma Symptom Checklist (TSC-40)." *Child Abuse and Neglect, 16*(3), 391ff.

Ellis, H. (1900). *Studies in the Psychology of Sex.* Philadelphia: F. A. Davis.

Ellis, H. (1938). *Psychology of Sex: A Manual for Students.* New York: Harcourt Brace Jovanovich.

Ellison, C. (1985). "Intimacy-Based Sex Therapy." In W. Eicher & G. Kockott (Eds.), *Sexology.* New York: Springer-Verlag.

Emanuele, M. A., Tentler, J., Emanuele, N. V., & Kelley, M. R. (1991). "In Vivo Effects of Acute ETOH on Rat Alpha-Luteinizing and Beta-Luteinizing Hormone Gene Expression." *Alcohol, 8*(5), 345–348.

Emery, A. F., & Rimarin, D. L. (Eds.).(1983). *Principles and Practices of Medical Genetics.* New York: Churchill Livingstone.

Emmanuel, N. P., Lydiard, R. B., & Ballenger, J. C. (1991). "Fluoxetine Treatment of Voyeurism." *American Journal of Psychiatry, 148,* 950.

Ephron, N. (1975). *Crazy Salad.* New York: Alfred Knopf.

Erikson, E. (1986). *Vital Improvements in Old Age: The Experience of Old Age in Our Time.* New York: Norton.

Erickson, P. I., & Rapkin, A. I. (1991). "Unwanted Sexual Experiences Among Middle and High School Youth." *Journal of Adolescent Youth, 12,* 319–325.

Ernster, V. L. (1975). "American Menstrual Slang." *Sex Roles, 5,* 1–13.

Espín, O. M. (1984). "Cultural and Historical Influences on Sexuality in Hispanic/Latin Women: Implications for Psychotherapy." In C. Vance (Ed.), *Pleasure and Danger: Exploring Female Sexuality.* New York: Routledge & Kegan Paul.

Essex, M., & Kanki, P. J. (1988, October). "The Origins of the AIDS Virus." *Scientific American, 259*(4), 64–71.

Evans, H. L., et al. (1981). "Sperm Abnormalities and Cigarette Smoking." *Lancet, 1*(8221), 627–629.

Ewell, M. (1993, January 9). "Anti-Gay Push in the Works." *San Jose Mercury News,* p. 3B.

Faderman, L. (1991). *Odd Girls and Twilight Lovers.* New York: Penguin Books.

Fagin, D. (1995, February 1). "DES Moms, Gay or Bisexual Daughters: Study Links Exposure to Sexual Orientation." *San Francisco Chronicle.*

Fagot, B., & Leinbach, M. (1987). "Socialization of Sex Roles Within the Family." In D. B. Carter (Ed.), *Current Conceptions of Sex Roles and Sex Typing.* New York: Praeger.

Falbo, T., & Peplau, L. A. (1980). "Power Strategies in Intimate Relationships." *Journal of Personality and Social Psychology, 38,* 618–628.

Falicov, C. (1982). "Mexican Families." In M. McGoldrick et al. (Eds.), *Ethnicity and Family Therapy.* New York: Guilford Press.

Falk, K. (1984). *How to Write a Romance and Get It Published.* New York: New American Library.

Faludi, S. (1991). *Backlash: The Undeclared War Against American Women.* New York: Crown.

Fang, R. H., Chen, C. F., & Imperato-McGinley, M. S. (1992). "A New Method for Clitoroplasty in Male-to-Female Sex Reassignment Surgery." *Plastic and Reconstructive Surgery, 89*(4), 179–182.

Farnsworth, C. H. (1992, January 14). "Homosexual Is Granted Refugee Status in Canada." *The New York Times,* p. A5.

Fathalla, M. F. (1992). "Reproductive Health in the World: Two Decades of Progress and the Challenge Ahead." In World Health Organization, *Reproductive Health.* Biennial Report 1990–1991. Geneva, Switzerland: World Health Organization.

Fausto-Sterling, A. (1985). *Myths of Gender: Biological Theories About Women and Men.* New York: Basic Books.

Fay, R., Turner, C., Klassen, A., & Gagnon, J. (1989). "Prevalence and Patterns of Same-Gender Sexual Contact Among Men." *Science, 243*(4889), 338–348.

Fazio, L. (1987). "Sexuality and Aging: A Community Wellness Program." Special Issue: Community Programs for the Health Impaired Elderly. *Physical and Occupational Therapy in Geriatrics, 6*(1), 59–69.

Fedora, O., Reddon, J. R., Morrison, J. W., & Fedora, S. T. (1992). "Sadism and Other Paraphilias in Normal Controls and Aggressive and Nonaggressive Sex Offenders." *Archives of Sexual Behavior, 21*(1), 1–15.

Fedora, O., Reddon, J. R., & Yendall, L. T. (1986). "Stimuli Eliciting Sexual Arousal in Genital Exhibitionists: A Possible Clinical Application." *Archives of Sexual Behavior, 15*(5), 417–427.

Fehr, B. (1988). "Prototype Analysis of the Concepts of Love and Commitment." *Journal of Personality and Social Psychology, 55*(4), 557–579.

Fein, R. (1980). "Research on Fathering." In A. Skolnick & J. Skolnick (Eds.), *The Family in Transition.* Boston: Little, Brown.

Feirstein, B. (1982). *Real Men Don't Eat Quiche.* New York: Pocket Books.

Feitl, L. F. (1990, April). "My Body, My Self." *Sesame Street Magazine Parents' Guide,* pp. 20–25.

Feray, J. C., & Herzer, M. (1990). "Homosexual Studies and Politics in the 19th Century: Karl Maria Kertbeny." *Journal of Homosexuality, 19*(1), 23–47.

Ferree, M. M. (1991). "Beyond Separate Spheres: Feminism and Family Research." In A. Booth (Ed.), *Contemporary Families: Looking Forward, Looking Back.* Minneapolis, MN: National Council on Family Relations.

Field, M. A. (1993). "Abortion Law Today." *Journal of Legal Medicine, 14*(1), 3–24.

Findlay, H. (1992). "Freud, Fetishism, and the Lesbian Dildo Debates." *Feminist Studies, 18*(3), 563–579.

Fine, M. (1988). "Sexuality, Schooling, and Adolescent Females: The Missing Discourse of Desire." *Harvard Education Review, 58*, 29–53.

Finkelhor, D. (1979). *Sexually Victimized Children.* New York: Free Press.

Finkelhor, D. (1984). *Child Sexual Abuse: New Theory and Research.* New York: Free Press.

Finkelhor, D. (1986a). "Prevention Approaches to Child Sexual Abuse." In M. Lystad (Ed.), *Violence in the Home: Interdisciplinary Perspectives.* New York: Brunner/Mazel.

Finkelhor, D. (1986b). "Sexual Abuse: Beyond the Family Systems Approach." *Journal of Psychotherapy and the Family, 2*, 53–65.

Finkelhor, D. (1990). "Early and Long-Term Effects of Child Sexual Abuse: An Update." *Professional Psychology: Research and Practice, 21*, 325–330.

Finkelhor, D., et al. (1990). "Sexual Abuse in a National Survey of Adult Men and Women." *Child Abuse and Neglect, 14*(1), 19–28.

Finkelhor, D., & Baron, L. (1986). "High-Risk Children." In D. Finkelhor (Ed.), *Sourcebook on Child Sexual Abuse.* Beverly Hills, CA: Sage Publications.

Finkelhor, D., Hotaling, G., Lewis, I. A., & Smith C. (1990). *Missing, Abducted, Runaway, and Throwaway Children in America.* Washington, DC: U.S. Department of Justice.

Finkelhor, D., Williams, L. M., & Burns, B. (1988). *Sexual Abuse in Day Care: A National Study.* Durham, NH: University of New Hampshire, Family Research Laboratory.

Finkelhor, D., & Yllo, K. (1985). *License to Rape: The Sexual Abuse of Wives.* New York: Holt Rinehart.

Fischhoff, B. (1992). "Giving Advice: Decision Theory Perspectives on Sexual Assault." *American Psychologist, 47*, 577–588.

Fischl, M. A., et al. (1987). "The Efficacy of Azidothymidine (AZT) in the Treatment of Patients with AIDS and AIDS-Related Complex." *Journal of Sex Research, 317*, 185–188.

Fischl, M. A., Dickinson, D. M., Scott, G. B., Klimas, N., Fletcher, M. A., & Parks, W. (1987). "Evaluation of Heterosexual Partners, Children, and Household Contacts of Adults with AIDS." *JAMA: Journal of the American Medical Association 257*(5), 640–644.

Fisher, B., et al. (1985a). "Five-Year Results of a Randomized Clinical Trial Comparing Total Mastectomy and Segmental Mastectomy with or without Radiation in the Treatment of Breast Cancer." *New England Journal of Medicine, 312*(11), 665–673.

Fisher, B., et al. (1985b). "Ten-Year Results of a Randomized Clinical Trial Comparing Radical Mastectomy and Total Mastectomy with or without Radiation in the Treatment of Breast Cancer." *New England Journal of Medicine, 312*(11), 674–681.

Fisher, W. (1983, March). "Why Teenagers Get Pregnant." *Psychology Today*, 70–71.

Fisher, W. (1986). "A Psychological Approach to Human Sexuality." In D. Byrne & K. K. Kelley (Eds.), *Alternate Approaches to Human Sexuality.* Hillsdale, NJ: Erlbaum.

Fisher, W., et al. (1988). "Erotophobia-Erotophilia as a Dimension of Personality." *Journal of Sex Research, 25*(1), 123–151.

Fisher, W., & Gray, J. (1988). "Erotophobia-Erotophilia and Sexual Behavior During Pregnancy and Postpartum." *Journal of Sex Research, 25*(3), 379–396.

Fitzgerald, L. F., & Ormerod, A. J. (1991). "Perceptions of Sexual Harassment: The Influence of Gender and Academic Context." *Psychology of Women Quarterly, 15*(2), 281–294.

FitzGerald, M., & FitzGerald, D. (1977). "Deaf People Are Sexual Too!" *SIECUS Report, 6*(2), 1, 13–15.

Flanigan, B. J. (1990). "The Social Context of Alcohol Consumption Prior to Female Sexual Intercourse." *Journal of Alcohol and Drug Education, 36*(1), 97–113.

Flor-Henry, P., Lang, R. A., Koles, Z. J., & Frenzel, R. R. (1991). "Quantitative EEG Studies of Pedophilia." *International Journal of Psychophysiology, 10*(3), 253–258.

Foa, U. G., Anderson, B., Converse, J., & Urbansky, W. A. (1987). "Gender-Related Sexual Attitudes: Some Cross-Cultural Similarities and Differences." *Sex Roles, 16*(19-20), 511–519.

Focus on the Family. (1993, February 11). "In Defense of a Little Virginity." *Good Times*, Santa Cruz, CA, pp. 30–31.

Follingstad, D. R., Rutledge, L. L., Berg, B. J., & Haure, E. S. (1990). "The Role of Emotional Abuse in Physically Abusive Relationships." *Journal of Family Violence, 5*(2), 107–120.

Fonow, M. M., et al. (1992). "Feminist Rape Education: Does It Work?" *Gender and Society, 6*(1), 108–121.

Foo, R. (1993, March 5). "U.S. Cracks Child Porn Ring." *San Jose Mercury News*, pp. 1A, 20A.

Ford, C., & Beach, F. (1951). *Patterns of Sexual Behavior.* New York: Harper & Row.

Fordyce, E. J., Blum, S., Balanon, A., & Stoneburner, R. L. (1991). "A Method for Estimating HIV Transmission Rates Among Female Sex Partners of Male Intravenous Drug Users." *American Journal of Epidemiology, 133*(6), 590–598.

Forgey, D. G. (1975). "The Institution of Berdache Among the North American Plains Indians." *Journal of Sex Research, 11*, 1–15.

Forrest, J. (1986). "The End of IUD Marketing in the United States: What Does It Mean for American Women?" *Family Planning Perspectives, 18*(2), 52–57.

Forrest, J. (1987). "Unintended Pregnancy Among American Women." *Family Planning Perspectives, 19*(2), 76–77.

Forrest, J. D., & Silverman, J. (1989). "What Public School Teachers Teach About Preventing Pregnancy, AIDS and Sexually Transmitted Diseases." *Family Planning Perspectives, 21*, 65–72.

Forrest, J. D., & Singh, S. (1990). "The Sexual and Reproductive Behavior of American Women, 1982–1988." *Family Planning Perspectives, 22*(5), 206–214.

Foucault, M. (1980). *The History of Sexuality: An Introduction. Vol. I.* New York: Pantheon Books.

Fowler, O. S. (1878). *Amativeness: or, Evils and the Remedies of Excessive Perverted Sexuality.* New York: Fowler & Wells.

Fox, B., & Joyce, C. (1991). "Americans Compete for Control Over Sex." *New Scientist, 12*, 23.

Fox, S. I. (1987). *Human Physiology.* Dubuque, Iowa: W. C. Brown.

Frable, D. E., & Bem, S. L. (1985). "If You Are Gender Schematic, All Members of the Opposite Sex Look Alike." *Journal of Personality and Social Psychology, 49*(2), 459–468.

Franco, E. L. (1991). "The Sexually Transmitted Disease Model for Cervical Cancer: Incoherent Epidemiologic Findings and the Role of Misclassification of Human Papillomavirus Infection." *Epidemiology, 2*(2), 98–106.

Franklin, D. L. (1988). "The Impact of Early Childbearing on Development Outcomes: The Case of Black Adolescent Parenting." *Family Relations, 37*, 268–274.

Franz, W., & Readon, D. (1992). "Differential Impact of Abortion on Adolescents and Adults." *Adolescence, 27*(105), 161–172.

Fraser, L. (1990, February). "Nasty Girls." *Mother Jones*, pp. 32–35, 48–50.

Frazier, P. A. (1991). "Self-Blame as a Mediator of Postrape Depressive Symptoms." *Journal of Social and Clinical Psychology, 10*(1), 47–57.

Freeman, E. (1980). "Adolescent Contraceptive Use." *American Journal of Public Health, 70*, 790–797.

French, J. P., & Bertram Raven. (1959). "The Bases of Social Power." In I. Cartwright (Ed.), *Studies in Social Power.* Ann Arbor, MI: University of Michigan Press.

Freud, S. (1938). "Three Contributions to the Theory of Sex." A. A. Brill (Ed.), *The Basic Writings of Sigmund Freud.* New York: Modern Library.

Freund, K., & Kuban, W. (1993). "Toward a Testable Developmental Model of Pedophilia: The Development of Erotic Age Preference." *Child Abuse and Neglect, 17*(2), 315–324.

Freund, K. (1988). "Courtship Disorder: Is This Hypothesis Valid?" In R. A. Prentky et al. (Eds.), *Human Sexual Aggression: Current Perspectives*. New York: New York Academy of Science.

Freund, K., & Blanchard, R. (1993). "Erotic Target Location Errors in Male Gender Dysphorics, Paedophiles, and Fetishists." *British Journal of Psychiatry, 162*, 558–563.

Freund, M., Leonard, T. L., & Lee, N. (1989). "Sexual Behavior of Resident Street Prostitutes with Their Clients in Camden, New Jersey." *Journal of Sex Research, 26*, 460–478.

Freund, K., Scher, H., & Hucker, S. (1983). "The Courtship Disorders." *Archives of Sexual Behavior, 12*, (369–379).

Freund, K., & Watson, R. J. (1993). "Gender Identity Disorder and Courtship Disorder." *Archives of Sexual Behavior, 22*(1), 13–21.

Freund, K., Watson, R., & Dickey, R. (1990). "Does Sexual Abuse in Childhood Cause Pedophilia: An Exploratory Study." *Archives of Sexual Behavior, 19*(6), 557–568.

Freund, K., Watson, R., Dickey, R., & Rienzo, D. (1991). "Erotic Gender Differentiation in Pedophilia." *Archives of Sexual Behavior, 20*(6), 555–566.

Freund, K., Watson, R., & Rienzo, D. (1988). "The Value of Self-Reports in the Study of Voyeurism and Exhibitionism." *Annals of Sex Research, 1*(2), 243–262.

Friday, N. *Men in Love*. (1980). New York: Delacorte Press.

Friedland, G. H. (1986). "Lack of Transmission of HTLV-III Infection to Household Contacts of Patients with AIDS or AIDS-Related Complex with Oral Candidiasis." *New England Journal of Medicine, 314*, 344–349.

Friedman, R., & Gradstein, B. (1982). *Surviving Pregnancy Loss*. Boston: Little, Brown.

Friedman, R. C. (1991). "Couple Therapy with Gay Couples." *Psychiatric Annals, 21*(8), 485–490.

Friend, R. (1980). "GAYging: Adjustment and the Older Gay Male." *Alternative Lifestyles, 3*(2), 231–248.

Fritz, G. S., Stoll, K., & Wagner, N. N. (1981). "A Comparison of Males and Females Who Were Sexually Molested as Children." *Journal of Sex and Marital Therapy, 7*, 54–58.

Fromm, E. (1974). *The Art of Loving*. New York: Perennial Library.

Frost, P. (1992, December 7). "Artichoke." *The New Yorker*, p. 66.

Fuller, A., Jr., et al. (1980). "Toxic-Shock Syndrome." *New England Journal of Medicine, 303*(15), 880.

Fullilove, R. E., Fullilove, M. T., Bowser, B. P., & Gross, S. (1990). "Risk of Sexually Transmitted Disease Among Black Adolescent Crack Users in Oakland and San Francisco, Calif." *JAMA: Journal of the American Medical Association, 263*(6), 851–855.

Furstenberg, F. K., Jr., et al. (1985). "Sex Education and Sexual Experience Among Adolescents." *American Journal of Public Health, 75*(11), 1331–1332.

Furstenberg, F. K., Jr., & Cherlin, A. (1991). *Divided Families*. Cambridge, MA: Harvard University Press.

Furstenberg, F. K., Jr., Lincoln, R., & Menken, J. (Eds.). (1981). *Teenage Sexuality, Pregnancy, and Childbearing*. Philadelphia: University of Pennsylvania Press.

Furstenberg, F. K., Jr., & Nord, C. (1985). "Parenting Apart: Patterns in Childrearing After Marital Disruption." *Journal of Marriage and the Family, 47*(4), 893–904.

Furstenberg, F. K., Jr., & Spanier, G. (1987). *Recycling the Family: Remarriage After Divorce* (rev. ed.). Newbury Park, CA: Sage Publications.

Gagnon, J. (1977). *Human Sexualities*. New York: Scott, Foresman.

Gagnon, J. (1985). "Attitudes and Responses of Parents to Pre-Adolescent Masturbation." *Archives of Sexual Behavior, 14*(5), 451–466.

Gagnon, J. (1986). "Sexual Scripts: Permanence and Change." *Archives of Sexual Behavior, 15*(2), 97–120.

Gagnon, J., & Simon, W. (1973). "Perspectives on the Sexual Scene." In J. Gagnon & W. Simon (Eds.), *The Sexual Scene* (2nd ed.). New Brunswick, NJ: Transaction Books.

Gagnon, J., & Simon, W. (1973). *Sexual Conduct: The Social Sources of Human Sexuality*. Chicago: Aldine.

Gagnon, J., & Simon, W. (1987). "The Sexual Scripting of Oral Genital Contacts." *Archives of Sexual Behavior, 16*(1), 1–25.

Gaines, J. (1990, October 7). "A Scandal of Artificial Insemination." *The Good Health Magazine/The New York Times Magazine*, p. 23ff.

Gallup, G. H., Jr., & Newport, F. (1990, June 4). "Parenthood: A Nearly Universal Desire." *San Francisco Chronicle*, p. 3.

Ganong, L., & Coleman, M. (1987). "Sex, Sex Roles, and Family Love." *Journal of Genetic Psychology, 148*, 45–52.

Gao, G. (1991). "Stability of Romantic Relationships in China and the United States." In S. Ting-Toomey & Felipe Korzenny (Eds.), *Cross-Cultural Interpersonal Communication*. Newbury Park, CA: Sage Publications.

Garber, L. (1991). *Vested Interests*. Boston: Little, Brown.

Garcia, L. T., & Milano, L. (1990). "A Content Analysis of Erotic Videos." *Journal of Psychology and Human Sexuality, 3*(2), 95–103.

Garner, D. M., Garfinkel, P. E., Schwartz, D., & Thompson, M. (1980). "Cultural Expectations of Thinness in Women." *Psychological Reports, 11*, 483–491.

Garnets, L., et al. (1990). "Violence and Victimization of Lesbians and Gay Men: Mental Health Consequences." *Journal of Interpersonal Violence, 5*, 366–383.

Garrison, J. E. (1989). "Sexual Dysfunction in the Elderly: Causes and Effects." *Journal of Psychotherapy and the Family, 5*(1-2), 149–162.

Garza-Leal, J., & Landron, F. (1991). "Autoerotic Asphyxial Death Initially Misinterpreted as Suicide and Review of the Literature." *Journal of Forensic Science, 36*(6), 1753–1759.

Gay, P. (1986). *The Bourgeois Experience: The Tender Passion*. New York: Oxford University Press.

Gebhard, P. (1976). "Fetishism and Sadomasochism." In P. Gebhard (Ed.), *Sex Research: Studies from the Kinsey Institute*. New York: Oxford University Press.

Gebhard, P. (Ed.). (1976). *Sex Research: Studies from the Kinsey Institute*. New York: Oxford University Press.

Gebhard, P., Pomeroy, W. B., & Christensen, C. V. (1965). "Situational Factors Affecting Human Sexual Behavior." In F. Beach (Ed.), *Sex and Behavior*. New York: John Wiley.

Gecas, V., & Seff, M. (1991). "Families and Adolescents." In A. Booth (Ed.), *Contemporary Families: Looking Forward, Looking Back*. Minneapolis, MN: National Council on Family Relations.

Geist, C. (1980). "Violence, Passion, and Sexual Racism: The Plantation Novel." *Southern Quarterly, 18*(2), 60–72.

Gelles, R. J., & Conte, J. R. (1991). "Domestic Violence and Sexual Abuse of Children: A Review of Research in the Eighties." In A. Booth (Ed.), *Contemporary Families: Looking Forward, Looking Back*. Minneapolis, MN: National Council on Family Relations.

Genevie, L., & Margolies, E. (1987). *The Motherhood Report: How Women Feel About Being Mothers*. New York: MacMillan.

George, L. K., Windfield, I., & Blazer, D. G. (1992). "Sociocultural Factors in Sexual Assault—Comparison of Two Representative Samples of Women." *Journal of Social Issues, 48*(1), 105–125.

Geraghty, C. (1990). *Women and Soap Opera: A Study of Prime Time Soaps*. London: Polity Press.

Gershman, K. A., & Rolfs, R. T. (1991). "Diverging Gonorrhea and Syphilis Trends in the 1980s: Are They Real?" *American Journal of Public Health, 81*(10), 1263–1267.

Getlin, J. (1989, July 24). "Legacy of a Mother's Drinking." *Los Angeles Times*, p. 1ff.

Gidyez, C. A., & Koss, M. P. (1990). "A Comparison of Group and Individual Sexual Assault Victims." *Psychology of Women Quarterly*, 14(3), 325–342.

Gilligan, C. (1982). *In a Different Voice*. Cambridge, MA: Harvard University Press.

Ginsburg, F. (1989). *Contested Lives: The Abortion Debate in an American Community*. Berkeley: University of California Press.

Glaser, J. B., Strange, T. J., & Rosati, D. (1989). "Heterosexual Human Immunodeficiency Virus Transmission Among the Middle Class." *Archives of Internal Medicine*, 149(3), 645–649.

Glasier, A., Thong, K. J., Dewar, M., Mackie, M., & Baird, D. T. (1992). "Mifepristone (RU-486) Compared with High-Dose Estrogen and Progesterone for Emergency Postcoital Contraception." *New England Journal of Medicine*, 327(15), 1041–1044.

Glass, R. H., & Ericsson, R. J. (1982). *Getting Pregnant in the 1980s*. Berkeley: University of California Press.

Glaus, K. O. (1988). "Alcoholism, Chemical Dependency and the Lesbian Client." Special Issue: Lesbianism: Affirming Nontraditional Roles. *Women and Therapy*, 8(1-2), 131–144.

Glazer-Malbin, N. (Ed.). (1975). *Old Family/New Family*. New York: Van Nostrand.

Glenn, J. (1981). "Penis Enlargement." *Medical Aspects of Human Sexuality*, 15(3), 23.

Glenn, N. (1991). "Quantitative Research on Marital Quality in the 1980s: A Critical Review." In A. Booth (Ed.), *Contemporary Families: Looking Forward, Looking Back*. Minneapolis, MN: National Council on Family Relations.

Glenn, N., & McLanahan, S. (1982). "Children and Marital Happiness: A Further Specification of the Relationship." *Journal of Marriage and the Family*, 43(1), 63–72.

Go, K. J. (1992). "Recent Advances in the Treatment of Male Infertility." *Naacogs Clinical Issues in Perinatal and Women's Health Nursing*, 3(2), 320–327.

Gochoros, J. S. (1989). *When Husbands Come Out of the Closet*. New York: Harrington Park Press.

Goetting, A. (1986). "The Developmental Tasks of Siblingship Over the Life Cycle." *Journal of Marriage and the Family*, 48(4), 703–714.

Goldberg, L. H., Kaufman, R., Kurtz, T. O., Conant, M. A., & Eron, L. J. (1993). "Long-Term Suppression of Recurrent Genital Herpes with Acyclovir." *Archives of Dermatology*, 129(5), 582–587.

Goldberg-Ambrose, C. (1992). "Unfinished Business in Rape Law Reform." *Journal of Social Issues*, 48(1), 173–175.

Golden, G. (1989, May). "Parental Attitudes to Infant's Sex Play Determine Child's Later Attitude to Sex." *Medical Aspects of Human Sexuality*, 73–97.

Goldman, A., & Carroll, J. L. (1990). "Educational Intervention as an Adjunct to Treatment in Erectile Dysfunction of Older Couples." *Journal of Sex and Marital Therapy*, 16(3), 127–141.

Goldmeier, D., & Hay, P. (1993). "A Review and Update on Adult Syphilis, with Particular Emphasis on Its Treatment." *International Journal of STD and AIDS*, 4(2), 70–82.

Golombok, S. (1992). "Psychological Functioning of Infertility Patients." *Human Reproduction*, 7(2), 208–212.

González, E. R. (1980). "New Era in Treatment of Dysmenorrhea." *JAMA: Journal of the American Medical Association*, 244, 1885–1886.

González, E. R. (1981). "Premenstrual Syndrome: An Ancient Woe Deserving of Modern Scrutiny." *JAMA: Journal of the American Medical Association*, 245(14), 1393–1396.

Goodman, E. (1985). *Keeping in Touch*. New York: Summit Books.

Goodman, W. (1992, August 4). "TV's Sexual Circus Has a Purpose." *The New York Times*, p. 2.

Gooren, L., & Cohen-Kettenis, P. T. (1991). "Development of Male Gender Identity/Role and a Sexual Orientation Towards Women in a 46,XY Subject with Incomplete Form of the Androgen Insensitivity Syndrome." *Archives of Sexual Behavior*, 20(5), 459–470.

Gordon, E. B. (1991). "Transsexual Healing: Medicaid Funding for Sex Reassignment Surgery." *Archives of Sexual Behavior*, 20(1), 61–74.

Gordon, S. (1984, March). "Parents as Sexuality Educators." *SIECUS Report*, 10–11.

Gordon, S. (1986, October). "What Kids Need to Know." *Psychology Today*, pp 46ff.

Gorman, C. (1992, January 20). "Sizing Up the Sexes." *Time*, pp. 42–51.

Gosselin, C., & Wilson, G. (1980). *Sexual Variations*. New York: Simon & Schuster.

"Gossypol: Effective Contraceptive, But Can Side Effects Be Overcome?" (1987, January). *Contraceptive Technology Update*, 8(1), 5–6.

Gostin, L. O. (1992). "Health Law." *JAMA: Journal of the American Medical Association*, 268(3), 364–366.

Gouchie, C., & Kimura, D. (1991). "The Relationship Between Testosterone Levels and Cognitive Ability Patterns." *Psychoneuroendocrinology*, 16, 323–334.

Gould, J. B., Davey, B., & Stafford, R. S. (1989). "Socioeconomic Differences in Rates of Cesarean Section." *New England Journal of Medicine*, 321(4), 233–239.

Grady, D. (1992, June). "Sex Test of Champions: Olympic Officials Struggle to Define What Should Be Obvious—Just Who Is a Female Athlete." *Discover*, pp. 78–82.

Grafenberg, E. (1950). "The Role of Urethra in Female Orgasm." *International Journal of Sexology*, 3, 145–148.

Graham, N. M., et al. (1992). "The Effects on Survival of Early Treatment of Human Immunodeficiency Virus Infection." *New England Journal of Medicine*, 326(16), 1032–1042.

Granberg, D. (1991). "Conformity to Religious Norms Regarding Abortion." *Sociological Quarterly*, 32(2), 267–275.

Green, R. (1987). *The "Sissy-Boy Syndrome" and the Development of Homosexuality*. New Haven, CT: Yale University Press.

Greenberg, B. S., & D'Alessio, D. D. (1985). "Quantity and Quality of Sex in the Soaps." *Broadcasting and Electronic Media*, 29, 309–321.

Greenberg, J., Magder, L., & Aral, S. (1992). "Age at First Coitus: A Marker for Risky Sexual Behavior in Women." *Sexually Transmitted Diseases*, 19(6), 331–334.

Greenberg, J., Schnell, D., & Conlon, R. (1992). "Behaviors of Crack Cocaine Users and Their Impact on Early Syphilis Intervention." *Sexually Transmitted Diseases*, 19(6), 346–350.

Greenburg, D., & Jacobs, M. (1966). *How to Make Yourself Miserable*. New York: Random House.

Greene, B. (1993). "The View from Schools." In S. Samuels & M. Smith (Eds.). *Condoms in the Schools*. Menlo Park, CA: Henry J. Kaiser Family Foundation.

Greensite, G. (1991). "Acquaintance Rape Clarified." *Student Guide*, Santa Cruz, CA, pp. 15, 68.

Greenwald, H. (1970). *The Elegant Prostitutes: A Social and Psychoanalytic Study*. New York: Walker.

Greenwood, S. (1992). *Menopause Naturally: Preparing for the Second Half of Life*. Volcano, CA: Volcano Press.

Gregersen, E. (1986). "Human Sexuality in Cross-Cultural Perspective." In D. Byrne & K. Kelley (Eds.), *Alternative Approaches to the Study of Sexual Behavior*. Hillsdale, NJ: Erlbaum.

Gregoire, A. (1992). "New Treatments for Erectile Impotence." *British Journal of Psychiatry*, 160, 315–326.

Gregor, T. (1985). *Anxious Pleasures: The Sexual Lives of an Amazonian People*. Chicago: University of Chicago Press.

Gressman, G. D., et al. (1992). "Female Awareness of University Sexual Harassment Policy." *Journal of College Student Development, 33*(4), 370–371.

Grimes, D. (1983). "Reversible Contraception for the 1980's." *Journal of the American Medical Association, 250,* 3081–3083.

Griswold Del Castillo, Richard (1984). *La Familia: Chicano Families in the Urban Southwest, 1848 to the Present.* Notre Dame, IN: University of Notre Dame.

Gritz, E. R., Wellisch, D. K., Wang, H. J., Siau, J., Landsverk, J. A., & Cosgrove, M. D. (1989). "Long-Term Effects of Testicular Cancer on Sexual Functioning in Married Couples." *Cancer, 64*(7), 1560–1567.

Gross, J. (1992, March 11). "Schools Are Newest Arena for Sex-Harassment Cases." *The New York Times,* pp. 1, 18.

Groth, A. N. (1979). *Men Who Rape: The Psychology of the Offender.* New York: Plenum Press.

Groth, A. N., & Birnbaum, H. J. (1978). "Adult Sexual Orientation and Attraction to Underage Persons." *Archives of Sexual Behavior, 7*(3), 175–181.

Groth, A. N., Burgess, A. W., & Holmstrom, L. L. (1977). "Rape: Power, Anger, and Sexuality." *American Journal of Psychiatry, 104*(11), 1239–1243.

Groth, A. N., Hobson, W. F., & Gary, T. (1982). "Heterosexuality, Homosexuality, and Pedophilia: Sexual Offenses Against Children." In A. Scacco (Ed.), *Male Rape: A Casebook of Sexual Aggression.* New York: AMS Press.

Grunfeld, L. (1989). "Workup for Male Infertility." *Journal of Reproductive Medicine, 43,* 143–149.

Gruters, R. A., et al. (1991). "Differences in Clinical Course in Zidovudine-Treated Asymptomatic HIV-Infected Men Associated with T-Cell Function at Intake." *AIDS, 5*(1), 43–47.

Gudjonsson, G. (1990). "Cognitive Distortions and Blame Attribution Among Paedophiles." *Sexual and Marital Therapy, 5*(2), 183–185.

Guerrero Pavich, Emma. (1986). "A Chicana Perspective on Mexican Culture and Sexuality." In L. Lister (Ed.), *Human Sexuality, Ethnoculture, and Social Work.* New York: Haworth Press.

Gump, J. (1980). "Reality and Myth: Employment and Sex Role Ideology in Black Women." In F. Denmark & J. Sherman (Eds.), *The Psychology of Women.* New York: Psychological Dimensions.

Gur, R., Mozley, L., Mozley, P., et al. (1995). "Sex Differences in Regional Cerebral Glucose Metabolism During a Resting State." *Science 267*(5197), 528–531.

Gutek, B. (1985). *Sex and the Workplace.* San Francisco: Jossey-Bass.

Gutin, J. C. (1992, June). "Why Bother?" *Discover,* pp. 32–39.

Gutman, H. (1976). *The Black Family: From Slavery to Freedom.* New York: Pantheon.

Guttentag, M., & Secord, P. (1983). *Too Many Women.* Newbury Park, CA: Sage Publications.

Gwartney-Gibbs, P. (1986). "The Institutionalization of Premarital Cohabitation: Estimates from Marriage License Applications." *Journal of Marriage and the Family, 48,* 423–434.

Haaga, D. A. (1991). "Homophobia?" *Journal of Behavior and Personality, 6,* 171–174.

Hafner, D. W. (1992). "From Where I Sit." *Family Life Educator, 11*(2), 14–15.

Hage, J. J., Bout, C. A., Bloem, J. J., & Megens, J. A. (1993). "Phalloplasty in Female-to-Male Transsexuals: What Do Our Patients Ask For?" *Annals of Plastic Surgery, 30*(4), 323–326.

Hahn, R. A. (1992). "The State of Federal Health Statistics on Racial and Ethnic Groups." *JAMA: Journal of the American Medical Association, 267*(2), 268–271.

Halikas, J. A., Weller, R. A., & Morse, C. (1982). "Effects of Regular Marijuana Use on Sexual Performance." *Journal of Psychoactive Drugs, 14,* 59–70.

Hall, C. (1980). *A Primer of Freudian Psychology.* New York: New American Library.

Hall, G. J. (1991). "Sexual Arousal as a Function of Physiological and Cognitive Variables in a Sexual Offender Population." *Archives of Sexual Behavior, 20*(4), 359–369.

Hall, J. G., & Gilchrist, D. M. (1990). "Turner Syndrome and Its Variants." *Pediatric Clinics of North America, 37*(6), 1421–1440.

Hällstrom, T., & Samuelsson, S. (1990). "Changes in Women's Sexual Desire in Middle Life: The Longitudinal Study of Women in Gothenburg [Sweden]." *Archives of Sexual Behavior, 19*(3), 259–267.

Hamer, D. H., et al. (1993). "A Linkage Between DNA Markers on the X-Chromosome and Male Sexual Orientation." *Science, 261*(5119), 321–327.

Hamilton, D. L. (1979). "A Cognitive-Attributional Analysis of Stereotyping." *Advances in Experimental Psychology, 12,* 53–81.

Hankinson, S. E., Colditz, G. A., Hunter, D. J., Spencer, T. L., Rosner, B., & Stampflau, M. J. (1992). "A Quantitative Assessment of Oral Contraceptive Use and Risk of Ovarian Cancer." *Obstetrics and Gynecology, 80*(4), 708–714.

Hanley, R. (1988, February 4). "Surrogate Deals for Mothers Held Illegal in New Jersey." *The New York Times,* p. 1ff.

Hansen, G. (1985). "Dating Jealousy Among College Students." *Sex Roles, 12*(7-8), 713–721.

Hansen, G. (1987). "Extradyadic Relations During Courtship." *Journal of Sex Research, 23*(3), 383–390.

Hansen, W. B., Wolkenstein, B. H., & Hahn, G. L. (1992). "Young Adult Behavior: Issues in Programming and Evaluation." *Health Education Research, 7,* 305–312.

Hanson, F. W., et al. (1990). "Ultrasonography—Guided Early Amniocentesis in Singleton Pregnancies." *American Journal of Obstetrics and Gynecology, 162*(6), 1381–1383.

Hanson, S. L., Myers, D. E., & Ginsburg, A. L. (1987). "The Role of Responsibility and Knowledge in Reducing Teenage Out-of-Wedlock Childbearing." *Journal of Marriage and the Family, 49*(2), 241–256.

Hare-Mustin, R. T., & Marecek, J. (1990a). "Beyond Difference." In R. T. Hare-Mustin & J. Marecek (Eds.), *Making a Difference: Psychology and the Construction of Gender.* New Haven, CT: Yale University Press.

Hare-Mustin, R. T., & Marecek, J. (1990b). "Gender and the Meaning of Difference." In R. T. Hare-Mustin & J. Marecek (Eds.), *Making a Difference: Psychology and the Construction of Gender.* New Haven, CT: Yale University Press.

Hare-Mustin, R. T., & Marecek, J. (Eds.). (1990c). *Making a Difference: Psychology and the Construction of Gender.* New Haven, CT: Yale University Press.

Hare-Mustin, R. T., & Marecek, J. (1990d). "On Making a Difference." In R. T. Hare-Mustin & J. Marecek (Eds.), *Making a Difference: Psychology and the Construction of Gender.* New Haven, CT: Yale University Press.

Hariton, E. B., & Singer, J. I. (1974). "Women's Fantasies During Sexual Intercourse." *Journal of Consulting and Clinical Psychology, 42,* 313–322.

Harlow, C. W. (1991). *Female Victims of Violent Crime.* Washington, DC: U.S. Department of Justice. (NCJ-126826).

Harriman, L. (1983). "Personal and Marital Changes Accompanying Parenthood." *Family Relations, 32,* 387–394.

Harris, M. B., & Turner, P. H. (1985). "Gay and Lesbian Parents." *Journal of Homosexuality, 12*(2), 101–113.

Harry, J. (1986). "Sampling Gay Men." *Journal of Homosexuality, 22*(1), 21–34.

Harry, J. (1988). "Decision Making and Age Differences Among Gay Male Couples." In J. De Cecco (Ed.), *Gay Relationships.* New York: Haworth Press.

Hart, J., Cohen, E., Gingold, A., & Homburg, R. (1991). "Sexual Behavior in Pregnancy: A Study of 219 Women." *Journal of Sex Education and Therapy, 17*(2), 88–90.

Harvard Law Review. (1991). "Constitutional Barriers to Civil and Criminal Restrictions on Premarital and Extramarital Sex." *Harvard Law Review, 104*(7), 1660–1680.

Harvey, S. (1987). "Female Sexual Behavior: Fluctuations During the Menstrual Cycle." *Journal of Psychosomatic Research, 31*, 101–110.

Haskell, M. (1976, November). "2000-Year-Old Misunderstanding: Rape Fantasy." *Ms.*, pp. 84–86ff.

Haskell, M. (1987). *From Reverence to Rape*. (2nd ed.). Chicago: University of Chicago Press.

Hass, A. (1979). *Teenage Sexuality: A Survey of Teenage Sexual Behavior*. New York: Macmillan.

Hassold, T., Arnovitz, K., Jacobs, P. A., May, K., & Robinson, D. (1990). "The Parental Origin of the Missing or Additional Chromosome in 45,X and 47,XXX Females." *Birth Defects Original Article Series, 26*(4), 297–304.

Hatcher, R., et al. (1986). *Contraceptive Technology: 1986–1988*. New York: Irvington.

Hatcher, R., et al. (1990). *Contraceptive Technology: 1990–1992*. New York: Irvington.

Hatcher, R., et al. (1994a). *Contraceptive Technology. Special Section: AIDS and Abnormal Pap Smears*. New York: Irvington.

Hatcher, R., Stewart, F., Trussel, J., Kowal, D., Guest, F., Stewart, G., & Cates, W. (1994b). *Contraceptive Technology: 1994–1995*. New York: Irvington.

Hatchett, S. J. (1991). "Women and Men." In J. S. Jackson (Ed.), *Life in Black America*. Newbury Park, CA: Sage Publications.

Hatfield, E., & Sprecher, S. (1986). *Mirror, Mirror: The Importance of Looks in Everyday Life*. New York: State University of New York.

Hatfield, E., & Walster, G. W. (1981). *A New Look at Love*. Reading, MA: Addison-Wesley.

Hausman, B. L. (1993). "Demanding Subjectivity: Transsexualism, Medicine, and the Technologies of Gender." *Journal of the History of Sexuality, 3*(2), 270–302.

Hawkins, R. O. (1990). "The Relationship Between Culture, Personality, and Sexual Jealousy in Men in Heterosexual and Homosexual Relationships." *Journal of Homosexuality, 19*(3), 67–84.

Hawton, K., Catalan, J., & Fagg, J. (1991). "Low Sexual Desire: Sex Therapy Results and Prognostic Factors." *Behavior Research and Therapy, 29*(3), 217–224.

Hayden, N. (1991). *How to Satisfy a Woman Every Time*. New York: Dutton.

Hays, D., & Samuels, A. (1989). "Heterosexual Women's Perceptions of Their Marriages to Bisexual or Homosexual Men." *Journal of Homosexuality, 18*, 81–100.

Hazan, C., & Shaver, P. (1987). "Romantic Love Conceptualized as an Attachment Process." *Journal of Personality and Social Psychology, 52*(3), 511–524.

Healy, J. M. (1988, November). "Preventing Birth Defects of the Mind." *Parents' Magazine*, p. 176ff.

Heath, D. (1984). "An Investigation of the Origins of a Copious Vaginal Discharge During Intercourse." *Journal of Sex Research, 20*, 194–215.

Heath, R. (1972). "Pleasure and Brain Activity in Man." *Journal of Nervous and Mental Disorders, 154*, 3–18.

Hefner, R., Rebecca, M., & Oleshansky. (1975). "Development of Sex-Role Transcendence." *Human Development, 18*, 143–158.

Heider, K. (1979). *Grand Valley Dani: Peaceful Warriors*. New York: Holt, Rinehart & Winston.

Heilbrun, C. (1982). *Toward a Recognition of Androgyny*. New York: Norton.

Heiman, J., LoPiccolo, L., & LoPiccolo, J. (1976). *Becoming Orgasmic: A Sexual Growth Program for Women*. Englewood Cliffs, NJ: Prentice-Hall.

Heiman, J., et al. (1986). "Historical and Current Factors Discriminating Sexually Functional from Sexually Dysfunctional Married Couples." *Journal of Marital and Family Therapy, 12*(2), 163–174.

Heiman, J., & LoPiccolo, J. (1988). *Becoming Orgasmic: A Sexual and Personal Growth Program for Women*. Englewood Cliffs, NJ: Prentice-Hall.

Heller, L., Keren, O., Aloni, R., & Davidoff, G. (1992). "An Open Trial of Vacuum Penile Tumescence: Constriction Therapy for Neurological Impotence." *Paraplegia, 30*(8), 550–553.

Hemminki, K., et al. (1983). "Spontaneous Abortion in an Industrialized Community in Finland." *American Journal of Public Health, 73*(1), 32–37.

Hendrick, C., & Hendrick, S. S. (1986). "A Theory and Method of Love." *Journal of Personality and Social Psychology, 50*, 392–402.

Hendrick, C., & Hendrick, S. S. (1988, May). "Lovers Wear Rose-Colored Glasses." *Journal of Social and Personal Relationships, 5*(2), 161–183.

Hendrick, S. S. (1981). "Self-Disclosure and Marital Satisfaction." *Journal of Personality and Social Psychology, 40*, 1150–1159.

Hendrick, S. S., & Hendrick, C. (1987). "Multidimensionality of Sexual Attitudes." *Journal of Sex Research, 23*(4), 502–526.

Hendrick, S. S., Hendrick, C., & Adler, N. L. (1988). "Romantic Relationships: Love, Satisfaction, and Staying Together." *Journal of Personality and Social Psychology, 54*, 980–988.

Henley, N. (1977). *Body Politics: Power, Sex, and Nonverbal Communication*. Englewood Cliffs, NJ: Prentice-Hall.

Henshaw, S., & VanVort, J. (1989). "Teenage Abortion, Birth and Pregnancy Statistics: An Update." *Family Planning Perspectives, 21*, 85–88.

Herbert, C. M. H. (1989). *Talking of Silence: The Sexual Harassment of Schoolgirls*. London: The Falmer Press.

Herbst, A. L., et al. (1980). "A Comparison of Pregnancy Experience in DES-Exposed and DES-Unexposed Daughters." *Journal of Reproductive Medicine, 24*, 62–68.

Herdt, G. (1984). "A Comment on Cultural Attributes and Fluidity of Bisexuality." *Journal of Homosexuality, 10*(3-4), 53–61.

Herdt, G. (1987). "Transitional Objects in Sambia Initiation." Special Issue: Interpretation in Psychoanalytic Anthropology. *Ethos, 15*, 40–57.

Herdt, G., & Boxer, A. (1992). "Introduction: Culture, History, and Life Course of Gay Men." In G. Herdt (Ed.), *Gay Culture in America: Essays from the Field*. Boston: Beacon Press.

Herek, G. M. (1984). "Beyond Homophobia: A Social Psychological Perspective on Attitudes Toward Lesbians and Gay Men." *Journal of Homosexuality, 10*(1-2), 1–21.

Herek, G. M. (1985). "On Doing, Being, and Not Being: Prejudice and the Social Construction of Sexuality." *Journal of Homosexuality, 12*(1), 135–151.

Herek, G. M. (1989). "Hate Crimes Against Lesbians and Gay Men: Issues for Research and Policy." *American Psychologist, 44*, 948–955.

Herek, G. M., Kimmel, D. C., Amaro, H., & Melton, G. B. (1991). "Avoiding Heterosexist Bias in Psychological Research." *American Psychologist, 46*(9), 957–963.

Herman, J. (1981). *Father-Daughter Incest*. Cambridge, MA: Harvard University Press.

Herold, E. E., Mantle, D., & Zemitis, D. (1979). "A Study of Sexual Offenses Against Females." *Adolescence, 14*, 65–72.

Herold, E. E., & Way, L. (1983). "Oral-Genital Sexual Behavior in a Sample of University Females." *Journal of Sex Research, 19*(4), 327–338.

Herzer, M. (1985). "Kertbeny and the Nameless Love." *Journal of Homosexuality, 12*(1), 1–26.

Hetherington, S. E. (1990). "A Controlled Study of the Effect of Prepared Childbirth Classes on Obstetric Outcomes." *Birth*, 17(2), 86–90.

Hewitt, J. (1987). "Preconceptional Sex Selection." *British Journal of Hospital Medicine*, 37(2), 149ff.

Heyl, B. (1989). "Homosexuality: A Social Phenomenon." In K. McKinney & S. Sprecher (Eds.), *Human Sexuality: The Societal and Interpersonal Context*. Norwood, NJ: Ablex.

Hibbard, R. A., & Hartman, G. L. (1992). "Behavioral Problems in Alleged Sexual Abuse Victims." *Child Abuse and Neglect*, 16(5), 755–762.

Hibbs, J. R., & Gunn, R. A. (1991). "Public Health Intervention in a Cocaine-Related Syphilis Outbreak." *American Journal of Public Health*, 8(10), 1259–1262.

Hill, I. (1987). *The Bisexual Spouse*. McLean, VA: Barlina Books.

Hilts, P. (1991, October 11). "Growing Concern Over Pelvic Infection in Women." *The New York Times*, p. B7.

Hilts, P. J. (1990, June 13). "Poorer Countries Are Hit Hardest by Spread of AIDS, U.N. Reports." *The New York Times*, p. A6.

Hines, M. (1982). "Prenatal Gonadal Hormones and Sex Differences in Human Behavior." *Psychological Bulletin*, 92, 56–80.

Hines, P. M., & Boyd-Franklin, N. (1982). "Black Families." In M. McGoldrick et al. (Eds.), *Ethnicity and Family Therapy*. New York: Guilford Press.

Hingson, R. W., Strunin, L., Berlin, B. M., & Heeren, T. (1990). "Beliefs About AIDS, Use of Alcohol and Drugs, and Unprotected Sex Among Massachusetts Adolescents." *American Journal of Public Health*, 80(3), 295–299.

Hirschfeld, M. (1978). *Research on Love Between Men*. Los Angeles: Urania Manuscripts.

Hirschfeld, M. (1991). *Transvestites: The Erotic Drive to Cross Dress*. Buffalo, NY: Prometheus Press.

Hite, S. (1976). *The Hite Report*. New York: Macmillan.

Ho, D. D., et al. (1985). "Infrequency of Isolation of HTLV-III Virus from Saliva in AIDS." *New England Journal of Medicine*, 313, 1606.

Ho, D. D., Bredesen, D. E., Vinters, H. V., & Daar, E. S. (1989). "The Acquired Immunodeficiency Syndrome (AIDS) Dementia Complex." *Annals of Internal Medicine*, 111(5), 400–410.

Hobart, C., & Griegel, F. (1992). "Cohabitation Among Canadian Students at the End of the Eighties." *Journal of Comparative Family Studies*, 23(3), 311–338.

Hochhauser, M. (1992). "Moral Development and HIV Prevention Among Adolescents." *Family Life Educator*, 10(3), 9–12.

Hockenberry, S. L., & Billingham, R. E. (1987). "Sexual Orientation and Boyhood Gender Conformity: Development of the Boyhood Gender Conformity Scale (BGCS)." *Archives of Sexual Behavior*, 16, 475–492.

Hoeffer, B. (1981). "Children's Acquisition of Sex-Role Behavior in Lesbian-Mother Families." *American Journal of Orthopsychiatry*, 51, 536–544.

Holcomb, D. R., et al. (1991). "Gender Differences Among College Students." *College Student Journal*, 25(4), 434–439.

Hollander, J. B., Gonzalez, J., & Norman, T. (1992). "Patient Satisfaction with Pharmacologic Erection Program." *Urology*, 39(5), 439–441.

Holman, P. B., Jenkins, W. C., Gayle, J. A., Duncan, C., & Lindsey, B. K. (1991). "Increasing the Involvement of National and Regional Racial and Ethnic Minority Organizations in HIV Information and Education." *Public Health Reports*, 106(6), 687–694.

Holmes, K. K., et al. (1990). "Future Directions." In K. K. Holmes et al. (Eds.), *Sexually Transmitted Diseases* (2nd ed.). New York: McGraw-Hill.

Holmes, K. K., et al. (Eds.). (1990). *Sexually Transmitted Diseases* (2nd ed.). New York: McGraw-Hill.

Holmes, R. M. (1991). *Sex Crimes*. Newbury Park, CA: Sage Publications.

Holtzen, D. W., & Agresti, A. A. (1990). "Parental Responses to Gay and Lesbian Children." *Journal of Social and Clinical Psychology*, 9(3), 390–399.

Hook, E. W., III, et al. (1992). "Herpes Simplex Virus Infection as a Risk Factor for Human Immunodeficiency Virus Infection in Heterosexuals." *Journal of Infectious Diseases*, 165(2), 251–255.

Hooker, E. (1957). "The Adjustment of the Overt Male Homosexual." *Journal of Projective Psychology*, 21, 18–31.

Hopson, J., & Rosenfeld, A. (1984, August). "PMS: Puzzling Monthly Symptoms." *Psychology Today*, 30–35.

Hort, B. E., Leinbach, M. D., & Fagot, B. I. (1991). "Is There Coherence Among the Cognitive Components of Gender Acquisition?" *Sex Roles*, 24(3-4), 195–207.

Hotelling, K. (1991). "Sexual Harassment: A Problem Shielded by Silence." *Journal of Counseling and Development*, 69(6), 497–501.

Houlberg, R. (1991). "The Magazine of a Sadomasochism Club— The Tie That Binds." *Journal of Homosexuality*, 21(1-2), 167–183.

Houseknecht, S. K. (1982). "Childlessness and Marital Adjustment." In J. Rosenfeld (Eds.), *Relationships: The Marriage and Family Reader*. Glencoe, IL: Scott, Foresman.

Houseknecht, S. K. (1987). "Voluntary Childlessness." In M. B. Sussman & S. K. Steinmetz (Eds.), *Handbook of Marriage and the Family*. New York: Plenum Press.

"How the Public Feels." (1986, November 24). *Time*, p. 58.

Howard, E. (1980, November). "Overcoming Rape Trauma." *Ms.*, p. 35.

Howard, J. (1988). "A Structural Approach to Interracial Patterns in Adolescent Judgments About Sexual Intimacy." *Sociological Perspectives*, 31(1), 88–121.

Howard, J. A., Blumstein, P., & Schwartz, P. (1986). "Sex, Power, and Influence Tactics in Intimate Relationships." *Journal of Personality and Social Psychology*, 51(1), 102–109.

Howard, L., et al. (1986). "Evaluation of Chlamydiazyme for the Detection of Genital Infection Caused by Chlamydia Trachomatis." *Journal of Clinical Microbiology*, 23, 329–332.

Hudson, B., Pepperell, R., & Wood, C. (1987). "The Problem of Infertility." In R. Pepperell, B. Hudson, & C. Wood (Eds.). *The Infertile Couple*. Edinburgh: Churchill Livingstone.

Humm, A. J. (1992). "Homosexuality: The New Frontier in Sexuality Education." *Family Life Educator*, 10(3), 13–18.

Humphreys, L. (1975). *Tearoom Trade: Impersonal Sex in Public Places*. Chicago: Aldine.

Hunt, M. (1974). *Sexual Behavior in the 1970s*. Chicago: Playboy Press.

Hunt, M., & Hunt, B. (1977). *The Divorce Experience*. New York: McGraw-Hill.

Hunter, A. G., & Davis, J. E. (1992). "Constructing Gender: An Exploration of Afro-American Men's Conceptualization of Manhood." *Gender and Society*, 6(3), 464–479.

Hupka, R. B. (1981). "Cultural Determinants of Jealousy." *Alternative Lifestyles*, 4(3), 310–356.

Hurst, M., & Summey, P. S. (1984). "Childbirth and Social Class: The Case of Cesarean Delivery." *Social Science and Medicine*, 18(8), 621–631.

Hutchins, L., & Kaahumanu, L. (Eds.). (1990). *Any Other Name: Bisexual People Speak Out*. Boston: Alyson Publications.

Imberti, L., Sottini, A., Bettinardi, A., Puoti, M., & Primi, D. (1991). "Selective Depletion in HIV Infection of T Cells That Bear Specific T Cell Receptor V Beta Sequences." *Science*, 254(5033), 860–862.

Imperato-McGinley, J. (1974). "Steroid 5'-reductase Deficiency in Man: An Inherited Form of Male Pseudohermaphroditism." *Science*, 186, 1213–1215.

Imperato-McGinley, J. (1979). "Androgens and the Evolution of Male Gender Identity Among Male Pseudohermaphrodites with 5'-reductase Deficiency." *New England Journal of Medicine, 300*, 1233–1237.

Imperato-McGinley, J., et al. (1991). "Cognitive Abilities in Androgen-Insensitive Subjects." *Clinical Endocrinology, 34*(5), 341–347.

Ingrassia, M., Springen, K., & Rosenberg, D. (1995, March 13). "Still Fumbling in the Dark." *Newsweek*, pp. 60–62.

Irvine, J. M. (1990). *Disorders of Desire*. Philadelphia: Temple University Press.

Isensee, R. (1990). *Love Between Men: Enhancing Intimacy and Keeping Your Relationship Alive*. New York: Prentice-Hall.

Israelski, D. (1992). "Current Issues in HIV/AIDS Research: A Report from the Amsterdam Conference." Talk given at Dominican Hospital, Santa Cruz, CA.

Israelstam, S. (1986). "Alcohol and Drug Problems of Gay Males and Lesbians: Therapy, Counseling and Prevention Issues." *Journal of Drug Issues, 16*(3), 443–461.

Jackson, J. S. (Ed.). (1991). *Life in Black America*. Newbury Park, CA: Sage Publications.

Jacobs, J. (1993, February 4). "Male GIs as Sexual Prey: Welcome to the Club." *San Jose Mercury News*, p. 7b.

Jacobs, S. E., & Cromwell, J. (1992). "Visions and Revisions of Reality: Reflections on Sex, Sexuality, Gender and Gender Variance." *Journal of Homosexuality, 23*(4), 43–70.

Jacoby, A., & Williams, J. (1985). "Effects of Premarital Sexual Standards and Behavior on Dating and Marriage Desirability." *Journal of Marriage and the Family, 47*(4), 1059–1065.

Jacques, J., & Chason, K. (1979). "Cohabitation: Its Impact on Marital Success." *Family Coordinator, 28*(1), 35–39.

James, C. (1992, November 22). "Dangerous Liaisons Are All the Rage." *The New York Times*, p. 13.

James, J., & Myerdling, J. (1977). "Early Sexual Experiences as a Factor in Prostitution." *American Journal of Psychiatry, 134*, 1381–1385.

James, N. J., Gillies, P. A., & Bignell, C. J. (1991). "AIDS-Related Risk Perception and Sexual Behaviour Among Sexually Transmitted Disease Clinic Attenders." *International Journal of STD and AIDS, 2*(4), 264–271.

Janus, S., & Janus, C. (1993). *The Janus Report on Sexual Behavior*. New York: John Wiley & Sons.

Jaschik, M. L., & Fretz, B. R. (1991). "Women's Perceptions and Labeling of Sexual Harassment." *Sex Roles, 25*(1-2), 19–23.

Jeffrey, T. B., & Jeffrey, L. K. (1991). "Psychologic Aspects of Sexual Abuse in Adolescence." *Current Opinion in Obstetrics and Gynecology, 3*(6), 825–831.

Jemmott, J. B. I., Jemmott, L. S., & Fong, G. T. (1992). "Reductions in HIV Risk-Associated Sexual Behaviors Among Black Male Adolescents: Effects of an AIDS Prevention Intervention." *American Journal of Public Health, 82*(3), 372–377.

Jenks, R. (1985). "Swinging: A Replication and Test of a Theory." *Journal of Sex Research, 21*(2), 199–210.

Jensen, M. A. (1984). *Love's Sweet Return: The Harlequin Story*. Toronto: Women's Press.

Jick, H., et al. (1981). "Vaginal Spermicides and Congenital Disorders." *JAMA: Journal of the American Medical Association, 243*(13), 1329–1332.

Joffe, G. P., et al. (1992). "Multiple Partners and Partner Choice as Risk Factors for Sexually Transmitted Disease Among Female College Students." *Sexually Transmitted Diseases, 19*(5), 272–278.

Johnson, C. (1993, June 5). "More Women-Controlled AIDS Prevention Methods Needed—WHO." *San Jose Mercury News*, p. 6.

Johnson, C. B., Stockdale, M. S., & Saal, F. E. (1991). "Persistence of Men's Misperceptions of Friendly Cues Across a Variety of Interpersonal Encounters." *Psychology of Women Quarterly, 15*(3), 463–475.

Johnson, G. T., & Goldfinger, S. (Eds.). (1981). *The Harvard Medical School Health Letter Book*. Cambridge, MA: Harvard University Press.

Johnston, D. (1992, April 24). "Survey Shows Number of Rapes Far Higher Than Official Figures." *The New York Times*, p. A9.

Jones, C. (1986, June). "Sharing the Childbearing Miracle." *Nurturing News, 8*(2), pp. 5, 18ff.

Jones, C. (1988). *Mind Over Labor*. New York: Penguin.

Jones, E. F., et al. (1985). "Teenage Pregnancy in Developed Countries: Determinants and Policy Implications." *Family Planning Perspectives, 17*(2), 53–63.

Jones, J. H. (1992). "Twenty Years After. The Legacy of the Tuskegee Syphilis Study. AIDS and the Black Community." *Hastings Center Report, 22*(6), 38–40.

Jones, J. H. (1993). *Bad Blood: The Tuskegee Syphilis Experiment* (rev. ed.). New York: Free Press.

Jones, M. (1989). *A Child by Any Means*. London: Piatkus.

Jones, R. W., & Bates, J. E. (1988). "Satisfaction in Male Homosexual Couples." In J. De Cecco (Ed.), *Gay Relationships*. New York: Haworth Press.

Jones, T. S., & Remland, M. S. (1992). "Sources of Variability in Perceptions of and Responses to Sexual Harassment." *Sex Roles, 27*(3-4), 121–142.

Jones, W., Chernovetz, M., & Hansson, R. (1978). "The Enigma of Androgyny: Differential Implications for Males and Females." *Journal of Consulting and Clinical Psychology, 46*, 298–313.

Jones, W., & Emerson, S. (1994, Spring). "Sexual Abuse and Binge Eating in a Nonclinical Population." *Journal of Sex Education and Therapy*, 47–55.

Jordan, W. (1968). *White Over Black: American Attitudes Toward the Negro*. Chapel Hill, NC: University of North Carolina Press.

Jorgensen, S., & Adams, R. (1988). "Predicting Mexican-American Family Planning Intentions: An Application and Test of a Social Psychological Model." *Journal of Marriage and the Family, 50*, 107–119.

Jurich, A., & Polson, C. (1985). "Nonverbal Assessment of Anxiety as a Function of Intimacy of Sexual Attitude Questions." *Psychological Reports, 57*(3, Pt. 2), 1247–1243.

Kagan, J. (1976). "The Psychological Requirements for Human Development." In N. Talbot (Ed.), *Raising Children in Modern America*. Boston: Little, Brown.

Kahn, Y. (1989). "Judaism and Homosexuality: The Traditionalist/Progressive Debate." *Journal of Homosexuality, 18*(3-4), 47–82.

Kalin, T. (1992, August). "Gays in Film: No Way Out." Special Issue: The Sexual Revolution in Movie, Music and TV. *US*, pp. 68–70.

Kalis, P., & Neuendorf, K. (1989). "Aggressive Cue-Prominence and Gender Participation in MTV." *Journalism Quarterly, 66*(1), 148–154, 229.

Kandel, D., Wu, P., & Davies, M. (1994). "Maternal Smoking During Pregnancy and Smoking by Adolescent Daughters." *American Journal of Public Health, 84*(9), 1407–1413.

Kantor, L. M. (1992). "Scared Chaste? Fear-Based Educational Curricula." *SIECUS Report, 21*(3), 1–13.

Kantrowitz, B. (1990, February 12). "The Crack Children." *Newsweek*, pp. 62–63.

Kantrowitz, B. (1992, August 3). "Teenagers and AIDS." *Newsweek*, pp. 44–49.

Kantrowitz, B., & Kaplan, D. A. (1990, March 19). "Not the Right Family." *Newsweek*, pp. 50–51.

Kantrowitz, B., Wingert, P., et al. (1992, January 13). "Breaking the Divorce Cycle." *Newsweek, 119*(2), 48.

Kaplan, A. (1979). "Clarifying the Concept of Androgyny: Implications for Therapy." *Psychology of Women, 3*, 223–230.

Kaplan, A., & Bean, J. P. (Eds.). (1979). *Beyond Sex-Role Stereotypes*. Boston: Little, Brown.

Kaplan, E. H. (1988). "Crisis? A Brief Critique of Masters, Johnson, and Kolodny." *Journal of Sex Research, 25,* 317–322.

Kaplan, G. T., & Rogers, L. J. (1984). "Breaking Out of the Dominant Paradigm." *Journal of Homosexuality, 10*(3-4), 71–75.

Kaplan, H. S. (1974). *The New Sex Therapy.* New York: Brunner/Mazel.

Kaplan, H. S. (1979). *Disorders of Desire.* New York: Brunner/Mazel.

Kaplan, H. S. (1983). *The Evaluation of Sexual Disorders: Psychological and Medical Aspects.* New York: Brunner/Mazel.

Kaplan, H. S. (1987). *Sexual Aversion, Sexual Phobias, and Panic Disorders.* New York: Brunner/Mazel.

Kaplan, H. S. (1992). "A Neglected Issue: The Sexual Side Effects of Current Treatment for Breast Cancer." *Journal of Sex and Marital Therapy, 18*(1), 3–19.

Kaplan, H. S., & Owett, T. (1993). "The Female Androgen Deficiency Syndrome." *Journal of Sex and Marital Therapy, 19*(1), 3–24.

Kaplan, M. (1992, August). "You Get What You Pay For: Cable TV and Sex." Special Issue: The Sexual Revolution in Movie, Music and TV. *US,* pp. 78–80.

Karenga, M. (1992). "Under the Camouflage of Color and Gender: The Dread and Drama of Thomas-Hill." In R. Chrisman & R. Allen (Eds.), *Court of Appeal: The Black Community Speaks Out on the Racial and Sexual Politics of Clarence Thomas vs. Anita Hill.* New York: Ballantine.

Kasl, C. D. (1989). *Women, Sex, and Addiction.* New York: Ticknor & Fields.

Kassler, W. J., & Cates, W. J. (1992). "The Epidemiology and Prevention of Sexually Transmitted Diseases." *Urological Clinics of North America, 19*(1), 1–12.

Katchadourian, H. (1987). *Midlife in Perspective.* New York: W. H. Freeman.

Katz, R., Gipson, M. J., Kearl, A., & Kriskovich, M. (1989). "Assessing Sexual Aversion in College Students: The Sexual Aversion Scale." *Journal of Sex and Marital Therapy, 15*(2), 135–140.

Kaufman, D., et al. (1980). "Decreased Risk of Endometrial Cancer Among Oral Contraceptive Users." *New England Journal of Medicine, 303,* 1045–1047.

Kayal, P. M. (1992). "Healing Homophobia: Volunteerism and Sacredness in AIDS." *Journal of Religion and Health, 31*(2), 113–128.

Kaye, K., et al. (1989). "Birth Outcomes for Infants of Drug Abusing Mothers." *New York State Journal of Medicine, 144*(7), 256–261.

Kehoe, M. (1988). "Lesbians Over 60 Speak for Themselves." *Journal of Homosexuality, 16,* 1–111.

Keim, J., Woodard, M. P., & Anderson, M. K. (1992). "Screening for Chlamydia Trachomatis in College Women in Routine Gynecological Exams." *Journal of American College Health, 41*(1), 17–19, 22–23.

Keller, D., & Rosen, H. (1988). "Treating the Gay Couple Within the Context of Their Families of Origin." *Family Therapy Collections, 25,* 105–119.

Keller, S. E., Bartlett, J. A., Schleifer, S. J., Johnson, R. L., Pinner, E., & Delaney, B. (1991). "HIV-Relevant Sexual Behavior Among a Healthy Inner-City Heterosexual Adolescent Population in an Endemic Area of HIV." *Journal of Adolescent Health, 12*(1), 44–48.

Kellett, J. M. (1991). "Sexuality of the Elderly." *Sexual and Marital Therapy, 6*(2), 147–155.

Kelley, H. (1983). "Love and Commitment." In H. Kelley et al. (Eds.), *Close Relationships.* New York: W. H. Freeman.

Kelly, M. P., Strassberg, D. S., & Kircher, J. R. (1990). "Attitudinal and Experiential Correlates of Anorgasmia." *Archives of Sexual Behavior, 19*(2), 165–167.

Kelly, T. E., et al. (1992). "Survival of Fetuses with 45,X: An Instructive Case and Hypothesis." *American Journal of Medical Genetics, 42*(6), 825–826.

Kelly, T. E., Ferguson, J. E., & Golden, W. (1992). "Survival of Fetuses with 45,X: An Instructive Case and Hypothesis." *American Journal of Medical Genetics, 42*(6), 825–826.

Kendall-Tackett, K., Williams, L. M., & Finkelhor, D. (1993). "Impact of Sexual Abuse on Children: A Review and Synthesis of Recent Empirical Studies." *Psychological Bulletin, 113*(1), 164 (17 pages).

Kendrick, W. (1987). *The Secret Museum: Pornography in Modern Culture.* New York: Viking Press.

Kendrick, W. (1992, May 31). "Increasing Our Dirty-Word Power: Why Yesterday's Smut Is Today's Erotica." *The New York Times Book Review,* pp. 3, 36.

Kenig, S., & Ryan, J. (1986). "Sex Differences of Tolerance and Attribution of Blame for Sexual Harassment on a University Campus." *Sex Roles, 15*(9-10), 535–549.

Kennedy, H. (1988). *Ulrichs: The Life and Works of Karl Heinrich Ulrichs, Pioneer of the Modern Gay Movement.* Boston: Alyson Publications.

Kensington, C. (1991). *Elise.* San Francisco: Spinsters Ink.

Kenyon, E. B. (1989). "The Management of Exhibitionism in the Elderly: A Case Study." *Sexual and Marital Therapy, 4*(1), 93–100.

Keuls, E. (1985). *The Reign of the Phallus: Sexual Politics in Ancient Greece.* New York: Harper & Row.

King, M. B. (1990). "Sneezing as a Fetishistic Stimulus." *Sexual and Marital Therapy, 5*(1), 69–72.

King, P. A. (1992). "Twenty Years After. The Legacy of the Tuskegee Syphilis Study. The Dangers of Difference." *Hastings Center Report, 22*(6), 35–38.

Kinsey, A., Pomeroy, W., & Martin, C. (1948). *Sexual Behavior in the Human Male.* Philadelphia: Saunders.

Kinsey, A., Pomeroy, W., Martin, C., & Gebhard, P. (1953). *Sexual Behavior in the Human Female.* Philadelphia: Saunders.

Kirby, D. (1993). "Research and Evaluation." In S. Samuels & M. Smith (Eds.) *Condoms in the Schools.* Menlo Park, CA: Henry J. Kaiser Foundation.

Kisker, E. (1984). "The Effectiveness of Family Planning Clinics in Serving Adolescents." *Family Planning Perspectives, 16*(5), 212ff.

Kisker, E. (1985). "Teenagers Talk About Sex, Pregnancy and Contraception." *Family Planning Perspectives, 17*(2), 83–89.

Kissman, K., & Allen, J. A. (1993). *Single-Parent Families.* Newbury Park, CA: Sage Publications.

Kite, M. (1984). "Sex Differences in Attitudes Toward Homosexuals: A Meta-Analytic Review." *Journal of Homosexuality, 10*(1-2), 69–82.

Kitzinger, S. (1989). *The Complete Book of Pregnancy and Childbirth.* New York: Knopf.

Kleczkowska, A., et al. (1990). "Turner Syndrome: The Leuven Experience (1965–1980) in 478 Patients." *Genetic Counseling, 1*(3-4), 235–240.

Klein, R. S., et al. (1988). "Low Occupational Risk of Human Immunodeficiency Infection Among Dental Professionals." *New England Journal of Medicine, 318,* 86–90.

Kline, A., Kline, E., & Oken, E. (1992). "Minority Women and Sexual Choice in the Age of AIDS." *Social Science and Medicine, 34*(4), 447–457.

Klinman, D., & Vukelich, C. (1985). "Mothers and Fathers: Expectations for Infants." *Family Relations, 34*(3), 305–313.

Knafo, D., & Jaffe, Y. (1984). "Sexual Fantasizing in Males and Females." *Journal of Research in Personality, 18,* 451–462.

Knapp, J., & Whitehurst, R. (1977). "Sexually Open Marriage and Relationships: Issues and Prospects." In R. Libby & R. Whitehurst (Eds.), *Marriage and Alternatives: Exploring Intimate Relationships.* Glenview, IL: Scott, Foresman.

Knopp, F. H. (1984). *Retraining Sex Offenders: Methods and Models*. Syracuse, NY: Safer Society Press.

Koblinsky, S. A., & Sugawara, A. I. (1984). "Nonsexist Curricula, Sex of Teacher and Children's Sex-Role Learning." *Sex Roles*, 10, 357–367.

Kockott, G., & Fahrner, E. M. (1988). "Male-to-Female and Female-to-Male Transsexuals: A Comparison." *Archives of Sexual Behavior*, 17(6), 539–546.

Koga, K. (1994, Autumn). "Run for Your Life: Exercise and Breast Cancer." *University of Southern California Trojan Family*, p. 18.

Kohen, J. A., et al. (1979). "Divorced Mothers: The Costs and Benefits of Female Family Control." In G. Levinger & O. C. Moles (Eds.), *Separation and Divorce*. New York: Basic Books.

Kohlberg, L. (1969). "The Cognitive-Development Approach to Socialization." In A. Goslin (Ed.), *Handbook of Socialization Theory and Research*. Chicago: Rand McNally.

Kolata, G. (1979, May). "Early Warnings and Latent Cures for Infertility." *Ms.*, pp. 86–89.

Kolata, G. (1988, April 22). "Anti-Acne Drug Faulted in Birth Defects." *The New York Times*, p. B: 1ff.

Kolata, G. (1990, May 31). "A Major Operation on a Fetus Works for the First Time." *The New York Times*, p. 1ff.

Kolata, G. (1992, March 17). "How AIDS Smolders: Immune System Studies Follow the Tracks of H.I.V." *The New York Times*, pp. B5, 8.

Kolker, A. (1989). "Advances in Prenatal Diagnosis: Social-Psychological and Policy Issues." *International Journal of Technology Assessment in Health Care*, 5(4), 601–617.

Kolodny, R., Masters, W., & Johnson, V. (1979). *Textbook of Sexual Medicine*. Boston: Little, Brown.

Komarovsky, M. (1985). *Women in College*. New York: Basic Books.

Konker, C. (1992). "Rethinking Child Sexual Abuse: An Anthropological Perspective." *American Journal of Orthopsychiatry*, 62(1), 147–153.

Koss, M. P. (1988). "Hidden Rape: Sexual Aggression and Victimization in a National Sample of Students in Higher Education." In A. W. Burgess (Ed.), *Rape and Sexual Assault II*. New York: Garland Press.

Koss, M. P. (1992). "The Underdetection of Rape: Methodological Choices Influence Incidence Estimates." *Journal of Social Issues*, 48, 61–75.

Koss, M. P., & Dinero, T. E. (1989). "Discriminant Analysis of Risk Factors for Sexual Victimization Among a National Sample of College Women." *Journal of Consulting and Clinical Psychology*, 57, 242–250.

Kotlowitz, A. (1991). *There Are No Children Here*. New York: Doubleday.

Kotulak, R. (1979, November 4). "Hopeful Forecast for Cancer Surgery." *San Francisco Chronicle*, p. 18.

Koziol, D. E., & Henderson, D. K. (1992). "Evolving Epidemiology of HIV Infection Among Adults." *Annals of Allergy*, 68(5), 375–385.

Krames, L., England, R., & Flett, G. (1988). "The Role of Masculinity and Femininity in Depression and Social Satisfaction in Elderly Years." *Sex Roles*, 19(11-12), 713–721.

Krauss, D. J., et al. (1990). "In Treating Impotence, Urology and Sex Therapy Are Complimentary." *Urology*, 36(5), 467–470.

Kreiss, J., et al. (1992). "Efficacy of Nonoxynol-9 Contraceptive Sponge Use in Preventing Heterosexual Acquisition of HIV in Nairobi Prostitutes." *JAMA: Journal of the American Medical Association* 268(4), 477–482.

Krettek, J. E., Arkin, S. I., Chaisilwattana, P., & Monif, G. R. (1993). "Chlamydia Trachomatis in Patients Who Used Oral Contraceptives and Had Intermenstrual Spotting." *Obstetrics and Gynecology*, 81(5, Pt. 1), 728–731.

Krieger, J. N., et al. (1993). "Clinical Manifestations of Trichomoniasis in Men." *Annals of Internal Medicine*, 118(11), 844–889.

Krieger, L. M. (1992, July 19). "Global Attack on AIDS." *San Francisco Examiner*, pp. A1, 10.

Kruesi, M. J., Fine, S., Valladares, L., & Philips, R. A. (1992). "Paraphilias: A Double-Blind Crossover Comparison of Clomipramine Versus Despiramine." *Archives of Sexual Behavior*, 21(6), 587–593.

Kruks, G. (1991). "Gay and Lesbian Homeless/Street Youth: Special Issues and Concerns." Special Issue: Homeless Youth. *Journal of Adolescent Health*, 12(7), 515–518.

Kulhanjian, J. A., et al. (1992). "Identification of Women at Unsuspected Risk of Primary Infection with Herpes Simplex Virus Type 2 During Pregnancy." *New England Journal of Medicine*, 326(14), 916–920.

Kupersmid, J., & Wonderly, D. (1980). "Moral Maturity and Behavior: Failure to Find a Link." *Journal of Youth and Adolescence*, 9, 249–261.

Kurdek, L. (1988). "Relationship Quality of Gay and Lesbian Cohabiting Couples." *Journal of Homosexuality*, 15(3-4), 93–118.

Kurdek, L. (1991). "Sexuality in Homosexual and Heterosexual Couples." In K. McKinney & Susan Sprecher (Eds.), *Sexuality in Close Relationships*. Hillsdale, NJ: Erlbaum.

Kurdek, L., & Schmitt, P. (1988). "Relationship Quality of Gay Men in Closed and Open Relationships." In J. De Cecco (Ed.), *Gay Relationships*. New York: Haworth Press.

Ladas, A., Whipple, B., & Perry, J. (1982). *The G Spot*. New York: Holt, Rinehart & Winston.

La Franchi, S. (1992). "Human Growth Hormone: Who Is a Candidate for Treatment?" *Postgraduate Medicine*, 91(5), 373–374, 380–382 passim.

Lamaze, F. (1970). *Painless Childbirth*. (1st ed., 1956). Chicago: H. Regnery.

Lamb, M. (1986). *The Father's Role: Cross-Cultural Perspectives*. Hillsdale, NJ: Erlbaum.

Lambert, B. (1990, September 6). "Despite Advice, Few Are Taking Drugs for AIDS." *The New York Times*, pp. A1, A18.

Lamontagne, Y., & Lesage, A. (1986). "Private Exposure and Covert Sensitization in the Treatment of Exhibitionism." *Journal of Behavior Therapy and Experimental Psychiatry*, 17(3), 197–201.

Landau, R. (1989). "Affect and Attachment: Kissing, Hugging, and Patting as Attachment Behaviors." *Infant Mental Health Journal*, 10(1), 59–69.

Landis, S. E., et al. (1992). "Results of a Randomized Trial of Partner Notification in Cases of HIV Infection in North Carolina." *New England Journal of Medicine*, 326(2), 101–106.

Laner, M. R. (1990). "Violence or Its Precipitators: Which Is More Likely to Be Identified as a Dating Problem?" *Deviant Behavior*, 11(4), 319–329.

Lang, R., Checkley, K. L., & Pugh, G. (1987). "Genital Exhibitionism: Courtship Disorder or Narcissism?" *Canadian Journal of Behavioural Science*, 19(2), 216–232.

Lang, R., & Frenzel, R. (1988). "How Sex Offenders Lure Children." *Annals of Sex Research*, 1(2), 303–317.

Langevin, R., Wright, P., & Handy, L. (1988). "Empathy, Assertiveness, and Defensiveness Among Sex Offenders." *Annals of Sex Research*, 1, 533–547.

Langevin, R., Wright, P., & Handy, L. (1989). "Studies of Brain Damage and Dysfunction in Sex Offenders." *Annals of Sex Research*, 2(2), 163–179.

Langhoff, E., & Haseltine, W. A. (1992). "Infection of Accessory Dendritic Cells by Human Immunodeficiency Virus Type 1." *Journal of Investigative Dermatology*, 99(5), 89S–94S.

Lantz, H. (1980). "Family and Kin as Revealed in the Narratives of Ex-Slaves." *Social Science Quarterly*, 60(4), 667–674.

La Torre, R., & Wendenburg, K. (1983). "Psychological Characteristics of Bisexual, Heterosexual, and Homosexual Women." *Journal of Homosexuality*, 9(1), 87–97.

Laube, D. (1985). "Premenstrual Syndrome." *The Female Patient*, 6, 50–61.

Laumann, E., Gagnon, J., Michael, R., & Michaels, S. (1994). *The Social Organization of Sexuality*. Chicago: University of Chicago Press.

Laurent, S. L., Thompson, S. J., Addy, C., Garrison, C. Z., & Moore, E. E. (1992). "An Epidemiologic Study of Smoking and Primary Infertility in Women." *Fertility and Sterility, 57*(3), 565–572.

Lavecchia, C., Negri, E., Bruzzi, P., & Franceschi, S. (1993). "The Impact of Mammography on Breast Cancer Detection." *Annals of Oncology, 4*(1), 41–44.

Lavee, Y. (1991). "Western and Non-Western Human Sexuality: Implications for Clinical Practice." *Journal of Sex and Marital Therapy, 17*(5), 203–213.

Lavrakas, P. (1975). "Female Preferences for Male Physiques." *Journal of Research in Personality, 9*, 324–334.

Lawrence III, C. (1992). "Cringing at the Myths of Black Sexuality." In R. Chrisman & R. Allen (Eds.), *Court of Appeal: The Black Community Speaks Out on the Racial and Sexual Politics of Clarence Thomas vs. Anita Hill*. New York: Ballantine.

Lawson, C. (1990, April 12). "Fathers, Too, Are Seeking a Balance Between Their Families and Careers." *The New York Times*, p. 1ff.

Lazarus, A. A. (1989). "Dyspareunia: A Multimodel Psychotherapeutic Perspective." In S. R. Lieblum & R. C. Rosen (Eds.), *Principles and Practice of Sex Therapy* (2nd ed.). New York: Guilford Press.

Leary, W. (1993, May 11). "Female Condom Approved for Market." *The New York Times*, p. C5.

Leavitt, F., & Berger, J. C. (1990). "Clinical Patterns Among Male Transsexual Candidates with Erotic Interest in Males." *Archives of Sexual Behavior, 19*(5), 491–505.

Ledwitz-Rigby, F. (1980). "Biochemical and Neurophysiological Influences on Human Sexual Development." In J. E. Parsons (Ed.), *The Psychobiology of Sex Differences and Sex Roles*. Washington, DC: Hemisphere.

Lee, A., & Scheurer, V. (1983). "Psychological Androgyny and Aspects of Self-Image in Women and Men." *Sex Roles, 9*, 289–306.

Lee, J. A. (1973). *The Color of Love*. Toronto: New Press.

Lee, J. A. (1988). "Love Styles." In R. Sternberg & M. Barnes (Eds.), *The Psychology of Love*. New Haven, CT: Yale University Press.

Leiblum, S. R. (1990). "Sexuality and the Midlife Woman." Special Issue: Women at Midlife and Beyond. *Psychology of Women Quarterly, 14*(4), 495–508.

Leifer, M. (1990). *Psychological Effects of Motherhood: A Study of First Pregnancy*. New York: Praeger.

Leigh, B. C. (1990). "Alcohol Expectancies and Reasons for Drinking: Comments from a Study of Sexuality." *Psychology of Addictive Behaviors, 4*(2), 91–96.

Leitenberg, H., Detzer, M. J., & Srebnik, D. (1993). "Gender Differences in Masturbation and the Relation of Masturbation Experience in Preadolescence and Early Adolescence to Sexual Behavior and Sexual Adjustment in Young Adulthood." *Archives of Sexual Behavior, 22*(2), 87–98.

Lemkau, J. P. (1988). "Emotional Sequelae of Abortion: Implications for Clinical Practice." Special Issue: Women's Health: Our Minds, Our Bodies. *Psychology of Women Quarterly, 12*, 461–472.

Lenz, R., & Chaves, B. (1981). "Becoming Active Partners: A Couple's Perspective." In D. Bullard & S. Knight (Eds.), *Sexuality and Disability: Personal Perspectives*. St. Louis, MO: Mosby.

Leo, J. (1986, November 26). "Sex and Schools." *Time*, pp. 54–63.

Leonard, A. S. (1991). "From Law: Homophobia, Heterosexism and Judicial Decision Making." *Journal of Gay and Lesbian Psychotherapy, 1*, 65–91.

Lerner, H. E. (1976). "Parental Mislabeling of Female Genitals as a Determinant of Penis Envy and Learning Inhibitions in Women." *Journal of the American Psychoanalytic Association, 24*, 269–283.

Lerner, H. E. (1993). *The Dance of Deception*. New York: HarperCollins.

"Lesbians' Cancer Risk Estimated to Be High." (1993, February 5). *San Jose Mercury News*, p. 8.

Lester, J. (1973, July). "Men: Being a Boy." *Ms.*, pp. 112–113.

Le Vay, S. (1991). "A Difference in Hypothalamic Structure Between Heterosexual and Homosexual Men." *Science, 253*, 1034–1037.

Levin, R. J. (1975). "The Redbook Report on Premarital and Extramarital Sex: The End of the Double Standard?" *Redbook*, 38–44, 190–192.

Levine, L., & Barbach, L. (1983). *The Intimate Male*. New York: Signet Books.

Levine, M. P., & Troiden, R. (1988). "The Myth of Sexual Compulsivity." *Journal of Sex Research, 25*(3), 347–363.

Levine, M. P. (1987). *How Schools Can Help Combat Student Eating Disorders: Anorexia Nervosa and Bulimia*. Washington, DC: National Education Association.

Levine, M. P. (1992). "The Life and Death of Gay Clones." In G. Herdt (Ed.), *Gay Culture in America: Essays from the Field*. Boston: Beacon Press.

Levine, M. P. (1993). "The Role of Culture in Eating Disorders." In D. N. Suggs & A. W. Miracle (Eds.), *Culture and Human Sexuality*. Pacific Grove, CA: Brooks/Cole.

Levine, S. (1987). "More on the Nature of Desire." *Journal of Sex and Marital Therapy, 13*(1), 35–44.

Levine, S. B., Risen, C. B., & Althof, A. E. (1990). "Essay on the Diagnosis and Nature of Paraphilia." *Journal of Sex and Marital Therapy, 16*(2), 89–102.

Levy, J. A. (1988). "Transmission of AIDS: The Case of the Infected Cell." *JAMA: Journal of the American Medical Association, 259*, 3037–3038.

Lewes, K. (1992). "Homophobia and the Heterosexual Fear of AIDS." *American Imago, 49*(3), 343–356.

Lewis, D. (1890). *Chastity: or, Our Secret Sins*. Philadelphia: G. Maclean.

Lewis, L. (1992). "Consumer Girl Culture: How Music Video Appeals to Girls." In M. E. Brown (Ed.), *Television and Women's Culture: The Politics of the Popular*. Newbury Park, CA: Sage Publications.

Li, C. K. (1990). "'The Main Thing Is Being Wanted': Some Case Studies in Adult Sexual Experiences with Children." *Journal of Homosexuality, 20*(1-2), 129–143.

Libman, E. (1989, July). "Sociocultural and Cognitive Factors in Aging and Sexual Expression: Conceptual and Research Issues." *Canadian Psychology, 30*(3), 560–567.

Lieberman, B. (1988). "Extrapremarital Intercourse: Attitudes Toward a Neglected Sexual Behavior." *Journal of Sex Research, 24*, 291–299.

Lieberson, S., & Waters, M. (1988). *From Many Strands: Ethnic and Racial Groups in Contemporary America*. New York: Russell Sage Foundation.

Lief, H. I., & Hubschman, L. (1993). "Orgasm in the Postoperative Transsexual." *Archives of Sexual Behavior, 22*(2), 145–155.

Lifson, A. R. (1988). "Do Alternative Modes for Transmission of Human Immunodeficiency Virus Exist?" *JAMA: Journal of the American Medical Association, 152*, 1353–1357.

Lifson, A. R., et al. (1990). "HIV Seroconversion in Two Homosexual Men After Receptive Oral Intercourse with Ejaculation: Implications for Counseling Concerning Safe Sex Practices." *American Journal of Public Health, 80*(12), 1509–1511.

Lindbohm, M. L., Hietanan, M., Kyronen, P., & Sallmen, M. (1992). "Magnetic Fields of Video Display Terminals and Spontaneous Abortion." *American Journal of Epidemiology, 136*, 1041–1051.

Lindemalm, G., Korlin, D., & Uddenberg, N. (1986). "Long-Term Follow-Up of 'Sex Change' in 13 Male-to-Female Transsexuals." *Archives of Sexual Behavior, 15*(3), 187–210.

Lino, M. (1990). "Expenditures on a Child by Husband-Wife Families." *Family Economics Review, 3*(3), 2–12.

Lipman, A. (1986). "Homosexual Relationships." *Generations, 10,* 51–54.

Lipman, M. (1994, May). "Office Visit: What Do Women Need?" *Consumer Reports on Health, 6*(5), 59.

Lips, H. (1992). *Sex and Gender.* Mountain View, CA: Mayfield.

Longo, R. E., & Groth, A. N. (1983). "Juvenile Sexual Offenses in the Histories of Adult Rapists and Child Molesters." *International Journal of Offender Therapy & Comparative Criminology, 27,* 150–155.

Lont, C. (1990). "The Roles Assigned to Females and Males in Non-Music Programming." *Sex Roles, 22*(9-10), 661–668.

LoPiccolo, J. (1991). "Counseling and Therapy for Sexual Problems in the Elderly." *Clinics in Geriatric Medicine, 7,* 161–179.

LoPresto, C., Sherman, M., & Sherman, N. (1985). "The Effects of a Masturbation Seminar on High School Males' Attitudes, False Beliefs, Guilt, and Behavior." *Journal of Sex Research, 21,* 142–156.

Lord, L. (1985, December 9). "Mortality." *U.S. News and World Report,* pp. 52–59.

Lord, L., et al. (1987, November 30). "Coming to Grips with Alcoholism." *U.S. News and World Report,* pp. 56–62.

Lorefice, L. (1991). "Fluoxitine Treatment of a Fetish." *Journal of Clinical Psychiatry, 52*(1), 41.

Losh-Hesselbart, S. (1987). "Development of Gender Roles." In M. Sussman & S. Steinmetz (Eds.), *Handbook of Marriage and the Family.* New York: Plenum Press.

Lott, B. (1990). "Dual Natures or Learned Behavior: The Challenge to Feminist Psychology." In R. T. Hare-Mustin & J. Marecek (Eds.), *Making a Difference: Psychology and the Construction of Gender.* New Haven, CT: Yale University Press.

Loulan, J. (1984). *Lesbian Sex.* San Francisco: Spinsters Book Company.

Lowry, D., & Towles, D. (1989). "Prime-Time TV Portrayals of Sex, Contraception, and Venereal Disease." *Journalism Quarterly, 66*(2), 347–352.

Lucas, V. A. (1992). "An Investigation of the Health Care Preferences of the Lesbian Population." *Health Care for Women International, 13*(2), 221–228.

Luker, K. (1975). *Taking Chances.* Berkeley: University of California Press.

Lunneborg, P. (1992). *Abortion: The Positive Decision.* New York: Bergin & Garvy.

Luria, Z., et al. (1987). *Human Sexuality.* New York: John Wiley.

Lynch, F. R. (1992). "Nonghetto Gays: An Ethnography of Suburban Homosexuals." In G. Herdt (Ed.), *Gay Culture in America: Essays from the Field.* Boston: Beacon Press.

Lyon, J. (1985). *Playing God in the Nursery.* New York: Norton.

Maccato, M. L., & Kaufman, R. H. (1992). "Herpes Genitalis." *Dermatologic Clinics, 10*(2), 415–422.

MacDonald, A., Jr. (1981). "Bisexuality: Some Comments on Research and Theory." *Journal of Homosexuality, 6,* 9–27.

Macdonald, P. T., Waldorf, D., Reinarman, C., & Murphy, S. (1988). "Heavy Cocaine Use and Sexual Behavior." *Journal of Drug Issues, 18*(3), 437–455.

Mackey, T., et al. (1992). "Factors Associated with Long-term Depressive Symptoms of Sexual Assault Victims." *Archives of Psychiatric Nursing, 6*(1), 10–25.

Macklin, E. (1987). "Nontraditional Family Forms." In M. Sussman & S. Steinmetz (Eds.), *Handbook of Marriage and the Family.* New York: Plenum Press.

Madaras, L., & Patterson, J. (1984). *Womancare: A Gynecological Guide to Your Body.* New York: Avon.

Maddock, J. W., et al. (1983). "Human Sexuality and the Family." New York: Haworth Press.

Madsen, W. (1973). *Mexican-American Youth of South Texas.* (2nd ed.). New York: Holt, Rinehart & Winston.

Major, B., & Cozzarelli, C. (1992). "Psychosocial Predictors of Adjustment to Abortion." *Journal of Social Issues, 48*(3), 121–142.

Malamuth, N. (1981). "Rape Fantasies as a Function of Exposure to Violent Sexual Stimuli." *Archives of Sexual Behavior, 10*(1), 33–47.

Malamuth, N., & Spinner, B. (1980). "A Longitudinal Content Analysis of Sexual Violence in Best-Selling Erotic Magazines." *Journal of Sex Research, 16*(3), 226–237.

Malatesta, V., Chambless, D., Pollack, M., & Cantor, A. (1989). "Widowhood, Sexuality, and Aging: A Life Span Analysis." *Journal of Sex and Marital Therapy, 14*(1), 49–62.

Mancini, J., & Bliezner, R. (1991). "Aging Parents and Adult Children: Research Themes in Intergenerational Relations." In A. Booth (Ed.), *Contemporary Families: Looking Forward, Looking Back.* Minneapolis, MN: National Council on Family Relations.

Mancini, J. A., & Blieszner, R. (1992). "Social Provisions in Adulthood: Concept and Measurement in Close Relationships." *Journal of Gerontology, 47*(1), P14–P20.

Mandoki, M. W., Sumner, G. S., Hoffman, R. P., & Riconda, D. L. (1991). "A Review of Klinefelter's Syndrome in Children and Adolescents." *Journal of the American Academy of Child and Adolescence Psychiatry, 30*(2), 167–172.

Mangasarian, L. (1993, June 5). "Experts Say AIDS Spreading into Adolescent Population." *San Jose Mercury News,* p. 6A.

Mann, J. M., et al. (1986). "Prevalence of HTLV-III/LAV in Household Contacts of Patients with Confirmed AIDS and Controls in Kinshasa, Zaire." *JAMA: Journal of the American Medical Association, 256,* 721–724.

Mansnerus, L. (1990, April 24). "The Cincinnati Case: What Are the Issues? What Is at Stake?" *The New York Times,* pp. B1, B3.

Marack, J., Finn, S. E., & Cardell, M. (1988). "Gender Roles in the Relationships of Lesbians and Gay Men." In J. P. DeCecco (Ed.), *Gay Relationships.* New York: Harrington Park Press.

Marcus, S. (1964). *The Other Victorians.* New York: Basic Books.

Marecek, J., et al. (1988). "Gender Roles in the Relationships of Lesbians and Gay Men." In J. De Cecco (Ed.), *Gay Relationships.* New York: Haworth Press.

Margiglio, W. (1991). "Male Procreative Consciousness and Responsibility: A Conceptual Analysis and Research Agenda." *Journal of Family Issues, 12,* 268–290.

Margiglio, W., & Donnelly, D. (1991). "Sexual Relations in Later Life: A National Study of Married Persons." *Journal of Gerontology, 46,* S338–S344.

Margolies, L., Becher, M., & Jackson-Brewer, K. (1988). "Internalized Homophobia: Identifying and Treating the Oppressor Within." In Boston Lesbian Psychologies Collective (Eds.), *Lesbian Psychologies.* Urbana, IL: University of Illinois Press.

Margolin, L. (1992). "Sexual Abuse by Grandparents." *Child Abuse and Neglect, 16*(5), 735–742.

Margolin, L., & White, L. (1987). "The Continuing Role of Physical Attractiveness in Marriage." *Journal of Marriage and the Family, 49,* 21–27.

Margolin, M. (1978). *The Ohlone Way.* Berkeley, CA: Heyday Books.

Marieb, E. N. (1992). *Human Anatomy and Physiology.* (2nd ed.). Redwood City, CA: Benjamin/Cummings.

Marin, R., Hannah, D., Colin, M., Annin, P., & Gegax, T. T. (1995, February 6). "Turning in the Badges of Rebellion." *Newsweek,* p. 45.

Marin, G., & Marin, B. V. (1989). "A Comparison of Three Interviewing Approaches for Studying Sensitive Topics with Hispanics." *Hispanic Journal of the Behavioral Sciences, 11*(4), 330–340.

Marin, G., & Marin, B. (1991). *Research with Hispanic Populations*. Newbury Park, CA: Sage Publications.

Marin, R., et al. (1995, February 6). "Turning in the Badges of Rebellion." *Newsweek*, p. 45.

Markman, H. (1981). "Prediction of Marital Distress: A Five-Year Follow-Up." *Journal of Consulting and Clinical Psychology, 49*, 760–761.

Markman, H., Duncan, W., Storaasli, R. D., & Howes, P. W. (1987). "The Prediction and Prevention of Marital Distress: A Longitudinal Investigation." In K. Hahlweg & M. Goldstein (Eds.), *Understanding Major Mental Disorders: The Contribution of Family Interaction Research*. New York: Family Process Press.

Markman, H., Floyd, F. J., Stanley, S. M., & Storaasli, R. D. (1988). "Prevention of Marital Distress: A Longitudinal Investigation." *Journal of Consulting and Clinical Psychology, 56*(2), 210–217.

Markowitz, L., et al. (1987). "Toxic Shock Syndrome: Evaluation of National Surveillance Data Using a Hospital Discharge Survey." *JAMA: Journal of the American Medical Association, 258*(1), 75–78.

Marmor, J. (1980a). "Homosexuality and the Issue of Mental Illness." In J. Marmor (Ed.), *Homosexual Behavior*. New York: Basic Books.

Marmor, J. (Ed.). (1980b). *Homosexual Behavior*. New York: Basic Books.

Marmor, J. (1980c). "The Multiple Roots of Homosexual Behavior." In J. Marmor (Ed.), *Homosexual Behavior*. New York: Basic Books.

Marrero, M. A., & Ory, S. J. (1991). "Unexplained Infertility." *Current Opinion in Obstetrics and Gynecology, 3*(2), 211–218.

Marshall, D. (1971). "Sexual Behavior on Mangaia." In D. Marshall & R. Suggs (Eds.), *Human Sexual Behavior*. New York: Basic Books.

Marshall, P., et al. (1981). "The Role of Nocturnal Penile Tumescence in Differentiating Between Organic and Psychogenic Impotence." *Archives of Sexual Behavior, 10*(1), 1–10.

Marshall, W. L. (1988). "The Use of Sexually Explicit Material by Rapists, Child Molesters, and Non-Offenders." *Journal of Sex Research, 25*, 267–268.

Marshall, W. L., Eccles, A., & Barabee, H. E. (1991). "The Treatment of Exhibitionism: A Focus on Sexual Deviance Versus Cognitive and Relationship Features." *Behaviour Research and Therapy, 29*(2), 129–135.

Marshall, W. L., Payne, K., Barabee, H. E., & Eccles, A. (1991). "Exhibitionism: Sexual Preference for Exposing." *Behaviour Research and Therapy, 29*(1), 37–40.

Marsiglio, W., & Donnelly, D. (1991). "Sexual Relations in Later Life: A National Study of Married Persons." *Journal of Gerontology, 46*(6), S338–S344.

Marsiglio, W., & Mott, F. (1986). "The Impact of Sex Education on Sexual Activity, Contraceptive Use and Premarital Pregnancy Among American Teenagers." *Family Planning Perspectives, 18*(4), 215ff.

Martens, M., & Faro, S. (1989, January). "Update on Trichomoniasis: Detection and Management." *Medical Aspects of Human Sexuality*, 73–79.

Martin, G. (1989). "Relationship, Romance, and Sexual Addiction in Extramarital Affairs." *Journal of Psychology and Christianity, 8*(4), 5–25.

Martin, G. (1992, October 16). "Justify Her Love." *San Jose Mercury News*, pp. 1, 4.

Martin, P. (1981). "Happy Sexless Marriages." *Medical Aspects of Human Sexuality, 15*(1), 25.

Martin, P. M., Gresenguet, G., Massanga, M., Georges, A., & Testa, J. (1992). "Association Between HIV1 Infection and Sexually Transmitted Disease Among Men in Central Africa." *Research in Virology, 143*(3), 205–209.

Martin, T. C., & Bumpass, L. L. (1989). "Recent Trends in Marital Disruption." *Demography, 26*, 37–51.

Martinez, F., Wright, A., Taussig, L., et al. (1994). "The Effect of Paternal Smoking on the Birthweight of Newborns Whose Mothers Did Not Smoke." *American Journal of Public Health, 84*(9), 1489–1491.

Marx, J. L. (1989). "Circumcision May Protect Against the AIDS Virus." *Science, 245*, 470–471.

Mason, K., & Lu, Y. H. (1988). "Attitudes Toward Women's Familial Roles: Changes in the United States, 1977–1985." *Gender and Society, 2*(1), 39–57.

Massa, G., Maes, M., Heinrichs, C., Vandeweghe, M., Craen, M., & Vanderschueren-Lodeweyckx, M. (1993). "Influence of Spontaneous or Induced Puberty on the Growth Promoting Effect of Treatment with Growth Hormone in Girls with Turner's Syndrome." *Clinical Endocrinology, 38*(3), 253–260.

"Massachusetts Midwife Curb Upheld." (1987, May 25). *The New York Times*, p. 5.

Masse, M., & Rosenblum, K. (1988). "Male and Female Created They Them: The Depiction of Gender in the Advertising of Traditional Women's and Men's Magazines." *Women's Studies International Forum, 11*(2), 127–144.

Massey, F. J., et al. (1984). "Vasectomy and Health: Results from a Large Cohort Study." *JAMA: Journal of the American Medical Association, 252*, 1023–1029.

Masters, W. H., & Johnson, V. E. (1966). *Human Sexual Response*. Boston: Little, Brown.

Masters, W. H., & Johnson, V. E. (1970). *Human Sexual Inadequacy*. Boston: Little, Brown.

Masters, W. H., & Johnson, V. E. (1974). *The Pleasure Bond*. Boston: Little, Brown.

Masters, W. H., & Johnson, V. E. (1979). *Homosexuality in Perspective*. Boston: Little, Brown.

Masters, W. H., Johnson, V. E., & Kolodny, R. C. (1985). *Human Sexuality* (2nd ed.). New York: Little, Brown.

Masters, W. H., Johnson, V. E., & Kolodny, R. C. (1986). *Masters and Johnson on Sex and Human Loving*. Boston: Little, Brown.

Masters, W. H., Johnson, V. E., & Kolodny, R. C. (1988). *Crisis: AIDS and Heterosexual Behavior*. New York: Grove Press.

Masters, W. H., Johnson, V., & Kolodny, R. C. (1992). *Human Sexuality* (3rd ed.). New York: HarperCollins.

Matek, O. (1988). "Obscene Phone Callers." In D. Dailey (Ed.), *The Sexually Unusual*. New York: Harrington Park Press.

Mathur, A., Stetol, L., Schatz, D., Maclaren, N. K., Scott, M. L., & Lippe, B. (1991). "The Parental Origin of the Single X Chromosome in Turner Syndrome: Lack of Correlation with Parental Age or Clinical Phenotype." *American Journal of Human Genetics, 48*(4), 682–686.

Matteo, S., & Rissman, E. (1984). "Increased Sexual Activity During Midcycle Portion of the Human Menstrual Cycle." *Hormones and Behavior, 18*, 249–255.

Mays, V. M., Cochran, S. D., Bellinger, G., & Smith, R. G. (1992). "The Language of Black Gay Men's Sexual Behavior: Implications for AIDS Risk Reduction." *Journal of Sex Research, 29*(3), 425–434.

Mays, V. M., & Jackson, J. S. (1991). "AIDS Survey Methodology with Black Americans." *Social Science and Medicine, 33*(1), 47–54.

Mazor, M., & Simons, H. (Eds.). (1984). *Infertility: Medical, Emotional and Social Considerations*. New York: Human Sciences Press.

Mazur, A. (1986). "U.S. Trends in Feminine Beauty and Overadaptation." *Journal of Sex Research, 22*(3), 281–303.

McAninch, J. (1989). "Editorial Comment on the Report of the Task Force on Circumcision." *Pediatrics, 84*, 667.

McCabe, M. P., & Collins, J. K. (1984). "Measurement of Depth of Desired and Experienced Sexual Involvement at Different Stages of Dating." *Journal of Sex Research, 20*, 377–390.

McCauley, E., & Ehrhardt, A. (1980). "Female Sexual Response." In D. Youngs & A. Ehrhardt (Eds.), *Psychosomatic Obstetrics and Gynecology*. New York: Appleton-Century-Crofts.

McClure, D. (1988, May). "Men with One Testicle." *Medical Aspects of Human Sexuality*, 22–32.

McClary, S. (1990). "Living to Tell: Madonna's Resurrection of the Fleshy." *Genders*, 7, 1–21.

McCormack, M. J., et al. (1990). "Patient's Attitudes Following Chorionic Villus Sampling." *Prenatal Diagnosis*, 10(4), 253–255.

McEwan, K. L., Costello, C. G., & Taylor, P. J. (1987). "Adjustment to Infertility." *Journal of Abnormal Psychology*, 96(2), 108–116.

McGoldrick, M. (1982). "Normal Families: An Ethnic Perspective." In F. Walsh (Ed.), *Normal Family Processes*. New York: Guilford Press.

McGoldrick, M., Pearce, J. K., & Giordano, J. (Eds.). (1982). *Ethnicity and Family Therapy*. New York: Guilford Press.

McIntosh, E. (1989). "An Investigation of Romantic Jealousy Among Black Undergraduates." *Social Behavior and Personality*, 17(2), 135–141.

McIntosh, E., & Tate, D. T. (1990). "Correlates of Jealous Behaviors." *Psychological Reports*, 66(2), 601–602.

McIntyre, I. (1980). "Victim Response to Rape: Alternative Outcomes." *Final Report to the National Institute of Mental Health* R01MH 29043, Rockville, MD: National Institute of Mental Health.

McIntyre, S. L., & Higgins, J. E. (1986). "Parity and Use-Effectiveness with the Contraceptive Sponge." *American Journal of Obstetrics and Gynecology*, 155, 796–801.

McKusick, L., Contes, T. J., Morin, S. F., & Pollack, L. (1990). "Longitudinal Predictors of Reductions in Unprotected Anal Intercourse Among Gay Men in San Francisco: The AIDS Behavioral Research Project." *American Journal of Public Health*, 80(8), 978–973.

McLaurin, M. (1991). *Celia: A Slave*. Athens, GA: University of Georgia Press.

McLeer, S. V., et al. (1992). "Sexually Abused Children at High Risk for Post-Traumatic Stress Disorder." *Journal of the American Academy of Child and Adolescent Psychiatry*, 31(5), 875–879.

McMahon, K. (1990). "The Cosmopolitan Ideology and the Management of Desire." *Journal of Sex Research*, 27(3), 381–396.

McMullen, R. (1987). "Youth Prostitution: A Balance of Power." *Journal of Adolescence*, 10, 35–43.

McNeeley, S. G., Jr. (1992). "Pelvic Inflammatory Disease." *Current Opinion in Obstetrics and Gynecology*, 4(5), 682–686.

McWhirter, D. (1990). "Prologue." In D. McWhirter, S. A. Sanders, & J. M. Reinisch (Eds.), *Homosexuality/Heterosexuality: Concepts of Sexual Orientation*. New York: Oxford University Press.

McWhirter, D., Sanders, S. A., & Reinisch, J. M. (Eds.). (1990). *Homosexuality/Heterosexuality: Concepts of Sexual Orientation*. New York: Oxford University Press.

Meacham, R. E., & Lipshultz, L. I. (1991). "Assisted Reproductive Technologies for Male Factor Infertility." *Current Opinion in Obstetrics and Gynecology*, 3(5), 656–661.

Mead, M. (1975). *Male and Female*. New York: William Morrow.

Meek, T. D., et al. (1990). "Inhibition of HIV-1 Protease in Infected T-lymphocytes by Synthetic Peptide Analogues." *Nature*, 343(6253), 90–92.

Meier, K. J., & McFarlane, D. R. (1993). "The Politics of Funding Abortion: State Responses to the Political Environment." *American Politics Quarterly*, 21(1), 81–101.

Mengel, M. B. (1989). "Diagnostic Criteria for Bacterial Vaginosis." *Journal of Family Practice*, 29, 359–360.

Menning, B. E. (1988). *Infertility: A Guide for Childless Couples*. Englewood Cliffs, NJ: Prentice-Hall.

Merson, M. H. (1993). "Slowing the Spread of HIV: Agenda for the 1990s." *Science*, 260(5112), 1266–1268.

Mertz, G. J., Benedetti, J., Ashley, R., Selke, S. A., & Corey, L. (1992). "Risk Factors for the Sexual Transmission of Genital Herpes." *Annals of Internal Medicine*, 116(3), 197–202.

Metts, S., & Cupach, W. (1989). "The Role of Communication in Human Sexuality." In K. McKinney & S. Sprecher (Eds.), *Human Sexuality: The Social and Interpersonal Context*. Norwood, NJ: Ablex.

Meuwissen, I., & Over, R. (1992). "Sexual Arousal Across Phases of the Human Menstrual Cycle." *Archives of Sexual Behavior*, 21, 101–119.

Michael, R., Gagnon, J., Laumann, E., & Kolata, G. (1994). *Sex in America: A Definitive Study*. Boston: Little Brown & Co.

Milan, R., Jr., & Kilmann, P. (1987). "Interpersonal Factors in Premarital Contraception." *Journal of Sex Research*, 23(3), 321–389.

Miller, B. (1986). *Family Research Methods*. Newbury Park, CA: Sage Publications.

Miller, B. C., Christopherson, C. R., & King, P. K. (1993). "Sexual Behavior in Adolescence." In T. P. Gullotta et al. (Eds.), *Adolescent Sexuality*. Newbury Park, CA: Sage Publications.

Miller, B. C., & Dyk, P. A. (1990). "Adolescent Fertility-Related Behavior in the 1990s: Risking the Future Continued." *Journal of Family Issues*, 11(3), 235–238.

Miller, B. C., & Fox, G. L. (1987). "Theories of Adolescent Heterosexual Behavior." *Adolescent Research*, 2, 269–282.

Miller, E. M. (1986). *Street Women*. Philadelphia: Temple University Press.

Miller, W. (1981). "Psychological Vulnerability to Unwanted Pregnancy." In F. Furstenberg et al. (Eds.), *Teenage Sexuality, Pregnancy, and Childbearing*. Philadelphia: University of Pennsylvania Press.

Mindel, C. H., Haberstein, R. W., & Wright, R., Jr. (Eds.). (1988). *Ethnic Families in America: Patterns and Variations* (3rd ed.). New York: Elsevier North Holland.

Minkoff, H. L. (1989). "AIDS in Pregnancy." *Current Problems in Obstetrics, Gynecology and Fertility*, 12, 205–228.

Minkoff, H. L., & Dehovitz, J. A. (1991). "Care of Women Infected with the Human Immunodeficiency Virus." *JAMA: Journal of the American Medical Association*, 266(16), 2253–2258.

Mio, J. S., & Foster, J. D. (1991). "The Effects of Rape Upon Victims and Families: Implications for a Comprehensive Family Therapy." *American Journal of Family Therapy*, 19(2), 147–159.

Mison, R. B. (1992). "Homophobia in Manslaughter: The Homosexual Advance as Provocation." *California Law Review*, 80(1), 133–178.

Moergen, S., Merkel, W. T., & Brown, S. (1990). "The Use of Covert Sensitization and Social Skills Training in Treatment of an Obscene Phone Caller." *Journal of Behavior Therapy and Experimental Psychology*, 21(4), 269–275.

Moffatt, M. (1989). *Coming of Age in New Jersey: College and American Culture*. New Brunswick, NJ: Rutgers University Press.

Mohr, J., & Beutler, I. (1990). "Erectile Dysfunction: A Review of Diagnostic and and Treatment Procedures." *Clinical Psychology Review*, 10, 123–150.

Moller, L. C., Hymel, S., & Rubin, K. H. (1992). "Sex Typing in Play and Popularity in Middle Childhood." *Sex Roles*, 26(7-8), 331–335.

Monat-Haller, R. K. (1982). *Sexuality and the Mentally Retarded: A Clinical and Therapeutic Guidebook*. San Diego, CA: College Hill Press.

Money, J. (1980). *Love and Lovesickness*. Baltimore: Johns Hopkins University Press.

Money, J. (1986). "Statements of the Shadow Commissioners." In P. Nobile (Ed.), *United States of America vs. Sex: How the Meese Commission Lied About Pornography*. New York: Minotaur Press.

Money, J. (1988). "Commentary: Current Status of Sex Research." *Journal of Psychology and Human Sexuality, 1*(1), 5–16.

Money, J. (1988). *Gay, Straight, and In-Between.* New York: Oxford University Press.

Money, J. (1990). "Forensic Sexology: Paraphilic Serial Rape (Biastophilia) and Lust Murder (Erotophonophilia)." *American Journal of Psychotherapy, 44*(1), 26–37.

Money, J., & Tucker, P. (1976). *Sexual Signatures: On Being a Man or a Woman.* London: Harrap.

Montagu, A. (1986). *Touching* (3rd ed.). New York: Columbia University Press.

Montauk, S., & Clasen, M. (1989, January). "Sex Education in Primary Care: Infancy to Puberty." *Medical Aspects of Human Sexuality,* 22–36.

Moore, L. J. (1988, May 9). "Protecting Babies from Hepatitis-B." *U.S. News & World Report,* p. 85.

Moore, M. M. (1985). "Nonverbal Courtship Patterns in Women: Context and Consequences." *Ethology and Sociobiology, 6*(2), 237–247.

Morales, A., Condra, M., Owen, J., Surridge, D., Fenemore, J., & Harris, C. (1987). "Is Yohimbine Effective in the Treatment of Organic Impotence? Results of a Controlled Trial." *Journal of Urology, 137,* 1168–1172.

Moran, J. S., et al. (1989). "The Impact of Sexually Transmitted Diseases on Minority Populations." *Public Health Reports, 104*(6), 560–564.

Moran, J. S., Janes, H. R., Peterman, T. A., & Stone, K. M. (1990). "Increase in Condom Sales Following AIDS Education and Publicity, United States." *American Journal of Public Health, 80*(5), 607–608.

Morawski, J. G. (1990). "Toward the Unimagined: Feminism and Epistemology in Psychology." In R. T. Hare-Mustin & J. Marecek (Eds.), *Making a Difference: Psychology and the Construction of Gender.* New Haven, CT: Yale University Press.

Morgenthaler, E. (1992, January 23). "These Thieves Are Partial to Sequins, and Pretty in Pink: Gangs of Florida Transvestites Steal Millions in Dresses." *The Wall Street Journal,* p. 1.

Morin, J. (1986). *Anal Pleasure and Health: A Guide for Men and Women.* Burlingame, CA: Yes Press.

Morokoff, P. (1986). "Volunteer Bias in the Psychophysiological Study of Female Sexuality." *Journal of Sex Research, 22*(1), 35–51.

Morse, E. V., et al. (1991). "The Male Street Prostitute: A Vector for Transmission of HIV Infection into the Heterosexual World." *Social Science and Medicine, 32*(5), 535–539.

Moser, C. (1988). "Sadomasochism." In D. Dailey (Ed.), *The Sexually Unusual.* New York: Harrington Park Press.

Mosher, D. L., & Tompkins, S. S. (1988). "Scripting the Macho Man: Hypermasculine Socialization and Enculturation." *Journal of Sex Research, 25,* 60–84.

Moss, G. B., et al. (1991). "Association of Cervical Ectopy with Heterosexual Transmission of Human Immunodeficiency Virus: Results of a Study of Couples in Nairobi, Kenya." *Journal of Infectious Diseases, 164*(3), 588–591.

Mota, R. G. (1991). "Project First Hand: The Power of HIV-Infected Educators in AIDS Prevention." *Exchange: World Health Organization Global Program on AIDS, 1,* 1–12.

Mota, R. G. (1992, July). "Breast-Feeding and HIV Transmission." *I.H.P.: International Health Programs Newsletter, 1,* 1ff.

Moultrup, D. J. (1990). *Husbands, Wives, and Lovers: The Emotional System of the Extramarital Affair.* New York: Guilford Press.

Muehlenhard, C. L. (1988). "Misinterpreted Dating Behaviors and the Risk of Date Rape." *Journal of Social and Clinical Psychology, 9*(1), 20–37.

Muehlenhard, C. L., & Cook, S. W. (1988). "Mens' Self-Reports of Unwanted Sexual Activity." *Journal of Sex Research, 24,* 58–72.

Muehlenhard, C. L., & Hollabaugh, L. C. (1988). "Do Women Sometimes Say No When They Mean Yes? The Prevalence and Correlates of Women's Token Resistance to Sex." *Journal of Personality and Social Psychology, 54,* 872–879.

Muehlenhard, C. L., & Linton, M. (1987). "Date Rape and Sexual Aggression in Dating Situations." *Journal of Consulting Psychology, 34,* 186–196.

Muehlenhard, C. L., & McCoy, M. L. (1991). "Double Standard/Double Bind." *Psychology of Women Quarterly, 15,* 447–461.

Muehlenhard, C. L., Ponch, I. G., Phelps, J. L., & Giusti, L. M. (1992). "Definitions of Rape: Scientific and Political Implications." *Journal of Social Issues, 48*(1), 23–44.

Muehlenhard, C. L., & Schrag, J. (1991). "Nonviolent Sexual Coercion." In A. Parrot & L. Bechhofer (Eds.), *Acquaintance Rape: The Hidden Crime.* New York: John Wiley.

Mueller, B. A., et al. (1992). "Risk Factors for Tubal Infertility: Influence of History of Prior Pelvic Inflammatory Disease." *Sexually Transmitted Diseases, 19*(1), 28–34.

Mulligan, T., & Moss, C. R. (1991). "Sexuality and Aging in Male Veterans: A Cross-Sectional Study of Interest, Ability, and Activity." *Archives of Sexual Behavior, 20*(1), 17–25.

Mulligan, T., & Palguta, R. (1991). "Sexual Interest, Activity, and Satisfaction Among Male Nursing Home Residents." *Archives of Sexual Behavior, 20*(2), 199–204.

Mulligan, T., Retchin, S. M., Chinchilli, V. M., & Bettinger, C. B. (1988). "The Role of Aging and Chronic Disease in Sexual Dysfunction." *Journal of the American Geriatrics Society, 36*(6), 520–524.

Mullins, L. L., Lynch, J., Orten, J., Youll, L. K., Verschraegen-Spae, Dypere, H., Speleman, F., Dhoult, M., & DePaepe, A. (1991). "Developing a Program to Assist Turner's Syndrome Patients and Families." *Social Work in Health Care, 16*(2), 69–79.

Muram, D., Miller, K., & Cutler, A. (1992). "Sexual Assault of the Elderly Victim." *Journal of Interpersonal Violence, 7*(1), 70–76.

Murnen, S. K., Perot, A., & Byrne, D. (1989). "Coping with Unwanted Sexual Activity: Normative Responses, Situational Determinants, and Individual Differences." *Journal of Sex Research, 26,* 85–106.

Murray, T. E. (1989). *The Language of Sadomasochism.* New York: Greenwood Press.

Murry, V. M. (1991). "Socio-Historical Study of Black Female Sexuality: Transition to First Coitus." In R. Staples (Ed.), *The Black Family* (4th ed.). Belmont, CA: Wadsworth.

Murstein, B. (1976). *Who Will Marry Whom: Theories and Research in Marital Choice.* New York: Springer.

Murstein, B. (1987). "A Clarification and Extension of the SVR Theory of Dyadic Pairing." *Journal of Marriage and the Family, 49,* 929–933.

Mydans, S. (1992, November 21). "Christian Conservatives Counting Hundreds of Gains in Local Votes." *The New York Times,* p. A1ff.

Nadelson, C. C. (1990). "Consequences of Rape: Clinical and Treatment Aspects." *Psychotherapy and Psychosomatics, 51*(4), 187–192.

Nadelson, C., & Sauzier, M. (1986). "Intervention Programs for Individual Victims and Their Families." In M. Lystad (Ed.), *Violence in the Home: Interdisciplinary Perspectives.* New York: Brunner/Mazel.

Nakamura, R. M., et al. (1988). "In Vitro Condom Testing." *IV International Conference on AIDS,* Stockholm, #6510.

National Victim Center. (1992). *Rape in America: A Report to the Nation.* Charleston, SC: Crime Victims Research and Treatment Center.

Nava, M. (1990). *How Town.* New York: Ballantine Books.

Navarro, M. (1992, November 23). "Trials and Triumphs Emerge for HIV-Infected Workers." *The New York Times,* pp. A1, A12.

Navarro, M. (1993, January 11). "Healthy, Gay, Guilt-Striken: AIDS' Toll on the Virus-Free." *The New York Times*, pp. A1, A16.

Neidigh, L., & Kinder, B. (1987). "The Use of Audiovisual Materials in Sex Therapy: A Critical Overview." *Journal of Sex and Marital Therapy*, 13(1), 64–72.

Nelson, K. E., Vlahov, D., Cohn, S., Odunmbaku, M., Lindsay, A., Antohony, J. C., & Hook, E. W. (1991). "Sexually Transmitted Diseases in a Population of Intravenous Drug Users: Association with Seropositivity to the Human Immunodeficiency Virus (HIV)." *Journal of Infectious Diseases*, 164(3), 457–463.

Nelson, R. (1988). "Nonoperatic Management of Impotence." *Journal of Urology*, 139, 2–5.

"Neonatal Herpes Is Preventable." (1984, February). *U.S.A. Today*, pp. 8–9.

Nestle, J. (1983). "The Fem Question." In C. Vance (Ed.), *Pleasure and Danger*. New York: Routledge & Kegan Paul.

Newcomb, M. (1979). "Cohabitation in America: An Assessment of Consequences." *Journal of Marriage and the Family*, 597–603.

Newcomb, M., & Bentler, P. (1980). "Assessment of Personality and Demographics Aspects of Cohabitation and Marital Success." *Journal of Personality Development*, 4(1), 11–24.

Newcomer, S., & Udry, R. (1985). "Oral Sex in an Adolescent Population." *Archives of Sexual Behavior*, 14(1), 41–46.

"New Policy Requires Abortion Training for Obstetrical Residents." (1995, March). *The Nation's Health*, p. 9.

Newton, N. (1955). *Maternal Emotions*. New York: Basic Books.

New York State Health Department (1992). "Methods of Personal Protection for Women to Reduce Transmission of HIV Through Vaginal Intercourse." Policy Statement, AIDS Institute.

NIAID/CDC. (1991). "U.S. Public Health Service National Conference: Women and HIV Infection." *Clinical Courier*, 9(6), 1–7.

Nichols, M. (1987). "Lesbian Sexuality: Issues and Developing Theory." In Boston Lesbian Psychologies Collective (Ed.), *Lesbian Psychologies: Explorations and Challenges*. Urbana, IL: University of Illinois Press.

Nichols, M. (1988). "Bisexuality in Women: Myths, Realities, and Implications for Therapy." Special Issue: Women and Sex Therapy. *Women and Therapy*, 7, 235–252.

Niebuhr, R. E., & Boyles, W. R. (1991). "Sexual Harassment of Military Personnel: An Examination of Power Differentials." Special Issue: Racial, Ethnic, and Gender Issues in the Military. *International Journal of Intercultural Relations*, 15, 445–457.

Nielson, J., & Wohlert, M. (1991). "Chromosome Abnormalities Found Among 34,910 Newborn Children: Results from a 13-Year Incidence Study in Arhus, Denmark." *Human Genetics*, 87(1), 81–83.

Nieman, L., et al. (1987). "The Progesterone Antagonist RU-486: A Potential New Contraceptive Agent." *New England Journal of Medicine*, 316(4), 187–191.

Nilsson Schonnesson, L. (1990). "Educational Requirements of Human Sexuality in the Counseling for and Prevention of Sexually Transmitted Diseases." *Seminars in Dermatology*, 9(2), 185–189.

Nock, S. (1987). "The Symbolic Meaning of Childbearing." *Journal of Family Issues*, 8(4), 373–393.

Noller, P. (1984). *Nonverbal Communication and Marital Interaction*. Oxford, England: Pergamon Press.

Noller, P., & Fitzpatrick, M. A. (1991). "Marital Communication." In A. Booth (Ed.), *Contemporary Families: Looking Forward, Looking Back*. Minneapolis, MN: National Council on Family Relations.

Norton, A. J. (1983). "Family Life Cycle: 1980." *Journal of Marriage and the Family*, 45, 267–275.

Nossiter, A. (1992, November 28). "Some Legal Experts See Intolerance as HIV and Sex are Linked to Crime." *The New York Times*, p. 6.

Notarius, C., & Johnson, J. (1982). "Emotional Expression in Husbands and Wives." *Journal of Marriage and the Family*, 44(2), 483–489.

Notman, M. T., & Lester, E. P. (1988). "Pregnancy: Theoretical Considerations." *Psychoanalytic Inquiry*, 8(2), 139–159.

Notzon, F. C., et al. (1987). "Comparisons of National Cesarean-Section Rates." *New England Journal of Medicine*, 316(7), 386–389.

Nugent, R., & Gramick, J. (1989). "Homosexuality: Protestant, Catholic, and Jewish Issues: A Fishbone Tale." *Journal of Homosexuality*, 18, 7–46.

Oakley, A. (1985). *Sex, Gender, and Society* (rev. ed.). New York: Harper & Row.

O'Carroll, R. (1989). "The Difficulty in Dealing with Deviance: An Illustrative Case Study." *Journal of Sex and Marital Therapy*, 4(2), 177–186.

Odent, M. (1984). *Birth Reborn*. New York: Pantheon.

Oehninger, S., & Alexander, N. J. (1991). "Male Infertility: The Focus Shifts to Sperm Manipulation." *Current Opinion in Obstetrics and Gynecology*, 3(2), 182–190.

O'Farrell, T. J., Choquette, K. A., & Birchler, G. R. (1991). "Sexual Satisfaction and Dissatisfaction in the Marital Relationships of Male Alcoholics Seeking Marital Therapy." *Journal of Studies on Alcohol*, 52(5), 441–447.

Ofman, U. S., & Auchincloss, S. S. (1992, August). "Sexual Dysfunction in Cancer Patients." *Current Opinion in Oncology*, 4(4), 605–613.

Okami, P. (1991). "Self-Reports of 'Positive' Childhood and Adolescent Sexual Contacts with Older Persons: An Exploratory Study." *Archives of Sexual Behavior*, 20(5), 437–457.

Olds, J. (1956). "Pleasure Centers in the Brain." *Scientific American*, 193, 105–116.

Olds, S. W. (1985). *The Eternal Garden: Seasons of Our Sexuality*. New York: Times Books.

Olshansky, E. F. (1992). "Redefining the Concepts of Success and Failure in Infertility Treatment." *Naacogs Clinical Issues in Perinatal and Women's Health Nursing*, 3(2), 343–346.

Olson, T., & Wallace, C. (1987). "Families, Decision-Making and Human Development." *Concerned Women of America*. Washington, DC.

Orbach, S. (1982). *Fat Is a Feminist Issue II: A Program to Conquer Compulsive Eating*. New York: Berkley Books.

O'Reilly, K. R., & Aral, S. O. (1985). "Adolescence and Sexual Behavior: Trends and Implications for STDs." *Journal of Adolescent Health Care*, 6(4), 262–270.

Orlofsky, J., & O'Heron, C. (1987). "Stereotypic and Nonstereotypic Sex Role Trait and Behavior Orientations: Implications for Personal Adjustment." *Journal of Personality and Social Psychology*, 52, 1034–1042.

Orten, J. L. (1990). "Coming Up Short: The Physical, Cognitive, and Social Effects of Turner's Syndrome." *Health and Social Work*, 15(2), 100–106.

Ortiz, M. E., & Croxatto, H. B. (1987). "The Mode of Action of IUDs." *Contraception*, 36(1), 37–53.

Ortiz, S., & Casas, J. M. (1990). "Birth Control and Low-Income Mexican-American Women: The Impact of Three Values." *Hispanic Journal of the Behavioral Sciences*, 12(1), 83–92.

Osborn, J. E. (1990). "Women and HIV/AIDS: The Silent Epidemic?" *SIECUS Report*, 19(2), 1–4.

Ostrow, D. G., Whitaker, R. E., Frasier, K., Cohen, C., Wan, J., Frank, C., & Fisher, E. (1991). "Racial Differences in Social Support and Mental Health in Men with HIV Infection: A Pilot Study." *AIDS Care*, 3(1), 55–62.

O'Sullivan, C. S. (1991). "Acquaintance Gang Rape on Campus." In A. Parrot & L. Bechhofer (Eds.), *Acquaintance Rape: The Hidden Crime*. New York: John Wiley.

O'Sullivan, L., & Byers, E. S. (1992). "College Students' Incorporation of Initiator and Restrictor Roles in Sexual Dating Interactions." *Journal of Sex Research, 29*(3), 435–446.

Padgett, V. R., Brislutz, J. A., & Neal, J. A. (1989). "Pornography, Erotica, and Attitudes Toward Women: The Effects of Repeated Exposure." *Journal of Sex Research, 26,* 479–491.

Padian, N. S., Shiboski, S. C., & Jewell, N. P. (1991). "Female-to-Male Transmission of Human Immunodeficiency Virus." *JAMA: Journal of the American Medical Association, 266*(12), 1664–1667.

Padilla, E. R., & O'Grady, K. E. (1987). "Sexuality among Mexican Americans: A Case of Sexual Stereotyping." *Journal of Personality and Social Psychology, 52,* 5–10.

Paludi, M. A. (1990). "Sociopsychological and Structural Factors Related to Women's Vocational Development." *Annals of the New York Academy of Sciences, 602,* 157–168.

Pan, L. Z., Sheppard, H. W., Winkelstein, W., & Levy, J. A. (1991). "Lack of Detection of Human Immunodeficiency Virus in Persistently Seronegative Homosexual Men with High or Medium Risk for Infection." *Journal of Infectious Diseases, 164*(5), 962–964.

Pang, S., Shlesinger, Y., Daar, E. S., Moudgil T., Ho, D. D., & Chen, I. S. (1992). "Rapid Generation of Sequence Variation During Primary HIV-1 Infection." *AIDS, 6*(5), 453–460.

Panuthos, C., & Romeo, C. (1984). *Ended Beginnings: Healing Childbearing Losses.* New York: Warner Books.

Panzarine, S., & Elster, A. B. (1983). "Coping in a Group of Expectant Adolescent Fathers: An Exploratory Study." *Journal of Adolescent Health Care, 4,* 117–120.

Parachini, A. (1987, February 3). "Survivorship: A New Movement Among Cancer Patients." *Los Angeles Times,* pp. 1, 2.

Parker, H., & Parker, S. (1984). "Cultural Rules, Rituals and Behavior Regulation." *American Anthropologist, 86*(3), 584–600.

Parker, H., & Parker, S. (1986). "Father-Daughter Sexual Child Abuse: An Emerging Perspective." *American Journal of Orthopsychiatry, 56*(4), 531–549.

Parker, P. (1983). "Motivation of Surrogate Mothers—Initial Findings." *American Journal of Psychiatry, 140*(1), 117–118.

Parker, R. G. (1991). *Bodies, Pleasures, and Passions.* Boston: Beacon Press.

Parrinder, G. (1980). *Sex in the World's Religions.* New York: Oxford University Press.

Parsons, T. (1955). "Family Structure and the Socialization of the Child." In T. Parsons & R. F. Bales (Eds.), *Family Socialization and Interaction Process.* Glencoe, IL: Free Press.

Patterson, C. J. (1992). "Children of Lesbian and Gay Parents." *Child Development, 63,* 1025–1042.

Patton, M. (1986). "Twentieth-Century Attitudes Toward Masturbation." *Journal of Religion and Health, 25*(4), 291–302.

Paul, J. P. (1984). "The Bisexual Identity: An Idea Without Social Recognition." *Journal of Homosexuality, 9,* 45–63.

Paul, J. P. (1993). "Childhood Cross-Gender Behavior and Adult Homosexuality: The Resurgence of Biological Models of Sexuality." *Journal of Homosexuality, 24*(3-4), 41–54.

Pauly, I., & Edgarton, M. (1986). "The Gender Identity Movement: A Growing Surgical-Psychiatric Liaison." *Archives of Sexual Behavior, 15*(4), 315–327.

Pauly, J. (1990). "Gender Identity Disorders: Evaluation and Treatment." *Journal of Sex Education and Therapy, 16*(1), 2–24.

Peacock, N. (1982). "Contraceptive Decision-Making Among Adolescent Girls." *Journal of Sex Education and Therapy, 8,* 31–34.

Pear, R. (1992, April 22). "U.S. Reports Rise in Low-Weight Births." *The New York Times,* p. A18.

Pear, R. (1993, February 7). "As AIDS Money Is Parceled Out, Political Questions." *The New York Times,* p. E3.

Pearson, L. (1992). "The Stigma of Infertility." *Nursing Times, 88*(1), 36–38.

Pelz, L., Sager, G., Hinkel, G. K., Kirchner, M., Kruger, C., & Verron, G. (1991). "Delayed Spontaneous Pubertal Growth Spurt in Girls with the Ullrich-Turner Syndrome." *American Journal of Medical Genetics, 40*(4), 401–405.

Peo, R. (1988). "Transvestism." In D. Dailey (Ed.), *The Sexually Unusual.* New York: Harrington Park Press.

Peplau, L. (1981). "What Homosexuals Want." *Psychology Today, 15*(3), 28–38.

Peplau, L. (1988). "Research on Homosexual Couples." In J. De Cecco (Ed.), *Gay Relationships.* New York: Haworth Press.

Peplau, L., et al. (1977). "Sexual Intimacy in Dating Relationships." *Journal of Social Issues, 33*(2), 86–109.

Peplau, L., & Cochran, S. (1988). "Value Orientations in the Intimate Relationships of Gay Men." In J. De Cecco (Ed.), *Gay Relationships.* New York: Haworth Press.

Peplau, L., & Gordon, S. (1982). "The Intimate Relationships of Lesbians and Gay Men." In E. Allgeier & N. McCormick (Eds.), *Gender Roles and Sexual Behavior.* Mountain View, CA: Mayfield.

Perez, E. (1990). "Why Women Wait to Be Tested for HIV Infection." *SIECUS Report, 19,* 6–7.

Perilstein, R., Lipper, S., & Friedman, L. J. (1991). "Three Cases of Paraphilias Responsive to Fluoxetine Treatment." *Journal of Clinical Psychology, 52*(4), 169–170.

Perkins, B., & Bennet, G. (1985). *Being a Prostitute: Prostitute Women and Prostitute Men.* Sydney, Australia: Allen & Unwin.

Perkins, J. L. (1991). "Primary Prevention of Adolescent Pregnancy." *Birth Defects Original Article Series, 27,* 9–28.

Perlez, J. (1990, January 15). "Puberty Rite for Girls Is Bitter Issue Across Africa." *The New York Times,* p. A4.

Perlman, D. (1990, March 5). "Brave New Babies." *San Francisco Chronicle,* p. 3ff.

Perry, J. D., & Whipple, B. (1981). "Pelvic Muscle Strength of Female Ejaculators: Evidence in Support of a New Theory of Orgasm." *Journal of Sex Research, 17*(1), 22–39.

Persky, H., et al. (1982). "The Relation of Plasma Androgen Levels to Sexual Behavior and Attitudes of Women." *Psychosomatic Medicine, 44,* 157–173.

Person, E. S., Terestman, N., Myers, W. A., & Goldberg, E. L. (1989). "Gender Differences in Sexual Behaviors and Fantasies in a College Population." *Journal of Sex and Marital Therapy, 15*(3), 187–214.

Petchesky, R. P. (1990). *Abortion and Woman's Choice: The State, Sexuality, and Reproductive Freedom.* (rev. ed.). Boston: Northeastern University Press.

Peters, K. (1992, October 15). "Gay Activists Denounce NAMBLA, Attempt to Highlight Differences." *Spartan Daily,* p. 1.

Peters, S., et al. (1986). "Prevalence of Child Sexual Abuse." In D. Finkelhor (Ed.), *Sourcebook on Child Sexual Abuse.* Newbury Park, CA: Sage Publications.

Peterson, H., et al. (1983). "Deaths Attributable to Tubal Sterilization in the United States, 1977–1981." *American Journal of Obstetrics and Gynecology, 146,* 131ff.

Peterson, J., Kretchmer, A., Nellis, B., Lever, J., & Hertz, R. (1983, March). "The *Playboy* Readers Sex Survey, Part 2." *Playboy,* 90–92, 178–184.

Peterson, J. L. (1992). "Black Men and Their Same-Sex Desires and Behaviors." In G. Herdt (Ed.), *Gay Culture in America: Essays from the Field.* Boston: Beacon Press.

Petit, C. (1990, May 9). "New Study to Ask Why So Many Infants Die." *San Francisco Chronicle,* p. 3.

Petit, C. (1992, April 2). "Why Both Parents Should Be Tested for Herpes." *San Francisco Chronicle,* p. D7.

Pfaus, J., Myronuk, & Jacobs. (1986). "Soundtrack Contents and Depicted Sexual Violence." *Archives of Sexual Behavior, 15*(3), 231–237.

Phelps, T. M., & Winternitz, H. (1992). *Capitol Games*. New York: Hyperion Books.

Phillips, G., & Over, R. (1992). "Adult Sexual Orientation in Relation to Memories of Childhood Gender Conforming and Gender Nonconforming Behaviors." *Archives of Sexual Behavior, 21*(6), 543–558.

Pies, C. (1987). "Considering Parenthood: Psychological Issues for Gay Men and Lesbians Choosing Alternative Fertilization." In F. W. Bozett (Ed.), *Gay and Lesbian Parents*. New York: Praeger.

Pincus, S. (1988). "Sexuality in the Mentally Retarded Patient." *American Family Physician, 37*(2), 319–323.

Pines, A., & Aronson, E. (1983). "Antecedents, Correlates, and Consequences of Sexual Jealousy." *Journal of Personality, 51*(1), 108–136.

Plato. (1961). "Protagoras." In E. Hamilton & H. Cairns (Eds.), *The Collected Dialogues of Plato*. New York: Bollengen Foundation.

Plummer, W., & Nelson, M. (1991, August 26). "A Mother's Priceless Gift." *People*, p. 18.

Pogrebin, L. C. (1982, February). "Are Men Discovering the Joys of Fatherhood?" *Ms.*, pp. 41–46.

Pogrebin, L. C. (1983). *Family Politics*. New York: McGraw-Hill.

Polit-O'Hara, D., & Kahn, J. (1985). "Communication and Contraceptive Practices in Adolescent Couples." *Adolescence, 20*(77), 33–43.

Pomeroy, W. (1972). *Dr. Kinsey and the Kinsey Institute*. New York: Harper & Row.

Pomice, E. (1990, April 2). "A Businesslike Approach to AIDS." *U.S. News & World Report*, p. 4.

Ponticas, Y. (1992). "Sexual Aversion Versus Hypoactive Sexual Desire: A Diagnostic Challenge." *Psychiatric Medicine, 10*(2), 273–281.

Popovich, P. M., et al. (1986). "Assessing the Incidence and Perceptions of Sexual Harassment Behaviors Among American Undergraduates." *Journal of Psychology, 120*, 387–396.

Popovich, P. M., et al. (1992). "Perceptions of Sexual Harassment as a Function of Sex of Rater and Incident Form and Consequence." *Sex Roles, 27*(11-1), 609–625.

Population Crisis Committee. (1985). "Issues in Contraceptive Development." *Population, 15*(3), 456ff.

Potterat, J. J., et al. (1985). "Gonorrhea as a Social Disease." *Sexually Transmitted Diseases, 12*, 25–32.

Potterat, J. J., Phillips, L., Rothenberg, R. B., & Darrow, W. V. (1985). "On Becoming a Prostitute: An Exploratory Case-Comparison Study." *Journal of Sex Research, 21*(3), 329–335.

Potterat, J. J., Woodhouse, D. E., Muth, J. B., & Muth, S. Q. (1990). "Estimating the Prevalence and Career Longevity of Prostitute Women." *Journal of Sex Research, 27*, 233–243.

Pozo, C., et al. (1992). "Effects of Mastectomy Versus Lumpectomy on Emotional Adjustment to Breast Cancer: A Prospective Study of the First Year Postsurgery." *Journal of Clinical Oncology, 10*(8), 1292–1298.

PPFA [Planned Parenthood Federation of America]. (1985, November). "They Did It 9000 Times on Television Last Year, How Come Nobody Got Pregnant?" *San Francisco Chronicle*, p. 14.

Pratt, C., & Schmall, V. (1989). "College Students' Attitudes Toward Elderly Sexual Behavior: Implications for Family Life Education." *Family Relations, 38*, 137–141.

Press, A. (1992). "Class, Gender, and the Female Viewer: Women's Responses to 'Dynasty'." In *Television and Women's Culture: The Politics of the Popular*. Newbury Park, CA: Sage Publications.

Price, D. (1993, January 14). "Twin Study Links Genetics, Gayness Closer." *San Jose Mercury News*, p. 2.

Price, J. (1982). "Who Wants to Have Children? And Why?" In J. Rosenfeld (Ed.), *Relationships: The Marriage and Family Reader*. Glenview, IL: Scott, Foresman.

Price, J. H., & Miller, P. A. (1984). "Sexual Fantasies of Black and White College Students." *Psychological Reports, 54*, 1007–1014.

Priest, R. (1992). "Child Sexual Abuse Histories Among African-American College Students: A Preliminary Study." *American Journal of Orthopsychiatry, 62*(3), 475–477.

Prober, C., et al. (1987). "Low Risk of Herpes Simplex Virus Infections in Neonates Exposed to the Virus at the Time of Vaginal Delivery to Mothers with Recurrent Genital Herpes Simplex Virus Infections." *New England Journal of Medicine, 316*, 129–138.

Project Inform. (1990a, March 27). "AZT—Retrovir." *Project Inform Fact Sheet*, 1–4.

Project Inform. (1990b, June 14). "ddI—Dideoxyinosine (VIDEX)." *Project Inform Fact Sheet*, 1–2.

Project Inform. (1991, May 1). "ddC—Dideocyctidine—HIVID." *Project Inform Fact Sheet*, 1–2.

Project Inform. (1992). "The Myth of 'Too Much Spending on AIDS'." *Project Inform Fact Sheet*, 1–2.

Pruett, K. (1987). *The Nurturing Father: Journey Toward the Complete Man*. New York: Warner Books.

Pryor, J. B., & Day, J. D. (1988). "Interpretations of Sexual Harassment: An Attributional Analysis." *Sex Roles, 18*(7-8), 405–417.

Puech-Leao, P. (1992). "Venous Surgery in Erectile Dysfunction." *Urologia Internationalis, 49*(1), 29–32.

Puglisi, J. T., & Jackson, D. W. (1981). "Sex Role Identity and Self-Esteem in Adulthood." *Journal of Aging and Human Development, 12*, 129–138.

Quackenbush, R. L. (1991). "Attitudes of College Men Toward Women and Rape." *Journal of College Students Development, 32*, 376–377.

Quadagno, D., et al. (1991). "Women at Risk for Human Immunodeficiency Virus." *Journal of Psychology and Human Sexuality, 4*(3), 97–110.

Quétel, C. (1990). *History of Syphilis*. Cambridge, England: Polity Press.

Raboch, J., & Raboch, J. (1992). "Infrequent Orgasms in Women." *Journal of Sex and Marital Therapy, 18*(3), 114–120.

Radway, J. A. (1984). *Reading the Romance*. Chapel Hill, NC: University of North Carolina Press.

Raisbaum, H. (1986). "El Rol Sexual Femenino en los Medios Comunicacion Masiva: Un Estudio Comparativo de Telenovelas Mexicanas y Estadounidenses." *Revista Mexicana de Psicología, 3*(2), 188–196.

Ramey, E. (1972). "Men's Cycles." *Ms.*, pp. 8ff.

Rando, R. (1988). "Human Papillomavirus: Implications for Clinical Medicine." *Annals of Internal Medicine, 108*, 628–630.

Randolph, E. (1988, March 9). "Critics Say Medical Journals Would Have Rejected AIDS Study." *Washington Post*, p. A7.

Rangaswamy, K. (1987). "Treatment of Voyeurism by Behavior Therapy." *Child Psychiatry Quarterly, 20*, 3–4.

Rao, K., et al. (1992). "Child Sexual Abuse of Asians Compared with Other Populations." *Journal of the American Academy of Child and Adolescent Psychiatry, 31*(5), 880–887.

Ratner, E. (1988). "A Model for the Treatment of Lesbian and Gay Alcohol Abusers." *Alcoholism Treatment Quarterly, 5*(1-2), 25–46.

Raven, B., et al. (1975). "The Bases of Conjugal Power." In R. Cromwell & D. Olson (Eds.), *Power in Families*. New York: Halstead Press.

Ravinder, S. (1987). "Androgyny: Is It Really the Product of Educated Middle-Class Western Societies?" *Journal of Cross-Cultural Psychology, 18*(2), 208–220.

Reamy, K., & White, S. (1987). "Sexuality in the Puerperium: A Review." *Archives of Sexual Behavior, 16*(2), 165–187.

Redfield, R. R., & Burke, D. S. (1988). "HIV Infection: The Clinical Picture." *Scientific American*, 90ff.

Reece, R. (1988). "Special Issues in the Etiologies and Treatments of Sexual Problems Among Gay Men." *Journal of Homosexuality, 15*, 43–57.

Reed, D., & Weinberg, M. (1984). "Premarital Coitus: Developing and Established Sexual Scripts." *Social Psychology Quarterly, 47*(2), 129–138.

Reeves, W. C., et al. (1989). "Human Papillomavirus Infection and Cervical Cancer in Latin America." *New England Journal of Medicine, 320*, 1437.

Reichel-Dolmatoff, G. (1971). *Amazonian Cosmos*. Chicago: University of Chicago Press.

Reid, P., & Comas-Diaz, L. (1990). "Gender and Ethnicity: Perspectives on Dual Status." *Sex Roles, 22*(7), 397–408.

Reid, R. (1986). "Premenstrual Syndrome: A Time for Introspection." *American Journal of Obstetrics and Gynecology, 155*(5), 921–926.

Reilly, M. E., et al. (1992). "Tolerance for Sexual Harassment Related to Self-Reported Sexual Victimization." *Gender and Society, 6*(1), 122–138.

Reinisch, J. (1986, August 26). "The Kinsey Report." *San Francisco Chronicle*, p. 16.

Reinisch, J., Ziemba-Davis, M., & Saunders, S. (1991). "Hormonal Contributions to Sexually Dimorphic Behavioral Development in Humans." *Psychoneuroendocrinology, 16*, 213–278.

Reiss, I. (1967). *The Social Context of Premarital Sexual Permissiveness*. New York: Irvington.

Reiss, I. (1980). "A Multivariate Model of the Determinants of Extramarital Sexual Permissiveness." *Journal of Marriage and the Family, 42*, 395–411.

Reiss, I. (1986). *Journey into Sexuality: An Exploratory Voyage*. Englewood Cliffs, NJ: Prentice-Hall.

Reiss, I. (1989). "Society and Sexuality: A Sociological Explanation." In K. McKinney & S. Sprecher (Eds.), *Human Sexuality: The Societal and Interpersonal Context*. Norwood, NJ: Ablex.

Reiss, I. (1990). *An End to Shame: Shaping Our Next Sexual Revolution*. Buffalo, NY: Prometheus Books.

Renshaw, D. (1988). "Short-Term Therapy for Sexual Dysfunction: Brief Counseling to Manage Vaginismus." *Clinical Practice in Sexuality, 6*(5), 23–29.

Renshaw, D. C. (1988). "Young Children's Sex Play: Counseling the Parents." *Medical Aspects of Human Sexuality, 22*(12), 68–72.

Resnick, H. S., et al. (1991). "Assessment of Rape-Related Post-traumatic Stress Disorder: Stressor and Symptom Dimensions." *Psychological Assessment, 3*(4), 561–572.

Resnick, H. S. (1972). "Eroticized Repetitive Hangings: A Form of Self-Destructive Behavior." *American Journal of Psychotherapy, 26*(1), 4–21.

Retik, A. B., & Bauer, S. B. (1984). "Infertility Related to DES Exposure in Utero: Reproductive Problems in the Male." In M. Mazor & H. Simons (Eds.), *Infertility: Medical, Emotional, and Social Considerations*. New York: Human Sciences Press.

Reuben, D. (1969). *Everything You Ever Wanted to Know About Sex—But Were Afraid to Ask*. New York: David McKay.

Rice, R. J., Roberts, P. L., Handsfield, H. H., & Holmes, K. K. (1991). "Sociodemographic Distribution of Gonorrhea Incidence: Implications for Prevention and Behavioral Research." *American Journal of Public Health, 81*(10), 1252–1258.

Rice, S. (1989). "Sexuality and Intimacy for Aging Women: A Changing Perspective." *Journal of Women and Aging, 1*(1-3), 245–264.

Rich, A. (1983). "Compulsory Heterosexuality and Lesbian Existence." In A. Snitow et al. (Eds.), *Powers of Desire: The Politics of Sexuality*. New York: Monthly Review Press.

Richards, E. P., & Bross, D. C. (1990). "Legal Aspects of STD Control: Public Duties and Private Rights." In K. K. Holmes et al. (Eds.), *Sexually Transmitted Diseases* (2nd ed.). New York: McGraw-Hill.

Richardson, D. (1983). "The Dilemma of Essentiality in Homosexual Theory." *Journal of Homosexuality, 9*(2-3), 79–90.

Ricketts, W., & Actenberg, R. (1989). "Adoption and Foster Parenting for Lesbians and Gay Men: Creating New Traditions in Family." *Marriage and Family Review, 14*, 83–118.

Rieff, P. (1979). *Freud: The Mind of a Moralist*. Chicago: University of Chicago Press.

Rieve, J. E. (1989). "Sexuality and the Adult with Acquired Physical Disability." *Nursing Clinics of North America, 24*(1), 265–276.

Riley, A. J. (1991). "Sexuality and the Menopause." *Sexual and Marital Therapy, 6*(2), 135–146.

Rio, L. M. (1991). "Psychological and Sociological Research and the Decriminalization or Legalization of Prostitution." *Archives of Sexual Behavior, 20*(2), 205–218.

Riseden, A. D., & Hort, B. E. (1992). "A Preliminary Investigation of the Sexual Component of the Male Stereotype." Unpublished manuscript.

Roan, S. (1994, October 31). "Young, Active, and Infected." *San Francisco Chronicle*, p. D-8.

Roberts, E. (1980). (Ed.). *Childhood Sexual Learning: The Unwritten Curriculum*. Cambridge, MA: Ballinger.

Roberts, E. (1982). "Television and Sexual Learning in Childhood." In *National Institute of Mental Health, Television and Behavior*. Washington, DC: U.S. Government Printing Office.

Roberts, E. (1983). "Childhood Sexual Learning: The Unwritten Curriculum." In C. Davis (Ed.), *Challenges in Sexual Science*. Philadelphia: Society for the Scientific Study of Sex.

Roberts, L., & Krokoff, L. (1990). "A Time Series Analysis of Withdrawal, Hostility, and Displeasure in Satisfied and Dissatisfied Marriages." *Journal of Marriage and the Family, 52*(1), 95–105.

Roberts, M. C., Alexander, K., & Fanurik, D. (1990). "Evaluation of Commercially Available Materials to Prevent Child Sexual Abuse." *American Psychologist, 45*(6), 782–783.

Robertson, D. (1990). "Counseling Women Who Have Been Sexually Assaulted." *Issues in Criminological and Legal Psychology, 19*, 46–53.

Robertson, M. M. (1992, April). "Lesbians as an Invisible Minority in the Health Services Arena." *Health Care for Women International, 13*(2), 155–163.

Robinson, B. (1987). *Teenage Fathers*. Lexington, MA: Lexington Books.

Robinson, B. (1988). "Teenage Pregnancy from the Father's Perspective." *American Journal of Orthopsychiatry, 58*(1), 46–51.

Robinson, H. (1992, December 14). "Sex, Marriage, and Divorce." *Christianity Today, 36*(15), 29–33.

Robinson, P. (1976). *The Modernization of Sex*. New York: Harper & Row.

Robinson, P. (1983). "The Sociological Perspective." In R. Weg (Ed.), *Sexuality in the Later Years: Roles and Behavior*. New York: Academic Press.

Rodabaugh, B., & Austin, M. (1981). *Sexual Assault*. New York: Garland Press.

Roen, P. (1974). *Male Sexual Health*. New York: William Morrow.

Roenrich, L., & Kinder, B. N. (1991). "Alcohol Expectancies and Male Sexuality: Review and Implications for Sex Therapy." *Journal of Sex and Marital Therapy, 17*, 45–54.

Rogers, M. F., et al. (1990). "Lack of Transmission of Human Immunodeficiency Virus from Infected Children to Their Household Contacts." *Pediatrics, 85*(2), 210–214.

Rogers, P. A., Murphy, C. R., Leeton, J., Hoise, M. J., & Beaton, L. (1992). "Turner's Syndrome Patients Lack Tight Junctions Between Uterine Epithelial Cells." *Human Reproduction, 7(6)*, 883–885.

Rogers, S. M., & Turner, C. F. (1991). "Male-Male Sexual Contact in the U.S.A.: Findings from Five Sample Surveys, 1970–1990." *Journal of Sex Research, 28(4)*, 491–519.

Romanowski, B., & Piper, G. (1988). "Sexually Transmitted Diseases: An Overview." Special Issue: Sociopsychological Aspects of Sexually Transmitted Diseases. *Journal of Social Work and Human Sexuality, 6(2)*, 7–20.

Romberg, R. (1985). *Circumcision: The Painful Dilemma*. South Hadley, MA: Bergin and Garvey.

Rome, E. (1992). "Anatomy and Physiology of Sexuality and Reproduction." In Boston Women's Health Book Collective, *The New Our Bodies, Ourselves*. New York: Simon & Schuster.

Rongen-Westelaken, C., Vanes, A., Wit, J., Otten, B. J., & Demuink Keizer-Schrama, C. (1992). "Growth Hormone Therapy in Turner's Syndrome." *American Journal of Diseases of Children, 146(7)*, 817–820.

Rooks, J., et al. (1989). "Outcomes of Care in Birth Centers." *New England Journal of Medicine, 321*, 1804–1811.

Roopnarine, J. L., & Mounts, N. S. (1987). "Current Theoretical Issues in Sex Roles and Sex Typing." In D. B. Carter (Ed.), *Current Conceptions of Sex Roles and Sex Typing: Theory and Research*. New York: Praeger.

Roos, P., & Cohen, L. (1987). "Sex Roles and Social Support as Moderates of Life Stress Adjustment." *Journal of Personality and Social Psychology, 52(3)*, 576–585.

Roper, W. L., Petersen, H. B., & Curran, J. W. (1993). "Commentary: Condoms and HIV/STD Prevention—Clarifying the Message." *American Journal of Public Health, 83(4)*, 501–503.

Roscoe, W. (1991). *The Zuni Man/Woman*. Albuquerque, NM: University of New Mexico Press.

Rosegrant, J. (1986). "Contributions to Psychohistory: Fetish Symbols in *Playboy* Centerfolds." *Psychological Reports, 59(2, Part 1)*, 623–631.

Rosen, M. P., et al. (1991). "Cigarette Smoking: An Independent Risk Factor for Artherosclerosis in the Hypogastric-Cavernous Arterial Bed of Men with Arteriogenic Impotence." *Journal of Urology, 145(4)*, 759–776.

Rosen, R. (1982). *The Lost Sisterhood: Prostitution in America, 1900–1918*. Baltimore, MD: Johns Hopkins University Press.

Rosenberg, M. J., Davidson, A. J., Chen, J. H., Judson, F. N., & Douglas, J. M. (1992). "Barrier Contraceptives and Sexually Transmitted Diseases in Women: A Comparison of Female-Dependent Methods and Condoms." *American Journal of Public Health, 82(5)*, 669–674.

Rosenblum, S., & Faber, M. (1979). "The Adolescent Sexual Asphyxia Syndrome." *Journal of the American Academy of Psychiatry, 18(3)*, 546–558.

Rosenfeld, R. G., Frane, J., Attie, L. M., Brasel, J. A., Bursten, S., & Clarer. (1992). "Six-Year Results of a Randomized, Prospective Trial of Human Growth Hormone and Oxandrolone in Turner Syndrome." *Journal of Pediatrics, 121(1)*, 49–55.

Rosenstock, I. (1974). "Historical Origins of the Health Belief Model." *Health Education Monographs, 2*, 328–335.

Rosenthal, E. (1990a, February 4). "When a Pregnant Woman Drinks." *The New York Times Magazine*, pp. 30ff.

Rosenthal, E. (1990b, August 28). "The Spread of AIDS: A Mystery Unravels." *The New York Times*, pp. B5–6.

Rosenthal, E. (1992, May 26). "Cost of High-Tech Fertility: Too Many Tiny Babies." *The New York Times*, pp. B5, B7.

Rosenzweig, J. M., & Dailey, D. M. (1989). "Dyadic Adjustment/ Sexual Satisfaction in Women and Men as a Function of Psychological Sex Role Self-Perception." *Journal of Sex and Marital Therapy, 15*, 42–56.

Rosman, J., & Resnick, P. J. (1989). "Sexual Attraction to Corpses: A Psychiatric Review of Necrophilia." *Bulletin of the American Academy of Psychiatry and the Law, 17(2)*, 153–163.

Ross, M. (1983a). "Femininity, Masculinity, and Sexual Orientation." *Journal of Homosexuality, 9(1)*, 27–36.

Ross, M. (1983b). "Homosexuality and Sex Roles: A Re-Evaluation." *Journal of Homosexuality, 9(1)*, 1–6.

Ross, M. W., & Need, J. A. (1989). "Effects of Adequacy of Gender Reassignment Surgery on Psychological Adjustment: A Follow-Up of Fourteen Male-to-Female Patients." *Archives of Sexual Behavior, 18(2)*, 145–153.

Ross, M. W., Wodak, A., Gold, J., & Miller, M. E. (1992). "Differences Across Sexual Orientation on HIV Risk Behaviors in Injecting Drug Users." *AIDS Care, 4(2)*, 139–148.

Rossignol, A. M., et al. (1989). "Tea and Premenstrual Syndrome in the People's Republic of China." *American Journal of Public Health, 79*, 67–69.

Roth, P. (1969). *Portnoy's Complaint*. New York: Random House.

Rothenberg, R. (1983). "The Geography of Gonorrhea." *American Journal of Epidemiology, 117(6)*, 688–694.

Rothenberg, R. B., & Potterat, J. J. (1990). "Strategies for Management of Sex Partners." In K. K. Holmes et al. (Eds.), *Sexually Transmitted Diseases* (2nd ed.). New York: McGraw-Hill.

Rotherman, M., & Weiner, N. (1983). "Androgyny, Stress, and Satisfaction." *Sex Roles, 9*, 151–158.

Rothschild, B. S., Fagan, P. J., & Woodall, C. (1991). "Sexual Functioning of Female Eating-Disordered Patients." *International Journal of Eating Disorders, 10*, 389–394.

Rotolo, J., & Lynch, J. (1991). "Penile Cancer: Curable with Early Detection." *Hospital Practice*, 131–138.

Rowan, E. L. (1988). "Pedophilia." In D. Dailey (Ed.), *The Sexually Unusual*. New York: Harrington Park Press.

Rowan, E. L. (1989). "Masturbation According to the Boy Scout Handbook." *Journal of Sex Education and Therapy, 15(2)*, 77–81.

Rowan, R., & Gillette, P. (1973). *Your Prostate*. New York: Doubleday.

Rowland, R. (1987). "Technology and Motherhood: Reproductive Choice Reconsidered." *Signs: Journal of Women in Culture and Society, 12(3)*, 512–528.

Rubenstein, C., & Tavris, C. (1987, September). "Special Survey Results: 26,000 Women Reveal the Secrets of Intimacy." *Redbook*, pp. 147–149ff.

Rubin, A. M., & Adams, J. R. (1986). "Outcomes of Sexually Open Marriages." *Journal of Sex Research, 22*, 311–319.

Rubin, L. (1976). *Worlds of Pain*. New York: Basic Books.

Rubin, L. (1990). *Erotic Wars*. New York: Farrar, Straus, & Giroux.

Rubin, R. T., Reinisch, J. M., & Haskett, R. F. (1981). "Postnatal Gonadal Steroid Effects on Human Behavior." *Science, 211*, 1318–1324.

Rubin, Z. (1970). "Measurement of Romantic Love." *Journal of Personality and Social Psychology, 16*, 265–273.

Rubin, Z. (1973). *Liking and Loving*. New York: Holt, Rinehart & Winston.

Rubin, Z., Provenzano, F., & Luria, Z. (1974). "The Eye of the Beholder: Parents' View of Sex of Newborn." *American Journal of Orthopsychiatry, 44*, 512–519.

Ruble, D. N. (1977). "Premenstrual Syndrome: A Reinterpretation." *Science, 197*, 291–292.

Rudolph, J. (1989a). "Effects of a Workshop on Mental Health Practitioners' Attitudes Toward Homosexuality and Counseling Effectiveness." *Journal of Counseling and Development, 68(1)*, 81–85.

Rudolph, J. (1989b). "The Impact of Contemporary Ideology and AIDS on the Counseling of Gay Clients." *Counseling and Values, 33*, 96–108.

Rush, D., et al. (1988). "The National WIC Evaluation." *American Journal of Clinical Nutrition, 48*(2), 439–483.

Rush, F. (1980). "Child Pornography." In L. Lederer (Ed.), *Take Back the Night: Women on Pornography*. New York: William Morrow.

Russell, D. (1984). *Sexual Exploitation: Rape, Child Sexual Abuse, and Workplace Harassment*. Newbury Park, CA: Sage Publications.

Russell, D. E. H. (1986). *The Secret Trauma: Incest in the Lives of Girls and Women*. New York: Basic Books.

Russell, D. E. H. (1990). *Rape in Marriage* (rev. ed.). Bloomington, IN: Indiana University Press.

Russell, S. (1991, December 3). "Women Fight Breast Cancer and the Health Care System." *San Francisco Chronicle*, pp. A1, A10.

Russo, N. F., Horn, J. D., & Schwartz, R. (1992). "U.S. Abortions in Context: Selected Characteristics." *Journal of Social Issues, 48*(3), 183–202.

Russo, V. (1987). *The Celluloid Closet*. New York: Harper & Row.

Safilios-Rothschild, C. (1970). "The Study of the Family Power Structure." *Journal of Marriage and the Family, 32*, 539–543.

Safilios-Rothschild, C. (1976). "Family Sociology or Wives' Sociology? A Cross-Cultural Examination of Decision-Making." *Journal of Marriage and the Family, 38*, 355–362.

Salgado de Snyder, V. N., Cervantes, R., & Padilla, A. (1990). "Gender and Ethnic Differences in Psychosocial Stress and Generalized Distress Among Hispanics." *Sex Roles, 22*(7), 441–453.

Salholz, E. (1992, August 10). "Deepening Shame." *Newsweek*, pp. 30–36.

Salovey, P., & Rodin, J. (1991). "Provoking Jealousy and Envy: Domain Relevance and Self-Esteem Threat." *Journal of Social and Clinical Psychology, 10*(4), 395–413.

Salsbury, K., & Johnson, E. (1981). *The Indispensable Cancer Handbook*. New York: Seaview Books.

Sampson, R. (1966). *The Problem of Power*. New York: Pantheon.

Samuels, M., & Samuels, N. (1986). *The Well Pregnancy Book*. New York: Summit Books.

Samuels, S., & Smith, M. (Eds.). (1993). *Condoms in the Schools*. Menlo Park, CA: Henry J. Kaiser Family Foundation.

Sanday, P. (1990). *Fraternity Gang Rape: Sex, Brotherhood and Privilege on Campus*. New York: New York University Press.

Sanders, J., & Robinson, W. (1979). "Talking and Not Talking About Sex: Male and Female Vocabulary." *Journal of Communication, 29*(2), 22–30.

Sanders, S. A., Reinisch, J. M., & McWhirter, D. P. (1990). "Homosexuality/Heterosexuality: An Overview." In D. P. McWhirter, S. A. Sanders, & J. M. Reinisch (Eds.), *Homosexuality/Heterosexuality: Concepts of Sexual Orientation*. New York: Oxford University Press.

San Jose Mercury News (1995, January 21). "Contraceptive Couldn't Pass FDS Inspection."

Santrock, J. (1983). *Life-Span Development*. Dubuque, IA. W. C. Brown.

Sarrel, L., & Sarrel, P. (1984). *Sexual Turning Points: The Seven Stages of Adult Sexuality*. New York: Macmillan.

Sarrel, P. M. (1990). "Sexuality and Menopause." *Obstetrics and Gynecology, 75* (4 Suppl.), 26S–30S.

Sarrell, P. M., & Johnson, W. H. (1982). "Sexual Molestation of Men by Women." *Archives of Sexual Behavior, 11*, 117–131.

Sarrel, P. M., Rousseau, M., Mazure, C., & Glazer, W. (1990). "Ovarian Steroids and the Capacity to Function at Home and in the Workplace. Multidisciplinary Perspectives on Menopause." *Annals of the New York Academy of Sciences, 592*, 156–161, 185–192.

Sarton, M. (1980). *Recovering: A Journal*. New York: Norton.

Satterfield, S. (1988). "Transsexualism." In D. Dailey (Ed.), *The Sexually Unusual*. New York: Harrington Park Press.

Saunders, E. (1989). "Life-Threatening Autoerotic Behavior: A Challenge for Sex Educators and Therapists." *Journal of Sex Education and Therapy, 15*(2), 77–81.

Saunders, E. B., & Awad, G. (1991). "Male Adolescent Sexual Offenders: Exhibitionism and Obscene Phone Calls." *Child Psychiatry and Human Development, 21*(3), 169–178.

Savin-Williams, R., & Rodriguez, R. G. (1993). "A Developmental, Clinical Perspective on Lesbian, Gay Male, and Bisexual Youths." In T. P. Gullotta et al. (Eds.), *Adolescent Sexuality*. Newbury Park, CA: Sage Publications.

Saviteer, S. M., White, G. C., & Cohen, M. S. (1985). "HTLV-III Exposure During Cardiopulmonary Resuscitation." *New England Journal of Medicine, 313*, 1607.

Savitz, L., & Rosen, L. (1988). "The Sexuality of Prostitutes: Sexual Enjoyment Reported by 'Streetwalkers'." *Journal of Sex Research, 24*, 200–208.

Sayers, J. (1991). *Mothers of Psychoanalysis*. New York: Norton.

Scanzoni, J. (1979). "Social Processes and Power in Families." In W. Burr et al. (Eds.), *Contemporary Theories About the Family, Vol. I*. New York: Free Press.

Schaap, C., Buunk, B., & Kerkstra, A. (1988). "Marital Conflict Resolutions." In P. Noller & M. A. Fitzpatrick (Eds.), *Perspectives on Marital Interaction*. Philadelphia: Multilingual Matters.

Schafer, J., & Brown, S. A. (1991). "Marijuana and Cocaine Effect Expectancies and Drug Use Patterns." *Journal of Consulting and Clinical Psychology, 59*(4), 558–565.

Schatzin, A., et al. (1987). "Alcohol Consumption and Breast Cancer in the Epidemiologic Follow-Up Study of the First National Health and Nutrition Examination Survey." *New England Journal of Medicine, 316*(1), 1169–1173.

Scherer, Y. K., Wu, Y. W., & Haughey, B. P. (1991). "AIDS and Homophobia Among Nurses." *Journal of Homosexuality, 21*(4), 17–27.

Schiavi, R. C., Schreiner-Engle, P., Mandeli, J., Schanzer, J., & Cohen, E. (1990). "Chronic Alcoholism and Male Sexual Dysfunction." *Journal of Sex and Marital Therapy, 16*(1), 23–33.

Schinke, S. P., Botvin, G. J., Orlandi, M. A., Schilling, R. F., & Gordon, A. N. (1990). "African-American and Hispanic-American Adolescents, HIV Infection, and Preventative Intervention." *AIDS Education and Prevention, 2*(4), 305–312.

Schlesselman, J. J. (1990). "Oral Contraception and Breast Cancer." *American Journal of Obstetrics and Gynecology, 163*(4:2), 1379–1387.

Schlesselman, J. J., et al. (1988). "Breast Cancer in Relation to Early Use of Oral Contraceptives: No Evidence of a Latent Effect." *JAMA: Journal of the American Medical Association, 259*, 1828–1833.

Schmalz, J. (1993, January 31). "Homosexuals Wake to See a Referendum: It's on Them." *The New York Times*, p. E1.

Schmidt, C. W. (1992). "Changes in Terminology for Sexual Disorders in DSM-IV." *Psychiatric Medicine, 10*(2), 247–255.

Schmitt, E. (1990, September 12). "2 Out of 3 Women in Military Study Report Sexual Harassment Incidents." *The New York Times*, p. A12.

Schneck, M. E., et al. (1990). "Low-Income Adolescents and Their Infants: Dietary Findings and Health Outcomes." *Journal of the American Dietetic Association, 90*(4), 555–558.

Schover, L. R., Fife, M., & Gershenson, D. M. (1989). "Sexual Dysfunction and Treatment for Early Stage Cervical Cancer." *Cancer, 63*(1), 204–212.

Schur, E. (1980). *The Politics of Deviance: Stigma Contests and the Uses of Power*. Englewood Cliffs, NJ: Prentice-Hall.

Schwanberg, S. (1985). "Changes in Labeling Homosexuality in Health Sciences: A Preliminary Investigation." *Journal of Homosexuality, 12*(1), 51–73.

Schwartz, I. D., & Root, A. W. (1991). "The Klinefelter Syndrome of Testicular Dysgenesis." *Endocrinology and Metabolism Clinics of North America, 20*(1), 153–163.

Schwarz, P. Interview with Bryan Strong, December 20, 1992.

Scott, J. (1986). "Gender: A Useful Category of Historical Analysis." *American Historical Review, 91,* 1053–1075.

Scott, J. (1986). "An Updated Longitudinal Content Analysis of Sex References in Mass Circulation Magazines." *Journal of Sex Research, 22*(3), 385–392.

Scott, J. (1990a, December 24). "Trying to Save the Babies." *Los Angeles Times,* pp. 1, 18ff.

Scott, J. (1990b, December 31). "Low Birth Weight's High Cost." *Los Angeles Times,* p. 1.

Scott, J., & Alwin, D. F. (1989). "Gender Differences in Parental Strain: Parental Role or Gender Role." *Journal of Family Issues, 10*(4), 482–503.

Scott, S. G., et al. (1990). "Therapeutic Donor Insemination with Frozen Semen." *Canadian Medical Association Journal, 143*(4), 273–278.

Seidman, S. (1989). "Constructing Sex as a Domain of Pleasure and Self-Expression: Sexual Ideology in the Sixties." *Theory, Culture, and Society, 6*(2), 293–315.

Senn, C., & Radtke, H. L. (1990). "Women's Evaluations of and Affective Reactions to Mainstream Violent Pornography, Nonviolent Pornography, and Erotica." *Violence and Victims, 5*(3), 143–155.

Serdahely, W., & Ziemba, G. (1984). "Changing Homophobic Attitudes through College Sexuality Education." *Journal of Homosexuality, 10*(1), 148ff.

Severn, J., Belch, G. E., & Belch, M. A. (1990). "The Effects of Sexual and Nonsexual Advertising Appeals and Information Level on Cognitive Processing and Communication Effectiveness." *Journal of Advertising, 19,* 14–22.

Shah, R., Woolley, M. M., & Costin, G. (1992). "Testicular Feminization: The Androgen Insensitivity Syndrome." *Journal of Pediatric Surgery, 27*(6), 757–760.

Shanis, B. S., et al. (1989). "Transmission of Sexually Transmitted Diseases by Donor Semen." *Archives of Andrology, 23*(3), 249–257.

Shannon, J. W., & Woods, W. J. (1991). "Affirmative Psychotherapy for Gay Men." *Counseling Psychologist, 19*(2), 197–215.

Shapiro, M. F., Hayward, R. A., Guillemot, D., & Jayle, D. (1992). "Residents' Experiences in, and Attitudes Toward, the Care of Persons with AIDS in Canada, France, and the United States." *JAMA: Journal of the American Medical Association, 268*(4), 510–515.

Sharlip, I. (1984). "Diagnosis and Management of Male Dysfunction." In J. Swanson & K. Forrest (Eds.), *Mens' Reproductive Health.* New York: Springer.

Shaver, P. (1984). *Emotions, Relationships, and Health.* Newbury Park, CA: Sage Publications.

Shaver, P., Hazan, C., & Bradshaw, D. (1988). "Love as Attachment: The Integration of Three Behavioral Systems." In R. Sternberg & M. Barnes (Eds.), *The Psychology of Love.* New Haven, CT: Yale University Press.

Shedler, J., & Block, J. (1990). "Adolescent Drug Use and Psychological Health: A Longitudinal Inquiry." *American Psychologist, 45,* 612–630.

Sheehan, W., & Garfinkel, B. (1988). "Adolescent Autoerotic Deaths." *American Academy of Child and Adolescent Psychiatry, 27,* 82–89.

Shelp, E. (1986). *Born to Die?* New York: Free Press.

Shepard, C. (1989). *Forgiven: The Rise and Fall of Jim Bakker and the PTL Ministry.* Boston: Atlantic Monthly Press.

Sherman, B., & Dominick, J. (1986). "Violence and Sex in Music Videos: TV and Rock 'n' Roll." *Journal of Communication, 36*(1), 79–93.

Shilts, R. (1987). *And the Band Played On: Politics, People, and the AIDS Epidemic.* New York: St. Martin's Press.

Shilts, R. (1993). *Conduct Unbecoming: Lesbians and Gays in the Military, Vietnam to the Persian Gulf.* New York: St. Martin's Press.

Shipp, E. R. (1985, December 18). "Curtailing Teen-Age Pregnancy." *The New York Times,* pp. 19, 22.

Shon, S., & Ja, D. (1982). "Asian Families." In M. McGoldrick et al. (Eds.), *Ethnicity and Family Therapy.* New York: Guilford Press.

Shostak, A. B. (1987). "Singlehood." In M. Sussman & S. Steinmetz (Eds.), *Handbook of Marriage and the Family.* New York: Plenum Press.

Shtarkshall, R. A., & Awerbuch, T. E. (1992). "It Takes Two to Tango but One to Infect (On the Underestimation of the Calculated Risk for Infection with HIV in Sexual Encounters, Arising from Nondisclosure of Previous Risk Behavior or Seropositivity)." *Journal of Sex and Marital Therapy, 18*(2), 121–127.

Shute, J. (1992). *Life-Size.* Boston: Houghton Mifflin.

Sigelman, C. K., et al. (1991). "Courteousy Stigma: The Social Implications of Associating with a Gay Person." *Journal of Social Psychology, 131,* 45–56.

Silbert, M., & Pines, A. (1981). "Child Sexual Abuse as an Antecedent to Prostitution." *Child Abuse and Neglect, 5*(4), 407–411.

Silver, D., & Campbell, B. K. (1988). "Failure of Psychological Gestation." *Psychoanalytic Inquiry, 8*(2), 222–223.

Simon, P. M., et al. (1992). "Psychological Characteristics of a Sample of Male Street Prostitutes." *Archives of Sexual Behavior, 21*(1), 33–44.

Simon, W. (1992). "Letters to the Editor: Reply to Muir and Eichel." *Archives of Sexual Behavior, 21*(6), 595–597.

Simon, W., & Gagnon, J. (1986). "Sexual Scripts: Permanence and Change." *Archives of Sexual Behavior, 15*(3), 97–120.

Simon, W., & Gagnon, J. (1987). "A Sexual Scripts Approach." J. H. Geer & W. O'Donohue (Eds.), *Theories of Human Sexuality.* New York: Plenum Press.

Simons, M. (1993, January 11). "France Jails a Gambian Woman Who Had Daughters Circumcised." *The New York Times,* p. A5.

Simons, R. L., & Whitbeck, L. B. (1991). "Sexual Abuse as a Precursor to Prostitution and Victimization Among Adolescent and Adult Homeless Women." *Journal of Family Issues, 12*(3), 361–380.

Simpson, J., Campbell, B., & Berscheid, E. (1986). "The Association Between Romantic Love and Marriage: Kephart (1967) Twice Revisited." *Personality and Social Psychology Bulletin, 12,* 363–372.

Simpson, W. S., & Ramberg, J. A. (1992). "Sexual Dysfunction in Married Female Patients with Anorexia and Bulimia Nervosa." *Journal of Sex and Marital Therapy, 18*(1), 44–54.

Singh, S. (1986). "Adolescent Pregnancy in the United States: An Interstate Analysis." *Family Planning Perspectives, 18*(5), 210–220.

Sinnott, J. (1986). *Sex Roles and Aging: Theory and Research from a Systems Perspective.* New York: Karger.

Skitka, L. J., & Maslach, C. (1990). "Gender Roles and the Categorization of Gender-Relevant Information." *Sex Roles, 22,* 3–4.

Slade, J. (1984). "Violence in the Hard-Core Pornographic Film: A Historical Survey." *Journal of Communication, 34*(3), 148–163.

Slater, P. (1974). *The Pursuit of Loneliness.* Boston: Beacon Press.

Sluzki, C. (1982). "The Latin Lover Revisited." In M. McGoldrick et al. (Eds.), *Ethnicity and Family Therapy.* New York: Guilford Press.

Smeltzer, S. C., & Whipple, B. (1991). "Women and HIV Infection." *IMAGE: Journal of Nursing Scholarship, 23*(4), 249–256.

Smith, D. K. (1992). "HIV Disease as a Cause of Death for African Americans in 1987 and 1990." *Journal of the National Medical Association, 84*(6), 481–487.

Smith, E. A., & Udry, J. R. (1985). "Coital and Non-Coital Sexual Behaviors of White and Black Adolescents." *American Journal of Public Health, 75,* 1200–1203.

Smith, E. J. (1982). "The Black Female Adolescent: A Review of the Educational, Career, and Psychological Literature." *Psychology of Women Quarterly, 6,* 261–288.

Smith, F. (1986, June 25). "Experimental AIDS Drug May Have Led to 3 Patients' Death." *San Jose Mercury News,* pp. 1, 6.

Smith, H., & Cox, C. (1983). "Dialogue with a Dominatrix." In T. Weinberg & G. W. L. Kamel (Eds.), *S and M: Studies in Sadomasochism.* Buffalo, NY: Prometheus Books.

Smith, J. E., & Krejci, J. (1991). "Minorities Join the Majority: Eating Disturbances Among Hispanic and Native American Youth." *International Journal of Eating Disorders, 10,* 179–186.

Smith, M. W., & Kronauge, C. (1990). "The Politics of Abortion: Husband Notification Legislation." *Sociological Quarterly, 31*(4), 585–598.

Smith, R. W. (1979). "What Kind of Sex Is Natural?" In V. Bullough (Ed.), *The Frontiers of Sex Research.* Buffalo, NY: Prometheus Books.

Snarey, J., et al. (1987). "The Role of Parenting in Men's Psychosocial Development." *Developmental Psychology, 23*(4), 593–603.

Snitow, A. (1983). "Mass Market Romance: Pornography for Women Is Different." In A. Snitow et al. (Ed.), *Powers of Desire: The Politics of Sexuality.* New York: Monthly Review Press.

Snitow, A., Stansells, C., & Thompson, S. (Eds.). (1983). *Powers of Desire: The Politics of Sexuality.* New York: Monthly Review Press.

Snyder, P. (1974). "Prostitution in Asia." *Journal of Sex Research, 10,* 119–127.

Soley, L., & Reid, L. (1986). "Taking It Off: Are Models in Magazine Ads Wearing Less?" *Journalism Quarterly, 85*(4), 960–966.

Sollom, T. (1991). "State Legislation on Reproductive Health in 1990: What Was Proposed and Enacted." *Family Planning Perspectives, 23,* 82–94.

Sondra, L., Mazo, R. & Chancellor, M. (1990). "The Role of Yohimbine for the Treatment of Erectile Impotence." *Journal of Sex and Marital Therapy, 16,* 15–21.

Sonenstein, F. L. (1986). "Rising Paternity: Sex and Contraception Among Adolescent Males." In A. B. Elster & M. E. Lamb (Eds.), *Adolescent Fatherhood.* Hillsdale, NJ: Erlbaum.

Sonenstein, F. L., et al. (1991). "Levels of Sexual Activity Among Adolescent Males in the United States." *Family Planning Perspectives, 23*(4), 162–167.

Sonenstein, F. L., & Pittman, K. (1984). "The Availability of Sex Education in Large City School Districts." *Family Planning Perspectives, 16*(1), 19–25.

Sonenstein, F. L., Pleck, J. H., & Ku, L. C. (1989). "Sexual Activity, Condom Use, and AIDS Awareness Among Adolescent Males." *Family Planning Perspectives, 21*(4), 152–158.

Sorenson, S. B., & Siegel, J. M. (1992). "Gender, Ethnicity, and Sexual Assault: Findings from a Los Angeles Study." *Journal of Social Issues, 48*(1), 93–104.

South, S., & Felson, R. (1990). "The Racial Patterning of Rape." *Social Forces, 69*(1), 71–93.

Spallone, P., & Steinberg, D. L. (1987). *Made to Order: The Myth of Reproductive and Genetic Progress.* New York: Pergamon Press.

Spanier, G. B., & Thompson, L. (1987). *Parting: The Aftermath of Separation and Divorce.* Newbury Park, CA: Sage Publications.

"Special Report: Sexuality and the Cardiovascular Patient." (1980, February). *The Female Patient,* 48–54.

Specter, M. (1988, March 8). "Heterosexual AIDS Study Denounced." *The Washington Post,* p. A3.

Spector, I. P., & Carey, M. P. (1990). "Incidence and Prevalence of the Sexual Dysfunctions: A Critical Review of the Empirical Literature." *Archives of Sexual Behavior, 19*(4), 389–408.

Spence, J., et al. (1985). "Sex Roles in Contemporary Society." In G. Lindzey & E. Aronson (Eds.), *Handbook of Social Psychology.* New York: Random House.

Spence, J., & Sawin, L. L. (1985). "Images of Masculinity and Femininity." In V. O'Leary et al. (Eds.), *Sex, Gender, and Social Psychology.* Hillsdale, NJ: Erlbaum.

Spencer, S. L., & Zeiss, A. M. (1987). "Sex Roles and Sexual Dysfunction in College Students." *Journal of Sex Research, 23,* 338–347.

Speroff, L., Glass, R. H., & Kase, N. G. (1989). *Clinical Gynecologic Endocrinology and Infertility.* (4th ed.). Baltimore, MD: Williams & Wilkins.

Spletter, M. (1982). *A Woman's Choice: New Options in the Treatment of Breast Cancer.* Boston: Beacon Press.

Spock, B., & Rothenberg, M. (1985). *Dr. Spock's Baby and Child Care.* New York: Pocket Books.

Sprecher, S. (1989). "Influences on Choice of a Partner and on Sexual Decision Making in the Relationship." In K. McKinney & S. Sprecher (Eds.), *Human Sexuality: The Social and Interpersonal Context.* Norwood, NJ: Ablex.

Sprecher, S., et al. (1989). "Sexual Relationships." In K. McKinney & S. Sprecher (Eds.), *Human Sexuality: The Societal and Interpersonal Context.* Norwood, NJ: Ablex.

Sprecher, S., & McKinney, K. (1993). *Sexuality.* Newbury Park, CA: Sage Publications.

Sprecher, S., McKinney, K., Walsh, R., & Anderson, C. (1988). "A Revision of the Reiss Premarital Sexual Permissiveness Scale." *Journal of Marriage and the Family, 50*(3), 821–828.

St. Lawrence, J. S., Husfeldt, B. A., Kelly, J. A., Hood, H. V., & Smith, Jr., S. (1990). "The Stigma of AIDS: Fear of Disease and Prejudice Toward Gay Men." *Journal of Homosexuality, 19*(3), 85–101.

St. Lawrence, J., & Joyner, D. (1991). "The Effects of Sexually Violent Rock Music on Male's Acceptance of Violence Against Women. *Psychology of Women Quarterly, 15*(1), 49–63.

St. Lawrence, J. S., & Madakasira, S. (1992). "Evaluation and Treatment of Premature Ejaculation: A Critical Review." *International Journal of Psychiatry in Medicine, 22*(1), 77–97.

Stack, C. B. (1974). *All Our Kin: Strategies for Survival in a Black Community.* New York: Harper & Row.

Stack, S., & Gundlach, J. H. (1992). "Divorce and Sex." *Archives of Sexual Behavior, 21*(4), 359–368.

Staggenborg, S. (1991). *The Pro-Choice Movement: Organization and Activism in the Abortion Conflict.* New York: Oxford University Press.

Stanton, M. C. (1985). "The Fetus: A Growing Member of the Family." *Family Relations, 34*(3), 321–326.

Staples, R. (1972). "Research on Black Sexuality: Its Implications for Family Life, Sex Education, and Public Policy." *Family Coordinator, 21,* 183–188.

Staples, R. (1988). "The Black American Family." In C. Mindel et al. (Eds.), *Ethnic Families in America: Patterns and Variations* (3rd ed.). New York: Elsevier North Holland.

Staples, R. (1991). "The Sexual Revolution and the Black Middle Class." In R. Staples (Ed.), *The Black Family* (4th ed.). Belmont, CA: Wadsworth.

Staples, R., & Johnson, L. B. (1993). *Black Families at the Crossroads: Challenges and Prospects.* San Francisco: Jossey-Bass.

Steck, L., Levitan, D., McLane, D., & Kelley, H. H. (1982). "Care, Need, and Conceptions of Love." *Journal of Personality and Social Psychology, 43,* 481–491.

Stein, J. A., Fox, S. A., & Murata, P. J. (1991). "The Influence of Ethnicity, Socioeconomic Status, and Psychological Barriers on Use of Mammography." *Journal of Health and Social Behavior, 32*(2), 101–113.

Stein, P. (1983). "Singlehood." In E. Macklin & R. Rubin (Eds.), *Contemporary Families and Alternative Lifestyles.* Newbury Park, CA: Sage Publications.

Steinberg, D. (Ed.). (1992). *The Erotic Impulse.* New York: Tarcher/Perigree.

Stelzer, C., Desmond, S. M., & Price, J. H. (1987). "Physical Attractiveness and Sexual Activity of College Students." *Psychological Reports, 60,* 567–573.

Stengel, R. (1985, December 9). "The Missing-Father Myth." *Time,* p. 90.

Stephen, T. D., & Harrison, T. M. (1985). "A Longitudinal Comparison of Couples with Sex-Typical and Non-Sex-Typical Orientation to Intimacy." *Sex Roles, 12*(1-2), 195–206.

Stephenson, P., Wagner, M., Badea, M., & Serbanescu, F. (1992). "Commentary: The Public Health Consequences of Restricted Induced Abortion—Lessons from Romania." *American Journal of Public Health, 82*(10), 1328–1331.

Stermac, L., Blanchard, R., Clemmensen, C. H., & Dickey, R. (1991). "Group Therapy for Gender-Dysphoric Heterosexual Men." *Journal of Sex and Marital Therapy, 17*(4), 252–258.

Stern, M., & Karraker, K. H. (1989). "Sex Stereotyping in Infants: A Review of Gender Labelling." *Sex Roles, 20,* 501–522.

Sternberg, R. (1986). "A Triangular Theory of Love." *Psychological Review, 93,* 119–135.

Sternberg, R. (1988). "Triangulating Love." In R. Sternberg & M. Barnes (Eds.), *The Psychology of Love.* New Haven, CT: Yale University Press.

Sternberg, R., & Barnes, M. (1985). "Real and Ideal Others in Romantic Relationships: Is Four a Crowd?" *Journal of Personality and Social Psychology, 49,* 1589–1596.

Sternberg, R., & Grajek, S. (1984). "The Nature of Love." *Journal of Personality and Social Psychology, 47,* 312–327.

Stets, J., & Pirog-Good, M. (1987). "Violence in Dating Relationships." *Social Psychology Quarterly, 50*(3), 237–246.

Stevens, P. E. (1992). "Lesbian Health Care Research: A Review of the Literature from 1970 to 1990." *Health Care for Women International, 13*(2), 91–120.

Stevenson, M. (1990). "Tolerance for Homosexuality and Interest in Sexuality Education." *Journal of Sex Education and Therapy, 16,* 194–197.

Stevens-Simon, C., & Beach, R. K. (1992). "School-Based Prenatal and Postpartum Care: Strategies for Meeting the Medical and Educational Needs of Pregnant and Parenting Students." *Journal of School Health, 62*(7), 304–309.

Stine, Gerald J. (1993). *Acquired Immune Deficiency Syndrome; Biological, Medical, Social and Legal Issues.* New Jersey: Prentice Hall.

Stockdale, M. S. (1993). "The Role of Sexual Misperceptions of Women's Friendliness in an Emerging Theory of Sexual Harassment." *Journal of Vocational Behavior, 42*(1), 84–101.

Stoller, R. J. (1975). *Perversion: The Erotic Form of Hatred.* New York: Pantheon.

Stoller, R. J. (1977). "Sexual Deviations." In F. Beach (Ed.), *Human Sexuality in Four Perspectives.* Baltimore, MD: Johns Hopkins University Press.

Stoller, R. J. (1982). "Transvestism in Women." *Archives of Sexual Behavior, 11*(2), 99–115.

Stoller, R. J. (1991). *Pain & Passion: A Psychoanalyst Explores the World of S & M.* New York: Plenum Press.

Stone, K. M., et al. (1989). "National Surveillance for Neonatal Herpes Simplex Virus Infections." *Sexually Transmitted Diseases, 16*(3), 152–160.

Stone, R. (1992). "Controversial Contraceptive Wins Approval from FDA Panel." *Science, 256,* 1754.

Straayer, C. (1992). "Redressing the Natural—The Temporary Transvestite Film." *Wide Angle: A Quarterly Journal of Film History, Theory, and Criticism, 14*(1), 36–55.

Strage, M. (1980). *The Durable Fig Leaf.* New York: William Morrow.

Strong, B. (1973, June). "Origins of the Sex Education Movement." *History of Education Quarterly,* 1–18.

Strong, B. (1973). "Toward a History of the Experiential Family: Sex and Incest in the 19th Century." *Journal of Marriage and the Family, 34,* 457–466.

Strong, B., & DeVault, C. (1992). *The Marriage and Family Experience.* St. Paul, MN: West.

Struckman-Johnson, D., & Struckman-Johnson, C. (1991). "Men and Women's Acceptance of Coercive Sexual Strategies Varied by Initiator Gender and Couple Intimacy." *Sex Roles, 25,* 661–676.

Studer, M., & Thornton, A. (1987). "Adolescent Religiosity and Contraceptive Use." *Journal of Marriage and the Family, 49,* 117–128.

"Study Relates Estrogen Levels to Breast Cancer." (1995, February 1). *Monterey Co. Herald.*

Sue, D. (1979). "Erotic Fantasies of College Students During Coitus." *Journal of Sex Research, 15,* 299–305.

Suggs, D. N., & Miracle, A. W. (1993). (Eds.). *Culture and Human Sexuality.* Pacific Grove, CA: Brooks/Cole.

Summers, R. (1991). "Determinants of Judgments of and Responses to a Complaint of Sexual Harassment." *Sex Roles, 25*(7-8), 379–392.

Surra, C. (1991). "Research and Theory on Mate Selection and Premarital Relationship in the 1980s." In A. Booth (Ed.), *Contemporary Families: Looking Forward, Looking Back.* Minneapolis, MN: National Council on Family Relations.

"Survey of 80,000 Cases Calls Birth-defect Test Safe." (1992, August 4). *San Jose Mercury News,* p. 3F.

Susser, M. (1992). "Induced Abortion and Health as a Value." *American Journal of Public Health, 82*(10), 1323–1324.

Sweet, J. A., & Bumpass, L. L. (1987). *American Families and Households.* New York: Russell Sage Foundation.

Sweet, R. (1986). "Pelvic Inflammatory Disease." *Sexually Transmitted Diseases, 13*(3), 192–198.

Swensen, C. H., Jr. (1972). "The Behavior of Love." In H. A. Otto (Ed.), *Love Today: A New Exploration.* New York: Association Press.

Symons, D. (1979). *The Evolution of Human Sexuality.* New York: Oxford University Press.

Szaz, T. (1990). *Sex by Prescription: The Startling Truth About Today's Sex Therapy.* Syracuse, NY: Syracuse University Press.

Szinovacz, M. (1987). "Family Power." In M. Sussman & S. Steinmetz (Eds.), *Handbook of Marriage and the Family.* New York: Plenum Press.

Talamini, J. T. (1982). *Boys Will Be Girls.* Washington, DC: University Press of America.

Tanfer, K. (1987). "Patterns of Premarital Cohabitation Among Never-Married Women in the United States." *Journal of Marriage and the Family, 49,* 683–697.

Tanfer, K., & Cubbins, L. A. (1992). "Coital Frequency Among Single Women: Normative Constraints and Situational Opportunities." *Journal of Sex Research, 29*(2), 221–250.

Tanfer, K., & Schoorl, J. J. (1992). "Premarital Sexual Careers and Partner Change." *Archives of Sexual Behavior, 21,* 45–68.

Tanke, E. D. (1982). "Dimensions of the Physical Attractiveness Stereotype: A Factor/Analytic Study." *Journal of Psychology, 110,* 63–74.

Tardif, G. S. (1989). "Sexual Activity After a Myocardial Infarction." *Archives of Physical Medicine and Rehabilitation, 70*(10), 763–766.

Tavris, C. (1992). *The Mismeasure of Woman*. New York: Norton.

Tavris, C., & Sadd, S. (1977). *The Redbook Report on Female Sexuality*. New York: Dell.

Tavris, C., & Wade, C. (1984). *The Longest War: Sex Differences in Perspective* (2nd ed.). New York: Harcourt Brace Jovanovich.

Taylor, E. (1989). *Prime-Time Families*. Berkeley, CA: University of California Press.

Taylor, R. J., Chatters, L. M., Tucker, B., & Lewis, E. (1991). "Developments in Research on Black Families." In A. Booth (Ed.), *Contemporary Families: Looking Forward, Looking Back*. Minneapolis, MN: National Council on Family Relations.

Teachman, J. D., & Polonko, K. A. (1990). "Cohabitation and Marital Stability in the United States." *Social Forces, 69*(1), 207–220.

"Teen-Age Fathers Now Getting Help." (1986, August 21). *The New York Times*, p. 24.

Templeman, T., & Stinnett, R. (1991). "Patterns of Sexual Arousal and History in a 'Normal' Sample of Young Men." *Archives of Sexual Behavior, 20*(2), 137–150.

Tessina, T. (1989). *Gay Relationships: For Men and Women. How to Find Them, How to Improve Them, How to Make Them Last*. Los Angeles: Tarcher.

Testa, R. J., Kinder, B. N., & Ironson, G. (1987). "Heterosexual Bias in the Perception of Loving Relationships of Gay Males and Lesbians." *Journal of Sex Research, 23*(2), 163–172.

Tharp, J. (1991). "The Transvestite as Monster: Gender Horror in 'The Silence of the Lambs' and 'Psycho'." *Journal of Popular Film and Television, 19*(3), 106–113.

Thayer, L. (1986). *On Communication*. Norwood, NJ: Ablex.

Thomas, S. B., & Quinn, S. C. (1991). "The Tuskegee Syphilis Study, 1932 to 1972: Implications for HIV Education and AIDS Risk Education Programs in the Black Community." *American Journal of Public Health, 81*(11), 1498–1504.

Thompson, A. (1983). "Extramarital Sex: A Review of the Research Literature." *Journal of Sex Research, 19*(1), 1–22.

Thompson, A. (1984). "Emotional and Sexual Components of Extramarital Relations." *Journal of Marriage and the Family, 46*(1), 35–42.

Thompson, B. W. (1992). "'A Way Outa No Way': Eating Problems Among African-American, Latina, and White Women." *Gender and Society, 6*(4), 546–561.

Thompson, C. E. (1990). "Transition of the Disabled Adolescent to Adulthood." *Pediatrician, 17*(4), 308–313.

Thompson, L., & Walker, A. J. (1989). "Gender in Families: Women and Men in Marriage, Work, and Parenthood." *Journal of Marriage and the Family, 51*, 845–871.

Thompson, M. E., Chaffee, S. H., & Oshagan, H. H. (1990). "Regulating Pornography: A Public Dilemma." *Journal of Communication, 40*(3), 73–83.

Thompson, S. (1986, December 23). "Pregnant on Purpose." *The Village Voice*, p. 28ff.

Thornton, A. (1989). "Changing Attitudes Toward Family Issues in the United States." *Journal of Marriage and the Family, 51*(4), 873–893.

Thornton, A. (1990). "The Courtship Process and Adolescent Sexuality." *Journal of Family Issues, 11*(3), 239–273.

Thornton, A., & Camburn, D. (1987). "The Influence of the Family on Premarital Sexual Attitudes and Behavior." *Demography, 24*, 323–340.

Tiefer, L. (1992). "Critique of the DSM-III-R Nosology of Sexual Dysfunctions." *Psychiatric Medicine, 10*(2), 227–245.

Tiefer, L., & Melman, A. (1989). "Comprehensive Evaluation of Erectile and Medical Treatments." In S. Leiblum & R. Rosen (Eds.), *Principles and Practices of Sex Therapy* (2nd ed.). New York: Guilford Press.

Tietjen, A., & Bradley, C. F. (1985). "Social Support and Maternal Psychosocial Adjustment During the Transition to Parenthood." *Canadian Journal of Behavioural Science, 17*(2), 109–121.

Timberlake, C., & Carpenter, W. (1986). "Adult Sexuality Training in the Black Church: An Approach Toward Combatting Teenage Pregnancy." *Journal of Home Economics, 78*, 29–31.

Ting-Toomey, S. (1983). "An Analysis of Verbal Communication Patterns in High and Low Marital Adjustment Groups." *Human Communications Research, 9*(4), 306–319.

Ting-Toomey, S., & Korzenny, Felipe. (1991). (Eds.). *Cross-Cultural Interpersonal Communication*. Newbury Park, CA: Sage Publications.

Toback, B. M. (1992). "Recent Advances in Female Infertility Care." *Naacogs Clinical Issues in Perinatal and Women's Health Nursing, 3*(2), 313–319.

Toback, J. (1992, August). "James Toback on 'The Hunger'." Special Issue: The Sexual Revolution in Movie, Music & TV. *US*, pp. 56–58.

Toomey, K. E., Oberschelp, A. G., & Greenspan, J. R. (1989). "Sexually Transmitted Diseases and Native Americans: Trends in Reported Gonorrhea and Syphilis Morbidity, 1984–1988." *Public Health Reports, 104*(6), 566–572.

Torres, A., & Forrest, J. D. (1988). "Why Do Women Have Abortions?" *Family Planning Perspectives, 20*, 7–9.

Torres, A., & Singh, S. (1986). "Contraceptive Practice Among Hispanic Adolescents." *Family Planning Perspectives, 18*(4), 193–194.

Trafford, A. (1980, November 10). "Medical Science Discovers the Baby." *U.S. News & World Report*, pp. 59–62.

Trall, R. T. (1853). *Home Treatment of Sexual Abuse*. New York: M. L. Holbrook.

Treiman, K., & Liskin, L. (1988). "IUDs: A New Look." *Population Reports*, Series B (No. 5), 1–31.

Tribe, L. (1992). *Abortion: The Clash of Absolutes*. New York: Norton.

Trippet, S. E., & Bain, J. (1992, April). "Reasons American Lesbians Fail to Seek Traditional Health Care." *Health Care for Women International, 13*(2), 145–153.

Troiden, R. (1988). *Gay and Lesbian Identity: A Sociological Analysis*. New York: General Hall.

True, R. H. (1990). "Psychotherapeutic Issues with Asian American Women." *Sex Roles, 22*(7), 477–485.

Trussell, J., Hatcher, R. A., Cates, W., Stewart, F. H., & Kost, K. (1990). "Contraceptive Failure in the United States: An Update." *Studies in Family Planning, 21*(1), Table 1.

Trussell, J., & Kost, K. (1987). "Contraceptive Failure in the United States: A Critical Review of the Literature." *Studies in Family Planning, 18*, 237–283.

Trussell, J., Stewart, F., Guest, F., & Hatcher, R. A. (1992). "Emergency Contraceptive Pills: A Simple Proposal to Reduce Unintended Pregnancies." *Family Planning Perspectives, 24*, 269–273.

Tsoi, W. F. (1990). "Developmental Profile of 200 Male and 100 Female Transsexuals in Singapore." *Archives of Sexual Behavior, 19*, 595–605.

Tsoukas, C., et al. (1986, June 23). "Risk of Transmission of HTLV-III/LAV from Human Bites." Paper presented at the Second International Conference on AIDS, Paris.

Tucker, M. B., & Taylor, R. J. (1989). "Demographic Correlates of Relationship Status Among Black Americans." *Journal of Marriage and the Family, 51*, 655–665.

Tucker, R. K., Marvin, M. G., & Vivian, B. (1991). "What Constitutes a Romantic Act?" *Psychological Reports, 89*(2), 651–654.

Tuleja, T. (1987). *Curious Customs*. New York: Harmony Books.

Tuller, N. R. (1988). "Couples: The Hidden Segment of the Gay World." In J. De Cecco (Ed.), *Gay Relationships*. New York: Haworth Press.

Tully, C. T. (1989). "Caregiving: What Do Midlife Lesbians View as Important?" *Journal of Gay and Lesbian Psychotherapy, 1*(1), 87–103.

Turner, P. H., et al. (1985, March). "Parenting in Gay and Lesbian Families." Paper presented at the first meeting of the Future of Parenting Symposium, Chicago.

Turner, R. J., & Avison, W. R. (1985). "Assessing Risk Factors for Problem Parenting: The Significance of Social Support." *Journal of Marriage and the Family, 47*(4), 881–892.

Turque, P. (1992, September 14). "Gays Under Fire." *Newsweek,* pp. 35–40.

Tuttle, G. E., & Pillard, R. C. (1991). "Sexual Orientation and Cognitive Abilities." *Archives of Sexual Behavior, 20*(3), 307–318.

Twinam, A. (1989). "Honor, Sexuality, and Illegitimacy in Colonial Spanish America." In A. Lavrin (Ed.), *Sexuality and Marriage in Colonial Latin America.* Lincoln, NE: University of Nebraska Press.

Ubell, E. (1994, September 11). "Stepping Up the Fight Against Breast Cancer." *San Francisco Chronicle, Parade Magazine,* pp. 24–27.

UCSF AIDS Health Project. (1991). "Risks of Oral Sex." *HIV Counselor Perspectives* (California Department of Health Services), 1(2), 1–8.

Ullman, S. E., & Knight, R. A. (1991). "A Multivariate Model for Predicting Rape and Physical Injury Outcomes During Sexual Assaults." *Journal of Consulting and Clinical Psychology, 59*(5), 724–731.

Unger, R. K. (1979). "Toward a Redefinition of Sex and Gender." *American Psychologist, 34,* 1085–1094.

Uribe, V., & Harbeck, K. M. (1991). "Addressing the Needs of Lesbian, Gay, and Bisexual Youth: The Origins of Project 10 and School Based Intervention." *Journal of Homosexuality, 22,* 9–28.

U.S. Bureau of the Census. (1990). *Statistical Abstract of the United States* (110th ed.). Washington, DC: U.S. Government Printing Office.

U.S. Bureau of the Census. (1991). "The Hispanic Population in the United States." *Current Population Reports,* Series P-20. Washington, DC: U.S. Government Printing Office.

U.S. Bureau of the Census. (1991). "Marital Status and Living Arrangements, 1990." *Current Population Reports,* Series P-20. Washington, DC: U.S. Government Printing Office.

U.S. Bureau of the Census. (1992). *Statistical Abstract of the United States* (112th ed.). Washington, DC: U.S. Government Printing Office.

U.S. Bureau of the Census. (1993). *Statistical Abstract of the United States* (113th ed.). Washington, DC: U.S. Government Printing Office.

U.S. Department of Justice. (1991). *Sourcebook of Criminal Justice Statistics.* Washington, DC: U.S. Government Printing Office.

Uslander, A., et al. (1973). *Their Universe: The Story of a Unique Educational Program.* New York: Delacorte Press.

U.S. News and World Report (1994, February 14). "Health Index: Condom Facts." *116,* 6.

Valentine, D. (1982). "The Experience of Pregnancy: A Developmental Process." *Family Relations, 31,* 243–248.

Van Buskirk. (1992, August). "Soap Opera Sex: Tuning In, Tuning Out." Special Issue: The Sexual Revolution in Movie, Music & TV. *US.,* pp. 64–67.

Vance, C. S. (1988). "Ordinances Restricting Pornography Could Damage Women." In R. T. Francoeur (Ed.), *Taking Sides: Clashing Views on Controversial Issues in Human Sexuality.* Guilford, CT: Dushkin Publishing Group.

Vance, C. S., & Pollis, C. (1990). "Introduction: Special Issue on Feminist Perspectives on Sexuality." *Journal of Sex Research, 27*(1), 1–5.

Van-de-Perre, P., Jacobs, D., & Sprecher-Goldberger, S. (1987). "The Latex Condom: An Efficient Barrier Against Sexual Transmission of AIDS-Related Viruses." *AIDS, 1,* 49–52.

Vanderford, M. (1989). "Vilification and Social Movements: A Case Study of Pro-Life and Pro-Choice Rhetoric." *Quarterly Journal of Speech, 75*(2), 166–182.

Vandewiel, H. B. M., Jaspers, J. P. M., Schultz, W. C. M. W., & Gal, J. (1990). "Treatment of Vaginismus: A Review of Concepts and Treatment Modalities." *Journal of Psychosomatic Obstetrics and Gynecology, 11,* 1–18.

Van Wyk, P. H., & Geist, C. S. (1984). "Psychosocial Development of Heterosexual, Bisexual, and Homosexual Behavior." *Archives of Sexual Behavior, 13,* 505–544.

Vasquez-Nuthall, E., Romero-Garcia, & DeLeon. (1987). "Sex Roles and Perceptions of Femininity and Masculinity of Hispanic Women: A Review of the Literature." *Psychology of Women Quarterly, 11,* 409–426.

Vaughan, D. (1986). *Uncoupling: Turning Points in Intimate Relationships.* New York: Oxford University Press.

Vaughter, R. M. (1976). "Psychology." *Signs, 2*(1), 120–146.

Veevers, J. (1980). *Childless by Choice.* Toronto, Canada: Butterworth.

Vega, W. (1991). "Hispanic Families." In A. Booth (Ed.), *Contemporary Families: Looking Forward, Looking Back.* Minneapolis, MN: National Council on Family Relations.

Ventura, J. N. (1987). "The Stresses of Parenthood Reexamined." *Family Relations, 36,* 26–29.

Verschraegen-Spae, M. R. (1992). "Familial Turner Syndrome." *Clinical Genetics, 41*(4), 218–220.

Verwoerdt, A., et al. (1969). "Sexual Behavior in Senescence." *Geriatrics, 24,* 137–157.

Verzaro-Lawrence, M. (1981, May). "Shared Childrearing: A Challenging Alternative Lifestyle." *Alternative Lifestyles, 4* (2), 205–217.

Vessey, M. P., et al. (1983). "Neoplasia of the Cervix Uteri and Contraception: A Possible Adverse Effect of the Pill." *Lancet, 2,* 930–934.

Vessey, M. P., Lawless, M., Yeates, D., & McPherson, K. (1985). "Progestin-Only Oral Contraception: Findings in a Large Prospective Study with Special Reference to Effectiveness." *British Journal of Family Planning, 10,* 117–121.

Vincent, R., et al. (1987). "Sexism on MTV: The Portrayal of Women in Rock Video." *Journalism Quarterly, 64*(4), 750–755, 941.

Virga, V. (1980). *Gaywyck.* New York: Avon.

Voeller, B. (1980). "Society and the Gay Movement." In J. Marmor (Ed.), *Homosexual Behavior.* New York: Basic Books.

Voeller, B. (1991). "AIDS and Heterosexual Anal Intercourse." *Archives of Sexual Behavior, 20*(3), 233–276.

Vogel, D. A., Lake, M. A., & Evans, S. (1991). "Children's and Adults' Sex-Stereotyped Perceptions of Infants." *Sex Roles, 24,* 605–616.

Voydanoff, P., & Donnelly, B. (1990). *Adolescent Sexuality and Pregnancy.* Newbury Park, CA: Sage Publications.

Wade, R. C. (1978). *For Men About Abortion.* Boulder, CO: R. C. Wade.

Walker, A. (1992). *Possessing the Secret of Joy.* New York: Harcourt Brace Jovanovich.

Walker, E. A., et al. (1992). "Medical and Psychiatric Symptoms in Women with Childhood Sexual Abuse." *Psychosomatic Medicine, 54*(6), 658–664.

Wallace, R. (1991). "Traveling Waves of HIV Infection on a Low Dimensional 'Socio-Geographic' Network." *Social Science and Medicine, 32*(7), 847–852.

Waller, W., & Hill, R. (1951). *The Family: A Dynamic Interpretation.* New York: Dryden Press.

Walling, M., Andersen, B. L., & Johnson, S. R. (1990). "Hormonal Replacement Therapy for Postmenopausal Women: A Review of Sexual Outcomes and Related Gynecologic Effects." *Archives of Sexual Behavior*, 19(2), 119–127.

Wallis, C. (1985, December 9). "Children Having Children." *Time*, pp. 78–79.

Wallis, C. (1986, April 28). "The Career Woman's Disease." *Time*, p. 62.

Wardle, F. (1989, December). "Helping Children Respect Differences." *PTA Today*, pp. 5–6.

Washton, A. M. (1989). *Cocaine Addiction: Treatment, Recovery, and Relapse Prevention*. New York: Norton.

Waterman, C. K., et al. (1989). "Sexual Coercion in Gay Male and Lesbian Relationships: Predictors and Implications for Support Services." *Journal of Sex Research*, 26(1), 118–125.

Waterson, E. J., & Murray-Lyon, I. M. (1990). "Preventing Alcohol-Related Birth Damage: A Review." *Social Science and Medicine*, 30(3), 349–364.

Watson, R. (1983). "Premarital Cohabitation vs. Traditional Courtship: Their Effects on Subsequent Marital Adjustment." *Family Relations*, 32(1), 139–147.

Webb, P. (1983). *The Erotic Arts*. New York: Farrar, Straus & Giroux.

Webb, T. (1992 August 2). "Rural Teen Who Got AIDS Warns Others They're at Risk." *San Jose Mercury News*, A2.

Weeks, J. (1985). *Sexuality and Its Discontents*. London: Routledge & Kegan Paul.

Weeks, J. (1986). *Sexuality*. New York: Tavistock Publications and Ellis Horwood, Ltd.

Weeks, J. (1993, February 11). "Someone Wicked This Way Comes." *San Jose Mercury News*, pp. 1C, 6C.

Weg, R. (1983a). "Introduction: Beyond Intercourse and Orgasm." In R. Weg (Ed.), *Sexuality in the Later Years: Roles and Behavior*. New York: Academic Press.

Weg, R. (1983b). "The Physiological Perspective." In R. Weg (Ed.), *Sexuality in the Later Years: Roles and Behavior*. New York: Academic Press.

Weidner, W., Weiske, W. H., Rudnick, J., Becker, H. C., Schroeder-Printzen, J., & Brahler, E. (1992). "Venous Surgery in Veno-Occulsive Dysfunction: Long-time Results after Dorsal Vein Resection." *Urologia Internationalis*, 49(1), 24–28.

Weinberg, M. S., & Williams, C. J. (1974). *Male Homosexuals: Their Problems and Adaptations*. New York: Oxford University Press.

Weinberg, M. S., & Williams, C. J. (1988). "Black Sexuality: A Test of Two Theories." *Journal of Sex Research*, 25(2), 197–218.

Weinberg, M. S., Williams, C. J., & Moser, C. (1984). "The Social Constituents of Sadomasochism." *Social Problems, 31*, 379–389.

Weinberg, M., Williams, C., & Pryor, D. (1994). *Dual Attraction: Understanding Bisexuality*. New York: Oxford University Press.

Weinberg, T. S. (1987). "Sadomasochism in the United States: A Review of Recent Sociological Literature." *Journal of Sex Research, 23*, 50–69.

Weinberg, T. S., & Kamel, G. W. L. (Eds.). (1983). *S and M: Studies in Sadomasochism*. Buffalo, NY: Prometheus Books.

Weir, J. (1992, March 29). "Gay-Bashing, Villany and the Oscars." *The New York Times*, p. 17.

Weis, D. (1985). "The Experience of Pain During Women's First Sexual Intercourse: Cultural Mythology About Female Sexual Initiation." *Archives of Sexual Behavior, 14*, 421–428.

Weisberg, D. K. (1985). *Children of the Night: A Study of Adolescent Prostitution*. Lexington, MA: Lexington Books.

Weiss, D. (1983). "Open Marriage and Multilateral Relationships: The Emergence of Nonexclusive Models of the Marital Relationship." In E. Macklin & R. Rubin (Eds.), *Contemporary Families and Alternative Lifestyles*. Newbury Park, CA: Sage Publications.

Weiss, D., & Jurich, J. (1985). "Size of Community as a Predictor of Attitudes Toward Extramarital Sexual Relations." *Journal of Marriage and the Family*, 47(1), 173–178.

Weiss, J. (1992). "Multiple Sclerosis: Will It Come Between Us? Sexual Concerns of Clients and Their Partners." *Journal of Neuroscience Nursing*, 24(4), 190–193.

Weiss, P. (1992, August 18). "The Bond of Mother's Milk." *San Jose Mercury News*, pp. 1–2E.

Weiss, R. (1975). *Marital Separation*. New York: Basic Books.

Weissbach, T. A., & Zagon, G. (1975). "The Effect of Deviant Group Membership Upon Impression of Personality." *Journal of Social Psychology, 95*, 263–266.

Weizman, R., & Hart, J. (1987). "Sexual Behavior in Healthy Married Elderly Men." *Archives of Sexual Behavior*, 16(1), 39–44.

Welch, M., & Herman, D. (1980, February). "Why Miscarriage Is So Misunderstood." *Ms.*, pp. 14–22.

Wenger, N. S., Linn, L. S., Epstein, M., & Shapiro, M. F. (1991). "Reduction of High-Risk Sexual Behavior Among Heterosexuals Undergoing HIV Antibody Testing: A Randomized Clinical Trial." *American Journal of Public Health*, 81(12), 1580–1585.

Wenz, P. S. (1992). *Abortion Rights as Religious Freedom*. Philadelphia: Temple University Press.

Wertz, R., & Wertz, D. (1977). *Lying-In: A History of Childbirth in America*. New York: Free Press.

Westheimer, R. (1988). *Dr. Ruth's Guide To Good Sex*. New York: Crown Publications Group.

Wheeless, L. R., Wheeless, V. E., & Baus, R. (1984). "Sexual Communication, Communication Satisfaction, and Solidarity in the Developmental Stages of Intimate Relationships." *Western Journal of Speech Communication, 48*, 217–230.

Whelan, E. (1986). *Boy or Girl?* New York: Pocket Books.

Whitam, F. L. (1977). "Childhood Indicators of Male Homosexuality." *Archives of Sexual Behavior, 6*, 89–96.

Whitbeck, L. B., & Hoyt, D. R. (1991). "Campus Prestige and Dating Behaviors." *College Student Journal*, 25(4), 457–469.

Whitbourne, S. K. (1990). "Sexuality in the Aging Male." *Generations, 14*(3), 28–30.

Whitbourne, S., & Ebmeyer, J. (1990). *Identity and Intimacy in Marriage: A Study of Couples*. New York: Springer-Verlag.

White, C. (1982). "Sexual Interest, Attitudes, Knowledge, and Sexual History in Relation to Sexual Behavior of the Institutionalized Aged." *Archives of Sexual Behavior, 11*, 11–21.

White, G. (1980a). "Inducing Jealousy: A Power Perspective." *Personality and Social Psychology Bulletin*, 6(2), 222–227.

White, G. (1980b, October). "Physical Attractiveness and Courtship Progress." *Journal of Personality and Social Psychology*, 39(4), 660–668.

White, G. (1981a). "Jealousy and Partner's Perceived Motives for Attraction to a Rival." *Social Psychology Quarterly*, 44(1), 24–30.

White, G. (1981b). "A Model of Romantic Jealousy." *Motivation and Education, 5*, 600–668.

White, J. W., & Farmer, R. (1992). "Research Methods: How They Shape Views of Sexual Violence." *Journal of Social Issues, 48*, 45–59.

White, J., & Parham, T. (1990). *The Psychology of Blacks: An African-American Perspective* (2nd ed.). Englewood Cliffs, NJ: Prentice-Hall.

White, P., & Rollins, J. (1981). "Rape: A Family Crisis." *Family Relations*, 103–109.

Whitehead, B. D. (1990, October 7). "How to Rebuild a 'Family Friendly' Society." *Des Moines Sunday Register*, p. 3.

Whiting, B. (1979). "Contributions of Anthropology to the Study of Gender Identity, Gender Role, and Sexual Behavior." In H. Katchadourian (Ed.), *Human Sexuality: A Comparative and Developmental Perspective*. Berkeley, CA: University of California Press.

"WHO Collaborative Study of Neoplasia and Steroid Contraceptives, Breast Cancer, Cervical Cancer, and Depot Medroxyprogesterone Acetate." (1984, November 24). *Lancet, 2*(8413) 1207–1208.

Why Gal. (1992, April 17). "Male Nipples Are Good for Something." *Seattle Times*, p. 6.

Wilcox, A., et al. (1988). "Incidents of Early Loss of Pregnancy." *New England Journal of Medicine, 319*(4), 189–194.

Wilkerson, I. (1987, June 26). "Infant Mortality: Frightful Odds in Inner City." *The New York Times*, p. 1ff.

Wilkinson, C. B. (1986). (Ed.). *Ethnic Psychiatry*. New York: Plenum Medical Book Company.

Wilkinson, C. B., & Spurlock, J. (1986). "The Mental Health of Black Americans: Psychiatric Diagnosis and Treatment." In C. B. Wilkinson (Ed.), *Ethnic Psychiatry*. New York: Plenum Medical Book Company.

Wilkinson, D., et al. (Eds.). (1992). "Transforming Social Knowledge: The Interlocking of Race, Class, and Gender." *Gender and Society*. Special issue.

Wilkinson, D., Zinn, M. B., & Chow, E. N. L. (1992). "Race, Class, and Gender: Introduction." *Gender and Society, 6*(3), 341–345.

Wilkinson, S., & Kitzinger, C. (Eds.). (1993). *Heterosexuality*. Newbury Park, CA: Sage Publications.

Willemsen, T. M. (1993). "On the Bipolarity of Androgyny: A Critical Comment on Kottke (1988)." *Psychological Reports, 72*(1), 327–332.

Willet, W. C., et al. (1987). "Moderate Alcohol Consumption and the Risk of Breast Cancer." *New England Journal of Medicine, 316*(19), 1174–1180.

Williams, D. M., Patterson, M. N., & Hughes, I. A. (1993). "Androgen Insensitivity Syndrome." *Archives of Disease in Childhood, 68*(3), 343–344.

Williams, E. A., et al. (1992). "The Impact of a University Policy on the Sexual Harassment of Female Students." *Journal of Higher Education, 63*(1), 50–64.

Williams, J. K. (1992). "School-Aged Children with Turner's Syndrome." *Journal of Pediatric Nursing, 7*(1), 14–19.

Williams, J. K., et al. (1991). "A Comparison of Memory and Attention in Turner Syndrome and Learning Disability." *Journal of Pediatric Psychology, 16*(5), 585–593.

Williams, J. K., Richman, L. C., & Yarbrough, D. B. (1992). "Comparison of Visual-Spatial Performance Strategy Training in Children with Turner Syndrome and Learning Disabilities." *Journal of Learning Disabilities, 25*(10), 658–664.

Williams, J., & Jacoby, A. (1989). "The Effects of Premarital Heterosexual and Homosexual Experience on Dating and Marriage Desirability." *Journal of Marriage and the Family, 51*, 489–497.

Williams, K. B., & Cyr, R. R. (1992). "Escalating Commitment to a Relationship: The Sexual Harassment Trap." *Sex Roles, 27*(1-2), 47–72.

Williams, W. L. (1985). "Persistence and Change in the Berdache Tradition Among Contemporary Lakota Indians." *Journal of Homosexuality, 11*(3-4), 191–200.

Wills, G. (1989, December 21). "The Phallic Pulpit." *The New York Review of Books*, pp. 20–26.

Wills, G. (1990). *Under God*. New York: Simon & Schuster.

Wilson, G. (1978). *The Secrets of Sexual Fantasy*. London: J. M. Dent.

Wilson, M. N., et al. (1990). "Flexibility and Sharing of Childcare Duties in Black Families." *Sex Roles, 22*(7-8), 409–425.

Wilson, P. (1986). "Black Culture and Sexuality." *Journal of Social Work and Human Sexuality, 4*(3), 29–46.

Wilson, S. M., & Medora, N. P. (1990). "Gender Comparisons of College Students' Attitudes Toward Sexual Behavior." *Adolescence, 25*(99), 615–627.

Wilson, W. (1988). "Rape as Entertainment." *Psychological Reports, 63*(2), 607–610.

Wincze, J., & Carey, M. (1991). *Sexual Dysfunction: A Guide for Assessment and Treatment*. New York: Guilford Press.

Wise, T. N., et al. (1991). "Personality and Sexual Functioning of Transvestitic Fetishists and Other Paraphilics." *Journal of Nervous and Mental Disease, 179*(11), 694–698.

Wise, T. N., et al. (1992). "Sexual Issues in the Medically Ill and Aging." *Psychiatric Medicine, 10*(2), 169–180.

Wise, T. N., & Meyer, J. K. (1980). "The Border Area Between Transvestism and Gender Dysphoria: Transvestitic Applicants for Sex Reassignment." *Archives of Sexual Behavior, 9*, 327–342.

Wishnietsky, D. H. (1991). "Reported and Unreported Teacher-Student Sexual Harassment." *Journal of Educational Research, 84*(3), 164–169.

Wolberg, W. H., Romsaas, E. P., Tanner, M. A., & Malec, J. F. (1989). "Psychosexual Adaptation to Breast Cancer Surgery." *Cancer, 63*(8), 1645–1655.

Wolf, D. (1980). *The Lesbian Community*. Berkeley, CA: University of California Press.

Wolf, M., & Kielwasser, A. (1991). "Introduction: The Body Electric: Human Sexuality and the Mass Media." *Journal of Homosexuality, 21*(1-2), 7–18.

Wolf, N. (1991). *The Beauty Myth: How Images of Beauty Are Used Against Women*. New York: Morrow.

Wolfe, L. (1981). *The Cosmos Report*. New York: Bantam.

Wolff, C. (1986). *Magnus Hirschfeld: A Portrait of a Pioneer in Sexology*. London: Quartet Books.

Wolinksy, S., et al. (1988, June 12). "Polymerase Chain Reaction (PCR) Detection of HIV Provirus Before HIV Seroconversion." Paper presented at the Fourth International Conference on AIDS, Stockholm, Sweden.

Wood, D. (1993, January 29). "Military Women Say Anti-Gay Rule Harms Heterosexuals' Careers, Too." *San Jose Mercury News*, p. 17.

Wood, F. G. (1990). *The Arrogance of Faith: Christianity and Race in America from the Colonial Era to the Twentieth Century*. New York: Knopf.

Woodhouse, A. (1985). "Forgotten Women: Transvestism and Marriage." *Women's Studies International Forum, 8*(6), 583–592.

Woodhouse, A. (1989). "Breaking the Rules or Bending Them: Transvestism, Femininity, and Feminism." *Women's Studies International Forum, 12*(4), 417–423.

Woods, N. F. (1984). *Human Sexuality in Health and Illness*. (3rd ed.). St. Louis, MO: Mosby.

Woods, S. C., & Mansfield, J. G. (1981, February 11). "Ethanol and Disinhibition: Physiological and Behavioral Links." In R. Room & Collins (Eds.), *Proceedings of Alcoholism and Drug Abuse Conference, Berkeley/Oakland* (pp. 4–22). Washington, DC: U.S. Department of Health and Human Services.

Woodward, K. (1987, March 23). "New Rules for Making Love and Babies." *Newsweek*, pp. 42–43.

Workman, J. E., & Johnson, K. K. (1991). "The Role of Cosmetics in Attributions About Sexual Harassment." *Sex Roles, 24*(11-12), 759–769.

World Health Organization. (1992). *Reproductive Health: A Key to a Brighter Future. Biennial Report, 1990–1991*. Geneva, Switzerland: World Health Organization.

Wormser, G. P., et al. (1992). "Absence of Infectious Human Immunodeficiency Virus Type 1 in 'Natural' Eccrine Sweat." *Journal of Infectious Diseases, 165*(1), 155–158.

Wright, J., Duchesne, C., Sabourin, S., Bissonnette, F., Benoit, J., & Girard, Y. (1991). "Psychosocial Distress and Infertility: Men and Women Respond Differently." *Fertility and Sterility, 55*(1), 100–108.

Wright, P., Nobrega, J., Langevin, R., & Wortzman, G. (1990). "Brain Density and Symmetry in Pedophilic and Sexually Aggressive Offenders." *Annals of Sex Research, 3*(3), 319–328.

Wyatt, G. E. (1991). "Examining Ethnicity Versus Race in AIDS Related Sex Research." *Social Science and Medicine, 33*(1), 37–45.

Wyatt, G. E. (1992). "The Sociocultural Context of African American and White American Women's Rape." *Journal of Social Issues, 48*(1), 77–91.

Wyatt, G. E., et al. (1988). "Kinsey Revisited II: Comparisons of the Sexual Socialization and Sexual Behavior of Black Women Over 33 Years." *Archives of Sexual Behavior, 17*(4), 289–332.

Wyatt, G. E., et al. (1992). "Differential Effects of Women's Child Sexual Abuse and Subsequent Sexual Revictimization." *Journal of Consulting and Clinical Psychology, 60*(2), 167–174.

Wyatt, G. E., & Lyons-Rowe, S. (1990). "African American Women's Sexual Satisfaction as a Dimension of Their Sex Roles." *Sex Roles, 22*(7–8), 509–524.

Wynn, R., & Fletcher, C. (1987). "Sex Role Development and Early Educational Experiences." In D. B. Carter (Ed.), *Current Conceptions of Sex Roles and Sex Typing.* New York: Praeger.

Yap, P. M. (1993). "Koro—A Culture-Bound Depersonalization." In D. N. Suggs & A. W. Miracle (Eds.), *Culture and Human Sexuality.* Pacific Grove, CA: Brooks/Cole.

Yarber, W. L., Torabi, M. R., & Veenker, C. H. (1989). "Development of a Three-Component Sexually Transmitted Diseases Attitude Scale." *Journal of Sex Education and Therapy, 15,* 36–49.

Yorke, J. A., et al. (1978). "Dynamics and Control of the Transmission of Gonorrhea." *Sexually Transmitted Diseases, 5,* 51–56.

Young, L. (1992). "Sexual Abuse and the Problem of Embodiment." *Child Abuse and Neglect, 16*(1), 89–100.

Yulsman, T. (1990, October 7). "A Little Help for Creation. The Good Health Magazine." *The New York Times,* p. 22ff.

Zabin, L. S., & Clark, S. D. (1981). "Why They Delay: A Study of Teenage Family Planning Clinic Patients." *Family Planning Perspectives, 13,* 205–217.

Zabin, L. S., Hardy, J. B., Smith, E. A., & Hirsch, M. B. (1986). "Substance Use and Its Relation to Sexual Activity Among Inner-City Adolescents." *Journal of Adolescent Health Care, 7*(5), 320–331.

Zabin, L. S., Hirsch, M. B., Smith, E. A., Street, R., & Hardy, J. B. (1986). "Evaluation of a Pregnancy Prevention Program for Urban Teenagers." *Family Planning Perspectives, 18,* 119–126.

Zacharias, L., et al. (1976). *Obstetrical and Gynecological Survey, 31*(4).

Zarit, S., et al. (1986). "Subjective Burden of Husbands and Wives as Caregivers: A Longitudinal Study." *Gerontologist, 26,* 260–266.

Zaslow, M., et al. (1981, April). "Depressed Mood in New Fathers." Unpublished manuscript, Society for Research in Child Development.

Zausner, M. (1986). *The Streets: A Factual Portrait of Sex Prostitutes as Told in Their Own Words.* New York: St. Martin's Press.

Zaviacic, M., et al. (1988). "Concentrations of Fructose in Female Ejaculate and Urine." *Journal of Sex Research, 24,* 319–325.

Zelnik, M. (1981). *Sex and Pregnancy in Adolescence.* Newbury Park, CA: Sage Publications.

Zelnik, M., & Kantner, J. F. (1972). "Probability of Premarital Intercourse." *Social Science Research, 1,* 335–341.

Zelnick, M., Kantner, J. F., & Ford, K. (1981). *Sex and Pregnancy in Adolescence.* Beverly Hills, CA: Sage.

Zelnik, M., & Shaw, F. (1983). "First Intercourse Among Young Adults." *Family Planning Perspectives, 15,* 64–70.

Zerbe, K. J. (1992). "Why Eating-Disordered Patients Resist Sex Therapy: A Response to Simpson and Ramberg." *Journal of Sex and Marital Therapy, 18*(1), 55–64.

Zevin, D. (1992, August). "The Pleasure Principle." Special Issue: The Sexual Revolution in Movies, Music & TV. *US.,* pp. 32–36.

Zilbergeld, B. (1992). *Male Sexuality.* Boston: Little, Brown.

Zimmerman, H. L., et al. (1990). "Epidemiological Differences Between Chlamydia and Gonorrhea." *American Journal of Public Health, 80*(11), 1338–1342.

Zinn, M. B. (1990). "Family, Feminism, and Race." *Gender and Society, 4,* 68–82.

Zinn, M. B., & Eitzen, D. S. (1990). *Diversity in Families* (2nd ed.). New York: HarperCollins.

PHOTO CREDITS

Chapter 1 p. 9 (top), © Joel Gordon 1993; p. 9 (bottom), © AP/Wide World Photos; p. 10, courtesy Christine DeVault; p. 11 (top), © Marc Bryan-Brown; p. 11 (bottom), © Joel Gordon 1992; p. 13, © D. McLaughlin/Motion Picture and Television Photo Archive; p. 14, © Capital Cities/ABC, Inc.; p. 16, © Mark Selinger/Outline Press Syndicate, Inc.; p. 20, © Motion Picture and Television Photo Archive; p. 21, © John Pearson; p. 25, © Scala/Art Resource, New York; p. 27, courtesy Smithsonian Institution, Negative # 85-8666; p. 30 (top left), © Tom McKitterick/Impact Visuals; p. 30 (top right), © Michael Newman/PhotoEdit; p. 30 (bottom left), R. Lord/The Image Works; p. 30 (bottom right), © Joel Gordon 1992 **Chapter 2** p. 37, © Oscar Abolafia/The Gamma Liaison Network; p. 38, © 1992 North America Syndicate, Inc.; p. 43, Swapan Parekh/Black Star; p. 51, © Mary Evans Picture Library; p. 52, © Mary Evans Picture Library; p. 54, © AP/Wide World Photos; p. 56, © The Bettmann Archive; p. 59, © Joel Gordon 1993; p. 61, © Kit Hedman/Jeroboam, Inc. **Chapter 3** p. 77, © C. Edelmann/La Vilette/Photo Researchers, Inc.; p. 86, © Michael Newman/PhotoEdit **Chapter 4** p. 94 (left), © David Ryan/Photo 20-20; p. 94 (right), © SIPA Press/Art Resource, New York; p. 97, © Joan Liftin/Actuality, Inc.; p. 100, © CNRI/Science Photo Library/Photo Researchers, Inc. **Chapter 5** p. 109, *Lisa Lyon*, 1981, © 1981 The Estate of Robert Mapplethorpe; p. 111, © Barbara Campbell/Liaison International; p. 113, © Evan Johnson/Jeroboam, Inc.; p. 114, © John Pearson; p. 118, © David Madison 1992; p. 122, © Suzanne Arms; p. 124, © Suzanne Arms; p. 126, © Ken Miller; p. 129, from *Man and Woman, Boy and Girl*, © 1972 Johns Hopkins University Press; p. 134, courtesy Dr. Donald Laub, Gender Dysphoria Program, Palo Alto **Chapter 6** p. 140, © Suzanne Arms/Jeroboam, Inc.; p. 142, © Ken Gaghan/Jeroboam, Inc.; p. 146 (top), © Thomas Conant; p. 146 (bottom), courtesy Christine DeVault; p. 149, © Ilene Perlman/Impact Visuals; p. 155, © Joel Gordon 1992; p. 160, © Catherine Smith/Impact Visuals; p. 165, © David Maung/Impact Visuals; p. 168, © Sara Krulwich/New York Times Pictures; p. 172, © David Sipress; p. 173, © Joel Gordon 1989; p. 182, © Joel Gordon 1990 **Chapter 7** p. 189, © Joel Gordon 1992; p. 191, © Tony Savino/The Image Works; p. 195, © Stephanie Rausser/Impact Visuals; p. 201, © Joel Gordon 1992 **Chapter 8** p. 213, © Alain McLaughlin/Impact Visuals; p. 214, reprinted from *Erotic by Nature: A Celebration of Life, of Love and of Our Wonderful Bodies*, David Steinberg, ed., Down There Press/Red Alder Books. © 1988 Tee Corinne. Reprinted by permission of the editor.; p. 217, © Joel Gordon 1990; p. 223, © Suzanne Arms; p. 229, © Joel Gordon 1992 **Chapter 9** p. 238, © 1990 Kevin Rolly; p. 243, © Mark Antman/The Image Works; p. 251, © Kit Hedman/Jeroboam, Inc. **Chapter 10** p. 267, © Joel Gordon 1992; p. 269, © Movie Star News; p. 273, © Porter Gifford/The Gamma Liaison Network; p. 275, © Design Conceptions/Timothy Healy 1988 **Chapter 11** p. 285, © Joel Gordon 1991; p. 291, © Jonathan A. Meyers/JAM Photography; p. 294 (left), © Joel Gordon 1990; p. 294 (right), © Robert Maas/SIPA Press; p. 296, © Jonathan A. Meyers/JAM Photography; p. 300, © Joel Gordon; p. 301 (top), © Joel Gordon; p. 301 (bottom), © Joel Gordon; p. 302, © Joel Gordon 1992; p. 303, © Joel Gordon; p. 305, © Joel Gordon **Chapter 12** pps. 328 & 329, © Lennart Nilsson, from *Behold Man*, courtesy Bonnierforlagen AB; p. 339 (top), © Suzanne Arms/Jeroboam, Inc.; p. 339 (bottom), © 1992 Custom Medical Stock Photo; p. 347, © Georges de Keerle/The Gamma Liaison Network; p. 350, © Suzanne Arms; p. 351 (top), © S.I.U. Medical School/Photo Researchers, Inc.; p. 351 (bottom), © Harriet Gans/The Image Works; p. 357, © Erika Stone; p. 359, *How the Husband Assists in the Birth of a Child* by Guadalupe, widow of Ramon Medina Silva, courtesy Photo Services Department, M.H. de Young Museum, San Francisco; p. 363, © Erika Stone **Chapter 13** p. 371, Reprinted with permission of High Self Esteem Toys Corp.; p. 373, © Suzanne Arms; p. 378, © Ellis Herwig/The Picture Cube; p. 384, *Deena Metzger, The Warrior*, © 1980 Hella Hammid, courtesy Tino Hammid; p. 393, © Ron Delaney/Jeroboam, Inc.; **Chapter 14** p. 402, © K. McGlynn/The Image Works; p. 405, © David Steinberg 1993; p. 422, © Alain McLaughlin/Impact Visuals **Chapter 15** p. 431, © Piet van Lier/Impact Visuals; pps. 435, 436, 439 & 443, courtesy the U.S. Center for Disease Control, Atlanta **Chapter 16** pps. 458 & 460, courtesy the U.S. Center for Disease Control, Atlanta; p. 466, courtesy Jon Stuen-Parker, National AIDS Brigade; p. 469, © Design Conceptions/Anita Bartsch 1989; p. 470, © Mark Phillips/Photo Researchers, Inc.; p. 472, © Roger Mastroianni; p. 477, © James D. Wilson/The Gamma Liaison Network **Chapter 17** p. 486, © Marilyn Humphries/Impact Visuals; p. 488 (left), © Scala/Art Resource, New York; p. 488 (top right), © The Bettmann Archive; p. 488 (bottom right), © James D. Wilson/The Gamma Liaison Network; p. 491, © Mark Peterson/SABA Press Photos, Inc.; p. 500, © Mary Ellen Mark/Library; p. 503, Reprinted with permission of ETR Associates. **Chapter 18** p. 509, © Joel Gordon 1992; p. 511, © Neal Boenzi/New York Times Pictures; p. 513, *Michael*, 1987, © The Estate of Robert Mapplethorpe; p. 514, © Michael Willhoite from *Daddy's Roommate*, Alyson Publications; p. 517 (left); © IPA/The Image Works; p. 517 (right), © Tom Batzdorff/Motion Picture and Television Photo Archive; p. 519, © 1987 Daniel Nicoletta

TEXT CREDITS

Pages 47–49 Copyright © 1990 The Kinsey Institute for Research in Sex, Gender, and Reproduction. From the book *The Kinsey Institute New Report on Sex* and reprinted by permission of St. Martin's Press, Inc., New York, NY. **Page 70** Reprinted by permission from *The Marriage and Family Experience* by Bryan Strong and Christine DeVault. Copyright © 1990 West Publishing Company. All rights reserved. **Page 100** Figure 4.4, From Stuart Ira Fox, *Human Physiology*, 4th ed. Copyright © 1993 Wm. C. Brosn Communications, Inc., Dubuque, Iowa. Reprinted by permission of Times Mirror Higher Education Group, Inc., Dubuque, Iowa. All rights reserved. **Page 315** Copyright © 1994, Los Angeles Times. Reprinted by permission. **Page 498** Copyright © San Francisco Chronicle. Reprinted by permission.

Index

Amnion, **326**
Amniotic fluid, **326**
Ampulla, **71, 96**
Amyl nitrate, 394–395
Anabolic steroids, 395
Anal eroticism, 259–261, 422
Analingus, **259**-260
Anal intercourse, 72, 98, **260**-261, 463–464
Anal stage, **53**
Anatomical sex, **110**
Anatomy. *See* Sexual physiology
Androgen, **98**, 131, 387
Androgen-insensitivity syndrome, 130, **131**
Androgen replacement therapy, **387**
Androgyny, **125**-129
Anger rape, 497
Anglo-Saxons. *See* Whites
Anorexia nervosa, **371**
Anorgasmia, **409**, 410, 417
Antibodies, **459**
Antidiscrimination laws, 487
Anti-gay prejudice, **487**-490
Antigens, **459**
Antihistamines, 411
Anus, 72
Anxiety, 53, 199, 202, 345, 413
Anxious/ambivalent attachment, **199**
Apgar score, **352**-353
Areola, **72**
Arthritis, 379–380
Artificial insemination (AI), **345**-346, 348
Asian Americans
    communication and, 210
    jealousy and, 201
    sampling in sex research and, 46
Asphyxia, autoerotic, **281**
Assigned gender, **110**, 111–112
Asymptomatic STDs, **431**, 440
Attachment, **198**-199, 201
Attitude, 62, 63
    defined, **42**
    gender-role, **110**
    HIV prevention and, 473
    love and, 189–190
    media and, 10–11
    self-assessment of, 22–23
    STDs and, 428–429
Atypical sexual behavior
    cross-dressing, 271, 272–273
    defined, **265**
    deviant sexual behavior and, 32–33, 51–52
    domination and submission, 268–270
    incidence of, 267–268
    paraphilic behavior vs., 265–267
    typical sexual behavior vs., 32–33
Autoerotic asphyxia, **281**
Autoeroticism
    defined, **244**
    Ellis's research on, 54
    erotic dreams and, 246
    masturbation and, 246–250
    sexual fantasies and, 244–246
Avoidant attachment, **199**
AZT (zidovudine or azidothymidine), 478

Babyism, 269
Bacterial pneumonia, 457
Bacterial vaginosis, **440**-441
Bactrim, 479
B&D (bondage and discipline), 267, **268**, 518
Bargaining, 232–233
Barrier methods of contraception
    cervical caps, 300–301
    condoms, 296–299. *See also* Condoms
    contraceptive sponges, 302
    diaphragms, 299–301
    female condoms, 301–302
Bartholin's glands, **68**
Basal body temperature (BBT) method, 307-**308**
B cells, **460**
Behavior, **42**, 110, 189–190. *See also* Sexual behavior
Benign prostatic hypertrophy, **376**
Benign tumors, **380**-381
Bestiality, 273
Bias, **41**, 50, 486. *See also* Discrimination; Stereotypes
Biased sample, **45**
Billings method, 308
Binge eating disorder, **371**-372
Biological sexism, 446
Biopsy, **385**
Birth canal, 68, **69**
Birth control
    contraception vs., 288–289
    defined, **288**
    postcoital, 313-316
    after thirty, 314
    See also Contraception
Birthing rooms or centers, 357
Bisexuality
    adolescence and, 162–163
    defined, **161**
    heterosexuality and, 163
    negativity toward, 163
    sexual attraction and, 237–238
Blacks. *See* African Americans
Blastocyst, **326**, 346
Blood analysis, 331
Blood cells, white, 459
Blood transfusions, 468
"Blue balls," 104
Body piercing, 266
Bondage and discipline (B&D), 267, **268**, 518
Bone loss, 374
Books, 514
Brain, 85
Braxton Hicks contractions, **350**
Breast(s)
    cancer of, 381–385
    female, 72, 73, 143, 144
    fibroadenomas and, 383
    fibrocystic disease and, 383
    lactation and, 72, 295, 359–360
    male, 97
    self-exam of, 382
Breast-feeding, 355, 359–361, 363
Brothels, 518
Brother-sister sexual abuse, 501
Bulbourethral glands, **97**
Bulimia, **371**

Calcium, 375
Calendar method, **307**
Call girls, 519
Cancer
    AIDS and, 458
    benign tumors and, 380–381
    malignant tumors and, 381
    in men
        checkups for, 387–388
        prostate, 388–389
        testicular, 389–390
    metastasis and, 381
    oral contraceptives and, 293
    in women
        breast, 381–385
        cervical, 385, 458
        hysterectomy for, 387
        ovarian, 385–386
        uterine, 386–387
        vaginal, 392
Candida albicans, 441, 445
Candidiasis, **441**-442, 458
Cantharides, 395–396
Capacitation, **326**
CAP (child abuse prevention) programs, 503
Cardiovascular disease, 379
"Career woman's disease" (endometriosis), 343, 390–391, 411
Castration anxiety, **53**
Catholics, 31, 62, 159
Caucasians. *See* Whites
CD4 protein receptor, 460
CD8 protein receptor, 460
Censorship, **513**
    of sexually oriented material, 513–515
    television and, 12, 148
Cervical cancer, 385, 458
Cervical caps, **300**-301
Cervical dysplasia, **385**, 458
Cervical intraepithelial neoplasia (CIN), **385**, 458
Cervix
    cancer of, 385, 458
    cervical caps and, 300–301
    defined, **71**
    in labor, 350, 352
    self-exam of, 386
    spotting and, 308
Cesarean section, **354**, 356
Chancre, **439**
Chancroid, 443
Chemicals, toxic, 335, 344
Chicanos (Mexican Americans), 62, 228, 248
Child abuse prevention (CAP) programs, 503
Childbirth
    in birthing rooms or centers, 357
    cesarean section and, 354, 356
    classes in, 356, 357
    delivery, 352–353
    at home, 357
    in hospital, 354
    labor, 350–353
    midwifery and, 358–359
    physiological changes during, 350–352
    plans for, 355
    prepared, **356**